DRAFTING TRUSTS

and

WILL TRUSTS

A Modern Approach

Hogarth: Marriage à la Mode: Plate 1 (detail)
Andrew Edmunds, London

AUSTRALIA
LBC Information Services
Sydney

CANADA and USA
The Carswell Company
Toronto

NEW ZEALAND
Brooker's
Auckland

SINGAPORE and MALAYSIA
Sweet & Maxwell Asia
Singapore and Kuala Lumpur

DRAFTING TRUSTS
and
WILL TRUSTS
A Modern Approach

Ninth Edition

by

JAMES KESSLER, QC

and

LEON SARTIN

SWEET & MAXWELL  THOMSON REUTERS

First Edition 1992
Second Edition 1995
Reprinted 1996
Third Edition 1997
Fourth Edition 1998
Reprinted 2000
Fifth Edition 2000
Reprinted 2001 (twice)
Sixth Edition 2002
Reprinted 2003
Seventh Edition 2004
Eighth Edition 2007

Published in 2008 by
Thomson Reuters (Legal) Limited
(Registered in England & Wales, Company No 1679046.
Registered Office and address for service:
100 Avenue Road, London, NW3 3PF) trading as Sweet & Maxwell
For further information on our products and services, visit
www.sweetandmaxwell.co.uk
Typeset by Servis Filmsetting Ltd, Stockport, Cheshire
Printed in Great Britain by TJ International, Padstow, Cornwall

No natural forests were destroyed to make this product;
only farmed timber was used and replanted.

A CIP record for this book is available from the British Library

ISBN 978-1-84703-582-0

All rights reserved. Crown copyright material is reproduced with the permission of the Controller of HMSO and the Queen's Printer for Scotland.

No part of this publication may be reproduced or transmitted in any form or by any means, or stored in any retrieval system of any nature, without prior written permission, except for permitted fair dealing under the Copyright, Designs and Patents Act 1988, or in accordance with the terms of a licence issued by the Copyright Licensing Agency in respect of photocopying and/or reprographic reproduction. Precedent material included in this publication may be used as a guide for drafting of legal documents specifically for particular clients, though no liability is accepted by the publishers or authors in relation to their use. Such documents may be provided to clients for their own use and to the solicitors acting for other parties to the transaction subject to acknowledgement of the source of the precedent. Precedents may not otherwise be distributed to other parties. Application for permission for other use of copyright material including permission to reproduce extracts in other published works shall be made to the publishers. Full acknowledgement of author, publisher and source must be given.
The authors assert their moral rights.

© James Kessler 2008

FOREWORD

While "Equity fashions a trust with flexible adaptation on the call of the occasion" (as Cardozo J. stated in *Adams v Champion* (1935) 294 U.S. 231, 237) so that Equity provides the flexible rules of the game, it is the drafter as player of the game who has to fashion the appropriate trust instrument for the settlor. The drafter needs to have a full critical understanding of these rules and the impact of tax law in order to facilitate the requisite endgame. His role is crucial because the execution of ideas is the essence of them.

Back in 1992 James Kessler produced the first edition of this innovative book providing the very assistance needed by drafters to fulfil their role in drafting settlements and will trusts—and I wrote the Foreword when the book contained 11 Chapters followed by illustrative Precedents. Since then, as a result of many changes in law, developments in practice and suggestions of readers, the book has expanded to 31 Chapters in going through nine editions. Moreover, James Kessler duly became a QC, reflecting his well-earned reputation in the field of tax and chancery practice. As a busy Silk and needing to deal with fundamental tax law changes in the Finance Acts 2006 and 2008 for the improved ninth edition, he has brought in a junior, Leon Sartin, as co-author.

His book has changed the mindset of many traditional prolix drafters and helped to produce a new breed of drafter focusing on the need for plain English but with a real understanding of the technical clauses necessarily employed in the drafts. As a reviewer wrote, the book is "full of erudition and insights imparted with a light touch and an engaging directness." The author's refreshingly forthright style makes the book eminently readable as well as soundly instructive. There is little doubt that his book has had the effect of improving the style and content of modern trust instruments. Perhaps this edition may contribute to reversal of Inheritance Tax changes in the FA 2006 discriminating against young and other vulnerable persons as spelled out in Chapter 1.

This book has now established for itself an indispensable place in the library of any serious trust lawyer.

The Honourable Mr Justice David Hayton, M.A., LL.B., LL.D.
Judge of the Caribbean Court of Justice,
Additional Bencher of Lincoln's Inn and
Fellow of King's College, London
Honorary Member of STEP
October 2008

PREFACE

Trust drafting is a professional skill. Trust drafting needs trust law, succession law, a considerable amount of tax law (and time and energy to keep up to date); some property law; and a dash of insolvency and family law. That is not all. Many laymen's wishes are unformulated beyond a general desire to put their affairs in order; conversely, some clients have firm ideas as to the disposition of their property which are far from suited to their circumstances. To deal with this calls for empathy and an ability to communicate.

The aim of this work is to aid the drafter by discussing all the issues which arise in drafting settlements and will trusts, and to provide precedents.

The precedents are accompanied with an explanation of why the text is there and the choices that have to be made. The explanation is of the essence; the adoption of a precedent without understanding it fully is a recipe for trouble. The precedents in this book adopt a drafting style which reads simply and naturally.

We also discuss many standard forms and questions which the reader of settlements in common use will often meet. This book will also serve as a guide to the interpretation of trust documentation. Obfuscatory formulae, which spring so lightly from the pen of the experienced practitioner, will baffle the less experienced. Here is some guidance for those who wish to understand their origin, meaning and effect, if any.

Although this book contains many precedents, we hope to persuade the reader to regard standard drafts with an independent eye; as a suggestion and not a solution. The solicitor does not serve his client well if he produces to him for execution any standard draft without consideration of individual circumstances.

It is unusual for a single work to discuss both settlements and will trusts. These topics are usually considered in isolation. More care is normally lavished on lifetime settlements than will trusts; this can be measured by the prolixity of a typical settlement, and the brevity of a typical will. But there are few differences of principle between them. If the will drafter took as much care as the trust drafter, then wills (if longer) would be better documents, and beneficiaries better provided for.

This is a practical book but it tries to address the hard questions which do arise in practice. Topics of trust and tax law are discussed so far as they impinge upon trust drafting. General questions of tax and tax planning are not developed here; the topic of drafting requires a book to itself. Drafting suffers if it is regarded as a mere afterthought to the more serious matter of tax planning. But some of the questions which arise are so interesting that this policy is adopted with regret, with the occasional lapse, and only by the exercise of considerable restraint.

Artificial tax avoidance schemes are beyond the scope of this book. When such arrangements are possible, this has sometimes been indicated. In such cases it would be necessary in any event to obtain independent and specialist advice.

Standard trust drafts need regular review, and so do books on the subject.[1] The authors owe to their readers an obligation to keep this work up to date.

We continue to apply to the text the test of practice at the chancery bar. The experience so gained enables us in each new edition to explain some matters a little more clearly, and investigate some problems a little more deeply. The task can never be accomplished to an author's total satisfaction.

Since the last edition Parliament has passed the Charities Act 2006. The Courts have decided many interesting cases including *AN v Barclays Private Bank* (no-contest clauses).

Reforms now in prospect are the abolition of the statutory rule against accumulations, simplification of the rule against perpetuities and new rules relating to the capital/income distinction. After these necessary reforms perhaps we can enjoy to a period of stable trust law.

Stability of tax law seems unattainable. The FA 2006 leaves the IHT treatment of trusts in a lamentable state. The FA 2008 introduces transferable nil-rate bands—a reform which this book has advocated since 2000—and will greatly simplify the drafting of wills and the administration of estates. The Act scraps the monstrous complexities of taper relief foolishly introduced without consultation in 1998.

We remain indebted to many friends and readers who have commented and continue to comment on the text. Responsibility for errors is, of course, our own. As to responsibility for errors in a document which draws on this book, see paragraph 30.2 (Use and misuse of precedents). We have enjoyed writing this book and will be happy if any readers enjoy reading it.

This book attempts to state the law as at August 1, 2008.

This book is gradually turning into a series covering Wills and Trusts in different jurisdictions, which now includes: Canada, Cayman Islands,

---

[1] "It is very strange that a clause should have been inserted in 1936 in this form. No doubt it was taken from some older and obsolescent precedent in a book of conveyancing precedents." (*Re Brassey* [1955] 1 All ER 577; the drafter had overlooked the Statute of Westminster 1931 in a trustee investment clause.)

Channel Islands, Northern Ireland, Singapore and Australia. Books for Bermuda and BVI are now underway. Any reader who is a trust practitioner in Bahrain, Cyprus, Dubai, Hong Kong, the Republic of Ireland, Mauritius, Scotland, or any other trust jurisdiction, who is sympathetic to the approach of this book, and interested in such a project, should please contact James Kessler.

James Kessler QC
15 Old Square
Lincoln's Inn
London WC2A 3UE

kessler@kessler.co.uk
www.kessler.co.uk

Leon Sartin
5 Stone Buildings
Lincoln's Inn
London WC2A 3XT

lsartin@5sblaw.com

TRUSTS DISCUSSION FORUM

Readers are invited to join the Trusts Discussion Forum, an internet discussion group dedicated to discussion of trust and will drafting and related private client topics, founded by the author in association with STEP and the Chancery Bar Association.

>To subscribe visit *www.trustsdiscussionforum.co.uk*
>There is no charge.

A NOTE TO THE LAY READER

Our advice is not to draft your own trust or will, but find a competent solicitor to advise you. Self-help guides extol "the benefit of bypassing expensive lawyers"; but the bypass may prove the more expensive route in the long run.

This book is not intended as a self-help guide, and is addressed to professional practitioners, but it is readable for a lay person. If you wish to research this subject in depth, and so take more control of your own legal affairs, read on.

DRAFTING QUOTATIONS[1]

He offered to read the draft to the plaintiff; but she refused, as she did not understand law terms; and at the time the deed was executed he repeated the offer with a similar result. It appeared that the plaintiff became acquainted with the effect of the settlement very soon after her marriage, and expressed her dissatisfaction therewith . . .

Wollaston v Tribe (1869)

Le style en doit être concis. Les lois des Douze Tables sont un modèle de précision: les enfants les apprenaient par cœur. Le style des lois doit être simple; l'expression directe s'entend toujours mieux que l'expression réfléchie.[2]

Montesquieu, *De l'Esprit des Lois*, L. XXIX, 1748

Words . . . are the wildest, freest, most irresponsible, most unteachable of all things. Of course, you can catch them and sort them and place them in alphabetical order in dictionaries. But words do not live in dictionaries; they live in the mind. . . . Thus to lay down any laws for such irreclaimable vagabonds is worse than useless. A few trifling rules of grammar and spelling are all the constraint we can put on them. All we can say about them, as we peer at them over the edge of that deep, dark and only fitfully illuminated cavern in which they live—the mind—all we can say about them is that they seem to like people to think and to feel before they use them, but to think and to feel not about them, but about something different. They are highly sensitive, easily made self-conscious. They do not like to have their purity or their impurity discussed. . . . Nor do they like being lifted out on the point of a pen and examined separately. They hang together, in sentences, in paragraphs, sometimes for whole pages at a time. They hate

---

[1] See *www.kessler.co.uk* for more drafting quotations.
[2] "The style ought to be concise. The laws of the Twelve Tables are a model of concision; children used to learn them by heart. The style should also be plain and simple, a direct expression being better understood than an indirect one."

being useful; they hate making money; they hate being lectured about in public. In short, they hate anything that stamps them with one meaning or confines them to one attitude, for it is their nature to change.

Virginia Woolf, *The Death of the Moth*

CONTENTS AT A GLANCE

	Page
Chapter 1—FA 2006: The Raid on Trusts	3
Chapter 2—First Principles	9
Chapter 3—Style	16
Chapter 4—Principles of Interpreting Trust Documents	34
Chapter 5—Beneficiaries	51
Chapter 6—Trustees	82
Chapter 7—Trustees' Powers	112
Chapter 8—Trust Property	141
Chapter 9—The Rule Against Perpetuities	143
Chapter 10—General Provisions of a Trust	149
Chapter 11—Drafting and Understanding Overriding Powers (Appointment, Re-settlement and Advancement)	173
Chapter 12—Exercising Overriding Powers	189
Chapter 13—Settlor Exclusion and Default Clauses	202
Chapter 14—Lifetime Interest in Possession Trusts	216
Chapter 15—Discretionary Trusts	230
Chapter 16—Provisions Inconsistent with IP and IHT Special Trusts	239
Chapter 17—Types of Will Trusts	252
Chapter 18—Will Drafting after the FA 2008-08-28	264
Chapter 19—Administration of Nil Rate Band Trusts	289
Chapter 20—Wills and Care Fee Planning	297
Chapter 21—Administrative Provisions	308
Chapter 22—Bare Trusts	354
Chapter 23—Trusts of Life Insurance Policies	359
Chapter 24—Charitable Trusts	368
Chapter 25—Trusts of Damages	378
Chapter 26—Trusts for Disabled Beneficiaries	385
Chapter 27—Governing Law, Place of Administration and Jurisdiction Clauses	397
Chapter 28—Restricting Rights of Beneficiaries	407
Chapter 29—Execution of Wills and Trust Deeds	417
Chapter 30—Appointment and Retirement of Trustees	427
Chapter 31—Indemnities for Trustees	435
Precedents	445
Appendices	523
Index	565

CONTENTS IN DETAIL

Foreword	v
Preface	vii
Trusts Discussion Forum	x
A Note to the Lay Reader	xi
Drafting Quotations	xii
Table of Cases	xxxi
Table of Statutes	xlv
Table of National (non UK) Statutes	li
Table of Abbreviations	liii
Trust Terminology	lv

PART 1 — TRUST DRAFTING

Chapter 1: The Finance Act 2006: The Raid on Trusts

Policy of FA 2006	1.1
Misconceptions	1.2
Policy issues	1.3
Trusts after the FA 2006	1.4
Existing trusts after the FA 2006	1.5

Chapter 2: First principles

Duty to the client	2.1
Elderly or ill client	2.2
Does drafting matter?	2.3
Flexibility	2.4
Simplicity	2.5
Sources for drafting	2.6
(1) Statute	2.7
(2) Law reports	2.8
(3) Company law	2.9
(4) Legal literature and precedent books	2.10
Formal qualifications for the drafter	2.11
Money laundering	2.12
Civil claims against the drafter	2.13

Chapter 3: Style

Introduction	3.1
Punctuation	3.2
Use of capitals	3.3
Sentence length	3.4
Must every clause be a single sentence?	3.5
Indentation	3.6
Passive voice	3.7
General comment	3.8
Numbers: words or figures?	3.9
Style of clause numbering	3.10
Dates	3.11
Addresses	3.12
Age	3.13
Singular and plural	3.14
Male and female	3.15
And/provided that/but	3.16
Deemed/treated as	3.17
Archaic and prolix expressions	3.18
Clause headings	3.19
Incorporation by reference	3.20
Artificial rules of construction	3.21
The class closing rule	3.22
The rule in *Lassence v Tierney* or *Hancock v Watson*	3.23
Cross-references	3.24
Obsolete forms	3.25
"For her separate use"	3.26
Entails	3.27
Trusts for sale	3.28

Chapter 4: Principles of interpreting trust documents

Introduction	4.1
General principle	4.2
Factual background/previous negotiations/declarations of intent	4.3
Meaning of words *v* meaning of document	4.4
The objective principle	4.5
Deemed intention	4.5.1
Intention irrelevant	4.5.2
Relationship between objective principle and inadmissibility rules	4.6
Relationship between objective principle and literal construction	4.7
Arguments for and against the objective principle	4.8
Relationship between objective principle and rectification	4.9
Precedent not the solution	4.10
Conclusion	4.11
Are principles of construction of wills or trusts the same as contracts or statutes?	4.12
"Construction not restricted by technical rules"	4.13

Chapter 5: Beneficiaries

Too much money	5.1
Profligacy	5.2
A protective trust?	5.3
A better solution	5.4
Insolvency of a beneficiary	5.5
Before or after the bankruptcy order is made	5.6
Before the bankruptcy order is made	5.7
Anti-creditor clauses	5.8
Divorce of beneficiaries	5.9
(1) Dealing with beneficiary's equitable interest	5.10
(2) Interest under the trust as a financial resource	5.11
(3) Variation of settlement on divorce	5.12–5.13
Divorce of beneficiaries: conclusions	5.14
Anti-alimony forms	5.15
Foreign domiciled beneficiary	5.16
Marriage under 18	5.17
Definition of "Beneficiaries"	5.18–5.19
Children and descendants	5.20
"Children of X and Y"	5.21
Illegitimate beneficiaries	5.22
Adopted beneficiaries	5.23
Stepchildren	5.24
Assisted reproduction	5.25
Children by surrogacy	5.26
Provisions distinguishing male/female	5.27
Spouses of beneficiaries	5.28
Civil partners	5.29
Spouses and civil partners of beneficiaries: drafting points	5.30
Settlor and spouse/civil partner as beneficiaries	5.31
Meaning of "spouse"/"civil partner" of settler	5.32
Settlor's surviving spouse/civil partner as beneficiary of lifetime trust	5.33
Testator's spouse/civil partner as beneficiary of will	5.34
Separated spouse/civil partner of settlor as beneficiary	5.35
Charities as beneficiaries	5.36
Non-charitable companies as beneficiaries	5.37
Foreign charities as beneficiaries	5.38
Power to add beneficiaries	5.39
Power to exclude beneficiaries	5.40
Other possible beneficiaries	5.41
Dependants	5.42
Employees of beneficiaries	5.43
Employees of family company	5.44
"Fall back" beneficiaries	5.45
Charity as "fall back" beneficiary	5.46
Distant relatives as "fall back" beneficiaries	5.47
Use of default clause	5.48
Simple addition to the class of beneficiaries	5.49

Limited extension of the class of beneficiaries	5.50
Tax and the class of beneficiaries	5.51

Chapter 6: Trustees

Number of trustees	6.1
Choice of trustees	6.2
Beneficiaries as trustees	6.3
Professional trustees	6.4
Corporate trustees	6.5
Accountants as trustees	6.6
Director of listed company as trustee	6.7
Insider dealing and trusteeship	6.8
Custodian trustees	6.9
Foreign trustees	6.10
Order of trustees' names	6.11
Flee clauses	6.12
Conflicts of interest	6.13–6.14
Distinguishing personal and fiduciary conflicts	6.15
Trustee-beneficiaries	6.16
Construction of trustee exemption clauses	6.17
"Free from responsibility for loss"	6.18
"No liability for loss"	6.19
"In the professed execution of the trusts and powers hereof"	6.20
"Absolute owner" "beneficial owner" clauses	6.21
Validity of exemption clauses	6.22
Should the drafter insert an exemption clause?	6.23
Duty to disclose exclusion clauses to settlor/testator	6.24
Drafting an exemption clause	6.25
Commentary: should exemption clauses be allowed?	6.26
What standard of care rests on trustees?	6.27
Excluding strict liability	6.28
Excluding claims by unknown beneficiaries	6.29
Relying on counsel's advice	6.30
Excluding duty to supervise family companies	6.31
Excluding duty to supervise parents and guardians	6.32
Appointment of new trustees	6.33
Who appoints trustees?	6.34
Appointment of foreign trustees	6.35
Retirement of trustees	6.36
Two trustees requirement	6.37
Further provisions concerning appointment of additional trustees?	6.38
Trustees' right to resign	6.39
Sections 19 and 20 Trusts of Land and Appointment of Trustees Act 1996	6.40
Power to dismiss trustees	6.41
Short form	6.42

Chapter 7: Trustees' powers
Introduction	7.1
Duties and powers distinguished	7.2
Duties or powers: does it matter?	7.3
Powers and duties: terminology	7.4
Drafting duties and powers	7.5
Other usage of "shall" and "may"	7.6
Provisions about how often and when powers are exercised	7.7
Should discretionary duties have time limits?	7.8
Powers exercisable "at any time" and "from time to time"	7.9
"Absolute discretion" and "as the trustees think fit"	7.10–7.11
Guidance and control of trustees	7.12
Majority decisions	7.13
Two-trustee rule	7.14
Statement of wishes	7.15
Drafting the statement of wishes	7.16
Power of appointment of new trustees	7.17
Consultation with beneficiaries	7.18
Control of trustees	7.19
What trustees' powers should be subject to control?	7.20
What sorts of checks can be made on trustees' powers and who exercises them?	7.21
Giving powers of appointment to beneficiaries personally	7.22
Giving powers of consent to beneficiaries	7.23
Giving powers of consent to the settler	7.24
Giving powers of appointment to a settlor	7.25
Better methods of controlling trustees	7.26
Settlor (or spouse) as sole trustees?	7.27
Weighted majority clause	7.28
Protectors	7.29
Power to dismiss trustees	7.30
Dealing with the former trustee	7.31–7.32
Nature of powers of consent and appointment	7.33

Chapter 8: Trust property
Particular assets	8.1
Shares and securities in a private company	8.2
Leasehold property	8.3
Land subject to mortgage	8.4
Life insurance policies	8.5
Chattels	8.6
Property qualifying for IHT business/agricultural property relief	8.7
Property situate outside England and Wales	8.8

Chapter 9: The rule against perpetuities
Introduction	9.1
Which perpetuity period?	9.2
Drafting	9.3
Confusion over dates	9.4

xx   CONTENTS IN DETAIL

Trust period and perpetuity period distinguished	9.5
(1) Dispositive powers	9.6
(2) Beneficiaries' interests	9.7
Effect of failure to remain within perpetuity period	9.8
Future of the rule against perpetuities	9.9

Chapter 10: General provisions of a trust

Order of provisions	10.1
Declaration of trust or transfer to trustees?	10.2
Title	10.3
Date	10.4
On what date does a trust take effect?	10.5
Backdating	10.6
Parties	10.7
Who should be parties?	10.8
Describing the parties	10.9
Form where settlor is one of the trustees	10.10
Form where trust made by joint settlers	10.11
Form where settlor is sole trustee	10.12
No named settlor	10.13
Nominal settlor	10.14
Recitals	10.15
Recital 1: A list of the principal beneficiaries of the trust	10.16
Recital 2: Name of trust	10.17
Power to change name of trust	10.18
Recital 3: Foreign domicile of settlor	10.19
Useless recitals	10.20–10.25
Testatum	10.26
Definitions	10.27
Beneficial provisions	10.28
Testimonium clause	10.29
Schedule of trust property	10.30
Schedule of administrative provisions	10.31
Schedule of beneficiaries?	10.32
Definitions	10.33
How to make definitions	10.34
"Define as you go"	10.35
A definition clause	10.36
"Means" and "includes"	10.37
Unnecessary forms in a definition clause	10.38
Some standard definitions	10.39
Definition of "the trustees"	10.40
Definition of "the trust fund"	10.41–10.42
Unnecessary definitions	10.43
Definitions implied by law	10.44
Definitions to break up text	10.45
Drafting successive interests	10.46–10.47
Irrevocability	10.48

Chapter 11: Drafting and understanding overriding powers (appointment, re-settlement and advancement)

Introduction	11.1
Power of appointment	11.2
Unnecessary provisions in the power of appointment	11.3–11.4
The problem of narrow powers of appointment	11.5
Power of resettlement	11.6
Power of resettlement and power of appointment compared	11.7
Power of advancement	11.8
Power to pay or transfer to beneficiary	11.9
Power of appointment used to make advance to beneficiary	11.10
Power of advancement used to create new trusts	11.11

Chapter 12: Exercising overriding powers

Who should draft deeds of appointment?	12.1
How to instruct counsel	12.2
Drafting deeds of appointment	12.3
Useful recitals	12.4
Appointment creating royal lives clause	12.5
Some points to watch in drafting deeds of appointment	12.6
Example deed of appointment	12.7
Points to watch in drafting transfers to another settlement	12.8
Example exercise of power to transfer to another settlement	12.9
Who should draft settled advances?	12.10
Drafting resolutions of advancement	12.11
Example resolution of advancement used to alter terms of trust	12.12
Example resolution of advancement used to transfer property to two separate settlements	12.13
Example resolution of advancement used to transfer property from one settlement to another	12.14
Procedure after execution of deed of appointment/resettlement/advancement	12.15

Chapter 13: Settlor exclusion and default clauses

Why exclude the settlor and spouse/civil partner?	13.1
CGT hold-over relief	13.2
Excluding the settlor: drafting	13.3
(1) Direct benefit	13.4–13.5
(2) Resulting trust	13.6
(3) Power to benefit settlor	13.7
(4) Actual benefit	13.8
(5) Reciprocal arrangements	13.9
Settlor exclusion clause	13.10
When is a settlor exclusion clause appropriate?	13.11
What does a settlor exclusion clause cover?	13.12
Drafting the settlor exclusion clause	13.13
Joint settlors	13.14
Exclusion of additional and indirect settlors	13.15
Reference to "spouse" in settlor exclusion clause	13.16

xxii CONTENTS IN DETAIL

Unnecessary provisions in settlor exclusion clause	13.17
No reservation of benefit	13.18–13.20
"No resulting trust for the settlor"	13.21
Dependent children exclusion clause	13.22
Default clause	13.23
Drafting the default clause	13.24
Unnecessary provisions in a default clause	13.25
Correcting errors in a default clause	13.26
An unnecessary default clause	13.27

Chapter 14: Lifetime interest in possession trusts

Introduction	14.1
Why use interest in possession trusts?	14.2
Interest in possession income clause	14.3
Structure of lifetime interest in possession trust	14.4
Income to the principal beneficiary for life	14.5
Provisions after death of the principal beneficiary	14.6
An alternative: beneficiary's power to appoint to widow/civil partner	14.7
Describing the widow	14.8
A perpetuity problem	14.9
Position after death of surviving spouse/civil partner	14.10
Future accumulation of income	14.11
IP forms for two life tenants	14.12
Commentary on straightforward flexible form	14.13
An inflexible form	14.14
Objection to simple accruer clause	14.15
Life tenant becomes entitled at specified age	14.16
Life tenant a minor	14.17
Interest in possession for settlor	14.18
Impeachment for waste	14.19

Chapter 15: Discretionary trusts

Meaning of discretionary trust	15.1
Why use discretionary trusts?	15.2
Discretionary trust: income clause	15.3
Distribution limb	15.4
Accumulation limb	15.5
The rule against accumulations	15.6–15.7
Other accumulation periods?	15.8
Strategies for trustees after accumulation period expires	15.9
Structure of discretionary trust	15.10
"Beneficiaries"	15.11
Powers of discretionary trusts	15.12

Chapter 16 : Provisions inconsistent with IP and IHT special trusts

Administrative, dispositive, beneficial: terminology	16.1
Significance of administrative/dispositive distinction	16.2
When is a provision administrative or dispositive?	16.3
Power to pay capital expenses out of income	16.4

Retention of income to provide for liabilities or depreciation of a capital asset	16.5–16.6
Capital/income and apportionment provisions	16.7
Power of appropriation	16.8
IP trusts: "departure" v "disqualifying" powers	16.9
Power to pay insurance premiums out of income	16.10
Power to permit beneficiary to occupy or use trust property rent free	16.11
Power to lend money interest free	16.12
Power to waive income	16.13
IHT special trusts	16.14
Power to permit beneficiary to occupy or use trust property rent free	16.15
Power to use income to pay life insurance premiums	16.16
Protection clauses	16.17
Drafting and construction of protection clauses	16.18
Interest in possession protection clause	16.19
"No conflict" clause	16.20
CGT protection clause	16.21
A & M protection clause	16.22

Chapter 17: Types of will trusts

Types of will trusts: terminology	17.1
Spouses : terminology	17.2
IPDI trusts: qualifying conditions	17.3
Why use IPDI trusts?	17.4
Terms of IPDI trust after death of life tenant	17.5
Age 18-to-25 trusts: qualifying conditions	17.6
Why use Age 18-to-25 trusts?	17.7
Bereaved Minors trusts	17.8
"Express Wills"	17.9
Will trusts and lifetime trusts: drafting differences	17.10
Foreign trustees	17.11
Survivorship clauses	17.12
Gift by will to existing trust	17.13

Chapter 18: Will drafting after the Finance Act 2008

Introduction	18.1–18.2
Classic NRB trusts?	18.3
Will drafting after the Finance Act 2008	18.4
How transferable NRBs work	18.5
NRB claims	18.6
Transfer of NRB in cases of remarriage	18.7
Untransferable NRB problems	18.8
Choice of will trusts: overview	18.9
Best form of will for single testator	18.10
Best form of will for testator who is married or a civil partner	18.11
Married testator: provision for children by will	18.12
The nil rate formula	18.13
Construction of traditional nil rate band formula where transferable NRB applies	18.14

xxiv   Contents in Detail

Terms of classic NRB trust	18.15
Alternatives to nil rate band trusts	18.16
Married testator with business or agricultural property	18.17
Best forms of will making substantial gifts to charity	18.18
Best form of will for foreign domiciled testator	18.19
Best form of will for UK domiciled testator with foreign domiciled spouse	18.20
Existing wills containing a classic NRB trust	18.21

Chapter 19: Administration of Nil Rate Band Trusts

Introduction	19.1
Appropriation of share of family home	19.2
Position if house worth less than nil rate sum	19.3
Trust law issues	19.4
Implementation of debt scheme	19.5
Administration of the NRB trust	19.6
Limitation considerations	19.7
Subsequent sale of property	19.8
Winding up the NRB trust after the death of the spouse	19.9
Tax implications of repayment or release of the debt	19.10

Chapter 20: Wills and care fee planning

Introduction	20.1
Why use will trusts?	20.2
Types of trust	20.3
Assessing liability to pay	20.4
Valuation	20.5
Capital disregards	20.6
Deprivation of capital	20.7
Administration of the will trust after the survivor goes into care	20.8

Chapter 21: Administrative provisions

Introduction	21.1
Unnecessary provisions	21.2
Power to insure	21.3
Power to vary investments	21.4
Power to add powers	21.5
Power to accept additional funds or onerous property	21.6
Powers relating to accounts and audits	21.7
Powers to deal with shares and debentures	21.8
Power to repair and maintain trust property	21.9
Unnecessary forms relating to administrative powers	21.10
Restricting administrative powers to perpetuity period	21.11
"In addition to the statutory powers"	21.12
Trustees entitled to expenses of exercising powers	21.13
Other provisions	21.14
Void powers	21.15
Power to determine questions of fact or law or "matters of doubt"	21.16
Power to make determinations subject to jurisdiction of court	21.17

Power exercisable with consent of court	21.18
Which powers should the drafter include?	21.19
STEP Standard Provisions	21.20
Standard administrative provisions	21.21
Power of investment	21.22–21.23
Power of joint purchase	21.24
General power of management and disposition	21.25
Power to improve trust property	21.26
Provisions relating to the income/capital distinction	21.27
Power to pay capital expenses out of income	21.28
Power to apply trust capital as income	21.29
Rent: income or capital receipt?	21.30
Sinking funds	21.31
Equitable apportionment	21.32
The balance between income and capital	21.33
Demergers	21.34
Occupation and use of trust property	21.35–21.36
Loans to beneficiaries	21.37–21.38
Trust property as security for beneficiaries' liabilities	21.39
Power to trade	21.40
Power to borrow	21.41
Delegation	21.42
Nominees and custodians	21.43
Power to give indemnities	21.44
Power to give security for trustees' liabilities	21.45
Power of appropriation	21.46
Receipt by charities	21.47
Release of rights and powers	21.48
Ancillary powers	21.49
Provisions relating to minors	21.50
Power to retain income of child	21.51
Administrative provision for mentally handicapped beneficiaries	21.52
Power to disclaim	21.53
Statutory apportionment	21.54
Trustee remuneration	21.55
Standard charges and conditions	21.56
Commissions and bank charges	21.57
Excursus: trustee charging clauses	21.58
Layman's work	21.59
Informing the client	21.60
Remuneration of corporate trustee	21.61
Trustee remuneration clause: dispositive or administrative	21.62
Status of remuneration clause for other purposes	21.63
Can the settlor charge if he is a trustee but there is a settlor exclusion clause?	21.64
Trustee/director remuneration	21.65

Chapter 22: Bare trusts
Terminology	22.1
Why use bare trusts?	22.2
Tax advantages	22.3
Non-tax aspects of bare trusts	22.4
Draft bare trust	22.5
Additions to bare trust	22.6

Chapter 23: Trusts of life insurance policies
Introduction	23.1
Insurance company standard form	23.2
Trusts created pursuant to contract of insurance	23.3
Trust created over existing policy	23.4
IHT implications of using a trust	23.5
Ten-year charges and exit charges during lifetime of settlor	23.6
Tax returns	23.7
Advantages of multiple discretionary trusts	23.8
Some drafting points	23.9
Precedent trust for life policy	23.10

Chapter 24: Charitable trusts
Introduction	24.1
Some general comments	24.2
Name	24.3
Trustees	24.4
Exclusion of settlor and non-charitable purposes	24.5
Rule against accumulation	24.6
Administrative provisions for charities	24.7
Trading	24.8
Remuneration of charity trustees	24.9
Procedure after execution of charitable trust	24.10
Charitable will trusts	24.11

Chapter 25: Trusts of damages
Benefit "disregard" of trust of damages	25.1
Trust of damages for adult with mental capacity	25.2
Jurisdiction to transfer child's damages to bare trust	25.3
A precedent bare trust for child	25.4
Consequences of using bare trust	25.5
Creation of a substantive trust of child's damages by compromise	25.6
Trusts for minors: commentary	25.7
Trusts of damages for person lacking mental capacity	25.8
Award under Criminal Injuries Compensation Scheme	25.9

Chapter 26: Trusts for disabled beneficiaries
Mentally handicapped beneficiaries	26.1
Choosing provisions for disabled beneficiaries	26.2
Welfare benefits	26.3
Tax reliefs for disabled beneficiaries	26.4

IHT dependent relative relief	26.5
Actual estate-IP for disabled beneficiary	26.6
Disabled Person Trap	26.7
Actual estate-IP for prospectively disabled settlor	26.8
IHT deemed IP for disabled beneficiary	26.9
IHT deemed IP for prospectively disabled settlor	26.10
CGT full annual allowance	26.11
Mixed trusts	26.12
CGT hold-over relief	26.13
Income tax/CGT transparency: disabled beneficiary	26.14
Drafting requirement	26.15
Income tax/CGT tax transparency: orphan beneficiary	26.16
Effect of income tax/CGT transparency relief	26.17
Disabled beneficiaries: conclusion	26.18
Small funds	26.19
Substantial funds: provision by will	26.20
Substantial funds: lifetime provision	26.21
Commentary	26.22

Chapter 27: Governing law, place of administration and jurisdiction clauses

The governing law	27.1
Selection of English governing law	27.2
Selection of foreign governing law	27.3
Power to change the governing law	27.4
Place of administration of trust	27.5
Exclusive jurisdiction clause	27.6
"Forum of administration"	27.7

Chapter 28: Restricting rights of beneficiaries

Restrictions on disclosure of information	28.1
Disclosure of Will	28.2
Beneficiary's right to trust information	28.3
No named beneficiaries or unascertainable default beneficiary	28.4
Extension of powers of disclosure	28.5
No-contest clauses	28.6
Non-assignment clauses	28.7

Chapter 29: Execution of wills and trust deeds

Review of draft	29.1
Review and approval by parties	29.2
Use and misuse of precedents	29.3
Caution! Word processor at work	29.4
Printing	29.5
Natural decay	29.6
Fraudulent alterations	29.7
Procedure on execution of a lifetime settlement	29.8
(1) Transfers of trust property to trustees	29.9
(2) Statement of wishes	29.10

xxviii   CONTENTS IN DETAIL

(3) Arrangements for payment of IHT on gift in case of death within seven years	29.11
(4) Arrangements for loss of nil rate band in case of death within seven years	29.12
(5) Return and other matters	29.13
Stamp duty and SDLT	29.14
Procedure on execution of a will	29.15
Tax reviews after execution of trust	29.16

Chapter 30: Appointment & retirement of trustees

Powers of appointment/retirement	30.1
Review by new trustees before accepting trusteeship	30.2
Review by appointor and retiring trustees before appointing new trustees or retiring	30.3
Drafting an appointment/retirement of new trustees	30.4
Provisions of deed	30.5
Unnecessary clauses in deed of appointment	30.6
Vesting trust property in new trustees	30.7
Stamp Duty and SDLT	30.8

Chapter 31: Indemnities for executors and trustees

Introduction	31.1
Trust law indemnities	31.2
Right of trustees to retain trust property as security.	31.3
Right of trustee to refuse to retire.	31.4
Right of executors	31.5
Right of former trustees	31.6
Limits on trust law indemnities	31.7
Are express indemnities needed?	31.8
Negotiating indemnities	31.9
Conflicts of interest	31.10
Indemnity from beneficiaries	31.11
Indemnity from new trustees	31.12
Indemnity for breach of trust	31.13
Time limit to indemnity	31.14
Cap on amount payable under indemnity	31.15
Death of new trustee	31.16
Retirement of new trustee	31.17
Multiple trustees	31.18
Security for indemnity	31.19
Proper law and jurisdiction clause	31.20

PART 2 — PRECEDENTS

Precedents for Lifetime Trusts
Interest in possession trust for adult beneficiary
Discretionary trust
Charitable trust

Precedents for Will Trusts
1. Discretionary will trust
2. Life interest for surviving spouse/civil partner
3. Life interest for surviving spouse/civil partner with absolute gift of nil rate sum
4. Life interest for surviving spouse/civil partner with nil rate band discretionary trust
5. Nil rate band discretionary trust; residue to surviving spouse/civil partner absolutely
6. NRB discretionary trust; residue to: (1) surviving spouse/civil partner absolutely (2) discretionary trust (if no surviving spouse/civil partner)
7. NRB discretionary trust; residue to partner (not spouse/civil partner) absolutely

Precedents for Administrative Provisions

Nil Rate Bank discretionary trusts: Supplemental documentation
NRB appointment 1: winding up unwanted NRB trust
NRB appointment 2: reducing gift to NRB trust to untransferable NRB
NRB appropriation and appointment (implementing NRB appropriation scheme)
NRB Spouse Undertaking
NRB Charge over half share of land

Appointments of New Trustees

Settlor appointor
   NT1 Retirement and appointment of new trustee
   NT2 Appointment of new trustee after death of trustee
   NT3 *Appointment of additional trustee* (Companion CD only)
   NT4 *Retirement without appointment of new trustee* (Companion CD only)

Trustees are appointors
   NT5 *Retirement and appointment of new trustee* (Companion CD only)
   NT6 *Appointment of new trustee after death of trustee*(Companion CD only)
   NT7 *Appointment of additional trustee* (Companion CD only)
   NT8 Retirement without appointment of new trustee

Appendix 1: STEP Standard Provisions
Appendix 2: Annotated Bibliography
Appendix 3: Useful Websites
Appendix 4: NRB Debt and charge arrangements: tax analysis
Appendix 5: Tax on payment of index linked nil rate sum
Appendix 6: Share of house in trust: CGT Private Residence Relief
Appendix 7: Definitions of "disabled" for tax purposes
Appendix 8: Notes on the translation of will precedents into Welsh

Index

Instructions on using the Companion CD are on the final page of this book

TABLE OF CASES

AN v Barclays Private Bank & Trust (Cayman) Ltd [2007] W.T.L.R. 565; (2006–07) 9 I.T.E.L.R. 630 Grand Ct (CI) 28.6
ATC (Cayman) Ltd v Rothschild Trust Cayman Ltd [2007] W.T.L.R. 951; (2006–07) 9 I.T.E.L.R. 36 Grand Ct (CI) 31.7, 31.12
Abacus Trust Co (Isle of Man) Ltd v Barr; sub nom. Barr's Settlement Trusts, Re [2003] EWHC 114 (Ch); [2003] Ch. 409; [2003] 2 W.L.R. 1362; [2003] 1 All E.R. 763 Ch D 12.6
Adam & Co International Trustees Ltd v Theodore Goddard (A Firm) [2000] W.T.L.R. 349; (1999–2000) 2 I.T.E.L.R. 634 Ch D 6.37
Agnew v Inland Revenue Commissioner. See Brumark Investments Ltd, Re
Air Jamaica Ltd v Charlton; Air Jamaica Ltd v Clarke; Air Jamaica Ltd v Goodall; Air Jamaica Ltd v Philpotts [1999] 1 W.L.R. 1399; [1999] O.P.L.R. 11 PC (Jam) 13.21
Ali v Lane [2006] EWCA Civ 1532; [2007] 1 P. & C.R. 26; [2007] 1 E.G.L.R. 71 CA (Civ Div) 4.6
Allen v Coster (139) 1 Beav. 202 .... 11.11
Allen v Distillers Co (Biochemicals) Ltd (Payment of Money in Court); Albrice v Distillers Co (Biochemicals) Ltd [1974] Q.B. 384; [1974] 2 W.L.R. 481; [1974] 2 All E.R. 365 QBD 25.3, 25.6
American Leaf Blending Co Sdn Bhd v Director General of Inland Revenue [1979] A.C. 676; [1978] 3 W.L.R. 985; [1978] 3 All E.R. 1185; [1978] S.T.C. 561 PC (Mal) 21.40
Andrews v Partington, 29 E.R. 610; (1791) 3 Bro. C.C. 401 Ct of Chancery 3.22
Anisminic Ltd v Foreign Compensation Commission [1969] 2 A.C. 147; [1969] 2 W.L.R. 163; [1969] 1 All E.R. 208 HL 3.8
Anker-Petersen v Christensen [2002] W.T.L.R. 313 Ch D 29.2
Armitage v Nurse [1998] Ch. 241; [1997] 3 W.L.R. 1046; [1997] 2 All E.R. 705 CA (Civ Div) 6.17, 6.18, 6.25, 6.26
Aspden v Seddon (1874–75) L.R. 10 Ch. App. 394 CA in Chancery 4.10
Aspden (Inspector of Taxes) v Hildesley [1982] 1 W.L.R. 264; [1982] 2 All E.R. 53; [1982] S.T.C. 206; 55 T.C. 609 DC 5.32
Attorney General v Great Eastern Railway Co (1879–80) L.R. 5 App. Cas. 473 HL 21.49
Attorney General v Munby (1816) 1 Merivale 327 .... 13.12
Baden's Deed Trusts (No.1), Re; sub nom. McPhail v Doulton; Baden v Smith (No.1) [1971] A.C. 424; [1970] 2 W.L.R. 1110; [1970] 2 All E.R. 228 HL ... 7.8, 15.11
Baden's Deed Trusts (No.2), Re; sub nom. Pearson v Smith; Baden v Smith (No.2); Baden (No.2), Re [1973] Ch. 9; [1972] 3 W.L.R. 250; [1972] 2 All E.R. 1304 CA (Civ Div) 5.42

Bank of Credit and Commerce International SA (In Liquidation) v Ali (No.1)
  [2001] UKHL 8; [2002] 1 A.C. 251; [2001] 2 W.L.R. 735; [2001] 1 All E.R.
  961 HL 4.2, 4.3, 4.10
Barclays Bank Ltd v Inland Revenue Commissioners [1961] A.C. 509; [1960]
  3 W.L.R. 280; [1960] 2 All E.R. 817 HL 6.11
Barclays Bank Trust Co Ltd v McDougall [2001] W.T.L.R. 23 Ch D 13.25, 13.27
Barr's Trustees v Inland Revenue Commissioners, 25 T.C. 72 .... 13.24
Bartlett v Barclays Bank Trust Co Ltd (No.2) [1980] Ch. 515; [1980] 2 W.L.R.
  430; [1980] 2 All E.R. 92 Ch D 6.21, 6.23, 6.31
Barton (Deceased), Re; sub nom. Tod v Barton [2002] EWHC 264 (Ch); [2002]
  W.T.L.R. 469; (2001–02) 4 I.T.E.L.R. 715 Ch D 27.2
Bassil v Lister, 68 E.R. 464; (1851) 9 Hare 177 QB 15.12, 16.16
Bathurst (Countess) v Kleinwort Benson (Channel Islands) Trustees Ltd; sub nom.
  Wesley v Kleinwort Benson (Channel Islands) Trustees Ltd [2007] W.T.L.R. 959
  Royal Ct (Gue) 28.3
Batty, Re [1952] Ch 250 .... 16.20
Beatty (Deceased), Re; sub nom. Hinves v Brooke [1990] 1 W.L.R. 1503; [1990]
  3 All E.R. 844 Ch D 5.29
Beatty (No.2), Re, Trusts Law International, Vol.11 (1997) 77 .... 6.35
Beautiland Co v Inland Revenue Commissioners [1991] S.T.C. 467 PC (HK) 10.33
Beddoe, Re; sub nom. Downes v Cottam [1893] 1 Ch. 547 CA 6.30
Berry, Re; sub nom. Lloyds Bank v Berry [1962] Ch. 97; [1961] 2 W.L.R. 329;
  [1961] 1 All E.R. 529 Ch D 21.40
Bevan Ashford v Geoff Yeandle (Contractors) Ltd (In Liquidation) [1999] Ch. 239;
  [1998] 3 W.L.R. 172; [1998] 3 All E.R. 238 Ch D 27.3
Blackwell's Settlement Trusts, Re ; sub nom. Blackwell v Blackwell [1952] 2 All
  E.R. 647; [1952] 2 T.L.R. 489 Ch D 16.3
Blandy Jenkins Estate, Re; sub nom. Blandy Jenkins v Walker [1917] 1 Ch. 46
  Ch D 22.1
Bogg v Raper (1998–99) 1 I.T.E.L.R. 267 .... 6.22
Bond (Inspector of Taxes) v Pickford [1983] S.T.C. 517 CA (Civ Div) 11.7
Bonham v Fishwick [2008] EWCA Civ 373; [2008] Pens. L.R. 289; [2008] 2 P. &
  C.R. DG6 CA (Civ Div) 6.30
Bonitto v Fuerst Bros & Co Ltd [1944] A.C. 75 HL 3.16
Bouch, Re; sub nom. Sproule v Bouch (1887) L.R. 12 App. Cas. 385 HL 21.34
Boulton's Settlement Trust, Re; sub nom. Stewart v Boulton [1928] Ch. 703 Ch D ... 14.19
Bradshaw v Pawley [1980] 1 W.L.R. 10; [1979] 3 All E.R. 273 Ch D 10.6
Breadner v Granville-Grossman [2001] Ch. 523; [2001] 2 W.L.R. 593; [2000]
  4 All E.R. 705 Ch D 7.5, 12.6
Breakspear v Ackland [2008] EWHC 220 (Ch); [2008] 2 All E.R. (Comm) 62;
  [2008] W.T.L.R. 777 Ch D 28.3
Brook's Settlement, Re; sub nom. Brook v Brook [1968] 1 W.L.R. 1661; [1968]
  3 All E.R. 416 Ch D 7.22
Brooks v Brooks; sub nom. B v B (Post Nuptial Settlements) (Pension Fund), Re
  [1996] A.C. 375; [1995] 3 W.L.R. 141; [1995] 3 All E.R. 257 HL 5.13
Brown's Estate, Re; sub nom. Brown v Brown [1893] 2 Ch. 300 Ch D 19.7
Browne v Browne [1989] 1 F.L.R. 291; [1989] Fam. Law 147 CA (Civ Div) 5.11
Brumark Investments Ltd, Re; sub nom. Inland Revenue Commissioner v Agnew;
  Agnew v Inland Revenue Commissioner [2001] UKPC 28; [2001] 2 A.C. 710;
  [2001] 3 W.L.R. 454; [2001] Lloyd's Rep. Bank. 251; [2001] B.C.C. 259; [2001]
  2 B.C.L.C. 188 PC (NZ) 10.41
Burden v United Kingdom (13378/05) [2007] S.T.C. 252; [2007] 1 F.C.R. 69
  ECHR 18.10

Burke, Re [1960] O.R. 26; 20 D.L.R. (2d) 396 .... 4.10
Butlin's Settlement Trusts (Rectification), Re; sub nom. Butlin v Butlin
    (Rectification) [1976] Ch. 251; [1976] 2 W.L.R. 547; [1976] 2 All E.R. 483
    Ch D 7.13
C v C (Ancillary Relief: Nuptial Settlement); sub nom. C v C (Financial Provision:
    Post Nuptial Settlements); C v C (Variation of Post Nuptial Settlement) [2004]
    EWCA Civ 1030; [2005] Fam. 250; [2005] 2 W.L.R. 241 CA (Civ Div) 5.13,
    13.12, 27.6
CD (A Child) v O. *See* D (A Child) v O
CI Law Trustees Ltd v Minwalla [2006] W.T.L.R. 807; (2006–07) 9 I.T.E.L.R.
    601 Royal Ct (Jer) 27.6
Cable (Deceased) Will Trusts, Re (Lord) (No.1); sub nom. Garratt v Waters; Lord
    Cable (Deceased), Re [1977] 1 W.L.R. 7; [1976] 3 All E.R. 417 Ch D 27.1, 27.6
Cameron (Deceased), Re; sub nom. Phillips v Cameron [1999] Ch. 386; [1999]
    3 W.L.R. 394; [1999] 2 All E.R. 924 Ch D 11.11, 15.9
Capricorn v Compass [2001] J.L.R. 205 .... 27.6
Carafe Trust, Re; sub nom. Guardian Trust Co Ltd v Louveaux [2006] W.T.L.R.
    1329; (2005–06) 8 I.T.E.L.R. 29; [2005] J.L.R. 159, Royal Ct (Jer) 31.7
Carnarvon's Chesterfield Settled Estates, Re (Earl of); Earl of Carnarvon's
    Highclere Settled Estates, Re [1927] 1 Ch. 138 Ch D 10.44
Carver v Duncan (Inspector of Taxes); Bosanquet v Allen [1985] A.C. 1082;
    [1985] 2 W.L.R. 1010; [1985] 2 All E.R. 645; [1985] S.T.C. 356; 59 T.C. 125
    HL 16.16, 21.28
Chapman's Settlement Trusts, Re; Blackwell's Settlement Trusts, Re; Downshire
    Settled Estates, Re; sub nom. Blackwell v Blackwell; Marquess of Downshire v
    Royal Bank of Scotland; Chapman v Chapman (No.1) [1954] A.C. 429; [1954]
    2 W.L.R. 723; [1954] 1 All E.R. 798 HL 16.3
Chapple, Re; sub nom. Newton v Chapman (1884) L.R. 27 Ch. D. 584 Ch D 21.60
Charalambous v Charalambous. *See* C v C
Charman v Charman [2005] EWCA Civ 1606; [2006] 1 W.L.R. 1053; [2006]
    2 F.L.R. 422 CA (Civ Div) 5.11
Charter Reinsurance Co Ltd (In Liquidation) v Fagan [1997] A.C. 313; [1996]
    2 W.L.R. 726; [1996] 3 All E.R. 46 HL 4.4
Chellaram v Chellaram (No.1) [1985] Ch. 409; [1985] 2 W.L.R. 510; [1985] 1 All
    E.R. 1043 Ch D 7.30, 27.2, 27.5, 27.7
Chellaram v Chellaram (No.2) [2002] EWHC 632 (Ch); [2002] 3 All E.R. 17;
    [2002] W.T.L.R. 675 Ch D 27.2, 27.4
Chen v Ling [2000] H.K.C.F.I. 1356; [2006] T.L.I. 262 .... 7.16
Chester, Re (1978) 19 S.A.S.R. 247 .... 28.6
Chief Commissioner of Stamp Duties (NSW) v Buckle (1998) 192 C.L.R. 226 .... 15.1
Chohan v Saggar [1994] B.C.C. 134; [1994] 1 B.C.L.C. 706; CA (Civ Div) 20.7
Chrimes, Re; sub nom. Locovich v Chrimes [1917] 1 Ch. 30 Ch D 10.8
Churston Settled Estates, Re [1954] Ch. 334; [1954] 2 W.L.R. 386; [1954] 1 All
    E.R. 725 Ch D 7.33
City of London Building Society v Flegg [1988] A.C. 54; [1987] 2 W.L.R. 1266;
    [1987] 3 All E.R. 435 HL 16.15
Clore's Settlement Trusts, Re; sub nom. Sainer v Clore [1966] 1 W.L.R. 955;
    [1966] 2 All E.R. 272; 21 A.L.R.3d 795 Ch D 11.11
Commissioner of Estate and Succession Duties (Barbados) v Bowring [1962] A.C.
    171; [1960] 3 W.L.R. 741; [1960] 3 All E.R. 188 PC (WI) 7.33
Commissioner of Stamp Duties v Bone [1977] A.C. 511; [1976] 2 W.L.R. 968;
    [1976] 2 All E.R. 354; [1976] S.T.C. 145 PC (Aus) 13.25
Coutts v Acworth (No.1) (1869) L.R. 8 Eq. 558 Ct of Chancery 10.48

Cowan v Scargill; sub nom. Mineworkers Pension Scheme Trusts, Re [1985] Ch. 270; [1984] 3 W.L.R. 501; [1984] 2 All E.R. 750 Ch D 21.23
Cowley (Earl) v Inland Revenue Commissioners; sub nom. Earl Cowley's Estate, Re [1899] A.C. 198, HL 3.17
Crowe v Appleby (Inspector of Taxes), 51 T.C. 457 .... 22.4
Customs and Excise Commissioners v Link Housing Association [1992] S.T.C. 718 .. 6.1
D (A Child) v O; sub nom. CD (A Child) v O [2004] EWHC 1036 (Ch); [2004] 3 All E.R. 780; [2004] 3 F.C.R. 195 Ch D 22.4, 25.5
Davis v FCT (2000) 44 A.T.R. 140 .... 10.6
Davis v Richards and Wallington Industries Ltd [1990] 1 W.L.R. 1511; [1991] 2 All E.R. 563 Ch D 6.39, 7.30, 13.21
De Vigier v Inland Revenue Commissioners [1964] 1 W.L.R. 1073; [1964] 2 All E.R. 907; 42 T.C. 25 HL 23.9
Deeny v Gooda Walker Ltd (No.2); Albert v Gooda Walker Ltd; Brownrigg v Gooda Walker Ltd [1996] 1 W.L.R. 426; [1996] 1 All E.R. 933; [1996] S.T.C. 299 HL 4.10
Delamere's Settlement Trusts, Re [1984] 1 W.L.R. 813; [1984] 1 All E.R. 584 CA (Civ Div) 11.3, 14.17
Derry v Peek; sub nom. Peek v Derry (1889) L.R. 14 App. Cas. 337; (1889) 5 T.L.R. 625 HL 6.17
Deutsche Morgan Grenfell Group Plc v Inland Revenue Commissioner; sub nom. Inland Revenue Commissioners v Deutsche Morgan Grenfell Group Plc; Deutsche Morgan Grenfell Group Plc v Revenue and Customs Commissioners [2006] UKHL 49; [2007] 1 A.C. 558; [2006] 3 W.L.R. 781; [2007] 1 All E.R. 449; [2007] S.T.C. 1; 78 T.C. 120 HL 4.6
Dick, Re. See Hume v Lopes
Dilke, Re; Verey v Dilke; sub nom. Dilke's Settlement Trusts, Re [1921] 1 Ch. 34 CA 7.33
Dilworth v Commissioner of Stamps; Dilworth v Commissioner for Land and Income Tax [1899] A.C. 99 PC (NZ) 10.37
DPP v Schildkamp [1971] A.C. 1; [1970] 2 W.L.R. 279; [1969] 3 All E.R. 1640 HL... 3.19
Dive, Re; sub nom. Dive v Roebuck [1909] 1 Ch. 328 Ch D 6.30
Dodwell & Co Ltd's Trust Deed, Re [1979] Ch. 301; [1979] 2 W.L.R. 169; [1978] 3 All E.R. 738 Ch D 15.6
Doe v Gwilum (1833) 5 B. & Ad. 122 .... 4.5.2
Doland's Will Trusts, Re; sub nom. Westminster Bank Ltd v Phillips; Doland, Re [1970] Ch. 267; [1969] 3 W.L.R. 614; [1969] 3 All E.R. 713 Ch D 4.4
Downshire Settled Estates, Re. See Chapman's Settlement Trusts, Re
Dowse v Gorton; sub nom. Gorton, Re [1891] A.C. 190 HL 21.13
Drew, Re; sub nom. Drew v Drew [1899] 1 Ch. 336 Ch D 14.8
Drexel Burnham Lambert UK Pension Plan, Re [1995] 1 W.L.R. 32 Ch D............. 6.16
Dunstan (Inspector of Taxes) v Young Austen & Young; sub nom. Young, Austen & Young v Dunstan [1989] S.T.C. 69; 62 T.C. 448; [1989] B.T.C. 77; (1989) 86(7) L.S.G. 41 CA (Civ Div) 10.37
Dutton v Thompson (1883) L.R. 23 Ch. D. 278 CA 10.48
E v E (Financial Provision) [1990] 2 F.L.R. 233; [1989] F.C.R. 591 .... 5.13
Edge v Pensions Ombudsman [2000] Ch. 602; [2000] 3 W.L.R. 79; [1999] 4 All E.R. 546 CA (Civ Div) 6.16
Edward's Will Trusts, Re; sub nom. Dalgleish v Leighton [1948] Ch. 440; [1948] 1 All E.R. 821 CA 17.13
Eland v Baker (1861) 29 Beav. 137; 54 E.R. 579 .... 7.33
Equity & Law Life Assurance Society Plc v Bodfield Ltd (1987) 54 P. & C.R. 290; [1987] 1 E.G.L.R. 124; (1987) 281 E.G. 1448 CA (Civ Div) 4.10

Esteem Settlement, The [2001] J.L.R. 7 .... 5.6
Esteem Settlement, The [2004] W.T.L.R. 1; [2003] J.L.R. 188 .... 7.30, 19.4
Esterhuizen v Allied Dunbar Assurance Plc [1998] 2 F.L.R. 668; [1998] Fam. Law
    527 QBD 29.15
Evans (Deceased), Re. *See* Evans v Westcombe
Evans v Westcombe; sub nom. Evans (Deceased), Re [1999] 2 All E.R. 777; (1999)
    96(10) L.S.G. 28 Ch D 24.9
Evanturel v Evanturel (1874–75) L.R. 6 P.C. 1 PC (Can) 28.6
Evered, Re; sub nom. Molineux v Evered [1910] 2 Ch. 147 CA 21.48
FJWT-M v CNRT-M [2004] I.E.H.C. 114 .... 5.13
Foster's Policy, Re; sub nom. Menneer v Foster [1966] 1 W.L.R. 222; [1966] 1 All
    E.R. 432 Ch D 23.3
Frankland v Inland Revenue Commissioners [1997] S.T.C. 1450; [1997] B.T.C.
    8045 CA (Civ Div) 18.11
Freeston, Re [1978] Ch 741 .... 16.8
Freke v Lord Carbery; sub nom. Freke v Lord Carberry (1873) L.R. 16 Eq. 461
    Lord Chancellor 27.3
Fuller v Evans [2000] 1 All E.R. 636; [2000] 2 F.L.R. 13 Ch D 13.12
Galmerrow Securities Ltd v National Westminster Bank Plc [2002] W.T.L.R. 125;
    (2000) 14 T.L.I. 158 Ch D 30.2
Gardiner (William), Re; sub nom. Gardiner v Smith [1901] 1 Ch. 697 Ch D 21.48
Gascoigne v Inland Revenue Commissioners, 13 T.C. 573 .... 14.17
Gates, Re [2003] 3 I.T.E.L.R. 113 .... 1.3, 11.11
Gaynor, Re [1960] V.R. 640, Sup.Ct (Vict) 28.6
Gee (Deceased), Re; sub nom. Wood v Staples [1948] Ch. 284; [1948] 1 All E.R.
    498 Ch D 21.65
Geering, Re; sub nom. Gulliver v Geering; Geering's Will Trusts, Re [1964] Ch.
    136; [1962] 3 W.L.R. 1541; [1962] 3 All E.R. 1043 Ch D 3.18
George, Re; sub nom. Francis v Bruce (1890) L.R. 44 Ch. D. 627 Ch D 19.7
George Drexler Ofrex Foundation Trustees v Inland Revenue Commissioners
    [1966] Ch. 675; [1965] 3 W.L.R. 1168; [1965] 3 All E.R. 529; 42 T.C. 524 Ch D .. 5.36
Gibson v South American Stores (Gath & Chaves) Ltd 80869 [1950] Ch. 177;
    [1949] 2 All E.R. 985; 66 T.L.R. (Pt. 1) 83; (1949) 93 S.J. 822 CA 10.37
Gilford Motor Co Ltd v Horne [1933] Ch. 935 CA 7.14
Gisborne v Gisborne (1876–77) L.R. 2 App. Cas. 300 HL 7.10
Glyn v Inland Revenue Commissioners [1948] 2 All E.R. 419; 30 T.C. 321
    KBD 13.12, 13.24
Green v Hoyle [1976] 1 W.L.R. 575; [1976] 2 All E.R. 633 DC 2.11
Green's Will Trusts, Re [1985] 3 All E.R. 455; (1984) 81 L.S.G. 3590 Ch D 9.3
Grunwick Processing Laboratories Ltd v Advisory, Conciliation and Arbitration
    Service (ACAS); sub nom. Advisory, Conciliation and Arbitration Service v
    Grunwick [1978] A.C. 655; [1978] 2 W.L.R. 277; [1978] 1 All E.R. 338 HL 7.5
Gulbenkian's Settlement Trusts (No.1), Re; sub nom. Whishaw v Stephens;
    Hacobian v Maun [1970] A.C. 508; [1968] 3 W.L.R. 1127; [1968] 3 All E.R.
    785 HL 2.3, 3.4, 7.10
Guthrie v Walrond (1883) L.R. 22 Ch. D. 573 Ch D 21.53
HSBC International Trustee Ltd v Wong Kit Wan; sub nom. Circle Trust, Re
    [2007] W.T.L.R. 631; (2006–07) 9 I.T.E.L.R. 676, Grand Ct (CI) 7.29
Hall v Hall; Hall v Hall (1872–73) L.R. 8 Ch. App. 430 CA in Chancery 10.48
Hamblett (Deceased), Re; sub nom. McGowan v Hamblett (2005–06) 8 I.T.E.L.R.
    943 HC (NZ) 18.17
Hambro v Duke of Marlborough [1994] Ch. 158; [1994] 3 W.L.R. 341; [1994]
    3 All E.R. 332 Ch D 7.22

Hampden's Settlement Trusts, Re [1977] T.R. 177; [2001] W.T.L.R. 195 Ch D 11.11, 12.11
Hancock v Watson; sub nom. Hancock, Re; Watson v Watson [1902] A.C. 14 HL... 3.23
Hanlon v Law Society [1981] A.C. 124; [1980] 2 W.L.R. 756; [1980] 2 All E.R. 199 HL 3.2
Harari's Settlement Trusts, Re; sub nom. Wordsworth v Fanshawe [1949] 1 All E.R. 430; [1949] W.N. 79 Ch D 21.22
Harding v Inland Revenue Commissioners [1997] S.T.C. (SCD) 321 .... 18.12
Hardy v Butler [1997] N.P.I.R. 643 .... 5.6
Hargreaves v Hargreaves [1926] P. 42 PDAD 5.13
Harris v Lord Shuttleworth (Trustees of the National & Provincial Building Society Pension Fund) [1994] I.C.R. 991; [1994] I.R.L.R. 547 CA (Civ Div) 7.10
Harrison v Tucker [2003] EWHC 1168 (Ch); [2003] W.T.L.R. 883; (2003) 147 S.J.L.B. 692 Ch D 4.10, 5.2
Hart (Inspector of Taxes) v Briscoe [1979] Ch. 1; [1978] 2 W.L.R. 832; 52 T.C. 53 Ch D 11.6
Hartigan Nominees Pty Ltd v Rydge (1992) 29 N.S.W.L.R. 405 .... 4.12
Harvey, Re [1941] 3 All E.R. 284 .... 21.24
Hastings-Bass (Deceased), Re; sub nom. Hastings-Bass Trustees v Inland Revenue Commissioners [1975] Ch. 25; [1974] 2 W.L.R. 904; [1974] 2 All E.R. 193; [1974] S.T.C. 211; CA (Civ Div) 11.3, 11.11
Hawkesley v May [1956] 1 Q.B. 304; [1955] 3 W.L.R. 569; [1955] 3 All E.R. 353 QBD 5.1
Hay's Settlement Trusts, Re; sub nom. Greig v McGregor [1982] 1 W.L.R. 202; [1981] 3 All E.R. 786 DC 11.5
Hazell v Hammersmith and Fulham LBC [1992] 2 A.C. 1; [1991] 2 W.L.R. 372; [1991] 1 All E.R. 545 HL 7.4
Henry v Armstrong (1880–81) L.R. 18 Ch. D. 668 Ch D 10.48
Hetherington (Deceased), Re; sub nom. Gibbs v McDonnell [1990] Ch. 1; [1989] 2 W.L.R. 1094; [1989] 2 All E.R. 129 Ch D 2.3
Hines v Willans [2002] W.T.L.R. 299 CA (Civ Div) 29.16
Holt's Settlement, Re; sub nom. Wilson v Holt [1969] 1 Ch. 100; [1968] 2 W.L.R. 653; [1968] 1 All E.R. 470 Ch D 1.3
Hooker's Settlement, Re; sub nom. Heron v Public Trustee [1955] Ch. 55; [1954] 3 W.L.R. 606; [1954] 3 All E.R. 321 Ch D 21.19
Hornsby v Playoust [2005] V.S.C. 107 .... 16.8
Hotchkys, Re; sub nom. Freke v Calmady (1886) L.R. 32 Ch. D. 408 CA 21.9
Houston v Burns [1918] A.C. 337 HL 3.2
Howell v Rozenbroek, December 14, 1999 .... 11.11
Hume v Lopes; Hume v Hume-Dick; sub nom. Dick, Re; Lopes v Hume-Dick [1892] A.C. 112 HL 10.41, 21.33
Hunter's Will Trusts, Re; sub nom. Gilks v Harris [1963] Ch. 372; [1962] 3 W.L.R. 1442; [1962] 3 All E.R. 1050 Ch D 11.3, 11.5
Hurlbatt, Re; sub nom. Hurlbatt v Hurlbatt [1910] 2 Ch. 553 Ch D 21.31
Inglewood (Lord) v Inland Revenue Commissioners; sub nom. Baron Inglewood v Inland Revenue Commissioners [1983] 1 W.L.R. 366; [1983] S.T.C. 133 CA (Civ Div) 16.3, 16.20
Ingram v Inland Revenue Commissioners [2000] 1 A.C. 293; [1999] 2 W.L.R. 90; [1999] 1 All E.R. 297; [1999] S.T.C. 37 HL 6.13
Inland Revenue Commissioners v Bernstein [1961] Ch. 399; [1961] 2 W.L.R. 143; [1961] 1 All E.R. 320; 39 T.C. 391 CA 11.8
Inland Revenue Commissioners v Berrill [1981] 1 W.L.R. 1449; [1982] 1 All E.R. 867; [1981] S.T.C. 784; 58 T.C. 429 DC 7.3, 21.51

Inland Revenue Commissioners v Botnar [1999] S.T.C. 711; 72 T.C. 205 CA (Civ Div) 4.12, 6.30, 10.21, 13.13
Inland Revenue Commissioners v Bullock [1976] 1 W.L.R. 1178; [1976] 3 All E.R. 353; [1976] S.T.C. 409; 51 T.C. 522 CA (Civ Div) 18.19
Inland Revenue Commissioners v Gaunt, 24 T.C. 69 .... 5.32
Inland Revenue Commissioners v Hawley, 13 T.C. 327 .... 10.6
Inland Revenue Commissioners v Lactagol, 47 R. & I.T. 397; 35 T.C. 230 .... 13.12
Inland Revenue Commissioners v Lithgows Ltd 1960 S.C. 405; 39 T.C. 270 IH (1 Div) 6.11
Inland Revenue Commissioners v Lloyds Private Banking Ltd [1998] S.T.C. 559; [1999] 1 F.L.R. 147 Ch D 16.2, 16.3, 16.11
Inland Revenue Commissioners v Raphael; Inland Revenue Commissioners v Ezra [1935] A.C. 96 HL 4.5
Inland Revenue Commissioners v Russell, 1955 S.C. 237; 1955 S.L.T. 255; 36 T.C. 83 IH (1 Div) 5.24
Inland Revenue Commissioners v Schroder [1983] S.T.C. 480; 57 T.C. 94 Ch D. 7.29, 7.30, 13.23, 27.4
Inland Revenue Commissioners v Stanley, 26 T.C. 12 .... 14.17
Inland Revenue Commissioners v Tennant, 24 T.C. 215 .... 5.32
Investors Compensation Scheme Ltd v West Bromwich Building Society (No.1); Investors Compensation Scheme Ltd v Hopkin & Sons; Alford v West Bromwich Building Society; Armitage v West Bromwich Building Society [1998] 1 W.L.R. 896; [1998] 1 All E.R. 98 HL 4.2
J v J (Minors) (Financial Provision); sub nom. Jones v Jones; J v J (C intervening) (Minors: Financial Provision) [1989] Fam. 29; [1989] 2 W.L.R. 852; [1989] 1 All E.R. 1121 CA (Civ Div) 5.11
Jackson's Trustees v Inland Revenue Commissioners, 25 T.C. 13 .... 21.29
James v Couchman (1885) L.R. 29 Ch. D. 212 Ch D 10.48
Jasmine Trustees Ltd v Wells & Hind (A Firm) [2007] EWHC 38 (Ch); [2008] Ch. 194; [2007] 3 W.L.R. 810; [2007] 1 All E.R. 1142; [2007] S.T.C. 660 Ch D 6.37
Joicey, Re; sub nom. Joicey v Elliot [1915] 2 Ch. 115 Ch D 11.5
Jones, Re; sub nom. Jones v Jones [1942] Ch. 328 Ch D 17.13
Julius v Lord Bishop of Oxford; sub nom. R. v Bishop of Oxford; Julius v Bishop of Oxford (1879–80) L.R. 5 App. Cas. 214 HL 7.11
K (Enduring Powers of Attorney), Re; F, Re [1988] Ch. 310; [1988] 2 W.L.R. 781; [1988] 1 All E.R. 358 Ch D 21.52
Kane v Radley-Kane; sub nom. Radley-Kane (Deceased), Re [1999] Ch. 274; [1998] 3 W.L.R. 617; [1998] 3 All E.R. 753; Ch D 21.46
Keech v Sandford, 25 E.R. 223; (1726) Sel. Cas. Ch. 61 Ct of Chancery 6.13, 6.14
Kemble v Hicks. *See* Scientific Investment Pension Plan (No.3)
Khoo Tek Keong v Ch'ng Joo Tuan Neoh [1934] A.C. 529 PC (Shanghai) .. 21.22, 21.38
Koonmen v Bender [2007] W.T.L.R. 293; (2003–04) 6 I.T.E.L.R. 568; 4 Butterworths Offshore Trust Cases 774; [2004] T.L.I. 44, CA (Jer) 10.33, 27.6
L Schuler AG v Wickman Machine Tool Sales Ltd; sub nom. Wickman Machine Tool Sales Ltd v L Schuler AG [1974] A.C. 235; [1973] 2 W.L.R. 683; [1973] 2 All E.R. 39 HL 4.5.1
Laing's Settlement, Re; sub nom. Laing v Radcliffe [1899] 1 Ch. 593 Ch D
Lassence v Tierney, 41 E.R. 1379; (1849) 1 Mac. & G. 551 Ct of Chancery 3.23
Latham, Re; sub nom. Inland Revenue Commissioners v Barclays Bank Ltd; Inland Revenue Commissioners v Latham [1962] Ch. 616; [1961] 3 W.L.R. 1154; [1961] 3 All E.R. 903 Ch D 27.1
Leedale (Inspector of Taxes) v Lewis; Toovey v Pepper (Inspector of Taxes); Southall v Pepper (Inspector of Taxes); Pearson (Inspector of Taxes) v Page

[1982] 1 W.L.R. 1319; [1982] 3 All E.R. 808; [1982] S.T.C. 835; 56 T.C. 501 HL 11.5
Leigh's Settlement Trusts, Re; sub nom. Farnsworth v Leigh [2006] W.T.L.R. 477; [2005] T.L.I. 109 Ch D... 11.11
Llewellin's Will Trusts, Re; sub nom. Griffiths v Wilcox [1949] Ch. 225; [1949] 1 All E.R. 487 Ch D 21.65
Lloyds Bank Plc v Duker [1987] 1 W.L.R. 1324; [1987] 3 All E.R. 193 Ch D 22.4
Locke v Camberwell HA [1991] 2 Med. L.R. 249; [2002] Lloyd's Rep. P.N. 23 CA (Civ Div)... 6.30
Locker, Re [1971] 1 W.L.R. 1323 .... 6.19, 7.8
London & County Banking Co v Goddard [1897] 1 Ch. 642 Ch D 7.30, 7.32
London County & Westminster Bank Ltd v Tompkins [1918] 1 K.B. 515 CA...........7.32
London Regional Transport Pension Fund Co Ltd v Hatt [1993] Pens.L.R. 227 .... 6.37, 10.40, 21.42
Lyon's Personal Representatives v Revenue and Customs Commissioners [2007] S.T.C. (S.C.D.) 675; [2007] W.T.L.R. 1257 Sp Comm 5.31
MacArthur (Inspector of Taxes) v Greycoat Estates Mayfair Ltd [1996] S.T.C. 1; 67 T.C. 598 Ch D..3.6
Macfarlane v Inland Revenue Commissioners, 14 T.C. 538.......................................21.41
MacKenzie, Re; sub nom. Bain v MacKenzie [1916] 1 Ch. 125 Ch D......................11.4
Mackie v BCB Trust Co Ltd [2006] W.T.L.R. 1253 Sup Ct (Ber).......................... 21.56
McPhail v Doulton. *See* Baden's Deed Trusts (No.1)
Mallinson's Consolidated Trusts, Re; sub nom. Mallinson v Gooley [1974] 1 W.L.R. 1120; [1974] 2 All E.R. 530; (1974) 118 S.J. 549 Ch D 10.46
Mander v O'Toole [1948] N.Z.L.R. 909; [1948] D.L.R. 445...................................... 5.24
Manisty's Settlement, Re; sub nom. Manisty v Manisty [1974] Ch. 17; [1973] 3 W.L.R. 341; [1973] 2 All E.R. 1203 Ch D.. 5.39
Mannai Investment Co Ltd v Eagle Star Life Assurance Co Ltd [1997] A.C. 749; [1997] 2 W.L.R. 945; [1997] 3 All E.R. 352 HL... 4.7
Marley v Mutual Security Merchant Bank & Trust Co Ltd [1995] C.L.C. 261; [2001] W.T.L.R. 483 PC (Jam) 21.57
Marshall v Cottingham [1982] Ch. 82; [1981] 3 W.L.R. 235; [1981] 3 All E.R. 8 Ch D..3.2
Marshall (Inspector of Taxes) v Kerr [1995] 1 A.C. 148; [1994] 3 W.L.R. 299; [1994] 3 All E.R. 106; [1994] S.T.C. 638; 67 T.C. 81 HL......................................4.13
Marson (Inspector of Taxes) v Morton [1986] 1 W.L.R. 1343; [1986] S.T.C. 463; 59 T.C. 381 Ch D...21.33
Mason v Farbrother [1983] 2 All E.R. 1078 Ch D 21.43
Master's Settlement, Re; sub nom. Master v Master [1911] 1 Ch. 321 Ch D..............11.3
Melville v Inland Revenue Commissioners [2001] EWCA Civ 1247; [2002] 1 W.L.R. 407; [2001] S.T.C. 1271; 74 T.C. 372; [2001] B.T.C. 8039; [2001] W.T.L.R. 887; (2001–02) 4 I.T.E.L.R. 231; [2001] S.T.I. 1106; (2001) 98(37) L.S.G. 39; [2001] N.P.C. 132 CA (Civ Div).. 10.38
Meredith, Re; sub nom. Davies v Davies [1924] 2 Ch. 552, Ch D.............................3.18
Mettoy Pension Trustees Ltd v Evans [1990] 1 W.L.R. 1587; [1991] 2 All E.R. 513 Ch D..7.4
Mewburn's Settlement, Re; sub nom. Perks v Wood [1934] Ch. 112 Ch D...............11.5
Miller v Farmer (1815) 1 Merrivale 55 .... 4.5.1
Miller v Inland Revenue Commissioners [1987] S.T.C. 108 CS 16.5, 16.20
Milner v Milner (1748) Ves. Sen. 1... 4.4
Molyneux v Fletcher [1898] 1 Q.B. 648 QBD 21.16
Morgan Trust Company of the Bahamas Ltd v DW, Butterworths Offshore Service Cases, Vol.2, 31, Sup. Ct (Bahamas) 21.27

Morley-Clarke v Jones (Inspector of Taxes) [1986] Ch. 311; [1985] 3 W.L.R. 749; [1985] 3 All E.R. 193; [1985] S.T.C. 660; 59 T.C. 567 CA (Civ Div) 10.6
Morris, Re; sub nom. Adams v Napier; Morris' Settlement Trusts, Re [1951] 2 All E.R. 528; [1951] W.N. 412 CA..11.5
Mourant v Magnus [2004] J.R.C. 056.. 7.29
Muir v Inland Revenue Commissioners [1966] 1 W.L.R. 1269; [1966] 3 All E.R. 38; 43 T.C. 367 CA 21.48
Murray v Inland Revenue Commissioners, 11 T.C. 133 ....21.41
Naas v Westminster Bank Ltd [1940] A.C. 366 HL 10.5
Nathan v Leonard [2002] EWHC 1701 (Ch); [2003] 1 W.L.R. 827; [2003] 4 All E.R. 198 Ch D 28.6
Nestle v National Westminster Bank Plc [1993] 1 W.L.R. 1260; [1994] 1 All E.R. 118 CA (Civ Div)..21.33
Nicholson, Re; sub nom. Eade v Nicholson [1909] 2 Ch. 111 Ch D........................21.32
Norfolk's Settlement Trusts, Re (Duke of); sub nom. Earl of Perth v Fitzalan-Howard [1982] Ch. 61; [1981] 3 W.L.R. 455; [1981] 3 All E.R. 220 CA (Civ Div)..16.2, 21.63
Orwell's Will Trusts, Re; sub nom. Dixon v Blair [1982] 1 W.L.R. 1337; [1982] 3 All E.R. 177 Ch D..21.60
Osborne v Steel Barrel Co Ltd, 24 T.C. 293 ....12.11
Padmore v Inland Revenue Commissioners [2001] S.T.C. 280; 73 T.C. 470 Ch D 13.11
Paget's Settlement, Re; sub nom. Baillie v De Brossard [1965] 1 W.L.R. 1046; [1965] 1 All E.R. 58 Ch D 27.6
Palmer v Locke (No.1) (1880) L.R. 15 Ch. D. 294 CA................................. 7.32, 11.11
Pappadakis v Pappadakis [2000] W.T.L.R. 719 Ch D.. 23.2
Parker's Trusts, Re [1894] 1 Ch. 707 Ch D 6.34
Pauling's Settlement Trusts (No.1), Re 9; sub nom. Younghusband v Coutts & Co (No.1) [1964] Ch. 303; [1963] 3 W.L.R. 742; [1963] 3 All E.R. 1 CA 6.32, 11.5, 31.4, 31.6
Pearson v Inland Revenue Commissioners; sub nom. Pilkington Trustees v Inland Revenue Commissioners [1981] A.C. 753; [1980] 2 W.L.R. 872; [1980] 2 All E.R. 479; [1980] S.T.C. 318 HL 7.5, 11.3, 16.2, 16.4
Peczenik's Settlement Trusts, Re; sub nom. Cole v Ingram; Peczenik's Settlement, Re [1964] 1 W.L.R. 720; [1964] 2 All E.R. 339 Ch D 21.22
Pedlar v Road Block Gold Mines of India Ltd [1905] 2 Ch. 427 Ch D...................... 4.10
Pennant's Will Trusts, Re; sub nom. Pennant v Rylands [1970] Ch. 75; [1969] 3 W.L.R. 63; [1969] 2 All E.R. 862 Ch D 12.7
Penrose, Re; sub nom. Penrose v Penrose [1933] Ch. 793 Ch D........................6.16, 7.22
Pepper (Inspector of Taxes) v Hart [1993] A.C. 593; [1992] 3 W.L.R. 1032; [1993] 1 All E.R. 42; [1992] S.T.C. 898 HL... 4.2, 4.13
Perpetual Executors and Trustees Association of Australia v Commissioner of Taxes of Australia [1954] A.C. 114; [1954] 2 W.L.R. 171; [1954] 1 All E.R. 339 PC (Aus) 6.2
Perpetual Trust Ltd v Roman Catholic Bishop of the Diocese of Christchurch; sub nom. Armstrong (Deceased), Re (2005–06) 8 I.T.E.L.R. 222 HC (NZ).............. 24.6
Perrin v Morgan; sub nom. Morgan, Re; Morgan v Morgan [1943] A.C. 399 HL 4.2
Peter Clay Discretionary Trust Trustees v Revenue and Customs Commissioners; sub nom. Revenue and Customs Commissioners v Peter Clay Discretionary Trust Trustees [2007] EWHC 2661 (Ch); [2008] 2 W.L.R. 1052; [2008] 2 All E.R. 283; [2008] S.T.C. 928 Ch D.. 21.28
Philean Trust v Taylor [2003] J.L.R. 61 .... 5.22
Philipson-Stow v Inland Revenue Commissioners [1961] A.C. 727; [1960] 3 W.L.R. 1008; [1960] 3 All E.R. 814 HL 27.1

Phillips, Re; Lawrence v Huxtable [1931] 1 Ch. 347 Ch D..7.33
Philpots (Woking) v Surrey Conveyancers [1986] 1 E.G.L.R. 97; (1985) 277 E.G. 61 CA (Civ Div) 4.8
Phipps v Ackers; sub nom. Phipps v Akers, 8 E.R. 539; (1842) 9 Cl. & F. 583 HL... 10.46
Pilkington v Inland Revenue Commissioners; sub nom. Pilkington's Will Trusts, Re; Pilkington v Pilkington [1964] A.C. 612; [1962] 3 W.L.R. 1051; [1962] 3 All E.R. 622; 40 T.C. 416 HL 11.8, 11.11, 21.42
Pope v DRP Nominees Pty Ltd, 74 S.A.S.R. 78; [1999] S.A.S.C. 337 .... 7.30
Pope's Contract, Re [1911] 2 Ch. 442 Ch D...21.4
Portland (Duke of) v Topham; sub nom. Portland v Topham, 11 E.R. 1242; (1864) 11 H.L. Cas. 32 HL... 7.33, 12.15
Power's Will Trusts, Re; sub nom. Public Trustee v Hastings [1947] Ch. 572; [1947] 2 All E.R. 282 Ch D..21.35
Prenn v Simmonds [1971] 1 W.L.R. 1381; [1971] 3 All E.R. 237 HL................. 4.2, 4.6
Prescott (otherwise Fellowes) v Fellowes [1958] P. 260; [1958] 3 W.L.R. 288; [1958] 3 All E.R. 55 CA..5.13
Prinsep v Prinsep (No.1) [1930] P. 35 CA 5.13
Public Trustee v Cooper [2001] W.T.L.R. 901 Ch D 6.16
Public Trustee v Inland Revenue Commissioners [1960] A.C. 398; [1960] 2 W.L.R. 203; [1960] 1 All E.R. 1 HL..3.17
RHB Trust Company v Butlin [1992–93] C.I.L.R. 219 ....5.22
Rank's Settlement Trusts, Re; sub nom. Newton v Rollo [1979] 1 W.L.R. 1242; (1979) 123 S.J. 720 Ch D 11.2
Recher's Will Trusts, Re; sub nom. National Westminster Bank Ltd v National Anti Vivisection Society [1972] Ch. 526; [1971] 3 W.L.R. 321; [1971] 3 All E.R. 401 Ch D 5.36, 5.37
Reddington v Macinnes [2002] ScotCS 46...18.19
Revenue and Customs Commissioners v Peter Clay Discretionary Trust Trustees. *See* Peter Clay Discretionary Trust Trustees v Revenue and Customs Commissioners
Richard v Mackay, Trusts Law International, Vol.11 (1997) 23................................. 6.35
Richardson v FCT (2001) 48 A.T.R. 101; [2001] F.C.A. 1354, Full Federal Court..21.15
Rickman v Carstairs (1833) 5 B. & Ad. 663 .... 4.5.2
Roberts (Deceased), Re; Public Trustee v Roberts [1946] Ch. 1 Ch D 23.9
Rochford's Settlement Trusts, Re; sub nom. Rochford v Rochford [1965] Ch. 111; [1964] 2 W.L.R. 1339; [1964] 2 All E.R. 177 Ch D.. 21.28
Ronbar Enterprises Ltd v Green [1954] 1 W.L.R. 815; [1954] 2 All E.R. 266 CA..21.55
Roome v Edwards (Inspector of Taxes) [1982] A.C. 279; [1981] 2 W.L.R. 268; [1981] 1 All E.R. 736; 54 T.C. 359 HL 11.6
Russell v Inland Revenue Commissioners [1988] 1 W.L.R. 834; [1988] 2 All E.R. 405; [1988] S.T.C. 195 Ch D 16.3, 16.8
Ryan v Liverpool Health Authority [2002] Lloyd's rep. Med, 23............................... 25.1
Rysaffe Trustee Co (CI) Ltd v Inland Revenue Commissioners; sub nom. Rysaffe Trustee Co (CI) Ltd v Customs and Excise Commissioners; Customs and Excise Commissioners v Rysaffe Trustee Co (CI) Ltd [2003] EWCA Civ 356; [2003] S.T.C. 536; [2003] B.T.C. 8021 CA (Civ Div) 23.8
Saunders v Vautier [1835]–42] All E.R. 58; 41 E.R. 482; 49 E.R. 282; (1841) 4 Beav. 115; (1841) Cr. & Ph. 240 Ct of Chancery 5.2, 6.40
Schintz, Re [1951] Ch 870..17.13
Schmidt v Rosewood Trust Ltd; sub nom. Angora Trust, Re; Everest Trust, Re; Rosewood Trust Ltd v Schmidt [2003] UKPC 26; [2003] 2 A.C. 709; [2003] 2 W.L.R. 1442; [2003] 3 All E.R. 76 PC (IoM)................5.39, 6.21, 10.14, 28.3, 28.4

Schuler v Wickman Machine Tool Sales. *See* L Schuler AG v Wickman Machine Tool Sales Ltd
Scientific Investment Pension Plan (No.3); sub nom. Re Kemble v Hicks (No.2) [1999] O.P.L.R. 1; [1999] Pens. L.R. 287 Ch D 24.9
Scott v National Trust for Places of Historic Interest or Natural Beauty [1998] 2 All E.R. 705 Ch D 28.3
Sergeant v National Westminster Bank (1990) 61 P.&C.R. 518 .... 6.14
Sharp v Cash (1879) 10 Ch D 468 .... 6.30
Sharp's Settlement Trusts, Re; sub nom. Ibbotson v Bliss [1973] Ch. 331; [1972] 3 W.L.R. 765; [1972] 3 All E.R. 151Ch D 11.3
Sifton v Sifton [1938] A.C. 656 PC (Can) 28.6
Simpson (Deceased), Re; sub nom. Schaniel v Simpson (1977) 121 S.J. 224 .... 2.2
Sinclair v Lee; sub nom. Lee (Deceased), Re [1993] Ch. 497; [1993] 3 W.L.R. 498; [1993] 3 All E.R. 926 Ch D 21.34
Skeats Settlement, Re (1889) L.R. 42 Ch. D. 522 Ch D 7.29
Skelton v Younghouse [1942] A.C. 571 HL 4.12
Skyparks Group Plc v Marks [2001] EWCA Civ 319; [2001] B.P.I.R. 683; [2001] W.T.L.R. 607, CA (Civ Div) 5.4
Smith, Re; sub nom. Eastwick v Smith [1904] 1 Ch. 139 Ch D 10.40, 20.5
Smith's Estate, Re; sub nom. Bilham v Smith [1937] Ch. 636 Ch D 23.9
Somech, Re; sub nom. Westminster Bank Ltd v Phillips [1957] Ch. 165; [1956] 3 W.L.R. 763; [1956] 3 All E.R. 523Ch D 21.50
Spence v Inland Revenue Commissioners, 24 T.C. 311 .... 10.6
Spencer, Re; sub nom. Lloyds Bank Ltd v Spencer [1935] Ch. 533 Ch D 11.8
Spens v Inland Revenue Commissioners, 46 T.C. 276 .... 21.51
Spurling's Will Trusts, Re; sub nom. Philpot v Philpot [1966] 1 W.L.R. 920; [1966] 1 All E.R. 745 Ch D 31.6
Star, Re, Knieriem v Bermuda Trust Co, Butterworths Offshore Cases Vol.1, 1996, 116 .... 7.29
Stein v Sybmorg Holdings Pty Ltd (2006) 64 A.T.R. 325; 2006 A.T.C. 4741; [2006] N.S.W.S.C. 1004 .... 4.12
Stevenson (Inspector of Taxes) v Wishart [1987] 1 W.L.R. 1204; [1987] 2 All E.R. 428; [1987] S.T.C. 266; 59 T.C. 740 CA (Civ Div) 14.17, 21.29, 21.51
Stirrup's Contract, Re; sub nom. Stirrup v Foel Agricultural Cooperative Society [1961] 1 W.L.R. 449; [1961] 1 All E.R. 805 Ch D 2.3
Stoneham's Settlement Trusts, Re; sub nom. Popkiss v Stoneham [1953] Ch. 59; [1952] 2 All E.R. 694 Ch D 30.4
Stott v Milne (1884) L.R. 25 Ch. D. 710 CA 6.30
Stratton's Disclaimer, Re; sub nom. Stratton v Inland Revenue Commissioners; Stratton's Executors v Inland Revenue Commissioners [1958] Ch. 42; [1957] 3 W.L.R. 199; [1957] 2 All E.R. 594 CA 10.6
Street v Mountford [1985] A.C. 809; [1985] 2 W.L.R. 877; [1985] 2 All E.R. 289 HL 16.3
Suenson-Taylor's Settlement Trusts, Re; sub nom. Moores v Moores [1974] 1 W.L.R. 1280; [1974] 3 All E.R. 397 Ch D 21.41
Sydall v Castings [1967] 1 Q.B. 302; [1966] 3 W.L.R. 1126; [1966] 3 All E.R. 770 CA 5.22
Sykes, Re; sub nom. Sykes v Sykes [1909] 2 Ch. 241 CA 21.60
T, Re [1964] Ch 158 .... 11.11
T v T (Joinder of Third Parties) [1996] 2 F.L.R. 357; [1997] 1 F.C.R. 98 Fam Div ... 27.6
Tankel v Tankel [1999] 1 F.L.R. 676; [1999] Fam. Law 93 Ch D 13.17
Taylor v Allhusen [1905] 1 Ch. 529 Ch D 6.16
Thomas, Re; sub nom. Thomas v Thompson [1930] 1 Ch. 194 Ch D 16.8

xlii TABLE OF CASES

Thompson's Settlement, Re [1986] Ch. 99; [1985] 3 W.L.R. 486; [1985] 3 All E.R. 720 Ch D 6.13, 6.14
Tod v Barton. *See* Barton (Deceased), Re
Triffitt's Settlement, Re; sub nom. Hall v Hyde [1958] Ch. 852; [1958] 2 W.L.R. 927; [1958] 2 All E.R. 299 Ch D 5.39, 7.33
Trow v Ind Coope (West Midlands) Ltd [1967] 2 Q.B. 899; [1967] 3 W.L.R. 633; [1967] 2 All E.R. 900 CA (Civ Div) 3.19
Tuck's Settlement Trusts, Re; sub nom. Public Trustee v Tuck; Tuck (Estate of Sir Adolph) (Deceased), Re [1978] Ch. 49; [1978] 2 W.L.R. 411; [1978] 1 All E.R. 1047 CA (Civ Div) 21.16
Tucker v Bennett (1888) L.R. 38 Ch. D. 1 CA 10.48
Turner's Will Trusts, Re; sub nom. District Bank Ltd v Turner [1937] Ch. 15 CA 21.42
Unit Construction Co Ltd v Bullock (Inspector of Taxes); sub nom. Bullock v Unit Construction Co [1960] A.C. 351; [1959] 3 W.L.R. 1022; [1959] 3 All E.R. 831; 38 T.C. 712 HL 27.5
Upton v National Westminster Bank [2005] EWCA Civ 1479 .... 5.22
Van Straubenzee, Re; sub nom. Boustead v Cooper [1901] 2 Ch. 779 Ch D 21.32
Vandervell's Trusts (No.1), Re; sub nom. White v Vandervell Trustees [1971] A.C. 912; [1970] 3 W.L.R. 452; [1970] 3 All E.R. 16; 46 T.C. 341 HL 2.3
Vestey v Inland Revenue Commissioners. 31 T.C. 1 .... 5.32, 13.16
Vickery, Re; sub nom. Vickery v Stephens [1931] 1 Ch. 572; [1931] All E.R. Rep. 562 Ch D 6.17
Vine v Raleigh (No.2) [1891] 2 Ch. 13 CA 21.26
Virani v Guernsey International Trustees Ltd 31.7
Von Brockdorff v Malcolm (1885) L.R. 30 Ch. D. 172 Ch D 16.1
Waddington v O'Callaghan, 16 T.C. 187 .... 10.6
Walker v Stones [2001] Q.B. 902; [2001] 2 W.L.R. 623; [2000] 4 All E.R. 412 CA (Civ Div) 6.17, 6.18, 6.20
Ward, Re; Public Trustee v Ward [1941] Ch. 308 CA 6.18
Watson v Holland (Inspector of Taxes) [1985] 1 All E.R. 290; [1984] S.T.C. 372 Ch D 3.23
Watts, Re; sub nom. Coffey v Watts [1931] 2 Ch. 302 Ch D 7.33
Webb v Jonas (1888) L.R. 39 Ch. D. 660 Ch D 21.24
Weightman's Settlement, Re; sub nom. Astle v Wainwright [1915] 2 Ch. 205 Ch D 11.5
Wellman, Re [2001] J.L.R. 218 .... 11.3
Wellsted's Will Trusts, Re; sub nom. Wellsted v Hanson [1949] Ch. 296; [1949] 1 All E.R. 577 CA 7.4
Wendt v Orr (Costs) [2004] WASC; [2005] W.T.L.R. 423; Sup Ct (WA) (Sgl judge) 21.15
West (Inspector of Taxes) v Trennery; sub nom. Tee v Inspector of Taxes; Trennery v West (Inspector of Taxes) ....
 [2005] UKHL 5; [2005] 1 All E.R. 827; [2005] S.T.C. 214; 76 T.C. 713 HL 13.12, 13.13
Westdeutsche Landesbank Girozentrale v Islington LBC; Kleinwort Benson Ltd v Sandwell BC; sub nom. Islington LBC v Westdeutsche Landesbank Girozentrale [1996] A.C. 669; [1996] 2 W.L.R. 802; [1996] 2 All E.R. 961 HL 13.21
Weston's Settlements, Re; sub nom. Weston v Weston [1969] 1 Ch. 223; [1968] 3 W.L.R. 786; [1968] 3 All E.R. 338 CA (Civ Div) 5.1
Whitehead's Will Trusts, Re; sub nom. Burke v Burke [1971] 1 W.L.R. 833; [1971] 2 All E.R. 1334 Ch D 6.35
Wight v Olswang (No.1) (1998–99) 1 I.T.E.L.R. 783; [1998] N.P.C. 111 CA (Civ

Div)	6.8, 6.18, 6.19
Wills Trust Deeds, Re; sub nom. Wills v Godfrey [1964] Ch. 219; [1963] 2 W.L.R. 1318; [1963] 1 All E.R. 390 Ch D	11.5, 12.5, 21.48
Wills Will Trusts, Re; sub nom. Wills v Wills [1959] Ch. 1; [1958] 3 W.L.R. 101; [1958] 2 All E.R. 472 Ch D	11.8, 11.11
Wilson v First County Trust Ltd (No.2); sub nom. Wilson v Secretary of State for Trade and Industry [2003] UKHL 40; [2004] 1 A.C. 816; [2003] 3 W.L.R. 568; [2003] 4 All E.R. 97 HL	4.13
Wilson (Inspector of Taxes) v Clayton [2004] EWCA Civ 1657; [2005] S.T.C. 157; 77 T.C. 1 CA (Civ Div)	13.12
Wolff v Wolff [2004] EWHC 2110 (Ch); [2004] S.T.C. 1633; [2004] W.T.L.R. 1349 Ch D	2.1
Wollaston v Tribe (1869–70) L.R. 9 Eq. 44 Ct of Chancery	10.48
Worsley v Worsley (1865–69) L.R. 1 P. & D. 648 Divorce Ct	5.13
Wynn's Will Trusts, Re (No.1); sub nom. Public Trustee v Baron Newborough [1952] Ch. 271; [1952] 1 All E.R. 341 Ch D	21.15, 21.17, 28.6
X v A [2000] 1 All E.R. 490; [2000] Env. L.R. 104 Ch D	7.18, 31.3
Young v Hansen, NZCA September 16, 2003	6.26
Yudt v Leonard Ross & Craig (A Firm), July 24, 1998, Ch	30.4
Yukong Line Ltd of Korea v Rendsburg Investments Corp of Liberia (The Rialto) [1998] 1 W.L.R. 294; [1998] 4 All E.R. 82 QBD (Comm)	7.14
Z, Re [1998] C.I.L.R. 248	6.16

TABLE OF STATUTES

Administration of Estates Act 1925 (15 & 16 Geo.5 c.23)
s.33 .... 6.19
s.39(1) 21.41
s.41 .... 3.20, 7.23, 21.46
s.46 .... 14.3
    (2) 14.3
s.47(1)(i) 5.17
    (ii) 11.8
    (iii) 6.19
    (iv) 21.38
s.48 .... 5.30
s.55 .... 3.20
Administration of Justice Act 1982 (c.53)
s.19 .... 5.20
s.20 .... 4.9
    (3) 6.28
Administration of Justice Act 1985 (c.61)
s.48 .... 6.30
Adoption and Children Act 2002 (c.38)
s.67(2) 5.23
Agricultural Holdings Act 1986 (c.5)
s.7 .... 21.20
Apportionment Act 1870 (33 & 34 Vict. c.35)
s.7 .... 21.54
Charities Act 1993 (c.10)
s.3(3) 24.3
s.6 .... 24.3
s.29 .... 6.30
s.73A 24.9
    (2)—(6) 24.9
    (7)(a) 24.9
s.73F 24.9
    (4) 24.9
    (5) 24.9
s.74F(2) 24.9
s.83 .... 24.4

Charities Act 2006 (c.50)
s.1 .... 5.36, 24.2
Children Act 1989 (c.41)
s.3 .... 25.5
    (3) 21.50
Civil Partnership Act 2004 (c.33)
s.212 .... 5.30
s.246 .... 5.24
Sch.5 para.7 .... 5.13
Common Law Procedure Amendment (Ireland) Act 1853 (16 & 17 Vict. c.113)
s.56 .... 3.1
Companies Act 1985 (c.6)
s.192 .... 7.4
Companies Act 2006 (c.46)
s.31(1) 21.39, 21.49
s.44 .... 10.29
    (6) 10.29
ss.44—48 .... 10.29
s.232 .... 6.26
s.750 .... 7.4
Conveyancing and Law of Property Act 1881 (44 & 45 Vict.)
s.43(1) 3.6
Sch.3 .... 3.1
Sch.4 .... 3.1
Copyright, Designs and Patents Act 1988 (c.48)
s.304 .... 27.1
Criminal Injuries Compensation Act 1995 (c.53)
s.3(1)(d) 25.9
Enduring Powers of Attorney Act 1985 (c.29)
s.3 .... 7.14
    (3) 21.42
Family Law Act 1996 (c.27)
Pt IV 5.13

Family Law Reform Act 1969 (c.46)
  s.12 .... 3.18
  s.15 .... 5.22
  s.17 .... 6.29
Family Law Reform Act 1987 (c.42)
  s.1 .... 5.22
  s.19 .... 5.22
  s.20 .... 6.29
Finance Act 1894 (57 & 58 Vict. c.30)
  s.2 .... 3.17
Finance Act 1940 (3 & 4 Geo.4 c.29)
  s.40 .... 6.3
  s.58(5) 6.3
Finance Act 1949 (12, 13 & 14 Geo.6 c.47)
  s.22 .... 27.1
Finance Act 1950 (14 Geo.6 c.15)
  s.44(2) 11.8
Finance Act 1984 (c.43)
  Sch.13 para.10(2) 3.4
Finance Act 1985 (c.54)
  s.85 .... 29.14
Finance Act 1986 (c.41)
  s.102 .... 6.2, 13.1, 13.18
  s.102A(4) 3.8
  s.103 .... 13.19, 19.2, 19.5
  Sch.20 ....
  3.18 ....
Finance Act 1989 (c.26)
  s.151 .... 30.2
Finance Act 1999 (c.16)
  Sch.13 para.7 .... 3.6
      para.16 .... 29.14
      para.17 .... 29.14
Finance Act 2000 (c.17)
  s.46 .... 24.8
Finance Act 2003 (c.14)
  s.53 .... 29.14
  s.54 .... 29.14
  s.77 .... 29.14
  s.125(1) 29.14
  Sch.3 para.3A 19.3
  Sch.16 para.5 .... 30.4
Finance Act 2005 (c.7)
  s.25 .... 26.17
  ss.26—32 .... 26.17
  s.34 .... 26.15
  s.35 .... 26.16
  s.37 .... 26.14
  s.38 .... 26.14
Finance Act 2008 (c.9)
  s.99 .... 29.14
  s.100 .... 29.14

Sch.32 .... 29.14
Financial Services Act 1986 (c.60)
  s.84 .... 7.4
Financial Services and Markets Act 2000 (c.8)
  s.253 .... 6.26
Fines and Recoveries Act 1833 (3 & 4 Will.4 c.74)
  s.36 .... 7.33
Gender Recognition Act 2004 (c.7)
  s.9 5,27
Health and Social Care Act 2001 (c.15)
  s.55 .... 20.5
Human Fertilisation and Embryology Act 1990 (c.37)
  ss.27—29 .... 5.25
  s.28 .... 5.25
  s.30 .... 5.25, 5.26
Income and Corporation Taxes Act 1988 (c.1)
  Pt IX 21.41
  s.213(3) 21.34
  s.279 .... 3.17
  s.343 .... 10.35
  s.698(3) 7.4
Income Tax Act 2007 (c.3)
  s.479 .... 16.2, 21.51, 21.54
  s.480 .... 7.4
  s.484 .... 16.2
  s.496 .... 14.16, 21.29, 21.51
  s.720 .... 13.19
  s.809M 5.51
  ss.811—812 .... 5.51
  s.812(2)—(5) 5.18
      (4) 7.4
  s.989 .... 5.36
Income Tax (Trading and Other Income) Act 2005 (c.5)
  s.538 .... 31.10
  s.624 .... 13.1, 24.5
  s.625(4) 5.32
  s.626 .... 13.2
  s.629 .... 21.51
  s.633 .... 13.19
  s.646 .... 31.10
Inheritance (Provision for Family and Dependants) Act 1975 (c.63)
  s.1 .... 5.42
  s.2(1)(f) 5.12
      (g) 5.12
Inheritance Tax Act 1984 (c.51) ....
  Ch.3 Pt 3 .... 17.1
  s.3(3) 22.4

s.3A	26.9
s.8A	18.2, 18.5, 18.6, 18.13
(2)	18.14
(3)	18.5, 18.6
(6)(a)	18.14
(7)	18.13
s.8B	18.6
(2)	18.7
s.11(3)	26.5
(6)	26.5
s.15	16.13
s.18	5.28, 18.11
(2)	18.11
s.21	23.5
s.39A	18.17
s.43	22.1
s.44	1.4
s.49A	17.1, 17.3
(2)	17.3
(3)	17.3
(5)	17.3
s.50	16.19
s.52(3A)(b)	26.6
s.58	17.1
s.60	23.8
s.62	23.8
s.64	19.6
s.65	19.9
(5)	16.2
s.66(4)(c)	23.8
s.67	23.5
s.71	3.13, 16.18
(1)	16.22
s.71A	16.18, 17.1, 17.8
s.71D	16.18, 17.1, 17.6
(6)	17.6
s.80	18.15
s.83	19.6
s.86	5.44
(1)(b)	5.42
s.88	5.3
s.89	26.9
(2)	26.9
(4)	26.6
s.89A	26.8
s.89B(1)(c)	26.6
(2)	26.6
s.90	21.63
s.92	17.12
s.93	21.53
s.112	18.17
s.113A	8.7, 31.9
s.124A	8.7, 31.9
s.142	10.6, 17.5
(5)	21.53
s.143	18.12
s.144	17.3, 17.5, 18.8, 18.10, 18.17, 18.20, 18.21, 19.2
(1)	18.11
(3)	17.6, 18.11
s.167	23.6
s.199	29.11
(1)	29.11
(c)	29.11
(d)	29.11
s.204(8)	10.47, 28.11
s.205	29.11
s.212	21.41, 28.11
s.216	29.13
s.218	29.13
s.245	23.7
s.272	10.36
Sch.4 para.2	7.14

Insolvency Act 1986 (c.45)
s.88	8.2
s.127	8.2
s.178	21.6
s.190(2)	3.5
s.283(4)	7.22
s.307	5.6
s.310	5.6
s.423(3)	20.7
Sch.1 para.23	21.49

Interpretation Act 1978 (c.30)
s.12	7.7
s.17	5.22, 16.19
s.23	16.19
Sch.1	5.22

Intestates' Estates Act 1952 (15 & 16 Geo.4 & 1 Eliz.2 c.64)
Sch.2 para.5(1)	6.14

Law of Property Act 1925 (15 & 16 Geo.5 c.20)
s.21	6.32, 21.50
s.25(2)	7.11
s.26(3)	7.18
s.27(2)	6.1
s.28	21.30
(4)	3.18
s.29	21.42
s.34	6.1
(2)	6.1
s.36	20.5
s.53	16.11
(1)(c)	10.13
s.57	10.3

s.61 .... 3.14, 10.44	Pensions Act 1995 (c.26)
(c) 15.4	s.22 .... 6.14
s.109(5) 7.32	s.23 .... 6.14
s.155 .... 21.48	s.33 .... 6.26
s.158 .... 11.3, 15.4	s.34 .... 21.22
s.164 .... 15.6	s.39 .... 6.14
s.179 .... 21.20	Perpetuities and Accumulations Act
s.188 .... 21.46	1964 (c.55)
s.205(1)(xii) 10.37	s.1 .... 9.3, 9.5, 12.5
Sch.3 .... 2.7	s.3 .... 9.8
Form 1 .... 3.3	(5) 11.3
Sch.4 .... 2.7	s.4(4) 3.17
Sch.5 .... 2.7, 3.1	s.8 .... 9.6, 16.2, 21.63
Law of Property (Amendment) Act	(1) 21.11
1926 (16 & 17 Geo.5 c.11)	s.13 .... 15.6
s.3 .... 7.14	s.15 .... 10.36
Law of Property (Miscellaneous	(4) 9.3
Provisions) Act 1989 (c.34)	Powers of Attorney Act 1971 (c.27)
s.1 .... 10.29	s.4 .... 7.31
Legal Services Act 2007 (c.29)	s.10 .... 21.42
s.13 .... 2.11	Public Trustee Act 1906 (6 Edw.7 c.55)
s.14 .... 2.11	s.4 .... 6.9
s.16 .... 2.11	(2)(h) 6.30
Sch.2 para.5 .... 2.11	School Standards and Framework Act
Limitation Act 1980 (c.58)	1998 (c.31)
s.6 .... 19.7	Sch.11 para.6 .... 21.55
s.8 .... 19.7	Settled Land Act 1882 (45 & 46 Vict.
s.29(5) 19.7	c.38)
Local Government Act 1972 (c.70)	s.55(1) 7.7
s.111 .... 21.49	Settled Land Act 1925 (15 & 16 Geo.5
Married Woman's Property Act 1882	c.18)
(45 & 46 Vict. c.75)	s.20 .... 10.44
s.11 .... 21.20, 23.2	s.29(1) 3.5
Matrimonial Causes Act 1859 (22 &	s.30(3) 6.34
23 Vict.)	s.39(2) 15.5
s.5 .... 5.13	s.47 .... 14.19, 16.2, 21.30
Matrimonial Causes Act 1973 (c.18)	s.55 .... 16.2, 16.3
s.24(1)(c)—(d) 5.12	s.64 .... 21.25
s.25 .... 5.11	s.66 .... 14.19, 16.2
s.34(1) 28.6	s.68 .... 6.14
Mental Capacity Act 2005 (c.9)	s.71 .... 21.41
s.2 .... 21.52	s.84(2) 21.26
s.3 .... 21.52	(a) 21.26
s.12 .... 5.36	s.94 .... 10.39
s.16 .... 25.8	s.95 .... 21.47
s.18(h) 25.8	s.102(3) 7.7
s.20(1) 29.15	s.105(1) 3.5
s.64 .... 7.14	Sch.1 .... 2.7
National Assistance Act 1948 (11 & 12	Form 1 .... 6.34
Geo.6 c.29)	Form, 2 .... 6.34
s.22(4) 20.4	Solicitors Act 1974 (c.47)
National Heritage Act 1983 (c.47)	s.22 .... 2.11
s.33(5)(d) 21.49	(1) 2.11

(2)	2.11
(2A)	2.11
(3)	2.11
s.90(4)	2.11

Solicitors (Scotland) Act 1980 (c.46)

s.32	2.11

Stamp Act 1891(54 & 55 Vict. c.39)

s.59(1)	3.6

Supreme Court Act 1981 (c.54)

s.114(1)	6.1
s.124	28.2

Supreme Court of Judicature Act 1875 (38 & 39 Vict. c.77)

Sch.1 Ord.19 r.4	3.9

Taxation of Chargeable Gains Act 1992 (c.12)

s.5	16.21
s.60	22.1
s.62	18.11
s.69(2)	7.14
s.71	11.7, 12.6, 16.8, 18.11
(1)	14.16
s.72	17.4
s.73	17.4
s.77	13.1
s.78	31.9
s.82	30.4
s.86	5.51, 13.1
s.163	3.13
s.168(7)	31.9
s.169B	13.2, 26.13
s.169C(2)(b)	13.2
s.169D	26.13
s.169F	13.22
s.169J	5.51
s.225	19.8
s.260	16.8, 17.7
s.274	18.6
Sch.1 para.1(1)	26.11
(6)	26.11
Sch.5 para.6	27.4, 31.10
para.9(3)	16.2
(10C)	5.18
Sch.5A	29.13
Sch.5B para.17	5.18, 5.51

Taxes Management Act 1970 (c.9)

s.4	6.30

Trustee Act 1925 (15 & 16 Geo.5 c.19)

s.1	10.41
s.3	7.11
s.10	6.21, 21.8
(3)	21.8
s.11	21.42
s.14	6.1, 21.47
s.15	7.11, 21.49, 31.12
(b)	21.2, 21.24, 21.46
(f)	31.12
s.16	11.8
(1)	21.41
s.18	7.4, 10.40
s.19	21.3
(5)	21.28
s.22(3)	18.13, 21.16, 21.46
(4)	21.7, 21.28
s.23(1)	21.13
(2)	21.42
s.25	7.4, 21.42, 21.42
s.26(1)	21.45
s.27	6.29, 24.9
(2)	7.4
s.28(3)	24.9
s.30(1)	6.17
s.31	3.6, 3.20, 7.4, 7.11, 10.46, 11.5, 14.3, 14.17, 15.9, 21.29
(2)	15.5
(i)	5.17, 21.50
s.32	3.17, 3.20, 7.7, 7.11, 7.33, 11.5, 11.8, 11.8, 22.4, 25.4
(1)	22.4
(a)	11.8
(c)	7.23, 7.24
s.33	5.3, 5.20, 7.11, 21.20, 26.15
(1)(ii)	5.7, 7.11, 15.4
s.34(2)	6.1, 6.11
s.36	30.4, 31.4
(1)	3.18, 6.34, 6.37, 6.38, 30.1, 30.4, 30.5
(a)	3.14, 6.35, 30.4
(b)	6.34, 30.4
(2)	7.30
(6)	6.34, 6.35, 6.38, 30.1, 30.5
(7)	7.4, 10.40
(8)	6.34
(9)	7.4, 14.2
(10)	31.5
s.37(1)(b)	11.4
(c)	6.37
(d)	30.4, 30.6
s.39	3.18, 6.37, 30.1, 30.4, 30.5
s.40	7.31, 23.4, 30.7
s.41	3.5
s.42	21.55
s.57	11.9, 16.2, 16.8, 21.24, 21.25, 21.43, 21.46
s.61	6.28, 21.48
s.63(2)	21.47

Table of Statutes

s.64(2) 6.34
s.68(13) 21.8
    (17) 6.34, 31.2
s.69(2) 7.4, 21.12
Trustee Act 2000 (c.29)
  s.1 ....6.21, 6.27, 6.28
    (1) 18.13
  s.3 .... 15.5, 21.22
  s.4(3)(a) 21.23
    (b) 21.22
  s.5 ....21.23
  s.8 .... 21.35, 21.38
    (1) 21.41
    (3) 16.2
  s.11 ....21.42
    (2)(a) 16.2
  ss.12—15 ....21.42
  s.15 ....21.42
  ss.16—20 ....21.43
  s.28 .... 6.1, 24.9
    (2) 21.59, 21.62
  s.29(1) 21.55
    (2) 21.55
    (3) 21.55
  s.30 ....24.9
  s.31 .... 13.12, 21.13, 21.28, 31.2
  s.39(1) 21.28
  Sch.1 para.7 .... 6.22
Trustee Investments Act 1961 (9 & 10 Eliz.2 c.62)
  s.1 .... 10.41
    (1) 21.4
  s.2(4) 7.4
  s.5 ....21.16
Trusts of Land and Appointment of Trustees Act 1996 (c.47)
  s.2 .... 3.28

s.4 ....21.35
s.6 .... 6.21
  (1) 21.25, 21.26, 21.31
s.7 ....21.46
  (5) 3.18
s.8 ....21.35
s.9 .... 6.3, 14.2, 21.42
s.11 ... 6.14, 7.18, 12.4, 14.2, 21.35, 23.10
s.12 .... 14.2, 21.35, 21.35
  (1) 20.5
    (a) 20.5
    (b) 20.5
s.13 ....21.35
s.19 .... 6.40
s.20 .... 6.40
s.22 ....5.18
Sch.3 .... 6.37, 7.4
Trusts (Scotland) Act 1921 (11 & 12 Geo.5 c.58)
  s.3 .... 6.39
  s.4(1)(m) 16.13
Value Added Tax Act 1994 (c.23)
  s.89(2) 3.8
  s.96 ....10.36
    (10) 3.19
Welsh Language Act 1976
  s.4 ....27.2
Wills Act 1837 (7 Will.4 & 1 Vict. c.26)
  s.1 ....10.36
  s.9 .... 17.10, 17.13
  s.15 ....16.2
  s.24 .... 17.13, 18.14
  s.33 ....5.20, 21.20

TABLE OF NATIONAL (NON-UK) STATUTES

Bahamas
Trusts (Choice of Governing Law) Act 1989
   s.4 ....
   27.3 ....

Bermuda
Trustee Act 1975
   s.24 .... 27.4

Cayman Islands
Legal Practitioners Law (2003 Revision)
   s.10 .... 2.11
   Trusts Law (2001 Revision)
   s.89(3) 27.7

Guernsey
Trusts (Guernsey) Law 1989
   art.33 .... 28.3

Jersey
Trusts (Jersey) Law 1984
   art.5(d) 27.5

   art.19 .... 6.39
   art.25 .... 21.42
   art.38 .... 15.5
     (5) 27.4

Liechtenstein
Personen und Gesellschaftrecht
   art.910 para.5 .... 27.4
   art.932a para.165 .... 27.4

South Africa
Trust of Property Control Act
   s.9 .... 6.26

United States of America
US Uniform Trust Code
   s.412(a) 27.4
   s.416 .... 27.4

TABLE OF ABBREVIATIONS

Statutes and Statutory Instruments

AEA:	Administration of Estates Act 1925
FA:	Finance Act
ICTA:	Income and Corporation Taxes Act 1988
IHTA:	Inheritance Tax Act 1984
ITTOIA:	Income Tax (Trading and Other Income) Act 2005
LPA:	Law of Property Act 1925
NAARR:	National Assistance (Assessment of Resources) Regulations 1992
PAA:	Perpetuities and Accumulations Act 1964
SLA:	Settled Land Act 1925
TA:	Trustee Act
TCGA:	Taxation of Chargeable Gains Act 1992
TLATA:	Trusts of Land and Appointment of Trustees Act 1996

Periodicals

BTR:	British Tax Review
LQR:	Law Quarterly Review
OITR:	Offshore & International Taxation Review (formerly OTPR)
OTPR:	Offshore Tax Planning Review[1]
PCB:	Private Client Business
PTPR:	Personal Tax Planning Review
TLI:	Trust Law International
WTLR:	Wills and Trusts Law Reports

---

[1] Renamed "Offshore Taxation Review" in 1997 and renamed (again) as OITR in 1999.

Other

A&M:	Accumulation and Maintenance
CGT:	Capital Gains Tax
CP:	Civil partner
IHT:	Inheritance Tax
IP:	Interest in Possession
IPDI:	Immediate post-death interest
NRB:	Nil rate band
PET:	Potentially Exempt Transfer
SDLT:	Stamp Duty Land Tax
SP:	Statement of Practice

An italic font is used to set out forms discussed but not adopted as precedents in this book; ordinary print is used for forms approved and adopted as precedents

TRUST TERMINOLOGY

Settlement

In general usage the word "settlement" describes the situation in which property is held in trust for a succession of interests, or the disposition creating that situation.[1]

In the Income Tax settlement provisions[2] (and other provisions which copy them), the term "settlement" is given an artificial meaning and includes any "arrangement". It is unfortunate that the Parliamentary Counsel used the word "settlement" as a label for this concept. The word "settlement" does not bear this wide meaning unless that is indicated.[3]

"Trust" and "settlement"

In general contemporary usage the term "trust" is used with exactly the same meaning as "settlement".[4]

---

[1] The statutory definitions of s.69 TCGA 1992 and s.43 IHTA 1984 correspond closely to this geeral sense. The word "settlement" is not a term of art, with one specific and precise meaning. Its meaning depends on the context in which it is being used; *Brooks v Brooks* [1996] AC 375 at 391. However this is also true of virtually all terminology relating to the law of trusts or anything else.

[2] Chapter 5 Part V ITTOIA

[3] Section 620 ITTOIA 2005. The criticism made by Lord Upjohn in relation to s.709 ICTA 1988 definitions applies here also: "They cannot possible be described as definition clauses; they are 'artificial inclusion' clauses. I say 'artificial' because the draftsman has paid no attention to the proper use of language . . ." *IRC v Cleary* 44 TC 399 at 428.

[4] e.g. s.69 TCGA 1992 where the usage varies between subsections (1) and (2). An even more striking example was s.5(2) TCGA 1992 (repealed) ("a trust is an accumulation or discretionary settlement where . . .").

The word "settlement" in the 1925 legislation means a Settled Land Act settlement, not any other kind of trust. But this is by virtue of a statutory definition of "settlement" so one cannot on that basis infer that the general usage is incorrect.

In some offshore jurisdictions, the word "trust" seems to be preferred to the exclusion of the word "settlement". This trend seems to be adopted in modern statutory drafting, such as the Trustee Act 2000.

Two doubtful linguistic distinctions

Sometimes a distinction is drawn under which the term "settlement" is used to refer to a settlement for the purposes of the (obsolescent) Settled Land Act 1925; anything else is referred to as a "trust".[5] But the distinction is "one sided": while a Settled Land Act settlement is properly called a "settlement" (not a "trust")[6] the word "settlement" is used indiscriminately, and refers to all settlements whether or not governed by the Settled Land Act. Therefore, if one needs to draw a distinction between the two, some more specific expression should be used.

Sometimes a distinction is drawn under which the term "trust" is used to refer to will trusts; and "settlement" refers to lifetime settlements. But this distinction is not firmly established and is not recommended.

"Trust" and "estate of deceased person"

The legal and equitable interest in the estate of a deceased person vests in the executors until the estate is administered and so an unadministered estate is not a "trust" if "trust" is understood to mean a situation where there is a separation of legal and equitable interests.[7] See *Commissioner of Stamp Duties (Queensland) v Livingston* [1965] AC 694. Executors are nevertheless often said to hold property on "trust" and the word "trust" is often used to refer to the way in which executors hold property in an estate. This usage is so common both in statutes[8] and in law reports[9] it cannot be described as improper or even loose language; it might perhaps be described as a non-technical usage.

Other usage of "trust"

"Trust" is also used as a synonym of "duty". This usage is confusing and best avoided.[10]

---

[5] e.g. the headnote of s.2 TLATA 1996 (abolishing SLA Settlements) reads: "Trusts in place of Settlements".
[6] Because this is the usage of the SLA 1925 itself.
[7] There is a debate between Lord Nicholls and Lord Millett whether the situation where legal and equitable interests are separated should always be described as a trust; see Millett, "Restitution and Constructive Trusts" (1998) 114 LQR 399. But happily the private client lawyer can leave that issue to the commercial lawyers.
[8] Section 33 AEA 1925 provides that on the death of a person intestate, his personal representatives hold his estate "upon trust" (in the original wording) and "in trust" (as amended by the TLATA 1996). Another example can be found in the Statutory Will Forms 1925, Form 8. Thus where necessary statute provides that personal representatives are not trustees: e.g. s.463(1) ITA. Failure to understand this has led to comical misunderstandings, such as the view that s.143 IHTA 1984 does not apply to unadministered estates. But this is not a drafting issue.
[9] See e.g. *Commissioner for Stamp Duties (Queensland) v Livingston* [1965] AC 694 at p.707.
[10] Para. 7.2 (Duties and powers distinguished).

"Trust" was used in the past to describe an equitable interest, but this usage is now archaic.[11]

The expression "trusts" is sometimes used simply to mean all the provisions of a settlement.[12] The word "terms" would often be clearer.

Types of trusts

Most family trusts fall into one of three categories:[13]

Interest in possession trust. An interest in possession trust is one where trust income must be paid to a particular beneficiary ("the life tenant"). There are two categories of this trust: "estate IP" and "non-estate IP". See 14.1 and Other Terminology below.

IPDI trusts. See 17.3 (IPDI Trusts)

Discretionary trust. In common parlance (and in this book) the expression "discretionary trust" is applied where trust income and capital may be paid to one or more of a class of beneficiaries, as the trustees think fit ("at their discretion"), without significant restrictions.[14] If it is desired to identify this type of trust more precisely, it may be called a "conventional discretionary trust"[15] or "a common form discretionary trust".

In contexts other than IHT, the expression "discretionary trust" is used to mean any settlement in which the trustees (or others) have powers ("discretions") over trust income, whether the property is or is "not relevant" property for IHT purposes. In this sense Age 18-to-25 trusts may be "discretionary", the trustees having some discretion over trust income.[16]

In the strictest and most literal sense the expression "discretionary trust" is taken to mean any trust in which the trustees (or others) have powers ("discretions") over trust income or trust capital. In this strict sense almost all trusts are "discretionary", since trustees will at least have the power over

---

[11] It was found in s.9 Statute of Frauds 1677 ("all grants and assignments of any trust or confidence shall be in writing..."). The usage survives in the successor to that section: s.53(1)(c) LPA 1925 ("a disposition of an equitable interest or trust... must be in writing").

[12] See e.g. s.3(1)(d) Criminal Injuries Compensation Act 1995.

[13] This is a loose categorisation. There is infinite potential for variety within each category. Settlements will change from one form to another through exercise of trustees' powers or change in the circumstances of the beneficiaries. A settlement may take partly one form and partly another.

[14] The Schedule to the IHT (Double Charges Relief) Regulations 1987 contains examples of this usage.

[15] The first recorded usage of this expression in the law reports is in *Kidson (Inspector of Taxes) v MacDonald* [1974] Ch 342, reflecting the rising popularity of this form in the 1960s.

[16] There are examples of this usage in s.5 TCGA 1992 (repealed); and in the sidenote to s.686 ICTA 1988 (repealed).

capital conferred by s.32 Trustee Act 1925. This usage is rare, confusing, and best avoided.[17]

Standard and special IHT trusts. See 17.1 (Terminology)

Other terminology

The following are not full definitions but brief explanations and, inevitably, over simplifications. So "except where the context otherwise requires...":

Administrative power: power to deal with the administration of a trust; such as a power to invest trust property. As opposed to dispositive power.

Advancement: see "power of advancement".

Appointment: see "power of appointment".

Bare Trust: see 22.1 (Bare trusts).

Closed class: a fixed class of beneficiaries; contrast "open class".

Default clause: provision in settlement directing who should become entitled to the trust property if all the other beneficiaries should die or the trusts fail.

Default beneficiary: beneficiary entitled under a default clause.

Disabled trust: trust satisfying conditions for IHT or CGT reliefs for disabled beneficiaries: see para.24.1 (Mentally handicapped beneficiaries).

Discretionary trust: see 15.1

Dispositive: see 16.1 (Administrative, dispositive, beneficial: terminology).

Duties and powers: see 7.2.

Estate IP: an interest in possession where property is treated for IHT purposes as if it belonged to the life tenant. Contrast "non-estate IP". See 14.1.

---

[17] The sidenote to s.689 ICTA 1988 (repealed) was an example of this usage. The expression "discretionary trust" is employed in the Income Support (General) Regulations 1987 in a manner which suggests that the drafter was not entirely familiar with trust terminology. It is thought that the term there is used in this wide sense.

Exit charge: IHT charge imposed under s.65 IHTA 1984 where property ceases to be held on standard IHT trusts.

Hold-over relief: relief from CGT charge (which may apply on lifetime gifts and on the termination of a settlement): see ss.165 and 260 TCGA 1992.

Interest in possession trust: see 14.1

Interest in possession: the right to the income from trust property.

Life tenant: person entitled to income of trust property.

Nil rate band: amount of chargeable transfer permitted before IHT becomes payable (2008/09 £312,000).

Non-estate IP: an interest in possession where property is not treated for IHT purposes as if it belonged to the life tenant. Contrast "estate IP". See 14.1.

Open class: a class of beneficiaries which might increase (e.g. "the Children of the Settlor" is an open class while the settlor is alive and capable of having more children). Contrast "closed class".

Overriding powers: term used in this book to refer to:
(i) power of appointment;
(ii) power to transfer property to a new settlement;
(iii) power of advancement.

Power of advancement: power to give a beneficiary trust capital or to apply it for his benefit. See 11.8 (Power of advancement).

Power of appointment: power to create new trusts for the benefit of beneficiaries.

Protection clause: clause to restrict a trust to ensure it satisfies the relevant tax conditions: see 16.17 (Protection clauses).

Protector: name given to a person who oversees trustees with power of consent and dismissal.

Settlement provisions: rules which apply (in short) where a settlor or spouse/civil partner has an interest in a settlement. See Chapter 5 Part 5 ITTOIA 2005; s.77 TCGA 1992.

Substantive trust: term used in this book to describe a trust other than a bare trust.

Ten-year charge: Inheritance tax charge on the 10-year anniversary of a standard IHT settlement. See IHTA 1984, s.64.

OTHER FORMS OF SETTLEMENT

It would not be possible to specify all the fanciful terminology sometimes used in connection with trusts.

Inheritance trust is a term propagated in marketed IHT avoidance arrangements. The expression has no settled meaning; indeed it has virtually no meaning. It generally involves insurance policies settled on some form of trust.

Asset protection trust is one in which the avoidance of insolvency legislation is a primary motive. The term (perhaps understandably) originates from America.

Marriage settlement. A settlement made in consideration of marriage or in contemplation of an intended marriage. The old form was: a life interest for husband and wife; with remainder to such of their issue as they might appoint; and in default of appointment for their children in equal shares. These forms are now obsolete[18] but any modern form of settlement may be a "marriage settlement". Marriage settlements enjoy two tax advantages of trivial importance:[19] no practitioner will waste much time on them.

---

[18] But financial negotiations prior to marriage, not dissimilar to those described in dusty textbooks on marriage settlements, may yet return in the guise of pre-nuptial agreements.

[19] 1. An IHT exemption for gifts to the settlement: s.22 IHTA 1984. The conditions for the relief are of a complexity quite out of proportion to the size of the relief, only £5,000 for a parent and £2,500 for a grandparent. An absolute gift is the only sensible way to take advantage of the relief.

2. A minor exemption from the Settlement Provisions: s.625 ITTOIA 2005.

PART 1

TRUST DRAFTING

CHAPTER 1

THE FINANCE ACT 2006: THE RAID ON TRUSTS

Policy of Finance Act 2006

The Finance Act 2006 makes revolutionary changes to the IHT treatment of trusts. Until 2006, the basic principle of tax policy has been that the tax system should not discriminate against trusts: **1.1**

> The government recognises the important role trusts play in society and has said that as far as possible it wants a tax system for trusts that does not provide artificial incentives to set up a trust, but equally avoids artificial obstacles to the use of trusts where their use would bring significant non-tax benefits.[1]

This policy has been completely reversed. The policy now is to impose additional charges on trusts, other than very limited, privileged trusts, with the result that:

(1) In most cases trusts will not be created. In particular a lifetime gift to another individual is a PET: a gift to a trust is generally chargeable.

(2) In most cases, where privileged trusts have been created, they will be wound up as soon as possible:

   (a) IPDI trusts will generally be wound up on the death of the life tenant. In particular, a gift to another individual may qualify for the spouse/civil partner exemption: the termination of an IPDI will not usually do so unless the trust then comes to an end.
   (b) Bereaved Minors trusts and Age 18-to-25 trusts will be wound up when the beneficiaries reach 18 or 25.

---

[1] "Modernising the Tax System for Trusts" HMRC, December 17, 2004.

4   THE FINANCE ACT 2006: THE RAID ON TRUSTS

Misconceptions

1.2   More striking than the revolutionary nature of these changes is the dishonesty used in their presentation. Fundamental misconceptions (a less charitable commentator would say, lies) were propounded by those pushing through the new law:

> (1) The changes "aligned" the formerly "privileged" tax treatment of IP and A&M trusts with the "normal" "mainstream" tax regime for discretionary trusts.[2] In fact, as any practitioner knew, substantial discretionary trusts, i.e. those paying any substantial IHT, were highly exceptional.[3]
>
> (2) The changes would only raise £15m per year.
>
> (3) Only a very small number of very rich people, quantified as 20,000, would be affected.
>
> (4) Wills made before the introduction of the new law would not need to be rewritten. (This was later made broadly true, by radical amendment of the Finance Bill in Committee; though accompanied by a false claim that those changes were only intended to clarify what the Government had always intended.)
>
> (5) Trusts of life insurance policies made before 2006 were not affected. (This was also later made true by amendments in Committee, accompanied by the false claim that those changes were not in fact necessary.)
>
> (6) That the new rules, requiring (on pain of penal tax charges) property to be distributed to children at the age of 18, had been supported by professional institutions in prior consultation.
>
> (7) The new rules offer a "modicum of simplification".[4]

To anyone knowledgeable in practice in this area, these statements are

---

[2] Standing Committee debate, June 13, 2006, HC Official Report, col. 569, 570, 633 (Dawn Primarolo).

[3] There was a good reason for this. The discretionary trust regime was designed in 1982 to impose on discretionary trusts a burden roughly equal to the burden of *capital transfer tax* on non-settled property. It achieved that. In 1986, CTT was then replaced by the much lighter IHT regime, under which tax was no longer charged on lifetime gifts. There is no obvious solution as to how to deal with discretionary trusts under an IHT regime. The solution adopted was to retain the old CTT rules, which then imposed a burden on discretionary trusts rather greater than that which applied to non-settled property, but allowing the alternative route of IP trusts (and A&M trusts) which were, broadly, treated in the same way as non-settled property. Thus the charges on discretionary trusts had something of the nature of anti-avoidance provisions. Although the tax charge could be unduly high, that did not matter at all because nobody needed to pay it, and very few actually did.

[4] Standing committee debate, col. 605 (Dawn Primarolo)

absurd and scarcely deserve refutation. But the formal evidence of refutation was in due course assembled, at short notice, and this was done with sufficient success to lead the Select Committee on Treasury to conclude:

> With respect to the new rules on the tax treatment of accumulation and maintenance and interest in possession trusts, we are concerned that estimates of the expected numbers of affected trusts vary so widely between Government and practitioners. If the Government's estimate, that the new rules will affect "only a very small number of very wealthy people" is correct, then the Government needs to provide much more detailed information about its estimates, in order to allay taxpayer and industry concerns. We are concerned that a legitimate measure designed to reduce tax avoidance may penalise trusts established to protect family members and consider that the issue merits further consideration. We recommend that the Government provide detailed information about how it has arrived at its estimate that the new rules on the tax treatment of certain trusts will affect only "a minority of a minority" of 100,000 discretionary trusts. This information should be provided prior to consideration in Committee of the House of Commons of Clause 57 of, and Schedule 20 to, the Finance Bill.[5]

No such evidence was ever produced (for the good reason that it did not exist).

Policy issues

Trusts offer important protection for beneficiaries as the Courts have often accepted: **1.3**

> Speaking in general terms, it is most important that young children should be reasonably advanced in a career and settled in life before they are in receipt of an income sufficient to make them independent of the need to work.[6]

Research by the Financial Services Authority shows (if proof was needed) that 18-year-olds are much less financially capable than 25-year-olds.[7]
Of course it is not just young persons who are particularly at risk:

---

[5] Select Committee on Treasury Fourth Report, para.109, accessible on *www.publications.parliament.uk/pa/cm200506/cmselect/cmtreasy/994/99407.htm#a46*.

[6] *Re Holt* [1969] 100 at p.122. Another example: *Re Gates* [2003] 3 ITELR 113, accessible *www.jerseylaw.je*, "It is not in our judgment generally in the interests of young persons to come into possession of large sums of money which might discourage them from achieving qualifications and from leading settled and industrious lives to the benefit of themselves and to the community."

[7] The report, "Levels of Financial Capability in the UK" concluded that 18-year-olds have a factor score of just 27 out of 100, while those aged 20 to 29 have a higher factor score of 40. See *www.fsa.gov.uk*. Dawn Primarolo's response was "I, for one, have more faith in our young people". During this *soi disant* debate, members of the standing committee passed the time reading "Private Eye": col. 710. Quote from website of "Rethink" (the Schizophrenia charity). Persons with mania or depression will often not qualify as "disabled persons" in the IHT sense.

People with mania sometimes believe they are rich and go on spending sprees and people with depression commonly spend money in an effort to make themselves feel better. Conversely, people with depressive symptoms may withdraw and ignore official letters, appointments and bills often leading to mounting debt.[8]

Until now the financial protection which trusts can confer has been available to everyone; it was one of the great benefits of living in a common law jurisdiction. The attack on trusts is a reform which in the long term (if it remains) has profound social implications. But the dishonest manner in which the changes were introduced effectively prevented any serious debate on the policy issues from taking place.

Does it now matter? Readers may think it pointless to cry "foul" in a game which has no referee, and whose result has now been declared. But the story does need to be recorded, for several reasons.

The UK tax system is notorious for its instability[9] and tax law which is not founded on proper debate and a modicum of consensus is not likely to prove stable.

The relationship between the individual and HMRC has in the past depended mainly on willing compliance. (A system based substantially or entirely on forced compliance could be created, and indeed we are presently moving in that direction, but no-one has ever openly advocated that.) HMRC rightly protest when they are cheated:

> HM Revenue & Customs expects professionals such as accountants who act on behalf of taxpayers to be entirely professional and honest. [The convicted defendant] has abused the trust of his clients and has failed in his legal and professional responsibilities to HMRC. He has cheated family, his friends, clients and all honest taxpayers.[10]

But honesty is a two-way street. Taxpayers should also expect HMRC to be "entirely professional and honest". In this matter HMRC have abused the trust of the public (which generally assumed that HMRC press releases are reliable). Settlors and beneficiaries of A&M trusts have been cheated. They have entered into arrangements which have never until now been regarded as tax avoidance and find themselves being penalised for having done so. The rank unfairness of some of the 2006 rules, combined with its dishonest presentation, will corrode the goodwill upon which HMRC has historically relied.

One can only hope that this proves to be a one-off and not a regular feature of future tax reform.

---

[8] Quote from website of "Rethink" (the Schizophrenia charity).
[9] Noted in *Taxation and Democracy*, Sven Steinmo, Yale University Press, 1993, p.44 but the instability has markedly increased since then.
[10] See Tax Bulletin 83 (2006).

Trusts after the Finance Act 2006

Wills trusts will still be used: see 17.1 (Types of Will Trusts). The usual situations in which lifetime trusts will be used by UK domiciliaries under the current law are as follows:

1.4

(1) If the value of the trust property falls within the nil rate band.

(2) If the trust property qualifies for 100% business or agricultural property relief.

These are of course significant categories. Basic IHT planning now will be for an individual to make a series of nil-rate band gifts every 7 years.[11]

In all other cases, the 20% IHT charge will rule out lifetime gifts to trusts. An individual who wishes to benefit his family should:

(1) Make absolute gifts, or gifts to bare trusts,[12] which will be PETs.

(2) Make interest free (or if desired, index linked) loans.[13]

(3) In the case of companies not qualifying for 100% BPR, deferred share arrangements should be considered (this topic is not discussed in this book).

A sensible course is to do nothing for now and wait for the fiscal climate to improve. Experience suggests that the pendulum swings to and fro, just as old Labour's capital transfer tax only lasted from 1974 to 1986. The present tax regime, founded on misconceptions and lies, is unlikely to last longer. At least the sensible advice for a client not in old age may be to wait and see.[14]

Existing trusts after the Finance Act 2006

Every A&M and IP trust in existence before 6 April 2008 needed review after the FA 2006.

1.5

---

[11] Spouses and civil partners may each make gifts to the same trust, as that trust will be treated as two separate trusts for IHT purposes: s.44 IHTA 1984.

[12] See Chapter 22 (Bare trusts).

[13] If desired:

(1) The loan (say, to a child) could be repayable only on the death of the borrower.
(2) The individual could give away the benefit of the loan to grandchildren.

[14] The life expectancy of an individual aged 60 is 21 years (male) and 26 years (female). See *www.gad.gov.uk*.

A&M Trusts

The choice for trustees of A&M trusts was a difficult and unpalatable one:

(1) To retain the trusts in their present form and pay 10-year and exit charges from 6 April 2008.

(2)(a) To wind up the trusts by 6 April 2008,[15] transferring property to beneficiaries absolutely or by transfers to bare trusts. If the transfer was to the A&M beneficiaries, this was straightforward. A transfer to other beneficiaries could also in principle[16] have been achieved by giving the A&M beneficiaries a short term interest in possession.

(b) If the A&M beneficiaries were under 18, to exercise the overriding power of appointment so that they would become absolutely entitled at the age of 18.

IP Trusts

The choices were:

(1) To leave the existing trust in its current form.

(2) To appoint a new life interest, before 6 October 2008, which took effect as a "transitional serial interest". This constituted a PET by the previous life tenant, and the GWR rules applied so it was normally necessary to exclude the previous life tenant.

Route (1) has the attraction that the spouse/CP exemption would apply more readily on the death of the life tenant.

---

[15] No action was needed before 6/4/2008 unless an A&M beneficiary would have become entitled to an IP before then (action had to be taken before the IP arose).

[16] The position depended on the extent of the trustees' powers of appointment. In the A&M trusts in earlier editions of this book, the trustees had sufficiently wide powers. Other trusts used were sometimes narrower.

CHAPTER 2

FIRST PRINCIPLES

Duty to the client

The purpose of drafting a settlement or will is to carry out the wishes of   2.1
the settlor or testator. The professional adviser will do more than this:
his duty is to advise, ascertain and carry out his client's wishes. This is a
matter of explanation and common sense. Suggestions of the solicitor or
textbook writer are often brushed aside by those wary or suspicious of
them. It is easy to let a client do what he wants; or what he thinks he wants.
Their families will pay the resulting bills in due course, probably without
complaint; almost certainly without redress. But the responsibility of the
adviser is to help his client whose basic wish will be to benefit his family
in the most appropriate way. Empathy and an ability to communicate are
called for; a little persuasion or cajolery may not be amiss.

A docile client may sign anything put in front of him. The professional
adviser does not serve that client well if he simply places before him the
firm's standard draft—even if settled by counsel—for execution without
discussion and explanation.

Consultation with the client comes at two stages. First, the general
strategy; at this stage consideration can be given to the nature of the trust
property, the tax position, the class of beneficiaries and the choice of trustees or executors. Later, when the draft is completed, it should itself be
explained to the settlor clause by clause. A modern style of drafting renders
this task much easier. The execution of a document which the client does
not understand is a recipe for disaster.[1]

Where the settlor is a trustee or a beneficiary—especially if he is both—
the solicitor has the difficult duty of explaining to the settlor the nature
of his rights and duties under the trust. Legal and equitable ownership
are subtle concepts. The client must not be left with the impression that
the trust fund is simply "his fund". The trustee acting on that assumption

---

[1] Is this so obvious that it does not need saying? Apparently not. For a recent example of such a disaster see *Wolff v Wolff* [2004] STC 1633.

Elderly or ill client

2.2 In the case of an aged testator or a testator who has suffered a serious illness, there is one golden rule which should always be observed, however straightforward matters may appear, and however difficult or tactless it may be to suggest that precautions be taken: the making of a will by such a testator ought to be witnessed or approved by a medical practitioner who satisfies himself of the capacity and understanding of the testator, and records and preserves his examination and findings.

There are other precautions which should be taken. If the testator has made an earlier will this should be considered by the legal and medical advisers of the testator and, if appropriate, discussed with the testator. The instructions of the testator should be taken in the absence of anyone who may stand to benefit, or who may have influence over the testator.

These are not counsels of perfection. If proper precautions are not taken injustice may result or be imagined, and great expense and misery may be unnecessarily caused.[3]

The same applies of course to a lifetime settlement made by such a client.

Does drafting matter?

2.3 Lord Reid said that the courts do not penalise the client for his lawyer's slovenly drafting.[4] It would be more accurate to say that the courts *try* not to penalise the client for bad drafting. If the meaning is clear, the court will "adopt methods of construction appropriate for documents *inter rusticos*". For instance, when a drafter uses the word "assent" when he means "convey" or says "Bishop of Westminster" instead of "archbishop" the intended meaning will be understood.[5] But slovenly drafting leads to ambiguity and sometimes invalidity. To ascertain the meaning of a badly

---

[2] James Kessler QC, "What is (and what is not) a Sham" (1999) OITR, vol.9, p.125 accessible on *www.kessler.co.uk*.
[3] *Re Simpson* (1977) 121 Sol. Jo. 224 (Templeman J.). See Ch.4 of the Mental Capacity Act Code of Practice, accessible on *www.justice.gov.uk*, and Assessment of Mental Capacity (2nd edn) published by the BMJ and written jointly by the BMA and the Law Society.
[4] *Re Gulbenkian* [1970] AC 508 at 517.
[5] The examples are from *Re Stirrup* [1961] 1 WLR 449 and *Re Hetherington* [1989] 2 All ER 129. Many illuminating and amusing examples can be found in Lewison, *Interpretation of Contracts* (4th edn, 2007), Ch.9.

drafted document can be a matter of great difficulty. Some apparently trivial drafting errors have disastrous tax consequences.[6] Drafting *does* matter.

Flexibility

A trust needs to be flexible. This means that trustees require overriding powers to enable them to rewrite the terms of the trust as appropriate. Beneficiaries' circumstances change in ways that are not possible to foresee. Trustees need to adapt to tax changes which are wholly unpredictable. "The major distinguishing feature of the British tax system is its instability."[7] 2.4

Simplicity

This book strives for simplicity of *style* and simplicity of *concept*. Simplicity of style is self-explanatory: a preference for the shorter formula over the longer; the use of aids to the reader such as punctuation and clause headings; and the rejection of material which is archaic or otiose. 2.5

Simplicity of concept calls for the broad structure of a trust to be simple and comprehensible. Provisions should be set out in a logical sequence. Vastly complicated settlements should not be employed where simpler provisions would be satisfactory.

Dense and obscure drafting carries a heavier price than may be realised. The more complex a draft, the more professional time must be spent studying it in order to ascertain its meaning, and the greater the chance of errors escaping observation.

---

[6] Although the courts may not penalise the client for his lawyer's slovenly drafting, HMRC (quite rightly) have no such scruple. A classic example is the *Vandervell* litigation [1971] AC 912. A modern example would be the inclusion of a power which might destroy an interest in possession.

[7] *Taxation and Democracy*, Sven Steinmo, Yale University Press, 1993, p.44. This was written in the light of the budgets of 1986, 1987, 1988, 1989 and 1992 which all contained fundamental changes; this under the administration of a single stable Conservative administration! Labour have brought in a new dividend regime in 1999, which is unlikely to endure; CGT taper relief in 1998 substantially amended in the Finance Acts 2000, 2001 and 2002; pre-owned assets rules, which are not likely to survive in their present form; and revolutionised IHT in the FA 2006, which should also be regarded as unstable.

Sources for drafting

2.6 The aim of the drafter is to keep so far as possible to familiar paths; to be unoriginal. He is happy to use well-worn phrases of established meaning and fearful to use novel forms. To this end the drafter may draw on many sources. Of course such sources should be used as a guide and not a crib. The wide variety of forms and styles employed in statute and published precedents force the drafter to some form of selection. Innovation is constantly required to meet changes in tax and trust law, circumstances of beneficiaries and wishes of settlors.

(1) Statute

2.7 Statute (and statutory instrument) should be the drafter's starting point: wording which the parliamentary drafter thought adequate can rarely be criticised as defective. This applies not only to the precedents thoughtfully set out by the parliamentary drafter for the benefit of the profession,[8] but to the vast body of statutory material. Many different styles of drafting are to be found in statutory precedent. This is hardly surprising when one bears in mind that many different hands may have been at work even in a single Act. English property legislation offers clearer sources of precedent than any precedent book. The precedents in this book have drawn whenever possible on statutory precedent.[9] Reference may also usefully be made to foreign trust laws.

(2) Law reports

2.8 In the law reports an immense number of precedents are discussed and analysed, and the adoption of a clause or formula which has the benefit of judicial consideration and approval may be attractive. Conversely, where the court has disapproved of a form, the drafter should take careful note.

(3) Company law

2.9 Precedents from a company law context may assist the trust drafter. This book makes occasional use of standard company articles in Table A form, the Companies Act 2006, and the Insolvency Act 1986.

---

[8] e.g. Sch.1 SLA 1925; Schs. 3 and 4 LPA 1925.
[9] This book specifies the statutory provisions which are used as the basis of its precedents. Also noted in footnotes are any other provisions which may also have served as precedents for the clause under discussion. This may serve as a starting point for research for the drafter creating a specific draft, or for a practitioner construing a particular clause in a document before him. It also illustrates the endless variety of formulae which may properly be used to achieve the same end and the different drafting styles used.

(4) Legal literature and precedent books

There is a large body of published precedents of varying age and authority. (For a selection, see the bibliography in appendix 2.) The authors of these works have naturally drawn from similar sources and each other. The forms proposed have a great deal in common; a review of any indenture from an earlier century will reveal phrases or entire clauses still familiar today. At the same time, copyright considerations may have led to an unnatural multiplicity in published precedents.

2.10

Formal qualifications for the drafter

Drafting requires formal qualifications. The rule (in short) is that drafting must be done by a solicitor, barrister or notary public. The unqualified person, who, for a fee, "draws or prepares an instrument relating to real or personal estate", directly or indirectly, commits an offence.[10] The restriction does not apply to:

2.11

(1) a will;

(2) an agreement not executed as a deed;

(3) a transfer of stock containing no trust;

(4) acts not done for a reward.[11]

The territorial limitations of the offence are not expressly stated. Section 90(4) Solicitors Act 1974 states (so far as relevant) that the provisions of the Act "extend to England and Wales only". It is suggested that the English offence applies only to a document governed by English law relating to property in England or Wales. Scotland, Northern Ireland, and many other jurisdictions have similar legislation: in particular the drafting of Scots/Northern Ireland law documents relating to property in those jurisdictions is restricted to lawyers locally qualified.[12]

Is a deed of appointment (or appointment of new trustees) a document "relating to real or personal estate" and if so, what (and where) is the property to which it relates? At first sight an appointment relates to the trust assets. But a trust fund may have assets all over the world. A better analysis would be that the document relates to the equitable interests of the beneficiaries. An equitable interest is probably situate where the trustees

---

[10] Section 22 Solicitors Act 1974. There are minor exceptions for certain employees and others: s.22(2), (2A).
[11] Section 22(1), (3) Solicitors Act 1974.
[12] Section 32 Solicitors (Scotland) Act 1980; art.23 Solicitors (Northern Ireland) Order 1976; s.10 Legal Practitioners Law (Cayman Island 2003 Revision).

are resident.[13] So an appointment governed by English law must be drafted by a qualified lawyer if the trustees are resident here.

An English law trust with English trustees must likewise be drafted by a qualified lawyer.

The transfer of property (except stock) to trustees (on the creation of a trust or on the appointment of new trustees) relates to the property transferred so an English law transfer of English property (except stock) must be drafted by a qualified lawyer.

Thus an offshore trust company may prepare a trust, in local form, if the initial trust property is local property. The trust company could also draft a transfer of shares or securities to the trustees; it should not prepare a transfer of land to the trustees if the land is situated in the United Kingdom. It is a criminal offence for a firm of accountants or a trust company to draft an English law trust relating to English property.

It is considered that the offence applies where drafting work is done by an employee of the firm who is a solicitor if the firm itself is a non-qualifying firm (e.g. accountants or a trust company). Although the qualified employee does the work, the unqualified firm has done it indirectly.[14]

Interesting questions arise where for the drafting the law is broken. Suppose an unqualified firm drafts a trust. Could it sue for its fees? Obviously not. Suppose the document was negligently drafted and the firm was sued for negligence. Would the firm be covered by its professional indemnity insurance? That would depend on the terms of the insurance cover. What would be the attitude of the appropriate regulatory body? Clearly, the penalty for breaking the solicitors' monopoly may extend further than the maximum statutory penalty, a fine at level three on the standard scale.

There is prospective legislation in this area. The Legal Services Act 2007 provides a new regulatory framework for "reserved legal activities" including provision for alternative business structures. Only authorised or exempt persons can carry out such activities.[15] It is an offence to carry out a reserved legal activity or to pretend to be authorised if not so authorised or exempt.[16]

"Reserved instrument activities" include "preparing any instrument relating to real or personal estate for the purposes of the law of England and Wales" but do not include: (a) a will or other testamentary instrument; (b) an agreement not intended to be executed as a deed, other than a contract for the sale or other disposition of land; (c) a letter or power of attorney; or (d) a transfer of stock containing no trust or limitation of the transfer".[17]

---

[13] See *Taxation of Foreign Domiciliaries*, 7th edn, 2008, James Kessler QC, para.55.25 (Situs of equitable interest).
[14] This view is supported by a comment in *Green v Hoyle* [1976] 1 WLR 575 at p.584.
[15] Section 13 Legal Services Act 2007.
[16] Section 14 Legal Services Act 2007. It is also an offence to carry out a reserved legal activity through a person who is not entitled: s.16.
[17] Paragraph 5, Schedule 2 Legal Services Act 2007.

No date has yet been fixed for the commencement of these provisions.

Money laundering[18]

2.12 The following is not a full discussion of the law, which goes beyond the scope of a book on trust drafting, but a summary in the nature of a checklist.

- Does the drafter suspect that the trust fund represents proceeds of criminal conduct? If so, drafting the trust may be an offence.
- The drafter must comply with the identification and record keeping procedures required by the Money Laundering Regulations 2007. These regulations apply regardless of whether the drafter has any suspicion of criminal conduct. Failure to do so may be an offence.

Civil claims against the drafter

2.13 A drafter may of course incur civil liabilities. In this work we need only mention the main heads of liability:

(1) in contract or negligence, to the client;

(2) in negligence, to beneficiaries or trustees;

(3) for dishonestly assisting a breach of trust even though the funds never pass into the drafter's hands;

(4) as constructive trustee for breach of trust, if the trust funds do pass through the drafter's hands as trustee or nominee (i.e. funds paid to a client account); and

(5) in due course, if the drafter becomes trustee, for actual breach of trust.

---

[18] On this topic see the Anti-money laundering practice note issued by the Law Society, accessible on *www.lawsociety.org.uk/productsandservices/practicenotes/aml.page*.

CHAPTER 3

STYLE

Introduction

3.1 The drafting style established in earlier centuries should be adapted to contemporary usage. The need for this is unquestionable. The drafter's aim should be to satisfy his client's wishes; and the general public wish to see plain English.[1]

To subject old precedents to critical review is not to disparage them. The old forms offer harmonious cadences which ravish the ear and intellect of the conveyancer; but they make little concession to the natural breaks and lucidities of the English tongue. There is nothing praiseworthy in practising the errors of one's forefathers.

This has for many years now been the establishment view. Lord Nicholls, then Vice-Chancellor, was asked at the Law Society's annual conference in 1993 what single change he would most like to see in the system of justice. He replied:

> If I could make one change, I would have the White Book rules rewritten in English, in a form that anyone can understand.[2] I would have orders drafted in a form that people can understand and recognise as being in English. That would make an improvement in the administration of justice but also in the impression that the consumer gets. Instead of thinking he's going into some strange world where people use language in documents and sometimes orally that people never use, he would actually be able to understand what was going on.

This comment drew spontaneous applause from the audience.

---

[1] This can hardly be doubted; but see the diatribe in *The Times'* leader November 30, 1990: "The Solicitors' word processors spew forth an ever-increasing flood of garbage. A clearer case of a profession 'conspiring against the public' is hard to imagine." In response to this pressure, the Law Society's Client's Charter (2003) (significantly) "backed by the Plain English Campaign", provides: "A solicitor will make every effort to explain things clearly, keeping jargon to a minimum".

[2] This comment can now be seen as a precursor of some of the Woolf reforms.

The modern drafting style adopted in this book, once revolutionary, is the present orthodoxy. The old controversy—whether mistakes are likely to be introduced by the adoption of a modern drafting style—is over.[3] Scarcely any law reform proposal nowadays fails to include "plain legal English" as one plank of its reforms.[4] Former President Clinton's *Memorandum on Plain Language* shows how far the movement has reached in the United States.[5] It is interesting to speculate as to the reason for this perceptible change of mood which may be dated to the early 1990s though its roots lie far earlier.[6] It is probably connected with the loss of respect for the professions generally and the assumption that they "know better"

---

[3] In this debate it was not always appreciated just how far the most "traditionalist" drafting style has advanced. For instance the modern practice of using separate clauses is innovatory: nineteenth-century documents contained no paragraph breaks and different sections were marked only by the use of capitalised words.

[4] Three examples will suffice:

1. *Goode Report on Pension Law Reform* Com. 2342 (1993), pp. 192–194:

    "The skilled draftsman produces text which is almost wholly unintelligible ... What concerns us is not particular infelicities of drafting, which are unavoidable, but a sense that clarity is not seen as important. Little thought seems to be given to the need of the user to be able to understand, at least in a broad sense, what it is that Parliament is saying. This results in professionals having to spend much more time than should be necessary trying to understand what the legislation is saying ... of course the paramount consideration must always be to produce the required legal effect; communication of that effect necessarily takes second place in the order of priorities. But the two are not incompatible. In recent years government departments had made substantial progress towards simplifying official forms and reducing the numbers in use. This has been widely welcome. We strongly urge a similar approach towards statutory and other rules affecting pension schemes."

2. One of the objects of the Civil Procedure Rules was "to remove verbiage and adopt a simpler and plainer style of drafting": *Woolf Report Access to Justice*, Ch.20.
3. The most extraordinarily ambitious project arising out of this trend is the current re-write of UK tax legislation in plain English.

    A striking reflection of this mood can be found in a *Hansard* debate of 26 June 1997 accessible on *www.kessler.co.uk*.

[5] Accessible on *http://govinfo.library.unt.edu/npr/library/direct/memos/memoeng.html*.

[6] Fierce dissatisfaction with legal drafting can be traced back at least to the Enlightenment:

"Lawyers ... charge exorbitant fees for piling up heaps of turgid documents couched in arcane terminology purposely incomprehensible to non-lawyers, rendering the public helpless victims of their wiles, a conceited, grasping clique, who, instead of serving the common good, cunningly exploit their supposed expertise to generate wealth and bogus status for themselves."

Adriaen Koerbagh (1664) cited in *Radical Enlightenment*, Jonathan Israel, OUP, 2001.

An early statutory example is s.56 Common Law Procedure Amendment (Ireland) Act 1853 ("Pleadings shall state all facts which constitute the Ground of the Defence or Reply in ordinary Language, and without Repetition, and as concisely as is possible consistent with Clearness").

The development of drafting styles can be traced to some extent in the drafting of Acts of Parliament which occasionally contain precedents. For instance, the precedents in Schs 3 and 4 of the Conveyancing and Law of Property Act 1881 are not divided into clauses; the only punctuation is a full stop at the end of the precedent. By the time of the LPA 1925, clauses are used, and, though sparingly, punctuation: see Sch.5. More recent important dates are: publication of Mellinkoff, *The Language of Law* (1963); foundation of the Plain English Campaign (1979) and Clarity (1983). For the history, see bibliography.

18 STYLE

than the layman; the commercial advantages offered by "plain English" in a competitive market[7]; that lawyers now learn no Latin in their childhood (or learn it to a low level and forget it); but ultimately it is because the arguments in favour of "plain legal English" are convincing.

In some areas plain English drafting is required by law. The Unfair Terms in Consumer Contracts Regulations 1999, only one example, require consumer contracts to be in "plain, intelligible language".

In the past, the style of drafting in the field of trusts and conveyancing fell behind the style of drafting in other areas of law; but this has changed; as witness the Law Society's Standard Conditions of Sale, the Charity Commissioners' model charitable trust, or the STEP Standard Provisions. There are still many who draft without punctuation, etc. but they are somewhat behind the curve.

Lastly, style is not a subject to which one should devote too much time! Many questions of style are matters of taste and discretion, and do not admit a right-or-wrong answer. Even where there is a right-or-wrong answer (such as to prefer *witnesses* to *witnesseth*) these are not issues of fundamental importance. Yet although literary style should not—legally—matter, it is a fact that where style is poor, more serious errors are often found.

Punctuation

3.2 Punctuation was traditionally omitted in legal documents. Many trust drafters still use no punctuation. If it is used, a sense of guilt or unease or tradition causes drafters (like children) to use it sparingly and in a manner quite distinct from ordinary English composition.[8]

The traditional practice rests on a precedent both ancient and authoritative. The Bible itself, in the original Hebrew, lacks punctuation and even paragraph breaks are rare; though the absence of punctuation adds little ease to its reading or interpretation.

Fortunately the old order has changed and punctuation has begun to appear in trust drafting. The parliamentary drafter led the way. Precedents in the Conveyancing Act 1881 have full stops at the end of them, though no other punctuation. This seems to have been the first concession to the

---

[7] Thus some insurance companies, banks and others boast in their advertising that their legal documentation, including trust documentation, is framed in plain English.

[8] Thus one sees underlining or absurd spaces to avoid the ordinary use of commas:

This Deed is made by John Adam Peter Jones and Adam West ...
This Deed is made by John Adam Peter Jones and Adam West ...

This is at least better than the older form:

This Deed is made by John Adam Peter Jones and Adam West ...

where it is not even clear how many parties there are to the deed.

rules of grammar as understood by the non-legal world. Precedents in the Law of Property Act 1925 use commas in addition, though sparingly. The Statutory Will Forms 1925 use punctuation in the manner of ordinary English prose. So do the Law Society's Standard Conditions of Sale. That is the approach adopted in this book.

Punctuation serves two functions: it will make a document easier to read; and it may convey meaning, showing which of two possible readings is correct. In the precedents in this book, punctuation is used only in the first of these ways. So the precedents would have the same meaning even if the punctuation were diligently abstracted by a drafter in time honoured tradition. However, this self-restraint is quite unnecessary: the courts will have proper regard to punctuation in the construction of a document. Thus Lord Shaw:

> Punctuation is a rational part of English composition ... I see no reason of depriving legal documents of such significance as attaches to punctuation in other writings.[9]

As Lord Shaw suggests, punctuation is an aid, and no more than an aid, towards revealing the meaning of a text. Punctuation is the servant and not the master of substance and meaning. Excessive reliance on punctuation to convey meaning is also contrary to good prose style.[10] For all these reservations, it remains plain that proper use of punctuation makes a document easier to read and understand and this is sufficient justification for its use in legal documents.

Use of capitals

In lieu of punctuation and paragraph breaks, the traditional style capitalised certain expressions to aid the reader to find his place. The few large

3.3

---

[9] *Houston v Burns* [1918] AC 337 at 348. Scots lawyers never adopted the English custom of drafting without punctuation. It is therefore significant that this was a Scottish case. Lords Finley and Haldane (whose practice had been at the English Bar) agreed, Lord Finley discussing earlier English case law, and drawing no distinction between English and Scots law on this point. So the principle became established in English law. The same rule applies for Acts of Parliament: *Hanlon v Law Society* [1981] AC 124 at 197–198; *Marshall v Cottingham* [1982] Ch 82 at 88 where Megarry V.C. sets out, with customary wit, the view which he expressed 20 years earlier: "Statutory Interpretation" (1959) 75 LQR 29. Likewise the EU Joint Practical Guide on the drafting of legislation (see appendix 3) para. 1.4.2 "Drafting which ... respects the rules of punctuation makes it easier to understand the text properly".

[10] *Fowler's Modern English Usage*: "Ambiguities may sometimes be removed by punctuation, but an attempt to correct a faulty sentence by inserting stops usually portrays itself as a slovenly and ineffective way of avoiding the trouble of re-writing. It may almost be said that what reads wrongly when the stops are removed is radically bad; stops are not to alter meaning but merely to show it up." But Fowler does not mean to say that one should try to write without meaningful use of punctuation. This is a feat difficult to achieve and quite contrary to English usage. One need only contrast *Don't Stop!* and *Don't! Stop!!*

letters offered, in Dickens' words: "a resting place in the immense desert of law hand and parchment, to break the awful monotony and save the traveller from despair". The main expressions put in capitals were as follows:

> the opening words: THIS SETTLEMENT
>
> the names of parties;
>
> the introduction to the body of the deed: NOW THIS DEED WITNESSETH ...
>
> words of action: DECLARE, APPOINT
>
> that the trustees hold ... UPON TRUST ...
>
> the first words of the "parcels" clause: ALL THAT ...
>
> provisos: SUBJECT TO ... PROVIDED THAT ...
>
> and finally: IN WITNESS ...

Some drafters capitalise the first word or two of every paragraph.

Now all this has lost its purpose with the introduction of paragraph breaks and numbering. The old practice is still common, perhaps because it is thought to give a pleasing legal feel to a document.[11]

One sometimes sees:

> the Trustees hold ... Upon Trust ... .

Wavering between legal usage (fully capitalised) and ordinary usage (uncapitalised) the drafter sought a compromise and capitalised the first letter only. The precedents set out in the 1925 property legislation do not adopt an entirely consistent practice. They have virtually abandoned the practice of full capitalisation.[12] They waver inconsistently between conventional usage and capitalisation of first letters. Thus in successive forms one sees " ... supplemental to a legal charge ..." and " ... Supplemental to a Legal Charge ... ." The drafter clearly gave little thought to the matter.

The initial letters of defined words should be capitalised. In other cases it is submitted that ordinary English usage should be adopted, and this is the practice adopted in this book.

---

[11] The pleasure may not be shared by non-lawyers. "The mutual massaging of the whole profession's ego. Give us capital letters and raise our status." See *Outrageous Fortune*, an autobiography by Terence Frisby, 1998 (recommended holiday reading for any lawyer). Frisby is unconsciously repeating criticism already made three centuries earlier: see fn.6.

[12] A stray "WITNESSETH" is found in Sch.3, Form 1 LPA 1925.

Sentence length

It is better to use a number of short sentences in preference to a single lengthy sentence. Short clauses help to produce a document which is easy to understand. The lengthy clause easily hides ambiguity or error. This has long been recognised.[13] A good example of the problems of an over-extended clause is to be found in the Finance Act 1984 Sch.13 para.10(2). Here the drafter failed to understand his own creation and omitted the word "not"! Parliament later inserted the word in the provision. That convenient remedy is not open to the trust drafter (except in accordance with an express power to vary, or under the expensive and embarrassing procedure of rectification). **3.4**

One could give countless examples of ambiguity arising from over-long clauses. But even when there is no ambiguity an over-loaded clause is best avoided. Take a clause such as this:

> The Trustees shall stand possessed of the trust fund on trust to sell call in or convert into money such part of the trust fund as shall not consist of money with power to postpone such sale calling in or conversion for so long as the trustees shall in their absolute discretion think fit without being responsible for loss and shall at the like discretion invest the monies produced thereby in the names or under the legal control of the trustees in or upon any investments hereinafter authorised with power at such discretion as aforesaid to vary or transpose any investment for or into others of any nature hereby authorised.

In this standard but tortuous provision are four elements: a trust for sale; a duty to invest trust money; a power to vary investments; and a power to use nominees. They could more clearly be contained in separate clauses. The drafter might then turn his mind to expressing the same thoughts more concisely; he might further consider where the provisions should most logically come; and even whether the provisions are needed at all.

Another example:

> The trustees shall stand possessed of the trust fund UPON TRUST to pay the income thereof to X during her lifetime Provided that the Trustees may at any time or times in their absolute discretion transfer the trust fund to X absolutely free and discharged from the trusts hereof...

This should be dealt with in two clauses: one conferring X's right to income, and the other dealing with the trustees' power to transfer capital. As the EU Joint Practical Guide on the drafting of legislation states:[14] "Sentences should express just one idea".

---

[13] "I have never understood why some conveyancers should regard it as beneath their dignity to employ sub-paragraphs in a clause so as to make their meaning plain": *Re Gulbenkian* [1970] AC 508 at 526 (Lord Donovan).
[14] Para.4.4; see *http://eur-lex.europa.eu./en/techleg/index.htm*.

22 STYLE

Must every clause be a single sentence?

3.5 Normally each clause is a single sentence. This has the practical advantage that references to the sentence concerned is easier. Nevertheless, it should not be regarded as an absolute rule and the tradition of one sentence clauses has often led to excessively long sentences. Standard Table A Company Articles set a good example here. It is sometimes convenient to divide a single clause into two paragraphs. This may be simpler than dividing the material into subclauses. There is statutory authority for this practice.[15]

Indentation

3.6 The parliamentary drafter is quite prepared to use indentation:

(1) to break up text into smaller pieces; and

(2) to carry meaning.

The 1925 property legislation makes considerable use of indentation and even introduces it when re-enacting older provisions where it was not found.[16] The courts take account of indentation to ascertain meaning.[17]

Passive voice

3.7 Plain English style guides agree that the active voice should be preferred to the passive.[18] The reason is that the passive can be used without specifying an agent, so it can be vague. However, this rarely causes difficulty. Sometimes the passive is appropriate because there is no need to specify the agent. The most that can be said is that "restraint" should be exercised in the use of the passive voice.[19]

---

[15] Examples are too numerous to compile a complete list; but see ss.29(1) and 105(1) SLA 1925 (which both contain three paragraphs); s.41 TA 1925; s.190(2) Insolvency Act 1986.
[16] See e.g. s.31 TA 1925 re-enacting material from s.43(1) Conveyancing and Law of Property Act 1881. This process of introducing indentation and modern punctuation when re-enacting old legislation offers the opportunity is still continuing: see e.g. Sch.13 para.7 FA 1999, re-enacting s.59(1) Stamp Act 1891. (Contrast again the Hebrew bible where the now familiar punctuation was introduced into MSS as recently as the 10th Century.)
[17] *Macarthur v Greycoat Estates Mayfair* 67 TC 598 at 613.
[18] The advice goes back to Orwell ("Never use the passive when you can use the active").
[19] The view taken in Uniform Drafting Convention of Canada, *www.ulcc.ca/en/home*; and Christopher Williams, *Tradition and Change in Legal English*, Peter Lang, 2005, p.159.

General comment

The guiding principles are simplicity and clarity. Ordinary English usage is the guideline. Double negatives and worse[20] should be avoided. **3.8**

Brevity is a merit, but not a central aim. Lord Reid deplored "the modern drafting practice" of compressing to the point of obscurity provisions which would not be difficult to understand if written out at rather greater length.[21] But it is considered the professional trust drafter is hardly ever guilty of causing obscurity by excessive brevity.

Generally, rules of style should be regarded as no more than guidelines. Fowler has discredited many silly schoolmaster's rules of style (such as that no sentence should begin with *and* or *but*).[22] It would be a pity to replace them with new ones (such as not to use the word "shall" or the passive voice).

Numbers: words or figures?

The authors favour the recommendation of Garner, to spell out numbers **3.9**
up to ten and to use numerals for numbers 11 and above. But numerals are used even for numbers below ten in the context of calculations, before units of measure, or if the numbers are frequent throughout the text.[23]

The use of figures alone is certainly a defensible practice. This has long been the case in court documents.[24]

To set out words and figures is an act of supererogation and in Garner's words "a noxious practice".[25]

Style of clause numbering

The choice lies between: **3.10**

(1) the style used in statutes and

(2) decimal numbering (so-called "legal numbering").

---

[20] Parliament sets a poor example: s.89(2) Value Added Tax Act 1994 is a simple triple negative; s.102A(4) FA 1986 (inserted by the FA 1999) is a quadruple negative.

[21] *Anisminic v Foreign Compensation Commission* [1969] 2 AC 147 at 171.

[22] See David Crystal's unputdownable history of the English language, *The Stories of English* (Allan Lane, 2004) esp. Ch.16 (Standard rules).

[23] *Dictionary of Modern Legal Usage*, 2nd edn, OUP, 1995, entry under *numerals*. This was the usage of the parliamentary drafter, until the regrettable change in the TCGA 1992; now the word *two* has become 2, etc. Perhaps this is an attempt to make the legislation appear shorter?

[24] CPR Pt 5, para.2.2(6) (All numbers including dates to be expressed in figures). In affidavits the change from words to numerals was made in 1923: [1923] W.N. 288. In pleadings the use of figures goes back to Sch.1 Ord.19 r.4 Supreme Court of Judicature Act 1875.

[25] There have been many cases where words and numbers failed to correspond. The mistake is easy enough to make in all conscience. Such errors arise from time to time in practice. Thus a drafting technique presumably intended to prevent ambiguity actually gives rise to new and quite unnecessary difficulties. For the construction of documents where numbers and figures conflict, see Lewison, *The Interpretation of Contracts* (4th edn, 2007, 9.11). The parliamentary drafter has never used both words and figures.

24   STYLE

The choice does not much matter. The latter though more cumbersome is gaining ground, and has the support of International Standard 1502145-1978.[26] This is used in the precedents in this book; though not quite consistently, as cross-references within a clause are easier to arrange with the other system and when one passes the level of sub-paragraphs, an (a) or (b) seems easier than a number such as 3.2.2.2.1.

Dates

3.11   The form "1st February 1991" is recommended.[27]

The form *"The first day of February 1991"* is unwieldy and *"The first day of February one thousand nine hundred and ninety one"* should certainly be avoided.

Addresses

3.12   Parties to a deed are identified by name and address:

> John Smith of 5 High Street, Topton, AB1 3XY.[28]

or

> X Limited of [address][29] ...

Two individuals with the same address

Where two individuals share the same address one could set it out twice in full, though this appears slightly clumsy. The traditional form was to abbreviate using the word "aforesaid", e.g.:

> This Deed is made [date] between
> John Smith of 21 High St, Topton, OX1 6LX and
> Lucy Smith of 21 High St *aforesaid*

This should be modernised: the following sets out formulae to suit all occasions. Where the two individuals are joint parties to a deed one can simply set out the single address:

> John Smith and Jane Smith both of 21 High Street, Topton, OX1 6LX ("the Trustees")

---

[26] Accessible on *www.kessler.co.uk*.
[27] The form: "1/2/1991" is best avoided as it would be read as Jan 2nd in the USA.
[28] It is sensible to use the conventional form of address with which the Post Office would be familiar rather than the archaic "in the county of Derby".
[29] Alternatively, "whose registered office is at ..."; but that is unnecessary. The address is after all only for identification.

Where the two individuals are separate parties say:

This Deed is made [date] between
John Smith of 21 High St, Topton, OX1 6LX ("the Settlor") of the one part and Lucy Smith also of 21 High St, Topton[30] ("the Trustee") of the other part.

In the case of husband and wife it is more elegant to state the relationship and omit the address of the second party mentioned. An address is included for purposes of identification and having stated the relationship nothing more is needed; thus:

This Deed is made [date] between:

(1) John Smith of 21 High St, Topton, OX1 6LX ("the Settlor") of the one part and
(2) the Settlor and Lucy Smith the wife of the Settlor ("the Trustees") of the other part.

Age

It is sufficient to say "the age of 25", not "the age of twenty-five years". There is statutory authority for the omission of the word "years".[31] No one will think it means months, lunar or solar. **3.13**

Singular and plural

The singular includes the plural.[32] So do not say "person or persons",[33] "by deed or deeds", "Trustee or Trustees",[34] "beneficiary or beneficiaries", "other or others". **3.14**

Male and female

There are three ways to deal with the issue of gender: **3.15**

(1) The drafter may seek circumlocutions appropriate to both genders. It is tiresome to have to avoid the convenient words "his" and "her". The cost is some inelegance of phrase:

The Trustees shall pay the income to the Principal Beneficiary during the life of the Principal Beneficiary and thereafter to the surviving spouse of the Principal Beneficiary during the life of that spouse.

---

[30] Give the first part of the address only; alternatively one could say: *of the same address*.
[31] Section 71 IHTA 1984 ("a specified age not exceeding eighteen"); s.163 TCGA 1992 ("the age of 50").
[32] Section 61 LPA 1925.
[33] Or worse, "person or persons or corporation or corporations" since the word "person" includes a corporation.
[34] Unfortunately the TA 1925 does not set a good example and often says "trustees or trustee", e.g. s.36(1)(a) TA 1925.

(2) The traditional approach is to use the masculine, which may be taken to include the feminine:

> The Trustees shall pay the income to the Principal Beneficiary during his life and thereafter to his widow during her life.

(3) Where the drafter knows the identity of the person referred to, he may select his/her, widow/widower as required:

> The Trustees shall pay the income to Jane during her life and thereafter to her widower during his life.

It is considered the choice is a matter of style and one should not be dogmatic.[35] This book adopts form (3) where possible. It is not too much trouble: every trust must be revised to some extent to the circumstances of the case. Where that is not possible, this book adopts form (2) for the sake of simplicity.

And/provided that/but

3.16 There is nothing wrong with the word "and". There is no harm in a proviso (a clause beginning "provided that ...") if used in moderation; but a separate sentence or clause would usually be clearer.

"And/or" generates strong feelings ("that bastard conjunction"[36]) and should be avoided.[37]

Deemed/treated as

3.17 The proper use of "deem" is to assume something to be a fact which is not, or may not be the case: to create a legal fiction. A piquant example is the rule, now abolished, that the income of a married woman living with her husband was:

> *deemed* for income tax purposes to be his income and not to be her income.[38]

The expression "treated as" is a modern equivalent of "deemed to be".[39]
Thankfully, deeming provisions are rarely if ever needed in trust drafting and the word "deemed" is not used in this book.

---

[35] It must be added that some do not see this as a question of style but as an issue of sexual politics on which views may be strongly held. For an introduction to this fraught topic see Garner, *Modern Legal Usage* (2nd edn, 1995), entry under "Sexism".
[36] *Bonitto v Fuerst Bros* [1944] AC 75 at 82 (Viscount Simon).
[37] For a discussion see Garner, *Modern Legal Usage* (2nd edn, 1995), entry under "and/or".
[38] Section 279 ICTA 1988. The rule survives in other jurisdictions, such as Jersey.
[39] e.g. s.4(4) PAA 1964, which the Law Commission propose in their report (Law Comm. No. 251) to re-enact as cl.8(2) of the draft Perpetuities and Accumulations Bill. The drafter has taken the opportunity to replace "deemed to be" with "treated as".

"Deemed" is sometimes employed as a verbose equivalent of the simple present tense. If the reader sees the word "deemed" in trust drafting he will almost always find it misused this way. The sort of sloppy usage one finds is:

> Section 32 Trustee Act 1925 shall be *deemed* to apply as if the provisos had been omitted.
>
> "X" shall be *deemed* to mean ...

These should read:

> Section 32 Trustee Act 1925 shall apply as if ...
>
> "X" means ...

The otiose "deemed" is used here merely to give a spurious legal feel to the text and should be omitted.[40] The parliamentary drafter adopts this approach.

Archaic and prolix expressions

Here are some archaic or prolix forms which can clutter legal documentation. It is not suggested that these forms should never be used: in normal circumstances, however, they add nothing and are best avoided. The list is not and cannot be comprehensive. **3.18**

ARCHAIC OR PROLIX FORM	SUGGESTED FORM
accretion e.g. holds as an accretion to	add to
as the case may be	[omit]
as the trustees shall/may think fit	as the trustees think fit
deemed	[generally, omit][41]
desirous of	desires to; wishes to[42]

---

[40] Of course where the word "deemed" is misused the context should govern the meaning. Thus the literal reading of "deemed" in s.2 FA 1894 accepted in *Earl Cowley v IRC* [1899] AC 19 was rejected in the striking judgment of Viscount Simonds in *Public Trustee v IRC* [1960] AC at 415. The language deserves to be remembered even though Estate Duty is now obsolete: "Observations so patently wrong (may I be forgiven for saying so) that they leave only a sense of wonderment—unnecessary to the decision, for, as Lord Davey pointed out, the same result could be reached by another route—by Lord Davey himself accepted and dissented from in the same breath—flatly contradicted in 1924 by Lord Haldane who in 1914 had adopted them—the source of endless doubt and confusion to all who have been concerned in the examination or administration of this branch of law...".

[41] 3.17 (Deemed/treated as).

[42] The 1925 property legislation uses "is desirous of" and "desires to" interchangeably and in about equal measure. Modern Parliamentary drafting generally adopts the advice of Garner's *Modern Legal Usage* (2nd edn, 1995), see e.g. ss.36(1), 39 TA 1925.

28 STYLE

ARCHAIC OR PROLIX FORM	SUGGESTED FORM
even date e.g. of even date herewith	at the same time as this settlement
hereby	[omit]
hereof e.g. clause 1 hereof clause 10 hereof the date hereof the trustees hereof	clause 1 above clause 10 below the date of this deed the trustees of this settlement
hereto e.g. the first schedule hereto	the first schedule below
irrevocably witnesses	witnesses[43]
infant	minor[44]
instrument	document
issue	descendant
it is hereby declared that	[omit]
it shall be lawful for the trustees to	the trustees may
the laws of England	English law *or* the law of England[45]
moiety	half
moneys	money
notwithstanding any rule of law or equity to the contrary	[omit]
notwithstanding that	even though; whether or not
or other the …	or
presents e.g. these presents	this deed

---

[43] 10.26 (Testatum)

[44] "Infant" has been archaic in English law since s.12 Family Law Reform Act 1969: "A person who is not of full age may be described as a minor instead of an infant …". This is the consistent usage in the TLATA 1996. e.g. s.7(5) TLATA 1996, re-enacting s. 28(4) LPA 1925, substitutes the word "minor" for "infant". The Children's Act 1989 and other legislation outside property law context (e.g. The Civil Procedures Rules 1998) prefer the term "child". But *child* can simply mean the son or daughter of a person rather than someone under the age of 18. In trust drafting "children" is usually used in that sense in the definition of Beneficiaries, so "minor" is the best word to refer to a person under 18.

[45] The plural form has scarcely been used by the Parliamentary Drafter since the 19th century. William Twining delightfully construes the plural *laws* as an affirmation of legal positivism: *Blackstone's Tower: The English Law School* (1994), p.68. But we may leave that to the dons as it would neither occur to, nor trouble, anyone else.

ARCHAIC OR PROLIX FORM	SUGGESTED FORM
provided always that	provided that; but
said	[omit]
stand possessed	hold
subject as aforesaid	subject to that
testatrix	testator[46]
the following, that is to say:	the following:
the trustees shall have power to/ the right to	the trustees may
upon the trusts and with and subject to the powers and conditions of	on the terms of …
the trust fund and the income thereof[47]	the trust fund
on trust as to both capital and income	on trust
will or codicil	Will[48]

Clause headings

Clause headings are widely used, and rightly so, since they greatly assist the reader of a document. In lifetime trusts they are standard. In wills they are less frequent; that only reflects the sad truth that less attention is lavished on a will (or that wills are often shorter). Nevertheless clause headings are still regarded with suspicion. It is common to see a provision to the effect that:

3.19

Clause headings are for convenience of reference only and shall not affect the construction hereof.

This is the wrong approach. In a well-drafted document there will be no conflict between the clause heading and the clause. If there were, the court

---

[46] 17.10 (Will trusts and lifetime trusts: drafting differences).
[47] This form is quite common, following the example of the Statutory Will Forms, accessible on *www.kessler.co.uk*. But in *Re Geering* [1964] Ch 136, concerning a deferred gift of "the trust fund and the income thereof", Cross J. held that (in the absence of a special context) no inference could be drawn from these words. In particular, the form did not shed any light on the question of whether the gift carried the intermediate income. So the words are plainly otiose.
[48] The word "will" (subject to context) is taken to include a codicil. This was accepted without argument in *Re Meredith* [1924] 2 Ch 552.

would not construe a clause heading so as to override an express provision in a clause. The clause heading would only be an aid to the construction of a clause.[49] A court should be encouraged to use that aid. Statutes, which have long had clause headings or side notes, do not use such a clause[50] and experience shows no difficulty has arisen. Where the clause is there, it is asking the judge to do something which is very difficult if not impossible: to disregard material on the same page as the substantive clause being interpreted.[51] Is that really what the drafter is trying to say with this clause? Who can unbite the apple of knowledge? It may be that the clause originated when clause headings were an innovation and before the judicial response to them had been ascertained. The clause has continued since then by the tradition of paying no attention to standard form clauses.

It is sometimes appropriate to give clause headings to sub-clauses.

Incorporation by reference

3.20 As a general rule it is better to set text out in full and not to incorporate text by reference. Rather than say:

> *the Trustees shall have the powers of appropriation and other incidental powers conferred on personal representatives by section 41 of the Administration of Estates Act 1925 ...*

it is better to set out a power of appropriation in full. Not everyone is familiar with the terms of s.41 of the Administration of Estates Act 1925.

To the general rule exceptions may be made of convenience or necessity. The majority of trust deeds incorporate s.32 of the Trustee Act 1925 by reference with slight amendment. In this book this is unnecessary, but no criticism could be fairly made of this drafting technique. Statute sometimes requires the incorporation by reference of s.31 of the Trustee Act 1925 (maintenance and accumulation). On a convenient short form of trustees' powers using the technique of incorporation by reference see 19.20 (STEP Standard Provisions). Wills in this book make gifts of personal chattels "as defined in section 55, Administration of Estates Act

---

[49] "The road north leads northwards even when the signpost has been turned round in the opposite direction", *Trow v Ind Coope (West Midlands) Ltd* [1967] 2 QB 899, at 929 (Salmon L.J.). *R v Schildkamp* [1971] AC 1 at p.28: "A side-note is a very brief precis of the section and therefore forms a most unsure guide to the construction ..." (Lord Upjohn). See further Lewison, *The Interpretation of Contracts* (4th edn, 2007).

[50] There are sporadic exceptions, e.g. s.96(10) Value Added Tax Act 1994. But the normal statutory practice has always been to omit this form ever since clause headings were first used in the 1845 Consolidation Acts. Nor is it found in that admirable example of modern drafting, the Law Society's Standard Conditions of Sale.

[51] In the Republic of Ireland, Judges have in practice had regard to clause headings despite a provision in their Interpretation Act which purports to prohibit that: see the Irish Law Commission Report, Statutory Drafting and Interpretation, 2000, para.4.11 ff accessible on *www.lawreform.ie*.

1925". This statutory definition corresponds to the ordinary meaning of the expression.

Artificial rules of construction

3.21 Some drafters like to take advantage of artificial rules of construction. There are two which are commonly used in trust drafting. They are best avoided.

The class closing rule

3.22 The class closing rule is also known as the rule in *Andrews v Partington*.[52] For instance: a gift is made to "such of my children as shall attain 21 absolutely". Once the first child has attained 21, the class closes so a child born later will not take a share in the gift. The trust lawyer should understand this. However, a document which does not spell out exactly what it means is confusing for the less experienced reader; the drafter should avoid such usage on principle.

The rule in Lassence v Tierney *or* Hancock v Watson

3.23 The form usually called *Lassence v Tierney* form (sometimes called *Hancock v Watson* form)[53] gives beneficiaries shares of capital which first appear to be absolute entitlements; and then (inconsistently) to provide that the shares do not belong to the beneficiary absolutely, but are held on trust. Thus:
   (1) The Trust fund shall be held on trust for such of the Principal Beneficiaries as shall attain the age of 25 and if more than one in equal shares.
   (2) On the Principal Beneficiary attaining the age of 25 his share shall be held on the following trusts ...

This is unnecessary and confusing, at least to the reader who is not a trust practitioner.

Cross-references

3.24 It is tempting when drafting one clause to refer to another; for instance:

   subject to the overriding powers conferred by clause ... hereof ...

---

[52] (1791) 3 Bro. C.C.401.
[53] *Lassence v Tierney* (1849) 1 Mac. & G. 551, 41 ER 1379; *Hancock v Watson* [1902] AC 14. For a discussion of this form see *Watson v Holland* [1984] STC 373.

It is best to avoid cross-reference by paragraph number. Any amendment to the draft will require consequent amendment to the clause references. Errors easily slip in. Where there are internal cross-references it is helpful to add in brackets a short explanation of the provision referred to, e.g. "subject to clause 4 (overriding powers)...".

Obsolete forms

Coverture

3.25   *The trustees shall pay the income to Mrs X during her life without power of anticipation during coverture.*[54]

This form prevented a married woman from disposing of her right to income. These restraints have long been abolished, and do not now take effect.[55]

"For her separate use"

3.26   *The trustees shall pay the income to Mrs X during her life for her separate use.*

This form protected a married woman's property from her husband. It has been unnecessary since 1882. The concept of "separate" property was abolished in 1935.[56]

Entails

3.27   Entails have been formally abolished by the Trusts of Land and Appointment of Trustees Act 1996, though they had been effectively obsolete for many years.

---

[54] "During coverture" means "during marriage". Sometimes the same point is made in a general clause (usually placed at the end of a Will or Trust) along these lines:

"*In every case in which any interest whether absolute or limited and whether in possession or remainder or in expectancy is given to or in trust for any female she shall not during any coverture have power to dispose of or charge the same or any part thereof by way of anticipation.*"

[55] The Married Women (Restraint Upon Anticipation) Act 1949. This law reform led to a Blimpian diatribe in *Key & Elphinstone* (14th edn) concluding with an (with hindsight) unfortunate recommendation for the use of protective trusts.

[56] Married Women's Property Act 1882; see now Law Reform (Married Women and Tortfeasors) Act 1935.

Trusts for sale

The trust for sale was required before January 1, 1997 to prevent trusts falling within the scope of the Settled Land Act 1925. The position now is that no new trust can be a settlement for the purposes of the SLA 1925.[57] Accordingly, it is not necessary to use a trust for sale of land. It has never been necessary to use a trust for sale of personal property. These clauses can now be regarded as completely obsolete.

3.28

Drafters are constantly adding to their drafts, but rarely deleting. The inclusion of additional material, it is thought, does no harm whereas (who knows?) any omission might be unfortunate. In this way much material is introduced where it serves no purpose. This book attempts to step back from that process. Whenever common forms are omitted, an attempt is made to give the basis and justification why such forms or expressions are considered to be unnecessary or otiose. Few questions are so difficult to prove as those to which the answer is obvious; sometimes the reasoning must end in an appeal to self-evidence.

---

[57] Section 2 TLATA 1996. For a discussion of the old forms, see the second edition of this work (1995) at 6.041 accessible on *www.kessler.co.uk*.

CHAPTER 4

PRINCIPLES OF INTERPRETING TRUST DOCUMENTS

Introduction

4.1 This subject is difficult and it is helpful at the start to say why. The problems lie partly in the topic and partly in the case law.

Any short formulation of the principles of interpretation[1] can only be expressed at a high level of generality which makes their application doubtful and their usefulness to the practitioner questionable. There is no single principle of interpretation, and anything which purports to be a short statement of principle immediately needs explanation and qualification. Interpretation issues which arise in practice are generally complex and cases cannot be briefly summarised or neatly categorised. The principles upon which cases are decided are often assumed or not clearly expressed. Cases are not consistent: different judges have applied different principles, or the same principles in different ways; or any principle available as an ad hoc rationalisation to justify a fair result on the facts of the case. When judges wish to change the law, precedent and the declaratory theory of law encourage them to deny that they are doing so. The total case law relating to interpretation of documents or statutes is so vast that no one can draw it all together into a coherent body of law. The only thing worse than too little data is too much data. Even now some important aspects are hotly debated.

In short, as Voltaire observed, language is difficult to put into words. Nevertheless it is worth persevering.

---

[1] The terms "construction" and "interpretation" are synonymous (but "interpretation" is clearer, not legalese and so perhaps preferable). Occasionally writers attempt to desynonynize the two terms, in order to clear out some distinction or other, but none of these suggestions have been generally accepted.

General principle

The starting point is Lord Hoffmann's much cited speech in *Investors*   **4.2**
Compensation Scheme v West Bromwich Building Society.[2]
Lord Hoffmann posits:

> I think I should preface my explanation of my reasons with some general remarks about the principles by which contractual documents are nowadays construed. I do not think that the fundamental change[3] which has overtaken this branch of the law ... is always sufficiently appreciated. The result has been, subject to one important exception, to assimilate the way in which such documents are interpreted by judges to the common sense principles by which any serious utterance would be interpreted in ordinary life. *Almost all the old intellectual baggage of "legal" interpretation has been discarded.*(1) Interpretation is the ascertainment of the meaning which the document would convey to a reasonable person having all the background knowledge which would reasonably have been available to the parties in the situation in which they were at the time of the contract.[4]

---

[2] [1998] 1 WLR 896 pp.912–913 affirmed *BCCI v Ali* [2002] 1 AC 251 at para.8. (The way that the majority applied the principles to the contract in *BCCI* was untenable, for reasons given in the dissenting speech of Lord Hoffmann, but what matters is that the principles themselves were accepted.) See Ewan McKendrick "The Interpretation of Contracts: Lord Hoffmann's Re-Statement" in *Commercial Law & Commercial Practice*, ed. Sarah Worthington, Hart Publishing, 2003 (hereafter "McKendrick"). There are similar trends in Canada: see *Drafting Trusts & Will Trusts in Canada*, James Kessler QC and Fiona Hunter, Butterworths, 2003, Ch.3.

[3] It is not possible to identify a precise date or single author of this "fundamental change." Of the two cases which Lord Hoffmann cites to, *Prenn v Simmonds* [1971] 1 WLR 1381 at 1384–1386 does contain a strongly worded passage ("The time has long passed when agreements ... were isolated from the matrix of facts in which they were set and interpreted purely on internal linguistic considerations"). But like many (perhaps most?) important changes, its roots can be traced much earlier:

> "It is difficult to measure what success the courts have achieved in attempting to give effect to the intentions of testators. One Chancery judge is reputed to have said 'I shudder to think that in the hereafter I shall have to meet those testators whose wishes on earth have been frustrated by my judgments.' [Attributed to Eve J., (1941) 60 *Law Notes* 26.] This dictum seems to have been in the mind of Lord Atkin when, in a case which did much to free the courts from some rather technical rules of construction, he said 'I anticipate with satisfaction that henceforth the group of ghosts of dissatisfied testators who, according to a late Chancery judge, wait on the other bank of the Styx to receive the judicial personages who have misconstrued their wills, may be considerably diminished'."

See Megarry's wonderful *Miscellany at Law*, 1955, p.162, citing *Perrin v Morgan* [1943] AC 399 at 415. *Pepper v Hart* [1993] AC 593 can be understood as reflecting the trend to search slightly harder for intention at the cost of convenience (though subsequent experience has shown the cost/benefit ratio to be so high that the Courts are now resiling from it).

[4] [1998] 1 WLR 912 (emphasis added).

Factual background/previous negotiations/declarations of intent

4.3 Lord Hoffmann continues:

> (2) The background was famously referred to by Lord Wilberforce as the "matrix of fact", but this phrase is, if anything, an understated description of what the background may include. Subject to the requirement that it should have been reasonably available to the parties and to the exception to be mentioned next, it includes absolutely anything which would have affected the way in which the language of the document would have been understood by a reasonable man.
>
> (3) The law excludes from the admissible background
>
>> [a] the previous negotiations of the parties and
>> [b] their declarations of subjective intent.
>
> They are admissible only in an action for rectification. The law makes this distinction for reasons of practical policy and, in this respect only, legal interpretation differs from the way we would interpret utterances in ordinary life.[5] The boundaries of this exception are in some respects unclear. But this is not the occasion on which to explore them.

We have here one rule of inclusion: the Court must consider what Lord Hoffmann terms "background"; and two exclusions—the Court will not consider previous negotiations or declarations of subjective intent. There are (as Lord Hoffmann suggests) a number of tensions in these principles. Some commentators advocate extending admissibility to include previous negotiations; others wish to restrict admissibility of evidence relating to background.[6] In construing wills and trusts, the tax background should certainly be taken into account.[7]

Separate from the question of what background the Court must "consider" is the question of what effect this considering should have on interpretation.[8] This takes us back to the problem of meaning.

---

[5] Literary criticism (or at least one school of it) adopts the same approach. See Wimsatt and Beardsley's essay, "The Intentional Fallacy" (reprinted in *The Verbal Icon*, Noonday Press, 1954):

> "The intention of the author is neither available nor desirable as a standard for judging the success of a work of literary art. ... Critical enquiries are not settled by consulting the oracle [the author]."

But interpretation of legal and literary documents is in this respect quite unlike the interpretation of less formal communications, and that is what Lord Hoffmann means by "utterances in ordinary life".

[6] See 4.6 (Inadmissibility rules).

[7] e.g. IR 12 is taken into account in construing pension schemes; the authorities are discussed in Keith Rowley QC, "The Interpretation of Scheme Deeds", [2003] TLI 129 at 134; likewise *BCCI v Ali* [2002] 1 AC 251 at [39].

[8] The questions overlap of course because it can only be right to consider background which may have an effect on the construction of a document.

Meaning of words *v* meaning of document

Continuing Lord Hoffmann's speech in *Investors Compensation Scheme*: **4.4**

> (4) The meaning which a document (or any other utterance) would convey to a reasonable man is not the same thing as the meaning of its words. The meaning of words is a matter of dictionaries[9] and grammars; the meaning of the document is what the parties using those words against the relevant background would reasonably have been understood to mean. The background may not merely enable the reasonable man to choose between the possible meanings of words which are ambiguous but even (as occasionally happens in ordinary life) to conclude that the parties must, for whatever reason, have used the wrong words or syntax ...
> (5) The "rule" that words should be given their "natural and ordinary meaning" reflects the common sense proposition that we do not easily accept that people have made linguistic mistakes, particularly in formal documents. On the other hand, if one would nevertheless conclude from the background that something must have gone wrong with the language, the law does not require judges to attribute to the parties an intention which they plainly could not have had.
> ... Leggatt LJ said that the judge's construction was not an "available meaning" of the words. If this means that judges cannot, short of rectification, decide that the parties must have made mistakes of meaning or syntax, I respectfully think he was wrong.

Lord Hoffmann draws a distinction between:

(1) the meaning of words[10] and

(2) the meaning which a document conveys.[11]

It is obvious that such a conflict may exist. It may arise in three different circumstances:

---

[9] Lawyers are not the only ones who may misuse dictionaries. Cf. the definition of "Dictionary" in Bierce's *Enlarged Devil's Dictionary*: "A malevolent literary device for cramping the growth of a language and making it hard and inelastic."

[10] Of course this begs the question of how one ascertains the meaning of words (isolated from background or context). The conceptual problem is not clarified but rather made even more obscure, by adding the epithet "natural", and seeking a "natural" meaning. Lord Hoffmann again:

> "I think that in some cases the notion of words having a natural meaning is not a very helpful one. Because the meaning of words is so sensitive to syntax and context, the natural meaning of words in one sentence may be quite unnatural in another. Thus a statement that words have a particular natural meaning may mean no more than that in many contexts they will have that meaning. In other contexts their meaning will be different but no less natural."

Charter Reinsurance Co Ltd v Fagan [1997] AC 313 at 391.
One sees how philosophers are drawn to the (non-intuitive) view that a word out of context has no meaning. If an exaggeration, this is at least a healthy reaction against over-emphasis on dictionary meaning.

[11] Of course this begs the question of how one ascertains "the meaning which a document conveys".

(1) The conflict may arise having regard only to the words of the document ("document context"). No-one has ever doubted that words must be construed with regard to document context[12] and in this sense the meaning of a document overrides the meaning of words in it.

(2) The conflict may arise having regard to background knowledge not stated in the document but which would be known to the parties and known to any reasonably well-informed reader (including a judge) without need for evidence. We refer to this as "intuitive context". In extreme cases no one has ever doubted that words must be construed with regard to intuitive context, and in this sense too the meaning of a document (if one can find it) may override the meaning of its words. Even the most ardent literalist would agree that, say, a gift expressed to be to the "National Society for the Promotion of Cruelty to Children" should take effect as a gift to the National Society for the *Prevention* of Cruelty to Children. Why is this? Because we know the background facts that the NSPCC exists and testators commonly make gifts to it; a National Society for the promotion of cruelty to children does not exist and no one would make a gift to it. But as soon as that is conceded, the extreme position that interpretation should *only* have regard to the plain meaning of words is lost. Lord Hoffmann is only expressing with more enthusiasm a principle which has for some time been observed by lawyers[13] and others.[14]

It is in this particular area of conflict that the distinction is drawn between a literal (or semantic) as opposed to a less literal (or purposive)[15] approach. The difference between the two is a matter of degree.

(3) The conflict may arise only when one has regard to evidence of background fact that would be known to the parties but not known to a judge (or others) unless additional evidence was provided. Lord

---

[12] See e.g. Lord Hardwicke, *Milner v Milner* (1748) Ves. Sen. 1 p.105, citing Roman law.

[13] For example, see *Re Doland* [1970] Ch 267 at 272:

"The point may be reached at which apparent caprice does become a warning signal that something may have gone awry with the testator's true expression of his intention. An error in drafting is sometimes clearly apparent from a grammatical defect, when for instance some word or words have been obviously omitted by accident. Or it may be manifest from the context that a testator has at a particular point used a mistaken word or a wrong name. In such cases if the court is clear about the true intention, it will, as an exercise of interpretation, give effect to that intention and for that purpose will remould the testator's language. Similarly, if the consequence of the language used by a testator, read in its primary and natural sense, is to produce a disposition or a series of dispositions which is so capricious as to be really irrational, the court may, in my judgment, be justified in concluding that the testator has failed to express himself adequately, and in such a case if, but only if, it can discern the true intention of the testator, it will give effect to it."

[14] E.g. C.S. Lewis, *Studies in Words*, 1960 Ch.1, Pt IV distinguishes "word's meaning" and "speaker's (or writer's) meaning". Wittgenstein, *Tractatus Logico-philosophicus* 5.4732: "we cannot give a sign a wrong sense". The battle between words and documents extends to biblical interpretation; see James Barr, *The Semantics of Biblical Language* (OUP, 1961).

[15] *Hawkins on the Construction of Wills,* 5th edn, 2000 uses the term "intentionalist".

Hoffmann's position (that this kind of background should be used to a greater degree than before in deciding issues of interpretation) is controversial.[16] This problem does not often arise in the interpretation of trusts.

The hard question in cases (1) and (2) and (if the evidence is admitted) in case (3) is not *whether* either kind of context can overturn the meaning of words but how easily or in what circumstances. In other words, how *does* one ascertain the meaning of a document?

The objective principle

The old style of legal interpretation had an answer to this problem. It drew a sharp distinction between: **4.5**

(1) subjective intention, i.e. the intention[17] in the mind of the author(s), the psychological data; and

(2) objective meaning, the objective[18] meaning of the words used.

Having drawn this distinction, the solution to the problem of interpretation was seen to lie in ignoring the subjective intention in favour of the objective meaning. This is here called "the objective principle".[19]

There are three ways that this principle has been expressed:

(1) The court seeks to find the intention of the parties but the expression "intention" actually *means* "the meaning of the document".

(2) The court seeks to find the intention of the parties but the meaning of the document is *deemed* to be the intention.

(3) The court seeks to find the meaning of the words and intention of the parties is irrelevant.

---

[16] See 4.6 (Inadmissibility rules).
[17] This begs the question of what we mean by "intention", but although there is much that could be said on the topic, "intention" is sufficiently clear to use for the purposes of this chapter without further analysis.
[18] "Objective meaning" is objective in the sense that it is independent of the mind of the individual *author(s)*. It is nevertheless often subjective in the sense that it will often depend on the mind of the *reader*, for the same text may convey different meanings to different minds. (It is submitted that meaning of a text may properly be called objective if all readers of the text in context would agree on the meaning even though the meaning is of course dependent on the minds of the readers as a community.)
[19] This expression is capable of various meanings and should not be used undefined. It has not been used in the law reports. The objective principle of interpretation is distinct from the objective principle of contract formation. Among other differences, the principle of interpretation extends beyond contracts and applies to other legal documents.

40   PRINCIPLES OF INTERPRETING TRUST DOCUMENTS

Identification of "intention" with "meaning"

Lewison enthusiastically supports the first view:

> For the purpose of the construction of contracts, the intention of the parties is the meaning of the words they have used. There is no intention independent of that meaning ... In other words "intention" is equivalent to "meaning".[20]

Lewison cites *IRC v Raphael*:[21]

> The fact is that the narrative [recitals] and operative parts of a deed perform quite different functions, and "intention" in reference to the narrative and the same word in reference to the operative parts respectively bear quite different significations. As appearing in the narrative part it means "purpose". In considering the intention of the operative part the word means significance or import—"the way in which anything is to be understood" (*Oxford English Dictionary*) supported by the illustration: "The intention of the passage was sufficiently clear".

This linguistic usage is to be utterly rejected for the following reasons:

(1) That is not the way the word "intention" is normally used.

(2) This usage is a sleight of hand giving the comforting impression that the reader or judge is seeking to find the true subjective intention; which is at best only partly the case.

(3) This usage makes a discussion of the subjective/objective aspects of construction impossible.

In short, this usage highjacks the meaning of "intention" in an Orwellian manner: contrast use of the word "democratic" in the *German Democratic Republic* or "trust" in *National Health Trust*.

Deemed intention

4.5.1 The second and more usual analysis is not to define (or misdefine) the word "intention" to mean "meaning" but to use the language of presumption or deeming:

> The question is not so much what was the intention, as what, in the contemplation of the law, must be presumed to have been the intention.[22]

---

[20] *Interpretation of Contracts*, 4th edn, 2007, 2.05. Some non-lawyers adopt the same approach: see Stanley Fish, *Doing What Comes Naturally*, 1989, p.116 (a surprisingly readable Derridian text).
[21] [1935] AC 96 at 135.
[22] *Miller v Farmer* (1815) 1 Merrivale 55 at 80 (Lord Eldon).

This view is taken in *Norton on Deeds*[23]:

> ... the question to be answered always is, "What is the meaning of what the parties have said?" not "What did the parties mean to say?" ... it being a presumption *juris et de jure* ... that the parties intended to say that which they have said.

This is distinct from the first approach, since it recognises that a distinction exists between the intention and that which is merely deemed (presumed) to be the intention; this is stressed because many cases and textbooks adopt both approaches in the same paragraph. The two are incompatible. The second approach is better than the first, but it is still to be rejected. The deeming is a fiction; all fictions are lies, and while they may have their purposes, the fiction is not needed here.

Intention irrelevant

The third and honest analysis is to forego the word "intention" altogether. Here are some examples from 19th-century case law: **4.5.2**

> The question in this and other cases of construction of written instruments, is, not what was the intention of the parties; but what is the meaning of the words they have used.[24] In expounding a will, the court is to ascertain, not what the testator actually intended, as contradistinguished from what his words express, but what is the meaning of the words he has used. I consider it doubtful what the testator actually meant should be done. But I have no doubt as to the meaning of the words used by him.[25]

Oliver Wendell Holmes, writing off the record, put the point more bluntly:

> We don't care a damn for the meaning of the writer, the only question is the meaning of the words.[26]

Relationship between objective principle and inadmissibility rules

The rule of inadmissibility of statements of intent/pre-contract negotiations is sometimes said to be founded on the objective principle.[27] This reasoning **4.6**

---

[23] (2nd edn, 1928), p.50 approved *Schuler v Wickman Machine Tool Sales* [1974] AC 235.
[24] *Rickman v Carstairs* (1833) 5 B. & Ad. 663 (Lord Denman).
[25] *Doe v Gwilum* (1833) 5 B. & Ad. 122 at 129 (Lord Wensleydale).
[26] Holmes–Pollock letters (9th December 1898).
[27] "The exclusion of the parties' subjective declarations of intent from the admissible material is a reflection of the principle that a contract must be interpreted objectively." Lewison, *The Interpretation of Contracts*, 4th edn, 2007, para.5.12.

is not just fallacious but pernicious. The reason for the inadmissibility rules is that they offer practical, pragmatic advantages. In particular:

(1) Cost saving: the cost of reviewing the additional evidence must be set against the number of occasions where it is significant. This applies not only to litigation but to every occasion where advice is given on construction. Some say that the cost/benefit ratio is very high.

(2) Admissibility is unfair to assignees and other third parties who may not be aware of this material.[28]

Where the balance of advantage lies is at present actively debated. Those who think the cost/benefit ratio is low (or can be reduced by case management) would favour a relaxation of the exclusory rules. Those who think the cost/benefit ratio is high will favour retention of strict inadmissibility rules. This debate cannot be carried out (and so a well grounded rule of law cannot be achieved) if the inadmissibility rules are said to be necessary consequences of an "objective principle" which is not open for debate. There is no reasoning with that and no arguing with it; it suppresses the policy debate which ought to be taking place.

In this debate the rules of inadmissibility of statements of intent and pre-contract negotiations should be considered separately. Everyone agrees that the rule excluding statements of intent is a sound rule.[29] The merit of the rule excluding prior negotiations is hotly contested.[30]

---

[28] There is obviously some strength in this objection but a workable solution is to restrict admissibility in the case of assets (such as leases) whose assignment is a substantial possibility. In these cases rectification is a better tool as it is a discretionary remedy which can be refused if necessary to protect third parties.

In *Prenn v Simmonds* [1971] 1 WLR 1381 at 1384, Lord Wilberforce offers a different reason:

"... such evidence is unhelpful. By the nature of things, where negotiations are difficult, the parties' positions, with each passing letter, are changing and until the final agreement, though converging, still divergent. It is only the final document which records a consensus."

Unfortunately this is not true: a consensus will usually be reached on some points well before the final agreement; otherwise the evidence would be equally unhelpful in rectification cases (which is not the case).

[29] "Once a judgment has been published, its interpretation belongs to posterity and its author and those who agreed with him at the time have no better claim to be able to declare its meaning than anyone else": *Deutsche Morgan Grenfell v HMRC* [2007] 1 AC 558 at [14].

[30] McMeel advocates extending admissibility of prior negotiations in his excellent article [2003] LQR 272: "Prior negotiations and subsequent conduct—the next step forward for contractual interpretation?" Lord Nicholls agrees: "My kingdom for a horse: the meaning of words" [2005] LQR 577. Sir Christopher Staughton calls for restrictions: "It is hard to imagine a ruling more calculated to perpetuate the vast cost of commercial litigation" [1999] CLJ 303 "How do Courts Interpret Commercial Contracts". Few advocate admissibility of simple declarations of intent by the parties (but even if officially excluded they may slip in under the guise of background fact). The current distinction between background (admissible) and previous negotiations (inadmissible) is also troublesome since previous negotiations will contain factual background. For the use of earlier agreements/trust documents to ascertain construction, see Paul Newman "Archaeology and construction: the use of predecessors to ascertain the meaning of a contract" [2006] TLI 115. Subsequent conduct raises similar problems: the traditional view is that it should not be relevant

Relationship between objective principle and literal construction

The approach of seeking objective meaning (as opposed to subjective intention) is often taken to be synonymous with a literal or semantic (as opposed to a less literal or purposive) approach. But this does not follow at all. It is true that a literal approach to construction is not consistent with a search for the subjective intention of the author. However, a less literal and more background-sensitive reading of the kind advocated by Lord Hoffmann can properly be described as a search for the author's subjective meaning. Lord Hoffmann said:

4.7

> It is of course true that the law is not concerned with the speaker's subjective intentions. But the notion that the law's concern is therefore with the "meaning of his words" conceals an important ambiguity. The ambiguity lies in a failure to distinguish between the meanings of words and the question of what would be understood as the meaning of a person who uses words. The meaning of words, as they would appear in the dictionary, and the effect of their syntactical arrangement, as it would appear in a grammar, is part of the material which we use to understand a speaker's utterance. But it is only a part; another part is our knowledge of the background against which the utterance was made. It is that background which enables us, not only to choose the intended meaning when a word has more than one dictionary meaning but also, in the ways I have expressed, to understand a speaker's meaning, often without ambiguity, when he has used the wrong words.
>
> When, therefore, lawyers say that they are concerned, not with subjective meaning but with the meaning of the language which the speaker has used, what they mean is that they are concerned with what he would objectively have been understood to mean. This involves examining not only the words and the grammar but the background as well.[31]

This takes us back to Lord Hoffmann's statement of general principle set out at 4.2 (General principle). He refers to "meaning which a document would convey to a reasonable person". However, a reasonable person looks for subjective intention of the author where possible, so it comes to the same thing. There is no practical difference between Lord Hoffman's approach and an approach expressly looking for subjective intention. They are two buses to the same destination. But the latter is to be preferred as it more accurately expresses the destination. Lord Steyn makes this point:

> In determining the meaning of the language of a commercial contract, and unilateral contractual notices, the law therefore generally favours a commercially sensible construction. The reason for this approach is that *a commercial*

---

to construction but some advocate that it should be. *Ali v Lane* [2006] EWCA Civ 1532 represents a somewhat illogical compromise between the conflicting authorities and is not likely to be the last word on the issue, in the absence of any consensus on what the law ought to be.

[31] *Mannai Investment Co v Eagle Star Life Assurance Society* [1997] AC 749 at 775.

construction is more likely to give effect to the intention of the parties. Words are therefore interpreted in the way in which a reasonable commercial person would construe them. And the standard of the reasonable commercial person is hostile to technical interpretations and undue emphasis on niceties of language.[32]

Arguments for and against the objective principle

4.8 We can and should distinguish between the objective principle[33] and the rules of inadmissibility of pre-contract negotiations and declarations of intent. They are completely separate rules and we can have one without the other. Having done so we can consider the merits of the objective principle.

The case against the objective principle is obvious and hardly needs to be stated. Those who sign legal documents have specific intentions in their mind and in principle they want *those* intentions to be acted on if possible and not any other.

The point is not theoretical. There is a good reason why a court should acknowledge that it is seeking to find the subjective intention of the parties. Disdain for subjective intention has pernicious consequences. It leads away from subjective intention where such intention does exist and can be found. Construction disassociated from the fetter of seeking subjective intention easily becomes very distant from it. Lewison quotes with approval the approach of Nourse L.J. (reversing the trial judge on the construction of a rent review clause):

> I think it very probable that, in accepting the landlord's construction, the learned judge has correctly assessed what the parties did indeed believe and desire to be the effect of [the clause]. But a court of construction can only hold that they intended it to have that effect if the intention appears from a fair interpretation of the words which they have used against the factual background known to them at or before the date of the lease ...[34]

Lewison defends this since:

> In the case of a lease there are potential successors in title of each party. Hence the court is right to insist that the intention must be made clear on the face of the contract.[35]

---

[32] *Mannai Investment Co v Eagle Star Life Assurance Society* [1997] AC 749 at 771 (emphasis added).
[33] By which is meant the principle that interpretation is the search for the objective meaning of the document and not the search for the intention in the mind of the writer.
[34] *Philpots (Woking) Ltd v Surrey Conveyancers Ltd* [1986] 1 EGLR 97. The decision of mainstream law reports not to report this case reflects tacit disapproval.
[35] *Interpretation of Contracts*, 4th edn, 2007, 2.05.

But if a judge can ascertain from the lease and intuitive context the "very probable" intention of the parties, so too can any other reasonably well informed reader of the lease.

What then is the argument for the objective principle?

The objective principle is said to be a logical consequence of the rule of inadmissibility of pre-contract negotiations and declarations of intent.[36] This reasoning is fallacious. There is a distinction between the aim of interpretation and the materials the Court uses to achieve that aim. It is consistent to say that the law *does* seek subjective intention where possible but for good reason imposes certain restraints on how it sets about its task (and so sometimes will fail to find the subjective intention correctly).[37]

The objective principle is said to be a logical consequence of those situations where a Court cannot find a subjective intention because none exists. There are circumstances where no subjective intention exists. One case is where the issue to be decided never came to the mind of the author. This can happen with wills and trusts, though it is more common in wider ranging documents (typically statutes). A related case is where one person adopts with minimal consideration a standard form drafted by another; e.g. an employee may pay money to a pension scheme without even seeing the trust deed. In this case the drafter may have subjective intentions where the employee has none. A second case is in a multilateral document where different parties may have agreed a form of words with different subjective intentions. An extreme example of this is a statute, where so many minds are involved (or half involved) that the concept "the intention of Parliament" might be regarded as a metaphor or legal fiction which may fall more distant from the subjective intentions of any of those who took a part in the process of passing the statute.[38] But even behind a statute there are human minds with subjective intentions, and it is usually reasonable to regard interpretation as the search for them.[39] However, although we cannot always find a subjective intention, it does not follow that we cannot or should not seek subjective intention *at all*.

Lewison says:

> The primary reason for adopting an objective approach to the interpretation of contracts is the promotion of certainty.[40]

---

[36] "If actual intent were the criterion, no reason can be given against admitting proof that the testator used every word in the language in a non-natural sense peculiar to himself. Short of that, we can only fall back on the objectively reasonable meaning of what the testator has said." (Holmes–Pollock letters, 22 February 1899.)
"The exclusion of the parties' subjective declarations of intent from the admissible material is a reflection of the principle that a contract must be interpreted objectively." Lewison, *The Construction of Contracts*, 5th edn, 2007, para.5.12.

[37] Contrast a trial which is generally and rightly regarded as a search for truth even though relevant evidence is excluded (so sometimes the court will reach a wrong conclusion).

[38] *Cross on Statutory Interpretation*, 3rd edn, 1995, Ch.2.

[39] The justification for regarding white papers, Law Commission reports and even *Hansard* as relevant background material is that it sheds light on those intentions.

[40] *Interpretation of Contracts*, 4th edn, 2007, 2.03.

If this were true it would be a powerful argument. Unfortunately, it is not true. It is based on the wishful thinking of Hawkins:

> The meaning of the words is, in theory at all events, a fixed one; it is independent of the writer, and capable of being known by the interpreter, not, like the writer's intent, with a greater or less degree of probability, but with certainty.[41]

This is fantasy. How one ascertains objective meaning (as distinct from seeking the subjective intention of the author) is more problematic (and more subjective, i.e. dependant on the mind of the reader) than proponents of the objective principle may realise.[42]

Admittedly, even when a subjective intention does exist, one cannot always expect to ascertain it from the materials available to the Court. But one can generally aim to find it, and in practice reach near it *if one tries*.

Moreover, in cases where a party had no specific subjective intention, his or her general intention would be that the matter should be decided in the manner most consistent with the documentation construed in its context. In this case the search for objective meaning *is* the subjective intention of the writer.

Relationship between objective principle and rectification

4.9 Rectification involves a search for the subjective intention of the author(s). The rejection (or reformulation) of the objective principle proposed in this article does not make the remedy of rectification redundant. For instance, if by accident a clause is omitted from a contract, correction of the error may be outside the scope of interpretation and require rectification. Kramer notes that in cases of mistaken drafting the Courts have two possible courses available: one solution is construction and the other is rectification.[43] Kramer states that "arguments from coherence and consistency of the law would suggest that only one response (probably rectification) should be used". However there is no reason why the two approaches make the law inconsistent or incoherent. Moreover this overlooks important classes of documents where rectification is not available.[44]

---

[41] *On the Principles of Legal Interpretation* (1860). The essay is reprinted in Thayer, *A Preliminary Treatise on Evidence*. But Hawkins himself resiles from this position later in his essay.
[42] Hence construction is often described by judges as "a matter of impression".
[43] "Common Sense Principles of Contract Interpretation" [2003] OJLS p.173 at p.191. But of course if construction is a solution it must have priority over rectification.
[44] In wills, rectification has strict time limits: s.20 Administration of Justice Act 1982. A company's memorandum and articles of association cannot be rectified.

Precedent not the solution

Precedent does not offer a solution to problems of construction. It has been tried and failed as it was bound to: **4.10**

> I think it is the duty of a Judge to ascertain the construction of the instrument before him, and not to refer to the construction put by another judge upon an instrument, perhaps similar, but not the same. The only result of referring to authorities for that purpose is confusion and error, in this way, that if you look at a similar instrument, and say that a certain construction was put upon it, and that it differs only to such a slight degree from the document before you, that you do not think the difference sufficient to alter the construction, you miss the real point of the case, which is to ascertain the meaning of the instrument before you. It may be quite true that in your opinion the difference between the two instruments is not sufficient to alter the construction, but at the same time the Judge who decided on that other instrument may have thought that that very difference would be sufficient to alter the interpretation of that instrument. You have in fact no guide whatever, and the result especially in some cases of wills has been remarkable. There is, first document A, and a Judge formed an opinion as to its construction. Then came document B, and some other Judge has said that it differs very little from document A—not sufficiently to alter the construction—therefore he construes it in the same way. Then comes document C, and the Judge there compares it with document B, and says it differs very little, and therefore he shall construe it in the same way. And so the construction has gone on until we find a document which is in totally different terms from the first, and which no human being would think of construing in the same manner, but which has by this process come to be construed in the same manner.[45]

We set this out at length (it deserves to be set out in stone) because it has not always been observed by judges. The use of precedent is part of the old legal baggage: it is inconsistent with the "common sense principles by which any serious utterance would be interpreted in ordinary life." The point is summed up succinctly by Lord Hoffmann:

> No case on the construction of one document is the authority on the construction of another, even if the words are very similar.[46]

---

[45] *Aspden v Seddon* (1875) LR 10 Ch App 394 at 398 (Jessel M.R.), approved by the Court of Appeal in *Equity and Law Life Assurance v Bodfield* (1987) 281 EG 1448. Likewise *Pedlar v Road Block Gold Mines of India Ltd* [1905] 2 Ch 427 "I remember hearing Sir George Jessel say that he should not regard himself as bound by the decision of a previous judge on the construction of the identical document and the identical passage of the document which he had to construe" (Warrington J.). The authorities are discussed in Lewison, *The Interpretation of Contracts* (4th edn, 2007), 4.07 and 4.11.
[46] *Deeny v Gooda Walker* [1996] STC 299 at 306. This is also the position in Canada: *Re Burke* [1960] O.R. 26 at 30, 20 DLR. (2d) 396 at 398 accessible on *www.kessler.co.uk*.

Precedent may however be relevant if parties use a word or phrase in what appears to have been a technical legal sense.[47]

Similar points apply to rules of construction[48] such as

(1) *ejusdem generis*

(2) *noscitur a sociis*

(the Latin tags themselves redolent of a past age).

These rules are useful in their spheres indeed they arise out of "common sense principles": it is their rigid or insensitive application (or misapplication) which Lord Hoffmann intended to reject. They mean us to use them as signposts and are not to blame if, in our weakness, we mistake the signpost for the destination.[49]

Conclusion

4.11 The modern approach to interpretation involves an extension of reliance on (and admissibility of) background fact; rejection of "old intellectual baggage" of precedents and rules of construction; and recognition of less literal readings. These are large steps away from the false god of objective meaning and towards seeking the author's subjective intention: they require the Court to try harder to put itself in the position of the author(s)[50] and the result is that the Court is more likely to find the subjective intention.

In summary, the correct answer to the objective meaning/subjective intention debate lies between the two extremes. It is not the case (or it is considerable oversimplification to say) that the aim of interpretation is to find the subjective intention *or* the objective meaning. In interpretation, the court should *aspire* to find the subjective intention, where possible, doing as best it can from limited information available. In the exceptional cases where there is (or appears to be) no subjective intention one

---

[47] *BCCI v Ali* [2002] 1 AC 251 para.51; McKendrick (op. cit.) p.152.
[48] Not discussed in this book; but see bibliography.
[49] *Harrison v Tucker* [2003] EWHC 1168; [2003] WTLR 883 makes this point and tacitly recognises the change in emphasis in modern times:

"These rules of construction are set out in relatively unequivocal terms and sometimes give the appearance of being almost absolute in nature. But it is important to remember that in wills, as in other instruments, the quest must always be to ascertain the intention of the maker of the document."

Lord Hoffmann is more blunt in *BCCI v Ali* [2002] 1 AC 251,at [55]:
"Books like *Jarman on Wills* are monuments to the rules of construction and a melancholy record of the occasions on which they have defeated the intentions of testators."

[50] The metaphor often used is being in the shoes or armchair of the author(s); if that means anything it means a search for subjective intentions.

should try to construe the document sympathetically, as if there were one (and of course one will not normally *know* that there is no subjective intention, that too requires one to look into the mind of the author). That is exactly what the modern law requires, and, surely, what the law ought to be.[51]

Are principles of construction of wills or trusts the same as contracts or statutes?

The principles are the same[52] but one must make allowance for the difference of context. **4.12**

One difference between wills and trusts on one hand, and contracts (and even more so, statutes) on the other, is that there are fewer occasions where there is any practical necessity to abandon the search for subjective intention. "A Will is a soliloquy, while the language of a contract is addressed to another".[53] Because a will or a trust is normally a unilateral document,[54] it is more often possible to find the subjective intention of the author if one looks for it sympathetically. In a contract one must assume that the parties are of one mind (which may not be the case) and seek a common intention.

A second difference is that, in the past, Chancery judges were generally more inclined to a literal rather than a purposive approach, and inclined to follow precedents, but both these approaches are now rightly out of favour.

---

[51] Article 5.101 of the Principles of European Contract Law provides: "A contract is to be interpreted according to the common intention of the parties even if this differs from the literal meaning of the words …". The approach of this book therefore offers a reconciliation of the EU and the common law approach to construction, which is another recommendation for it. The modern Canadian position is the same: "the Court should attempt to ascertain, if possible, the testator's actual or subjective intent, as opposed to an objective intent presumed by law". Feeney's *Canadian Law of Wills*, 4th edn, para.10.1. See *Drafting Trusts & Will Trusts in Canada*, James Kessler QC and Fiona Hunter, Butterworths, 2003, Ch.3. For the background of linguistics and philosophy of language see Adam Kramer's "Common Sense Principles of Contract Interpretation" [2003] Oxford Journal of Legal Studies 173.

[52] *Investors Compensation Scheme* principles were applied by the Court of Appeal to the trust in *Botnar v IRC* [1999] STC 711 and have subsequently been applied in many wills, trust and pension cases: Keith Rowley QC, "The Interpretation of Scheme Deeds and Rules" [2003] TLI 129 at 134.

[53] *Skelton v Younghouse* [1942] AC 571 at 579.

[54] In the case of a trust, there will usually be two parties but the intention of the trustees is to carry out the intention of the settlor, they generally have no independent intentions, except in relation to a few provisions (e.g. trustee remuneration and exoneration clauses). Note that in the case of a trust established by a nominal settlor the relevant intention may be that of the "instigator": see *Hartigan Nominees Pty Ltd v Rydge* (1992) 29 NSWLR 405 and *Stein v Sybmorg Holdings Pty Ltd* (2006) 64 ATR 325; 2006 ATC 4741; [2006] NSWSC 1004. "Nominal" settlors are discussed in 10.14 (Nominal settlor).

"Construction not restricted by technical rules"

4.13 One sometimes sees this form:

> *These powers shall not be restricted by any technical rules of interpretation. They shall operate according to the widest generality of which they are capable.*

The point that this clause is probably trying to make is to echo or seek to apply Lord Hoffmann's sentiment, that the interpretation of the document should not be governed by the "old intellectual baggage of legal interpretation". Since this is what the Courts are now supposed to do, the clause has no effect.[55]

Further, the wording that the clause employs in order to make its point is not very happy. Which rules of interpretation are "technical"? For example, suppose trustees have powers "of a beneficial owner". It is nevertheless a clear inference that the powers are fiduciary.[56] Can trustees argue[57] that this is a "technical" rule of construction which should not restrict the power when this form is used? The word "technical" used (as here) pejoratively is hopelessly imprecise. A construction which gives a result one does not like can usually be castigated as "technical".[58] "Technical" (in this sense) is not a technical term! It is merely a term of abuse.

So this form is not used in this book. Nor are we able to offer any better wording. The difficulty the drafter faces here is he is attempting to prescribe a principle of interpretation which acts at such a high level of generality that it is impossible to reduce it to a formula which assists when any hard, stubborn, practical issue of interpretation arises. For a more modest form which achieves all that this form could hope to achieve see 19.49 (Ancillary powers).

---

[55] A further reason why the clause has no effect in practice is that a trust with such a clause almost always confers very wide powers.

[56] 6.21 ("Absolute owner" and "beneficial owner" clauses).

[57] Or is it the trustees' argument which is the "technical" one?

[58] *Pepper v Hart* [1993] AC 593, rejecting the rule preventing Courts referring to *Hansard*, described it as "a technical rule of construction". In *Wilson v First Country Trust* [2004] 1 AC 816 para.67 (qualifying if not rejecting the *Pepper v Hart* approach) the same rule was "a cardinal constitutional principle"! For another example of (mis)describing an otherwise unanswerable argument as "technical", in order to summarily reject it, see *Marshall v Kerr* [1995] 1 AC 148 at 157.

CHAPTER 5

BENEFICIARIES

Too much money

It is generally agreed, among adults of mature age, that young people should be settled in life before they receive an income sufficient to make them independent of the need to work. "Many a child has been ruined by being given too much."[1] **5.1**

No difficulty should arise here, no matter how large the trust fund. There are many possible strategies. The terms of the trust may allow trustees to pay out only as much income or capital as they think fit, always with power to accumulate income rather than paying it to the beneficiaries. The trustees may reduce the amount of income by investing trust funds in investment products which yield little or no income (such as an insurance bond, capital growth unit trust or OEIC) or (if tax considerations permit) by acquiring a company themselves for this purpose and arranging that trust income accrues to it. The trustees should have appropriate powers[2] to revoke a child's interest and so to reduce the child's income or capital receipts to an appropriate amount.[3]

A related concern is that the beneficiaries should be encouraged to take an active interest in their own affairs and should not be passive recipients of trust income. The solution here may be to appoint the beneficiary trustee, so as to give him a direct interest in his financial affairs.

---

[1] *Re Weston* [1969] 1 Ch 223 at 245 (Lord Denning in good form).
[2] In desperate cases a power of advancement will suffice: see 11.11 (Power of advancement used to create new trusts).
[3] Another response to this problem is not to inform the beneficiary of his right to the income! Instead the trustees apply the income for his benefit or retain and invest it. There may be a duty of disclosure, but the duty is not accompanied by any sanction: see generally *Hawkesley v May* [1956] 1 QB 304. This does not work in theory but it may work in practice. One difficulty with concealment is that an adult beneficiary may need to complete a tax return which must disclose the trust income (but the trustees may be able to arrange that there is no income). In some circumstances concealment may be evidence of sham, on which see 2.1 (Duty to the client). A solution may be to invite the beneficiary voluntarily to consent, or even covenant, to allow surplus income to be retained by the trustees on his behalf or re-settled (watch undue influence).

Profligacy

5.2 The financially irresponsible beneficiary, do what he may, cannot squander the trust fund of a well-drafted trust. This is one of the great advantages of trusts.

Where a trust has minor beneficiaries—which is virtually all trusts—it is wise to bear in mind that a child may turn out to be insufficiently mature to handle capital; at the age of 18 or 25 or 40 or at all. Conceivably, the receipt of a large sum of money may be most unwelcome to him, e.g. on insolvency. If the beneficiary has a vested and indefeasible interest, one cannot say that he must wait until a specified age before the trustees pay income or capital to him. Such a clause does not bind the beneficiary.[4] How should the trust be drafted so as to secure against a beneficiary's profligacy or insolvency? The following methods do not give complete protection:

> The trustees shall stand possessed of the trust fund upon trust for X on attaining the age of 25.

This confers little protection. As soon as X attains the age of 18 he can sell his contingent interest. Alternatively, if he became insolvent, the interest would be transferred to his trustee in bankruptcy.

> The trustees shall hold the trust fund upon trust for X if he attains the age of 40 absolutely.

This is little better. X may only become absolutely entitled to the trust property at the age of 40; but, again, he could sell his contingent interest at the age of 18. If he became insolvent, the interest would be transferred to his trustee in bankruptcy.

> The trustees shall stand possessed of the trust fund upon trust to pay the income to X during his life with remainder to such of his children as shall attain the age of 21.

This gives X a life interest; he might sell that life interest for a capital sum. Again, on his insolvency the interest would become transferred to his trustee in bankruptcy and the income would accrue for the benefit of his creditors.

---

[4] *Saunders v Vautier* (1841) 4 Beav 115. In order to defeat the somewhat undesirable consequence of this rule, the trust in *Harrison v Tucker* [2003] WTLR 883 was (implausibly) construed to say that the beneficiary did not have a vested interest.

A protective trust?

5.3 The old-fashioned solution is a protective trust.[5] This is a particular form of interest in possession trust. Trustees are directed to pay income to the life tenant, but if he should sell his right to trust income or become insolvent then his interest ceases and the income becomes held on discretionary trusts for the beneficiary and his family.

The laudable purpose of a protective trust is to prevent a prodigal beneficiary selling his income interest for a lump sum which might be dissipated, and to protect the trust fund from his creditors.

The terms of the protective trust may be written out in full in the trust deed, but the usual form is to provide that:

The income of the Trust Fund shall be held on protective trusts for the benefit of X for his life.

This shorthand form incorporates by reference the standard provisions of s.33 of Trustee Act 1925.[6]

The standard form protective trust has significant disadvantages. There may sometimes be doubts whether the life tenant's interest has been forfeit. More significantly, under the standard form, a discretionary trust arises automatically if the beneficiary tries to dispose of his interest. A life tenant may have good reasons to dispose of his interest (for instance IHT planning) but the "protection" makes this difficult. In the 1940s and 1950s protective trusts were created as a matter of routine; they caused such difficulties that the Variation of Trusts Act 1958 was required to allow the protection to be overridden, though at considerable trouble and expense. The necessity for the 1958 Act reflects a failure of vision of that generation of drafters; or a failure of the then state of trust law or trust draftsmanship to provide them with appropriate tools for their work. Special provisions govern the taxation of protective trusts but overall they do not enjoy tax advantages of any value.[7]

A better solution

5.4 What, then, is the answer to the problem of the profligate beneficiary? The best solution is also a simple one: the beneficiary's interest should be *terminable at the trustees' discretion*. The interest of the beneficiary is then

---

[5] Where the settlor was intended to be the principal beneficiary, this was not possible and the standard form was a discretionary trust during the life of the settlor, with gifts over to his children and issue.

[6] If the drafter is minded to use protective trusts, it is advisable to provide that acts done with consent of the trustees do not cause a forfeiture. Underhill and Hayton, *The Law Relating to Trusts and Trustees* (17th edn, 2006) para.11.66 also criticise the standard form and suggest amendments if a protective trust is to be used.

[7] Section 88 IHTA 1984. On the cessation of an estate-IP, the principal beneficiary is treated for IHT purposes as if his interest continued. The trust thus faces a tax charge on his death without the usual CGT uplift applicable to an estate-IP trust.

transferable but unsaleable. No purchaser would pay a penny for it: it could be terminated by the trustees the next day. If the beneficiary became insolvent the interest could be terminated and the trust fund applied for his benefit in the most appropriate way.[8] Wherever a trust contains overriding powers in the form of this book, the beneficiary's interest will be terminable, and the problem is solved.

Insolvency of a beneficiary

5.5 Let us look ahead to the time when a beneficiary (who is, let us assume, the life tenant of a trust but not the settlor) has become insolvent. A bankruptcy order will shortly be made. The trustees have the usual overriding powers. What steps can they take? The trustees have two problems. The first is to prevent the property becoming available to the creditors. We shall call this "the insolvency problem". The second is to minimise the tax costs. We shall call this "the tax problem".

The trustees have available to them a number of solutions to the insolvency problem. The reader will not be surprised to find that these all have different tax consequences; and the task for the trustees is to select the most attractive of them. One must consider IHT, CGT and income tax.

Before or after the bankruptcy order is made

5.6 The trustees may use the overriding power to create a discretionary trust for a class which include the insolvent life tenant. Thereafter trust assets can be used for the benefit of the insolvent beneficiary or for other beneficiaries who are prepared to help the insolvent.[9] Tax consequences:

(a) *IHT.* If the IP is an estate-IP for IHT purposes there will be a chargeable transfer and the GWR rule may apply. This may or may not rule out this option. That will depend on the value of the trust property, and whether or not it qualifies for any relief.

---

[8] For an example see *Skyparks Group v Marks* [2001] WTLR 607 (judgment debt against beneficiary with revocable life interest; no charging order against trust land).

[9] Capital receipts from a trust may be after-acquired property: a beneficiary who is an undischarged bankrupt must declare them and the trustee in bankruptcy may claim them: s.307 Insolvency Act 1986. This applies to a loan from trustees: *Hardy v Butler* [1997] NPIR 643. Income receipts may fall within s.310 Insolvency Act 1986 (Income Payment Orders). In *The Esteem Settlement* [2001] JLR 7 the trustee sought an order that trust funds be distributed to a bankrupt beneficiary in reduction of a debt. The Jersey Court of Appeal held that a person cannot be forced to accept a direct gift and that therefore a direct distribution could not be forced upon a beneficiary. A trustee can make a distribution for the benefit of a beneficiary, contrary to his objections, when such benefit was conferred by means of a payment to a third party. However, in the circumstances of that case it was held that there would be no material benefit to the beneficiary in the (proportionately) small reduction of his total debt.

(b) *Income tax.* The income may continue to be taxed effectively as income of the insolvent life tenant, though the trustees have the tiresome administration of a discretionary trust and additional problems for dividend income.

Before the bankruptcy order is made

The trustees may convert the life tenant's interest into a protective trust (subject to the further exercise of the overriding powers). That will be tax neutral. Then on the making of the bankruptcy order, the life tenant's interest will cease, and the discretionary trusts of s.33(1)(ii) Trustee Act 1925 take effect. Tax consequences: **5.7**

(a) *IHT.* There is relief from the IHT charge which might otherwise arise on the termination of the estate-IP.[10] For this reason, this route will sometimes be more attractive than routes (1) or (2) above.

(b) *Income tax.* The trust income (except dividends) may continue to be taxed effectively as income of the insolvent life tenant, which may be helpful.

(c) *CGT.* There will be no tax free uplift on the death of the life tenant, even though there will be an IHT charge at that time.[11]

It is easy to envisage the different circumstances in which any of these routes would be best.

This route requires action before the bankruptcy order is made, but the trustees should have time to consider the position before the order is made.

As far as the drafting is concerned, the important point which arises from the discussion is that there will be no need to put any particular provision in a draft in normal circumstances. The problems can be dealt with when they arise.

Anti-creditor clauses

These raise problems similar to anti-alimony clauses: see 5.15 (Anti-alimony forms).   **5.8**

---

[10] See fn.7.
[11] The rule that the life tenant is treated as having an interest in possession in the fund applies for IHT only. Here, as so often in the tax code, Parliament has failed to carry the implications of a policy through the various taxes that apply. (Contrast instruments of variation, which apply for IHT, in part for CGT, and not at all for income tax.) This is not the result of policy, but chance and legislative neglect. It would be possible to overcome this difficulty by giving a new life interest to the life tenant. This requires the consent of the trustee in bankruptcy, but the trustee in bankruptcy could not reasonably refuse.

Divorce[12] of beneficiaries

5.9 This is a common concern of settlors and a very real one: that a beneficiary, perhaps the son-in-law or daughter-in-law of the settlor, might claim trust property in the event of divorce. What steps can be taken to prevent that?

Where a beneficiary under a trust is party to a divorce, the court has three possible courses:

(1) The court may deal with an equitable interest as property of the spouse.

(2) The court may regard the trust as a financial resource.

(3) The court may vary the terms of a marriage settlement.

(1) Dealing with beneficiary's equitable interest

5.10 In the event of a divorce the court may divest the beneficiary of his property, including an interest under a trust. In the precedents used in this book, that interest will be of no value. The beneficiary's interest will be subject to an overriding power of appointment. A court order to transfer any revocable interest is impractical: the trustees would exercise their power to revoke the interest. In practice such an order would not be made.

(2) Interest under the trust as a financial resource[13]

5.11 In making financial provision the court has regard to the "financial resources" of the divorcing beneficiary.[14] Any interest under a trust may be a financial resource, even an interest under a discretionary trust, or an interest subject to an overriding power.

In assessing this "resource", the court will ask what the beneficiary may reasonably expect to receive from the trust.[15] Where the beneficiary has a fixed interest, this may be easy enough to determine. With flexible trusts like those in this book the position is not so straightforward. A life interest may be revoked; a beneficiary may only be the object of discretion, so that he has only the hope that the trustees might exercise their powers in his favour. In such cases the courts will "look at the reality". Where history shows that a beneficiary has had "immediate access" to funds in

---

[12] The word "divorce" here includes dissolution of a civil partnership.
[13] On this topic see Gareth Miller "Third Party Control of Resources" [1996] PCB 190 accessible on *www.kessler.co.uk*.
[14] Section 25 Matrimonial Causes Act 1973.
[15] *J v J* [1989] 1 All ER 1121. *Charman v Charman* [2006] 1 WLR 1053.

a discretionary trust, the court may treat the beneficiary as if the funds were his own.

Once the court has assessed this "financial resource" it can proceed to make a financial provision order. The consequence of the trust is that a beneficiary will face a greater lump sum order or greater maintenance payments than would have been the case in the absence of the trust.

In theory the trustees might exercise their powers so that the beneficiary no longer receives anything from the trust. In practice the trustees can hardly reduce the beneficiary to penury. The courts may commit the divorcing beneficiary to prison for non-payment. This puts such pressure on the trustees that there is little alternative but to fund the beneficiary's liabilities.[16]

Despite all these powers, the bargaining position of a beneficiary under a trust is perhaps somewhat stronger than if the beneficiary had owned the trust property absolutely. Is there anything the drafter can do to improve the situation? The reader will not expect to find a simple drafting solution and there is none. The courts are less concerned with the drafting than with the actual use to which the settled funds have been put.

If divorce of a beneficiary is foreseen, the best solution may be not to make trusts of any kind, but simply to make loans of money, or allow rent-free use of assets (appropriately documented); but this is a course of despair.[17]

(3) Variation of settlement on divorce

The court may vary certain settlements (here called "marriage settlements") for the benefit of a divorcing spouse or the children of the family. The court may also reduce or extinguish the interest of a divorcing spouse under such a settlement.[18] This is different from treating the settlement as a financial resource: here the court order does not only affect the property

5.12

---

[16] *J v J*, above; *Browne v Browne* [1989] 1 FLR 291 accessible on *www.kessler.co.uk*. The Court of Appeal described the trust in such loose layman's language that the report is distressing for a trust lawyer to read. For instance, we are told that the spouse was the "sole beneficiary" of the trust. The lesson to be drawn is that in a family law context courts not only refuse to be bound by technicalities of trust law; they may not recognise their existence. The approach is described by those who approve of it as "robust". This may be regarded as analogous to the company law concept of "lifting the corporate veil". There is, however, an important distinction. A company belongs to its shareholders and to regard a company's assets as belonging to its shareholders does not ignore the rights of any third parties. Trust property belongs to all the beneficiaries and to regard it as belonging to *one* beneficiary is to ignore and override the rights of the others. (The position is of course different if there is a sham in the true sense.)

[17] The courts may regard gifts and loans from a parent as a financial resource; but plainly only very limited weight can be given to that "resource". The courts will not blackmail a parent in the way that they blackmailed the trustees in *Browne v Browne*, above. See fn.16.

[18] Sections 24(1) (c)–(d) Matrimonial Causes Act 1973. (The Family Law Act 1996 would have modernised the wording (without any change of substance). It now seems unlikely that this part of the Act will ever come into force.) A marriage settlement may also be varied under s.2(1)(f) (g) Inheritance (Provision for Family and Dependants) Act 1975.

of the divorcing beneficiary, it expropriates property of third parties (other beneficiaries).

The jurisdiction of the court to vary settlements was formerly of the greatest importance, and attracted a substantial case law. Then in the Matrimonial Causes Act 1973 the court acquired broader powers to order financial provision, and the power to vary settlements ceased to be much used. There is no need to vary a settlement if the spouses have enough property of their own for the court to share out between the parties to the marriage. The power to vary settlements remains important if the bulk of the family wealth is settled, and nowadays such settlements have become more common.

Fortunately the courts cannot vary every settlement of which a divorcing spouse is a beneficiary. The jurisdiction is limited to two classes of settlement. Firstly:

> any ante-nuptial or post-nuptial settlement (including such a settlement made by will or codicil) made on the parties to the marriage other than one in the form of a pension arrangement.[19]

5.13 There are two conceptually distinct (perhaps overlapping) requirements here: the settlement must be "made on the parties to the marriage" and it must be "ante-nuptial or post-nuptial".

This terminology originates from s.5 Matrimonial Causes Act 1859. At that time a settlement on marriage was a standard procedure taking a standard form, and no-one would have had much difficulty in classifying a settlement as a marriage settlement. Now social conditions and drafting styles have changed and that kind of marriage settlement is a matter of history. The term has lost its original reference[20] and the courts have had to do the best they can to invent a new one.

Some test must be framed to decide if a settlement is a marriage settlement. A measure of guidance can be drawn from the old case law; but the cases need careful evaluation, as times have changed, and the text of the statutory provision has also changed.

Often the test is said to be whether the settlement is "upon the husband in the character of husband or upon the wife in the character of wife, or upon both in the character of husband and wife"; whether it benefits them "with reference to their married state"; or whether the settlement is made "in respect of the marriage".[21] These formulae (which should be regarded as three ways of expressing the same test) made sense in relation to the old marriage settlements in which the parties to the marriage were described

---

[19] Pensions are excluded here because they are covered by other legislation.
[20] Contrast Frege's distinction between sense and reference discussed in Appendix 2 (Annotated Bibliography).
[21] *Prinsep v Prinsep* [1929] P. 225. The test goes back to *Worsley v Worsley* (1869) LR 1 P&D 648 and has often been cited since.

as "the Husband" and "the Wife". It is submitted that this test is not now of much practical use. How does one decide if a settlement in a modern form is made on the husband in his own character or in the character of husband? [22]

Sometimes the test is said to be whether the settlement has a "nuptial element" and this, it is submitted, offers a more satisfactory approach. A variety of factors will be relevant in determining whether a settlement has the requisite nuptial element:

(1) The existence of a marriage or proposed marriage at the time the settlement is made. A settlement made for the principal benefit of a beneficiary who is neither married nor contemplating marriage at the time of the settlement is not a marriage settlement.[23] Conversely "a settlement made on the parties to a marriage during the marriage" is almost bound to be a marriage settlement.

(2) The terms of the settlement. The settlement must be "made on the parties to the marriage". This expression is not used by trust lawyers today. In the past, a settlement "made on X" meant specifically one under which X had a life interest with very standard provisions for X's family thereafter. But now it seems that a settlement is "made on the parties to the marriage" if it contains any provisions which benefit either party; even a provision benefiting the widow of a settlor will suffice.[24] A discretionary settlement may be caught.[25] A settlement genuinely for the benefit of parties to more than one marriage is not, it is submitted, a marriage settlement. Presumably a settlement for the children of the marriage, from which the parents are wholly excluded, is not a marriage settlement.

(3) The nature of the trust property. A settlement holding the family home is almost bound to be a marriage settlement.[26]

Some general points can be made.

---

[22] Contrast the test for employment income, whether a person receives funds "in his capacity as employee": a test easy to state, but often impossible to apply. Occasionally this test may help; for instance, it suggests that an employee benefit trust will not be a marriage settlement: it is made on the beneficiaries as employees.

[23] *Hargreaves v Hargreaves* [1926] P. 42 is an example. A settlement not made in contemplation of marriage was held not to be a nuptial settlement, even though the beneficiary had powers of appointment in favour of a future spouse. (The finding of fact in this case, that the settlement was not made in anticipation of marriage, was surprising: the settlement was made 28 April 1914, and the marriage was agreed before 25 May! But that cannot affect the authority of the case.)

[24] See *FJWT-M v CNRT-M* [2004] IEHC 114. "Broadly stated, the disposition must be one which makes some form of continuing provision for both or either of the parties to a marriage, with or without provision for their children": *Brooks v Brooks* [1996] AC 375 at 391.

[25] *E v E* [1990] 2 FLR 233. Here it was conceded that the settlement was a marriage settlement, and the court held that the concession was "plainly right".

[26] In the case of the family home, the Family Law Act 1996 Pt IV also needs to be considered, especially if the spouses are trustees.

The substance matters more than the form. So the addition of potential beneficiaries not intended to benefit at all (or only intended to benefit as fall back beneficiaries if the husband and wife die childless) would not preclude "marriage settlement" status. A declaration that the settlement is not a marriage settlement will not carry any weight.[27] A settlement with a foreign governing law may be a marriage settlement.

It is arguable that the settlement must be a marriage settlement at the time when the settlement is made.

If so, where there is an existing settlement, and a subsequent appointment is made for the benefit of parties to a marriage, the appointment cannot turn the settlement into a marriage settlement. This is so whether the appointment deals with all the property or only part.[28]

The settlement must certainly be a marriage settlement at the time of the court order. A marriage settlement can cease to be a marriage settlement; a clear case is if spouses and issue are excluded.[29]

Special considerations apply to will trusts. The original legislation referred simply to "ante-nuptial or post-nuptial settlements" without reference to wills. It was held that will trusts were not within its scope. Then the statute was amended in a curious way: it now says that "marriage settlements" means an ante- or post-nuptial settlement (including one made by will). The settlement made by will can only be varied if it is a nuptial settlement; but marriage settlements in the old sense were never made by will and settlements made by will were not nuptial settlements. The present position could be that will trusts can be marriage settlements if they contain the requisite "nuptial element"; but it is less likely that they will do so. The better view is that there is no difference now between will trusts and lifetime settlements.

The second type of settlement which the Courts can vary on divorce is the civil partnership equivalent of a marriage settlement. In the legislation this is unhelpfully called "a relevant settlement". The drafter had the challenge of encapsulating the marriage settlement concept in this new context, and he came up with this:

> "relevant settlement" means, in relation to a civil partnership, a settlement made, during its subsistence or in anticipation of its formation, on the civil partners including one made by will or codicil, but not including one in the form of a pension arrangement.[30]

---

[27] In *Prescott v Fellows* [1958] P. 260 a document which described itself as "settlement on marriage" was held not to be a marriage settlement.
[28] *Hargreaves v Hargreaves* [1926] P. 42 might be taken as authority to the contrary. There an appointment under a non-nuptial settlement created an annuity which was a nuptial settlement. But the annuity was regarded as a separate settlement.
[29] *C v C* [2005] Fam 250 para.44.
[30] Para.7, Sch.5 Civil Partnership Act 2004. "Pension arrangements" are excluded because of the separate provisions for pension sharing orders.

Divorce of beneficiaries: conclusions

What conclusions can be drawn from this discussion? The first is that it may not much matter whether or not a settlement is a marriage settlement. For even if the drafter succeeds in creating a non-marriage settlement, so the court could not vary the settlement, the settlement may remain a "financial resource": see 5.11 (Interest under the trust as a financial resource). Nevertheless, a settlor will often not wish to create a marriage settlement if it is possible to create a non-marriage settlement. The best time to provide for one's family is well before a marriage. Settlements made when the marriage is contemplated, or made after the marriage, for the benefit of the parties of the marriage, are the ones at risk. One can avoid or reduce the risk of a settlement being varied by the court by making it as "un-nuptial" as circumstances allow. For instance, consider a settlor with two married children. He may create two separate settlements for each family. Those might each be "a marriage settlement". He may alternatively create a single trust for the benefit of his whole family, and others whom he wishes to benefit. The settlement could not so easily be described as a marriage settlement.

5.14

Anti-alimony forms

One sometimes sees (particularly in offshore trusts) a provision that trustees' powers are not exercisable in favour of a beneficiary if sums paid to him would substantially accrue to satisfy the claims of a divorcing spouse. This form ("an anti-alimony form") raises significant practical difficulties and is not recommended.

5.15

If the form is used, how would it work in practice? The following general comments are subject to the point that much in any particular case would depend on the precise circumstances and especially the drafting. It is assumed that H is regarded by the trustees as the principal beneficiary, and W is not.

Suppose H has assets of £5m in his own estate, and a trust fund of £5m. Plainly the court could order him to transfer his own £5m to W. Could the trustees subsequently appoint the trust fund to H? Obviously, yes. In other words, the court may regard H's interest under the trust as a financial resource and the anti-alimony form cannot prevent that.

Suppose now that H has no significant assets in his estate at all, but £10m in the trust fund. Assuming that the court would order half of whatever H receives from the fund to be transferred to W, the form read literally may seem to say that nothing can ever be paid to H at all! In result it could be a breach of trust to transfer funds to a beneficiary at a time when access to funds is needed. Probably, the anti-alimony form would be construed as imposing no more than the usual rules relating to fraud on a power. In that case the apparently disastrous effect of the anti-alimony form is avoided, but the form achieves nothing.

62 BENEFICIARIES

If the settlement is a marriage settlement, another approach for W is to seek to vary the settlement by deleting the anti-alimony clause.

One may say of course that the anti-alimony form will help the negotiating position of H in the divorce proceedings; but it may require the trustees to seek the guidance of the court in order to be secure from possible claims later of breach of trust.

Similar points arise on anti-creditor clauses.

Foreign domiciled beneficiary

5.16 A United Kingdom domiciled settlor may wish to make a trust for persons who are not domiciled here. Special consideration must then be given to United Kingdom tax law and any restrictions imposed by the law of the beneficiary's home country. These questions are beyond the scope of this book.[31]

Marriage under 18

5.17 A traditional form is:

> *In trust for [my children] who being male attain the age of 21 years or being female attain that age or marry ...* [32]

This is not a point of much importance; marriage under 21 is relatively uncommon. However, clauses of this kind are not recommended.

Definition of "Beneficiaries"

5.18 Anyone interested in a trust may be called a "beneficiary".[33] However the term "Beneficiaries" is used in a defined sense in the precedents in

---

[31] James Kessler QC, *Taxation of Foreign Domiciliaries* (7th edn, 2008, Key Haven Publications).

[32] Under the intestacy rules, an intestate's estate is held in trust for [the children] who attain the age of 18 years or marry under that age: s.47(1)(i) AEA 1925; s.31(2)(i) TA 1925. Sexual equality was a general principle of the 1925 legislation; as in the abolition of male preference in the descent of land.

[33] The word "beneficiary" is not a term of art. In common parlance it means:

1. a person with an equitable interest under a settlement; and
2. an object of trustees' powers over income or capital.

Views may differ on whether a person who the trustees may add to the class of objects is to be described as a beneficiary in the general sense of the word or merely a potential beneficiary. The distinction may be a wholly formal one in circumstances where there is no realistic prospect of a beneficiary who is an object of trustees powers receiving anything; and every prospect of a person later being added and receiving something. In practice where it matters the word is usually defined, e.g. s.22 TLATA 1996; s.812(2)–(5) ITA 2007; Sch.5 para.9(10C) TCGA 1992. Without a definition there is ambiguity, e.g. in the ill-thought out Sch.5B, para.17 TCGA 1992.

this book. The term is used in this book in the overriding powers and in discretionary trusts:

> The Trustees may appoint that they hold the Trust Fund for the benefit of any Beneficiaries on such terms as the Trustees think fit.
> The Trustees may pay the income of the Trust Fund to such of the Beneficiaries as they think fit.

Other terms are sometimes used in such clauses, such as:

> Appointed Class
>
> Appointable Class
>
> Specified Class
>
> Wider Class
>
> Discretionary Class
>
> Discretionary Beneficiaries[34]

However the term "Beneficiaries" seems quite apt.

5.19 The definition of the term "Beneficiaries" is an important issue in the drafting of a trust. The definition should be set out in full in the definition clause (not relegated to a schedule, forcing every reader to leaf through many pages to find the meat).

The draft must try to reconcile two contradictory considerations. On the one hand, it is desirable to compile a list of everyone who it might in any circumstances be desired to benefit from the trust fund; not just the persons expected to benefit. On the other hand, a wide class will enable the trustees to benefit those whom the settlor would not normally wish to benefit, and the settlor may be unhappy with that result even allowing for the comfort of a statement of wishes. It can also make life difficult for trustees who may feel obliged to consider the needs and interests of those who are remote from the settlor and his family, and who may not even know that they are beneficiaries. This can be dealt with by drafting techniques of fall-back beneficiaries, and powers to add beneficiaries subject to safeguards.

The starting point is usually the family of the settlor. Before the introduction of civil partnerships this book used the following form:

> **"The Beneficiaries"** means:
>
> (i) The children and descendants of the Settlor
> (ii) The spouses, widows and widowers (whether or not remarried) of (i) above and
> (iii) The widow (whether or not remarried) of the Settlor.[35]

---

[34] This appears to be a novel coinage of the 1997 edition of the *Encyclopaedia of Forms and Precedents*, and has a great deal to be said for it.
[35] Some add: "and 'Beneficiary' has a corresponding meaning." This only expresses an inference

The expansion of this form to include civil partners is described at 5.30 (Spouses and civil partners) but the above form would still be appropriate where a settlor did not wish to make any provision for civil partners.

Children and descendants

5.20 There are of course a number of ways to describe children and descendants. Statutory precedents include:

> ... children or more remote issue ...[36]
> ... children or remoter descendants ...[37]
> ... the issue, whether children or remoter descendants ...[38]

The terms "issue" and "descendants" are in this context synonymous. The term "descendants" is preferred here as it is in common usage. It is sufficient to say "the descendants of the Settlor"; the term "descendants" connotes descendants of any degree.[39]

"Children of X and Y"

5.21 The clause used in this book would include all the children of the settlor, including children of a remarriage. It is not usually desired to restrict the trust to children of an individual and his present spouse. If such a case does arise the recommended form is:

> The children of X born to Y.
> or: The children of the marriage between X and Y.
> or: The children of X who are also children of Y.

---

which would be made in any event. The use of the word "**Beneficiary**" with a capital "B" is sufficient indication that the word is used in its defined sense. Some restrict the class to beneficiaries born before the end of the Trust Period. This is not necessary. All that matters is that the power of appointment is properly restricted: see 9.6 (Remaining within the perpetuity period).

[36] Section 33 TA 1925.
[37] Section 33 Wills Act 1837, as amended by s.19 Administration of Justice Act 1982. This modernised the 1837 wording ("children and other issue").
[38] Statutory Will Forms 1925, Form 9 accessible on *www.kessler.co.uk*.
[39] The form "children and descendants" was used in the precedents in earlier editions of this book as the more readily understood. However, following the introduction of Civil Partnerships, this usage would lead to references to "the spouses and civil partners of the children and descendants of the settlor" which seems excessively clumsy.
It is plainly unnecessary to refer to "children or *remoter* descendants". The word "remoter" should only be used where it adds to the meaning. For instance "grandchildren and remoter descendants of the Settlor" where the word "remoter" is apt as the children of the settlor are excluded.

The form *"the children of X and Y"* is not suitable. This seemingly innocuous form hides three ambiguities. It may mean:

(1) the children whose parents are both X and Y.

(2) the children whose parents include either X or Y.

(3) the children of X, and Y himself (not Y's children.)[40]

Illegitimate beneficiaries[41]

Illegitimacy raises a question of principle and a technical point of drafting. Should illegitimate descendants of the settlor be included as beneficiaries under the trust? This is a matter for the settlor. If the drafter may offer tentative advice, the preference should be to include the illegitimate children, not to exclude them. This is an assessment of the spirit of the times[42] and a matter of practical advantage. Parents are under a legal obligation to maintain their children legitimate or not. A family trust is a natural source of funds for that purpose, and the exclusion of illegitimate children from the trust may cause inconvenience. Trustees should not be deterred by the fear that unknown illegitimate beneficiaries might later emerge with claims against them; appropriate protection can be given by the trust deed.[43]

5.22

If it is desired to include the illegitimate beneficiaries then nothing need be done. The words "child", "descendant" and so forth are understood to include children and descendants born outside marriage.[44]

If it is desired to exclude illegitimate children then what form of words should the drafter use to achieve that end? A traditional formula is as follows:

---

[40] The ambiguous form has often been used and has given rise to considerable litigation. *Williams on Wills* (8th edn, 2002), p.720 cites no less than a dozen authorities. The ambiguity is exploited in a parody reprinted in Megarry's wonderful *Miscellany at Law*, Stevens & Sons (1955) pp.298–301 (Bequest of "all my black and white horses". Did this include the pied horses?) A traditional and somewhat archaic form is "the children of X by Y".

[41] For a more detailed discussion see James Kessler, Drafting Trusts: Illegitimacy Issues, accessible www.kessler.co.uk.

[42] In 2006, 43.7% of births in the UK were outside marriage: Social Trends Report 2008, accessible www.statistics.gov.uk.

[43] 6.29 (Excluding claims by unknown beneficiaries).

[44] Sections 1, 19 Family Law Reform Act 1987, re-enacting (and slightly extending) s.15 Family Law Reform Act 1969.
  Trusts made before 1 January 1970 are governed by the old rule that expressions such as "children" do not include illegitimate children. The common law rule survived an attack by Lord Denning in *Sydall v Castings* [1967] 1 QB 302 and has been followed in trust jurisdictions where no statutory provision applies: *Philean Trust v Taylor* [2003] JLR 61; *RHB Trust Company v Butlin* [1992–93] CILR 219. The rule survived a Human Rights challenge in *Upton v National Westminster Bank* [2005] EWCA Civ 1479.

In this settlement references to family relationships shall be construed as if the Family Law Reform Acts 1969 and 1987 had not been enacted.

The Family Law Reform Acts reversed the common law rule, that reference to relationships did not in principle include the illegitimate. The effect of this provision is thus to restore the former position. The form of wording used has the advantage of seemliness; avoiding the word "illegitimate" let alone any more offensive synonym. But the wording is unintelligible to the layman and indeed to a lawyer or accountant unfamiliar with finer points of trust law. There is then scope for misunderstanding and the form is not recommended.[45]

The obscurity may be a virtue in a case where a settlor wished to exclude his illegitimate children from the trust without openly admitting their existence: an example of Talleyrand's epigram that *la parole a été donnée à l'homme pour déguiser sa pensée.*[46] But that is exceptional. This book proposes a more explicit clause for general use:

(1) "Children" does not include illegitimate children.

(2) References (however expressed) to any relationship between two persons do not include anything traced through an illegitimate relationship.[47]

A fair but complex set of rules takes effect to determine whether a person is legitimate, but that need only be considered in the rare cases where legitimacy matters.[48]

We have occasionally seen trusts taking a middle way between excluding and including illegitimate beneficiaries:

(1) illegitimate beneficiaries are prima facie excluded from benefit; but trustees are given power to add them in as beneficiaries; or

(2) illegitimate beneficiaries are included as a fall back if and only if there are no legitimate ones.

These are rather complex solutions but they might appeal to some settlors.

---

[45] A minor disadvantage with this form is the need to keep the statutory references up to date. Sooner or later the 1987 Act will be repealed and replaced by new legislation and the form will need amending. Fortunately it will not usually matter if out of date forms are used (for instance a form referring to the 1969 Act which omits to refer to the 1987 Act): s.17 Interpretation Act 1978.

[46] Franz Rosenzweig makes a similar point in language which could serve as an epigram for this book: "Words are bridges over chasms. One usually walks across without looking down. If one looks down one is liable to feel giddy. Words are also boards laid over a shaft, concealing it. To be a philosopher [or a lawyer] is to look into abysses, climb down shafts."

[47] The drafting is loosely derived from Sch.1 Interpretation Act 1978.

[48] They are well set out in Barlow "Children and Issue: Some Lingering Growing Pains" (1993) PCB 99 accessible on *www.kessler.co.uk*. These rules could of course be amended in a particular case; but it is suggested that in normal cases they should be regarded as quite satisfactory.

Adopted beneficiaries

When a child is adopted by a couple or by one of a couple (whether or not married and irrespective of the sex of the couple), he is treated as the legitimate child of the couple. A child adopted by a single person is treated as a legitimate child of the adopter.[49] The settlor would not normally wish to provide otherwise. Complicated provisions apply to ascertain the age and birth date of the adopted child for the purpose of the trust.[50]

5.23

Stepchildren

The term "children" does not include stepchildren (unless context shows otherwise). This rule could be reversed by the drafter if the settlor so desired. In practice most settlors wish to benefit their own children to the exclusion of their stepchildren. Accordingly, unless the settlor so requests, there should not be any general form to the effect that "children" include "stepchildren" or that relationships include step-relationships.[51] If, later, it is in fact desired to benefit stepchildren, this could in principle be done later using the power to add beneficiaries.

5.24

Assisted reproduction

If an embryo or egg is placed in a woman the position (simplifying slightly) is as follows:

5.25

(1) The woman who gives birth to a child is regarded as the mother.

(2) Where donor sperm (or an embryo created from it) is used and the woman is married, the husband is regarded as the father unless it is shown that he did not consent to his wife's treatment.

---

[49] Section 67(2) Adoption and Children Act 2002.
[50] The rules could in theory give rise to difficulty, but problems in practice are rare. See again Barlow "Children and Issue: Some Lingering Growing Pains" [1993] PCB 99 accessible on *www.kessler.co.uk*.
[51] The meaning of the word "stepchild" is not always clear. In *IRC v Russell* 36 TC 83 a child of the wife of A was held to be A's stepchild even though the child's father was still living: that is surely now part of the ordinary meaning. In *Mander v O'Toole* [1948] NZLR 909; [1948] DLR 445 accessible at *www.kessler.co.uk* the child of the ex-wife of A ceased to be A's stepchild after divorce; that too is probably the natural meaning but views might differ. By s.246 Civil Partnership Act 2004, A's stepchild for many statutory purposes includes a child of civil partner who is not A's child. This would not apply to the construction of trust documentation but in the course of time this may come to be the natural meaning of the word "stepchild". An express definition addressing all these points would be desirable if the term is used in trust documentation.

68 BENEFICIARIES

(3) Where donor sperm (or an embryo created from it) is used and the woman is unmarried, but a man was being treated together with her at a licensed centre, then that man is regarded as the father.

References to relationships in a trust are construed accordingly.[52] While these rules could be reversed by the drafter, it is not thought that a settlor would usually wish to provide otherwise. The female partner of a woman who gives birth to a child following assisted reproduction cannot become a parent in the way that a male partner currently can;[53] and neither opposite-sex nor same-sex cohabitants can apply for parental orders following surrogacy.[54] However, if reforms contained in the Human Fertilisation and Embryology Bill[55] are enacted, couples using those techniques in future would be able to become joint parents as a matter of law, and so become automatically eligible under our precedents.

Children by surrogacy

5.26 There are two types of surrogacy. In host surrogacy, which dates from 1989, the surrogate mother carries an embryo derived from the egg and sperm of an infertile couple. The surrogate has no genetic relationship with the baby but acts as a host for the pregnancy. In traditional surrogacy, the egg is derived from the surrogate mother while the sperm is from the male partner of the infertile woman. In either case, s.30 Human Fertilisation and Embryology Act 1990 allows for fast track adoption of a surrogate baby for married couples.[56] However, until a Court order is obtained, the child is regarded as the child of the woman who gives birth and not of the genetic mother. About 50 parental orders are made each year.[57] In some cases it might be appropriate to provide a definition of "children" specifically to include children by surrogacy even before a parental order is made. The drafting should copy the language of the 1990 Act.

---

[52] For full details see ss.27–29 Human Fertilisation and Embryology Act 1990.
[53] See Human Fertilisation and Embryology Act 1990 s.28.
[54] Nor, at present, can civil partners: see Human Fertilisation and Embryology Act 1990 s.30.
[55] Available online at http://services.parliament.uk/bills/2007-08/humanfertilisationandembryology.html.
[56] If reforms contained in the Human Fertilisation and Embryology Bill are enacted, civil partners and two persons "living as partners in an enduring family relationship" (not within prohibited degrees of relationship) will also be able to apply.
[57] Review of the Human Fertilisation and Embryology Act, 2006, para.2.61.

Provisions distinguishing male/female

5.27 The precedents in this book do not discriminate between male and female beneficiaries. Where such forms are used, note s.9 Gender Recognition Act 2004: where a full gender recognition certificate is issued to a person, the person's gender becomes the acquired gender. This could be reversed by appropriate drafting. Since in practice discrimination between male/female beneficiaries is rare in modern trust drafting, the many problems potentially raised by the 2004 Act will rarely if ever arise.

Spouses of beneficiaries

5.28 The class of beneficiaries should normally include the spouses of the settlor's descendants. This is done for two reasons. First, there is a practical advantage. It may be desired to benefit a spouse: a beneficiary might die and leave an impecunious widow. Second, there are possible tax advantages. Spouses are taxed separately from each other. It will be desirable to arrange that they receive an independent income so each can use their personal relief and lower rates of tax.[58] The trust is a convenient source of income for this purpose. It may still be possible to salvage some of these advantages where the spouse is not a beneficiary.[59] On settlors who object to including spouses of beneficiaries, see 14.6 ("Provisions after death of the prinicpal beneficiary").

Civil partners

5.29 The word "spouse" in its normal sense does not include a civil partner. So in the absence of specific words or a special context, a definition of "beneficiaries" which includes spouses of beneficiaries (the common form before the Civil Partnership Act 2004) would not include civil partners of beneficiaries.

The terms of a trust or will are a matter for the settlor to decide, and the drafter should obtain and follow instructions. However, it is thought that the better course (for IHT planning reasons), and the more commonly

---

[58] Further, in the case of an interest in possession arising before 22 March 2006, inheritance tax may be avoided or deferred by arranging for a beneficiary's interest in possession to be followed by a short term interest in possession for his spouse or civil partner: s.18 IHTA 1984. Note the exemption does not apply if the beneficiary is UK domiciled (for IHT purposes) and the spouse is not UK domiciled.

[59] Either by appointing a beneficiary an interest for more than his life, which he may leave by will to a surviving spouse or by exercise of power of advancement, see 12.12 (Example resolution of advancement used to alter terms of trust).

desired course, would be to treat civil partners in the same way as spouses; this is the form used in this book.

Spouses and civil partners of beneficiaries: drafting points

5.30 There are two ways to extend the class of beneficiaries to include civil partners as well as spouses. The first is to include them expressly:

> **"The Beneficiaries"** means:
> (a) The descendants of the Settlor.
> (b) The spouses and Civil Partners of the descendants of the Settlor.
> (c) The surviving spouses and surviving Civil Partners[60] of the descendants of the Settlor (whether or not they have remarried or entered into another Civil Partnership).
> (d) The surviving spouse[61] or surviving Civil Partner[62] of the Settlor (whether or not he or she has remarried or entered into another Civil Partnership).

The alternative is to define the expression "spouse" to include a civil partner; and to define "widow/widower" of a person to include the surviving civil partner; now that civil partnerships are becoming more familiar, we think this shorter form is easier to understand.

The expression "civil partner" should be defined and the following is suggested:

> "Civil Partner" and "Civil Partnership" have the same meaning as in section 1 Civil Partnership Act 2004.

This definition includes civil partnerships registered in the UK, and "overseas relationships"—civil partnerships under foreign law—within the meaning of s.212 Civil Partnership Act 2004. But if "civil partner" is used without being defined, it would in principle carry that same meaning in a document governed by English law.

An alternative form is:

> **"The Beneficiaries"** means:
> ...
> (c) The *former* spouses and Civil Partners of the descendants of the Settlor (whether or not they have remarried or entered into another Civil Partnership).

---

[60] The term "surviving civil partner" (meaning, the person who was civil partner of a person at the time of that person's death) is taken from the Civil Partnership Act 2004.

[61] Until the Civil Partnership Act, the form used in this book was "widow" or "widower". However the term "surviving spouse" (meaning, widow or widower) is more convenient in this context. The term was first used in the side note to s.48 Administration of Estates Act 1925, and is now standard statutory usage.

[62] The words "Civil Partner" are of course unnecessary here if the Settlor will not contemplate entering into a civil partnership, and so some settlors may prefer to delete them; but they can do no harm.

The alternative form is wider as it includes not only a widow[63] (and surviving civil partner) of a deceased beneficiary, but also the divorced spouse (and ex-civil partner) of a living beneficiary. But under the form used in this book such persons can in principle be added as beneficiaries. The difference between the two forms is little more than one of style, or at most, one of emphasis. The form now[64] used in this book reflects what is understood to be the more common preference or perception of settlors.

An interesting question arises with the form used here. Suppose trustees appoint a life interest to a spouse within limb (b) of the definition (e.g. a spouse of a child of the settlor). Suppose the spouse subsequently divorces and ceases to be a Beneficiary. Does the life interest automatically terminate on the divorce? The answer is, no. Provided that the spouse is a Beneficiary at the time the appointment is made, the life interest continues after a divorce.[65]

Settlor and spouse/civil partner as beneficiaries

5.31 It is usual to exclude the settlor, spouse and civil partner from benefit under their trust:

(1) they will not be included in the class of beneficiaries (which is the subject of this section); and

(2) a settlor exclusion clause will expressly exclude settlor, spouse and civil partner from benefit.

If this is not done, then trust income and capital gains may be taxed at the settlor's rate and the settlor may be subject to inheritance tax on the settled property as if he had never given it away.[66]

---

[63] Is it possible that "former spouse" might be construed to refer to a divorced spouse but not a widow or widower? Since a widow is someone who was formerly a spouse, it is considered that the expression "former spouse" can only reasonably be taken to refer to widows and widowers as well as divorcees. In the context any other interpretation would be perverse.
 The alternative form is not wide enough to cover the situation where:
 1. a beneficiary ("A") marries a person ("B");
 2. the marriage comes to an end;
 3. B marries a third person ("C").

 Even though B is a beneficiary, C is not. This may be tax-inefficient; but one has to stop somewhere. C will be very far from the benevolent intentions of the settlor. This unusual case may be dealt with by the use of the power to add beneficiaries, if appropriate.

[64] A change from the fourth edition.

[65] At first sight this seems doubtful: the ex-spouse has ceased to be a "Beneficiary", so how can she continue to receive income from the trust? The paradox resolves when one recalls that the term "Beneficiary" here is used in a defined sense. It means objects of the power of appointment. Thus it is quite consistent to say that (i) the ex-spouse is not a Beneficiary in the defined sense, being no longer an object of the power of appointment; but at the same time (ii) the ex-spouse is a beneficiary in the general sense of that word, having a beneficial life interest.

[66] See *Lyon's PRs v HMRC* [2007] STC (SCD) 675 and 13.1 (Why exclude settlor and spouse/civil partner?).

This is not necessary for a will trust; a testator cannot benefit under his own will.

The income tax and CGT Settlement Provisions have six exceptions, the IHT Gifts with Reservation rule, ten. In particular, it is possible to arrange that trust property should revert to the settlor on the bankruptcy of a beneficiary, or, in some cases, on the death of beneficiaries. It is not thought worthwhile to take advantage of these in a standard draft. But where a settlor wishes specifically to be able to recover the trust property in the event that her children should die before her, that can be done.

Meaning of "spouse"/"civil partner" of settlor

5.32 Statute gives a restricted definition to the terms "spouse"/"civil partner" for the purposes of the Settlement Provisions rules which require the spouse/civil partner to be excluded. Three categories of person are stated not to be a spouse or civil partner for this purpose:

(1) The widow, widower or surviving civil partner of the settlor does not count. This merely codifies the long established rule, that the word "spouse" in its natural sense does not include a widow.[67]

(2) A potential spouse[68] or potential civil partner does not count as a spouse or civil partner. This appears to be otiose: no one could contend that a potential spouse or civil partner should count as a "spouse" or civil partner.[69]

(3) A separated spouse or civil partner[70] does not count as a spouse or civil partner.

---

[67] Section 625(4) ITTOIA 2005. Different rules apply to non-resident trusts, but this is outside the scope of this book. The House of Lords held that the term "spouse" did not include a widow or widower: *Vestey v IRC* 31 TC 1, reversing *IRC v Gaunt* 24 TC 69. *Gaunt*, though obsolete, deserves a mention in a footnote as an exemplar of judicial mentality. Reversing the decision of the High Court, Goddard L.J. said the point was "clear". Clausen L.J. thought it was "perfectly clear". Scott L.J. thought it was "obvious". Yet only six years later, the House of Lords held their view to be wrong.

[68] In the words of the statute, "a person to whom the settlor is not for the time being married but may later marry".

[69] In HMRC's view this reverses the decision in *Tennant v IRC* 24 TC 215: see CG Manual 34753. This might be doubted but that is not a drafting issue.

[70] In the words of the statute, "a spouse or civil partner from whom the settlor is separated under an order of a court, or under a separation agreement" or "where the separation is likely to be permanent". As a matter of general law, a marriage continues until dissolved by decree absolute. Until decree absolute, therefore, the parties to a marriage are still "spouses", except where the word is given an artificial definition. This proposition is obvious; but if authority is needed see *Aspden v Hildesley* 55 TC 608.

The practical consequence of this definition for trust drafting is that it is possible to include in the class of beneficiaries:

(1) the widow, widower or surviving civil partner of the settlor; and

(2) a separated spouse/civil partner.

Settlor's surviving spouse/civil partner as beneficiary of lifetime trust

It is recommended that the surviving spouse/civil partner of the settlor should be included in the class of beneficiaries in a lifetime trust. The intended beneficiaries of the trust may be children and descendants of the settlor; there may be no intention to use the funds to benefit the settlor's widow or civil partner. Nevertheless, there are advantages in including him or her in the class of beneficiaries. It is to be stressed that we are not necessarily concerned with any actual benefit, but to retain the opportunity of benefiting him or her. It is conceivable that a widow might find herself in need after the death of the settlor. More significantly, the existence of the power to benefit may be a comfort to him or her; and specifically it may enable the survivor to make lifetime gifts, confident in the knowledge that the trust fund is there to fall back on in case of unforeseen need. The inclusion of the surviving spouse or civil partner of the settlor in the class of beneficiaries may therefore be an important aid to long-term inheritance tax planning. 5.33

Testator's spouse/civil partner as beneficiary of will

A testator will normally include his wife/civil partner[71] in the class of beneficiaries under his will as a matter of course. The will of a testator who is single should not include any reference to a wife or civil partner since (1) if the testator does not marry or enter into a civil partnership, there will be no wife/civil partner and (2) if he does marry or enter into a civil partnership the will is revoked by the marriage or civil partnership! So the reference to "wife" or "civil partner" in such a will can never take effect and may cause confusion. (A will expressed to be in contemplation of marriage or civil partnership may include in the class "my intended wife or civil partner [Jane]".) 5.34

---

[71] It makes no difference whether one refers in a will to a "wife", "spouse" or "widow" of the testator. The term "wife" or "spouse" is preferred in the wills in this book since (at the time the will is written) it is more apt than "widow" and more cheerful.

Separated spouse/civil partner of settlor as beneficiary

5.35 The next question is whether a typical settlor will want to include his separated spouse/civil partner as a beneficiary. The answer, in general, is that he will not; so it is suggested that it is not appropriate in a standard draft to include the separated spouse/civil partner expressly as a beneficiary. (It may be possible later to add the spouse/civil partner as a beneficiary after divorce or, if the settlor exclusion clause permits, after separation.)

Charities as beneficiaries

5.36 No drafting problem should arise if the settlor wishes to include specific charities by name. The charity should be identified by name, address, and charity registration number if it has one. **It is the duty of the drafter to check that:**

(1) the name given by the client is correct,

(2) the body is still in existence when the will or trust is made.[72]

The register of English charities is accessible on *www.charitycommission.gov.uk* and an index of Scottish Charities is on *www.oscr.org.uk*. The Institute of Legacy Management keep a register which gives previous and alternative names and addresses of charities: *www.ilmnet.org*. Until the Northern Ireland Charity Commission is established (this was expected to be in 2008) some help may be obtained from the Northern Ireland Council for Voluntary Action (NICVA)[73] which maintains a voluntary database of many Northern Ireland voluntary associations (not just charities).[74] There is no enforceable obligation for charities to file annual reports and no requirement to notify that a charity has been wound up so entries are often out of date. NICVA staff are pleased to take telephone enquiries from

---

[72] *Re Recher* [1972] Ch 526. Bold print should not be needed to emphasise this "most elementary" duty but this is sometimes overlooked (a fault perhaps attributable to cut price will drafting). It is not sufficient to check in published reference books. In *Recher* the drafter was criticised for drafting a will which made a gift to an association less than six months after the association was wound up. A phone call would have identified the problem but most reference books would have been out of date. Fortunately, well advised bodies do not disband on a reorganisation or merger: they continue a dormant existence in order to receive future legacies.

[73] NICVA promotes good practice among voluntary organisations and assists them to become formally established within an appropriate legal framework. It provides a charity Advice Service which makes available information on matters such as drawing up a Constitution and claiming tax exemption. It has no regulatory responsibilities. NICVA's telephone number is 0028 9087 7777.

[74] It includes non-charitable voluntary groups and purely contemplative religious groups which would fail the public benefit test.

solicitors who are seeking current information about charities within the jurisdiction.

If a settlor has set up a private charitable trust then that trust may conveniently be named as one of the class of beneficiaries.

If it is desired to benefit any charity, define "Beneficiaries" to include:

> any company, body or trust established for charitable purposes only.

One sometimes sees the definition:

> any institution which is a charity for the purposes of the Charities Act 2006.

The second definition is narrower as it would not include charities governed by Scottish, Northern Irish or foreign laws, even if their objects are charitable in the English law sense. So the first definition is better.[75]

"Any charity" would be sufficiently precise[76] but the common practice is to define the term.

Where a trust wishes to make a gift to charity, it will usually be more tax efficient in practice to transfer funds to a beneficiary who (independently) makes a donation to charity which qualifies for income tax relief.[77]

Non-charitable companies as beneficiaries

No difficulty arises where non-charitable companies (e.g. campaigning organisations such as the National Anti-Vivisection Society) are to be beneficiaries. The drafter should check that the name given by the client is correct and that the body is still in existence when the will or trust is made, and that a non-charitable institution is not mis-described in the documentation as a charity. The drafting should not create a trust for the purposes of the institution, but simply a gift to the company.[78]

Subject to the same checks, no problem should arise with a gift to an unincorporated non-charitable body.

5.37

---

[75] This wording is loosely derived from statutory precedent: s.989 ITA 2007; s.1 Charities Act 2006. The expression "company, body or trust" is preferred to the statutory phrase "body of persons" with its archaic Taxes Act definition; or "undertaking", the (deliberately wide) Charities Act expression. It is unnecessary to say that "charitable" means "charitable according to English law": see 24.2 (Some general comments). It is equally unnecessary to say that charitable means "exclusively charitable". The court would not give the word any other meaning unless the context so required; in which case something has gone very wrong with the drafting. For an example see *George Drexler Ofrex Foundation v IRC* 42 TC 524.

[76] In the CGT and VAT legislation, the statute contentedly uses the word "charity" without definition; likewise s.12 Mental Capacity Act 2005 and the Law Commission draft Perpetuities Bill.

[77] *Taxation of Charities* (Kessler and Kamal, Key Haven Publications, 6th edn, 2007); s.1 Charities Act 2006. For charities as default beneficiaries see 13.23 (Default clause).

[78] A gift to the company is not regarded as a trust for the purposes of the company: *Re Recher* [1972] Ch 526.

Foreign charities as beneficiaries

5.38 Foreign charities are not "charities" for UK tax and English charity law purposes.[79] Foreign charitable trusts may nevertheless be beneficiaries of an English law trust. While English law would not recognise a non-charitable purpose trust as valid, it will recognise a power or duty for trustees to transfer property to foreign trustees to hold on the terms of foreign trust law. This does not breach the English law rule which is based on propositions that a trust must be enforceable by beneficiaries: the foreign trustees are the "beneficiaries" for this purpose.

Power to add beneficiaries

5.39 A settlor who specifies even a very wide class of beneficiaries may later regret that the trustees cannot benefit some other persons. Hence the popularity of powers to add beneficiaries, which arm the trustees with a weapon which will enable them to consider all developments and respond to all future mishaps and disasters. It is a convenient way to provide for unmarried cohabitees of beneficiaries. The power can simplify the drafting of a trust: it may become unnecessary to include some classes of beneficiaries "just in case". The power to add beneficiaries could, however, be used to frustrate the wishes of the settlor. The authors would not confer a power to add beneficiaries unless it is subject to constraints to prevent abuse. The obvious restraint is to require the consent of the settlor during his life. That is straightforward, but what should be done after his death? One does not want the power to lapse. The proposed solution is to require the consent of two beneficiaries after the death of the settlor. It is unlikely that two beneficiaries and the trustees should all conspire to defeat the intentions of the settlor. It may occasionally happen that there is only one adult beneficiary; the power to add beneficiaries would then be suspended until such time as there are two adult beneficiaries available.

The wording formerly adopted in this book was to say that "the Beneficiaries" include:

> *any person or class of persons nominated to the Trustees by:*
>
> > *(i) the Settlor, or*
> > *(ii) two Beneficiaries (after the death of the Settlor)*
>
> *and whose nomination is accepted in writing by the Trustees.*

---

[79] See Ch.1, *Taxation of Charities* (Kessler and Kamal, Key Haven Publications, 6th edn, 2007).

The reason was that it had been (implausibly[80]) suggested that a power for trustees to add anyone in the world to a class of beneficiaries was too wide to be a valid fiduciary power. That objection would not have applied to the narrower power to add nominated persons. But now it is clear that a power to add anyone in the world is valid.[81] The wording can therefore be simplified.

The power to add beneficiaries may be treated either as a separate power in a clause of its own; or it may be included in the definition of "Beneficiaries." The latter course is adopted in this book, since the form used is short and concise.

> Any person[82] or class of persons added to the class of Beneficiaries by the Trustees by deed with the consent in writing of:
> (i) the Settlor or
> (ii) two Beneficiaries (if the Settlor has died or has no capacity to consent).

If there is a protector, one can simplify the form by requiring his consent instead of that of the settlor or two beneficiaries.

Power to exclude beneficiaries

This is not needed as the overriding powers can be used to exclude any beneficiary if desired. 5.40

Other possible beneficiaries

In drafting any trust, the drafter should as a matter of course ask the settlor whether it is desired to include any other particular beneficiaries. There may be other specific individuals or members of his family whom he wishes to keep in mind; and there are certain categories of beneficiaries to which we can now turn. These are not for inclusion in a standard draft. 5.41

Dependants

It is certainly possible to include in the class of beneficiaries the dependants of any person. It is a matter of fact and degree what constitutes "dependence" but the courts have held the concept to be sufficiently certain for 5.42

---

[80] See the 6th edition of this book at 4.38.
[81] *Re Manisty* [1974] Ch 17 approved *Schmidt v Rosewood* [2003] 2 AC 709. *Lewin on Trusts* agrees: 18th edn, 4–32. The same applies to will trusts: *Re Beatty* [1990] 3 All ER 844.
[82] This term would include charitable trusts and charitable purposes generally: *Re Triffitt* [1958] Ch 852 at 862.

trust law requirements.[83] The inclusion of dependants may be desirable for both practical and tax reasons. The precedents in the book do not include dependants in a standard form as the power to add beneficiaries ought to be sufficient.

Although it would be satisfactory to use the bare term "Dependants", we would prefer to use the wording from s.1 Inheritance (Provision for Family and Dependants) Act 1975. This is slightly more precise and has the benefit of some discussion in the case law. The class of dependants of a testator would be defined in these terms:

> Any person who immediately before the death of the testator was being maintained, either wholly or partly, by the testator. For this purpose a person shall be treated as being maintained, either wholly or partly, by the testator if the testator, otherwise than for full valuable consideration, was making a substantial contribution in money or money's worth towards the reasonable needs of that person.

It is better practice where possible to name specific dependants as beneficiaries, and not to leave them to qualify under this clause. That saves the trustees from having to satisfy themselves that such persons qualify as dependants.

Employees of beneficiaries

5.43 It may be convenient to include employees in the class of beneficiaries, especially where employees may live on trust property. This also offers the prospect of substantial tax savings, conceivably for income tax, CGT and IHT. The employee could be added by name. Otherwise the following form is proposed:

> **"The Beneficiaries"** means ... [children, etc.]; and (iv) any employee or former employee of the above.

Employees of family company

5.44 Where the trust property is shares in a family company it should be considered whether employees of that company might be added to the class of beneficiaries. This gives the trustees flexibility to convert the trust, or any part of it, into an employee trust enjoying significant IHT advantages.[84]

---

[83] *Re Baden (No.2)* [1973] Ch 9. Section 86(1)(b) IHTA 1984 is also drafted on the basis that "dependancy" is sufficiently certain to satisfy trust law requirements, and the law on this point must be regarded as settled.
[84] Section 86 IHTA 1984.

"Fall back" beneficiaries

A settlor will generally want his trust fund to be used in the first instance for his children and their families. They may all die: what should happen to the fund then? **5.45**

This is of course a matter for the settlor to decide: the drafter should seek instructions.

Charity as "fall back" beneficiary

The settlor may wish the trust fund to pass to charity absolutely. This is straightforward and can be dealt with in the default clause. The settlor may wish the trust fund to pass either to charity or (at the discretion of the trustees) to some other beneficiaries. Careful drafting is needed to ensure that, if the gift to charity takes effect, the IHT charity exemption applies.[85] **5.46**

Distant relatives as "fall back" beneficiaries

The common and understandable wish is that if the settlor's own family die out, the fund should pass to the nearest surviving family: brothers or sisters and their families; or nephews and nieces and their families. (For the purpose of this discussion we shall refer to "direct family" and "distant relatives".) How is the drafter to achieve this? **5.47**

Use of default clause

It is possible to name some distant relatives in the default clause. Then on the death of the direct family, the trust fund passes to the named relative; if he is dead, the fund passes with his estate, on the terms of his will. This is a crude and unsatisfactory solution. The default clause is too inflexible. Who is to be specified? At the time the trust is made, the only practical course may be to name (say) the brothers or sisters of the settlor; but by the time of the death of the direct family, it may be desired to pass the fund not to the siblings of the settlor, but to their children or grandchildren. **5.48**

Simple addition to the class of beneficiaries

A better course is to expand the class of beneficiaries, the objects of the overriding powers, to include the distant relatives as well as the direct family. Thus: **5.49**

---

[85] See *Taxation of Charities* (Kessler and Kamal, Key Haven Publications, 6th edn, 2007) Chapters 22 (IHT Reliefs) and 23 (Will Drafting).

80 BENEFICIARIES

"The Beneficiaries" means:

(a) The descendants of the Settlor.
(b) The spouses and Civil Partners of the descendants of the Settlor.
(c) The surviving spouses and surviving Civil Partners of the descendants of the Settlor (whether or not they have remarried or entered into another Civil Partnership).
(d) The surviving spouse or surviving Civil Partner of the Settlor (whether or not he or she has remarried or entered into another Civil Partnership).
(e) The descendants of [*name and address ("Name")*].
(f) The spouses and Civil Partners of the descendants of [*Name*].
(g) The surviving spouses and surviving Civil Partners of the descendants of [*Name*] (whether or not they have remarried or entered into another Civil Partnership).

This is superior to the use of a default clause alone. On the failure of the direct family, the trustees have the discretion they need to benefit the more distant relatives in the most appropriate way.

This clause does give the trustees an unnecessarily wide discretion. They could use their overriding powers to cut out the settlor's direct family in order to benefit the distant relatives. That may not matter too much, since the trustees will not, in practice, behave in such an irrational manner. However, the settlor may not want the trustees to possess such a power and even if he is content to leave the matter to the good sense of the trustees it raises the problem mentioned in 5.19 (Definition of "Beneficiaries").

A general power to add beneficiaries could also be used to solve this problem, but should not be regarded as satisfactory: something more specific is needed.[86]

Limited extension of the class of beneficiaries

5.50   The intention of the settlor is likely to be that the distant relatives become beneficiaries on the death of all the direct descendants of the settlor. While the form is slightly more complicated, there is no reason why this should not be expressed in the trust. The following is proposed:

"The Beneficiaries" means:

(a) The descendants of the Settlor.
(b) The spouses and Civil Partners of the descendants of the Settlor.
(c) The surviving spouses and surviving Civil Partners of the descendants of the Settlor (whether or not they have remarried or entered into another Civil Partnership).
(d) The surviving spouse or surviving Civil Partner of the Settlor (whether or not he or she has remarried or entered into another Civil Partnership).
(e) At any time when there is no Beneficiary within (a) above:
   (i) The descendants of [*name and address ("Name")*].
   (ii) The spouses and Civil Partners of the descendants of [*Name*].
   (iii) The surviving spouses and surviving Civil Partners of the descendants of

---

[86] The power to add beneficiaries in the form used in this book would not be exercisable unless the settlor or two adult beneficiaries were living and willing to give consent to the exercise of the power.

[Name] (whether or not they have remarried or entered into another Civil Partnership).

Tax and the class of beneficiaries

Apart from the exclusion of the settlor and spouse, are other exclusions from the class of beneficiaries are sometimes needed for tax reasons? **5.51**

Offshore trusts. A settlor may wish to exclude "defined persons" from the class of beneficiaries to avoid the CGT charge on the settlor of an offshore trust.[87] Non-resident trusts do not qualify for the income tax relief for "disregarded income" if there is a beneficiary who is ordinarily resident in the UK or is a UK resident company.[88]

Remittance basis planning. Foreign domiciled settlors transferring income or gains to a trust may wish to exclude "relevant persons" in order to avoid a charge under the remittance basis.[89]

Re-investment relief. There are (somewhat curious) restrictions on beneficiaries in certain cases where trustees wish to claim CGT re-investment relief.[90] All that matters however is that the relevant conditions are satisfied when the trustees realise a gain on which they want to claim the relief. Accordingly, the drafter need not be concerned with this at the time he makes the trust. If need be, beneficiaries can be excluded at some later time, so as to qualify for the relief.

Entrepeneurs' Relief. This new relief applies to a trust if the life tenant is a "qualifying beneficiary" (in short an employee with 5% of the shares).[91] Trusts holding business property should review their position to ensure that this relief (which is worth up to £80k) applies if possible.

---

[87] Section 86 TCGA 1992.
[88] Sections 811–812 ITA 2007. See *Taxation of Foreign Domiciliaries*, James Kessler QC (7th edn, 2008, Key Haven Publications) Chapters 29 and 30.
[89] Section 809M ITA 2008; see *Taxation of Foreign Domiciliaries*, James Kessler QC (7th edn, 2008, Key Haven Publications) Chapter 9 (The Meaning of Remittance).
[90] Schedule 5B, para.17 TCGA 1992.
[91] Section 169J TCGA 1992.

CHAPTER 6

TRUSTEES

Number of trustees

6.1 The minimum number of trustees is one.[1] There is no maximum, though minor complications arise if trustees of personal property exceed four in number[2]; and considerable complications arise if trustees of land exceed four.[3]

---

[1] A sole trustee is competent in every respect with the following exceptions:

(1) A sole trustee cannot give a valid receipt for capital sums derived from land: TA 1925 s.14; LPA 1925 s.27(2).
(2) Two trustees are needed to discharge a retiring trustee under the statutory power.
(3) A sole professional trustee cannot charge under the statutory power: TA 2000 s.28.

These three restrictions do not apply to a trust corporation. Rules (2) and (3) are excluded in the precedents in this book; see 6.37 (Two trustees requirement); 21.55 (Trustee remuneration).

(4) The drafter may require that two trustees are required to exercise certain powers: see 7.14 (Two-trustee rule).

[2] On the appointment of additional trustees bringing the total above four, see 6.38 (Further provisions concerning appointment of additional trustees?) and its footnotes.

Under standard company articles the directors may refuse to register a transfer of shares to more than four transferees, see Table A Art. 24. But if necessary the shares could be vested in nominees for the trustees.

[3] TA 1925, s.34(2) as amended by the TLATA 1996 provides:

In the case of ... dispositions creating trusts of land ...

(a) the number of trustees thereof shall not in any case exceed four, and where more than four persons are named as such trustees, the four first named (who are able and willing to act) shall alone be the trustees, and the other persons named shall not be trustees unless appointed on the occurrence of a vacancy;
(b) the number of the trustees shall not be increased beyond four.

Let us consider a number of situations:

(1) S creates a trust of land which purports to appoint more than four trustees at the outset: only four trustees are validly appointed.
(2) S creates a trust of land, and later purports to appoint trustees (in excess of four): the appointment is invalid.

Situations (1) and (2) are plain cases. In other circumstances the position is less clear, and the inadequate drafting of the section is exposed:

(3) S creates a trust of land, the trustees then sell the land and hold only personal property. Can more than four trustees be appointed subsequently? It is submitted that the answer is, yes.
(4) S creates a trust of personalty, with four trustees, and the trustees acquire land. Can more than four trustees be appointed subsequently? It is submitted that the answer is, no.

The maximum number of personal representatives is also four.[4]
There should normally be two trustees:

(1) A professional trustee who should be a partner in a firm of solicitors or accountants. This gives slightly more security than a sole practitioner.

(2) The settlor, or a friend or member of the family.

There may be more than two trustees, though trust administration becomes more cumbersome. In older precedents one occasionally sees requirements that there should be at least two or even three trustees at all times. This seems unnecessary and has rightly fallen out of favour.

Choice of trustees

Settlor and spouse as trustees

The settlor may be a trustee and so may his spouse/civil partner. The appointment of the settlor (or spouse/civil partner) as trustee does not have any tax drawback.[5] The prejudice sometimes met against the settlor- 6.2

    The question in cases (3) and (4) is whether one has had a disposition "creating" a trust of land, for the purposes of s.34(2) TA 1925. Inference from tenses is notoriously imprecise. It is submitted that in these cases the question is whether trusts of land subsist at the time of the appointment of new trustees. Contrast *Customs and Excise Commissioners v Link Housing Association Ltd* [1992] STC 718. This view leads to a sensible state of the law, and is at least consistent with the language of the statute. It is also consistent with the law before the amendment by TLATA 1996.

(5) S creates a trust of personalty with five trustees, as is plainly permitted. The trustees purchase land. Are there (i) still five trustees, or (ii) only four trustees, or (iii) five trustees in relation to personalty and four in relation to the land?

    There is something to be said for each of these answers, but answer (i) seems best. So in this case one can have more than five trustees of land. The land cannot be conveyed to all five trustees: s.34 LPA 1925. But that is only a matter of conveyancing. The land must be conveyed to nominees for the five trustees. To avoid uncertainties, it is suggested that where there are more than four trustees, the number should be reduced to four before the trust purchases land.

    If it were desired to create a trust with more than four trustees, and the trust may hold land, a better course would be to constitute a committee or protectorship under the trust deed, and direct the trustees (four or less) to follow the decisions of the committee on key points of trust administration.

    The case for repeal of s.34(2) TA 1925 seems very strong. The section does not apply to charities, and no difficulty seems to have arisen; it is difficult to see why it should apply to private trusts. Canada and Northern Ireland have no equivalent. In practice trusts with more than four trustees would be very infrequent and no difficulty would arise.

[4] Section 114(1) Supreme Court Act 1981.
[5] A settlor may be a trustee (or the sole trustee) without transgressing s.102 FA 1986 (gifts with reservation): *Perpetual Executors & Trustees Association of Australia Ltd v The Commissioner of Taxes of the Commonwealth of Australia* [1954] AC 114. HMRC accept this: IHT Manual 14394. On trustee remuneration, where the settlor is trustee see 19.62 (Trustee remuneration clause: dispositive or administrative?) and 21.64 (Can the settlor charge if he is a trustee?).

trustee probably reflects a distant memory of Estate Duty provisions which discouraged the appointment of a settlor as trustee.[6] On the settlor as sole trustee, see 7.27 (Settlor (or spouse) as sole trustee?).

Beneficiaries as trustees

6.3 Old precedents sometimes direct that a beneficiary may not be appointed trustee. This is entirely the wrong approach.[7] The appointment of a beneficiary as trustee gives him a direct interest and involvement in his or her family's financial affairs, and may be highly advantageous.

The appointment of a beneficiary as trustee does, however, give rise to a possible conflict of interest. There are various ways to minimise the problems which may arise. First, of course, no one will appoint a beneficiary trustee unless confident that he will act properly. Second, the beneficiary should not be the sole trustee. There should be a professional trustee to hold the balance. A settlor creating a trust for his two children and their respective families might appoint each child trustee to safeguard each family interest. Third, the trust can provide that a beneficiary who is a trustee cannot exercise powers in his own favour without the concurrence of an independent trustee. See 6.13 (Conflicts of interest).

In short, it is thought that the conflict of interest will be manageable and should not be a serious objection to the appointment of a beneficiary as trustee. There are many cases where the law accepts an element of conflict of interest.[8] Given the advantages of a beneficiary acting as trustee, the rigorous exclusion of the possibility of conflicts of interest carries too high a price.

Professional trustees

6.4 The aim in combining family and professional trustees is that the trust should be administered both with technical expertise and an understanding of the needs of the beneficiaries.

Professional trustees will be reluctant to act if they may incur personal liabilities unless indemnified. Trustees may incur liabilities to third parties (e.g. loans to acquire trust property, leases with onerous covenants, sale or purchase agreements or shareholder agreements). Here, with care, it should be possible to arrange that the professional trustees are not personally liable beyond the extent of any trust property. This, therefore,

---

[6] Sections 40, 58(5) FA 1940. There is no equivalent in current tax legislation.

[7] This may in the past have been done for Estate Duty reasons doubtful then and now obsolete. See 13.17 (Extending the settlor exclusion clause to exclude trustees). Where an existing trust has this or any other inappropriate prohibition on the choice of trustees, it would be possible to override it, if there was a good reason, by an application to the Court.

[8] The concept of a trustee-beneficiary was enshrined in the Settled Land Act scheme, under which many trustee powers were given to the tenant for life. For further cases where a sensible conflict of interest is accepted see s.9 TLATA 1996; Table A, art.85.

should not cause the trust to be deprived of the benefit of a professional trustee. Tax liabilities (and liability for breach of trust) are inescapably joint and several liabilities of trustees. These may be liabilities for which trustees cannot be suitably indemnified. The solution may be for a professional trustee to retire in favour of a family trustee before any liability accrues.[9]

Corporate trustees

There is a choice between professional individuals, and trust companies. Trust companies will neither die nor retire. On the other hand, if a trust corporation is appointed trustee, the personnel actually managing the trust may and usually will change from time to time, without the consent and perhaps even without the knowledge of the settlor. It is also common offshore for trust companies to be sold, in which case effective management and even the jurisdiction of administration may change. This is a good reason for the settlor or protector to have power to dismiss trustees. **6.5**

If the trust holds land, the use of a corporate trustee may raise SDLT problems; see 29.14 (Stamp duty and SDLT).

Accountants as trustees

An accountant may be unable to act as trustee if his firm also audits a company held by the trust. See ICAEW Code of Ethics section 290 and the APB Ethical Standards 2 and 5.[10] These rules have caused some accountancy firms to hive off their trust companies or to dispose of them altogether. **6.6**

Director of listed company as trustee

If a director of a listed company acts as trustee, disposals of a trust's shareholding in that company must be in accordance with the Stock Exchange Listing Rules.[11] **6.7**

Insider dealing and trusteeship

Similarly, any person who may obtain inside information relating to trust property may be constrained by the Insider Dealing legislation and unable **6.8**

---

[9] However, a retirement in order to facilitate a breach of trust may itself be a breach of trust.
[10] Accessible on *www.icaew.co.uk* and *www.frc.org.uk/APB/publications*.
[11] Ch.16 of the Listing Rules. The restrictions may apply in any event, if the director or his minor children are beneficiaries, in which case the appointment of the director as trustee may make no practical difference.

to deal with trust property. Such a person may be unsuitable to act as trustee.[12]

Custodian trustees

6.9 A custodian trustee holds the trust fund on behalf of active trustees, known as managing trustees.[13] The custodian trustee is similar to a nominee but with rather greater powers and responsibilities. Custodian trustees are more trouble than they are worth, and in practice they are not and should not be used either for private trusts or for charitable trusts.[14]

Foreign trustees

6.10 If it is desired to appoint non-resident trustees the choice is generally restricted to professional trustees. The disadvantages of non-resident trustees in terms of additional expense and inconvenience is one factor to be balanced against the tax advantages; the tax advantages were reduced but by no means eliminated by the reforms in the Finance Acts 1991 and 1998.

If offshore trustees are appointed it is recommended that the settlor (i) should find a firm with professional liability insurance and (ii) should insist that there is no wide indemnity clause. An anxious settlor who cannot satisfy his concerns might set up his own offshore trustee company.

Order of trustees' names

6.11 The order in which the trustees' names appear is of little significance.[15] The idea that the first named trustee is in a special position is a fallacy. This misconception is based on a confusion with the company law rule that, in the case of joint shareholders, the company has regard to the vote of the first named on the register.[16] There is no reason why the first name on the register should be the first named trustee. Moreover, while the company will only regard the first named on the register, the first so named may only act with the concurrence of his co-trustees.[17]

---

[12] *Wight v Olswang No.1* [1998] NPC 111 accessible on *www.kessler.co.uk* illustrates these difficulties.
[13] Section 4 Public Trustee Act 1906.
[14] They raise a number of doubtful questions. For instance Hallett (*Conveyancing Precedents*, p.782) questions whether a custodian trustee can retire without a Court Order. It is considered he can; but how much better not to have to consider these obscure questions.
[15] For an exception see s.34(2) TA 1925 (more than four trustees of land appointed; only the first four named are validly appointed).
[16] Table A of the Companies (Tables A to F) Regulations 1985, art.55.
[17] *IRC v Lithgows Ltd* 39 TC 270. Although a Scottish case, the same principles will apply in England. The order of trustees may matter for tax (e.g. *Barclays Bank v IRC* [1961] AC 509) but in practice that will only exceptionally be the case.

Flee clauses

The purpose of "flee clauses" is to facilitate the appointment of new trustees if, where the old trustees reside, there is a breakdown of law and order, or confiscation of private property. These are sometimes seen in offshore trusts, but they fall outside the scope of this book. Milton Grundy comments on such clauses: "I myself have never seen a draft which I regard as wholly satisfactory".[18] If Milton Grundy has not seen a satisfactory draft, it is unlikely that anyone else has. But a settlor may take the view that a not wholly satisfactory clause is better than nothing at all.

6.12

Conflicts of interest

The general rule is that a trustee cannot enter into any transaction which might conflict with his duty as trustee. Trustees cannot purchase trust property, or sell property to the trust, nor can property be sold between trusts which share a trustee. Trustees cannot take a lease of property which was formerly let to the trust.[19] A trustee-landlord cannot consent to the assignment of the lease of his land to a property company of which he is director.[20] The prohibition is not absolute: such acts may be carried out with the consent of the court, or may be authorised in the trust deed.

6.13

The aim of the rule is the prevention of fraud; but the rule is too strict: one independent person would be sufficient to safeguard the interests of the trust.[21] That is the aim of this clause:

(1) In this clause:
  (a) "**A Fiduciary**" means a Trustee or other Person[22] subject to fiduciary duties under the Settlement.
  (b) "**An Independent Trustee**", in relation to a Person, means a Trustee who is not:
    (i) a brother, sister, ancestor, descendant or dependant of the Person;
    (ii) a spouse or Civil Partner of (i) above or a spouse or Civil Partner of the Person;
    (iii) a company controlled by one or more of the above.

---

[18] *Essays in International Taxation* (2001), Key Haven Publications p.201.
[19] *Keech v Sandford* (1726) Sel Cas Ch 61.
[20] *Re Thompson* [1986] Ch 99.
[21] This is the view of Millett L.J.:

"The rule has been thought in modern times to operate harshly where one of several trustees purchases the trust property at a fair price properly negotiated with his co-trustees."

Ingram v IRC [1997] STC 1234 at p.1260.

[22] The expression "Person" is defined in the precedents in this book to include any person in the world, and to include a trustee.

(2) Subject to sub-clause (3) below a Fiduciary may:

    (a) enter into a transaction with the Trustees, or
    (b) be interested in an arrangement in which the Trustees are or might have been interested, or
    (c) act (or not act) in any other circumstances;

even though his fiduciary duty under the Settlement conflicts with other duties or with his personal interest.

(3) Sub-clause (2) above only applies if:

    (a) the Fiduciary first discloses to the Trustees the nature and extent of any material interest conflicting with his fiduciary duties, and
    (b) there is in relation to the Fiduciary an Independent Trustee in respect of whom there is no conflict of interest, and he considers that the transaction arrangement or action is not contrary to the general interest of the Settlement.

6.14 This draft is loosely based on statutory precedent.[23] It is sometimes said that clauses of this type should be strictly construed. But it is submitted that these clauses should be construed fairly and naturally, according to their terms, like any other clause.[24]

The aim is to cover all eventualities. This has led to a fairly complex draft; though not so complex, it is hoped, that it needs reading more than once to be understood. The clause is in three respects more widely drawn than others in use.

(1) The clause authorises a wide range of transactions. A common form which simply authorises trustees to purchase trust property would not solve many difficulties which arise in practice.[25]

(2) The clause defines in detail the qualifications of an independent trustee. The definition is not wholly comprehensive; there may be occasions where it is doubtful whether there is a "conflict of interest" or what is meant by "control of a company". This should not matter in practice, where there will generally be a professional trustee of undoubted independence. Further refinements (such as defining "control") are thought unnecessary. The short-cut of incorporating statutory rules[26] is rejected. The statutory rules are too cumbersome,

---

[23] Section 68 SLA 1925; Table A art.85 Companies (Tables A to F) Regulations 1985; Sch.2, para.5(1) Intestates' Estates Act 1952.

[24] This was the approach of the Court of Appeal in *Sergeant v National Westminster Bank* (1990) 61 P. & C.R. 518 accessible on *www.kessler.co.uk*.

[25] For instance, such a limited form would not have helped the trustees in *Re Thompson* [1986] Ch 99, where a trustee breached the self-dealing rule when he consented (in his capacity as trustee) to the assignment of a lease to a company of which he was a director. Nor would the limited form help the trustees in *Keech v Sandford* (1726) Sel Cas Ch 61, where the trustees took a new lease of property after an earlier lease to the trustees had expired. Nor would the limited form help where trust property is to be sold from one trust to another, and the same person was a trustee of both trusts.

[26] Such as ss.22 and 23 Pensions Act 1995 (independent trustee) or tax provisions defining "control".

and the trust may need to be read and understood many years after those provisions have become obsolete.

(3) The clause applies to trustees and other persons subject to fiduciary duties. If it applied only to trustees then others (e.g. former trustees and the protector if there is one) might remain subject to the self-dealing rule.

The clause specifies that the transaction is only to proceed if the trustees consider it to accord with the general interest of the settlement. This phrase "the general interest of the settlement" has statutory authority.[27] It would be possible simply to require the independent trustee's "consent"; but it seems better to spell out the circumstances in which consent is to be granted.

Distinguishing personal and fiduciary conflicts

Some drafters distinguish between: 6.15

(1) *Fiduciary* conflicts of interest, for instance, where it is desired to sell assets from one trust to another, and the same persons are trustees of both trusts.

(2) *Personal* conflicts of interest, for instance, where a trustee wishes to purchase property himself from a trust of which he is a trustee.

The distinction is a real one and, strictly, rather more protection is needed in the case of a personal conflict of interest. This school of drafting therefore sets out different rules to govern the dealings of trustees in the two situations. For instance, trustees may be authorised to act in all situations where there is merely a fiduciary conflict of interest; and an independent trustee is required only in cases of personal conflict. It is considered that the matter is not of sufficient practical importance to be worth taking the trouble to make these distinctions in a standard draft.

Trustee-beneficiaries

> The powers of the Trustees may be used to benefit a Trustee (to the same extent as if he were not a Trustee) provided that there is an Independent Trustee in respect of whom there is no conflict of interest.

6.16

A trustee is not, generally speaking, able to exercise a fiduciary[28] power

---

[27] Section 11 TLATA 1996.
[28] Different considerations apply to powers vested in individuals, not trustees; see *Taylor v Allhusen* [1905] 1 Ch 529 and *Re Penrose* [1933] Ch 793 but these powers are not used in the precedents in this book.

of appointment in his own favour unless expressly or implicitly authorised to do so.[29]

It is a matter of construction whether the exercise of a power is implicitly authorised.[30] In the absence of an express clause the answer may not be entirely clear. Even where there is no implicit authority to act in conflict of interest, there are cases where trustees are nevertheless able to exercise their power.[31] That is, the rule prohibiting exercise of trustees' powers in cases of conflict is not always an inflexible rule. In appropriate cases the exercise of the power will be valid. (The onus of proof may rest on the trustees if challenged but that does not ultimately matter.) Once again, however, the extent of that leniency is not entirely clear.

All these problems should be avoided by a clause which addresses the point directly.

The course adopted here is to say that this can be done with the approval of an independent trustee.[32]

Another possible course is to provide that the beneficiary could appoint property to himself even if there is no independent trustee, provided there is at least a second trustee. This would be more appropriate where a settlor wanted all the trustees to be members of the family, so there would be no independent trustee (as defined). A precedent is:

(1) In this paragraph **"a Fiduciary"** means a Trustee, or other person subject to fiduciary duties under this Settlement.
(2) Subject to (3) below a Fiduciary may:

   (a) enter into a transaction with the Trustees, or
   (b) be interested in an arrangement in which the Trustees are or might have been interested, or
   (c) act (or not act) in any other circumstances;

   even though his fiduciary duty under the Settlement conflicts with other duties or with his personal interest.
(3) Sub-clause (2) above only has effect if there is at least one other Trustee and the Fiduciary first discloses to the Trustee(s) the nature and extent of any material interest conflicting with his fiduciary duties
(4) The powers of the Trustees may be used to benefit a Beneficiary who is a Trustee (to the same extent as if he were not a Trustee) provided there is at least one other trustee.

---

[29] *Public Trustee v Cooper* [2001] WTLR 901 at p.933.
[30] In the context of pension funds the Courts have held after some vacillation that a trustee-beneficiary can exercise powers in his own favour; *Edge v Pensions Ombudsman* [2000] Ch 602 at 621–622 not following *Re Drexel Burnham Lambert UK Pension Plan* [1995] 1 WLR 32. For private trusts, one case where a conflict is implicitly authorised is that of the original trustees (the trust deed shows the intention that those particular trustees should be able to exercise the power in their own favour). See Re Z [1998] CILR 248 accessible on *www.kessler.co.uk*; John Mowbray "Choosing Among the Beneficiaries of Discretionary Trusts" [1998] PCB 239 accessible on *www.kessler.co.uk*; *Thomas on Powers*, 11.14–11.33; *Lewin on Trusts* (18th edn, 2008) 20-122-134 (interest of trustees in exercise of dispositive powers).
[31] *Public Trustee v Cooper* [2001] WTLR 901 at p. 933–934.
[32] For a statutory precedent see s.39 Pensions Act 1995.

Another course is to provide that the beneficiary could appoint property to himself even if he is sole trustee. This raises a number of difficulties, and is not recommended.[33]

Alternative form where there is a "protector"

Where there is a protector, he is an ideal person to authorise a breach of the self-dealing rule. This allows the form to be simplified:

(1) In this paragraph **"a Fiduciary"** means a Trustee, or other person subject to fiduciary duties under this Settlement, but not the Protector.
(2) Subject to (3) below a Fiduciary may:

   (a) enter into a transaction with the Trustees, or
   (b) be interested in an arrangement in which the Trustees are or might have been interested, or
   (c) act (or not act) in any other circumstances;

   even though his fiduciary duty under the Settlement conflicts with other duties or with his personal interest.
(3) Sub-clause (2) above only has effect if:

   (a) the Fiduciary first discloses to the Protector the nature and extent of any material interest conflicting with his fiduciary duties, and
   (b) the Protector considers that the transaction arrangement or action is not contrary to the general interest of the Settlement.
(4) The powers of the Trustees may be used to benefit a Beneficiary who is a Trustee (to the same extent as if he were not a Trustee) with the consent in writing of the Protector.

Construction of trustee exemption clauses[34]

6.17 This section considers the meaning of the wide range of expressions used in exemption clauses.

"Actual fraud"

The leading case *Armitage v Nurse*[35] discussed the following clause:

   No Trustee shall be liable for any loss or damage which may happen to the Trust Fund or any part thereof or the income thereof at any time or from any

---

[33] *Drexel Burnham Lambert UK Pension Plan*; *Re Penrose* [1933] Ch 793.
[34] A note on terminology. The terms "exemption clause" "exoneration clause" "exclusion clause" and "exculpation clause" "indemnity clause" are all used interchangeably. "Indemnity clause" means a clause which provides an indemnity for an extant liability, rather than a clause which prevents a liability arising, but the end result may be the same.
For a discussion, see Trustee Exemption Clauses, Law Com No.301, 2006, accessible on *www.lawcom.gov.uk*.
[35] [1998] Ch 241.

cause whatsoever unless such loss or damage shall be caused by his own actual fraud.

It was held that the expression "actual fraud" means dishonesty.[36] "Dishonesty" connotes action by the trustee:

(1) knowing that it is contrary to the interests of the beneficiaries (in the discussion below, "knowing dishonesty");

(2) recklessly indifferent whether it is contrary to their interests or not ("reckless indifference"); or

(3) with the honest belief that it is proper, but which is objectively so unreasonable that no reasonable professional trustee could have thought it for the benefit of beneficiaries. This category may not apply to non-professional trustees.[37]

"Wilful fraud" " dishonesty"

These expressions have the same meaning as "actual fraud".[38]

"Wilful default"

Some exemption clauses exclude liability for loss unless due to the "wilful default" of the trustee.[39] The expression "wilful default" has two meanings. It sometimes means want of ordinary prudence (i.e. negligence); or any breach of fiduciary duty (for instance in the phrase "liable to account on the footing of wilful default"). In the context of a trustee exemption clause, however, wilful default means fraud: knowing dishonesty or reckless indifference.[40]

It is submitted that "wilful misconduct" has the same meaning.

---

[36] The word "actual" excluded an extended meaning of "fraud" (known as "constructive fraud" or "equitable fraud") with the vague definition (or non-definition) of "a breach of duty, falling short of deceit, to which equity attached its sanction".

[37] The concept of dishonesty in categories (1) and (2) is derived from *Armitage v Nurse*. It is consistent with the definition of "fraud" for the purposes of the tort of deceit (fraudulent misrepresentation). See *Derry v Peek* (1889) 14 App. Cas. 337; the headnote reads: "In an action of deceit the Plaintiff must prove actual fraud. Fraud is proved when it is shown that a false representation has been made knowingly, or without belief in its truth, or recklessly, without caring whether it be true or false." *Walker v Stones* [2001] QB 902 at 937 adds category (3). A layman using ordinary language would not describe category (2) or (3) as "dishonesty", so "dishonesty" is being used in an artificial, technical sense. This is unfortunate but understandable. The court's regrettable ruling that exclusion clauses are effective (except for dishonesty) causes injustice which the court mitigates by giving an unnaturally wide meaning to "dishonesty".

[38] *Walker v Stones* [2001] QB 902.

[39] Section 30(1) TA 1925 (repealed) was the pattern for such clauses.

[40] *Armitage v Nurse* [1998] Ch 241 at 252, approving *Re Vickery* [1931] 1 Ch 572. This view of "wilful default" seems well grounded in the natural sense of the expression, and settled in law, despite severe academic disapproval illustrated, for instance, by the *Trust Law Committee Consultation Paper on Trustee Exemption Clauses*, para.3.10 ff accessible on *www.kcl.ac.uk/schools/law/research/tlc*.

"Conscious wrongdoing"

Some exemption clauses exclude liability for loss unless due to "conscious wrongdoing" on the part of the trustee. It is suggested that "conscious wrongdoing" is best construed to mean the same as "actual fraud", that is, both knowing dishonesty and reckless indifference.[41]

"Free from responsibility for loss"

A clause discussed in *Armitage v Nurse* provided: 6.18

> The Trustees may carry on the business of farming *and the Trustees shall be free from all responsibility and be fully indemnified out of the Trust Fund in respect of any loss arising in relation to the business.*

Millett L.J. commented:

> In the absence of the clause, the trustees would have no power to carry on a farming business. If they did so, however prudently, they would commit a breach of trust. The concluding words of the clause confer upon the trustees a consequential exemption from liability for trading losses incurred in the carrying on of the farming business. It does not exonerate them from liability for imprudently investing in a farming business yielding poor returns or from failing to ensure that the business is properly managed.[42]

The words in italics appear at first sight to be an exemption clause. But on this (slightly forced) construction, the words are not an exemption clause at all: they simply spell out the implications of the power to carry on the business of farming; the words are in fact completely otiose. This should be regarded as an application of the principle of construction that exemption clauses are to be narrowly construed[43] (overriding the weaker principle of construction that words in a document should not be regarded as otiose).[44]

It would be better drafting not to use this form of words.

---

[41] Millett L.J. in *Armitage v Nurse* [1998] Ch 241 at 252 referred to both "knowing dishonesty" and "reckless indifference" as "conscious and wilful misconduct." He also expressed the view that the prolix exemption clause in *Key & Elphinstone* (15th edn, 1953) vol.2, p.695 had the same meaning as an exemption clause referring to actual fraud. The *Key & Elphinstone* clause referred to "personal conscious bad faith of the trustee sought to be made liable."
[42] [1998] Ch 241 at 260.
[43] *Wight v Olswang (No.1)* [1998] NPC 111 accessible on www.kessler.co.uk; cf. *Walker v Stones* [2001] QB 902 at 941; exclusion clauses to be construed "no more widely than a fair reading requires".
[44] "There is no canon of construction which denies to a testator the privilege of indulging, to some extent, in tautology": *Re Ward* [1941] Ch 308 at 318 (Luxmore J.).

"No liability for loss"

6.19 *Wight v Olswang (No.1)*[45] considered the following common form:

> (1) Every discretion or power hereby conferred on the trustees shall be an absolute and uncontrolled discretion or power and
> (2) no trustee shall be held liable for any loss or damage accruing as a result of his concurring or refusing or failing to concur in any exercise of any such discretion or power.[46]

The second part seems like an exemption clause, but it is not. The Court of Appeal held that its purpose was "to make clear that the trustee would not be liable for exercising or not exercising a discretion or power merely because the court considered the trustees' grounds unreasonable or merely because the court would not have exercised the discretion or power in the same way." The court continued:

> Whilst on its face exempting every trustee from liability it does so only in relation to loss or damage accruing as a result of the trustees concurring or failing to concur in the exercise of the absolute and uncontrolled discretion or power. It is significant that there is no reference to, for example, a breach of trust or other impropriety in the exercise or non-exercise of the power ... the loss or damage, liability for which is exempted, is that which accrues merely as a result of the trustee concurring or failing to concur.

It follows that the words in the second part of the clause are not only otiose, but misleading (since there could be no liability in any event in the absence of a breach of trust). Forms of this kind should generally not be used. It may be appropriate if the drafter wishes to authorise some exercise of a power that could cause a loss and which might (in the absence of these words) be regarded as a negligent exercise of the power. The wording must describe the act specifically, not in general terms.

"In the professed execution of the trusts and powers hereof"

6.20 These words add nothing.[47]

"Absolute owner" and "beneficial owner" clauses

6.21 In *Bartlett v Barclays Trust Co (No.1)* Brightman J. considered the following clause:

---

[45] [1998] NPC 111 accessible on *www.kessler.co.uk*.
[46] Needless to say, sub-paragraphing here added for clarity. The first part of the clause is discussed briefly in *Re Locker* [1971] 1 WLR 1323. The parliamentary drafter used similar forms: ss.33, 47(1)(iii) AEA 1925.
[47] *Walker v Stones* [2001] QB 902 at 935.

The Trustees may act in relation to the Bartlett Trust Ltd. or any other company and the shares securities and properties thereof in such way as it shall think best calculated to benefit the trust premises and *as if it was the absolute owner* of such shares, securities and property.

This was rightly held merely to confer on the trustee power to engage in a transaction which might otherwise be outside the scope of its authority; it was not an exemption clause protecting the trustee against liability for breach of trust (or authorising a transaction that a prudent man of business would have eschewed). The power was fiduciary.[48]

Validity of exemption clauses

It is now settled, at all levels below the House of Lords, that one can exclude liability except for fraud, in the wide sense of "knowing dishonesty" and "reckless indifference".[49] **6.22**

Plainly one cannot exclude liability for "knowing dishonesty". That is inconsistent with any trust at all.

Can one accept liability for "knowing dishonesty", but at least exclude liability for mere "reckless indifference"? Millett L.J. said:

> There is an irreducible core of obligations owed by the trustees to the beneficiaries and enforceable by them which is fundamental to the concept of a trust. If the beneficiaries have no rights enforceable against the trustees there are no trusts. But I do not accept that these core obligations include the duties of skill and care, prudence and diligence. The duty of the trustees to perform the trusts honestly and in good faith for the benefit of the beneficiaries is the minimum necessary to give substance to the trusts, but in my opinion it is sufficient.

Since honesty is a "core obligation" and reckless indifference is regarded as a form of dishonesty, the natural reading of the passage is that one cannot exclude liability for reckless indifference; and this is considered to be the

---

[48] [1980] Ch 515 at 536. Likewise *Schmidt v Rosewood* [2003] 2 AC 709 para.36:

> "Even if . . . the discretions are expressed in the deed as equivalent to an absolute owner of the trust fund, a trustee is still a trustee."

The same applies if the reference is to a "beneficial" owner (the form used in s.10 TA 1925). Some even say: "absolute beneficial owner" (synonymy). These words "as absolute owner" mean no more or less than the expression "as the trustees think fit". Cf. the cases cited in 19.22 (Power of investment).

It might be said that if a power is fiduciary, and so restricted, it is not the power of an absolute owner, so the terms of the clause are misleading. But then a power to invest "as the trustees think fit" is equally misleading. There are a number of occasions where the parliamentary drafter uses the expression "as absolute owner" to confer wide fiduciary powers: see, e.g. s.1 TA 2000, s.6 TLATA 1996.

[49] In conformity with the common law approach, the new statutory duty of care is subject to contrary intent: Sch.1, para.7 TA 2000.

law. Nor can one exclude liability for an act which no reasonable solicitor/trustee could have thought proper—another category of "dishonesty".[50]

A clause purporting to exclude liability for reckless indifference would be wholly void, unless its invalidity could be severed so the clause could be taken as void so far as it purported to exclude liability for reckless indifference, but nevertheless valid so far as it deals with other matters (e.g. excluding negligence).

The Court of Appeal, surprisingly, upheld the validity of an exemption clause in a will even in circumstances where:

(1) the clause was inserted by a drafter who, in a conflict of interest, acted for the testator and was a trustee (or partner of a trustee); and

(2) the clause was not expressly brought to the testator's attention.[51]

Where a drafter is acting for the settlor, and the drafter (or a partner in the same firm) will be a trustee, there is an apparent conflict of interest. In practice, this is regarded as resolved by appropriate disclosure.

Should the drafter insert an exemption clause?

6.23 The blanket exemption clause has no place in a standard draft. Exemption for trustees' negligence is wrong in principle because it would directly contravene the wishes of the settlor, if he were fairly asked. It should not need saying, but if it does it should be shouted from the rooftops: *the duty of the drafter is to advise, ascertain and carry out the wishes of his client the settlor*. The most respected textbooks all take this view. Prideaux states "the form should only be used in special circumstances". Hallett advises that the relieving clause should only be used for unpaid trustees. The *Encyclopaedia of Forms & Precedents* adopts the same approach: the proposed exemption clause does not apply to professional trustees.[52] Waters states "The wisdom of such a provision is itself questionable, since it weakens the trust machinery available to the beneficiary".[53] Some firms are unwilling to listen to that note of caution, and routinely insert the widest possible trustee exemption clauses for the benefit of themselves as professional trustees.

---

[50] This view is supported by comments on the meaning of "dishonesty" in other cases, discussed in Simon Gardner "Knowing Assistance and Knowing Receipt: Taking Stock" (1996) 112 LQR 56 accessible on *www.kessler.co.uk*.

[51] *Bogg v Raper* (1998/9) 1 ITELR 267. The failure of mainstream law reports to report this decision may be taken as tacit disapproval. Even *Bogg v Raper* recognises at para.53 that an exclusion clause is not effective "if the draftsman inserted the provision without calling the settlor's intention to it and knowing that the settlor did not realise its effect".

[52] Prideaux, *Forms and Precedents in Conveyancing* (25th edn, 1959) Vol.3, p.158; Hallett, *Conveyancing Precedents* (1965) p.801, n.30; *Encyclopaedia of Forms & Precedents* (5th edn) Vol.40, p.512.

[53] *Law of Trusts in Canada*, 3rd edn.

Others, to their credit, do not, and a fair indication of a firm of integrity is that they do not take that course.

Suppose there are non-professional, unpaid trustees. Certainly less can reasonably be expected of them. The law already recognises this; or, more positively, it may be said that more is expected of the professional trustee.[54] Moreover, in the usual case, where there are professional and family trustees, the professional (and his firm) will act for the trustees as a whole; so in the event of professional incompetence, the professional will carry the liability. The settlor may well want to authorise lay trustees to be negligent. However, it should not be assumed that he will do so in the absence of express instructions, and a wide exemption clause, even for the unpaid trustee, should not be a standard form.

The reason sometimes put forward is that professional trustees refuse to act where there is no exemption clause. This is true only in exceptional cases: most trustees will not so lightly turn away good business.

There are circumstances where a wide exemption clause may properly be inserted by the drafter. For example:[55]

1. Where the settlor (or members of the settlor's family) are trustees. Here the settlor may indeed wish for a low standard of duty to rest on the trustees, because he may like the trustees as much as, or more than, he likes the beneficiaries. It is suggested that an exemption clause in such a case should be limited to unpaid trustees.

2. Where a drafter is acting for the trustees and is not acting for the settlor. The clause is in the interest of the drafter's client. It would be good practice to require the settlor to be separately advised.

Duty to disclose exceptions clause to settlor/testator

Members of STEP who draft a will or trust are subject to a duty to disclose trustee exemption clauses.[56] The duty is to notify the settlor or testator of **6.24**

---

[54] *Bartlett v Barclays Trust Co (No.1)* [1980] Ch 515.
[55] This list is not comprehensive. Another example may be artificial tax avoidance schemes, under which the client may not mind (or may even (dangerously) desire) that trustees are not diligent in carrying out their functions as trustees.
[56] See *www.step.org/attach.pl/1622/2894*. Strictly, the duty applies:
"Where a member prepares, or causes to be prepared, a will or other testamentary document or a trust instrument (each an "Instrument"), or is aware of being named as an original trustee or executor in an Instrument:
  a) i) in which he, or any trustee or executor, is entitled to remuneration under the terms of the Instrument; or
     ii) where he has, or may expect to have, a Financial Interest in the trusteeship or executorship of the trust or will or the preparation of the Instrument".
However it will (almost) always be the case that a trustee or executor is entitled to remuneration so the duty will (almost) always apply.

"the existence of provisions in the Instrument... the effect of which would limit or exclude the liability of a trustee or executor for negligence".[57]

A full and fair explanation is that, in Lord Millett's words, the clause "exempts the trustee from liability for loss or damage to the trust property no matter how indolent, imprudent, lacking in diligence, negligent or wilful he may have been, so long as he has not acted dishonestly". However the STEP guidance (which is for all practical purposes authoritative) states that it is in principle sufficient to write to the settlor saying:

> I should also draw your attention to clause [X]. This clause provides that no executor of your will/trustee will be personally liable for any act by them in that capacity unless they are guilty of fraud. If you have any queries in relation to this, then please let me know.

The Solicitors' Code of Conduct[58] contains a similar rule, but categorised as guidance:

> 66. Where you are preparing a trust instrument for a client and that instrument includes a term or terms which has or have the effect of excluding or limiting liability in negligence for a prospective trustee, you should take reasonable steps before the trust is created to ensure that your client is aware of the meaning and effect of the clause. Extra care will be needed if you are, or anyone in or associated with your firm is, or is likely later to become, a paid trustee of the trust.
> 67. Where you or another person in, or associated with, your firm is considering acting as a paid trustee you should not cause to be included a clause in a trust instrument which has the effect of excluding or limiting liability for negligence without taking reasonable steps before the trust is created to ensure that the settlor is aware of the meaning and effect of the clause.
> It would be prudent to ensure both that:—
> (a) there is evidence that you have taken the appropriate steps; and
> (b) that evidence is retained for so long as the trust exists and for a suitable period afterwards.

This is strictly guidance, not mandatory, but in practice it should be followed. There are minor differences between the STEP rule and the Law Society guidance, but in practice they are the same and anyone who satisfies one code will satisfy the other.

---

[57] Strictly, the duty is:

> "such member shall use his reasonable endeavours to ensure:
> (i) that he or another shall have notified the Settlor of the provisions in the Instrument or the original trustee or executor's terms and conditions relating to the Disclosable Circumstances; and
> (ii) that he has reasonable grounds for believing that the Settlor has given his full and informed acceptance of such provisions prior to his execution or approval of the Instrument."

But normally notification will be all that is needed.

[58] Accessible on *www.sra.org.uk/code-of-conduct.page*.

Drafting an exemption clause

6.25 There are many statutory precedents, but in drafting it would be best now to use a form based on that approved in *Armitage v Nurse*.

Commentary: should exemption clauses be allowed?

6.26 In *Armitage v Nurse*, Millett L.J. said:

> The view is widely held that these clauses have gone too far, and that trustees who charge for their services ... should not be able to rely on a trustee exemption clause excluding liability for gross negligence.

Exemption clauses are outlawed in England for directors (whose position is analogous to trustees) and in some investor protection legislation;[59] and in many foreign jurisdictions.[60] Yet if settlors genuinely wish their trustees to have the benefit of an exemption clause, it is hard to see why they should not be allowed to do so. Moreover, statutory reform would bring additional problems and complications to the law. For instance, if reform prohibited exclusion of liability for gross negligence, the courts would have to identify what is "gross" negligence. It would not be easy to frame legislation in a manner which a careful drafter cannot evade, and yet which does not outlaw reasonable, targeted, exemption clauses such as those mentioned below.

In most cases the firm of the solicitor-trustee will act for the trust (and submit invoices accordingly). So the trustees (or beneficiaries) will have a right to sue the firm for breach of contract (or negligence). The exclusion clause in the settlement will not affect that.[61]

In the 7th edition of this book I concluded:

> The problem with exemption clauses, it is submitted, is not one of trust law but of trust draftsmanship. The solution is not law reform, but a drafting solution;

---

[59] Section 232 Companies Act 2006; s.33 Pensions Act 1995; s.253 Financial Services and Markets Act 2000.

[60] Foreign jurisdictions use the full gamut of solutions. Some prohibit exclusion of liability for negligence or failure to act with reasonable care: s.9 Trust of Property Control Act 1988 (South Africa). The position is similar in the Turks and Caicos Islands. Others, e.g. Jersey, more tentatively, prohibit exclusion of liability for gross negligence (so the Jersey Trustee may act negligently, so long as he takes care not to be grossly negligent). Belize prohibits exclusion of liability for fraud or wilful misconduct; a provision which merely codifies the common law rule.

[61] However, in *Young v Hansen* (NZCA 16 September 2003 accessible on *www.ipsofactoj.com*) a claim in contract against a negligent solicitor-trustee failed, because a narrow view was taken of the scope of the solicitor's firm's contractual duties. The firm was not (on the facts) retained to act generally in administering the estate.

to require appropriate use of such clauses in trust drafting. A strengthening of the rules of professional conduct—or a greater recognition of the implications of existing rules—would be the best solution to the problem.

The Law Commission has gone down this road; it will be interesting to see if it works.

What standard of care rests on trustees?

6.27 The form used in this book is as follows:

> The duty of reasonable care (set out in s.1 Trustee Act 2000) applies to all the functions of the Trustees.

The duty is expressed at length in the statute but amounts effectively to "reasonable care".

This applies to powers relating to investment, acquisition of land, agents, nominees and custodians and insurance. It is submitted that case law imposes the same duty in the exercise of trustee functions generally but it is best to say so expressly.

Excluding strict liability

6.28 Trustees have the benefit of what may be regarded as a statutory exemption clause. They are not liable if they have acted honestly and reasonably and ought fairly to be excused for any breach of trust.[62] Do they need any more than this? It is considered some slight tinkering is desirable to get the fairest balance between the needs of trustees and beneficiaries.

The first concerns no-fault liability. Trust law sometimes imposes liabilities for innocent and non-negligent errors, for instance where trustees act outside the powers conferred on them. It seems fair that personal liability should be restricted to negligence:[63]

---

[62] Section 61 TA 1925. See also s.20(3) Administration of Justice Act 1982.
[63] The Charity Commission Model Charitable Trust adopts this idea:

> "**8 Duty of care and extent of liability.**
> When exercising any power (whether given to them by this deed, or by statute, or by any rule of law) in administering or managing the charity, each of the trustees must use the level of care and skill that is reasonable in the circumstances, taking into account any special knowledge or experience that he or she has or claims to have ("the duty of care").
>
> No trustee, and no one exercising powers or responsibilities that have been delegated by the trustees, shall be liable for any act or failure to act unless, in acting or in failing to act, he or she has failed to discharge the duty of care."

It is submitted that the law ought to develop in this direction and impose the simply stated duty of reasonable care in relation to all trustee liability. The rules of breach of trust should in many

> A Trustee shall not be liable for a loss to the Trust Fund unless that loss was caused by his own actual fraud or negligence.

Trustees may object that the duty of care is so vague that they may always feel at risk; no matter how carefully they act it is easy with hindsight to allege an innocent error was negligent. The higher standard of care may increase the costs of running the trust. However, money spent on careful (i.e. non-negligent) administration of a trust is not wasted. While one certainly wishes to make the administration of the trust as easy and as cheap as possible, this must be balanced against the hazards of authorising sloppy practice. Solicitors and accountants are generally subject to a duty of care for their work in contract or in negligence. There is no reason why trust administration should be different.

Moreover the professional trustee will be insured. So the effect of the trustee exemption clause is to lighten the burden on the trustees' insurer.

There is a respectable argument that trustee liability should be limited to the amounts for which the trustees can reasonably obtain insurance cover. The drafting would be tricky. This course is not pursued in practice.

Excluding claims by unknown beneficiaries

There is a fear that unknown beneficiaries may emerge with claims against the trustees, who (unaware of their existence) may have distributed the trust fund on the wrong basis. **6.29**

When the Family Law Reform Act 1969 first extended the rights of illegitimate beneficiaries, special protection was provided by statute.[64] Unfortunately for trustees, the statutory protection was repealed.[65] The trustees may already have the protection of the general clause above, and statute provides some general protection, especially s.27 Trustee Act 1925 (Protection by means of advertisements)[66]; but something specific is probably appropriate.

The following is based on the original statutory wording:

> The Trustees may distribute Trust Property or income in accordance with this Settlement but without having ascertained that there is no person who is or may be

---

respects be assimilated with those of professional negligence. Section 1 TA 2000 is a step in this direction.

[64] Section 17 Family Law Reform Act 1969.
[65] Section 20 Family Law Reform Act 1987.
[66] But advertising is hardly appropriate in small cases. Further, and importantly, s.27 only applies to (i) trustees of a settlement (within the meaning of the SLA 1925); (ii) trustees of land (within the meaning of the TLATA 1996); (iii) trustees for sale of personal property; and (iv) personal representatives. Thus there is a lacuna, and the section would not normally apply to a trust holding only personal property, in the absence of a trust for sale. (This seems to be one of the few situations after the TLATA 1996 where a trust for sale may still have significance, and must be an unintended quirk of the drafting of the 1996 Act.)

entitled to any interest therein by virtue of a relationship unknown to the Trustees. [67] The Trustees shall not be liable to such a person unless they have notice of his claim at the time of the distribution. This clause does not prejudice the right of any person to follow property or income into the hands of any person, other than a purchaser in good faith, who may have received it.

Relying on counsel's advice

Counsel's advice generally

6.30 The relevant principles of professional negligence are as follows[68]:

(1) In general, a solicitor is entitled to rely upon the advice of counsel properly instructed.

(2) For a solicitor without specialist experience in a particular field to rely on counsel's advice is to make normal and proper use of the Bar.

(3) He must not do so blindly but must exercise his own independent judgment. If he reasonably thinks counsel's advice is obviously or glaringly wrong, it is his duty to reject it. The more specialist the nature of the advice, the more reasonable it is likely to be to follow it.

It is submitted that exactly the same rules should apply to trustees who rely on counsel even in the absence of anything dealing with the matter in the trust deed; and a fortiori if there is a clause (as in this book) restricting trustees' liability to cases of negligence.[69]

However, dicta in some antique cases[70] might be taken to suggest that trustees who (acting reasonably) rely on counsel may nevertheless be liable for breach of trust in some circumstances. It is best for an express clause to

---

[67] In the 8th edition of this book I referred to "an illegitimate relationship" rather than "a relationship unknown to the Trustees". But now that births out of wedlock have reached 43% in the UK, 2008 Social Trends Report, accessible on *www.statistics.gov.uk*, this has ceased to be an appropriate wording (though no difficulty should arise where it has been used in the past).

[68] *Locke v Camberwell Health Authority* [1991] 2 Med LR 249 at 254 accessible at *www.kessler.co.uk*. See *Cordery on Solicitors*, Butterworths looseleaf, J553, citing nearly a dozen more cases.

[69] See *Bonham v Fishwick* [2008] EWCA Civ 372 in which an allegation of "wilful wrongdoing" was struck out where the trustees had heeded the legal advice given by their counsel and solicitor so that the exoneration clause was a complete defence.

[70] "The advice of counsel is not an absolute indemnity to trustees in bringing an action, though it may go a long way towards it": *Stott v Milne* (1884) 25 Ch D 710 at 714, approved *Re Beddoe* [1893] 1 Ch 547 at 558. Relying on a solicitor (as opposed to Counsel) was thought no excuse for a breach of trust in *Re Dive* [1909] 1 Ch 328 at 342: "Although no doubt it seems hard to hold a trustee liable where he has followed the advice of his solicitor, I do not think I can allow the trustee to be excused where, if he had with reasonable care considered the authority under which he was acting, he would have found that it did not authorize that which he was doing."

make the position clear. An express clause may save the costs of cautious trustees who might otherwise seek directions from the court.

Counsel's advice on litigation

Where trustees propose to be involved in litigation, they should (under the general trust law) apply to the court for prior approval.[71] In 1893 it was said to be a matter of ease and comparatively small expense for trustees to obtain the opinion of a judge on the question whether an action should be brought or defended at the expense of the trust.[72]

Nowadays the procedure is slow and expensive; moreover a Chancery Master or judge (in a difficult case) will not be in a good position to second guess counsel's advice. In these cases it is suggested that the opinion of counsel is as much protection for the trust as can reasonably be provided. Counsel owes a duty of care to the trustees and could be sued if negligent. This is the background to the following clause:

> (1) A Trustee shall not be liable for acting in accordance with the advice of counsel, of at least ten years' standing, with respect to the settlement. The Trustees may in particular conduct legal proceedings in accordance with such advice without obtaining a Court Order. A Trustee may recover from the Trust Fund any expenses where he has acted in accordance with such advice.
> (2) The above paragraph does not apply:
>> (a) if the Trustee knows or has reasonable cause to suspect that the advice was given in ignorance of material facts;
>> (b) if proceedings are pending to obtain the decision of the court on the matter;
>> (c) in relation to a Trustee who has a personal interest in the subject matter of the advice; or
>> (d) in relation to a Trustee who has committed a breach of trust relating to the subject matter of the advice prior to obtaining the advice.

This follows the precedent of s.29 Charities Act 1993 (which provides that charity trustees are not liable if they follow the advice of the charity commissioners).[73] The clause does not state expressly that the trustee

---

[71] Failure to do so may result in the trustees being personally liable for the costs: *Re Beddoe* [1893] 1 Ch 547. Hence the application is called a *Beddoe* application.

[72] *Re Beddoe* [1893] 1 Ch at 558. Jessel M.R. considered "It very often is cheaper to take the opinion of the Court than even the opinion of counsel"; *Sharp v Cash* (1879) 10 Ch D 468 at 471. One can only conclude that the operation of the Courts and the legal profession as recently as the late 19th century was amazingly different from today. It is important to bear this in mind in considering the relevance of these antique cases to the law today.

[73] For other statutory precedents, see s.48 Administration of Justice Act 1985; r.200 Land Registration Rules 2003; s.4(2)(h) Public Trustee Act 1906. The form used in this book may be contrasted with that in *IRC v Botnar* [1999] STC 711:

> "The Trustees may take the opinion of counsel locally or where appropriate elsewhere concerning any difference arising under this Settlement or any matter in any way relating to the Trust or to their duties in connection with the trusts hereof and in all matters may act in accordance with the opinion of such counsel."

> The form in this book merely saves trustees from personal liability: the *Botnar* form is wider as it authorises trustees to act in a manner which would bind the beneficiaries. In *Botnar* the trustees

should refuse to follow counsel's advice if "glaringly wrong". However, this must be implied, as no exclusion clause will relieve a trustee for reckless indifference.

"Ten years' standing" would mean ten years since call to the Bar.[74] Younger practitioners may feel that five years is sufficient.[75]

Excluding duty to supervise family companies

6.31 Where the trust property includes a controlling shareholding in a family company it is the duty of trustees under the general law to keep a close eye on the company's activities. A trustee may run the business himself; or become a non-executive director; or appoint a nominee on the board to report to him. Alternatively the trustee may be able to oversee the company's affairs by studying the agenda and minutes of board meetings if regularly held, or management accounts, or quarterly reports. A trustee should not sit back and allow the company to be run by its directors, receiving no more than statutory accounts. If he does so, he is at risk if things go wrong.[76] The same principle applies where the trustees hold a substantial minority interest, if their holding gives them effective power to interfere in the company's business.

Now, where the trust property is shares in the family company, the last thing that the settlor wants is his professional trustees on the board or interfering in any way with his management of his company. Professional trustees—not by training or temperament qualified to run a business[77]—will not want to undertake this duty of oversight. Here, then, is a case where too much is expected of trustees, under the general law, and some relaxation may be thought appropriate.

The proposed form is:

> The Trustees are under no duty to enquire into the conduct of a company in which they are interested, unless they have knowledge[78] of circumstances which call for enquiry.

---

had been advised that they may use the trust fund to benefit the settlor (the unusually worded settlor exclusion clause was ambiguous). It was stated (obiter, but rightly) that the settlor had an interest in the settlement, regardless of the true construction of the settlor exclusion clause, because of the effect of the *Botnar* form combined with the advice the trustees had received. However, it is unlikely that there will be many, if any, cases like *Botnar*.

[74] Parliamentary counsel often use this phrase (e.g. s.4 Taxes Management Act 1970) and it is not necessary to be more specific.
[75] That was the view of the STEP Standard Provisions (1st edn). Parliament thought 10 years appropriate: s.48 Administration of Justice Act 1985 (action taken in reliance on Counsel's Opinion).
[76] *Bartlett v Barclays Trust Co (No.1)* [1980] Ch 515 at p.533.
[77] This accords with the principle that a solicitor's duty "is to advise on matters of law and the solicitor is under no duty to advise on matters of business, unless he specifically agrees to do so" (*Cordery on Solicitors*, J354).
[78] On the concept of "knowledge" (to be contrasted with "notice") see an illuminating article by Simon Gardner, "Knowing Assistance and Knowing Receipt; Taking Stock" (1996) 112 LQR 56 accessible on *www.kessler.co.uk*.

This clause does not prevent trustees from interfering in the company's business; but it allows them to do very little; this they will normally prefer. A common form allows trustees to do nothing until they have notice of acts of dishonesty: under the suggested clause, the trustees should interfere if they have knowledge of directors' negligence or incompetence; and they may do so even if they do not. This is thought to strike a fair balance.

Excluding duty to supervise parents and guardians

The proposed form is: **6.32**

> The Trustees are under no duty to enquire into the use of income paid to a parent or guardian on behalf of a minor, unless they have knowledge[79] of circumstances which call for enquiry.

Where a payment is made to a parent for the benefit of a beneficiary, trustees are obliged to take reasonable care to ensure that that sum is properly applied for the beneficiary's benefit, not misappropriated by the parent or misapplied by the beneficiary.[80]

The common practice is to exclude this duty. Is this advisable? On one hand, it eases the burden of the trustees, and reduces administrative costs of the trust. On the other hand, the wider power would permit negligent trustees to dissipate trust funds.

This clause confers a carefully circumscribed freedom on the trustees. They may make regular payments of income to the parents. If they are dealing with capital—the sums will usually be greater—they must take proper care. (This follows the example of s.21 LPA 1925, which allows a beneficiary who is unmarried but under 18 to give a good receipt for income but not capital.) Moreover, if their suspicions are aroused at any time, the trustees are expected to investigate. It is thought that this is as much relief as the settlor would normally wish the trustees to have.

Appointment of new trustees

The Trustee Act 1925 provides a detailed code of rules to regulate the **6.33**
appointment and retirement of trustees. The usual practice is to adopt the statutory rules with slight amendments. The approach in this book is to specify in the main part of the deed the person who has power to appoint

---

[79] See above footnote.
[80] *Re Pauling* [1964] Ch 303.

new trustees; that is an important matter. Points of detail are placed in the Schedule.

Who appoints trustees?

6.34 The form used in this book is as follows:

> The power of appointing trustees[81] is exercisable by the Settlor during his life and by will.

This form is self-explanatory.[82]

Obviously the settlor will want the power of appointment of new trustees during his life. (Under the forms in this book he can release or delegate the power if desired.) It is less clear who should have the power to appoint new trustees after the settlor's death.

In the absence of specific provisions in the trust, the power to appoint new trustees will vest in the continuing trustees. This is the most satisfactory general solution and it is adopted in the precedents in this book. Where this course is adopted, it does not seem necessary to spell the position out in full.[83] Occasionally the surviving spouse of the settlor is given the power; that is:

> The power of appointing trustees is exercisable by the Settlor during his life, *and after his death by his widow during her life.*

Is this desirable? In an age where one third of marriages end in divorce—the proportion may still be rising—it is quite possible that the widow of the settlor will not be the mother of the main beneficiaries, the settlor's children. In such cases this form might be a recipe for trouble.

If the settlor wants to decide trustees in the event of his death, he should have an express power to appoint new trustees by will.[84] It is suggested

---

[81] The small "t" is appropriate here: see 10.33 (Definitions).
[82] Three minor variants of wording may be noted here:

(1) Some drafters refer to "the *statutory* power of appointing new trustees ..." but the clause can hardly be read as referring to anything else.
(2) Some refer to a power to appoint "new *or additional* trustees". Section 36(1) TA 1925 confers a power to appoint a "new" trustee in place of a retiring trustee; s.36(6) confers power to appoint "another person ... to be an additional trustee." There is statutory authority for the phrase "new or additional trustees": ss.64(2) and 68(17) TA 1925; but elsewhere statute is content to use the shorter form: see, e.g. s.30(3) SLA 1925; and the precedents in Forms Nos. 1 and 2 of Sch. 1 to SLA 1925.
(3) Some refer to the power as "vested in" the Settlor; "exercisable by" the Settlor seems more lucid.

It is not necessary to say: "will or codicil": see 3.18 (Archaic or prolix expressions).
[83] If the drafter does wish to set the position out in full, it would be best to set out the relevant parts of s.36(1) and (8) TA 1925 more or less in full. This of course is not impractical, but the form becomes complicated.
[84] The position in the absence of an express power is unclear. *Re Parker* [1894] 1 Ch 707 decided that (what is now) s.36(1)(b) TA 1925 did not permit an appointment of new trustees by will. It is arguable that s.36(1)(a) or s.36(6) TA 1925 would authorise such an appointment.

that most settlors would like this power so it should be a standard form. (A more complex solution is to provide that a "protector" should appoint new trustees. The settlor can appoint his wife, or child, or whoever, to be protector and can have power to revoke that appointment and appoint a different protector. The advantage of this course is that the protector's powers continue after the death of the settlor. The protector can (if desired) appoint his own successor in due course. See 7.29 (Protectors).)

Where there are two settlors, see 10.11 (Form where trust made by joint settlors).

Appointment of foreign trustees

A person may be appointed trustee of the Settlement even though he has no connection with the United Kingdom. **6.35**

Is it possible to use the statutory power to appoint foreign trustees? A cryptic passage in *Re Whitehead* states that this is not generally right or proper.[85] If that were right, it would be a serious deficiency in the statutory power. No-one seriously thinks that the obiter dicta in *Re Whitehead* represent the law,[86] but still, the drafter can and should avoid the issue: the form in this book therefore sets out an express power to appoint foreign trustees. This is generally desirable even if the appointment of foreign trustees is not contemplated; one can never anticipate the future needs of beneficiaries.

There is no reported case in which a clause of this kind has been considered. The drafter has no judicial guidance as to what form of words is required. It would be sufficient to give power to appoint trustees "not resident in the United Kingdom" or "anywhere in the world". This precedent adopts a slightly wider formula.

---

[85] [1971] 1 WLR 837. The *Whitehead* principle did not apply where (a rare case) the beneficiaries have themselves become resident in a foreign jurisdiction.

[86] For the following reasons:

(1) *Whitehead* gives insufficient weight to the tax advantages which may be enjoyed by beneficiaries of offshore trusts. If the duty of trustees is to secure the maximum benefit for beneficiaries, then in some cases it should be a breach of trust *not* to retire in favour of non-resident trustees.

(2) There is little cause for indiscriminate jurisdictional chauvinism: in some jurisdictions professional trustees are at least as well regulated as in the United Kingdom.

(3) The law is influenced by the practice of the profession. *Whitehead* is ignored in practice: non-resident trustees are frequently appointed under the statutory power.

(4) The case was not followed in two cases in 1987: *Richard v Mackay* and *Re Beatty (No.2)*, belatedly reported in Trust Law International, Vol.11 (1997) pp.23 and 77 accessible on www.kessler.co.uk.

If *Whitehead* were correct, interesting questions would arise as to the consequences of an "improper" appointment. The fourth edition of this book touched on these; but the discussion is wholly theoretical, except so far as it supplies further reasons why *Whitehead* cannot be good law.

The clause does not affect the duty to consider the suitability of any new trustees before making an appointment. This may be especially important when foreign trustees are to be appointed.

The statutory power allows a trustee to be replaced if he remains out of the United Kingdom for more than a year. It is fairly standard practice, where the appointment of foreign trustees is permitted, to amend this rule so that:

> ... *remaining out of the United Kingdom shall not be a ground for the replacement or removal of a trustee.*

However, there is something to be said for retaining what is effectively a power of dismissal over foreign trustees. This can do no harm: the non-resident trustee does not have to be replaced so in this book the statutory rule is not amended in this way. Of course, the statutory power to replace non-resident trustees is nugatory if the power of appointing new trustees is vested in trustees who are all non-resident.

Mandatory retirement of trustees

6.36 The 8th and earlier editions of this book included a provision that a trustee who has reached the age of 65 shall retire if requested to do so.[87] Such a provision is still valid under current age discrimination law.[88] However, we do not consider that it complies with the spirit of the times (or perhaps with the spirit of the legislation) so we have removed it from the precedents in this edition.

Two trustees requirement

6.37 A Trustee may be discharged even though there is neither a trust corporation nor two persons to act as trustees provided that there remains at least one trustee. A trustee may be appointed under s.36(1) Trustee Act 1925 in place of more than one trustee.

This clause reverses the rule of trust law that a retiring trustee is not discharged from the trust unless there remain two persons to act as trustees, or

---

[87] Drafting Trusts and Will Trusts, 8th edn, para.6.35.
[88] The Employment Equality (Age) Regulations 2006 covers equal treatment in employment and occupations.
   Regulation 12 sets out the application of the Age Regulations to "office-holders"—the only category under which a trustee could fall. This provision prohibits discrimination in the context of any post "to which persons are appointed to discharge functions personally *under the direction of another person*, and in respect of which they are entitled to remuneration" (Reg.12(8)(a)).
   Trustees are not under the direction of another person. They must exercise their powers and discretions independently. They do not therefore fall within the category of officer-holder so that the Age Regs do not apply. This view is consistent with DTI Guidance Notes.

a trust corporation.[89] Thus if a foreign trust company[90] is appointed to be trustee in place of United Kingdom trustees, the United Kingdom trustees would not generally be discharged, unless the trust provided otherwise. The second sentence resolves a somewhat theoretical doubt whether a single trustee can be appointed in place of more than one trustee without satisfying the conditions of s.39 Trustee Act 1925.

The drafter can alter the general rule if he wishes to do so.[91] The rule now offers little protection to the trust.[92] It is considered that the rule serves no real purpose, and for ease of trust administration it should be excluded.

Further provisions concerning appointment of additional trustees?

In practice, new trustees are usually needed to replace trustees who have died or wish to retire. Under the statutory code a new trustee may also be appointed to boost the number of trustees, without a retirement. The power to appoint additional trustees has two somewhat senseless restrictions.[93] Fortunately, they can in practice be avoided.[94] The question for

6.38

---

[89] Sections 37(1)(c) and 39 TA 1925, as amended by Sch.3 TLATA 1996. Prior to the 1996 reforms, there had to be two *individuals* or a trust corporation to act as trustees. This led to disaster in *Jasmine Trustees v Wells* [2008] Ch 194 in which it was held that the term "individuals" in s.37(1)(c) meant natural persons and did not include a body corporate so that two individuals had not retired when they thought they did and subsequent appointments of trustees in which they did not participate were invalid. Similar rules apply where a trustee retires without the appointment of a new trustee: s.39 TA 1925 (likewise amended).

[90] A foreign trust company is not generally a "trust corporation" as defined, see 7.14 (Two-trustee rule).

[91] *LRT Pension Fund Trustee Co Ltd v Hatt* [1993] Pensions Law Reports 227. This was followed without discussion in *Adam v Theodore Goddard* [2000] WTLR 349 where the issue was whether a particular clause had the effect of reversing the normal rule. (Both cases are accessible on *www.kessler.co.uk*.) Prior to 1993 it was unclear whether the rule could be amended. Accordingly the STEP provisions (1st edn, 1992) did not deal with this point. Failure to exclude the rule matters less after the TLATA 1996 reforms.

[92] The second company to act as trustee may be a subsidiary of the first, with nominal share capital. See 7.14 (Two-trustee rule).

[93] 1. The person holding the power to appoint trustees cannot appoint himself.
2. One cannot add trustees so as to increase the number beyond four trustees, even if the general law permits more than four trustees (because the trust does not hold land or is a charity).

[94] Suppose a trust has four trustees, and the settlor, having the power to appoint additional trustees, wishes to appoint himself as fifth trustee. This cannot be done directly under s.36(6) TA 1925. Instead:

(1) One of the present trustees retires, and the settlor and another trustee is appointed in his place, under s.36(1) TA 1925 (which is wider than s.36(6)).
(2) Then the other trustee retires, and the first mentioned trustee is appointed in his place.

This was in fact a common practice before 1925: see Wolstenhome and Cherry, *Conveyancing Statutes* (13th edn, 1972), Vol.4, p.60. Where the trust holds land, see 6.1 (Number of trustees).

the drafter is whether he should leave the (slightly odd) statutory rules to apply, or whether he should, as he could, delete the restrictions. It is suggested that in a private trust, the drafter should leave matters as they stand. It is not worth the trouble to deal with these points. However in a charitable trust, the position is different. Here it will often be desirable to have more than four trustees, and the restricted power to add trustees may well cause inconvenience.

Trustees' right to resign

6.39 Trustees are sometimes given a right to resign. The statutory provision, under which a trustee can retire with the consent of his co-trustees, is generally thought to be sufficient. In the case of a charity, where there may be a large number of unpaid trustees, a right to resign without the consent of fellow trustees would be appropriate. The following form is suggested:[95]

> A Trustee may resign by giving notice in writing to the other Trustees. On receipt of such notice the retiring Trustee shall cease to be a Trustee provided that there shall be remaining at least two persons to act as Trustees or a Trust Corporation (within the meaning of the Trustee Act 1925).

Sections 19 and 20 Trusts of Land and Appointment of Trustees Act 1996

6.40 Sections 19 and 20 TLATA 1996 give beneficiaries powers to dismiss trustees where beneficiaries are all adult and absolutely entitled to trust property. It is considered that it is not appropriate to exclude these sections in a standard form for two reasons:

> (1) It is relatively rare that all the beneficiaries will be of full age and (taken together) absolutely entitled to the trust property. In particular, that would not be the case in any of the precedents in this book.
>
> (2) In the simple case where the beneficiaries are so entitled, the power conferred by ss.19 and 20 is appropriate. For the beneficiaries could in any event direct the trustees to transfer the trust property to other trustees, by virtue of the rule in *Saunders v Vautier*.[96] Sections 19 and 20 only allow them to achieve the same result without a possible capital gains tax difficulty.

---

[95] For statutory precedents see art.19 Trusts (Jersey) Law 1984 and s.3 Trusts (Scotland) Act 1921. For a case (of construction) where a right to retire was inferred from exiguous wording see *Davis v Wallington* [1990] 1 WLR 1511 at p.1528.

[96] [1835–42] All ER 58.

Power to dismiss trustees

On this topic see 7.30 (Power to dismiss trustees). **6.41**

Short form

In short forms (e.g. a declaration of trust for an insurance policy) it would **6.42** be simplest to adopt the statutory rules without amendment. In that case the trustees will have the power to appoint their successor. When that is done, nothing need be put into the trust deed at all. It is quite unnecessary to say (as one sometimes sees) that:

> *The statutory power of appointing new trustees shall apply hereto.*

CHAPTER 7

TRUSTEES' POWERS

Introduction

7.1 This chapter considers some general questions relating to powers of trustees: the drafting of specific powers is considered at 12.1 (Overriding powers) and 21.1 (Administrative provisions).

Duties and powers distinguished

7.2 Trust law distinguishes between:

(i) A power conferred on trustees, which permits them to act.

(ii) A duty imposed on trustees, which obliges them to act.

There is also a hybrid between the ordinary power and a duty, a form such as:

The trustees shall pay the income to A, B, or C.

Here trustees have a duty to act—to pay the income to somebody—but a choice as to which of A, B or C is to receive it. In this book this is referred to as a "discretionary duty" or a "discretionary trust of income".

Duties or powers: does it matter?

7.3 The distinction between a duty and a power seems crucial. If one reads "The trustees *shall* pay the income to X" then X will receive the income. If one reads that "The trustees *may* pay the income to X" then he may or may not do so.

However, when duties and powers are combined together, the formal distinction loses most of its significance. Contrast:

(i) The trustees may accumulate any income and shall pay the remainder to X.

(ii) The trustees may pay any income to X and shall accumulate the remainder.

(iii) The trustees shall either accumulate the income or pay it to X.

The first of these clauses confers a power to accumulate income, with a duty to pay unaccumulated income to X. The second confers a power to pay income to X, with a duty to accumulate the remainder. The third imposes a discretionary duty to do one or the other. The practical differences between them all are very small and only rarely is the distinction important.[1] The drafter will not usually mind which form is used but there should be no ambiguity. The drafter should be aware whether he is creating a duty or a power.

Powers and duties: terminology

Terminology in this area is something of a headache. 7.4

Terms to describe "duties"

The modern approach—much to be encouraged—is to use the word "duty".[2] The traditional term for this was the word "trust". That usage was unfortunate. Nowadays the word "trust" is more commonly used as a synonym of "settlement"—except in a few stylised phrases, such as "trust for sale" (meaning a duty to sell).[3]

---

[1] There are different results if the trustees cannot agree about the exercise of the power; or if they delay before its exercise. The clauses would have different results in the event of a breach of the rule against accumulations. The distinction also affects income accruing but not paid on the death of X or on an assignment of X's interest: *IRC v Berrill* [1981] 1 WLR 1449. The distinction may remain of some significance for the rule relating to "administrative workability" of a trust. These differences savour more of academic than practical interest and need not concern the trust drafter.
[2] An early statutory example was in s.2(4) Trustee Investments Act 1961 ("the exercise of any power or duty of a trustee"). There are many examples in the updating provisions of Sch.3 Trusts of Land and Appointment of Trustees Act 1996, where the word "trust" in the old legislation is replaced by the word "duty".
[3] Also see the discussion of *trust* in *Terminology*.

Terms to describe powers

The words "power" and "discretion" are used indiscriminately to refer to both true powers and discretionary duties.[4] The usage is understandable and (it is submitted) acceptable. "True powers" and "discretionary duties" are best regarded as two types of power.[5] Where (as is almost always the case) the difference does not matter, it is not realistic to expect any precision in normal use.

Statute and drafters often use the phrase "powers and discretions".[6] Here it could be that "power" refers to true powers; and "discretions" refers to discretionary duties; but in view of the vagaries of usage, the better view must be that the two terms are used as synonyms.

The phrase is sometimes expanded to "powers, authorities and discretions".[7] This is mere synonymy: the word "authorities" adds style but contributes nothing to the sense. Thoughtful drafters in the modern style need not use this expression.

The best and modern term to describe duties, powers and discretionary duties of trustees is "functions".[8]

Drafting duties and powers

7.5 The best approach is to adopt the well settled rule that the word "may"

---

[4] On use of "power" in this wide sense, see for instance, *Re Wellsted* [1949] Ch 296 at 308 (where Lord Greene said the word power could "properly" be used to describe an obligation to choose between a number of objects, i.e. a discretionary trust). Statutory examples of this usage are: ss.18, 30(2) (repealed), 31, 69(2) TA 1925.
   Statutory examples of "discretion" in this wide sense are s. 698(3) ICTA 1988 and ss.480 and 812(4) ITA 2007.

[5] *Mettoy Pension Trustees Ltd v Evans* [1991] 2 All ER 513 at 545. Something should be done on those occasions (rare outside textbooks) when one does need to distinguish between true powers and discretionary duties. One must use some special phrase but at present there is no agreed terminology. One sometimes finds "powers" or "powers in the strict sense" to describe powers; and "imperative trusts" "trust powers" or a whole variety of other expressions to describe discretionary duties. Perhaps one day a decision of the higher courts will prescribe some terminology. We need better descriptive labels than those adopted by Warner J. in *Mettoy*: "Categories 1, 2, 3 & 4."

[6] For instance, s.25 TA 1925 as amended.

[7] For instance, s.36(7) TA 1925.

[8] e.g. s.36(9) TA 1925 (which dates from 1959). An early triumph of the term "functions" in modern statutory usage is illustrated by s.84 Financial Services Act 1986 (which makes void certain exclusion clauses). Here the parliamentary drafter had before him the precedent of s.192 Companies Act 1985 (now s.750 Companies Act 2006); but he substituted the word "functions" for the traditional phrase "powers, authorities or discretions". The term is ubiquitous in the TLATA 1996. In *Hazell v Hammersmith LBC* [1992] 2 AC 1 at p.29 the House of Lords held that the word "functions" in Local Authority legislation "embraces all the duties and powers of a Local Authority, the sum total of the activities Parliament has entrusted to it". The word is (rightly) undefined in the TLATA 1996 though (unnecessarily) given a partial definition in the TA 2000.

confers a power: the word "shall" imposes a duty.[9] Thus we simply say as required:

> The trustees may ... *or* The trustees shall ... .

The alternative methods of imposing duties and powers are innumerable. For duties:

> *The Trustees shall hold the trust property on trust to ...*
> *It shall be the duty of the Trustees to ...*
> *The Trustees shall be bound to ...*
> *The Trustees must ...*

For powers:

> *The Trustees shall have full power to ...*
> *The Trustees shall have the right to ...*
> *It shall be lawful for the Trustees to ...*
> *The Trustees shall be entitled and are hereby authorised to ...*
> *The Trustees shall be at liberty to ...*
> *I empower my Trustees to ...*
> *The Trustees shall ... if they think fit ...*[10]

It is better to use a simple and consistent form.

Other usage of "shall" and "may"

A draft should be composed in the simple present tense. Unless one is conferring a duty or a power, it is best not to use the modal auxiliaries "may" or "shall". Thus for:

> *...as the Trustees **may** think fit; or*
> *...as the Trustees **shall** think fit;*

---

[9] Of course the context may show that the word "may" or "shall" has been used wrongly, and the context governs the sense; this is self-evident but for an example see *Grunwick Processing Laboratories Ltd v ACAS* [1978] AC 655 at 698: "Prima facie the word 'shall' suggests that it is mandatory but that word has often been rightly construed as being directory. Everything turns upon the context in which it is used—the subject matter, the purpose and effect of the section in which it appears." (Lord Salmon.)

[10] Thus (as in *Pearson v IRC* [1980] STC 318) a direction that:

> "the trustees shall accumulate so much of the income of the Trust Fund as they shall think fit"

confers a power to accumulate income. Likewise, in a normal context (as in *Breadner v Granville-Grossman* [2001] Ch 523), a provision that:

> "The Trustees stand possessed of the Trust Fund and the income thereof upon trust for the Principal Beneficiaries or any one or more of them exclusive of the other or others in such shares as the Trustees shall from time to time by deed appoint"

confers a power of appointment (not a discretionary duty). See 7.10 ("Absolute discretion "and" as the trustees think fit").

Read:

> ... as the Trustees think fit

Again, for:

> "The Trust Fund" **shall** mean ...

Read:

> "The Trust Fund" means ...

The word "shall" should be used in legal drafting primarily in this mandatory sense of imposing a duty. Some say the word should not be used at all.[11] A blanket application of that rule is contrary to ordinary English usage and common legal usage.[12] While no doubt it would always be possible to paraphrase, the word "shall" does in some contexts serve as well as any other. So this approach has not been completely adopted in this book.

Provisions about how often and when powers are exercised

Should true powers have time limits?

7.7 Consider a simple power such as:

> The Trustees may pay the income of the trust fund to X.

Such powers must be exercised within a reasonable time. If it is not exercised within a reasonable time, the power will lapse. What is a "reasonable time" is uncertain and will vary according to the circumstances. Some drafters would specify a time limit (typically 12 months). This avoids the uncertainty which might otherwise arise: in the event of some delay trustees may not know whether their power remains exercisable or has lapsed. This book does not impose any time limit. The "reasonable time" period raises little difficulty in practice; a fixed and inflexible time limit may cause greater difficulty. In this we follow the example of the statutory power of maintenance; indeed there is no statutory trustee power for which a fixed time limit is imposed.

---

[11] *Garner's Modern Legal Usage* (2nd edn, 1995) entry under Words of Authority contains a good discussion of the possible ambiguities of the word "shall".
[12] Likewise the EU Joint Practical Guide on the Drafting of Legislation 2.3.2:

> "In the enacting terms of binding acts, French uses the present tense, whilst English generally uses the auxiliary 'shall'. In both languages, the use of the future tense should be avoided wherever possible."

Should discretionary duties have time limits?

Suppose trustees hold income on discretionary trusts: **7.8**

the Trustees shall pay the income to any Beneficiaries as the Trustees think fit.

The trustees should, within a reasonable time, decide who to pay the income to. The drafter could if he wished specify some time limit. There seems little point in doing this. The discretionary duty will never lapse.[13]

Powers exercisable "at any time" and "from time to time"

A common formula provides that trustees' powers may be exercised "at any time". The purpose of this must be to make it clear that the power will not lapse during the life of the trust. **7.9**

A related and equally common formula is to direct that the power may be exercised "at any time or times", or "at any time and from time to time …". This emphasises that the power can be exercised more than once. Another form to the same effect is to say that the trustees may exercise a power "by deed or deeds".

These forms are not usually necessary. In most cases it is obvious from the nature of the power concerned whether any sort of time limit is implied. It is also obvious whether the power may be exercised more than once. The forms are considered undesirable. To specify on every occasion that powers are exercisable "at any time and from time to time" would be inordinately repetitive; to scatter the phrase here and there might give an entirely misleading impression that the omission of the phrase in other contexts is significant.

The solution adopted in this book is to set out a general provision that trustees' powers in general may be exercised "from time to time as occasion requires". It is then unnecessary to say anywhere else in the document that the trustees' powers are exercisable "from time to time" or "at any time or times". This is in fact the approach adopted by the parliamentary drafter as long ago as 1882.[14] A drafter seeking brevity could safely omit the clause.

---

[13] *Macphail v Doulton* [1971] AC 424; *Re Locker* [1977] 1 WLR 1323. For completeness it should be said that the time limit does have one consequence. Suppose the trustees failed to distribute the income, in breach of trust. The beneficiaries could take action (i) after the fixed time, if there was a fixed time; but (ii) only after a "reasonable time" if no time was fixed. But this is not important in practice.

[14] Section 55(1) SLA 1882 provided that: "Powers and authorities conferred by this Act … are exercisable from time to time." Then the Interpretation Act 1889 introduced a general principle, now found in s.12 Interpretation Act 1978. Where any Act confers a power or imposes a duty then (subject to contrary intention): "the power may be exercised, or the duty is to be performed, from time to time as occasion requires". So when the SLA 1882 was recast as the SLA 1925 the drafter was able to jettison s.55(1) SLA 1882; its work was done by the Interpretation Act provision. (Inconsistently, the form "at any time or times" surfaces in s.32 TA 1925; and the form "from time to time" is in s.102(3) SLA 1925. The words must be considered otiose as the context could hardly supply the contrary intention.) The clause in the book is of course modelled on s.12 Interpretation Act 1978. It is unnecessary to refer to duties.

The provision is included in the absolute discretion clause, to which we can now turn.

"Absolute discretion" and "as the trustees think fit"[15]

7.10 In general it should be the trustees—and no one else—who decide how their powers should be exercised. The "absolute discretion" clause is intended to make this clear:

> The trustees may ... in such manner as they may *in their absolute discretion think fit.*

It is reasonably clear that the absolute discretion clause has no effect whatsoever. If trustees act improperly they may be restrained even if their powers are said to be "uncontrollable".[16] Conversely beneficiaries cannot control trustees acting properly. This is so even in the absence of an "absolute discretion" clause. Trustees' freedom of action is not increased by including an "absolute discretion" provision, and not decreased by its omission.[17] The clause can be justified as for the avoidance of doubt or as a statement of what might not be obvious to the layman. For these rather marginal reasons, the precedents in this book include an absolute discretion clause.

7.11 Parliamentary drafters have used a variety of formulae:

> The trustees may
>> ... as they shall in their absolute discretion think fit
>> ... as the trustees in their absolute discretion, without being liable to account for the exercise of such discretion, think fit.
>> ... at their sole discretion ...
>> ... if and as they think fit ...
>
> The power shall be exercised according to the discretion of the trustees.[18]

These expressions are all equally efficacious; the drafter may take his choice.

What, then, is the drafter to do? One could specify whenever trustees

---

[15] A note on terminology. We have seen the term "Gisborne clause" used to describe what is here called an "absolute discretion" clause; but the more transparent term is to be preferred.

[16] *Re Gulbenkian* [1970] AC 508; *Harris v Lord Shuttleworth* [1994] ICR 991. For a discussion see *Thomas on Powers* (1st edn, 1998).

[17] In the leading case *Gisborne v Gisborne* (1877) 2 App.Cas. 300, the Court refused to interfere with the trustees' decisions even though it would have exercised the power differently. The House of Lords drew some comfort from the use of the word "uncontrollable" in the trust concerned, but see Parry, "Control of Trustee Discretions", [1989] *The Conveyancer* 244 accessible on *www.kessler.co.uk*; Underhill and Hayton, *The Law Relating to Trusts and Trustees* (17th edn, 2006) para.61.46.

[18] The examples are from ss.3, 15, 31, 32, 33 TA 1925. We have even seen the form "fullest, widest and most unfettered discretion".

are given a power that such power is to be "absolute"; that would be inordinately repetitive. The usual approach is to scatter a variety of "absolute discretion" formulae intermittently throughout a trust.[19] This is not an attractive course; it sets in defiance the usual principle of interpretation which would suggest that where the words were omitted, trustees' powers were intended to be less than absolute.[20]

The preferred approach is to insert in the trust a general provision, expressed to apply to every power of the trustees:

> Powers of the Trustees are exercisable at their absolute discretion.

It is then unnecessary to provide anywhere else that trustees' powers are "uncontrollable" or exercisable at the trustees' "absolute discretion", or "exercisable at any time or times". The clause may be omitted where brevity is desired.

The clause should be amended where trustees' powers are made subject to the consent of a "protector". The following is proposed:[21]

> Subject to obtaining the consent of the Protector when necessary, the powers of the Trustees may be exercised:
>
> (a) at their absolute discretion and
> (b) from time to time as occasion requires.

Guidance and control of trustees

7.12 This section is concerned with methods of controlling trustees. First, however, a short note on how trustees make decisions in the absence of any form of control in the trust deed.

Majority decisions

7.13 Trustees' decisions must be unanimous unless the trust directs otherwise.

---

[19] The favourite place for "absolute discretion" formulae is in discretionary trusts of income and trust for sale clauses (now obsolete); perhaps this shows the influence of the statutory precedents: s.33(1)(ii) TA 1925 (discretionary trust of income); s.25(2) LPA 1925; s.33 AEA 1925 (trusts for sale).

[20] An argument of this kind was rejected in *Julius v Lord Bishop of Oxford* (1880) 5 App.Cas. 214. Here the words "if he shall think fit" qualified one power but not another. The House of Lords refused to draw any inference from this; the words were "mere surplusage". The litigation would have been unnecessary had the words been omitted.

[21] But it would not matter if there was no reference to the Protector.

The usual practice is to leave the rule of unanimity to apply and this is the course taken in the forms in this book.[22]

If majority rule is desired the drafting is simple enough:

> The functions of the Trustees may be exercised by a majority of them.[23]

Some drafters add that the trustees in the minority must join in the execution of documents in accordance with the decision of the majority but that is plainly implied.

Two-trustee rule

7.14 A sole trustee can generally exercise all the powers of the trustees.[24] It is quite common to specify that powers of appointment should only be exercised by two trustees or a trust corporation.[25]

This restriction may formerly have been imposed for estate duty reasons which are long obsolete. The requirement does impose some restraint on wayward acts of a sole trustee but only a limited restraint. One point may be made in particular. Generally a sole trustee has (after the death of the settlor) the power to appoint additional trustees. So a sole trustee can side-step the restriction by the simple means of appointing a like-minded co-trustee, if he can find one.[26] For what it is worth, however, the restriction is applied to the overriding powers in this book.

If the trustee is a substantial trust company the requirement of a second trustee is not necessary and may be inconvenient. Accordingly the precedents in this book provide that the requirement of two trustees does not apply if the trustee is a company carrying on a business which consists of

---

[22] Where two or more family members are to be trustees, and their relationship may be inharmonious a majority clause may be an effective solution so long as there is a third trustee to hold the balance. But a better course may be the creation of two or more separate trusts, one for each member of the family; or to use professional trustees alone. Majority rule applies in the case of charitable trusts.

[23] The draft is loosely based on that approved in *Re Butlin* [1976] Ch 251. A variant sometimes used is that the power may be exercised by a majority so long as a Professional Trustee is one of the majority. There should be a consequential amendment in the conflict of interest clause, so that where a trustee was under a conflict of interest, his vote could not override his co-trustee.

[24] Subject to minor exceptions: see 6.1 (Number of trustees).

[25] The Parliamentary drafter has occasionally adopted this approach: see 6.1 (Number of trustees). A more drastic version of the same idea is to require at least two (or even three) trustees at all times.

[26] An individual could not avoid a two-trustee rule simply by appointing as a second trustee an "off the shelf" company, of which he was sole director. In *Gilford Motor Co v Horne* [1933] Ch 935 (as explained in *Yukong Line Ltd v Rendsburg Investments Corp (No.2)* [1998] 1 WLR 294 at 307) a one-man company was held to be ineffective as a device to avoid a restraint of trade clause. It is suggested that similar reasoning applies in the case of a one-man company used as a device to avoid a two-trustee rule.

or includes the management of trusts.[27] A simpler course, which would work in practice, would be for the draft just to say that the requirement of two trustees does not apply if the trustee is a company.

Another course would be for the draft to say that the requirement of two trustees does not apply if the trustee is a *trust corporation* and to define that expression to have the same meaning as in the Trustee Act 1925. This could be inconvenient if a foreign trust company is appointed trustee as it would not normally be a trust corporation within this definition. (This inconvenience is avoided by widening the definition but the drafting becomes more complicated.)

A course to avoid is for the draft to say that the requirement of two trustees does not apply if the trustee is a *trust corporation* and to leave that expression undefined. When the parliamentary drafter uses the expression he always takes care to define it.[28] Without a definition it is ambiguous.[29] The drafter is best advised to avoid the expression *trust corporation* altogether.

Statement of wishes

7.15 Where trustees have wide powers, it is always desirable to record the settlor's wishes as to how they should be exercised. The settlor's wishes were conventionally recorded in a document addressed to the trustees and called a "letter". Perhaps the epithet "letter" was adopted to emphasise the informal and non-binding nature of the statement of wishes but an epistolary form is artificial. The document should more aptly be titled: "statement of wishes" or perhaps "memorandum of wishes".

---

[27] The wording is derived from s.69(2) TCGA 1992.
[28] "Trust Corporation" for the purposes of the TA 1925 means (i) the Public Trustee; (ii) a corporation appointed by the court to be a trustee; (iii) a corporation entitled under Rule 30 Public Trustee Rules 1912 to act as custodian trustee; or (iv) a list of persons (not all corporations!) set out in s.3 Law of Property (Amendment) Act 1926. There are identical definitions in the other 1925 property statutes and (with slightly different wording) in the Supreme Court Act 1981. Modern statutes incorporate this definition by reference. There are occasionally non-standard definitions, e.g. s.3 Enduring Powers of Attorney Act 1985 (but s.64 Mental Capacity Act 2005 reverts to the standard definition); and Sch.4, para.2 IHTA 1984 (Maintenance funds for historic buildings). Companies incorporated outside the EU or with less than £250,000 share capital are not generally "Trust Corporations" within these definitions.
[29] There are three possible meanings:

1. *Trust corporation* may have its TA 1925 meaning. (An objection to this solution is that there are various statutory definitions but the one in the TA 1925 is the standard one which will immediately come to the mind of a trust lawyer.)
2. *Trust corporation* may mean any company carrying on trust business.
3. *Trust corporation* may mean any company which is a trustee.

The better view is that the expression (if written in lower case letters and assuming no guidance from the context) should be taken to have the second of these meanings but in practice one should proceed on the most cautious view.

Drafting the statement of wishes

7.16 The statement of wishes may be put in a recital or in the body of the trust itself, but it is more appropriately put in a separate document. This is because it is non-binding, it may be changed, and it may be confidential. On rights of beneficiaries to see the statement of wishes see 28.3 (Beneficiary's right to trust information).

The important drafting point is to state that the wishes are not binding on the trustees, so the status of the memorandum of wishes is clear. A statement of wishes expressed in imperative terms may be construed to be binding and override the terms of the trust instrument.[30]

This is the sort of precedent one might use:

> Joan Smith Will Trust: Statement of Wishes
>
> This note sets out my wishes for my will trust. I express these wishes only for the guidance of the trustees. It is not intended to bind them. They must use their own discretion. They should also have regard to any change in circumstances of my family and of course to any wishes which I may record for their guidance in the future.
>
> My wishes are as follows:
>
> (1) My trustees should ensure that my husband is reasonably provided for.
> (2) Subject to that, I would like my trustees to regard my children (and if the fund is not distributed, their families in due course) as the principal beneficiaries of the residuary estate.
> (3) Subject to that I would like my trustees to regard my nephews and nieces as the principal beneficiaries per stirpes [or per capita].

The statement of wishes must not be peremptory but can, if appropriate, be strongly worded. This is not always appreciated and may be helpful for settlors reluctant to create wide powers or trusts of long duration. Some examples:

> I wish to express my firm desire (without binding the trustees) that they should transfer the Trust Fund to my son Adam absolutely, on attaining the age of 25, unless there are overpowering reasons for not doing so.
>
> I have accepted the advice of my solicitors that the most tax efficient form of will is a discretionary will trust, but (tax apart) I would rather have made an absolute gift to my son Adam. I request the trustees (without binding them) to give weight to Adam's wishes accordingly.
>
> I wish to express my desire (without binding the trustees) that the trustees should regard my son Adam as the principal beneficiary of the Trust Fund.

---

[30] For an example see *Chen v Ling* [2000] HKCFI 1356 belatedly reported [2006] TLI 262 accessible on *www.hklii.org.hk*.

A statement of wishes (however expressed) could not override the terms of a will, unless executed in accordance with the formalities required for a will, though it could form the basis of an application to rectify the will.

The statement of wishes should give reasons (if not obvious). It should be reviewed periodically and best practice would be for the trustees to seek confirmation that the wishes are unaltered every few years as appropriate.

The settlor's signature is normally witnessed, and this is good practice, though not strictly essential. The statement should be dated.

Some drafters put into the trust a clause requesting the trustees to have regard to any statement of wishes, but this is plainly unnecessary and best omitted.

When should the statement of wishes be executed?

Some commentators advise that the statement of wishes should not be executed at the time of the trust. The reason is to make the non-binding nature of the statement even clearer. Of course, this will not help if the facts are that the settlor gives binding oral directions to trustees at the time of the settlement, and merely delays putting them into writing to avoid giving the *appearance* of a sham. Conversely, if the statement of wishes is non-binding, as it should be, there is absolutely no need to wait until after executing the trust. It is considered that the better practice is to execute the statement of wishes at the same time as the trust. In practice the settlor *will* indicate his wishes to the trustees (no other course is really practical) and formal legal documentation should accord with the reality.

Power of appointment of new trustees

The power of appointment of new trustees gives considerable power to the appointor. If trustees propose to do something of which the appointor disapproves, he can frustrate their intention by appointing a trustee opposed to the idea. The consent of existing trustees is not required for that appointment. Trustees can refuse to disclose certain confidential documents[31] but the appointor can bypass that restriction by appointing a sympathetic trustee, who will have much greater rights to see trust documents. Offshore, institutional trustees may require the appointment of additional trustees to be subject to their consent. However, that is not thought appropriate as a standard form.

7.17

---

[31] See 26.3 (Beneficiary's right to trust information)

Consultation with beneficiaries

7.18 Should the drafter impose a duty on trustees to consult with beneficiaries and if so what duty? There are four options:

(1) Say nothing, so the default rules apply.

(2) Exclude the statutory duty of consultation and say nothing more.

(3) Exclude all duties of consultation.

(4) Replace the default rules with an express duty of consultation.

Default rules

Section 11 TLATA 1996 provides:

> The trustees of land shall in the exercise of any function relating to land subject to the trust—
>
> (a) so far as practicable, consult the beneficiaries of full age and beneficially entitled to an interest in possession in the land, and
> (b) so far as consistent with the general interest of the trust, give effect to the wishes of those beneficiaries, or (in the case of dispute) of the majority (according to the value of their combined interests).[32]

This imposes two duties, here called "the statutory duty to consult" and "the statutory duty to obey". Unfortunately this provision does not make good sense when applied to substantive trusts.[33] It is arbitrary, as the duties depend on the nature of the trust property, and come and go as the trustees buy or sell land. It is limited, as the duties are only to consult and obey the life tenant, whereas the interest of the remainderman may actuarially be much more valuable. But in practice no difficulty would arise because it is so circumscribed ("so far as practicable ... so far as consistent with the general interest of the trust") that trustees can ignore it (as in practice they do, and for the most part they must). The general law, which includes some reasonable duty of consultation,[34] is not excluded by the statutory duty to consult, but only (imperceptibly) modified by it.

---

[32] This replaced s.26(3) LPA 1925 which imposed a duty of consultation only where the trust instrument expressly so directed, so in practice it could be ignored. The only comparable statutory precedent is Form 6 Statutory Will Forms 1925 (notice of intended appropriation) accessible on www.kessler.co.uk.

[33] The provision was drafted with bare trusts of land in mind. It makes some sense if the trust property is the residence of the life tenant, but not for land held as an investment. It may introduce uncertainty into the administration of the trust, because it is debatable what is "the best interest of the trust". In the event of a dispute, it is unclear who decides what is in the best interest of the trust. Would the court accept the trustees' view, unless no reasonable body of trustees would reach that view? Or would the court form its own view? But in practice no difficulty seems to arise.

[34] This proposition is self-evident, but if authority is needed, see *X v A* [2000] 1 All ER 490.

Exclude the duty

The obvious form would be:

> Section 11 Trusts of Land and Appointment of Trustees Act 1996 (consultation with beneficiaries) shall not apply.

This restores the pre-TLATA position, under which trustees must act reasonably, including consultation where reasonable, but have no duty to obey. This is a satisfactory result, but no-one other than a trust lawyer would understand the drafting, so it is not the preferred course.

A form used in the STEP Standard Provisions is:

> *The powers of the Trustees may be exercised ... at their absolute discretion ...*[35]

This form of words, devised before the TLATA, excludes the (almost illusory) statutory duty to obey the life tenant; though not the statutory duty to consult.

The form used in this book is as follows:

> The Trustees are not under any duty to consult with any Beneficiaries or to give effect to the wishes of any Beneficiaries. The powers of the Trustees may be exercised at their absolute discretion.

The intention is to maximise trustees' freedom of action, and not to stop or discourage trustees from consulting with beneficiaries where appropriate. However some clients (i.e. testators or settlors) might feel it sent the wrong message to their trustees, seemingly encouraging them to act in a high-handed or paternalistic manner.

An express duty

Clients of this mind would prefer to set out an express duty (excluding s.11 TLATA expressly or by implication). The following draft is based on s.11 TLATA:

> The Trustees shall, so far as appropriate, consult with Beneficiaries who have reached the age of 25 (but there is no duty to consult with Beneficiaries who are not in practice likely to receive substantial benefits from the Trust). The powers of the Trustees may be exercised at their absolute discretion.

The clause is of course somewhat vague, but it has to be so.[36]

---

[35] Standard Provision 10. The Provisions are in Appendix 1.
[36] If the client wants more than that, he needs to consider the other methods of influencing trustees discussed in this book. A very concerned client might wish to add:
  The Trustees shall so far as consistent with the general interest of the Trust, give effect to the wishes of those Beneficiaries, or (in case of dispute) of the majority (according to the value in the opinion of the Trustees of the Beneficiaries' anticipated receipts from the Trust Fund).
  But this clause is a rather unhappy compromise between the two more effective options of (i)

Which route?

It actually makes little if any difference in practice what the drafter says. Of course trustees should where appropriate consult with beneficiaries, without express provision directing them to do so. But some choice needs to be made about the drafting. In this book the standard form is to exclude the duty to consult and to obey, but that may be replaced by the express duty if the settlor or testator prefers it.

Control of trustees

7.19   Most settlors will be content to select trustees whom they trust and to guide them if necessary with a statement of wishes. In the precedents in this book the only important controls are the restraints on adding beneficiaries, the power to dismiss a trustee after retirement age, and the conflict of interest clause.[37]

Human nature being what it is, some settlors seek further methods of controlling their trustees. This is particularly common where shares in the settlor's family company are held in a trust.

It is no answer to say that the settlor should find trustees in whom he has complete faith.[38]

Of course it is possible as a matter of trust law to provide a variety of checks on trustees' powers. Three related sets of questions arise here: (i) what powers of trustees should be subject to control; (ii) what methods of control should be applied; (iii) to whom should these powers of control be given?

What trustees' powers should be subject to control?

7.20   A list of important powers can easily be drawn up.

(1) The most important are the overriding powers of appointment, resettlement and advancement.

(2) Power to lend interest-free to a beneficiary. Money lent to a beneficiary is rarely repaid.

---

giving powers to trustees and (ii) giving powers to beneficiaries. It is almost entirely ineffective, since, in practice, if the trustees did not want to adopt the beneficiaries' wishes, they would maintain that this was contrary to the "interests of the trust".

[37] 5.39 (Power to add beneficiaries); 7.30 (Power to dismiss trustees); 6.13 (Conflicts of interest).
[38] "... *There is no art/to find the mind's construction in the face* ..." (Macbeth) .

(3) Power to allow beneficiaries to use trust property, and power to charge trust property for their benefit and power to apply capital as if it is income. These may have a similar effect to a power of appointment.

(4) Power to release powers and power to change the governing law may be used to change the effect of a trust.

In the discussion below we shall refer for the sake of brevity to restrictions on "the power of appointment, etc.".

What sorts of checks can be made on trustees' powers and who exercises them?

The sorts of checks which may be made on trustees are as follows: 7.21

(1) powers of consent: so the trustees cannot exercise powers of appointment, etc. without consent;

(2) giving powers of appointment, etc. to other persons instead of the trustees;

(3) power to dismiss trustees.

These powers may be given to:

(1) Beneficiaries

(2) The settlor

(3) A protector.

We will discuss in turn the possible role of beneficiaries, settlors and protectors. The power to dismiss trustees is in a category of its own and will be considered separately. One general comment may be made at this point. Of course whoever is given these powers of control may act wrongly. This is not a problem of trust law or drafting, but an aspect of the human condition: at some point someone must be trusted.

Giving powers of appointment to beneficiaries personally

A traditional approach is to give powers of appointment, etc. to a beneficiary, rather than to the trustees. One occasionally still sees trusts for a beneficiary for life, with remainder to such of his issue as *he* may appoint, and in default of appointment, for the beneficiary's children at 21.[39]   7.22

---

[39] This form was so common that a precedent was provided in the Statutory Will Forms 1925: see Forms 7 and 9 accessible on *www.kessler.co.uk*. The form formerly had some advantages for the rule against perpetuities. This has not been the case since the reforms of the PAA 1964.

This sort of provision may be thought of not so much as controlling the trustees, but conferring rights on the beneficiary for his own benefit, making his position slightly closer to beneficial ownership. This is why such powers are here classified as semi-fiduciary. See 7.33 (Nature of powers of consent and appointment).

The use of personal powers of appointment remains an acceptable drafting technique. However it has a few disadvantages.

The personal power would, in absence of specific provision, lapse on the death of the beneficiary. The exercise of the power in the course of winding up a trust may sometimes be frustrated by the doctrine of a fraud on a power.[40] There are further complications if the beneficiary could appoint the property to himself.[41]

These problems may be solved if the drafter confers overlapping powers, i.e. a beneficiary has a personal power of appointment and the trustees have a second (usually wider) fiduciary power of appointment. This is quite often seen. There can be no harm in this practice beyond the complications of drafting. Yet there is no obvious advantage to be gained from it. (Possibly, it might be thought to give the beneficiary greater involvement in the devolution of his trust fund? But that is little more than cosmetic.)

Personal powers might be supported on the grounds that a beneficiary is the best qualified person to have the powers. Who better to decide how to appoint property to his children? The argument is wrong. Some beneficiaries may not have the best understanding of their financial affairs.[42] The trustees will in practice consult the beneficiary and the beneficiary may be appointed trustee.

In conclusion, there is little merit in personal powers of appointment, and they are not used in the forms in this book.

Giving powers of consent to beneficiaries[43]

7.23 The next possibility is to direct that the trustees can only exercise a power of appointment with the consent of a particular beneficiary (typically the

---

[40] *Re Brook* [1968] 1 WLR 1661. See *Thomas on Powers* (1st edn), para.9–53.
[41] Such a power may not be a fiduciary power: *Re Penrose* [1933] Ch 793. See also s.283(4) Insolvency Act 1986. It can, however, be argued that there was no reason in principle to support the dictum in *Penrose* that a power cannot be fiduciary if the donee is an object. On the contrary, such a power may be fiduciary or not: it is a matter of construction. A full discussion, which would require a review of many authorities and statutory provisions, falls outside the scope of this book; see John Mowbray QC, "Choosing Among the Beneficiaries of Discretionary Trusts" [1998] PCB 239 accessible on *www.kessler.co.uk*.
[42] The technique of the (now obsolete) SLA 1925, giving administrative powers to the life tenant, is also in this category. *Hambro v Duke of Marlborough* [1994] Ch 158 is a poignant example of why the form is not desirable.
[43] *Thomas on Powers* (1st edn), Ch.5 has a good general discussion on consents to powers; for pensions cases see Keith Rowley QC, "The Interpretation of Pension Scheme Deeds" [2003] TLI 129 at 140.

life tenant).[44] If the power of consent is a wholly personal one,[45] this route raises some intriguing tax questions.[46] If the reader uses the forms in this book the questions do not arise (but of course the questions do arise with less carefully drafted trusts).

Giving powers of consent to the settlor

7.24 A common and practical course is to provide that powers of appointment, etc. should only be exercisable with the consent of the settlor. This normally[47] raises no tax problems thought the simpler course in these cases would be to make the settlor a trustee. The drafting is straightforward:

> The Trustees may *with the consent in writing of the Settlor during his life* and afterwards at their discretion ...

This echoes a statutory precedent.[48] The need for written consent is obvious. Some say "with the *prior* written consent ..."; but "prior" in this context is unnecessary.[49]

A power exercisable "with the consent of the settlor" lapses after the death; but a power exercisable "with the consent of the settlor *during his life*" will be exercisable after the death of the settlor without any consent.

Giving powers of appointment to a settlor

7.25 This is a possible course, but not often adopted in practice. Plainly, some provision would be needed to ensure that the power does not lapse at the death of the settlor, and the benefits would not justify the drafting complications.

Better methods of controlling trustees

7.26 Imposing the requirement for settlor consent is a practical step, as far as it goes. It is of course a limited control on trustees. The settlor can prevent the trustees taking some step of which he disapproves but cannot require them to take any action when he wishes. What, then, can be done for a settlor who wishes to possess effective control over his trust fund?

---

[44] For statutory examples see s.32(c) TA 1925 (power of advancement), s.41 AEA 1925 (power of appropriation).
[45] On this terminology see 7.33 (Nature of powers of consent and appointment).
[46] See James Kessler QC, *Taxation of Foreign Domiciliaries* (7th edn, 2008, Key Haven Publications), para.54.12 (Consent to exercise of trustees' powers).
[47] A CGT problem might arise in the case of a non-resident trust.
[48] Section 32(1)(c) TA 1925.
[49] The statutory powers of consent mentioned above do not use the word "prior".

Settlor as one of the trustees. If the settlor is one of the trustees, he will in principle have a power of veto, for (in the absence of contrary provision) trustees' powers must be exercised unanimously. This may be sufficient for most settlors.

Settlor (or spouse) as sole trustees?

7.27 One obvious suggestion is that the settlor should be the sole trustee. As a matter of trust law there is little difficulty.[50] Alternatively the settlor and his spouse/civil partner may wish to be the only trustees. This is particularly common when the trust property is the family company, and the settlor is not prepared to contemplate the possibility of interference. However, it is not desirable for the settlor (or spouse) to act as sole trustees. A trust will benefit in practice from having a professional trustee to keep an eye on administration and the exigencies of tax planning from time to time. Yet although undesirable in principle, this may be done. The professional adviser should stress the need to seek regular professional advice and the difficulties which may arise if this is not done. Alternative possibilities to this are to be preferred where possible.

For those who want a greater measure of control, there are two recommended solutions. The first is the use of a weighted majority clause. The second is the use of a protector.

Weighted majority clause

7.28 Under this route, the settlor will be a trustee, jointly with a single professional trustee. In addition there will be a clause providing that trustees' decisions are made by a majority; *and in the case of equality of votes, the settlor should have a second and casting vote.*

So provided that there are only two trustees, the settlor's wishes must prevail. The settlor should be advised that he will not own the trust property. He must act in good faith in the best interest of the trust and its beneficiaries.[51] Nevertheless for many practical purposes the settlor will have the control which he desires.

A precedent is:

> The functions of the Trustees shall be exercisable by a majority of them, each trustee to have one vote. In the case of an equality of votes, the Settlor (if a trustee) shall have a casting vote in addition to his first vote.[52]

---

[50] See 6.1 (Number of trustees). If the settlor is a beneficiary, problems may arise if he wishes to appoint trust property to himself: see 6.16 (Trustee-beneficiaries).
[51] In addition, if the settlor is a beneficiary, he may require the consent of his co-trustee to appoint the fund in his own favour: see 6.16 (Trustee-beneficiaries).
[52] There should be a consequential amendment in the conflict of interest clause, so that where there was a conflict of interest, a settlor could not override his co-trustee.

This draws on familiar company law precedent.[53]

Sometimes the settlor may wish control to pass to some other person on his death. The easiest solution here is to use a protector.

Protectors[54]

The solution of a weighted majority vote only works if the settlor can be a trustee. That is not possible where non-resident trustees are to be appointed. The now traditional solution is to create an office of "protector".

7.29

In practice protectors are used principally for offshore trusts. They may have a useful role for United Kingdom trusts.

The word "protector", as a term of property law, was first used in the Fines and Recoveries Act 1833, in relation to entails. That area of law is obsolete, but its nomenclature of "protector" survives to the modern law of trusts.

The protector is commonly given the following powers:

(1) The protector's consent is required to the exercise of powers of appointment, etc. by the trustees.
(2) The protector is given power to appoint new trustees; to dismiss trustees; and to authorise breach of the self-dealing rule.

The following precedent is proposed as a definition of "protector" where the settlor is the initial protector.[55]

The Protector

(1) The Settlor shall be the first Protector.
(2) [The widow of the Settlor][56] shall be the next Protector.
(3) The Protector for the time being may appoint one or more persons to be Protector for such period as the Protector shall specify. All the powers of the Protector (including this power of appointment) shall be vested in the new Protector accord-

---

[53] Article 50 of Table A of the Companies (Tables A to F) Regulations 1985.
[54] On this topic, see Deborah Hartnett and William Norris "The Protector's Position" (1995) PCB 109 accessible on www.kessler.co.uk; John Mowbray QC, "Protectors" OTPR, Vol.5, p.151 accessible on www.kessler.co.uk; Antony Duckworth "Protectors—Fish or Fowl?" (1996) PCB 169 accessible on www.kessler.co.uk; and Ch.4, *Contemporary Trends in Trust Law* (Oakley ed., OUP, 1996).
[55] It is clear that the settlor may be a protector: Law Commission Consultation Paper No.171, Trustee Exemption Clauses, para.4.8; *The Esteem Settlement* [2003] JLR 188 [2004] WTLR 1 accessible on www.jerseylaw.je at para.205(viii). The appointment of settlor as protector is possible but less than ideal where the settlor is also the principal beneficiary. The main problem is the conflict of interest: see 7.30 (Power to dismiss trustees). Sham also needs consideration: see Kessler, "What is (and what is not) a Sham" (2000) OITR, Vol.9, p.125 accessible on www.kessler. co.uk.
[56] The trust will name here the person provisionally intended to be protector after the death of the settlor. This need not be the widow of the Settlor: it might for instance be a child of the Settlor.

ingly. The appointment shall be made by will or by deed. The appointment may be revocable or irrevocable. The appointment has priority to sub-clause (2) above.
(4) A Person ceases to be Protector in the event of the following:

   (a) death;
   (b) execution by the Protector of a deed of retirement;
   (c) refusal or incapacity to act.

(5) If at any time there is no Protector able or willing to act, the Trustees shall appoint a new Protector.
(6) A Protector shall not be appointed trustee. A Trustee shall not be appointed Protector.

A slight variation is needed where the settlor is not the first protector:

The Protector

(1) [Name and address] shall be the first Protector.
(2) [Name and address] shall be the next Protector.
(3) [As (3) above]
(4) [As (4) above]
(5) If at any time there is no Protector able and willing to act:

   (a) The Settlor if able and willing to act, and subject to that
   (b) the Trustees
   shall appoint a new Protector.

(6) [As (6) above]

The draft should make provision for the death or retirement of the first protector. The usual form is to provide that the protector may select his successor. A provisional successor is named in this draft. This is more convenient than an immediate exercise of the power of appointment (or the risk that the protector may die without having appointed a successor). The protector may alter the position later if desired.

The drafter must cater for the possibility that there is no protector. One course is to allow all the trustees' powers which require the protector's consent to lapse permanently. That could be most unsatisfactory. The course adopted here is to rely on the trustees to appoint their new protector.[57] The only objection is that the checks intended to restrict the trustees will not at that moment be fully operative. It might be best to say that the power to add beneficiaries should lapse or become further restricted.

One could add further precautions to try to ensure a suitable person is chosen as a new protector. For instance, one could direct the trustees to appoint a new protector being a solicitor of, say, ten years' standing and nominated by two beneficiaries or by the President of the Law Society. The form adopted here is slightly simpler; and is not likely to give rise to any problems in practice.

---

[57] The power to appoint a new protector is fiduciary: see *Re Circle Trust, HSBC v Wong* [2007] WTLR 631 (Cayman Islands Grand Court).

Occasionally a grander precedent is seen where the protector is not an individual but a committee.[58] The charging clause should if appropriate be extended to allow a protector to charge. It is not necessary to make the protector a party to the trust deed.[59]

Nature of protector's powers and duties

It is a question of construction of any particular trust to determine the nature of a protector's powers and duties. If the trust does not contain anything to answer the question expressly, the gap must be filled by a legal presumption or principle of construction. In the absence of anything unusual in the trust, the protector's powers will be understood to be fiduciary and not personal powers.[60]

One could provide that the powers conferred on the protector are personal and not fiduciary. The typical settlor would want the protector to exercise the powers in the interest of the trust, and not in his own interest.

The description of the powers as "fiduciary" does not answer all the questions which may arise. In particular:

(1) Suppose a protector has a power to dismiss trustees. Is the protector obliged to review the trust regularly, to satisfy himself that the trustees are doing a good job, and should not be removed? Or may he wait until something comes to his attention to suggest that action is needed?

(2) Suppose the protector has power to consent to appointments by the trustees. Is this subject only to the requirements of honesty and proper motive (summarised as "good faith"); or must the protector consider whether the proposed appointment is desirable?

The question is whether the protector's duties are fully fiduciary, or semi-fiduciary.[61] It is best to deal with these matters expressly:

Duties of Protector

(1) The powers of the Protector must be exercised in good faith and in the interests of the trust.
(2) The Protector is under no duty to enquire into or interfere with the management or conduct of this Trust, unless he has actual knowledge of circumstances which call for enquiry.

---

[58] For an example see *IRC v Schroder* 57 TC 94. But *quaere* whether a committee is likely to reach wiser decisions than an individual.
[59] 10.8 (Who should be parties?).
[60] See *Re Star, Knieriem v Bermuda Trust Co*, Butterworths Offshore Cases Vol.1, 1996, p.116 (Supreme Court of Bermuda); for English authorities see *Re Skeats* (1889) 42 Ch D 522, which was cited in the Bermudan case; *IRC v Schroder* 57 TC 94 and *Mourant v Magnus* [2004] JRC 056.
[61] On this terminology see 7.33 (Nature of powers of consent).

(3) The Protector shall consider the appropriateness of any act before exercising his powers.[62]

It is unnecessary to provide any further indemnity for a protector, or provision for access to trust documents. If trustees refuse to supply documents the protector would exercise his power to remove them.

Where trustees have power subject to consent of the protector it is implicit that the protector cannot be a trustee. It is desirable to say this expressly so that the position is made clear.

Protectors: tax implications

This topic has been considered in detail elsewhere[63] and it is concluded that the use of a protector has no significant tax implications. In particular:

1. A protector cannot normally be regarded as a trustee for tax purposes.

2. A trust with a UK resident protector may nonetheless be non-UK resident for tax purposes. The most that can be said is that where there is a UK protector, care is needed to ensure that the protector is not a branch, agency or permanent establishment of the trustees.

The position could be different if the protector was given unusually wide powers.

Power to dismiss trustees

7.30 It is common for offshore trusts to confer powers to remove trustees. Such powers are valid as a matter of trust law.[64] It is considered that a will cannot confer a power to appoint or dismiss executors.

It is considered that a power to dismiss trustees is not normally appropriate for United Kingdom trusts and should not be a standard form. The appointment of the settlor as trustee, backed with a weighted majority

---

[62] What would the position be in the absence of express provision? This is a matter of construction of each individual trust. In the absence of any indication in the trust, it is submitted that the protector's power of consent is semi-fiduciary only. The protector is not usually expected to involve himself actively in the affairs of the trust. This view is based on the general practice in the profession, a relevant matter in construction.

[63] James Kessler QC, *Taxation of Foreign Domiciliaries* (7th edn, 2008, Key Haven Publications); 4.13 (UK protector and trust residence).

[64] The power was accepted as valid in *London & County Banking Co v Goddard* [1897] 1 Ch 642; and in *Davis v Richards and Wallington Industries* [1990] 1 WLR 1511 the power was held to be exercised by mere implication. See also *Chelleram v Chelleram* [1985] Ch 409 at 432. The validity of the power is assumed in s.36(2) TA 1925.

clause is sufficient. The following discussion is therefore principally of importance for offshore trusts. It is also relevant to trustees in the United Kingdom or elsewhere considering whether to accept an appointment to a trust containing a power of dismissal.

A power of removal does not operate retrospectively. If the trustees have done an act of which the person with the power to dismiss disapproves, the subsequent dismissal of trustees may come too late. The power to dismiss trustees should therefore be seen as ancillary to the other controls on trustees' powers.

Who will exercise the power? A trust with power to dismiss trustees will generally have a protector who will be given the power. The protector should ideally not be a principal beneficiary.

The power of removal would be a fiduciary power. If the settlor was a protector, it could not be used for the private benefit of the protector. The proper course for trustees is to ignore the existence of the power while acting as trustee.[65] Suppose the trustees refused to transfer trust funds to the settlor; and the settlor (having the power of dismissal) then dismissed them and appointed more amenable trustees. This would probably be an invalid exercise of the power.[66] The power to dismiss trustees may, for this reason, fail when the person with the power most wants to use it. The drafter should warn the settlor of the problem; or he may seriously misunderstand his rights under the trust. For all this, the power may offer a solution to a settlor's fears that trustees may refuse to resign or will resign only on unacceptable terms.

A precedent is:

The Protector may remove any trustee by giving notice in writing to that and the other trustees. On receipt of such notice the removed trustee shall cease to be a trustee provided there remains at least two trustees.

Dealing with the former trustee

It is not enough to dismiss a recalcitrant trustee. One must also recover the trust property which was vested in him. Suppose the trustee refused to part with it; which, in the context of a dispute, is likely to happen. **7.31**

---

[65] *The Esteem Settlement* [2004] WTLR 1 at para.204(viii) accessible on *www.jerseylegalinfo.je*.
[66] *IRC v Schroder* [1983] STC 480 at 500; *The Esteem Settlement* [2004] WTLR 1 at para.204(viii) accessible on *www.jerseylaw.je*. *Pope v DRP Nominees Pty Ltd* 74 SASR 78; [1999] SASC 337 provides a good illustration of the dangers of assuming that a protector with power to appoint new trustees has control of the trust. In that case, on the application of one of the beneficiaries, the Supreme Court ordered the removal of the trustee because of irregularities in the administration of the trust. Under the trust deed there was an "appointor" who had power to appoint a new trustee. On appeal, the Full Court held that the appointor (who as director of a corporate trustee had also controlled the trustee) was in a position of conflict and was therefore under a duty *not* to exercise the power of appointing a new trustee. Instead, the Court appointed professional trustees nominated by the applicant beneficiary (who was also the appointor's son).

Obviously the new trustees could take proceedings; but is there some short cut which might avoid that process?

There are three methods of extracting trust property from an ex-trustee without his consent:

(1) *Use of Trustee Act 1925, section 40*

Suppose that on the dismissal of the ex-trustee a new trustee is appointed by deed. This automatically vests many types of property in the new trustees without any need for a conveyance or assignment. The dismissed trustee does not need to be a party to the deed.

Section 40 does not apply to certain types of property, of which the most important category is company shares; and such property cannot be dealt with in this way.

(2) *Use of power of attorney*

A trustee on his appointment might give the protector an irrevocable power of attorney authorising the protector to execute a transfer of the trust property. Appropriate provision would be needed in the trust deed and in every appointment of new trustees. While possible in theory, this is a somewhat impractical solution.[67]

(3) *Use of nominees*

If at the time of the dismissal the trust fund is vested in nominees. The problem does not arise provided the nominee is not a subsidiary of the ex-trustee. After the dismissal of the ex-trustee, the nominees will hold the fund for the new trustees. In anticipation of such problems, it would be possible to provide in the trust deed that the trust fund should at all times be held by nominees on terms approved by the protector.

7.32 So it is possible, by one method or another, to arrange that trust property can be wrested from an ex-trustee without his co-operation. However, there is a difficulty. These methods allow the protector to override what may be reasonable needs of the trustees. Trustees may incur substantial liabilities—particularly tax liabilities—to which they will generally remain liable even if they are later removed from their trust. Trustees need recourse to the trust fund to meet those liabilities and while they may have other remedies, they may not so easily be enforced.

The problem here is not the mechanisms of trust or property law. It

---

[67] The power would have to satisfy the conditions of s.4 Powers of Attorney Act 1971 if it is to be irrevocable. A related idea is to have the trustees execute blank transfers of the trust property and hand them to the protector or settlor. Besides the obvious problem that the trust property may change, the trustees might counteract this by a transfer of trust property to a nominee prior to their dismissal.

is more fundamental: the drafter must find a fair balance between the conflicting interests of trustees on the one hand, and beneficiaries on the other. It is submitted that there is no objection to powers to dismiss trustees. However, the more extreme routes, which allow the protector to divest ex-trustees of the trust property, do not find the right balance. They should not form part of a standard draft or standard administrative provisions. Otherwise careful trustees will refuse to act without an appropriate indemnity.

The approach of this book is to have the power of dismissal only where there are foreign trustees. Provision is made to provide fair protection for trustees.

Case law offers some precedents of far-reaching powers to dismiss trustees and recover trust property.[68]

Nature of powers of consent and appointment

Where a person has a power of consent under a trust, what rights and duties does this impose on him? This is a question of construction of the trust concerned. In general, however, the trust will not contain anything which expressly answers the question, so the gap must be filled by legal presumptions or principles of construction.   **7.33**

There are three broad categories of power of appointment. There is general agreement as to their characteristics, but no agreed terminology. In this area "a great deal of inaccurate argument arises from expressions undeveloped and not explained which may bear two senses."[69] In particular the expressions "fiduciary" or "as trustee" in isolation are unhelpful, as they are applied to many quite different types of powers. If a power is not "fiduciary" that is an end of the matter. But if the power is "fiduciary", that is only the beginning of the enquiry: one has to go on and ask what are the duties which attach to it. The following terminology is proposed:

(1) *Completely Beneficial* Powers of Appointment. Here the appointor is not subject to any legal restraint in the motive or purpose for which the power is exercised. The appointor may exercise the power (or refuse to exercise it) for his own benefit. The classic example is an unrestricted power to appoint to anyone in the world, including the appointor: a general power.

(2) *Semi-Fiduciary* Powers of Appointment. Here the appointor is not under any obligation to exercise the power; but if he exercises it, he

---

[68] *London & County Banking Co v Goddard* [1897] 1 Ch 642 and *London County and Westminster Bank v Tompkins* [1918] 1 KB 515. For a statutory precedent see s.109(5) LPA 1925.
[69] *Palmer v Locke* 15 Ch D 294 at 303.

is subject to requirements of good faith and proper motive (failing which it will constitute a "fraud on a power"). That is, "the appointor under the power, shall, for any purpose for which it is used, act with good faith and sincerity, and with an entire and single view to the real purpose and object of the power, and not for the purpose of accomplishing or carrying into effect any bye or sinister object (sinister in the sense of its being beyond the purpose and intent of the power) which he may desire to effect in the exercise of the power". In the same leading case, Lord St Leonards observed: "A party having a power like this must fairly and honestly execute it without having any ulterior object to be accomplished. He cannot carry into execution any indirect object, or acquire any benefit for himself, directly or indirectly. It may be subject to limitations and directions, but it must be a pure, straightforward, honest dedication of the property, as property, to the person to whom he affects, or attempts, to give it in that character."[70] The classic example is a power of appointment exercisable by a beneficiary in favour of his issue.

(3) *Wholly Fiduciary* Powers of Appointment: powers where the appointor is under an obligation to consider whether or not to exercise the power. The classic example is a common form power of appointment exercisable by the trustees.

It is submitted that the same framework should be applied to powers of consent. There are then three categories of powers of consent:

(1) *Wholly Personal* Powers of Consent. An example is the power under s.32 Trustee Act 1925 to consent to the exercise of the power of advancement. Another example is a will trust, letting the widow live in the matrimonial home, the trustees to sell only with the consent of the widow. Obviously, the person with this power may consult his own interests: that is what the power of consent is for. Another example is the protector's power of consent under the (obsolete) law of entails.[71]

(2) *Semi-Fiduciary* Powers of Consent. Here the consentor has a power of veto, which he may exercise or not subject only to the requirements of good faith and proper motive (summarised as "fraud on a power").

(3) *Wholly Fiduciary* Powers of Consent. Here the consentor must consider whether the proposed action is desirable.

---

[70] *Portland v Topham* (1864) 11 HLC 32, 54 accessible on *www.kessler.co.uk*.
[71] Section 36 Fines and Recoveries Act 1833 (a useful precedent for a draft to make a power of consent a wholly personal one).

The question of which category any particular power falls in can only be a question of construction. In principle, it is submitted:

(1) Trustees' powers of consent should prima facie be considered to be wholly fiduciary.

(2) Beneficiaries' powers of consent which do not affect their own interests should prima facie be considered to be semi-fiduciary.

(3) Beneficiaries' powers of consent which do affect their own interests should be considered to be wholly personal.

This is consistent with powers of appointment.

Does it matter which category a power falls into? The distinction between wholly personal and fiduciary powers is obviously important. The distinction between semi and wholly fiduciary powers is not important in practice. What does it matter if a person is not obliged to consider whether an appointment to which he consents is suitable? In practice, he will surely do so.

The distinction does not matter for other trust law purposes.[72]

Unfortunately the authorities in this area are extremely difficult.

First, they treat the question as one to be decided by authority. The better view should be that it is a question of construction, in which authority offers relatively little guidance. See 11.5 (Narrow powers of appointment).

The law got off to the right start in *Eland* v *Baker*.[73] Trustees' powers of consent were held to be wholly fiduciary. Trustees were required to consider the interests of beneficiaries affected by the appointment.

The next case is *Re Dilke*.[74] A power of appointment was subject to trustees' consent. The appointor appointed that the trust fund should be held on such trusts as he appointed. This was (rightly) held to be valid; for the trustees could properly consent to such an appointment, if they thought it appropriate.

The law took a wrong turn, it is submitted, with *Re Phillips*.[75] Here, it was deduced from *Dilke* the remarkable proposition that trustees had no duty to the persons appointed. The better view of that case was that the trustees did have a duty, but exercised it. As often happens to wrongly decided cases, *Phillips* was subsequently distinguished on wholly illusory grounds: *Re Watts*.[76] The nakedness of the attempted distinctions

---

[72] It does not matter for the rule against perpetuity: *Re Churston* [1954] Ch 334, as explained in *Commissioners of Estate & Succession Duties v Bowring* [1962] AC 171. *Re Phillips* [1931] 1 Ch 347, if correctly decided, is an exceptional case. (Unfortunately, a full discussion is beyond the scope of this book.)
[73] (1861) 29 Beav. 137; 54 E.R. 579
[74] [1921] 1 Ch 34
[75] [1931] 1 Ch 347.
[76] [1931] 2 Ch 302.

was cruelly exposed in *Re Churston*.[77] But both those cases concerned a different point—the rule against perpetuities—and did not have to decide the point now being discussed. Conversely, it must be admitted, *Phillips* obtained obiter dicta support in other cases.[78]

For all practical purposes, however, the drafter may simply impose a power of consent, and need not concern himself with the nature of the power.

---

[77] [1954] Ch 334 at 342 "I cannot think why... With all respect, I cannot agree... Again, I cannot appreciate the bearing of that." (Roxburgh J.)

[78] *Re Triffit* [1958] Ch 852; *Commissioner of Estate & Succession Duties v Bowring* [1962] AC 171, PC.

CHAPTER 8

TRUST PROPERTY

Particular assets

Special considerations arise where the trust property takes the form of certain assets. **8.1**

Shares and securities in a private company

The normal procedure is to transfer the shares from the settlor to the trustees. It must be checked that the company's articles and any shareholder agreement permits the settlor to do this. The consent of the settlor's co-shareholders may be needed. Where company articles do not permit a transfer of the shares, it may be possible for the shareholder to create a trust by declaring himself sole trustee or nominee for the trustees. This involves no transfer of the legal title to the shares. This would need careful consideration in the light of the individual case. Where the company is in voluntary liquidation, the liquidator must sanction the transfer.[1] **8.2**

Similar considerations and restrictions may apply to unlisted debentures or loan notes.

Leasehold property

Similarly, if the trust property is a lease it may be necessary to obtain the landlord's consent to any transfer to trustees. **8.3**

Land subject to mortgage

If land subject to mortgage is to become trust property, the consent of the mortgagee will usually be required: standard mortgage deeds prohibit disposals of the mortgaged property without consent. A reasonable **8.4**

---

[1] Section 88 Insolvency Act 1986. If the company is being wound up by the court, the consent of the court is required: s.127 Insolvency Act 1986.

lender should readily grant consent, as his position is not prejudiced by the making of the trust.

There are further questions to be addressed. Are the donees—the trustees—to assume liability for the mortgage debt, or are they not? Whichever is decided there should be an agreement between the trustees and the settlor so the position is clear. If the trustees assume liability to pay the mortgage debt, they will need to satisfy themselves that the property is worth more than the mortgage; and that they have sufficient funds (and if necessary indemnities) to pay interest and capital. There are tax complications which cannot be fully discussed here.[2]

Life insurance policies

8.5 See 23.1 (Trusts of life insurance policies)

Chattels

8.6 Trusts in this book are drafted with a view to holding land or investments. Further consideration may be needed where the trust property will consist of chattels. Form 3 of the Statutory Will Forms 1925 (text available on *www.kessler.co.uk*) will provide some ideas.

Property qualifying for IHT business/agricultural property relief

8.7 On will drafting for an estate containing business or agricultural property, see 18.21 (Married testator with business or agricultural property).
Consider IHT problems of ss.113A and 124A IHTA 1984 if the property may be sold by the donees.

Property situate outside England and Wales

8.8 Where property is situate outside the United Kingdom the tax and other requirements of the domestic law will need consideration. When property is situate outside England but in other parts of the United Kingdom non-tax aspects of the domestic law might still need consideration.

---

[2] Where the donees (the trustees) assume the mortgage debt, a charge to SDLT and capital gains tax may arise as the gift may be treated like a sale for consideration. Where the trustees do not assume liability for the mortgage debt that problem is avoided but others arise. How will interest on the debt be paid? If it is paid by the trustees, one must ensure that the terms of the trust permit this. The capital gains tax position is interesting: what is the trustees' base cost? Is there a reservation of benefit problem for inheritance tax? Will the interest qualify for income tax relief?

CHAPTER 9

THE RULE AGAINST PERPETUITIES

Introduction

The rule against perpetuities is designed to prevent a trust from lasting indefinitely. **9.1**

In outline, the rule prescribes a maximum period within which the interest of a beneficiary is required to vest. This period is:

(1) the period of the lifetimes of one or more persons living when the trust is created, and 21 years; or

(2) a fixed period of up to 80 years.

The fixed period only applies if specified in the trust.

A simple trust may satisfy the perpetuity rule without any express provisions. The terms of the trust may be such that no beneficiary has an interest which could possibly vest outside the permitted period.[1] In practice such simple trusts are unduly restrictive. The drafter must therefore:

(1) direct that an appropriate perpetuity period applies to his trust; and

(2) take care to arrange that all beneficiaries' interests do vest within that period.

---

[1] For instance:
  (1) For A for life with remainder to such of his children as attain the age of 21.
  (2) For A for life, with the remainder to such of A's issue as A should appoint, and in default of appointment, to such of his children as attain 21.

Which perpetuity period?

9.2 Until 1964 the perpetuity period could only be defined by reference to lifetimes of persons alive when the trust was made. Often use was made of the "Royal lives" clause; this would specify as a perpetuity period:

> *The period ending 21 years after the death of the last survivor of the issue living on the date of this Settlement of his late Majesty King George V.*

It is now possible to specify a fixed period of up to 80 years and this is far preferable. The Royal Lives clause may allow a perpetuity period exceeding 80 years, but the period is uncertain. How are trustees to keep track of all those royal lives? If there is a fixed period the trustees will know exactly where they stand.

It is suggested that the drafter should specify the maximum possible fixed period, which is 80 years. Statute permits shorter periods (one occasionally sees 60 years selected) but it must be best to take advantage of the longest possible period. The trust can of course end sooner if desired.

Different rules apply to a non-charitable purpose trust (exceedingly rare in England);[2] the period cannot be used.[3]

Drafting

9.3 It is helpful for the draft to coin a term to describe the perpetuity period or the day on which it ends. This term will be used later in the trust. The following terms are commonly used:

> The Trust Period; The Trust Date
>
> The Perpetuity Period; the Perpetuity Date; the Perpetuity Day
>
> The Vesting Date; the Vesting Day

The following are also seen:

> The Specified Period
>
> The Distribution Date; The Termination Date[4]
>
> The Ultimate Date[5]

---

[2] Upkeep of grave clauses are common in the different culture of Ireland; see *Drafting Northern Ireland Trusts & Will Trusts*, Kessler and Grattan (Roundall, 2003), para.8.2.

[3] Section 15(4) PAA 1964.

[4] These two terms are appropriate to trusts under laws like that of Guernsey where the trust comes to an end on the expiry of the perpetuity period. They are strictly less appropriate to English trusts which do not, or at least need not, come to an end on the expiry of the perpetuity period. The rule is that interests must vest within that period.

[5] This apocalyptic term seems to be a novel coinage in the *Encyclopedia of Forms & Precedents* (5th edn); the 4th edn used the more usual term "perpetuity period".

The choice hardly matters and the term used in this book is "the Trust Period". The form is simple:

"The Trust Period" means the period of 80 years beginning with the date of this Deed. That is the perpetuity period applicable to this settlement under the rule against perpetuities.

This clause does two things:

(1) The first sentence defines the expression "trust period", which is used elsewhere in the settlement: powers are restricted so they must be exercised in that period; contingent interests are drafted so they will vest in that period.

(2) The second sentence specifies the perpetuity period which applies for the rule against perpetuities, in words modelled on the statute.[6]

Normally one would deal with two such separate matters in separate clauses or sub-clauses and purists do so here. A combined clause is adopted in this book in deference to the more common practice and the reader's expectations; of course no difficulty can arise either way.

Confusion over dates

The manner of specifying the perpetuity period has given rise to some confusion; this is caused by applying (or misapplying) two rules of law:

9.4

(1) The law may ignore parts of a day. Suppose a trust is executed on 1 January 1992. The 80-year perpetuity period would expire on 31 December 2071. It would not matter what time on 1 January the trust was made; the law does not usually take notice of fractions of a day.

(2) The word "from" may be understood to be exclusive of the *terminus a quo*.[7]

Consider a trust executed 1 January 2000, using this form:

The Perpetuity Period applicable to this settlement is the period of 80 years from the date of this deed.

---

[6] Section 1 PAA 1964. Some add "instead of being of any other duration", echoing the section exactly. This is clearly unnecessary; if there could be any doubt, *Re Green* [1985] 3 All ER 455 confirms the point. One could delete the words "under the rule against perpetuities" but they do help to explain the effect of the clause to the general reader. One could delete the second sentence altogether as a trust may validly specify a perpetuity period by implication. However, it is better to specify the period expressly.
[7] See the fine discussion on this point in Elizabeth Cooke, "Touching the time of the beginning of a lease for years", *The Conveyancer* [1993] 206 accessible on *www.kessler.co.uk*.

In this case, it might perhaps be argued that the perpetuity period began on 2 January continuing until 1 January 2080, or even continuing to 2 January. If so, the perpetuity period would exceed 80 years, which is not permitted. That view does not survive examination. The true meaning would obviously be that the period begins on the day of the trust and ends on the last moment of December 31. It must be intended that the perpetuity period begins as soon as the trust begins. This may however have been the fear which led some drafters to direct the perpetuity period to be a day or two less than 80 years.[8]

In this book the perpetuity period is expressed to "begin with" the day of the trust, so it is plain that the perpetuity period includes the day of the trust, and the problem does not arise.

Trust period and perpetuity period distinguished

9.5 One sometimes sees this form:

(1) *The perpetuity period applicable to this settlement is the period of 80 years from the date of this deed.*
(2) *"The Trust Period" means the period ending on the earlier of*
   (a) *the perpetuity period or*
   (b) *such date as the Trustees by deed determine (not being earlier than the date of the deed).*

This distinguishes between the perpetuity period (which applies for the purpose of the rule against perpetuities) and "the Trust Period". It gives the trustees power to curtail the "Trust Period".[9] The power is valid as a matter of trust law.[10] However, this power is not needed. The conventional overriding powers can be used to the same effect. Accordingly the power is not used in this book.

---

[8] The form is not much used now, but survives in some older trusts. In the early years of the PAA 1964 some drafters apparently believed that the perpetuity period must be a whole number of years. (The reason is difficult to fathom. A fraction is a "number".) Hence (perhaps) the occasional use of a 79-year period.
[9] The significance of curtailing the Trust Period would depend on how the term "Trust Period" was used in the trust. Generally the ending of the "Trust Period" will bring forward the end of the trust.
[10] A power to alter the perpetuity period (for the purposes of the rule against perpetuities) may arguably be invalid. One argument is based on s.1 PAA 1964 which requires that the perpetuity period must be "specified" in the trust. That argument is not convincing as a matter of linguistics alone, but the general scheme of the rule against perpetuities does not fit comfortably with a power to shorten the perpetuity period. However, the matter is academic. The objection does not apply to the type of power set out in the text. Here the perpetuity period (for the purposes of the law against perpetuities) remains fixed. All that is varied is the "Trust Period", a term specific to the trust, to which the drafter is free to give any kind of definition. Perhaps the expression "Specified Period" would be a more accurate label.

Effect of failure to remain within perpetuity period   147

Remaining within the perpetuity period

(1) Dispositive powers

All dispositive powers must be restricted so that they can only be exercised in the perpetuity period. Thus in the case of a power of appointment, it is necessary to say: **9.6**

> The Trustees shall hold the Trust Fund on such trusts as they may during the Trust Period appoint.

In the case of a discretionary trust or power over income:

> During the Trust Period the Trustees may pay the income of the Trust Fund to such of the Beneficiaries as they think fit.

Administrative powers are not affected by the rule against perpetuities and do not need such restrictions.[11]

Powers of appointment and resettlement must of course be *exercised* in a manner which complies with the rule against perpetuities. This is not, however, a matter for the drafter of the trust itself.

(2) Beneficiaries' interests

> The Trustees shall hold the Trust Fund on trust for the Beneficiary during his life.   **9.7**

The position here depends entirely on the definition of "the Beneficiary". If the beneficiary is born before the expiry of the trust period there will be no difficulty. It may be that "Beneficiary" is a defined term, under which a "Beneficiary" may be born after the trust period expires; then there is a potential difficulty. So to avoid the problem the drafter must either restrict the definition of "Beneficiary" to exclude beneficiaries born after the trust period expires; or else put the limitation in the clause giving an interest to the beneficiaries.[12]

Effect of failure to remain within perpetuity period

If the drafter does not follow these guidelines the trust he produces will confer interests which might vest outside the perpetuity period. This may not matter too much since the trust remains valid during a lengthy "Wait   **9.8**

---

[11] Section 8 PAA 1964.
[12] See 14.9 (A perpetuity problem) for an illustration of this technique.

and See" period.[13] Nevertheless it is better for the drafter not to rely on the "Wait and See" rule. There are some uncertainties as to how it operates; and a trust where the "Wait and See" rule applies may mislead the reader: it will not take effect according to its tenor.

Future of the rule against perpetuities

9.9 In 1998 the Law Commission issued an admirable Report[14] to simplify the law. The proposed reforms are highly desirable, welcomed by all concerned, and the delay in implementing the proposals is regrettable. However, in April 2008 the House of Lords approved a new procedure to deal with the backlog of uncontroversial Law Commission Bills, and it is hoped that the Perpetuities & Accumulations Act will be implemented by the time of the next edition of this book.

---

[13] Section 3 PAA 1964.
[14] The Rules against Perpetuities and Excessive Accumulations, Law Com. No.251 (1998) accessible on *www.lawcom.gov.uk*.

CHAPTER 10

GENERAL PROVISIONS OF A TRUST

Order of Provisions

Blackstone introduces our subject: 10.1

> The matter written must be legally and orderly set forth. ... It is not absolutely necessary in law to have all the formal parts that are usually drawn out in deeds, so long as there are sufficient words to declare legally the party's meaning. But, as these formal and orderly parts are calculated to convey that meaning in the clearest, distinctest, most effectual manner, and have been well considered and settled by the wisdom of successive ages, it is prudent not to depart from them without good reason or urgent necessity .... [1]

The following order is fairly standard:

1. Title, date and parties: "This settlement is made ..."
2. Recitals: "Whereas ..."
3. Testatum: "Now this deed witnesses ..."
4. Definitions
5. Beneficial provisions
6. Overriding Powers[2]
7. Appointment of new trustees[3]
8. Incorporation of schedule (administrative provisions)
9. Settlor exclusion clause[4]

---

[1] *Commentaries* Book II (1st edn, 1766) p.297.
[2] Para.11.1 (Drafting and understanding overriding powers).
[3] Para.6.33 (Appointment of new trustees).
[4] Para.13.10 (Settlor exclusion clause),

10. Default Clause[5]

11. Irrevocability clause

12. Testimonium clause: "In witness ..."

13. Schedule: Administrative Provisions

These forms are discussed in this chapter except where footnotes give another reference.

A lengthy document results: it is helpful to furnish it with a contents page.[6]

Declaration of trust or transfer to trustees?

10.2   There are two ways to create a lifetime settlement:

(1) A settlor may declare himself trustee (acting as sole trustee unless and until another trustee is appointed).

(2) The settlor may:

(a) transfer trust property to trustees;
(b) direct the trustees to hold on the appropriate trusts.

The second is the normal route and adopted in the precedents in this book. The first route, the declaration of trust, may be convenient if for any reason it is difficult to transfer property to trustees. For instance, in the case of shares, if there are restrictions on transfers; or foreign land (especially if there is no time to seek local advice); or certain pension policies.

Of course, a declaration of trust may also be used for the different reason that the settlor wants to be sole trustee.

See also 10.12 (Form where settlor is sole trustee).

On the consequential amendment of the definition of "the trustees": see 10.40 (Definition of "the trustees"). Either in the body of the trust or in a separate document there will need to be a declaration of trust by which the settlor declares that he holds the intended trust property on the terms of the trust.[7]

---

[5] Para.13.23 (Default clause).
[6] Some drafters subdivide their settlement into "parts" like a statute. The precedents in this book are simple enough to render this unnecessary.
[7] If the latter, the document might begin "This Declaration of Trust is made ...". However the term "settlement" is just as apt and it is preferred to retain it for the sake of uniformity.

Title

> This settlement is made ...

10.3

The title is self-explanatory.[8]

Date

A document should be dated, though the absence of a date or even a wrong date does not invalidate it.[9] It only means that there may be doubts as to when it was made. For the style of writing a date, see 3.11 (Dates).

10.4

On what date does a trust take effect?

The date is important for tax and property law purposes (e.g. if the settlor wishes to resile from his gift). The position is complex, because several distinct sets of rules interact:

10.5

(1) Rules as to when a transfer of assets to a trustee takes effect. As every student learns, a trust cannot take effect until the trust property is vested in the trustee, or the settlor has done what he can to transfer it.

(2) Rules as to when a settlor becomes bound by a deed he has executed, but which other parties have not.[10]

(3) Rules as to when a deed signed by a settlor binds him: the law of "delivery" (a confusing and unfortunate term) and escrow.[11]

---

[8] The custom before 1925 was to begin all deeds with the words "this Indenture" (if more than one party) or "this Deed Poll" (if only one party). Section 57 LPA 1925 put an end to that unhelpful practice.

[9] Lewison discusses dates in *The Interpretation of Contracts* 4th edn (London: Sweet & Maxwell, 2007), 10.02–10.03. Law Commission Report No. 253, Cm 4026, 1998, *The Execution of Deeds and Documents by or on behalf of Bodies Corporate*, accessible at www.lawcom.gov.uk, also has a discussion at para.6.6.

[10] Perhaps surprisingly, a settlor is in principle bound by a settlement which he has executed, even if the trustees are parties and have not executed it: *Lady Naas v Westminster Bank* [1940] AC 366.

[11] *Emmet on Title* is a good starting point for research on this subject.

152   General Provisions of a Trust

Backdating

10.6   "Even the gods cannot alter the past."[12] The same principle holds in English law: a document cannot be back-dated. If it is back-dated it does not alter anything that has happened in the past; the document can only take effect from the date of execution.[13] In this the law only reflects the human condition, inconvenient though it may sometimes be.[14] And yet the clear spring of principle is muddied by many real or apparent exceptions.[15]

---

[12] Agathon, *cit.* Aristotle, *Nicomachean Ethics,* Vol.6, Ch.2.

[13] Many cases could be cited (as is usually the case for basic principles). For examples of private agreements failing to alter the past see *Waddington v O'Callaghan* 16 TC 187; *Bradshaw v Pawley* [1980] 1 WLR 10.

[14] Thus, the non-judicial dictum of Edward Fitzgerald: "The moving finger writes; and, having writ/ Moves on: nor all thy piety and wit/ Shall lure it back to cancel half a line/ Nor all thy tears wash out a word of it." The inconvenience extends beyond the law. "Reminded of the President's previous statements that the White House was not involved in the Watergate affair, Ziegler [government spokesman] said that Mr Nixon's latest statement is the Operative White House Position ... and all previous statements are inoperative." (Cited in the *Oxford Dictionary of Quotations,* 4th edn.)

[15] There are seven categories of exception:

(1) Parliament can enact retrospective legislation.

(2) Parliament sometimes empowers private persons to make arrangements which are wholly or partly retrospective. (Retrospectivity is not all or nothing, but a matter of degree.) One example is s.142 IHTA 1984 (deeds of variation). A deed of variation which purports to vary past dispositions does not do so for the general purposes of the law, but is treated for some tax purposes as if it had that effect. Again, an election for hold-over relief and indeed most tax elections have some retrospective fiscal effect.

(3) The courts sometimes have power to make orders which are wholly or partly retrospective. For instance, the statutory powers to set aside transactions under insolvency or matrimonial legislation. There are dicta suggesting that the jurisdiction for rectification is in this category. There is a better argument of principle that rectification ought to fall in category (4) below (this is the view expressed by Hill J. in *Davis v FCT* (2000) 44 ATR 140 at [56]). The issue will probably never be resolved.

(4) The courts have no general inherent jurisdiction to change the past: *Morley Clarke v Jones* 59 TC 567. But some judgments are effectively backdated: e.g. in *Spence v IRC* 24 TC 311 where a party to a contract exercised his right to set it aside for fraud. The *restitutio in integrum* represented by the court order obtained some years later did not reconstruct history: it recognised and declared that which had been the legal position before the judgment, although until the order the parties were in a state of some uncertainty as to what their rights were. So the court order in this case was not retrospective in the strict sense; but the distinction requires a legal microscope. Likewise new judge-made law, such as the *Ramsay* principle, is harshly retrospective in reality, if not in legal theory.

(5) A few legal acts have some retrospective effect at common law (without any court order). Examples include disclaimers, assents, escrows (said to "relate back"); the exercise of a right to render a voidable disposition void will sometimes make it void ab initio. Whether these acts are retrospective for fiscal purposes has been decided on an ad hoc basis. A disclaimer was held not to have retrospective fiscal effect but an assent does: *Re Stratton* [1958] Ch 42; *IRC v Hawley* 13 TC 327. In *Spence v IRC* 24 TC 311, T sold shares under a contract completed in 1933. T rescinded the contract (for fraudulent misrepresentation) in 1936. The House of Lords ordered the fraudulent purchaser to transfer the shares back to T in 1939. It was held that T was rightly assessed on dividends from the shares for the years 1936 to 1939. That was obviously correct: this is a category (4) case. More interestingly, it was said that the effect of the exercise of T's right of rescission was retrospective (for income tax) back to the date of contract. (But this was obiter since dividends were only assessed from after the date of the rescission.)

In view of the exceptions it is not surprising that the general principle itself is occasionally overlooked. A surprising number of practitioners do not regard backdating as wrong. So it should be well noted that the execution of a backdated document with a view to mislead may involve criminal offences, inter alia, forgery and fraud on HMRC.

Parties

10.7

This settlement is made [date] between

(1) X of [address] ("the Settlor") of the one part and

(2) (a) Y of [address] and
    (b) Z of [address]

("the Trustees") of the other part

The form is so standard that it is rare to stop to consider whether these words are all necessary or indeed what they may mean. In fact the words "of the one part" and "of the other part" have no significance in the context of a deed of settlement.

Who should be parties?

10.8

It is not strictly necessary that the trustees should be parties to the trust deed. All that matters is that the trust property is vested in the trustees.[16] The only significance of making trustees a party is that (since they sign the deed) (1) they cannot disclaim trusteeship; and (2) they cannot deny that they have notice of the trust. It is, however, the standard practice to include them. The practice in will drafting is a striking contrast: trustees of a will trust are not made a party to the will. Likewise it is not necessary that a Protector should be a party to the trust deed, and it is better practice that he should not be a party, though no harm is done if he is a party. The same applies to a beneficiary (of a bare trust or otherwise). All the parties should execute the deed (and if they do not they should not be parties).

---

(6) Private persons may agree between themselves that a document should have effect from an earlier date. But this is not true retrospectivity, and only parties to the agreement are affected. For instance, HMRC will not be bound.

(7) Samuel Butler observed that although God cannot alter the past, historians can. Accountants—financial historians—enjoy some similar licence.

[16] *Re Chrimes* [1917] 1 Ch 30. If trustees are made parties, it does not matter if they do not sign the trust deed: see 10.5 (On what date does a trust take effect?).

Describing the parties

10.9 Full names and addresses should be given so that there can be no doubt as to identity. For the style of writing the address, see 3.12 (Addresses). Further details should be given in unusual situations where ambiguity may still remain (e.g. where an individual uses two names, where two individuals in the same family share the same name or where a person has changed his name).

The traditional practice was to specify the occupation and (for women only) marital status of each party. This usually is (and should be) omitted as unnecessary and (to some) offensive. It would be convenient to give former names, if a person is referred to in an earlier relevant document by a different name, as this avoids confusion.

Each name should begin on a separate line.

Form where settlor is one of the trustees

10.10 The settlor is commonly one of the trustees. The use of a definition conveniently shortens the text:

> This Deed is made the ..... day of ..... between
>
> 1. John Smith of [address] ("the Settlor") of the one part and
>
> 2. (a) The Settlor and
>   (b) Peter Smith of [address]
>   ("the Trustees") of the other part.

It was formerly the practice for the person to sign twice, once in each capacity, but this is not necessary and not recommended.

Form where trust made by joint settlors

10.11 It happens occasionally that two settlors (usually husband and wife) contribute funds to a single trust. (Two separate trusts may be advantageous for tax,[17] but the administrative convenience of a single trust may outweigh any tax considerations.)

The form hardly needs to be spelt out:

> This Settlement is made [date] between
>
> 1. John Smith and Jane Smith both of [address] ("the Settlors"), etc.

Note that consequential amendments must be made elsewhere in the trust.

Amendments are usually needed for the following:

---

[17] Two separate trusts will qualify for two separate CGT annual exemptions

(1) The definition of Beneficiaries.

(2) The power to appoint new trustees.

(3) The settlor exclusion clause.

This seems, and indeed is, obvious; but it is easy to forget and therefore not infrequently overlooked in practice.[18]

Form where settlor is sole trustee

The form is self-explanatory: 10.12

> This Settlement is made [date] by [name] ("the Settlor").
> Whereas...

It is wrong to say:

> *This Settlement is made [date] between*
>
> *(1) John Smith of [address] ("the Settlor") of the one part and*
> *(2) John Smith ("the Original Trustee") of the other part*

But no harm is done (save as to reputation) if this uncouth form is used.

No named settlor

It is possible for a settlor to convey his property to trustees and for the   10.13
trustees then to declare appropriate trusts at his direction[19]: there is then no need to name the settlor in the trust deed. This may be done for confidentiality which may be desired for reasons proper or improper. Bearing in mind the risk that an uncharitable or cynical court may infer that the reasons are improper, it seems a wiser policy to name the settlor in the trust deed. This is, however, a better course than to use a nominal settlor.

Nominal settlor

It is the custom in some offshore jurisdictions to arrange for a lawyer or   10.14
trust company to settle an initial nominal trust fund.[20] This is correctly

---

[18] Interesting questions can arise where this mistake is made. For instance: suppose there are two settlors, Mr and Mrs X. The Beneficiaries are defined as "the children of the Settlor". Y is the child of Mr X but not of Mrs X. Is Y a beneficiary?
[19] A written and signed direction would be needed in English law, or in a jurisdiction which has an equivalent of the English rules concerning formalities: s.53(1)(c) LPA 1925.
[20] This practice is recognised in *Schmidt v Rosewood* [2003] 2 AC 709.

referred to as a nominal settlor;[21] though others may use pejorative terms such as dummy, puppet or stooge. The real settlor then adds the substantial trust fund. It goes without saying that the person who provides trust property directly or indirectly will be the "settlor" for tax purposes[22] and likewise for insolvency and matrimonial law purposes. This style of drafting may have the pernicious result of leading a court to infer an intention to mislead the reader into thinking that the nominal settlor is the only and real settlor. (Though the true explanation may be that the parties are seeking lawful confidentiality and mistakenly believe that every trust deed ought to specify a named settlor; or the drafter adopted the common form without any thought on the subject at all.)

Recitals

10.15　Before the operative part of the deed there are traditionally inserted a series of statements known as "recitals." Their function—in a trust context—is to assist the reader of the deed by explaining its background and purpose. They are not intended to have legal effect and do not normally have any.[23] The use of recitals to instruct or entertain has fallen into sad decline.[24]

Recitals are traditionally introduced by the word "whereas". Sometimes the heading "Recitals" is used. A radical drafter might replace this with the word "Background" which describes precisely the place and function of the recitals.

A glance at different trusts encountered in practice or in precedent books shows that a wide variety of recitals are used. The approach of this book is to include recitals which will be of assistance to the reader or user of the deed. These are as follows.

---

[21] This is the expression used in *Schmidt v Rosewood* [2003] 2 AC 709 para.8.
[22] See James Kessler QC, *Taxation of Foreign Domiciliaries* (7th edn, Key Haven Publications, 2008), Ch.54 ("Who is the Settlor").
[23] Recitals occasionally serve a legal function, operating to supply evidence or to form an estoppel. None of these are normally relevant to a deed of trust. In addition, of course, recitals will have a legal effect if the context shows that that is the intention. The correct practice is to put such material into the body of the deed. For a couple of examples of erroneous recitals disregarded, see 12.11 (Drafting resolutions of advancement).
[24] But note the preamble to A.P. Herbert's Spring (Arrangements) Bill (which did not pass into the statute book):

"Whereas on every lawn and bed
The plucky crocus lifts his head,
And to and fro the sweet birds go,
The names of which we do not know ..."

(Cited in the biography by R. Pround, Michael Joseph, 1976).

Recital 1: A list of the principal beneficiaries of the trust

> The Settlor has two children, namely:
>   (i) Adam Smith, who was born on [date] and
>   (ii) Daniel Smith, who was born on [date]

10.16

The names and dates of birth will be convenient to later users of the deed. The layout—each name on a separate line—adds greatly to the clarity of the precedent. Dates of birth may be omitted if irrelevant to the trust; this will usually be the case where the beneficiaries are adult.

Recital 2: Name of trust

> This settlement shall be known as the John Smith 1997 Settlement.

10.17

A trust does not need a name to be valid, but a name is necessary for convenient administration, e.g., as a designation for a trust bank account and a heading in correspondence and tax returns. It seems appropriate for the drafter to supply the name in the draft (though no harm can arise if this is not done; the trust will be named in due course).

It is suggested that the name belongs logically in the recitals. The body of the trust should contain the provisions which have legal effect.

The choice of name hardly matters. It is usually taken from the name of the settlor and the year. Where the settlor creates a number of trusts in one year, they may be distinguished by number, or by the type of trust ("John Smith Grandchildren Settlement 1994"). Sometimes a trust is named after the principal beneficiary, or the trust property ("the Green Farm Trust").

Will trusts (which lack recitals) are not usually given a name in the will; the trust will no doubt be called "the John Smith Will Trust" without the benefit of an express name clause. If a will creates two separate trusts (not a course adopted in this book), the drafter should provide two names.

Power to change name of trust

Occasionally trusts confer a power to change (by deed!) the name of a trust; this is based on a misconception. A name is only a label and trustees may name and rename a trust at their pleasure. Power to do so derives not from the terms of the trust, but from the nature of human language. Individuals commonly change their name by deed poll, but the deed is merely evidence of the intention to change a name.[25]

10.18

---

[25] *Halsbury's Laws of England* (1994), vol.35, para.1279. The form has also been seen:
> "*For the purposes of identification* this settlement shall be known as ..."

One wonders what purposes a name can serve other than identification.

Recital 3: Foreign domicile of settlor

10.19 It may be helpful to state in a recital where the settlor is domiciled (if not in the United Kingdom).[26]

Useless recitals

10.20 Recitals are strictly unnecessary: they have no legal effect. The will drafter manages without them. The justification for the recitals included in our standard precedents is that they assist the reader. Others serve no purpose whatsoever, in normal circumstances, and should be omitted. This includes some quite common recitals. The following list is not exhaustive.

10.21 (1) Statement of purpose of the trust:

> *The Settlor wishes to provide for his family and others.*

This is innocuous; but it must be admitted to be completely unnecessary.[27] At any rate, this form would be preferable to grandiloquent forms such as:

> *The Settlor is desirous of making such provision as hereinafter appears for the benefit of the persons hereinafter specified ...*

10.22 (2) Transfer of trust property to trustees

It is common to recite that the settlor has transferred the trust property to the trustees. Thus:

> *The Settlor has transferred the property specified in the first schedule below to the Original Trustees.*

This may conceivably serve as a useful reminder to ensure that the trust property is in fact transferred to the trustees.[28] But would advisors who need the reminder read or act on the recital? One frequently turns to the schedule and finds a reference to a nominal sum. No harm is done if the recital is omitted, and it is not used in this book.

There is certainly no point in elaborations; such as:

---

[26] For precedents, see 18.19 (Best form of will for foreign domiciled testator).

[27] The vacuity of this recital is illustrated by *IRC v Botnar* [1998] STC at 61. This records a submission that a recital in this form was relevant to the construction of a power to transfer to a new trust. The submission (rightly) raised no ripple of response before the Special Commissioners or on appeal.

[28] See 29.9 (Transfers of trust property to trustees).

The Settlor has paid or caused to be transferred to or otherwise caused to be vested in the joint names of the Original Trustees the investments and other property specified in the schedule hereto to be held on the trusts declared by this deed and for the purposes hereinafter appearing ...

(3) Intention to transfer additional property to trustees 10.23

It is apprehended that further moneys, property or investments may from time to time be assigned delivered transferred to or otherwise vested in the name or control of the trustees to be held on the trusts declared by this deed.

If the initial trust fund is a nominal sum this is obvious. If the trust fund is substantial, and it is *actually* intended to increase the trust fund, then the recital may serve some purpose. The recital serves no purpose in standard precedents.

(4) Consent of Trustees 10.24

The trustees have consented to act as trustees of this settlement.

Would the trustees execute the deed if they did not consent?

(5) Irrevocability 10.25

On this see 10.48 (Irrevocability).

Testatum

Now this deed[29] witnesses as follows: 10.26

This introduces the body of the deed. It serves as a marker, and has no other purpose. The radical would omit the phrase altogether, as meaning no more than "this document says what it says". Others modernise the language and say "this deed therefore provides as follows..." or use the heading "Operative Provisions". There is a lot to be said for this. At any rate, the drafter should avoid embellishment such as:

Now in consideration of the premises[30] this deed witnesseth ...;
Now this deed made in pursuance of the said desire[31] witnesseth ...
Now this deed witnesseth and it is hereby declared as follows ...

---

[29] Some say: "this *settlement* witnesses. ...". The word "deed" is preferable: it is the document which is doing the "witnessing".
[30] "Premises" is an archaic term referring to the body of the deed before the "habendum". The reference is to a recital that the settlor intends to benefit his family.
[31] This refers to the recited desire of the settlor to create the settlement.

The additional words add nothing. If the drafter is tempted to add words to the testatum, he should consider whether they should better be placed in recitals or in the body of the deed.

Witnesseth is dying a surprisingly gradual death, but is now rare.

"*Irrevocably* witnesses" is a neologism based on a twofold misunderstanding of the need to state that a deed is irrevocable, and the nature of a witness, whose testimony can never be revoked (though it might be contradicted). The form should not be used.

Definitions

10.27 For this topic see 10.33 (Definitions).

Beneficial provisions

10.28 Clauses appropriate to IP trusts and discretionary trusts are discussed in the chapters on these topics.

It is common to preface the beneficial provisions with a general declaration of trust such as this:

> The Trustees shall hold the Trust Fund upon the trusts and with and subject to the powers and provisions hereinafter declared concerning the same.

Sometimes this is followed by a direction that property added is held on the same trusts.[32]

This is the drafter clearing his throat. He is politely requesting his reader's attention to what follows. The formula is omitted from the precedents in this book.

In our precedents the beneficial provisions are normally contained within three clauses:

(1) Trust Income
(2) Overriding Powers
(3) Default Clause

This division provides conceptual simplicity. It is better style not to mix income and capital powers in one single clause such as:

> The Trustees shall pay the income of the Trust Fund to X during her life but with power to pay or apply the capital thereof to or for her benefit during her life.

---

[32] Para. 19.6 (Power to accept additional funds).

Testimonium clause

10.29 The practice is to make a lifetime trust by deed. There is no legal requirement to use a deed: any signed document would have the same effect; a trust (except of land) can even be made orally. The formalities of a deed[33] (signature, witness, delivery "as a deed")—though unnecessary—are appropriate; a deed being, in Blackstone's words, "the most solemn and authentic act that a man can possibly perform with relation to the disposal of his property."[34]

> The form for an individual is:
> Signed as a deed and delivered by
> *(full name of individual)*   *Signature*
> in the presence of
>
> Signature of witness ....
> Name (in BLOCK CAPITALS) ....
> Address ....
> ....

The precedent is based on that used in Land Registry forms, except that we have retained the word "delivered". This is not strictly necessary, for delivery will be implied. But since a deed must be "delivered", it seems better to say so.

The two simplest ways for a company to execute a deed are:

(1) signature by two authorised signatories; authorised signatories are the director(s) and the company secretary (if any); or

(2) signature by a director in the presence of a witness who attests the signature.[35]

Accordingly there are two alternative forms for a company testimonium clause. Either:

> Signed as a deed and delivered by
> *(name of company)* acting by
> [a director and its secretary]
> [two directors]
>   *Signature*
>   [Director]
>
>   *Signature*
>   [Secretary] [Director]

---

[33] For individuals: s.1 Law of Property (Miscellaneous Provisions) Act 1989. For companies: ss.44–48 Companies Act 2006.

[34] *Commentaries* Book II (1st edn, 1766) p.297.

[35] Section 44 Companies Act 2006. A deed could alternatively be executed with the company seal, but we see no advantage in this. Where a document is to be signed by a person on behalf of more than one company, he must sign it separately in each capacity: s.44(6) CA 2006.

Alternatively:

>Signed as a deed and delivered by
>(*name of company*) acting by a director
>
>Signature of Director ....
>
>In the presence of
>Signature of witness ....
>Name (in BLOCK CAPITALS) ....
>Address ....

Every party should execute the deed.

The Land Registry Guide 8 (Execution of Deeds)[36] has useful precedents for rarer execution clauses, including:

- person is physically unable to sign
- person signs in foreign (i.e. non-Roman) characters
- company executing has a corporate secretary/director
- foreign company
- execution by trustees of charities
- execution under power of attorney.

Schedule of trust property

10.30 It was conventional to set out a list of the original trust property in a schedule to the trust deed. There is little point in this: the relevant information will be provided in the trust accounts.

The old practice was to create an initial trust with a nominal sum of cash, formerly £5 and nowadays £100, and to transfer the real settled property to the trust immediately afterwards. The good reason for this curious arrangement was the avoidance of stamp duty on gifts. Stamp duty on gifts was abolished in 1985, and this practice should now be abandoned.

Schedule of administrative provisions

10.31 The form used in this book is:

>The provisions set out in the schedule shall have effect.

---

[36] Practice Guide 8 accessible on *www1.landregistry.gov.uk/assets/library/documents/lrpg008.pdf*.

The practice of placing administrative provisions in a schedule at the end of a trust is a modern innovation and a welcome one. These provisions are of some length, but are of secondary importance. This may assist the client who will wish to understand the beneficial provisions, but who may be content to rely on his advisers to supply a suitable collection of administrative provisions. The schedule allows the matters which are of no interest to the lay client to be tucked away in decent obscurity; and has become established practice. This book adopts a fairly rigorous policy here: all routine provisions are excluded from the body of the trust. The draft is based on standard statutory precedent.

Schedule of beneficiaries?

In some foreign jurisdictions drafters have the tiresome habit of defining "Beneficiaries" as the persons listed in the third or fourth schedule, so the reader has to stop and locate the schedule, only to find a few lines of text which would be more conveniently placed in the definitions clause.

10.32

Definitions

Definitions are used in various ways. A definition may serve to identify the status of an individual ("the Settlor", "the Trustees", "the Principal Beneficiary"). It may be used simply to avoid repeating a full name ("Adam" or "Mr Smith" instead of "Adam Philip Newbury Smith"). A definition may serve as a label for the complex concept (e.g. "the Beneficiaries"). It is a useful tool for dividing text into pieces of manageable size. The use of a definition may ease the adoption of a standard precedent to its specific circumstances. The first letter of defined terms should be capitalised whenever used in the defined sense: "the Trustees"; "the Trust Fund". This reminds the reader that the term is defined.[37] This practice is generally adopted in lifetime trusts but often ignored in wills; the distinction is not justifiable and only reflects the lower quality of will drafting.[38]

10.33

A modish fad is to italicise or even capitalise every letter of defined expressions wherever used. The result is rather messy typography.

---

[37] This rule of construction was adopted without comment in *Beautiland Co Ltd v IRC* [1991] STC 467 PC Lord Keith, at 471, said: "The context of the reference to 'the properties' (with a small 'p') ... makes it clear that the definition of 'the Properties' is not imported."

[38] In drafting statutes, defined terms are not capitalised. But there the reader should be alert to the use of definitions; and to capitalise every defined expression (there are so many) would irritate rather than aid the reader. Moreover the reader will find editions of the statutes which will direct his attention to the defined terms at the end of each section. The reader of a private trust will not have that aid.

A defined expression should only be used in its defined sense. Occasionally it may be convenient to breach this rule. The drafter should signal this by using a small initial letter instead of the usual capital letter. There is only one example of such latitude in this book. The expression "the Trustees" is defined to mean the trustees of the trust for the time being. This book nevertheless refers to:

> a former trustee
> a new trustee
> the trustees of another settlement

in each case the small "t" is appropriate.

The words "said" or "aforesaid" are not used in this book. If they are used, be it noted that they are not appropriate where an expression has been defined. It is a solecism to say:

> *Hereinafter called "the said trustees".*

It is generally undesirable to incorporate substantive provisions in a definition clause,[39] but this is a rule of style and not inflexible.

How to make definitions

10.34 There are two common ways to make definitions. The first, one might call "define as you go"; the second uses a formal definition clause.

"Define as you go"

10.35 This is established practice in the introductory paragraph of a trust. The modern practice—sanctioned by Parliament[40]—is to signify the definition by use of quotation marks and brackets alone. Thus:

> This Settlement is made on the 6th April 1991 between Mr. John Smith ("the Settlor")
> ...

The traditional formula was grander:

> *Jack Spratt (hereinafter called "the Settlor")*

or the plural form:

> *Adam Smith and Barry Jones (hereinafter together[41] called the "Trustees")*

---

[39] *Koonmen v Bender* 6 ITELR 568 (accessible on *www.jerseylaw.je*) is an example of confusion caused by breaching this rule: see 25.6 (Exclusive jurisdiction clause).
[40] e.g. s.343 ICTA 1988.
[41] Of course it would not matter if the word "together" is omitted, as the sense is clear enough.

"Hereinafter" is unattractive legalese. One could say:

> *"here called. . . ."*
> *"in this Deed called . . ."*

It seems safe enough to omit the tiresome word altogether. Indeed, the time may come when even the quotation marks are abandoned.

A definition clause

Except for the parties to a settlement (where the above form is well established) it is helpful to assemble the principal definitions in a definition clause at the beginning[42] of the trust. A definition clause in a trust is a fairly recent innovation though now standard practice. **10.36**

The drafter has a variety of statutory precedents to choose from. The form used in the 1925 property legislation is:

> In this Act unless the context otherwise requires, the following expressions have the meanings hereby assigned to them respectively, that is to say:

This wordy form is an abbreviation of even lengthier nineteenth-century forms.[43] It has been shortened to:

> In this Act, except where the context otherwise requires:[44]

Or concisely:

> In this Act . . .[45]

The form used in this book follows this:

> In this Settlement,[46] **"the Trustees"** means . . .

It is kind on the eye to print the expression being defined in bold type. There is, however, no need to embolden the word where used throughout the document.

---

[42] Curiously the general practice in drafting Acts of Parliament (though not statutory instruments or in schedules to an Act) is to place the definitions at the end. Each practice, now established, is best adhered to; the experienced reader will know where to turn.
[43] Section 1 Wills Act 1837.
[44] Section 272 IHTA 1984.
[45] Section 15 PAA 1964; s.96 VATA 1994.
[46] "In this *Deed*" would do just as well but the word "settlement" is better as the same form can be used without amendment in lifetime settlements and will trusts. One occasionally sees the archaic form, "in these presents . . .".

"Means" and "includes"

10.37 *Means* is the appropriate word for an exhaustive definition. *Includes* is the appropriate word for an inclusive, non-comprehensive definition.[47] An inclusive definition is usually imprecise and not generally appropriate in trust drafting because a comprehensive definition is possible. To say "X means and includes Y" is a contradiction in terms.[48] Of course where the wrong word is used the courts will allow the context to govern the sense.[49]

It is better to say:

X means ...

not:

X *shall* mean ...

In this context "shall" is purely ornamental. Its omission is more in accordance with ordinary English usage;[50] it is also the more standard practice of the parliamentary drafter.

Grammarians may debate whether the singular or plural verb is appropriate where the term being defined is in the plural. Does one say **"the Trustees"** *means* ... or **"the Trustees"** *mean* ... ? The 1925 property legislation employs the plural verb (with a slip in s.205(1)(xii) Law of Property Act 1925). Since one is defining a single expression, the singular seems more correct; this is now the practice in modern statutory and trust drafting.

The word "comprises" is best avoided in a definition clause.

Unnecessary forms in a definition clause

10.38 The traditional form provides that definitions apply "except where the context otherwise requires" or (more tentatively) "where the context so permits".[51] A well-drafted trust will use defined terms in their defined meanings. The form was included perhaps to cover the exceptional case,

---

[47] Four cases on different nuances of "include" are summarised in *Dunstan v Young Austen Young* [1987] STC at 721.
[48] It can be proper usage to say:
X means 'a' *but* includes 'b'; or
X means 'a' *and* includes 'b'.
[49] No authority is needed for this self-evident proposition, but the point is made in *Dilworth v Commissioner of Stamps* [1889] AC 99 at p.105. For an example see *Gibson v South American Stores (Gath and Chaves) Ltd* [1950] Ch 177 at 184: "the class of beneficiaries shall include ..." held to form a comprehensive definition.
[50] Para. 7.6 (Other usage of "shall" and "may").
[51] In *Melville v IRC* [2000] STC 628 at 634, Lightman J. recognises the difference in nuance between the two formulas; while linguistically this seems right, it is difficult to conceive (1) that any drafter ever ponders carefully on the choice between the two wordings; or (2) that any case of construction in practice is ever so finely balanced as to turn upon this distinction. Even the form "where the context so permits or requires" has been seen.

or to allow for drafting oversights. In either case the words are unnecessary: the context will always govern the meaning. In the first edition of this book these words were retained "to serve as a ritual confession of the drafter's fallibility" but the value of ritual confessions is perhaps open to question. So this book now follows the example of more concise drafters[52] and omits these words altogether.

It is plainly unnecessary to say: "the following terms have the following meanings". The heading "Definitions" is sufficient indication of what is to come.

Some standard definitions

"The Settlor" should be defined by name. Trusts occasionally use this form: **10.39**

> *"The Settlor" means the Original Settlor and any person who shall make any addition to the trust fund.*

The consequence is that the settlor exclusion clause will exclude not only the original settlor but all the contributor settlors. This form is not satisfactory for the reasons set out in 13.15 (Exclusion of additional and indirect settlors).

"The Original Trustees" are also defined by name.

Definitions of "Accumulation Period", "Beneficiaries", "Charities", "Interest in Possession" and "Trust Period" are considered elsewhere.[53] If the term "Trust Corporation" is used it should be defined.[54] We here consider other commonly defined expressions.

Definition of "the trustees"

> *"The Trustees"* means the Original Trustees or other the trustees or trustee[55] *for the time being of this Settlement.*[56]   **10.40**

Until quite recently this appeared to be an almost universally adopted form; so common, perhaps, that few drafters pause to ponder its significance

---

[52] e.g. the Law Society's Standard Conditions of Sale. The parliamentary drafter occasionally omits this form in a definition clause governing an entire Act. In providing definitions for a schedule or a particular section, on the other hand, the form "unless the context otherwise requires" is almost invariably omitted.
[53] 15.7 (The rule against accumulations); 5.18 (Definition of "Beneficiaries"); 5.36 (Charities as beneficiaries); 16.19 (IP protection clause); 9.3 (Drafting).
[54] 7.14 (Two-trustees rule).
[55] Note the use of the small "*t*" is appropriate.
[56] More traditionally "hereof" stood for "of this settlement"; or even, wrongly, "of this deed".

or syntax. The purpose may be: (i) to confirm the appointment of the "Original Trustees" (defined by name) as the trustees of the trust; (ii) to confirm that the trustees' powers are given to them ex officio, and pass on to succeeding trustees. The clause is not strictly necessary: both inferences would be made quite naturally in the absence of indications to the contrary.[57] The archaism in the traditional formula, "other the trustees" is a particularly unhappy one: the expression is dismissed by laymen as a typographical error.

In will drafting, a different formula is generally used to make these two points:

> *I appoint X and Y to be the executors and trustees of my will (hereinafter called "my[58] trustees" which expression includes the trustees for the time being).*

Some lifetime trusts use this approach too.[59]

Statute provides two precedents:

> "The Trustees" means the trustees appointed by the Testator ... and the persons who by appointment by the court or otherwise become the trustees.[60]
>
> The provisions of this Act referring to the trustees of a settlement apply to the surviving or continuing trustees or trustee of the settlement for the time being.[61]

This is the basis for the definition used in this book:

> **"The Trustees"** means[62] the Original Trustees or the trustees of the settlement for the time being.

The best approach would possibly be to abandon the definition altogether, as Prideaux did a generation ago;[63] though it would be a bold drafter who is prepared to step this far out of line with conveyancing practice.

The draft needs amendment where the Settlor is the sole Trustee. The term "Original Trustees" will not have been used. Thus:

> **"The Trustees"** means the Settlor or the trustees of this Settlement for the time being.

---

[57] *Re Smith* [1904] 1 Ch 139; see also ss.18 and 36(7) TA 1925. *LRT Pension Trustees v Hatt* [1993] PLR 227 at 257 (accessible on *www.kessler.co.uk*) is a further authority that "the Trustees" will be taken to mean the trustees for the time being. Wolstenholme and Cherry, *Conveyancing Statutes* (13th edn, 1972) Vol.4, p.6 goes so far as to say that the definition is undesirable; though it does not seem to do any harm.

[58] It is a curious custom that the form "*my* trustees" is used in a will, while the form "*the* trustees" is used in a lifetime trust. It is convenient to use the form "the trustees" generally

[59] e.g. Potter and Monroe, *Tax Planning with Precedents* (11th edn), contrast the 10th edn; *Kelly's Draftsman*.

[60] Statutory Will Forms 1925, para.3(1)(iii), accessible on *www.kessler.co.uk*. Extraneous material has been omitted.

[61] Section 94 SLA 1925.

[62] "includes" is not the appropriate word here (it is occasionally used by confusion with the form used in wills, set out above, where "includes" is the appropriate word).

[63] *Prideaux's Forms and Precedents in Conveyancing* (25th edn, 1959).

Definition of "the trust fund"

A common form is: 10.41

"*The Trust Fund*" *means:*
   (i) *the property specified in the First Schedule hereto; and*
   (ii) *all accretions thereto by way of further settlement, accumulation of income or otherwise,*[64] *and*
   (iii) *all property from time to time representing the above.*

This is another standard and self-evident definition. In this book, a simplified version is proposed:

"**The Trust Fund**" means:
   (i) property transferred to the Trustees to hold on the terms of this Settlement[65]; and
   (ii) all property representing the above.

This definition is not necessary[66] but it is universal practice to include this form, and it is included in deference to the reader's expectation.

It is plainly not necessary to say that the trust fund includes property which shall be added to the trust fund. If property is subsequently transferred to the trustees with the intent that it should be added to the trust fund, then the trustees can hardly be heard to say the added property is not held on the terms of the original trust. It is not necessary to refer to accumulated income here, since the provision dealing with accumulation states it is to be added to the trust fund.[67]

A further definition is also introduced here: 10.42

"**Trust Property**" means any property comprised in the Trust Fund.

---

[64] This is about as common as the grander form with the same meaning: "*all other property investments or money* [as if investments or money were not "property"!] *hereinafter transferred or paid to, or under the control of the Trustees as additions to the Trust Property.*" This is plainly unnecessary; see 21.6 (Power to accept additional funds or onerous property).

[65] This form avoids the unnecessary chore of specifying the trust property in a schedule: see 10.30 (Schedule of trust property).

[66] This proposition is self-evident but support for it can be found if needed in statutory drafting practice and case law. The Parliamentary drafter uses the terms "trust funds", "trust property" and "trust money" without any definition. In *Hume v Lopes* [1892] AC 112 at p.115 Lord Watson said: " the expression 'trust funds' ... signifies funds belonging to the trust, including money invested on security or otherwise, as well as uninvested cash. I do not doubt that such is the ordinary and natural meaning of the words." (When s.1 TA 1925 was re-enacted as s.1 of the Trustee Investments Act 1961 (now repealed) the Parliamentary drafter preferred the word "property" to "trust funds" but that is a stylistic change only.) *Agnew v IRC* [2001] 2 AC 710, paras. 42–47 raised in another context the question whether an asset and its proceeds were to be regarded as separate assets. The answer given, correctly, was that (1) they are separate assets but (2) the latter is merely traceable proceeds of the former so (3) an attempt to separate the ownership of the two (even if conceptually possible) will "make no commercial sense".

[67] See 21.6 (Power to accept additional funds or onerous property); 15.7 (The rule against accumulations).

The additional definition of "Trust Property" facilitates drafting the trustees' administrative powers, where references to "property comprised in the trust fund" are otherwise very frequent.

Unnecessary definitions

10.43   *"This Settlement" means the Settlement created by this Deed.*
"The settlor", and "the trustees" have the respective meanings hereinbefore assigned to these expressions.

Comment seems unnecessary. Enthusiasm for definitions can be taken to excess and, having already two redundant definitions in this text, one is reluctant to admit more.

Where a word is used once or twice, a definition may be more trouble than it is worth. Thus, in a straightforward trust for a named beneficiary on attaining the age of 40, there is little advantage in providing that the trust fund is held on trust for "the principal beneficiary" on attaining the "specified age", and then separately defining these expressions to be the beneficiary concerned and the age of 40 years.

Definitions implied by law

10.44   The following definitions are implied by statute into every document[68]:

(1) "Month" means calendar month.

(2) "Person" includes a corporation.

(3) The singular includes the plural and vice versa.

(4) The masculine includes the feminine and vice versa.

These definitions need not and should not be repeated by the drafter of any particular document.

There is no need to introduce the anatomical curiosity that "references to one gender include all genders"; the court will not infer from the use of the masculine word "he" or "his" that the reference is intended to exclude a company (even though a company is referred to by the neuter "it" or "its").[69]

---

[68] Section 61 LPA 1925. See also 3.14 (Singular and plural); and 3.15 (Male and female).
[69] In *Re Carnarvon* [1927] 1 Ch 138 a company was held to be entitled to powers conferred by s.20 SLA 1925 on a person "of full age". The argument that the words "of full age" excluded companies was rejected. A similar argument based on the words *he* or *his* must be rejected a fortiori.

Definitions to break up text

A definition may be used to break up text into manageable parts. In this context a defined term may be used once only, and it may be more convenient to define the term where used, rather than to place the definition in the definition clause.[70]

10.45

Drafting successive interests

The practice in this book is to employ a chain of clauses linked with the words "subject to that". Thus:

10.46

(1) The Trustees shall pay the income of the Trust Fund to John during his life.
(2) **Subject to that** the Trustees shall pay the income to John's widow during her life.

An alternative approach is to specify the starting point of each sub-clause more precisely:

(1) The Trustees shall pay the income of the Trust Fund to John during his life.
(2) On the death of John, the Trustees shall pay the income to his widow during her life.

This is considered to be an inferior approach. Using the phrase "subject to that", each sub-clause forms, as it were, a slat which rests firmly on that which has gone before. The structure will be sound: there can be no gaps. If, however, each sub-clause stands independently, there is a risk of an omission. What happens, for instance, in the example above, if John should surrender or disclaim his interest? Who is then entitled to the income during John's life?[71]

"Subject to that" is adopted in this book as synonymous for the more archaic "subject as aforesaid". The form has the sanction of Parliamentary usage.[72] It is common to find grander forms with the same meaning, for instance, following a power of appointment:

10.47

in default of and until and subject to any such appointment . . .[73]

or in a Default Clause:

---

[70] 3.5 (Must every clause be a single sentence?).
[71] The answer is supplied by the presumptions of the doctrine of acceleration; like all the artificial rules of construction this involves some difficult case law. Another advantage of this form is that it avoids the rule in *Phipps v Ackers*, which turns a contingent into a vested interest, with unfortunate consequences for income accumulated under s.31 TA 1925; see *Re Mallinson* [1974] 1 WLR 1120.
[72] Section 204(8) IHTA 1984.
[73] This form is used in Statutory Will Forms 1925, Form 9 accessible on *www.kessler.co.uk*.

> *in default of and subject to the trusts and powers hereinbefore declared and to the extent that the same shall not extend or take effect. ...*

But the modest phrase "subject to that" is equal to them all.

Irrevocability

10.48   This settlement is irrevocable.

In the mid-nineteenth century a power of revocation was standard form. (Of course the powers caused no tax problems in those days.) If the power was, exceptionally, omitted, the court might set aside or rectify a settlement unless the settlor had "distinctly repudiated and refused to have a power of revocation".[74] This explains the origin of the recital that:

> *The Settlor has been advised that unless a power of revocation is reserved the Settlement will be irrevocable but well understanding such advice he had decided to reserve no power of revocation whatsoever and the settlement is irrevocable.*

This is sometimes shortened to a recital that:

> *It is intended by the Settlor that this settlement shall be irrevocable.*

This approach was reversed in the 1880s and the omission of a power of revocation ceased to be a reason for setting aside a trust.[75] Nowadays a UK trust hardly ever has a power of revocation. A trust will therefore be irrevocable unless it actually reserves a power of revocation.[76]

Irrevocability forms have accordingly been unnecessary in English law for more than a century. They were not used in this book until the 6th edition. However, in some American jurisdictions[77] trusts are revocable unless stated to be irrevocable. So it is (just) worthwhile to state the point expressly, not because there would otherwise be any doubt, but because some readers unfamiliar with the law might possibly misunderstand the position.

The appropriate place to put this form is in the body of the deed, not a recital.

---

[74] Many cases could be cited, but since they are now obsolete it is sufficient to refer to *Hall v Hall* (1871) LR 14 Eq. 365; *James v Couchman* (1883) 29 Ch D 212; *Coutts v Acworth* (1869) LR 8 Eq. 558; *Wollaston v Tribe* (1869) LR 9 Eq. 44.
[75] *Henry v Armstrong* (1881) 18 Ch D 668; *Dutton v Thompson* (1883) 23 Ch D 278; *Tucker v Bennett* (1887) 38 Ch D 1.
[76] No authority is needed for this self-evident proposition (which is of course the basis on which the cases in the two footnotes above were decided). See however, *Farwell on Powers* (3rd edn, 1916), p.306: "A deed once executed cannot be revoked unless it reserves a power of revocation".
[77] Following the American Uniform Trust Code s.602; accessible on *www.nccusl.org*.

CHAPTER 11

DRAFTING AND UNDERSTANDING OVERRIDING POWERS (APPOINTMENT, RE-SETTLEMENT AND ADVANCEMENT)

Introduction

The fundamental desire of the settlor, in creating his trust, is this: to benefit the beneficiaries of his trust in the most appropriate way. It is impossible for settlor or drafter to anticipate in advance exactly what that will be. Drafts in this book are based on the premise that the trustees should be trusted—as their name suggests—and they may be given wide powers to achieve the settlor's intention. This is the principal function of the overriding powers.

There is a further advantage: the existence of the overriding powers effectively prevents a profligate beneficiary from selling his interest in a trust. He will not find a purchaser for an interest subject to the overriding power: the interest could and probably would be revoked the day after the sale. This, in turn, has an incidental tax advantage. Any tax charge based on the market value of the equitable interest is effectively avoided.

These powers raise questions of principle. The flexibility intended to satisfy the wishes of the settlor may be used to frustrate them. The question of who should exercise the powers, and with what constraints, is discussed at 7.12 (Guidance and control of trustees). This chapter is devoted to the technical drafting issues.

Overriding powers may be divided into three categories.

Power of appointment: Power to create new trusts for the beneficiaries.

Power of resettlement: Power to transfer funds to a new settlement for the beneficiaries.

Power of advancement: Power to apply capital for the benefit of a beneficiary.

11.1

Power of appointment

11.2 The power of appointment may take the form of a true power to terminate existing provisions and create new ones; or it may take the form of a discretionary duty, the trustees being (in theory) required to appoint new provisions. The distinction is of little importance.[1] In this book the form used is a true power: this corresponds more closely to the reality.

The clause must, obviously, specify the form of the new trusts which may be created and the objects who may benefit. In this book the objects are simply described as "the Beneficiaries" and the definition of the term is considered at 5.18 (Definition of "Beneficiaries").

The parliamentary drafter provides one influential precedent:

> The capital and income of the trust fund shall be held in trust for all or any one or more exclusively of the other or others of the Beneficiaries, and if more than one in such shares, with such provisions for maintenance, education, advancement and otherwise, at the discretion of any person or persons, and with such gifts over, and generally in such manner, for the benefit of such Beneficiaries, or some or one of them, as the Appointor shall, by deed, revocable or irrevocable, or by will appoint.[2]

This precedent will be known to anyone familiar with trust deeds. Old style precedents take this material, delete the punctuation, and expand it in a single clause of extraordinary length. The single clause has become unwieldy: Hallett led the way and divided the power into separate clauses, with a view to greater comprehensibility. The clause used in our precedents is a simpler version of the statutory precedent:

> The Trustees shall have the following powers:
>
> (1) Power of Appointment[3]
>
>   (a) The Trustees may appoint that they shall hold any Trust Property[4] for the benefit of any Beneficiaries, on such terms as the Trustees think fit.
>   (b) An appointment may create any provisions and in particular
>
>   (i) discretionary trusts
>   (ii) dispositive or administrative powers
>   exercisable by the Trustees or any other person.

---

[1] 7.2 (Duties and powers distinguished).
[2] Statutory Will Forms 1925, Forms 7 and 9 (here slightly amended to stand in isolation), accessible on www.kessler.co.uk.
[3] The words "appointment" and "appoint" are the appropriate technical term. Plain English enthusiasts may prefer to call the power of appointment, a "power of variation" and substitute "direct" or "declare" for "appoint". Some old precedents use the formula "direct and appoint". Occasionally one sees: "appoint direct and declare"; pointless collecting of synonyms.
[4] Until the 9th edition the text read "the Trust Fund". This old wording follows the example of the Statutory Will Forms. But the other overriding powers use the expression "any Trust Property"; and experience showed that the inconsistency in the wording occasionally caused confusion. The change does not make any difference in the meaning. In particular, just as the power in the SWF could by used over part of the Trust Fund, so the power of appointment in the wording formerly used in this book could be used over part of the Trust Fund.

(c) An appointment shall be made by deed and may be revocable or irrevocable.

The draft refers to "such terms as the Trustees think fit", which covers all the various terms used in the Statutory Will Forms precedent.

It is usual to require an appointment to be made by deed. This is not essential, but a deed is appropriate since an appointment is a formal legal document.

The power of appointment can be used to alter administrative provisions as well as beneficial provisions.[5]

Sub-clause (b) is essential. A stumbling block for older powers of appointment was the court's view that a power of appointment was (in the absence of clear words) a power to create fixed interests and could not be used to create dispositive trusts and powers. This clause makes the position clear.[6]

It is normal to state that an appointment may be revocable or irrevocable, though strictly even without those words an appointment may be made which is revocable within the time that the power of appointment may be exercised. There is no particular reason why trustees need make revocable appointments when they have a wide flexible power, but it may be convenient to do this.

Unnecessary provisions in the power of appointment

Some drafters refer not just to "the Beneficiaries" but to   **11.3**

... all or any one or more exclusively of the other or others of the Beneficiaries

This has been unnecessary since 1874.[7]

Some drafters do not refer to trusts for the benefit of the Beneficiaries, but to:

Such trusts *in favour or* for the benefit of the Beneficiaries

It is submitted that the extra words add no meaning. The expression "favour or benefit" is a pointless use of synonyms.[8]

Occasionally drafters use the word "respective" thus:

The Trustees shall hold the trust fund on trust for the Beneficiaries ... with such trusts for their *respective* benefit ... as the Trustees shall appoint.

---

[5] In the standard overriding powers in this book, this is stated expressly, though it would in principle be implied: *Re Rank* [1979] 1 WLR 1242. In consequence, a power to add administrative powers is unnecessary: see 21.5 (Power to add powers).

[6] For the position in the absence of such a clause see 11.5 (The problem of narrow powers of appointment).

[7] Section 158 LPA 1925, re-enacting the Powers of Appointment Act 1874. See 3.14 (Singular and plural).

[8] In s.3(5) PAA 1964 the expression used is "a power of appointment exercisable in favour of members of a class" (without the word "benefit").

In one case it was held that this word "respective" suggested that the creation of discretionary trusts was not permitted.[9] In practice the trustees will expressly be permitted to create such trusts. So the word "respective" is either erroneous (if Cross's comments in *Hunter* are correct) or superfluous (if they are not.) Plainly no one who cares about accurate language will use the word here.

It is common to add a requirement that any appointment must observe the rules against accumulation and perpetuities. This has no legal effect, and may be omitted. (The form might conceivably serve as a reminder to the person who drafts the deed of appointment; but a person who needs that reminder is unlikely to be capable of drafting the necessary deed in any event.)[10]

Some drafters add a provision saying that to the extent that the power of appointment is not exercised, the original trusts continue to apply. This is implied in any case, and is unnecessary.[11]

Some drafters add a provision that the power of appointment cannot be operated retrospectively. For instance:

> No exercise of this power shall reduce the amount of any accrued benefit to which a beneficiary shall have become entitled under this settlement.
> No appointment shall affect income payable to the Trustees before the date of that appointment.

A provision of that type will be understood by necessary implication and is therefore unnecessary.[12]

11.4 Hallett[13] added two further provisions not generally found in modern powers of appointment, but which should be mentioned for completeness. The Hallett precedent directed that the power of appointment may be used to:

> provide for the appointment or remuneration of trustees on any terms and conditions whatever.

---

[9] Cross J. said that a discretionary trust is not for the respective benefit of the beneficiaries: it is a trust for the *collective* benefit of all of them under which none has any separate benefit: *Re Hunter* [1963] Ch 372. Is this convincing? The word "respective" is vacuous in this context. It does not carry the inference which Cross J. put upon it. But this makes no practical difference. Either the power of appointment will expressly permit the creation of discretionary trusts; or else it will be silent and (as the authorities now stand) discretionary trusts will not be permitted in any event. See the excursus at 11.5 (The problem of narrow powers of appointment).

[10] See 9.6 (Remaining within the perpetuity period). In one unfortunately worded trust (perhaps drafted for an economically minded settlor) the overriding power was subject to "the rules against excessive accumulations and gratuities".

[11] *Re Hastings Bass* [1975] Ch 25; *Re Master* [1911] 1 Ch 321 followed in *Re Sharp* [1973] Ch 331.

[12] This was accepted without argument in *IRC v Pearson* [1981] AC 753 (confirming the view taken in the HMRC Press Release of 12 February 1976). It is apparent that the power of appointment in that case contained no such proviso: see at first instance [1980] Ch 1. This view is also supported by *Re Delamere* [1984] 1 WLR 813; *Re Master* [1911] 1 Ch 321 followed *Re Wellman* [2001] JLR 218 accessible on www.jerseylaw.je.

[13] Hallett's *Conveyancing Precedents* (1st edn, 1965), p.772.

There is no need to make an express provision here for remuneration of trustees, since the normal trustee remuneration clause is sufficient.[14]

The Hallett precedent provided that the power of appointment may be used to:

> direct that the Trust Fund shall be transferred or paid to and held by any persons as trustees ...

The power of appointment (as drafted in this book or in any common form) cannot itself be used to transfer the fund to new trustees.[15] However there is the usual power to appoint new trustees, power to appoint separate trustees of separate funds[16] and (in precedents in this book) a separate express power of re-settlement. That seems comprehensive enough.

The problem of narrow powers of appointment[17]

Modern powers of appointment are generally widely drawn and give rise to no difficulty, but there are many older trusts with powers more narrowly drawn. It is worth considering these in some detail. The reader who is not familiar with the case law may go wrong here: if the old cases are still good law, these powers of appointment do not have the effect which a simple reading would suggest.

Let us start with an example. In *Re Joicey*,[18] property was held on trust for the beneficiaries:

> for such interests in such proportions and in such manner in all respects as the appointor should appoint.

An appointment was made for children who attained a certain age. Trustees were given power to transfer capital to them under that age (a dispositive power). This power was void. This was said to follow from the rule against delegation.

In the following discussion, powers of appointment which allow the

11.5

---

[14] For good measure, the overriding power in the precedents in this book could be used to make further provision for remunerating trustees. Such provision is an administrative provision. Of course this could only be done if (i) this was for the benefit of the beneficiaries and (ii) there was an independent trustee who did not benefit from the new remuneration clause. See 6.13 (Conflicts of interest). It seems unlikely that this would ever need to be done.
[15] This proposition is self-evident, but if authority is needed see *Re Mackenzie* [1916] 1 Ch 125. Happily there is a solution to problems when such powers are lacking. A power of appointment in common form will generally be wide enough to confer upon trustees a power of resettlement.
[16] Section 37(1)(b) TA 1925.
[17] See Richard Oerton, *Trusts and Estates* [1994] pp.317 and 402.
[18] [1915] 2 Ch 115. In other cases the invalid power was a power of maintenance (which would from 1926 be implied by s.31 TA 1925) and a power arising under a protective trust. This is just an early example of a long line of cases, of which the most recent is *Re Hay* [1982] 1 WLR 202. Here Megarry J. took the principle to a new height of absurdity by holding that the trustees had wrongly delegated their discretions to themselves.

appointor to create dispositive powers are described as wider powers; and powers which do not are called narrower powers. The effect of *Joicey* therefore, is to hold that the power considered in that case was a narrower and not a wider power.

It is submitted that the law has taken a wrong turning here.

An issue of delegation. First, this line of cases has treated the matter as one of delegation. It need not and (it is submitted) should not be put that way. The appointor is not delegating his existing power of appointment: he is exercising it so as to create new dispositive powers.[19]

A matter of construction. The question whether a power of appointment is narrower or wider is a question of construction. That is not in dispute. The correct question to ask is not whether the power contains within it a right to delegate, but whether it was to be construed widely enough to permit the creation of new dispositive powers. The difference is one of nuance, but it is a significant nuance.

Let us return to the *Joicey* power, and consider whether it should be construed as wider or narrower. Property was held on trust for the beneficiaries:

> for such interests in such proportions and in such manner in all respects as the appointor should appoint.

The phrase "in such manner in all respects" points to the wider construction. In the nineteenth century the courts would nevertheless give it the narrower meaning; for flexible trusts were then unusual. In the present time, a natural reading would apply the wider meaning; for flexible trusts are common; it is most unlikely that a settlor now intends the power to be so limited.[20]

What has happened is that the courts have followed the nineteenth-century approach—summed up in *Joicey*—to the present day. This is why such powers are given such a limited meaning. This is a misuse of precedent, which should not be regarded as binding in matters of construction. Unfortunately the Court of Appeal missed the opportunity to correct these errors in *Re Morris*.[21] Evershed M.R. preferred to follow the old authorities, more or less conceding that they were wrong, than to construe the document according to its plain language. The complaint about the state of the law was repeated in *Re Hunter*.[22] If the matter came to be

---

[19] The point was accepted in *Re Wills* [1964] Ch 219 at 237 and in *Re Weightman* [1915] 2 Ch 205; (A power of revocation "in no sense" a delegation of a power of appointment).

[20] Another way to reach the same conclusion is to rely on the phrase "for such interests". The word "interests" may be used to mean only fixed equitable interests; nowadays it is used more often used to mean interests under true powers or trust powers: *Leedale v Lewis* 56 TC 501. But often the wording of the power does not include that phrase.

[21] [1951] 2 All ER 528.

[22] [1963] Ch 372.

reviewed by the courts, it is submitted that principle should take priority over precedent. This, indeed, is what precedent requires.[23] Of course, for the time being, one should act on the cautious view that the old cases might still be followed.

Happily, there is a solution to the problems presented by these narrow powers of appointment. Such powers can in principle be used to confer on the trustees a power of advancement, being either the statutory power (which is exercisable over half the trust fund) or a power of advancement extended over the entire trust fund.[24] Once that is done, of course, the trustees can if appropriate use their power of advancement to achieve results beyond the scope of their narrow power of appointment: see 11.8 (Power of advancement).

Power of resettlement

The form used in this book is as follows: 11.6

(1) The Trustees may by deed declare that they hold any Trust Property on trust to transfer it to trustees of another settlement, wherever established, to hold on the terms of that settlement, freed and released from the terms of this Settlement.
(2) The Trustees shall only exercise this power if:

    (a) every Person who may benefit is (or would if living be) a Beneficiary; or
    (b) with the consent of

        (i) the Settlor, or
        (ii) two Beneficiaries (after the death of the Settlor).

The wording makes it clear that the new settlement will be a separate trust from the existing trust, as intended. The reported cases indicate what is needed. The phrase "freed and released from the terms of this settlement"

---

[23] See 4.10 (Precedent not the solution).
[24] In *Re Mewburn* [1934] Ch 112 the Court approved of the exercise of a power of appointment (in relatively standard narrower form) to create a power of advancement exercisable over one half the trust fund. The judge noted that a power of advancement would (after 1926) be implied by s.32 TA 1925 so it cannot exceed the power of appointment to create it. The case was approved by the Court of Appeal in *Re Morris* [1951] 2 All ER 528 at 533 where the principle was held to apply

> "... at all events where the instrument creating the power [of appointment] enables any appointment to be made 'in such manner and form in every respect' or 'generally in such manner for the benefit of' the objects of the power, as the donee of the power may appoint."

If it is permissible to create a power of advancement over one half the trust fund, it must logically be permissible to create a power over the whole, especially since the extension of s.32 to cover the whole is a standard form. The opposite conclusion was apparently reached in *Re Joicey* [1915] 2 Ch 115. There an appointor tried unsuccessfully to use a narrower power of appointment to create a power which (at first sight) appears an ordinary power of advancement. But this case no longer represents the law. That decision was based on the view that the (to modern eyes unexceptional) power which the appointor attempted to create was *not* an ordinary power of advancement. That view could not now be sustained in the light of (i) s.32 TA 1925 and (ii) current drafting practice and (iii) the comments in *Re Pauling* [1964] Ch 303 at 333 (which contradict the view of the power taken at [1915] 2 Ch 123).

could be omitted, but it spells out the effect of the transfer clearly, and has judicial approval.[25]

Trustees are sometimes given power to transfer the trust fund to any trust if only one beneficiary of the present trust happens also to be a beneficiary of the new trust. That is equivalent to authorising trustees to add beneficiaries; a serious proposition if the power is exercisable without restraint. The form used here brings in the same safeguards as the power to add beneficiaries; see 5.39 (Power to add beneficiaries).

Power of resettlement and power of appointment compared

11.7 A power of appointment can vary the terms of a trust. The power of resettlement may effectively achieve the same result, but will also result in trust property being held by a different trust (perhaps, but not necessarily, with different trustees and a different governing law). As a matter of trust law there may not be much difference between altering the terms of an existing trust (in a power of appointment) and transfers to a new trust (by a power of re-settlement). There are, however, important differences for tax purposes:

(1) The transfer to another trust is a disposal for CGT purposes; an exercise of a power of appointment does not normally involve a disposal.[26]

(2) If only part of the trust fund is transferred to a new trust, the result is two separate trusts. The trustees of one trust are not subject to liabilities of the second, and that may obviously be more convenient when different branches of a family wish to go separate ways. It would then be possible to appoint foreign trustees for one trust but not for the other.

(3) Many tax planning arrangements require transfers of funds to new trusts. A discussion of such planning is beyond the scope of this book: sufficient to say that a well drafted trust should give scope to make such arrangements in case it becomes appropriate.

Tax aside, this power may also be useful to combine trusts with similar terms, so as to reduce administrative costs; or to split up one trust with several sub-funds into separate trusts with separate classes of beneficiary.

---

[25] *Hart v Briscoe* 52 TC 53. The leading cases are *Roome v Edwards* 54 TC 359; and *Bond v Pickford* [1983] STC 517.
[26] Section 71 TCGA 1992. This may be undesirable if a CGT charge would arise. For this reason trustees will generally prefer the power of appointment to the power of resettlement if the aim is only to vary the terms of the trust. However there will be occasions when trustees want a disposal of trust property; for instance, to realise losses.

Power of advancement

The term "power of advancement" is used to describe a power to transfer trust property to a person, or apply it for his "advancement or benefit".[27] The person for whose benefit the trust property may be applied (or to whom the property may be transferred) is called the "object" of the power.

11.8

Trustees have a power of advancement by statute. The statutory power is however subject to three important restrictions[28]:

(1) Only a beneficiary with some interest in trust capital is an object of the power. Thus a life tenant is not an object of the power.

(2) The power only extends over one-half of the object's share in the trust fund.[29]

(3) The trustees can only exercise the statutory power with the consent of any beneficiary with a prior interest.

It is standard practice to override the second of these restrictions, by a form such as:

> Section 32 TA 1925 (Power of Advancement) shall apply with the following modification: the words "one-half of" in section 32(1)(a) shall be deleted.[30]

This book adopts a different approach. The form used in this book is:

> The Trustees may pay or apply Trust Property for the advancement or benefit of any Beneficiary.

None of the restrictions which inhibit the statutory power of advancement apply:

---

[27] This is the usage of the Parliamentary drafter, who describes the power conferred by s.32 TA 1925 as "the statutory power of advancement"; e.g. s.47(1)(ii) AEA 1925; likewise s.44(2) FA 1950 (an estate duty provision).

[28] And for completeness three minor restrictions:

    (1) The power does not apply to Settled Land Act settlements (now obsolescent).
    (2) The power does not apply where there is an expression of contrary intent; it seems that a very shadowy one will suffice.
    (3) Where the beneficiary is to become entitled to a share (and not the whole) of the trust property, any advance is to be brought into account as part of that share (the hotchpot rule).

(s.32 TA 1925.)

[29] It is possible (if expensive) to apply to the Court to extend this power to the entire trust property.

[30] This is the STEP standard provision. Some use the form:

> *S. 32 TA 1925 shall apply with the deletion of proviso (a) thereof.*

Note that this is arguably wider than the STEP form. For example consider a trust for A and B contingently upon attaining the age of 21 in equal shares. The statutory power of advancement allows one-quarter of the trust fund to be used for the benefit of A and one-quarter for the benefit of B. The STEP form allows one-half to be used for A and one-half for B. The form set out in this footnote arguably allows the *entire* fund to be used for A or B.

(1) All beneficiaries are objects of the power.

(2) The entire trust fund may be advanced.

(3) Consents of beneficiaries are not needed.

This is in line with the approach of this book, that trustees should be trusted with wide powers and that beneficiaries' consents are not desirable.[31] The restrictions which apply to the statutory power raise some difficult questions of trust law.[32] An advantage of our approach is that none of these difficulties can arise.

The form adopts unabridged the statutory phrases "pay or apply", and "advancement or benefit." The full form is used to display the clause's parentage, s.32 Trustee Act 1925, so as to suggest that the useful case law giving a wide meaning to "benefit" should apply.

It is intended that trustees should be able to use their power of advancement informally, so no deed or written document is required. This rather simplifies the administration of the trust. The statutory power takes the same approach.

Where there is a wide power of advancement, as in our draft, there is clearly no call for the statutory power. In the lifetime trusts in this book it is therefore not necessary to provide that the statutory power should apply (with or without amendment). In the Will Trusts it is also unnecessary, except that it might be useful in Wills 5 and 7, which contain an absolute gift of residue. So the wide power is included in the administrative forms for wills but not for lifetime trusts. Although strictly only needed for Will forms 5 and 7, it does no harm in the other cases.

Other forms in powers of advancement

The statutory power of advancement is a power to pay or apply capital *money*. However, the power nevertheless applies to trust funds not in the form of money.[33] In drafting a power of advancement it is more apt to refer to trust property (or trust capital) than to "money".

Older trust precedents gave trustees power to *raise money* and pay or apply the trust money. This has been unnecessary since 1925.[34]

Another precedent gives power to *raise a share* in the trust fund and pay

---

[31] See 7.23 (Giving powers of consent to beneficiaries).
[32] How is the fraction of one-half to be calculated? What is a "prior" interest? (A question "of great difficulty" according to Clausen J. in *Re Spencer* [1935] Ch 533; in *IRC v Bernstein* 39 TC 391 at 403 Lord Evershed M.R. was "glad" to follow authority which refrained from expressing a view on the question. Such authorities are of more assistance to the Bench than to practitioners.) The hotchpot rule does not work well since no account is taken of inflation.
[33] *Pilkington v IRC* [1964] AC 612 at 639.
[34] Section 16 TA 1925 (power to raise money by sale, mortgage, etc.). Hence the word "raise" is not used in the statutory power of advancement. In a modern trust there would also be an express power to borrow.

or apply that share for the advancement or benefit of a beneficiary. Here the word "raise" adds nothing but a puzzle of what it might mean.[35]

Power to pay or transfer to beneficiary

A common form in older trusts is: 11.9

> The Trustees may pay or transfer trust funds to [a Beneficiary] for his own use and benefit absolutely.

This power is narrower than the common form power of advancement, since it does not allow funds to be applied for the benefit of the beneficiary but only to be paid or transferred to him absolutely.[36] The power is unnecessary where (as in the drafts in this book) there is a wide power of advancement.

Power of appointment used to make advance to beneficiary

The power of appointment (or indeed the power of resettlement) may be used so as to transfer trust capital to a beneficiary. But it may be easier to use the power of advancement for this purpose, since no formal deed is required. Trust money can simply be transferred by cheque or wire transfer.   11.10

---

[35] It has been said that "raise" in this context has "a broad sense" and means no more than identify or set aside trust capital for the purpose of the exercise of the power: *Re Wills* [1959] Ch 1 at 14. This does however give the word a sense which it does not normally have. When one talks in ordinary usage of "raising funds", "raising" means obtaining money, either by loan, or by issuing shares for cash, or by any other method (as in charity "fundraising"). So another interpretation is suggested. A power of advancement of this kind might be read with a comma after the word "pay" so it empowers trustees to do one of two things:

 (1) "Raise" trust capital (i.e. raise money, by borrowing, mortgage, or sale of trust assets) and pay the money to or for the benefit of beneficiaries; or
 (2) apply trust capital *in specie* (without "raising" money) for the benefit of beneficiaries.
    Whichever is the right approach does not in practice matter: the trustees can exercise a power of advancement without troubling themselves about any requirement of "raising" capital.

[36] The words "pay or transfer *to*" do not in their normal sense mean "pay to or apply *for the benefit of*". Of course the context may show that an extended sense is meant: for examples see the 7th edn of this book at 14.7. But here the words "for his own use and benefit absolutely" require that the object becomes absolutely and beneficially entitled to the property paid or transferred to him. If appropriate, the Court may extend a narrow power to "pay or transfer" into a wider power to "apply for the benefit" under s.57 TA 1925; this may solve the problem of the narrow power. Another solution is to transfer to the beneficiary and let the beneficiary re-settle; but of course that has possible tax and property law problems.

Power of advancement used to create new trusts

11.11 The power of advancement in a trust may be used:

(1) to transfer trust property to a new trust where it may be held on terms wholly[37] or partly[38] different from the original trust;

(2) to alter the terms of the existing trust so as to create new beneficial interests which may wholly or partly replace the existing beneficial interests;[39] or

(3) to alter administrative provisions.[40]

Thus the power of advancement may be used broadly to the same effect as powers of appointment or resettlement.

This is particularly important where a trust is drafted badly, or inflexibly, because even badly drafted trusts generally contain a full power of advancement, which should allow terms of the trust to be altered where necessary.

In the following discussion:

(1) It is assumed that under a trust ("the Original Settlement") trustees have power to apply capital for the benefit of an object, "O".

(2) The exercise of the power of advancement which results in a settlement of the funds advanced is called a "settled advancement" and the trusts created are called "advanced trusts".

(3) The beneficiaries of the trusts created by the settled advancement are called "Advanced Beneficiaries."

A typical case is where trustees, having power of advancement for the benefit of O, exercise that power by a settled advancement, in such a way that the trust fund is held on trust for O for life, with remainder over to O's family.

The starting point is to note that the Advanced Beneficiaries include persons other than the object, O—in this example, his family. The

---

[37] As in *Re Clore* [1966] 1 WLR 955 (transfer to charity).
[38] In *Re Hastings-Bass* the trustees transferred trust property to a new trust but created only a limited beneficial interest in income and no exhaustive beneficial trust of capital of the funds advanced. The new trustees held on the terms of the old trusts, which remained in effect to the extent that the new trusts were not comprehensive. See [1975] Ch 25 at 42. In the leading case of *Pilkington v IRC* 40 TC 416 the new trusts were nearly, but not quite, exhaustive.
[39] In *Re Hampden* the new trusts were nearly but not quite exhaustive. This important case is reported in [1977] TR 177 and also, belatedly, reported in [2001] WTLR 195 and accessible at *www.kessler.co.uk*.
[40] *Howell v Rozenbroek* (14 December 1999, accessible at *www.kessler.co.uk*).

advance must be for the benefit of O; but it is easy to see that this settled advancement may be an application of the trust fund for the benefit of O, since it will usually be for O's benefit that there should be funds to maintain his family after his death. It is not relevant whether or not O's family are beneficiaries under the original settlement. They may be or they may not be; but the reason they become Advanced Beneficiaries is because this is for the benefit of O, and not because of their status under the original settlement. O himself need not be an Advanced Beneficiary at all. All that matters is that the settled advancement is for the benefit of O.[41]

A settled advancement can only create new trusts in a manner which is specifically for the benefit (albeit "benefit" in the wide sense) of the object, O.[42] If there is a power to advance for the benefit of O, one cannot normally create new[43] trusts giving trustees a wide power of appointment in favour of O's siblings, or cousins, or more remote family, as that will not normally be for the benefit of O. The test is whether the trustees have O's interest and O's interest only, in mind. By contrast, the normal power of appointment can be used to create any type of trusts so long as the beneficiaries of the created trusts are objects of the power of appointment.[44] Where it is not obvious that a proposed advance is for the benefit of the object, a possible course may be to exercise the power of advancement so as to confer powers of appointment which are exercisable by the object or which are exercisable with his consent or for his benefit. This brings out more clearly the benefit for the object. The next chapter sets out some precedents.

The commonest examples are a settled advance:

(1) to make provision for O's family; or

(2) to prevent O from becoming absolutely entitled to trust capital because:

   (a) O is immature and irresponsible as regards money so it is a benefit to retain the capital in the trusts;[45] or

---

[41] Striking examples are *Re Clore* [1966] 1 WLR 955—transfer to charity favoured by object of power of advancement; *Re Hampden* [1977] TR 177, also belatedly reported in [2001] WTLR 195, accessible at www.kessler.co.uk: transfer to trust for benefit of children of object of power of advancement.

[42] "Under such a power the trustees can deal with capital in any way which, viewed objectively, can fairly be regarded as being to the benefit of the object of the power, and subjectively they believe to be so." *Re Hampden*, above.

[43] It is different if such trusts already exist and the exercise of the power of advancement merely preserves them.

[44] This is all that Upjohn J. meant in *Re Wills* [1959] Ch 1 at 14: "Trustees cannot under the guise of making an advancement create new trusts merely because they think that they can devise better trusts than those which the settlor has chosen to declare. They must honestly have in mind some particular circumstances making it right to apply funds for the benefit of an object or objects of the power."

[45] This was grudgingly accepted in *Re T* [1964] Ch 158 "only because a strong case on the facts is made out for protection of this nature". But attitudes have changed. In Jersey:

(b) this avoids a tax charge on O becoming entitled to the trust fund;

(3) to transfer to another trust for the reasons discussed at 11.7 (Resettlement and appointment compared).

It is considered that similar principles govern a common form power of *appointment*. For instance, a power of appointment for the benefit of the children of the settlor may be used to create trusts for the children for life with remainder to the grandchildren (not objects of the power, but assuming the provision for the grandchildren is regarded as a benefit to the children who are objects).[46]

"It is not in our judgment generally in the interests of young persons to come into possession of large sums of money which might discourage them from achieving qualifications and from leading settled and industrious lives to the benefit of themselves and of the community."

See Re Gates [2003] 3 ITELR 113 accessible at *www.jerseylaw.je*. This view would be accepted now in England. Lord Eldon shared this sentiment: see Campbell's anecdote of Lord Eldon accessible on *www.kessler.co.uk*.

[46] The word "benefit" has two distinct meanings, a narrow meaning and a wide meaning:

(1) *Direct Financial Advantage only* In the narrow sense, "benefit" means only a direct pecuniary benefit. In this sense it is not a "benefit", say, to a person to pay his children's school fees.

(2) *Intangible Non-financial Benefit also* In the wide sense, "benefit" includes not only direct financial advantage, but also intangible non-pecuniary advantages including mental satisfaction. In this sense (only) it is for the benefit of a person:

(a) to pay his children's school fees (assuming the person wishes to see his children privately educated); or
(b) to provide a fund for their use (assuming the person wishes to see his children financially secure); or
(c) to make a contribution to a charity which that person wishes to support.

A similar distinction is made in the law relating to a fraud on a power. An appointment with the motive of securing a financial benefit to the appointor is void: but an appointment satisfying an appointor's *moral* obligation is valid. See *Palmer v Locke* (1880) 15 Ch D 294 at 303.

Confusion can be caused by failing to ask which of these meanings applies. The context must decide which meaning is intended.

In general fiscal legislation the narrow meaning is normal and the wide meaning is exceptional. For instance, the word "benefit" in the context of the income tax or CGT settlement provisions or the IHT gifts with reservation provisions has the narrow meaning and refers to direct financial benefits only. No-one has ever suggested that a payment to a person's minor children is a "benefit" to the parent, so as to bring those sections into application.

In the context of a power of advancement, a power to apply for the advancement or "benefit" of O, the word "benefit" bears the wide meaning and includes any intangible non-financial advantage. This construction is perhaps suggested by the phrase "advancement or benefit" showing that a wider sense of "benefit" is intended; but in any event it is long settled by the authorities cited above.

In the context of a common form power of appointment, a power to appoint on trusts for the "benefit" of O, it is considered that the word "benefit" has the same wide sense. This was accepted without argument in *Re Leigh* (1980) belatedly reported [2005] TLI 109 [2006] WTLR 477. The position is exactly the same if the power of appointment refers to "trusts *in favour* or for the benefit of the Beneficiaries", i.e. the words "in favour of" are mere synonym and do not extend the width of the power.

In the context of a common form power to apply income for the benefit of a beneficiary, it is again suggested that the word "benefit" has the same wide sense. A little support for this view might be gained from the old case of *Allen v Coster* (1839) 1 Beav 202, accessible on *www.kessler.co.uk*. In this remarkable case a fund of £6,000 was held (in short) for the benefit of two minors.

Under the statutory power of advancement the trustees need the consent of a beneficiary with a prior interest. The consent of O is not needed however,[47] though in practice trustees should take his views into account and circumstances where the trustees can properly act contrary to O's views (if adult) will be rare.

O is not the settlor of the advanced trusts for any tax purposes.

The statutory power of advancement can only be used for the benefit of an object or objects individually, and not for the benefit of two or more objects as a class.[48]

The statutory power of advancement can only be used in favour of living beneficiaries, and not in favour of unborn beneficiaries.[49]

There has been some debate whether, under the statutory power of advancement, the terms of the Advanced Trusts can include any dispositive powers for the trustees or others. That is said by some to amount to a delegation of the power of advancement, and so prima facie not permitted. After some disagreement in the lower courts, this view has been rejected by the House of Lords and does not represent the law.[50] In the precedents

---

The parents "were in a state of great indigence, and kept from the parish by a person who charitably allowed them 10s. a week". Lord Langdale said: "I think this is a case in which the Court can increase the maintenance of the children for the support of their parents ... I may give to the infants the benefit of the property, so as to assist the parents: To do so is evidently for the benefit of the infants themselves."

In any particular case, regard must be given to the exact wording of the power concerned.

[47] "It is no bar to an exercise of the power of advancement that the primary object neither requested nor consented to it"; *Re Cameron* [1999] Ch 386 para.77; *Pilkington v IRC* 40 TC 416 at p.439.

[48] Suppose a trust fund is held on trust for A and B contingently upon attaining the age of 25 in equal shares; and the trustees have the statutory power to apply capital for the benefit of "any person contingently entitled to the capital". They can apply half the trust fund for the benefit of A; and they can apply the other half for the benefit of B separately. They cannot create discretionary trusts for the class of A and B; or create a trust of the whole fund for A for life with power to appoint to B. This is an application of capital for the benefit of A and B, collectively, as a class. Even applying the Interpretation Act principle that the singular includes the plural, it does not seem correct to construe the section to mean that this is permissible.

It is considered that the wide power of advancement in the form in this book could be exercised in favour of a class of Beneficiaries.

[49] In relation to the statutory power this is clear. An unborn beneficiary cannot be said to be "entitled" to trust property, even contingently, and so is not an object of the statutory power. It is considered that the wide power of advancement in the form used in this book could be exercised in favour of unborn beneficiaries.

[50] The view that the power of advancement is restricted in this way was championed by Lord Upjohn. He expressed this view in *Re Wills* [1959] Ch 1. The view was criticised in strong language by Dankwerts J. in *Pilkington v IRC* ("I am not quite sure what the learned Judge had in his mind ...") but repeated by Upjohn in *Pilkington* in the Court of Appeal. The law was definitively settled by the House of Lords in *Pilkington* 40 TC 416. For the terms of the advanced trusts approved by the House of Lords included protective trusts, i.e. they included discretionary trusts. This is absolutely right in principle, it is respectfully submitted, because any powers exercised by the trustees of a new trust are not the powers of advancement, delegated; they are new powers created by the exercise of the powers of advancement. See 11.5 (The problem of narrow powers of appointment). Many of the other cases also authorised settled advances with dispositive powers of some kind. *Lewin on Trusts* agrees: (18th edn, 2008) para.32–20. The contrary view must necessarily involve the conclusion that the decision of the House of Lords was *per incuriam*.

in this book, however, the question does not arise since trustees have a wide power of delegation.

The advanced trusts are governed by the perpetuity and accumulation rules as they apply to the original trust.[51]

One conclusion to draw from all this is that the drafter should include in a trust all three overriding powers: powers of appointment, resettlement and advancement. He should not rely on one to do the work of the others.

A narrowly drafted trust will generally include a power of advancement but no power of appointment or resettlement. In such a case the trustees still have some scope to alter the terms of the trust, or to transfer to a new trust, by use of the power of advancement. This is a matter of considerable practical importance.

---

[51] However, where a common law perpetuity period applies, the advanced trusts can include an appropriate "Royal Lives" period even if this was not found in the original trust. See 12.5 (Appointment creating royal lives clause).

CHAPTER 12

EXERCISING OVERRIDING POWERS

Who should draft deeds of appointment?

The drafting of deeds of appointment (and other documentation supplemental to existing trusts) is more difficult than drafting a new trust. Save for more straightforward deeds, such as absolute appointments to a beneficiary, or appointments of new trustees, the practitioner who does not have considerable experience of trust documentation should delegate the work to specialist Chancery Counsel.[1] The same applies to the drafting of new trusts in non-standard form. A fair test of competence is whether the drafter has a working knowledge of *Thomas on Powers*.[2] In the words of a leading practitioner:

12.1

> The reality is that the use of defective or inadequate trust instruments produces far more work for the specialist Bar, when things go wrong (or, rather, when it is appreciated that they are going wrong) than if a suitable trust instrument had been settled in the first place.[3]

Drafting is deceptively difficult: an inexpert drafter skates on thin ice, the more innocent of danger, the more at risk.

How to instruct counsel

Where counsel is instructed it is almost always best to send the relevant information and instruct counsel to prepare the draft. It is more time-consuming, more costly and ultimately less satisfactory for counsel to settle another person's draft than to start afresh.

12.2

---

[1] A list can be obtained from the Chancery Bar Association *www.chba.org.uk*.
[2] 1st edn, 1998.
[3] Robert Venables QC, *Non-Resident Trusts* (8th edn, 2000), para.3.1.1.

Drafting deeds of appointment

Parties

12.3 The trustees jointly form one party to the deed. The drafting may need to distinguish between (1) the trustees who make the appointment and (2) the trustees from time to time (i.e. including future trustees). The precedents in this book refer to the former as "the Present Trustees". The more cumbersome title is "the Appointors". There will not usually be any other party to the deed except where a consent is needed to the appointment.

If a Deed of Appointment has only one party it is said to be made "by" that party. If two or more, it is said to be made "between" the parties. It is a solecism to say:

> This appointment is made [date] between A, B and C ("the Trustees")...

Useful recitals

12.4 The recommended practice is to give recitals setting out the following:

(1) The appointment is supplemental to:

    (a) the settlement (or the will and relevant codicils);
    (b) relevant deeds of appointment (but not irrelevant ones such as those which have been revoked or absolute appointments of capital).

The form is as follows:

> This deed is supplemental to the following:
>
> (1) The settlement ("the Settlement") made [date] between (1) ... and (2)(a) ... (b) ...
> (2) The Deed of Appointment ("the 1994 Appointment")[4] made [date] between, *etc.*

(Add the numbering for ease of reading and avoid the words "one part" "other part".) When there are a large number of supplemental deeds, it is easiest to set out the list in a schedule.

(2) The power being exercised. This saves readers from looking back, concentrates the drafter's mind on what he is doing and satisfies the requirement of showing intention to exercise the power.[5]

---

[4] It is a matter of style whether to describe earlier deeds as "the 1994 Appointment", etc. or "the First Appointment", etc.

[5] Of course "An express reference to the power, though much to be preferred, is not essential, provided that an intention to exercise that power is manifested in substance"; *Thomas on Powers* (1st edn, 1998) pp. 236–238.

(3) The identity of the trustees. It is not necessary to recite all the deeds of appointment of new trustees.

(4) If s.11 TLATA 1996 (consultation with beneficiaries) applies, which is unusual,[6] that the trustees have acted in accordance with its requirements—copy the statutory wording.

Useless recitals

Do not bother to say:

The Trustees wish to exercise the power of appointment in the following manner.

It is not usually necessary or useful to set out a schedule of the assets of the trust fund. (In complex cases it is not uncommon to find an asset accidentally omitted, thus raising an obvious question of the extent of the appointed fund.)

The deed is not subject to stamp duty, SDRT or SDLT.[7]

Appointment creating royal lives clause

12.5 A full discussion of perpetuities is outside the scope of this book. One common question arises where a power of appointment or advancement is exercised under a settlement governed by the *common law* rule against perpetuities (either a pre-1964 settlement or a post-1964 settlement which does not specify a fixed perpetuity period). It is sometimes desired to create a new perpetuity period consisting of "royal lives" in being at the date of the original settlement. This is plainly permissible.[8] It is not possible

---

[6] This arises in relation to an interest in possession trust whose trust property includes land:

(1) If the trust is made on or after 1 January 1997 *and* s.11 is not excluded. It is usually excluded: see 7.18 (Consultation with beneficiaries).

(2) If the trust is made before 1 January 1997 *and* the settlor has directed s.11 to apply. (But this never happens in practice.)

[7] See 29.16 (Stamp duties).

[8] (1) The common law rule is that every interest must vest within 21 years after the determination of lives in being at the date of the trust. The "royal lives" will satisfy this because they were in being at that time. It is not the case that the lives in being must be specified at the date of the trust and an appointment or advancement could not bring in other lives in being. That is often done with other lives and "royal lives" can be no different. See, generally, Maudsley, *The Modern Law of Perpetuities*, 1979, page 94ff. (2) Even if that were wrong, the appointment or advancement is valid under the so-called "second look" principle: see *Thomas on Powers*, 1st edn, para.4-31. (3) This is the general practice of conveyancers. See e.g. *Re Wills* [1964] Ch 219 where a "royal lives" clause was inserted without criticism from the judge.

I add for completeness that the Law Commission Report No.251 (Rules against Perpetuities and Excessive Accumulations) accessible on *www.lawcom.gov.uk* para.4.30 does describe this issue as never having been "finally settled". However that is only because no one has seriously argued the contrary view.

to specify a fixed perpetuity period by an appointment, even under a post-1964 settlement. That can only be done in the original settlement.[9]

Some points to watch in drafting deeds of appointment

12.6 These include:

(1) time limits imposed by the trust;[10]

(2) the rules against perpetuities and accumulations;

(3) in discretionary will trusts, appointment within three months of death;[11]

(4) self-dealing rule, if appointment may benefit the trustee;

(5) fraud on a power, if a non-beneficiary may benefit directly or indirectly;

(6) the width of the power: see 11.5 (Narrow powers of appointment), check there are no restrictions tucked away, e.g. in a settlor exclusion clause[12] or conflict of interest clause;[13]

(7) inheritance tax:

(a) the burden and incidence of IHT on any transfer of value made by the appointment; loss of life tenant's nil rate band;
(b) insurance against IHT;
(c) notice under s.57(3) IHTA 1984 (to use transferor's annual IHT exemptions);[14]

---

[9] Section 1 PAA 1964.
[10] Is this unnecessary to say? It is not. A time limit was overlooked with the consequence of invalidity despite ingenious arguments in *Breadner v Granville-Grossman* [2001] Ch 523.
[11] See 18.11 (Best form of will for testator who is married or a civil partner).
[12] See 13.15 (Exclusion of additional and indirect settlors), 13.17 (Extending the settlor exclusion clause to exclude trustees).
[13] See 6.13 (Conflicts of interest). If the STEP Standard Provisions apply, note the conflict of interest rule in cl.9.
[14] HMRC practice is set out in the IHT Manual 14170:

"The form for giving the notice is form 222. It does not have to be sent to this office, but the trustees are instructed on the form to retain it in case it is subsequently required by the IR."

The former CTO Advanced Instruction Manual continued:

"You should not ask for the notice unless you suspect abuse—e.g. where the annual exemption is claimed twice for the same year. Although the notice should be given within six months of the transaction, you need not check this. You should not disallow the exemption solely for the reason that it was given out of time."

This is no doubt the text which in the published IHT Manual "has been withheld because of exemptions in the Freedom of Information Act 2000". Accordingly, it should be safe in practice not to complete this form in straightforward cases.

(d) if the trust holds business or agricultural property, the effect of s.113A and s.124A IHTA 1984 on earlier transfers of value within the last seven years.

(8) CGT: possible charge under s.71 TCGA 1992; possibility of hold-over relief;

(9) trustee liabilities:

(a) if the appointment transfers assets to a beneficiary absolutely, consider the need for (i) expressly preserving a trustee lien; (ii) an indemnity from the beneficiary; and (iii) perhaps, security for that indemnity;[15]

(b) if the appointment creates separate sub-funds, and the trustees have existing liabilities, consider how the separate funds are to share the burden of the liabilities; this arises especially in appointments in the course of administration of an estate of a deceased person;

(10) if a living person has made a gift to the trust by will, a codicil to the will is needed: see 17.13 (Gift by will to existing trust).

It is good practice to send a draft to the settlor and beneficiaries concerned, to give them the opportunity to comment or clear misunderstandings.[16]

Example deed of appointment

This is an example of an appointment with the following characteristics: **12.7**

(1) it divides a trust fund into two shares each held on IP trusts

(2) the trust retains a wide power of appointment.[17]

It is assumed the power of appointment is wide, as in the forms in this book.

This deed of appointment is made [date] by

(1) [Name] of [address] ("the Settlor")[18] and
(2) [Name] of [address]

(together called "the Present Trustees").

---

[15] See Chapter 31 (Indemnities for trustees).
[16] This might have avoided the problem which arose in *Abacus v Barr* [2003] Ch 409 at [27] where "the trustees perhaps surprisingly failed to seek from the settlor an expression of his wishes in documentary form or provide him with a copy of the proposed appointment before it was executed".
[17] See 14.12 (IP forms for two life tenants).
[18] It is assumed in this draft that the settlor is one of the two trustees: the definition of settlor is used in recital A(1). Contrast the draft resolution at 12.12 which concerns a will trust and at 12.13 (where the settlor is not one of the trustees).

WHEREAS:

(A) This deed is supplemental to the following:

(1) A settlement ("the Settlement") made [date] between (1) the Settlor and (2)(a) the Settlor (b) [name of other original trustee].
(2) An appointment ("the First Deed of Appointment") made [date] by the Present Trustees.

(B) Clause ... of the Settlement confers on the Trustees the following power ("the Power of Appointment"):
[set out power]

(C) The Present Trustees are the present trustees of the Settlement.

Now this deed witnesses as follows:

1. In this deed:

    (1) "**Gillian**" means [name] of [address].
    (2) "**Giles**" means [name] of [address].
    (3) Words defined in the Settlement have the same meaning in this deed.

2. In exercise of the Power of Appointment[19] the Present Trustees irrevocably appoint[20] that they hold the Trust Fund on the following terms.
3. Subject to the Overriding Powers conferred below the Trustees shall divide the Trust Fund into two equal shares ("Gillian's Fund" and "Giles' Fund").
4. **Gillian's Fund**

    Subject to the overriding powers conferred below:

    (1) The Trustees shall pay the income of Gillian's Fund to Gillian during her life.
    (2) Subject to that, if Gillian dies during the Trust Period, the Trustees shall pay the income of her fund to her widower during his life.
    (3) Subject to that, during the Trust Period, the Trustees shall pay or apply the income of Gillian's Fund to or for the benefit of any Beneficiaries as the Trustees think fit.

5. **Giles' Fund**

    [Repeat clause 4 with appropriate modifications]

6. **Overriding Powers**

    [set out the standard overriding powers in this book]

8. This appointment shall carry all the income payable after the date of this deed and no apportionment shall be made.[21]
9. Subject to that the Settlement as amended by the First Deed of Appointment shall stand.[22]

In witness *etc*

---

[19] Do not add: *... or any other power enabling them* ... . The trustees should usually know which power they are exercising! Where there is doubt these words may be appropriate; but a power will in appropriate circumstances be taken to be exercised by implication, so even then it makes no difference whether these words are added or not; see, e.g. *Re Pennant* [1970] Ch 75.

[20] Do not say: "... appoint *and declare*"; or "... appoint *and direct*", this is pointless synonymy.

[21] This clause is not strictly necessary if the trust excludes the statutory apportionment rule, which is usually the case: 21.54 (Statutory apportionment) but it is better to make it plain.

[22] This would of course be implied, but it is better to make it plain.

Points to watch in drafting transfers to another settlement

12.8 The points at 12.6 (Some points to watch in drafting deeds of appointment) apply here, but in addition:

(1) It may be necessary first to alter the terms of the transferor or transferee settlement to ensure that there is no breach of the rules against perpetuities and accumulations, to satisfy the settlor exclusion clause of the transferor settlement, or to satisfy restrictions on the power of transfer (see the draft below for an example).

(2) Especially for pre-1970 settlements, watch out for illegitimate/adopted beneficiaries who may not be "beneficiaries" under the old settlement and may easily and unexpectedly be "beneficiaries" under the transferee settlement.

(3) The transfer will govern trust capital (including accumulated income) but some income of discretionary trusts may be received and not yet distributed or accumulated. There are two ways to deal with such income:

   (a) The trustees may resolve to accumulate the income just before executing the transfer (so the accumulated income passes with the rest of the trust capital).
   (b) The income may be distributed (before or after the execution of the transfer) under the terms of the old settlement.

Example exercise of power to transfer to another settlement

12.9 *This deed illustrates a transfer of funds from one settlement (conveniently defined in the draft as "the Old Settlement") to another.*

   This deed is made [date] between
   (1) [name] of [address] ("the Settlor") of the one part and
   (2) (a) the Settlor and
       (b) [name] of [address]
   ("the Trustees") of the other part.

   WHEREAS:

   (A) This deed is supplemental to a Settlement ("the Old Settlement") made *etc*
   (B) The Trustees are the trustees of the Old Settlement.
   (C) Under clause 1.6 of the Old Settlement "the Beneficiaries" includes:

"1.6.4 Any Person or class of Persons nominated to the Trustees by:
1.6.4.1 the Settlor or
1.6.4.2 two Beneficiaries (after the death of the Settlor)
and whose nomination is accepted in writing by the Trustees."

(D) Clause 3.2 of the Old Settlement confers on the Trustees the following power ("the Power of Resettlement"):

"The Trustees may by deed declare that they hold any Trust Property on trust to transfer it to trustees of a Qualifying Settlement, to hold on the terms of that Qualifying Settlement, freed and released from the terms of this Settlement.

"A Qualifying Settlement" here means any settlement, wherever established, under which every Person who may benefit is (or would if living be) a Beneficiary of this Settlement."[23]

Now this deed witnesses as follows:

1. In this deed

    (1) Terms defined in the Old Settlement have the same meaning in this deed.
    (2) "**The 1996 Settlement**" means the settlement made *etc*

2. In exercise of the power conferred by clause 1.6 of the Old Settlement the Settlor nominates and the Trustees accept as Beneficiaries the class of beneficiaries of the 1996 Settlement (so far as not already Beneficiaries).
3. In exercise of the Power of Resettlement the Trustees declare that they hold the Trust Fund on trust to transfer it to the trustees of the 1996 Settlement, to hold on the terms of the 1996 Settlement as one fund for all purposes, freed and released from the terms of the Old Settlement.

In witness *etc*

Who should draft settled advances?

12.10 The point made at 12.1 (Who should draft deeds of appointment?) applies even more to the drafting of settled advances:

> It cannot be sufficiently stressed that this is highly technical work which requires the advice of a trusts and tax expert. The penalty for failing to take such advice could well be nullity.[24]

Quite true; but the heavier penalty is likely to be a fiscal one.

---

[23] This is the form used in the first five editions of this book. The form in subsequent editions is slightly wider.
[24] Robert Venables QC, *Non-Resident Trusts* (8th edn, 2000), para.10.6.3.

Drafting resolutions of advancement

12.11 The exercise of a power of advancement in the standard form does not need a deed. In the case of a simple advance of capital, all that is needed is a cheque (or transfer of an asset) though a written trustee resolution would be good practice. In the case of a settled advance, a trustee resolution is the appropriate form. The content will be similar to a deed of appointment.

It is good practice to say for whose benefit the power is being exercised.[25]

The points at 12.6 (Points to watch in drafting appointments) and 12.8 (Points to watch in drafting transfers to another settlement) apply here too. In addition, consider whether it is desired to transfer funds to a new settlement for CGT, and review SP 7/84 to ensure the draft has the desired effect.

Example resolution of advancement used to alter terms of trust

12.12 *The following example was drafted for a trust under which a share was held for John for life, with remainder to his children absolutely. This poor form would leave John's widow unprovided for, incur an IHT charge on his death which could be deferred or avoided if he left a widow, and give the children absolute interests at too young an age. There was fortunately a power of advancement for the benefit of John which is used here to give John power to create more appropriate trusts.*

The form illustrates the slight variants appropriate to a will trust.

This Trustee Resolution is made [date] by

(1) [Name] of [address] and
(2) [Name] of [address]
("The Present Trustees").

Whereas:

(A) This Resolution is supplemental to the will ("the Will") made [date] by [name] ("the Testator").
(B) The Testator died on [date] and probate was granted on [date] by the [name] registry.
(C) The Present Trustees are the present trustees of the Settlement constituted by the Will.

---

[25] In *Re Hampden* [1977] TR 177 also belatedly reported in [2001] WTLR 195 accessible on www.kessler.co.uk the advance contained a "slightly unfortunate" recital stating that the trustees intended to benefit A. In fact they intended to benefit A's father. The Judge accepted affidavit evidence to this effect and (correctly) disregarded the erroneous recital. For another example see *Osborne v Steel Barrel Co Ltd* 24 TC 293 at p.305: "As between the Crown and the Appellant company neither is bound by an untrue recital".

(D) Clause 6(6) of the Will confers on the Trustees the following power ("the Power of Advancement"):
"The Trustees may in their uncontrolled discretion from time to time during the lifetime of John by mortgage or sale of the share or any part thereof or assets comprised therein raise any monies (up to the total value of the share) and pay or apply the same to or for the benefit of John in such manner as the Trustees shall think fit".
(E) The Present Trustees now wish to exercise the Power of Advancement by applying John's Share for the benefit of John so as to enable John to make the most appropriate provision for John's family.

The Present Trustees hereby resolve as follows:

1. In this Resolution:
   (1) Terms defined in the Will have the same meaning in this Resolution.
   (2) "**John**" means [full name]
   (3) "**The Family of John**" means

   (a) the children and remoter issue of John.
   (b) the spouses and former spouses (whether or not remarried) of (a) above and
   (c) the widow of John.

   (4) "**John's Share**" means the share of the Trust Fund the income of which is payable to John under the terms of clause 6 of the Will.

2. In exercise of the Power of Advancement, the Present Trustees apply John's Share for the benefit of John by declaring that they hold John's Share in their capacity as the Trustees upon the terms of the Settlement, but as if clause 6(2) of the Will provided as follows:

   "From and after the death of John the capital and income of the said share or so much thereof respectively as shall not have become vested or been paid or applied under any trust or power affecting the same shall be held upon trust for all or any one or more of the Family of John at such time and if more than one in such shares with such provision for maintenance education advancement and otherwise at the discretion of the Trustees or any persons and with such gifts over and generally in such manner for the benefit of the Family of John or some or one of them as John shall by deed or deeds revocable during the Trust Period or irrevocable or by will or codicil taking effect during the Trust Period appoint and it is declared for the avoidance of doubt that this power extends to the creation of discretionary trusts and powers for the benefit of the Family of John and in default of and subject to any such appointment upon trust for all or any the children of John born within the Trust Period who shall attain the age of twenty one or who (without attaining that age) shall be living at the expiration of the Trust Period if more than one in equal shares."

   This is emphatically not the "plain English" form which would have been preferred. It is however the wording used elsewhere in the documentation of this trust, and it is probably better in supplemental documentation to use consistent forms throughout.

3. Subject to that, the Will shall stand.

Signed by the Present Trustees

....

....

[date]

Example resolution of advancement used to transfer property to two separate settlements

This resolution illustrates a power of advancement used to transfer separate funds to two separate settlements. The terms of the new settlements would need careful consideration to ensure that the transfer was for the benefit of the objects of the power of advancement.

12.13

This Trustee Resolution is made [date] by

(1) [Name] of [address] and
(2) [Name] of [address]
("the Present Trustees")

Whereas

(A) This Resolution is supplemental to a Settlement (**"the Old Settlement"**) made [date] between (1) [name of settlor] and (2) [name of trustees].
(B) Clause 6 of the Old Settlement confers on the Trustees the following power ("the Power of Advancement"):

"NOTWITHSTANDING anything to the contrary hereinbefore contained the Trustees may at any time in their absolute discretion apply for the benefit of any Beneficiary the whole or any part of the capital of his or her share (and any accumulations added thereto) freed and discharged from the provisions of this Deed ..."

(C) The Trustees now wish to exercise the Power of Advancement by applying each Beneficiary's share for his benefit by transferring that share to a settlement in which that Beneficiary shall be entitled to an interest in possession.
The trustees hereby resolve as follows:

1. Definitions

In this Resolution:

1.1 Terms defined in the Old Settlement have the same meaning in this Resolution.
1.2 **"Adam"** means [full name].
1.3 **"Danny"** means [full name].
1.4 **"The Adam Smith Settlement 2008"** means the settlement of that name made the same date as this resolution by [parties].
1.5 **"The Danny Smith Settlement 2008"** means the settlement of that name made the same date as this resolution by [parties].[26]

2. Advancement

2.1 In exercise of the Power of Advancement the Trustees resolve to apply Adam's Share for the benefit of Adam by declaring that they hold the same on trust to transfer it to the Trustees of the Adam Smith Settlement 2008 on the terms of that Settlement as an accretion to the Trust Fund

---

[26] "Adam's Share" and "Danny's Share" would also need to be defined unless those terms are already defined in the Old Settlement.

of that Settlement freed and discharged from the terms of the Old Settlement.

2.2 In exercise of the Power of Advancement the Trustees resolve to apply Danny's Share for the benefit of Danny by declaring that they hold the same on trust to transfer it to the Trustees of the Danny Smith Settlement 2008 on the terms of that Settlement as an accretion to the Trust Fund of that Settlement freed and discharged from the terms of the Old Settlement.

Signed by the Trustees [*etc*]

Example resolution of advancement used to transfer property from one settlement to another

12.14 The difference between this form and the above is that the trust funds become held as separate sub-funds of a single new settlement. Replace clause 2 above with the following:

2 Advancement

2.1 In exercise of the Power of Advancement the Trustees resolve to apply Adam's Share for the benefit of Adam by declaring that they hold the same on trust to transfer it to the Trustees of the William Smith Grandchildren Settlement 2008 to hold as an accretion to the share of Adam under that Settlement freed and discharged from the terms of the Old Settlement.

2.2 In exercise of the Power of Advancement the Trustees resolve to apply Danny's Share for the benefit of Danny by declaring that they hold the same on trust to transfer it to the Trustees of the William Smith Grandchildren Settlement 2008 to hold as an accretion to the share of Danny under that Settlement freed and discharged from the terms of the Old Settlement.

Procedure after execution of deed of appointment/resettlement/advancement

12.15 The following is a checklist of possible issues (which will all not arise in every case):

(1) Transfer legal title to beneficiaries/new trustees (if appropriate).

(2) Insurance against IHT risk (if appointment is a PET).

(3) Arrangements for loss of nil rate band; contrast 28.12 (Loss of NRB).

(4) Returns and other matters:

    (a) IHT account if appointment is a chargeable transfer.
    (b) CGT claim for holdover relief or for losses.

(c) Inform beneficiaries. Concealment may be taken as evidence of a fraud on a power.[27] Contrast 29.13 (Returns and other matters).

---

[27] As in *Duke of Portland v Topham* (1864) 11 HLC 32.

CHAPTER 13

SETTLOR EXCLUSION AND DEFAULT CLAUSES

Why exclude the settlor and spouse/civil partner?

13.1 The position is complicated, because there are at least three different sets of anti-avoidance provisions to consider. The rules are internally inconsistent and sometimes irrational. Discussion is also made more difficult because the drafter uses the same term "interest in the settlement" in two[1] different senses, which I shall call "the income tax sense" and "the CGT sense". The following sets out the main points for the trust drafter, but is not comprehensive.

(1) If the settlor has an "interest in the settlement" (for income tax purposes) trust income will in effect be taxed at the settlor's rates. See s.624 ITTOIA. This rule may increase the IT due. It is usually desired to avoid this rule, so it is necessary to exclude the settlor (and the settlor's spouse/civil partner) from benefit under the trust.[2] However, since trusts which accumulate income pay income tax at the top rate (a stealth tax increase of 2004) this rule may make no difference (except for deductible expenses). Further, dividend income of discretionary trusts which is distributed to higher rate taxpayers effectively bears tax at more than the settlor's top rate, so the application of this rule may actually reduce tax rates.

(2) If the settlor has an "interest in the settlement" (for CGT purposes) capital gains will in effect be taxed at the settlor's rates. See s.77 TCGA 1992. Since the trust rate is 18% apart from the almost trivial trust CGT exemption, this can only reduce the rate of tax, it will not

---

[1] In fact the expression "interest in the settlement" is used in three different senses, as it has different definitions for the purposes of the income tax settlement provisions, s.77 and s.86 TCGA 1992. However, s.86 only concerns offshore trusts and is not discussed here.
[2] 5.31 (Settlor and spouse/civil partner as beneficiaries).

increase it. It is not worthwhile arranging that the settlor does not have an "interest in the settlement" (for CGT purposes) merely to avoid s.77. But see below on CGT hold-over relief.

(3) If (in short) overriding powers may benefit the settlor, the settlor may be subject to IHT on the settled property as if he had never given it away. See s.102 FA 1986.

(4) If the settlor has an interest in the settlement (for IT purposes) the pre-owned assets rules need consideration. However, in practice a problem here would be exceptional.[3]

None of these problems arise for a will trust; a testator cannot benefit under his own will.

CGT hold-over relief

Further restrictions may be necessary if it is desired to claim CGT hold-over relief on the gift to the trust. This relief is not available if the settlor has an "interest in the trust" for CGT purposes.[4] A settlor has an interest in the settlement (for CGT purposes) if he, his spouse/civil partner, or *dependent children* may benefit. The daft rule excluding hold-over relief if dependent children may benefit was introduced in the FA 2006. It is supposedly justified by a (misconceived) analogy with s.626 ITTOIA, but it rests, perhaps, on a general desire to discriminate fiscally against the use of trusts. But there it is.

The position depends on whether or not the settlor has any dependent children.[5]

13.2

Settlor has dependent children

It is necessary to exclude the settlor, spouse/civil partner and dependent children of the settlor. The dependent children need only be excluded while they are dependent: they can benefit once they reach the age of 18.[6]

---

[3] See Chapter 51, *Taxation of Foreign Domiciliaries*, 7th edn, 2008, Key Haven Publications (Pre-owned Assets).
[4] Section 169B TCGA 1992.
[5] We adopt the terminology of the TCGA, under which "dependent child" means a child or step-child who:
    (a) is under the age of 18 years,
    (b) is unmarried, and
    (c) does not have a civil partner.
[6] Or (for completeness) if they become married/civil partners under 18, but in practice that is almost wholly academic. Out of 248,000 marriages in 2005, 335 bridegrooms and 1420 brides were under the age of 18; (National Statistics Series FN2, no.231, Marriage Divorce and adoption statistics table 3.18, 3.19).

Settlor has no dependent children

The position is different if the settlor does not have dependent children and is not expected to have any dependent children shortly. Here there is a choice:

(1) Exclude all future dependent children (while they are dependent children).

(2) Not to exclude future dependent children.

The second course is more trouble, but more flexible. If, adopting the second course, the settlor actually acquires dependent children within six years, CGT hold-over relief is lost.[7] However, if the children are acquired later, no tax problem arises.[8] A settlor may acquire dependent children in one of two ways:

(1) Becoming a parent.

(2) Becoming a step-parent of a dependent child (marrying the actual parent).

In either case, the settlor will have notice of what is about to happen. Provided the trustees act before the settlor acquires a dependent child, by excluding the dependent child (during dependency), no clawback charge arises.

Excluding the settlor: drafting

(1) Direct benefit

13.3 The exclusion of the settlor is not as straightforward as one might have thought. There are five ways by which settlors may benefit under their trust; each requires separate means to counteract it.

13.4 The trust may make express provision for the benefit of the settlor. This should be easy enough to avoid. The following should be noted.

Trustees to pay the costs of setting up the trust. This is not permitted. These costs will usually be liabilities of the settlor; a provision of this kind operates for

---

[7] See s.169C(2)(b) TCGA 1992.
[8] It is assumed that there is no arrangement within s.169C(2)(b) TCGA 1992.

the benefit of the settlor. Until the costs are paid, income tax, CGT and IHT anti-avoidance provisions may apply.

Trustees to pay tax on gift to trust. A gift to a disabled trust is a PET and so an IHT charge may arise if the donor does not survive seven years. This tax charge is primarily the liability of the trustees.[9] Accordingly it is unnecessary to say that the trustees shall pay the tax. The same applies to the additional IHT payable on a chargeable transfer (such as a gift to a discretionary trust) which may arise if the donor dies within seven years of the gift.[10]   **13.5**

A provision that the trustees *may* pay the IHT if the donor dies within seven years raises a number of difficulties and is not recommended.

The trustees should not be directed or empowered to pay CGT arising on the transfer to the trust; HMRC take the view that this allows the settlor to benefit from the trust.

(2)   Resulting trust

The settlor may benefit under a resulting trust. This is prevented by an effective Default Clause: see 13.23 (Default clause).   **13.6**

(3)   Power to benefit settlor

The settlor may benefit if the trustees have any powers which may be used to benefit him. It does not matter whether the power is in fact exercised so as to benefit the settlor; the mere possibility of benefit is disastrous. This possibility is averted by a Settlor Exclusion Clause: see 13.10 (Settlor exclusion clause).   **13.7**

(4)   Actual benefit

The settlor may benefit directly or indirectly from trust property, despite everything in the trust, by the consent of beneficiaries or through breach of trust. No feat of draftsmanship can prevent this: this problem must be dealt with through careful trust administration.   **13.8**

(5)   Reciprocal arrangements

The settlor may be excluded from his own trust, but may benefit from another trust under a reciprocal arrangement. The solution of this problem   **13.9**

---

[9] See 29.11 (Arrangements for payment of IHT on gift in case of death within seven years).
[10] The position is more complicated for IHT immediately payable on a gift to a discretionary trust (which is a chargeable transfer). This is discussed in the first edition of this book at para.4–071. However, the point is fairly academic: in practice a well advised settlor will not normally make gifts which give rise to an immediate charge to IHT.

does not lie in the trust drafting; but in the careful avoidance of arrangements which have an element of reciprocity.

It sometimes happens that spouses (or other members of one family) make trusts at the same time, and each settlor may benefit under the other's trust. It is considered that these are not (normally) "reciprocal settlements" because (normally) one trust is not made in return for the other.[11]

Settlor exclusion clause

13.10 Notwithstanding anything else in this settlement, no power conferred by this settlement shall be exercisable, and no provision shall operate so as to allow Trust Property or its income to become payable to or applicable for the benefit of the Settlor or the spouse or Civil Partner of the Settlor in any circumstances whatsoever.

This "settlor exclusion clause" is a convenient drafting technique to help to ensure that the requirements of the settlement provisions are satisfied:

(1) Trustees might have some power which could be used to benefit the settlor (or spouse or civil partner) as well as others. If all the powers are made subject to the settlor exclusion clause, it is unnecessary to exclude the settlor (or spouse) from benefit specifically under each individual power.

(2) If by some error any clause in a settlement directs a benefit be provided to the settlor (or spouse or civil partner), the settlor exclusion clause should prevent the erroneous clause from taking effect.[12]

---

[11] There is an interesting discussion of the concept of reciprocity from a sociological perspective in Zygmunt Bauman, *Postmodern Ethics*, 1993, pp.56–58, accessible on *www.kessler.co.uk*. There is no discussion in the cases, but it is suggested that Bauman is right that the essential element of reciprocity is that it affects motive. The distinction is between disinterested generosity on the one hand and conduct inspired by considerations of self-interest on the other. Reciprocity (like so much in life) offers delicate shades of grey, matters of fact and degree, which the tax system must resolve into black or white.

HMRC do not take a GWR point in these circumstances. See IHT Manual para.14453:

"Example 6
A husband and wife jointly settle an insurance policy on trusts under which there is an immediate interest in possession. The trustees have a power of appointment over the whole fund in favour of a number of persons including the settlors but each settlor is specifically excluded from benefiting from the part which (s)he settled.

The inclusion of each settlor's spouse or civil partner as an object of the trust affecting the settlor's share would not of itself make either gift a GWR."

[12] At least if it is clear which clause is erroneous: see 13.11 (When is a settlor exclusion clause appropriate?)

When is a settlor exclusion clause appropriate?

A settlor exclusion clause is usually needed whether the settlor is single, married or a civil partner; it is of course unnecessary in a will trust. Where, exceptionally, the settlor (or his spouse or civil partner) are intended to benefit under a trust it is essential to amend or omit the settlor exclusion clause as appropriate.[13]

13.11

What does a settlor exclusion clause cover?

The words of the common form settlor exclusion clause "are so wide that everyone agrees there must be some limitation placed upon them".[14] There are a number of situations where it has been held not to apply.

13.12

An obvious case is where the benefit to the settlor is "a mere voluntary application of income by a beneficiary to the settlor, outside the provisions of the trust itself".[15] For the same reason, a common form clause excluding the settlor does not prevent trustees paying capital to a child of the settlor who is a minor, even though the settlor would benefit on the intestacy of the child (and of course the child could not make a will to prevent this).

The clause does not exclude the settlor's right to reimbursement for tax paid by him on trust income or gains, under the settlement provisions.[16] This is because that right does not arise under the settlement: it arises under the statute The settlement cannot exclude a right which does not

---

[13] It happens occasionally that a settlor exclusion clause is accidentally retained in a trust intended for the principal benefit of the settlor; so in one clause the trustees are directed to pay the income to the settlor; and in another clause they are prohibited from doing so. Which clause prevails? Applying a literal construction the answer would be the settlor exclusion clause, which is stated to apply "notwithstanding anything else in the Settlement". It is suggested that a literal construction should not be applied, see 4.4 (Meaning of words v meaning of document). A similar argument was accepted in *Padmore v IRC (No.2)* [2001] STC 280. Here it was rightly held that the context showed that one provision overrode a second, even though the second provision was stated to apply "notwithstanding anything in any enactment". Rectification may be available to put matters right, if construction cannot do so.

[14] *Glyn v IRC* 30 TC 321 at 329.

[15] *Glyn v IRC* 30 TC 321 at p.329; *West v Trennery* [2003] STC 580 at para.51 (point not discussed on appeal). HMRC accept this. Helpsheet IR270 for 2005/06 provides:

"Because the words 'in any circumstances whatsoever' are so wide there are certain circumstances in which you will not be treated as having an interest even though you may have.[!] These are

- where you give money to another person absolutely (in other words, you give up any rights or control over the money). That person could decide of their own accord to give the money back to you. You will not be regarded as having an interest because the person has complete freedom to do what they want with the money."

[16] HMRC accept this: SP5/92 paras 8–10.

arise under the settlement.[17] (Suppose, for instance, that the trustees owed money to a creditor, and the creditor assigned the right to that debt to the settlor. No-one could possibly suggest that a settlor could not (as a matter of property law) enforce the debt, just because there was a settlor exclusion clause.) It may also fairly be said that reimbursement is not a "benefit" for the settlor because (looking at the matter broadly) the settlor has gained no advantage.[18] Likewise the clause does not exclude the right of a settlor-trustee to reimbursement of expenses under s.31 TA 2000.[19] For similar reasons it is considered that the clause does not exclude the settlor's right to trustee remuneration.[20]

A common form clause excluding the settlor does not prevent trustees benefiting beneficiaries who are dependents of the settlor (e.g. school fees for the settlor's children). One reason is that such a payment is generally merely an intangible, non-financial benefit to the settlor, not a "benefit" within the sense of the clause (a direct financial benefit).[21] But the same applies where the settlor is under a direct legal obligation to maintain and pay school fees for his children (such as may arise on a divorce or in other family law proceedings). Here, there is a benefit to the settlor but the benefit is not prohibited by a standard form settlor exclusion clause because it is unintended, merely incidental.[22] Likewise the clause does not prevent trustees making a payment to a divorced spouse of the settlor, even though an incidental and unintended effect may be to increase the settlor's claim for financial relief in divorce proceedings. In these cases special consideration must be given to the doctrine of fraud on a power.

Drafting the settlor exclusion clause

13.13   The draft echoes the relevant statutory provisions.[23] The words "notwithstanding anything else in this settlement" are traditional, though

---

[17] Contrast *C v C* [2005] Fam 250 para.30 also reported under the name *Charalambous v Charalambous* [2004] WTLR 1061: power to vary nuptial settlement not excluded by Jersey proper law and exclusive jurisdiction clauses because "the power to vary is derived not from the settlement but from the matrimonial regime of the state".

[18] See (if authority is needed) *IRC v Lactagol* 35 TC 230 and *Wilson v Clayton* [2005] STC 157. A third reason for reaching this conclusion is that the payment is merely administrative and the settlor exclusion clause applies only to dispositive matters: see 16.2 (Significance of administrative/dispositive distinction).

[19] *West v Trennery* [2003] STC 580, paras 41–44 (point not discussed on appeal).

[20] 21.64 (Can the settlor charge if he is a trustee but there is a settlor exclusion clause?).

[21] On this distinction see 11.11 (Power of advancement used to create new trusts).

[22] *Fuller v Evans* [2000] 1 All ER 636, [2000] WTLR 5, accessible on *www.kessler.co.uk*. It is interesting (and relevant, because some have doubted the correctness of *Fuller v Evans*) to note that the courts reached exactly the same conclusion two centuries ago in relation to comparable wording in the Mortmain Acts: *Att.-Gen. v Munby* (1816) 1 Merivale 327, accessible on *www.kessler.co.uk*.

[23] For an example of a (perhaps deliberately) botched settlor exclusion clause see *IRC v Botnar* [1999] STC 711. *Botnar* turns on the trust's unusually worded settlor exclusion clause, It has no

unnecessary; Potter and Monroe's *Tax Planning with Precedents* (looseleaf) omits them.

Joint settlors

13.14 Where one trust is made by joint settlors (most commonly husband and wife), each must be excluded (together with their spouses or civil partners and, if hold-over relief is desired, dependent children). See 10.11 (Form where trust made by joint settlors).

Exclusion of additional and indirect settlors

13.15 Our draft assumes the term "the Settlor" is defined elsewhere in the trust, and excludes only the person so defined.

However, for tax purposes, any person who (in short) provides funds for the purposes of a settlement is a "settlor". To avoid the income tax and CGT settlement provisions every such "settlor" must be excluded from benefit under the settlement. Some drafters therefore extend the settlor exclusion clause so as to exclude not only the settlor named in the trust, but also any other person who provides any funds, directly or indirectly, and their spouses/civil partners. This has the attraction of possibly[24] defeating HMRC arguments that a beneficiary has provided property indirectly for the trust and so is taxed under the income tax or CGT settlement provisions.

The drawbacks, however, are considerable. There may be uncertainty as to whether a person has "provided funds" for the purposes of the settlement. The concept of "providing funds" is difficult and has generated a substantial case law.[25] Perhaps it is necessary to use vague language in anti-avoidance provisions. The trust drafter should hesitate to follow that lead. There may be substantial tax charges and disastrous practical consequences if any funds were inadvertently "provided" by a beneficiary or spouse/civil partner. Paying trustees' fees, or some minor expenditure on trust property, may suffice. So might working for less than full remuneration for a company owned by the trust. An interesting (one hopes theoretical) question arises if the default beneficiary provides funds for the trust. Does

---

general importance. This is obvious but if authority is needed see *West v Trennery* [2003] STC 580, paras 45–51. The point was not discussed on appeal. However, *Botnar* illustrates the danger of not following the wording of a statutory provision, where it is intended to satisfy that statutory provision.

[24] Whether or not this argument will be valid depends on the circumstances. The point is too theoretical to justify a full discussion here, but the conclusion of any detailed analysis must be that in many, if not most, cases an extended settlor exclusion clause would not avail the taxpayer.

[25] This is discussed in detail in James Kessler QC, *Taxation of Foreign Domiciliaries*, 7th edn (2008), Key Haven Publications, Ch.54 (Who is the Settlor?).

the default trust then fail, and if so, is there a resulting trust to the settlor or *bona vacantia*?[26]

A variant is to exclude anyone who "adds" property to the trust fund. This raises the same problems, with the further problem of what is meant by "adding". Does it mean the same as the statutory wording ("providing property directly or indirectly"), or is it narrower? There is plenty of scope for litigation on that point.

This book does not extend the settlor exclusion clause to exclude anyone who adds or provides funds. If such a clause is used, it is recommended that each settlor is only excluded from the property he actually adds or provides. Otherwise a trivial provision of property to the trust may have drastic repercussions. The drafting becomes complex and is rarely attempted.

Reference to "spouse" in settlor exclusion clause

13.16 It is necessary to refer to the "spouse" or "civil partner" of the Settlor in the settlor exclusion clause and wrong to identify the individual who is the spouse/civil partner by name. This is for two reasons. First, so that after the death of the settlor, the surviving spouse/civil partner, no longer a "spouse/civil partner", falls outside the clause. The widow may then benefit under the trust.[27] Second, in case the settlor should remarry or enter into a new civil partnership: it is necessary to exclude future spouses/civil partners.

The standard settlor exclusion clause before 1995 provided simply that the trust property should not be used to benefit:

> The settlor or the spouse of the settlor.

This form was apt to exclude the settlor's wife or husband. It did not exclude the settlor's widow or widower, since a widow or widower was not a spouse.[28] Nor would it exclude a divorcee or a civil partner.

Since the Finance Act 1995 the term "spouse" in the settlement provisions is defined: see 5.32 (Meaning of "spouse"/"civil partner"). This will not affect the construction of the standard form settlor exclusion clause because the statutory definition will not apply for the purposes of the trust.

---

[26] 13.21 ("No resulting trust for the settlor").
[27] 5.33 (Settlor's surviving spouse/civil partner as beneficiary).
[28] *Vestey v IRC* 31 TC 1.

Unnecessary provisions in settlor exclusion clause

Extending the settlor exclusion clause to exclude trustees

13.17 In the days of estate duty, some practitioners extended the settlor exclusion clause to exclude trustees, but even then this was "unnecessary and overly restrictive".[29] See 6.3 (Beneficiaries as trustees).

No reservation of benefit

13.18 Some drafters provide that:

> The Trust Fund shall be possessed and enjoyed to the entire exclusion of the Settlor and of any benefit to him by contract or otherwise.

This echoes the IHT Gift with Reservation provision.[30] There is no advantage in this form: the drafting cannot alter one way or another the question of whether the settlor actually enjoys any direct or indirect benefit from the trust fund. The conventional form, excluding entitlement to benefit, does all that documentation can do. This particular form does not even accurately reproduce the IHT rules (unless a further clause is put in to incorporate the rules in FA 1986, Sch. 20, para. 6 but that is never done in practice).

13.19 The effect of the standard settlor exclusion clause is to prohibit the trustees making a loan to the settlor (or spouse or civil partner) on beneficial or favourable terms. In the drafts in this book, it remains possible for trustees to lend money to the settlor on commercial terms as an investment. Some drafters prohibit this. This course is not taken here: the existence of the power to make the loan has no adverse tax consequences (though tax problems may arise if such a loan is actually made).[31]

13.20 One occasionally sees this form:

> If any person who enjoys any benefit hereunder or under any exercise of any power conferred by this settlement should marry the Settlor then this settlement and any appointment made pursuant to any power hereby conferred shall upon such marriage take effect as if such person were dead.

---

[29] *Tankel v Tankel* [1999] 1 FLR 679; [1999] Fam. Law 93 accessible on *www.kessler.co.uk*. In this amusing (except to those concerned) case the clause excluding trustee-beneficiaries from benefit was later overlooked and subsequent appointments were void. An attempt to rectify the clause rightly failed on the facts.

[30] Section 102 FA 1986. This is a different rule than that adopted by the Income Tax settlement provisions. The CGT settlement provision is different again.

[31] In brief:
  (1) If the trust has "undistributed income", s.633 ITTOIA 2005
  (2) If the trust is non-resident: s.720 ITA 2007.
  (3) The loan may not be deductible from the settlor's estate for IHT: s.103 FA 1986.

It is considered that the standard settlor exclusion clause would in principle exclude any beneficiary who married the settlor. So a provision of this kind is not necessary to satisfy the tax requirements. Moreover the possibility that the settlor should marry a person who enjoys some benefit under the trust seems exceedingly remote. Accordingly this provision is unnecessary.

"No resulting trust for the settlor"

13.21   Some drafters provide in the settlor exclusion clause that:

> *There shall be no resulting trust to the Settlor;* or
> *Under no circumstances shall any interest be taken under this deed by the Settlor.*

The correct way to avoid a resulting trust is to use an effective default clause; see 13.23 (Default clause). If this is done there can be no resulting trust, and it is not necessary or appropriate to exclude one. Accordingly this form is not used in this book.

If a badly drafted trust does have not have a proper default clause, and does exclude resulting trusts with a form like the above, what (to the extent that the validly declared trusts do not take effect) is the result? Some say that there is nonetheless a resulting trust and a form of words simply purporting to prevent a resulting trust do not take effect. So the form is totally ineffective[32]. Another view is that the clause takes effect as it says, and the trust property becomes property of the Crown as *bona vacantia*.[33] That might or might not suit the settlor, depending on the attitude of the Crown, the value of the property forgone, and the tax position. It is tentatively suggested that neither extreme view should be adopted, but the question should be regarded as one of construction, turning like all questions of construction, on the circumstances of the individual case.[34]

---

[32] This is the view taken by Robert Chambers, *Resulting Trusts* (1997) pp.64–66 and supported by *Air Jamaica Ltd v Charlton* [1999] 1 WLR 1399.
[33] *Davis v Richards & Wallington Ltd* [1990] 1 WLR 1511 at 1538; *Westdeutsche Landesbank Girozentrale v Islington LBC* [1997] AC 669 at 708.
[34] Faced with inconsistent case law, it is helpful to stand back and ask what the law should be (as opposed to what it actually is). It is suggested that the answer to this question is as follows:

  (1) The law ought to permit a person to abandon property if he wishes. "Abandonment" meaning that the property passes to the Crown as *bona vacantia*. After all, any person can give his property to the Crown (subject of course to a disclaimer). It would be foolish to draw a distinction which gives effect to words of assignment and not to words of abandonment.
  (2) A fortiori the law ought to permit a settlor to abandon an interest under a resulting trust.
  (3) Effect should only be given to a desire to abandon property if expressed in clear words. One does not lightly abandon. The words must be especially clear if the property abandoned is of considerable value, and if the settlor would not have appreciated the value of what he is said to have abandoned.

  It is further suggested that this sensible position is more consonant with the authorities than either extreme; but a full discussion is beyond the scope of this book.

Dependent children exclusion clause

13.22 If it is desired to exclude dependent children of the settlor, to obtain CGT hold-over relief,[35] the draft should based on s.169F TCGA 1992:

(1) Notwithstanding anything else in this settlement, no power conferred by this settlement shall be exercisable, and no provision shall operate so as to allow Trust Property or its income to become payable to or applicable for the benefit of a Dependent Child of the Settlor, at a time when the child is a Dependent Child of the Settlor, in any circumstances whatsoever.

(2) In this clause "Dependent Child" means a child or stepchild who—

   (a) is under the age of 18 years,
   (b) is unmarried, and
   (c) does not have a Civil Partner.

(3) This clause does not apply at any time when the Settlor has no Dependent Child.

It would also be necessary to ensure that a dependent child is not a default beneficiary.[36]

Default clause

13.23 The clause used in this book is as follows:

Subject to that, the Trust Fund shall be held on trust for
[a named living individual] absolutely.
or [two or more named living individuals] in equal shares[37] absolutely.
or [a named charity] absolutely.
or such charities as the Trustees shall determine.[38]

The default clause (sometimes called a "longstop provision") has a general purpose and a specific tax function.

The general purpose is to specify who should become entitled to the trust property, should the other terms of the trust fail (e.g. if all beneficiaries die). The trust should state how the trust property should pass in that event. (Even though it is unlikely or almost inconceivable that the default clause will ever come into effect.)

---

[35] See 13.2 (CGT hold-over relief)
[36] See 13.23 (Default clause)
[37] The words "in equal shares" are significant: they ensure that the individuals hold as tenants in common and not as joint tenants (so there is no right of survivorship).
[38] This trust could not fail since it would be administered by the court in default of the performance of the trustees' duty to select objects. Authority is scarcely needed but see *IRC v Schroder* [1983] STC 480 at 489; the Crown quite rightly did not appeal on that point. A definition of "charity" is usual but not strictly necessary: see 5.36 (Charities as beneficiaries).

The tax function relates to the settlement provisions. In the absence of a default clause, on the death of all the beneficiaries, the trust fund would revert to the settlor under a resulting trust. It is usually desired to exclude the settlor from all benefit under the trust to avoid the settlement provisions. The drafter must provide that the trust property will have a clear destination in all circumstances, so the trust fund cannot revert to the settlor. (The tax function does not apply to a will trust, but it is better to have a default clause even in a will trust, if only for tidiness, to avoid a remote possibility of a partial intestacy.)

Drafting the default clause

13.24 The usual practice is to direct that the property should pass to named children or grandchildren of the settlor or more distant relatives. If these have died, the trust property will then pass according to the terms of their wills or intestacies.[39] An alternative is that the trust property should pass to charity or a more distant relative. The person who receives the trust property in these circumstances is sometimes called "the Default Beneficiary."

The following clauses fail to satisfy the tax requirement:

Subject as aforesaid the trust property shall be held on trust for X if he is then living.

This fails to satisfy the tax function: X may not then be "then" living; so the trust fund may revert to the settlor.

Subject to that, the Trust Fund shall be held upon trust absolutely for such of them the Beneficiaries[40] as shall then be living.

This is no better. It is possible that none of the "Beneficiaries" may then be living.

Subject as aforesaid the trust property shall be held on the trusts of [another] settlement.

This is only satisfactory if the second trust has an adequate default clause, and entirely excludes the settlor (and spouse or civil partner). Where the second trust is made later than the first, care must be taken that the arrangement does not breach the rules against accumulation or perpetuities.

Unnecessary provisions in a default clause

13.25 It is unnecessary to say that the trust fund should be held on trust for:

---

[39] It is then possible that the property will revert to the settlor, under the will or intestacy of the default beneficiary. That does not matter for the purposes of the settlement provisions. This has never been judicially decided, but only because it has never been challenged: see *Barr's Trustees v IRC* 25 TC 72 (where this was assumed without argument) and *Glyn v IRC* 30 TC 321 at 329.
[40] Assume this is a defined term.

[a named individual] *or his estate or assigns* absolutely.
or [a named individual] *or his personal representatives* absolutely[41]

The clause is sometimes expanded to read:

> Subject to that, *and if and so far as not wholly disposed of by the above provisions the capital and income of* the Trust Fund shall be held on trust for X absolutely

The italicised addition is harmless but plainly unnecessary.

Correcting errors in a default clause

Where a default clause is not exhaustive, it is possible to set the matter right for the future. The settlor may assign his interest to some other person or the trustees may exercise their overriding powers. **13.26**

An unnecessary default clause

Where the provisions of a trust are exhaustive, a default clause is not strictly needed; but if the clause is included, no harm is done (save as to the reputation of the drafter). In *Barclays Bank v McDougall*[42] Rimer J. rightly rejected a fanciful construction intended to give effect to an obviously redundant default clause. **13.27**

---

[41] Authority is not needed for this proposition, but see *Commissioners of Stamp Duties v Bone* [1976] STC 145. For an example of a case where this was held to be the correct construction, see *Barclays Bank v McDougall* [2001] WTLR 23
[42] [2001] WTLR 23.

CHAPTER 14

LIFETIME INTEREST IN POSSESSION TRUSTS

Introduction

14.1 The IP trust is one where trustees are to pay trust income to a particular beneficiary. In the discussion below that beneficiary is called "the life tenant"; in the drafting he is usually identified by name or given the title of "the Principal Beneficiary".

For IHT purposes there are two categories of IP trust:

(1) Estate-IP: These are:

    (a) IPDI trusts
    (b) disabled actual estate-IP trusts
    (c) pre-22 March 2006 IP trusts and
    (d) transitional serial interests.

(2) Non-estate IP trusts (IP disregarded for IHT and taxed as standard IHT trusts).

Why use interest in possession trusts?[1]

14.2 The reason may simply be that it is desired to pay all the income to the life tenant: but the following outline tax points may also be noted here. For IHT there is from 22 March 2006 no difference between a discretionary trust and a non-estate IP trust. However, IP status remains important for income tax. An IP trust is not subject to income tax at the rate applicable to trusts.

The administration of an IP trust is therefore much easier and unless the

---

[1] See also 15.2 (Why use discretionary trusts?); 22.2 (Why use bare trusts?). The existence of an interest in possession is occasionally relevant for trust law purposes, e.g. s.36(9) TA 1925; ss.9, 11, 12 TLATA 1996, but these will not concern the drafter.

amounts involved are large this should be a significant factor. IP trusts are also much more tax-efficient for beneficiaries who pay tax at the basic rate when the trust receives dividend income.

Interest in possession income clause

14.3 The income clause of an IP trust must give the life tenant the right to trust income as it arises.

Drafting the income clause seems a straightforward matter. Statutory precedents provide a choice of forms:

> The trustees shall stand possessed of the trust fund upon trust to pay the income thereof ...
> ... to X during his life[2]
> ... to X for life[3]
> The trust fund shall be held on trust ...
> ... for X during his life.[4]
> ... for Z during the residue of his or her life.[5]

The form adopted in this book is:

> The Trustees shall pay the income of the Trust Fund to X during his life.[6]

The drafter must also omit provisions inconsistent with an interest in possession: see Chapter 16 (Provisions inconsistent with IP and IHT special trusts).

Structure of lifetime interest in possession trust

14.4 The form proposed in this book is as follows:

(1) income is paid to the life tenant for life;

(2) income is then paid to his widow or surviving civil partner for life (unless the disabled person trap applies);

(3) there is then a discretionary trust over income;

(4) the trustees have the standard overriding powers which may override any of the above;

(5) lastly there is a standard default clause.

---

[2] The Statutory Will Forms 1925, Form 7 accessible on *www.kessler.co.uk*.
[3] The Statutory Will Forms 1925, Form 9 accessible on *www.kessler.co.uk*.
[4] Section 46(2) Administration of Estates Act 1925.
[5] Section 46 AEA 1925 (original form). The word "residue" was omitted when the section was re-written in 1952.
[6] The form is loosely derived from s.31 Trustee Act 1925.

These five limbs are contained in three clauses. The first deals with trust income. The second contains the overriding powers. The third is the default clause.

1. Trust Income
Subject to the overriding powers below:

(1) The Trustees shall pay the income of the Trust Fund to the Principal Beneficiary[7] during his life.
(2) Subject to that, if the Principal Beneficiary dies during the Trust Period, the Trustees shall pay the income of the Trust Fund to the Principal Beneficiary's surviving spouse or surviving Civil Partner during his or her life.
(3) Subject to that, during the Trust Period, the Trustees shall pay or apply the income of the Trust Fund to or for the benefit of any Beneficiaries as the Trustees think fit.

2. Overriding Powers
[Here set out the standard Overriding Powers of this book.]

3. Default Trusts
Subject to that, the Trust Fund shall be held on trust for the Principal Beneficiary absolutely.

Income to the principal beneficiary for life

14.5 The settlor may prefer that the beneficiary should become absolutely entitled to the trust property on attaining the age of (say) 25, 30, 40; as to which see 14.16 (Life tenant becomes absolutely entitled at specified age).

Provisions after death of the principal beneficiary

14.6 What should happen after the principal beneficiary dies? This section considers the position for non-estate IP trusts (IHT standard trusts). (Entirely different considerations apply to an estate-IP trusts. We discuss this under Will Trusts[8] because the most common type of estate-IP trust (from 22 March 2006) will be an IPDI, but the discussion there would also apply to estate-IP disabled trusts.)

The main choices are:

(1) Discretionary trusts.

(2) Life interest to the widow, surviving civil partner or children.

From an IHT viewpoint (for standard IHT trusts made after 22 March 2006) it makes no difference.[9] If the life tenant relies on the income from

---

[7] The "Principal Beneficiary" will be defined in the definition clause. Where the Principal Beneficiary is female, it is good practice to replace "his" with "her" as appropriate in this clause.
[8] See 17.3 (IPDI trusts: qualifying conditions) and 17.5 (Terms of IPDI trust after death of life tenant).
[9] Provided that the surviving spouse/civil partner is not disabled (in the IHT sense) on the death of the principal beneficiary: see 26.6 (Actual estate-IP for disabled beneficiary).

the trust for his living expenditure, or resides in trust property, then his surviving spouse/civil partner usually needs a similar interest after the survivor's death; otherwise she will face some financial difficulty.

The drafts in this book provide that the surviving spouse/civil partner takes a life interest.

The reversionary interest of the spouse/civil partner in the trust fund is actually a precarious one. It need confer no real or valuable rights as it may be revoked at any time before or after the death of the original life tenant, the principal beneficiary. The trustees can respond to the beneficiaries' needs and changes in tax law.

An alternative: beneficiary's power to appoint to widow/civil partner

14.7 There is an alternative course which is quite common in practice. This is to give the principal beneficiary a power to confer (technically "to appoint") a life interest on his surviving spouse/civil partner. This is well enough in theory. The principal beneficiary can review the position and give the interest, or refrain from doing so, as he thinks best. This solution is less satisfactory in practice. The power is as likely as not to be overlooked. Assuming it is not overlooked the power will in most cases be exercised with concomitant expense. It is easier all round to start off as one means to go on: give the reversionary interest to the principal beneficiary's surviving spouse/civil partner and not merely empower the principal beneficiary to do so. This alternative course might be adopted when a particular settlor has a rooted objection to giving the spouse or civil partner an interest directly under the trust.[10]

It is said that this power gives the life tenant a measure of power over his or her spouse or civil partner. So it does; but just how conducive that may be to family harmony must be open to question.

Describing the widow

14.8 [Subject to the Principal Beneficiary's life interest] the Trustees shall pay the income of the Trust Fund to his surviving spouse or surviving Civil Partner during his or her life.

In the event of divorce or dissolution of civil partnership during the lifetime of the principal beneficiary, the ex-spouse/civil partner will not take any interest under this clause. However a person who is the spouse/civil partner of the principal beneficiary at the time of his death acquires an IP and will continue to receive the income even if she later remarries or enters into a new civil partnership.

---

[10] For a precedent see Statutory Will Forms 1925, form 7(6) accessible on *www.kessler.co.uk*.

Three bad forms

The drafter should not identify the spouse/civil partner of the principal beneficiary by name, saying:

> [Subject to Mr Jones' interest] the trustees shall pay the income of the Trust Fund to Mrs Pauline Jones during her life.

For then, if Mr Jones (the principal beneficiary) should divorce and remarry, the first Mrs Jones will still receive a life interest after his death; which will not at all be the intended result.

The use of the word "wife" (rather than "widow" or "surviving spouse") can introduce an element of doubt where the beneficiary remarries. Consider:

> [Subject to the Principal Beneficiary's life interest] the trustees shall pay the income to his *wife* during her life.

It may be doubtful whether a first or second wife is intended to benefit.[11]

What is the position if the drafter combines the two forms above, and says:

> [Subject to Mr Jones' life interest] the trustees shall pay the income to his *wife Mrs Pauline Jones* during her life.

If the Principal Beneficiary should divorce and remarry and then dies, there are three theoretical possibilities:

(1) Mrs Pauline Jones, the first wife, receives the income: since she is expressly named in the clause.
(2) The second wife receives the income, since she is the "wife" at the time of the Principal Beneficiary's death.
(3) The clause does not take effect, since there is no person who satisfies the description "his wife Mrs Pauline Jones" at the time of the death of the Principal Beneficiary.

There are rules of construction which can resolve such questions, but it is better that the drafter should not require beneficiaries (and their lawyers) to consider them.

---

[11] For a case where such confusion arose, see *Re Drew* [1899] 1 Ch 336.

A perpetuity problem

The reversionary life interest also causes a perpetuity difficulty.[12] Assume the 80-year perpetuity period is selected. One cannot simply say:

> *[Subject to L's life interest] the trustees shall pay the income to L's surviving spouse or surviving Civil Partner during his or her life.*

14.9

The objection is that if L dies after the expiry of the 80-year perpetuity period, then the reversionary interest will breach the rule against perpetuities.

Where L is married or a civil partner at the time the trust is made, one could avoid this difficulty by naming his wife or civil partner expressly, e.g.:

> *[Subject to L's life interest,] the trustees shall pay the income to Mrs Pauline L during her life.*
> ...

But this is unsatisfactory for the reason already mentioned: L may divorce.

What, then, can be done? There are various possibilities. The solution adopted here is to say:

> ... **If A dies during the Trust Period,** the trustees shall pay the income of the trust fund to the surviving spouse or surviving Civil Partner of A during his or her life.

The interest of the spouse/civil partner must vest within the perpetuity period. Note that it is not appropriate to say:

> *During the trust period:*
> *(1) The trustees shall pay the income of the trust fund to L during his life.*
> *(2) Subject to that, the trustees shall pay the income of the trust fund to the surviving spouse or surviving Civil Partner of L during her life.*

This form would terminate both interests on the expiry of the perpetuity period, which is unnecessary: the requirement is that the interests must vest (begin) within that period.

Alternatively one could select a different perpetuity period. It would be permissible to choose a perpetuity period of the lifetime of the principal beneficiary, L, and 21 years.[13] This solves the problem. L must die within the perpetuity period; so the reversionary interest must vest in that time. The cost is the introduction of artificiality into the trust; so this is not adopted in this work.

---

[12] For a general discussion of the perpetuity rule, see 9.1 (The rule against perpetuities).
[13] There could be a longer period, being the lifetimes of the principal beneficiary and "royal lives", and 21 years.

The drafter searching for simplicity may be very tempted to ignore the problem. If L is aged 30 at the time the trust is made, it is inconceivable that he should still be living in 80 years' time when the perpetuity period ends; he would then be 110! So it is tempting to ignore the problem and say:

> *[Subject to L's life interest]* the trustees shall pay the income from the trust fund to the surviving spouse or surviving Civil Partner of L during his or her life.

This approach is not wholly satisfactory. The fear is not so much that the life tenant will outlive the perpetuity date; though who knows what life expectancies will be in the future; but rather the reliance on the "wait and see" rule; this is not entirely certain or satisfactory in its operation. The drafter should not leave this problem for the next generation to sort out.

Position after death of surviving spouse/civil partner

14.10 The drafter must lastly make appropriate provision for the time after the death of the principal beneficiary and spouse/civil partner. This is to look far into the future; it is impossible to decide what form the trust should best take. For trusts made after 22 March 2006, it usually makes no difference for IHT.

A traditional solution is to direct the trust property to pass absolutely to the children of the principal beneficiary who attain 21. That course is too inflexible; it should be rejected out of hand. A refinement which allows some flexibility is to give the principal beneficiary power, during his lifetime, to appoint appropriate trusts for his children and remoter issue. But this course would vest an important power in the beneficiary which is considered undesirable.[14]

A discretionary trust over income offers the best solution. This—combined with the overriding powers in the trust—gives the trustees complete flexibility to do what seems best at the time. The drafting is pleasingly simple.

Alternatively the trust may provide that after the death of the life tenant

---

[14] 7.22 (Giving powers of appointment to beneficiaries personally). If for some specific reason such a form is desired, the following form is proposed (to be inserted after the sub-clause giving the life tenant his interest and before the sub-clause giving his widow a reversionary life interest):

  (1) Subject to that, the Principal Beneficiary may appoint that the Trustees shall hold the Trust Fund for the benefit of any Beneficiaries other than the Principal Beneficiary, on such terms as the Principal Beneficiary thinks fit.
  (2) An appointment may create any provisions and in particular:
    (a) discretionary trusts;
    (b) dispositive or administrative powers;
      exercisable by any Person.
  (3) An appointment shall be made by deed during the Trust Period and may be revocable or irrevocable.

and his spouse/civil partner, the trust property is held on trust for the children who reach the age of (say) 18, absolutely, but subject to the trustees' overriding power of appointment. This is likely to be perfectly satisfactory, at least for smaller funds. It may be easier for clients to accept than the discretionary trusts preferred here.

Future accumulation of income

While the trust is interest in possession in form, income will not of course be accumulated. However, the form of the trust may change, after which the trustees may wish to accumulate. **14.11**

The difficulty is caused by the drafter's bane, the rule against accumulations. Only one of the six accumulation periods is permitted. If none is expressly selected, it will be unclear which will apply. It is desirable to specify that one of the accumulation periods should apply. Which one should the drafter select? The best choice seems to be the period of 21 years from the date of the trust[15] and this is adopted in sub-clause (4) of the overriding power of appointment.[16]

IP forms for two life tenants

The settlor may wish to make an interest in possession trust for the benefit of two or more life tenants. One course is to create a separate trust, one for each; but it may be more convenient to create one trust for all the life tenants. **14.12**

A straightforward and flexible form

The following is the structure of a straightforward and flexible form of trust:

(1) trust fund to be divided into shares;

(2) income of each share to be paid:

---

[15] Of course by the time the trustees decide they wish to accumulate, there may be few (or no) years left out of the 21-year period. An alternative is 21 years from the death of the settlor. The time when this period starts to run is uncertain, and no more likely to suit the needs of the trust. (The accumulation period cannot begin on the death of the survivor of the life tenant and his spouse; that is not one of the permitted periods.) For a general discussion of the rule against accumulations see 15.6 (The rule against accumulations).

[16] There is of course no equivalent of (4) in the overriding powers in the discretionary trust in this book because there are other provisions which specify that the 21-year accumulation period applies.

(a) to each life tenant for life,
(b) subject to that, to his surviving spouse/civil partner for life,
(c) subject to that, there are discretionary trusts over income;

(3) the trustees have the standard overriding powers which may override any of the above.

The central parts of the draft are as follows. The two life tenants are here called Adam and Danny.

1. Subject to the overriding powers below the Trustees shall divide the Trust Fund into two equal shares "Adam's Share" and "Danny's Share".

2. **Adam's Share**
Subject to the overriding powers below:

   (1) The Trustees shall pay the income of Adam's Share to Adam during his life.
   (2) Subject to that, if Adam dies during the Trust Period, the Trustees shall pay the income of Adam's Share to his surviving spouse or surviving Civil Partner during his or her life.
   (3) Subject to that, during the Trust Period, the Trustees shall pay or apply the income of Adam's Share to or for the benefit of any of *the Beneficiaries* as the Trustees think fit.

3. **Danny's Share**
[Text same as Adam's Share saying "Danny" for "Adam".]

4. **Overriding Powers**
Here come the overriding powers in this book: see 11.1 (Drafting and understanding overriding powers (appointment, re-settlement and advancement). The objects of the Overriding Powers will be Adam *and* Danny and their families.]

Commentary on straightforward flexible form

14.13 In the following discussion the two life tenants are called A and B.

Under the straightforward flexible form, as the italicised words make clear, A's share could be used (if the trustees think fit) to benefit B and his family; and vice versa. This may happen by exercise of the overriding powers, or after the death of a life tenant and spouse, when the discretionary trusts of income take effect. It may be the intention of the settlor that the trustees should have this flexibility. If not, a letter of wishes will guide the trustees against that course; but the wishes do not bind the trustees. This is a theoretical rather than a practical problem. In practice, trustees may be expected to act in accordance with the settlor's wishes so far as it is appropriate to do so. If that is thought to be insufficient then A's family and B's family may be represented as trustees, or a protector may be used.

An inflexible form

14.14 An alternative approach is to provide that A's share cannot be used for the benefit of B and his family, and vice versa. The drafting is rather more complicated and the flexible form set out above is better. But it can be done. The central parts of the draft are as follows:

1 Definitions
In clauses [2] to [5] below

(1) **"Adam's Fund"** means:

    (a) Adam's Share and
    (b) All property from time to time representing the above.

(2) **"Trust Property"** means any property comprised in Adam's Fund.

(3) **"Adam's Family"** means:

    (a) Adam and his children and descendants;
    (b) The spouses and Civil Partners of (a) above;
    (c) The surviving spouses and surviving Civil Partners of (a) above (whether or not they have remarried or entered into another Civil Partnership);
    (d) Any Person or class of Persons nominated to the Trustees by:

        (i) Adam, or
        (ii) two members of Adam's Family (after the death of Adam)

    and whose nomination is accepted in writing by the Trustees.

    (e) At any time during which there are no members of Adam's Family within (a) above:

        (i) Danny and his children and descendants;
        (ii) the spouses and former spouses of (i) above; and
        (iii) any company body or trust established for charitable purposes only.

(4) **"Adam"** means [full name].
(5) **"Danny"** means [full name].
(6) **"Person"** includes a person anywhere in the world and includes a Trustee.

2 Division of Trust Fund into Shares
The Trustees shall divide the Trust Fund into two equal shares ("Adam's Share" and "Danny's Share").

3 Trust Income
Subject to the Overriding Powers below:

    (1) The Trustees shall pay the income of Adam's Fund to Adam during his life.
    (2) Subject to that, if Adam dies during the Trust Period, the Trustees shall pay the income of Adam's Fund to Adam's surviving spouse or surviving Civil Partner during his or her life.
    (3) Subject to that, during the Trust Period, the Trustees shall pay or apply the income of Adam's Fund to or for the benefit of any of Adam's Family as the Trustees think fit.

4 Overriding Powers
[Here set out the standard overriding powers.]

5 Default Clause
Subject to that, Adam's Fund shall be held on trust for Adam absolutely.

6 Danny's Fund[17]

Clauses [1] to [5] shall apply to Danny's Share with the following modifications:

(1) "Danny" shall replace "Adam" wherever it occurs except in clause [1(4)] (definition of "Adam")

(2) "Adam" shall replace "Danny" wherever it occurs except in clause [1(5)] (definition of "Danny")

Objection to simple accruer clause

14.15 A common form where there are two life tenants is to provide:

(1) A's share to be held on trust for A for life, then A's widow/civil partner for life, then for A's issue;

(2) B's share to be held on trust for B for life, then B's widow/civil partner for life, then for B's issue;

(3) In default each share will accrue to the other share.

It is better to have a simple discretionary trust on the death of the spouse/civil partner of A and B. Appropriate trusts can then be appointed, either before or after the time of the deaths, in the light of the then circumstances.

Life tenant becomes entitled at specified age

14.16 A trust should usually be drafted so that it may continue for as long as possible. It is far preferable to arrange that beneficiaries need not become absolutely entitled to the trust property. This offers many advantages. Trust property is safe in the trust. It should be secure from creditors in the event of insolvency; and secure from a spouse in the event of divorce. The trust property may be better administered by the trustees than by the

---

[17] There are three ways to deal with the drafting of trusts containing multiple funds for different primary beneficiaries. (1) One can set out each fund at length. That is best if the total length is not too great to bear. (2) One can use a substitution clause like the clause set out in the text. That becomes complicated if the beneficiaries are of both sexes as "his" and "her" becomes messy. (3) One can set out a single standard anonymised form:

1. The Primary Beneficiaries means [specify]
2. The Trust Fund shall be divided into one share for each Primary Beneficiary.
3. Subject to the Overriding Powers below:

   (1) The Trustees shall pay the income of the share of the Primary Beneficiary to the Primary Beneficiary during his life, *etc.*

beneficiary, were he to become absolutely entitled. The termination of a trust will often lead to tax difficulties.[18]

On this point the views of the client may be far from those of his professional adviser. The client may prefer his children or grandchildren to become absolutely entitled to the trust property on attaining the age of 25, or 35 or 40. It should be pointed out that the trustees may transfer the trust fund to the beneficiaries at the desired age. There are many methods of controlling trustees to comfort a nervous or reluctant settlor. See 7.12 (Guidance and control of trustees). If that course is not acceptable to the settlor, one may resort to the following precedent.

1. **Trust Income**
   Subject to the following clauses:
   (1) The Trustees shall pay the income of the Trust Fund to the Principal Beneficiary[19] until he attains the age of 40.
   (2) Subject to that, if the Principal Beneficiary dies before attaining the age of 40, the Trustees shall pay the income of the Trust Fund to his surviving spouse or surviving Civil Partner during his or her life.
   (3) Subject to that, during the Trust Period, the Trustees shall pay or apply the income of the Trust Fund to or for the benefit of any Beneficiaries[20] as the Trustees think fit.
2. [Here come the standard overriding powers of this book as in 10.1.]
3. **Principal Beneficiary to receive Trust Fund at 40**
   Subject to any prior exercise of the overriding powers, the Trustees shall transfer the Trust Fund to the Principal Beneficiary when he attains the age of 40 free from the terms of this settlement.
4. **Default Trusts**
   Subject to that, the Trust Fund shall be held on trust for the Principal Beneficiary [OR: specify default trusts as appropriate] absolutely.

The purpose of this form is that the trustees can review the position before the principal beneficiary attains the age of 40. If they consider that tax or other considerations make it desirable to do so, they can take action to prevent him becoming entitled by exercising their overriding power.

Life tenant a minor

For child beneficiaries, the normal course was to use A&M or discretionary trusts, i.e. to direct that the income may be accumulated or applied for the child's benefit. But now that undistributed income is taxed at the top rates, this is a very unattractive course. It is usually better to give a minor

14.17

---

[18] One possible problem is the CGT disposal on the termination of the trust: s.71(1) TCGA 1992. Hold-over relief is not always available. Also, if income has been accumulated, termination of the trust may lose a valuable "tax pool" of credit which could be utilised under s.496 ITA 2007.
[19] The "Principal Beneficiary" will be defined in the definition clause. Where the principal beneficiary is female, it is good practice to replace "his" with "her" as appropriate in clause 1 and "he" with "she" in clause 3.
[20] The term "Beneficiaries" would of course be defined.

an interest in possession.[21] This is better for will trusts as the interest will be an IPDI.

To give a minor an interest in possession, the following form is proposed:

> The Trustees shall pay or apply the income of the Trust Fund to or for the benefit of [Georgina] during her life.[22] Section 31 of the Trustee Act 1925 shall not apply to this Settlement.[23]

No other amendment is needed to the standard IP form.

Interest in possession for settlor

14.18 There are various reasons why a settlor might transfer his assets to a trust under which he has an interest in possession, rather than retaining them in his absolute ownership:

(1) Anticipation of mental incapacity of the settlor (avoiding the need to invoke the Court of Protection or the rather more restricted regime under the Mental Capacity Act 2005).

(2) For those who plan well ahead, the trust allows the ability in the future to make a gift without CGT.

(3) Avoidance of the Inheritance (Provision for Family and Dependants) Act 1975.

---

[21] Where the trust produces a very substantial income, this may be unwise for practical (non-tax) reasons: any income not applied for the child's benefit will be retained and paid to him on his 18th birthday; that may not be a satisfactory state of affairs. In the normal case the annual trust income will be consumed on the child's education and maintenance; so this difficulty does not arise.

[22] This clause confers on a minor beneficiary an interest in possession for income tax and IHT purposes because income applied for the benefit of a beneficiary is regarded as income of the beneficiary: *Gascoigne v IRC* 13 TC 573, *IRC v Stanley* 26 TC 12 *Stevenson v Wishart* 59 TC 740 at 757. HMRC rightly accept this: see (for income tax) Tax Bulletin 26 ("Trusts—liability at the rate applicable to trusts") and discussion paper on Trust Management Expenses (Sept 2004) para.9-25 ff; (for IHT) Press Notice 12/2/1976, reprinted in HMRC Booklet IHT 16, and IHT Manual 16062. See also 21.51 (Power to retain income of child).

[23] The second sentence is probably not strictly necessary since the first sentence by implication excludes the operation of s.31 TA 1925. There is a contrary argument. The section applies to vested annuities "as if the annuity were the income of property held by trustees *in trust to pay the income* thereof" to the annuitant. This (arguably) suggests that s.31 is intended to apply to trusts to pay income to a minor and that the words "to pay the income" are insufficient to exclude the operation of that section. On any view, it should be included for the avoidance of doubt. "The draftsman may be well advised out of caution either expressly to provide that section 31 is to apply, or expressly to exclude its application altogether": *Re Delamere* [1984] 1 WLR 813 at 823.

In practice the main use is for foreign domiciled settlors.[24] In other contexts these settlements have always been rare; except for property qualifying for 100% BPR/APR, the FA 2006 has made them impractical.

The trust will take the form set out above; appropriate amendments will be made in the definition of "the Beneficiaries", and the settlor exclusion clause.[25] The most appropriate accumulation period would usually be 21 years from the death of the settlor (rather than 21 years from the date of the settlement) assuming that the named settlor is the only settlor. Part 2 of this book has a precedent.

Impeachment for waste

Occasionally one sees trusts where the interest of a life tenant was expressed to be "without impeachment for waste". The form related to SLA Settlements[26] and so is now obsolete. **14.19**

---

[24] See James Kessler QC, *Taxation of Foreign Domiciliaries* 7th edn, 2008, Key Haven Publications. Outside England and Wales there are other uses. One is to avoid Scots forced heirship rules (a well established practice which is another accidental victim of the 2006 reforms). Another is to ease administration of US estates (Grantor trusts).
[25] 13.10 (Settlor exclusion clause).
[26] See s.47 SLA 1925 discussed at 20.30 (Rent: income or capital receipt?) and s.66 SLA 1925. The formula only makes sense in the context of a SLA settlement, where the life tenant had power to commit "waste". In *Re Boulton* [1928] Ch 703 at 708 Eve J. admitted disarmingly, "I cannot see what those words ('without impeachment for waste') mean".

CHAPTER 15

DISCRETIONARY TRUSTS

Meaning of discretionary trust

15.1 A discretionary trust is one where trust income and capital may be paid to one or more of a class of beneficiaries, as the trustees think fit.[1] The discretionary trust is simple in concept and there are no exacting tax requirements to satisfy. The drafting is relatively easy.

Why use discretionary trusts?[2]

15.2 The simple reason may be that it is desired to give trustees the flexibility to pay income to different beneficiaries (or accumulate it). In practice tax considerations are often paramount. The following outline tax points may also be noted here:

IHT advantages There is no tax charge on the death of any beneficiary. Instead the trust will be subject to the IHT discretionary trust regime; for small trusts (in particular those under the nil rate band) this is not harsh.

CGT advantages Gifts to the trust will usually qualify for CGT hold-over relief.

Income tax The appalling reforms of dividend taxation (a stealth tax increase of 1997) make it unattractive to use discretionary trusts to receive and distribute dividend income to basic rate taxpayers; IP trusts are preferable.[3]

---

[1] More accurately, the expression "discretionary trust" does not have a constant, fixed normative meaning: see *Chief Commr of Stamp Duties (NSW) v Buckle* (1998) 192 CLR 226 at [8] accessible on *www.austlii.org*. However the definition given above reflects the way the expression is used by private client practitioners.
[2] See also 14.2 (Why use interest in possession trusts?); 22.2 (Why use bare trusts?).
[3] See Appendix 5 of the 5th edition of this book.

Discretionary trust: income clause

15.3 In the discretionary trust the trustees may have power either to distribute income to any beneficiaries, or to retain and accumulate it.[4]

Income clauses in discretionary trusts therefore contain two limbs: distribution and accumulation. These are very much bound together, and are often to be found in the same clause. In this book, they are placed in two separate sub-clauses. We shall discuss the distribution limb before turning to the question of accumulation.

Distribution limb

15.4 Distribution of income under a discretionary trust is simple. There is a statutory precedent:

> The income shall be held upon trust for the application thereof for the maintenance or support, or otherwise for the benefit of, all or any one or more exclusively of the other or others of the [Beneficiaries].[5]

The form used in this book says the same more simply:

> The Trustees shall pay or apply the income of the Trust Fund to or for the benefit[6] of any Beneficiaries.

A traditional form prefers:

> ... such one or more of the Beneficiary or Beneficiaries exclusive of the others or other of them.

That clumsy syntax has been unnecessary since 1874.[7]

Accumulation limb

15.5 How should one draft the second part of the income clause, dealing with accumulation? There is a statutory precedent:

---

[4] There are, strictly, three possibilities: (i) a power to distribute the income with a duty to accumulate any undistributed income (ii) a power to accumulate and a duty to distribute unaccumulated income (iii) a duty either to distribute or to accumulate. There is little practical difference. See 7.2 (Duties and powers distinguished).
[5] Section 33(1)(ii) TA 1925.
[6] On the wide meaning of "benefit", in this context, see 11.11 (Power of advancement used to create new trusts).
[7] Section 158 LPA 1925 re-enacting the Powers of Appointment Act 1874. See also s.61(c) LPA 1925: the singular includes the plural and vice versa.

> The trustees shall accumulate all the residue of the income [by investing it and any profits of so investing it][8] from time to time in authorised investments, and shall hold those accumulations ... as an accretion to the capital of the trust fund, and as one fund with such capital for all purposes, ... but the trustees may, at any time ... apply those accumulations, or any part thereof, as if they were income arising in the then current year.[9]

This is often adopted verbatim (but with the punctuation deleted!). That it is not necessary to do so can be seen by comparing another statutory precedent:

> The Trustees shall ... accumulate the profits from the capital money by investing them and the resulting profits under the general power of investment in section 3 of the TA 2000 and shall add the accumulations to capital.[10]

The basic form used in this book is as follows:

> The Trustees may accumulate the whole or part of the income of the Trust Fund. That income shall be added to the Trust Fund.

This draws on the statutory language, but considerably simplifies it. It is, of course, unnecessary to direct the trustees to invest the accumulated income: the trustees will have a power of investment, and no one expects that they will place accumulated income in a current account.[11] The power to deal with accumulated income as income is important; but it is best relegated to the schedule of trustees' powers.

The basic form must be reviewed in the light of the rule against accumulations.

The rule against accumulations

15.6 The rule against accumulations is intricate and arbitrary; it strikes down provisions which seem and which are unobjectionable; it extends further than the mischief it was meant to prevent. For good measure the statutory language "is some of the less well drafted in the statute book, and that is really saying something."[12] The Law Commission recommended effective abolition of the statutory rule against accumulations in 1998.[13] In 2002 the Government promised legislation "as soon as Parliamentary

---

[8] Words inserted by the TA 2000 to replace "*in the way of compound interest by investing the same and the resulting income thereof*". The only purpose of the change seems to be to modernise the language. The old words will remain familiar as they are found in many precedents.
[9] Section 31(2) TA 1925.
[10] Section 39(2) SLA 1925 as amended by the TA 2000.
[11] This was recognised by the drafter of Trusts (Jersey) Law 1984 art.38.
[12] *Re Dodwell* [1979] Ch 301 at 309.
[13] The Rules against Perpetuities and Excessive Accumulations, Law Com 251, accessible *www.lawcom.gov.uk*.

time allowed". Unfortunately, Parliamentary time has not allowed. In the meantime the labour and resources which were invested in the Law Commission are wasted, and the law is much more complicated and less satisfactory than it need be. In most of the common law world comparable reforms the rule has been abolished (if it every applied) and its survival in the UK is shameful.

The rule is that income can only be accumulated in a trust for a limited period. After this period, neither a duty nor a power to accumulate income is valid.[14]

There are six permitted periods of accumulation. Only one of these is normally appropriate: this is the period of 21 years from the date of the trust (in the case of a will trust, 21 years from the death of the testator).

The following apparently innocuous clauses are all in breach of the rule:

> (1) The trustees may accumulate the trust income until X attains 25.

This will breach the rule unless X is aged four or more at the time the trust is made.

> (2) The trustees may accumulate the trust income until X attains 21.

This will breach the rule if X is unborn at the time the trust is made.

> (3) The trustees may accumulate the trust income during the life of X.

This will breach the rule unless X is the settlor.[15]

> (4) The trustees may accumulate the trust income for 21 years from the date of this Appointment.

This will breach the rule: time runs from the date of the original trust.

The provision for accumulation is often bound up in a long and turgid clause, which makes the accumulation aspect easy to overlook. In the following clause, the accumulation problem is plain to see:

> The Trustees shall accumulate the income of the trust fund for twenty five years.

Now compare this clause (from a trust once met in practice):

> The Trustees shall deal with the income of the presumptive share in the Trust Fund of any Beneficiary by paying or applying the same or so much thereof as the Trustees may in their absolute discretion think fit to or for the maintenance education or benefit of the Beneficiary from whose share the income arose or of any other Beneficiary for the time being under the age of 25 and shall accumulate and capitalise all such income not so paid or applied as an accretion to the share from which the same arose.

Such a clause will usually breach the rule against accumulations; but the eye may emerge from the verbal quagmire without spotting the error.

15.7

---

[14] Section 164 LPA 1925; s.13 PAA 1964.
[15] The lifetime of the settlor is one of the permitted accumulation periods, but it is not usually practical to use it.

A common mistake is to alter an existing precedent by replacing the age of 18 with the age of 21 or 25. This almost invariably leads to breaches of the rule.

The misunderstanding may cause tax problems because the invalidity of a power to accumulate may significantly affect the tax position, e.g. it may cause an interest in possession to arise.

The drafter must therefore ensure that the trust does not permit accumulation in breach of the rule. This requires amendment of the basic form set out above:

> The Trustees may accumulate the whole or part of the income of the Trust Fund during the Accumulation Period. That income shall be added to the Trust Fund.

The accumulation period must be defined:

> "The Accumulation Period" means the period of 21 years beginning with the date of this Settlement.

Other accumulation periods?

15.8 There are no less than six permitted accumulation periods: the reader may wonder whether any of the other five can be of service. They are as follows:

(1) *The lifetime of the settlor.* A middle-aged person in good health is likely to live for far longer than 21 years.[16] While tempting, it would be unwise to set the accumulation period as the lifetime of the settlor; the uncertainty involved makes it impractical.

(2) *Twenty-one years from the death of the settlor.* This is not normally appropriate for a trust made in the lifetime of the settlor. The period does not begin until the settlor has died: one could not accumulate income (except under the statutory power) until the settlor's death. In exceptional cases where there would be no wish to accumulate income during the settlor's life,[17] one may wish to use this period.

(3) *The minorities of persons in being at the time the trust is made.* This period is shorter than the period of 21 years from the time the trust is made.

---

[16] The mean life expectancy for a 40-year-old male is 39 years; for a 40-year-old female, 43 years (see *www.statistics.gov.uk*).

[17] Examples are:

(1) a trust of an insurance policy on the life of the settlor. The policy would produce no income during the settlor's life.
(2) a trust under which the settlor has a life interest.

(4) *The minority of the persons living or en ventre sa mere at the death of the settlor.* This period is shorter than the period of 21 years from the death of the settlor.

(5) *The minorities of any person or persons who would, for the time being, if of full age, be entitled to the income directed to be accumulated.* The difficulty with this period is that it would not permit accumulation after a beneficiary attains the age of 18. It is also doubtful whether this period can apply if the trustees have an overriding power of appointment.

In conclusion: none of these accumulation periods are of much practical use. Note that only one of the permitted accumulation periods can be chosen. For instance, it is not possible to specify a period of accumulation beginning at the time of the settlement and continuing until 21 years after the settlor's death.

Extension of accumulation period for added property?

The following form has been seen:

> During the period of twenty one years after any money or property shall become part of the Trust Fund (otherwise than by accumulation of income) the trustees shall have power as respects any income derived therefrom to accumulate it ...

This form is only significant in a case where property has been added to a trust after it has been made. The advantage is that income from such property may be accumulated for 21 years from the date that the property was given to the trust, and not from the date of the original trust. The disadvantage is that trustees must maintain separate funds (or at least separate accounting records) for all the added property. The form is not recommended as a standard form. (If there are substantial additions of funds, and it is desired to extend the accumulation period, this can of course be dealt with at the time either by making the gift to a new trust or by an appropriate appointment under an existing trust, prior to the gift.)

Strategies for trustees after accumulation period expires

The expiry of the accumulation period is not necessarily too serious a problem for the discretionary trust. The trustees will have to distribute all their income; but there will usually be adult beneficiaries to whom income can sensibly be distributed.

15.9

There are a number of colourful but impractical exceptions to the rule against accumulations.[18]

Trustees might retain income in breach of trust. Adult beneficiaries could of course require distributions but generally will not choose to do so. This strategy can be expected to work in practice, but the possible difficulties are just sufficiently real that it is not recommended.[19]

The trustees might accept that income cannot be accumulated, and invest or manage the trust fund so as to produce little or no income; but this may be unattractive from a tax and investment point of view.

There are solutions to this problem. The preferred solution would be to change the governing law to a jurisdiction (e.g. Northern Ireland or the Isle of Man) which has no equivalent to the English statutory rule against accumulations. This has been possible since the enactment of the Recognition of Trusts Act 1987.[20]

Another solution is clumsy and artificial, but it was often done before 1987. This is to appoint a contingent interest in the whole of the trust fund to a minor. In this way, income may be accumulated under s.31 Trustee Act 1925 until the child attains the age of 18.[21]

A third solution is an application under the Variation of Trusts Act 1958; this is possible but expensive.

Another solution (if the trustees have or can be given the necessary powers) is to pay the income to another (younger) trust which has power to accumulate. If trust B receives income from trust A, the question whether trust B can accumulate the income depends on the accumulation period of trust B, not of trust A.

Another solution is to use the income to pay insurance premiums.[22]

---

[18] The rule against accumulations does not apply to trusts of woodland; or trusts for the payment of debts. Also, it does not apply to trusts for the raising of "portions". It is not worthwhile to create "portions" (the meaning of which is discussed in *Re Cameron* [1999] Ch 386) merely to avoid the rule against accumulations.

There are also a number of routes round the rule which are possibly effective, but which raise sufficient doubts that the drafter is advised to avoid them. It may be that one can avoid the rigour of the rule against accumulations by a trust to distribute income within a very extensive time limit. For instance the trustees may be directed to distribute the income among the beneficiaries within 10 years of the time the income accrues to the trustees. Such a provision is arguably not caught by the rule against accumulations, for the income is not being accumulated.

[19] Retained income could not properly be used for beneficiaries born (a reasonable time) after the income has accrued.

[20] Assuming the trustees have (or can create) power to change the governing law, see 27.4 (Power to change the governing law).

[21] *Thomas on Powers* expresses doubts about this solution (1st edn, paras 9–39). But the doubt assumes that the purpose of such an appointment is "foreign" to the purpose of the power; which is not the case. It is submitted that the Court, having regard to the practice of trust drafters, should and would not strain the doctrine of fraud on a power so as to make void appointments made for the benefit of objects of the power, according to the best judgment of the trustees.

The drafting needs great care. For a discussion of the issues, see the 7th edition of this book, para.15.21, accessible on *www.kessler.co.uk*.

[22] See 16.10 (Power to pay insurance premiums out of income).

Structure of discretionary trust

This is the structure of the discretionary trusts in this book: **15.10**

(1) there is the income clause already discussed: the trustees have a power to accumulate income during an accumulation period and the trustees are directed to pay income to any beneficiaries they wish;

(2) the trustees have the standard overriding powers which may override the above;

(3) lastly, there is a standard default clause.

This is contained in three clauses. The first deals with trust income. The second contains the overriding powers. The third is the default clause. The draft is as follows:

1. Trust Income

(1) The Trustees may accumulate the whole or part of the income of the Trust Fund during the Accumulation Period. That income shall be added to the Trust Fund.

(2) The Trustees shall pay or apply the remainder of the income to or for the benefit of any Beneficiaries, as the Trustees think fit, during the Trust Period.

2. Overriding Powers[23]
[Here follow the standard overriding powers in this book.]

3. Default Clause[24]
Subject to that, the Trust Fund shall be held on trust for [specify name] absolutely.

"Beneficiaries"

For the definition of "Beneficiaries", see 5.18. **15.11**

Some discretionary trusts specify two classes of beneficiaries: a narrow class to whom income is to be distributed: and a wider class who may benefit under the overriding powers.[25] There was once a good reason for this. To satisfy the requirement of certainty, it was once thought that the objects of the discretionary trust over trust income had to be a narrow class: a class of whom a complete list could be drawn up. The object of a power of appointment (over capital) could be a wider class. It was worth

---

[23] For a discussion of this clause see 11.1 (Drafting and understanding overriding powers: appointment, re-settlement and advancement).
[24] For a discussion of this clause see 13.23 (Default clause).
[25] These might be called "the Beneficiaries" and "the Appointed Class".

having two classes, a narrow one for the discretionary trust of income, and a wide one for the power of appointment over trust capital. In 1970 the House of Lords decided that the broader test applied to discretionary trusts as well as to powers.[26] Accordingly, it has long been unnecessary to create two separate classes of beneficiaries.

Powers of discretionary trusts

15.12   There is no restriction on the powers of discretionary trusts. One may include powers not permitted in IP trusts. The additional powers include the following:

Power to pay insurance premiums out of income

The following form is used in this book:

> The Trustees may pay premiums of any insurance policy out of income.

It has been held in an old case that the use of income to pay insurance premiums is not "accumulation".[27] Thus, trust law does not require that a power to pay insurance premiums out of trust income need be restricted to any accumulation period. This may allow an effective form of accumulation after the accumulation period has expired.

Waiver of income

The following form is used in this book:

> The Trustees may waive the payment of income before it becomes due.

There may from time to time be situations where it would be convenient or tax efficient for trustees to waive the payment of rent, interest or dividends. In the case of the discretionary trust, this could only be possible if the trustees were expressly authorised.

---

[26] *McPhail v Doulton* [1971] AC 424. Another solution to this trust law difficulty would have been to confer on trustees a mere power over trust income, not a discretionary trust in the strict sense. (On the distinction see 7.2 (Duties and powers distinguished)). But this was not possible for estate duty reasons.

[27] *Bassil v Lister* (1851) 9 Hare 177; 68 ER 464. Some doubt whether this case would be followed today; it is hoped that respect for its age would overcome any disrespect for its reasoning.

CHAPTER 16

PROVISIONS INCONSISTENT WITH IP AND IHT SPECIAL TRUSTS

Administrative, dispositive, beneficial: terminology

The provisions of a settlement may be classified as: **16.1**

(1) "administrative" (sometimes called "managerial");

(2) "dispositive" (sometimes called "beneficial"[1]).

The distinction is broadly as these labels suggest: administrative provisions relate to trust administration; dispositive provisions deal with beneficial ownership.

Significance of administrative/dispositive distinction

The administrative/dispositive distinction arises for a number of purposes of trust law.[2] These are interesting, but only rarely of concern to the trust practitioner. **16.2**

---

[1] The word "beneficial" when applied to powers is ambiguous and may mean:
  (1) the power is dispositive (not merely administrative) or
  (2) the power is neither fiduciary nor semi-fiduciary (on this terminology see 7.33 (Nature of pow ers of consent and appointment)) so the appointor is not subject to any legal restraint in the motive or purpose for which the power is exercised, and may exercise the power to suit himself.

  Accordingly it is best not to describe powers as "beneficial" but to use some more precise description. For an example of the ambiguity see *Von Brockdorff v Malcolm* (1885) 30 Ch D 172: "All the real and personal estate ... over which at the time of my decease, I shall have any *beneficial disposing power* by this my will"—held in context to include a power of appointment which the testator could not exercise for the benefit of himself or his estate.

[2] This common thread is slightly disguised as different statutory provisions use different expressions to describe the administrative/dispositive distinction (although the underlying concept is the same or substantially the same).

The distinction is of considerable importance for tax purposes, and especially for the drafting of IHT Special Trusts.

Existence of interest in possession. A beneficiary has an "interest in possession" where (in short) he is entitled to trust income as it arises. Yet it is rare for a beneficiary to receive all the income of a trust. Some is spent on "administration", for instance, trustees' and accountancy fees. The fact that income may in fact be withheld from a beneficiary by virtue of administrative provisions is ignored in deciding whether an interest in possession exists.[3]

Special trusts. The income condition of a disabled deemed IP trust or an Age 18-to-25 trust requires that income must be applied for the beneficiary or accumulated. Again, it is rare that all the trust income is so applied. Income may be spent on "administration" for instance, trustees' and accountancy fees. Such income is not necessarily spent for the benefit of the beneficiary and is certainly not accumulated. These matters of administration are ignored in deciding whether the income condition is satisfied. The capital condition of an Age 18-to-25 trust requires that the beneficiary must become entitled to the trust property. Here too administrative powers are ignored in deciding whether this condition is satisfied. A striking example is the old statutory power to transfer some trust land to charity.[4] If this power is used, the beneficiaries will not become entitled to all the trust property. The Court of Appeal have said that this power did not breach the capital condition formerly applicable to an A&M trust because it is administrative.[5]

---

(1) *Perpetuities.* The rule against perpetuities does not affect a power to do any act in the administration (as opposed to the distribution) of any trust property: s.8 PAA 1964. (The same distinction should apply in deciding whether any provision offends against the rule against accumulations; but see 21.28 (Power to pay capital expenses out of income)).

(2) *Jurisdiction of Court.* The inherent jurisdiction of the Court to secure the proper administration of the trust fund is said to allow the Court to deal with administrative matters, but not to deal with beneficial interests: Re Duke of Norfolk [1982] Ch 61. Likewise jurisdiction under s.57 TA 1925 applies only to "management and administration".

(3) *Section 15 Wills Act 1837.* A "beneficial interest" given to a witness of a will (or his spouse) is (generally) void.

(4) *Power of delegation.* Trustees do not have power to delegate "any function relating to whether or in what way any assets of the trust should be distributed"; s.11(2)(a) TA 2000.

(5) *Insolvent estates.* Funeral, testamentary and administration expenses have priority over other debts: Administration of Insolvent Estates of Deceased Persons Order 1986.

(6) *Construction of particular trust.* If any particular trust document refers to administrative or dispositive powers, it then becomes necessary for the purpose of understanding that document to decide which is which. Such clauses are unnecessary and slightly imprecise.

[3] *Pearson v IRC* [1980] STC 318; *Lloyds Private Banking v IRC* [1998] STC 559.
[4] The power was formerly conferred by s.55 SLA 1925. (Since the TLATA 1996 the power is not expressly conferred on trusts of land, but it is suggested it can be spelt out of s.8(3) TA 2000. The power is rarely used but this does not spoil the force of the example.)
[5] See fn.7.

Tax law generally

These are only two instances of a broader principle. Tax law lays down rules or exemptions which apply if income or capital are treated in a particular way under a trust. In general, one should ignore "merely" administrative provisions in deciding whether these rules or exemptions apply.[6]

When is a provision administrative or dispositive?

The administrative/dispositive question arises most commonly in connection with trustees' powers, but it may also be applied to other provisions of the trust.

In general it is clear whether a provision is dispositive or administrative. For example:

(1) A direction to pay income to a beneficiary is a dispositive provision; a power to accumulate income is a dispositive power.

(2) A provision that trustees are not required to supervise companies is an administrative provision; a power of investment is an administrative power.

Yet there are borderline cases. Provisions may be administrative in character even though they impinge on or affect beneficial interests.[7] In

16.3

---

[6] The administrative/dispositive distinction arises in many tax contexts. Sometimes the statute sets out rules which expressly depend on whether an expense is administrative. There are too many to give a complete list, but for example, see: s.484 ITA 2007 (referring to "expenses"); s.65(5) IHTA 1984 ("costs or expenses"), Sch.5, para.9(3) TCGA 1992 ("expenses relating to administration and taxation"). Often the rule to ignore merely administrative matters is left to be implied. For instance for the purpose of:

(1) s.479 ITA 2007: Income which is retained under an administrative provision is not subject to the tax charge on income which is "accumulated". This (it is submitted) is the basis of the HMRC practice that income from mineral rents and timber crops, capitalised under ss.47, 66 SLA 1925, is not regarded as "accumulated" for the purposes of s.479 ITA 2007.
(2) IHT exemptions: A gift of a residuary estate by will qualifies for the IHT charity or spouse exemption in whole, even though part of the estate is spent on administration and never reaches the spouse or charity.
(3) CGT private residence relief: "If trustees allow a beneficiary to occupy a trust property, by the use of their discretionary [i.e. dispositive] power, private residence relief may be due … If the trustees allow any third party to occupy trust property, by exercise of their managerial [i.e. administrative] powers, the relief is not due." (CG Manual 65454.)

[7] *Inglewood v IRC* [1983] STC at 139:

"Some administrative powers (e.g. the power conferred by s.55 of the SLA 1925 to give away small parts of the trust land for public purposes or a power to trustees to apply income for capital purposes) do affect beneficial interests but they are not truly dispositive in nature."

Russell v IRC [1988] STC 195 at 203:

"… a power of appropriation is only ancillary and administrative although its exercise can, in times of fluctuating values, have a considerable impact on beneficiaries' rights inter se."

such cases it is not obvious whether the provision should be regarded as administrative or not. "The boundary between administrative action and rewriting the trusts ... is incapable of precise definition."[8] The approach of the courts may be summed up as pragmatic.

In general, the same line is drawn in all the areas where the distinction is relevant. A provision which is administrative for the purposes of the perpetuity rule is administrative for the purposes of deciding whether a beneficiary has an interest in possession. However, this is not invariably the case, and provisions may be classified as administrative for one purpose and not for another. So they should: different policy considerations may apply in the different cases.[9] A provision for trustee remuneration is in this special category.[10]

In a borderline case, how does one categorise a provision as administrative or dispositive? It has been said that "what is decisive is the substance of the provision and not the clothes or label which it wears".[11] That observation, while undoubtedly true, does not take us very far.

There is no single test to determine the question; but a number of relevant factors. Powers conferred by general trust law (except for powers of maintenance and advancement) are administrative. Another consideration is whether a power could consume all the income—no matter how much income there is; if so it is a dispositive power. Provisions which can only affect limited amounts of income are likely to be administrative. On this basis the following are all to be considered as administrative.

Power to pay capital expenses out of income

16.4 This is an administrative power permitted in IP and special trusts.[12] This power is a very useful one. Trustees often find that they cannot easily realise trust capital to pay capital expenses. (In practice trust income is often used for the purpose, in conscious or unconscious breach of trust.) Trustees can and should be given power to pay capital expenses out of income.

---

[8] *Re Blackwell* [1952] 2 All ER 647. This part of the judgment was approved on appeal in *Re Downshire Settled Estates* [1953] Ch 218.
[9] Further, of course, the terms of the relevant statutory provisions are all slightly different. In the same way, the question whether a power is to be classified as "general" or "special" may be answered differently for different trust law purposes.
[10] 21.62 (Trustee remuneration clause: dispositive or administrative?).
[11] *IRC v Lloyds Private Banking* [1998] STC 559 at 566. *Street v Mountford* [1985] AC 809 at 819 contains a felicitous and often cited statement of the Courts approach to categorisation issues: "The manufacture of a five-pronged implement for manual digging results in a fork even if the manufacturer, unfamiliar with the English language, insists that he intended to make and has made a spade."
[12] *Pearson v IRC* [1980] STC 318 at p.325. HMRC accept this: ICEAW Guidance Note, 14 December 1992 "If the trust deed contains a power to pay capital expenses out of income, exercise of this power will not cause the trust to lose interest in possession status for inheritance tax purposes." See 21.29 (Power to apply trust capital as income).

Retention of income to provide for liabilities or depreciation of a capital asset

16.5 This rather less important power is administrative and so permitted in IP and special trusts.[13]

16.6 On the other hand the following powers are not merely administrative: Power to:

- apply income in the purchase or subscription of partly paid shares ...
- use income to pay life assurance premiums ...
- apply income in purchasing any annuity ...
- apply income to improve or develop trust property.

Capital/income and apportionment provisions

16.7 A second general point: trust law lays down various prima facie assumptions sometimes—somewhat arbitrary—which regulate the thorny question of whether a receipt is income or capital; or whether it accrues at one moment of time or another. These assumptions take effect subject to contrary provisions in the trust. Such provisions are administrative, not dispositive, if the drafter has merely adopted a different definition of the amorphous concept "income" (or "accrual"), which in principle is as legitimate as the general trust law definition. Here are common examples. Exclusion of the statutory apportionment rules is a matter of administration.[14] This is an important provision and should not be omitted out of a super-abundance of caution. The exclusion of the equitable apportionment rules is also an administrative provision.[15] A provision that a dividend in the course of an exempt demerger is capital is likewise an administrative provision.[16]

Power of appropriation

16.8 It is considered that the power of appropriation should be regarded as administrative.[17] In practice it rarely matters.[18]

---

[13] *Miller v IRC* [1987] STC 108.
[14] The arguments to this effect, which are overwhelming, are set out in detail in Kessler, PTPR (Vol.2), p.171 accessible on *www.kessler.co.uk*. This view was evidently shared by the drafter of Form 8 of the Statutory Will Forms 1925 accessible on *www.kessler.co.uk* who described such forms as "*administration trusts*". For the drafting of the provision, see 21.54 (Statutory apportionment).
[15] 21.32 (Equitable apportionment).
[16] See 21.34 (Demergers).
[17] It has been held to be administrative for the purposes of s.57 TA 1925: *Re Thomas* [1930] 1 Ch 194; *Hornsby v Playoust* [2005] VSC 107. Likewise *Russell v IRC* [1988] STC 195 at 203. In *Re Freeston* [1978] Ch 741, the Court of Appeal did say the opposite, at p.752, but this comment was obiter, the relevant cases were not cited or discussed, so it is considered that notwithstanding this comment the position is reasonably clear.
[18] The question arises where one beneficiary becomes entitled to a share of a trust fund, (the other shares being held on continuing substantive trust). According to HMRC CG Manual 37530,

IP trusts: "departure" v "disqualifying" powers

16.9 Any administrative provision can be included in an IP trust. We can now turn to consider what non-administrative powers may safely be included in IP trusts. Non-administrative (i.e. dispositive) powers must themselves be divided into two categories:[19]

(1) Trustees may have some power which allows them to withhold trust income from the beneficiary as it arises. The beneficiary cannot then have an interest in possession. This is here called a *Disqualifying* Power. An example is a common form power of accumulation.

(2) Trustees may have some power which may allow them to withhold trust income from the beneficiary at some time in the future. The beneficiary has an interest in possession until that time comes. For the beneficiary is in the meantime entitled to trust income as it arises. This is here called a *Departure* Power. Standard form powers of appointment, advancement and resettlement are clear examples of departure powers.[20] Such powers are consistent with an interest in possession: the life tenant is entitled to all income until the power is exercised.

Thus an IP trust may include departure powers. It may not include disqualifying powers. Whether a power is a disqualifying power or a departure power is sometimes difficult to discuss in the abstract: a great deal depends on the words used in each case.

Power to pay insurance premiums out of income

16.10 There are two types of policy. *Administrative* policies (our terminology). For instance:

(a) a term policy used to cover an IHT liability;

(b) a policy used as a sinking fund against a wasting asset.

---

there is in principle no CGT disposal, under s.71 TCGA 1994, if the trustees have a power of appropriation. The commonest case is a trust for a class of beneficiaries absolutely at 25; and one beneficiary reaches 25, but others are younger. If HMRC's view is right it is best regarded as an exceptional case where the power of appropriation, an administrative provision, has substantial tax consequences; (or else perhaps the power is not merely administrative: see the above footnote). If HMRC's view is right, it will very often prevent a claim for hold-over relief under s.260 TCGA 1992. It is considered that HMRC's view is right, though the arguments are finely balanced, and despite the terms of the Manual, HMRC do not seem to take that view in practice.

[19] This important distinction was first clearly drawn in Richard Oerton "Safety Net Clauses" (1992) Trusts & Estates 66.

[20] See 11.3 (Unnecessary provisions in power of appointment).

Power to pay premiums on an administrative policy out of income is administrative.[21]

Investment policies (purely investments). A power to pay premiums on such policies out of income is a dispositive power. This power may be framed as a departure power, or a disqualifying power, depending on the words used. The actual effect of old common form clauses is uncertain.[22] The drafter should avoid these problems by ensuring that the interest in possession trust does not contain a wide power to pay life insurance premiums out of income.

Power to permit beneficiary to occupy or use trust property rent free

A power to allow a beneficiary to reside in trust property rent free is obviously a dispositive power. It is a departure power rather than a disqualifying power. Suppose X is entitled to an interest in possession, and the power is then exercised so as to allow Y to occupy property rent free: 16.11

(1) X's interest in possession will normally come to an end; and

(2) Y may acquire an interest in possession.[23]

---

[21] HMRC accept this: IHT Manual 16067 provides:

"Examples of administrative powers include ... a power to pay premiums on a life assurance policy designed to cover any claim to IHT on the fund. These expenses are capital expenses, but if the trust deed permits them to be paid out of income then the trustees may do so. Such payments do not defeat an interest in possession although, as a practical matter, there will be less income to give to the beneficiary."

[22] Older trusts often provided that trustees may pay life assurance premiums out of trust income. What is the effect of this if included in an ordinary interest in possession trust? At least three views are possible:

(1) The power is exercisable at any time. In this case, the power is in principle a disqualifying power and the beneficiary does not have an interest in possession.
(2) The power is only exercisable if the trustees hold a life assurance policy, and only to the extent that there are premiums payable under the policy. In this case, the beneficiary has an interest in possession until the trustees acquire a life assurance policy. Thereafter his interest in possession will be restricted in part or in whole.
(3) The power is only exercisable if the trustees hold a life assurance policy, and only in respect of income arising after the trustees have resolved to make payments out of income. In this case, the beneficiary has an interest in possession until the trustees resolve to use the power.

The point is not covered by authority. In practice, according to the old CTO Advanced Instruction Manual E.61ff, HMRC officially take view (2) but might be persuaded not to take the point. This would normally benefit the taxpayer and so it will not often be challenged. The new IHT Manual seems to shift to view (1): para.42810. But some text has been withheld (supposedly) because of "exemptions in the Freedom of Information Act 2000" and it is very likely that the text formerly published in the CTO Manual survives as a secret instruction to HMRC staff in the IHT Manual.

[23] However Y may not acquire an IP, either because the rights conferred on Y are too precarious to count as an interest in possession (so the position is analogous to a common form discretionary trust), see SP 10/79; or because the formalities required by s.53 LPA 1925 are not met (the creation of an interest in land must be in writing and signed by the person creating it). On the position where the trustees have a share in the land, see 19.2 (Appropriation of share of family home). The

The best course, in drafting an IP trust, is to restrict the power so only the life tenant can be allowed rent free occupation of trust property. Then no difficult questions arise.

The same considerations apply to powers to allow beneficiaries to enjoy chattels or other trust property *in specie*.

Power to lend money interest free

16.12 A power to lend money interest free is not a disqualifying power. It is probably a departure power and arguably may be exercised so as to confer an interest in possession on the borrower. The best course in drafting an IP trust is to restrict the trustees' powers so that they can only lend interest free to the life tenant. Then no difficult questions can arise.

Power to waive income

16.13 Trustees sometimes have power to waive income before that income falls due. It is suggested that this should in principle be construed as an administrative power.[24] However, for safety's sake, it is recommended that such a power should not be included in an IP or other special trust. The omission should not cause difficulties. Trustees could of course waive the income with the consent of the life tenant.

IHT special trusts

16.14 Any administrative power may be included in an IHT special trust. We can now turn to consider what non-administrative (i.e. dispositive) powers may safely be included in special trusts.

"Departure" *v* "disqualifying" powers

The same terminology can be used: dispositive powers in a special trust can be divided into two categories:

---

issue in *IRC v Lloyds Private Banking* [1998] STC 559 was one of construction, whether the words used in the will had the effect of conferring a right to occupy.

[24] In Scotland, a similar power is conferred by statute: s.4(1)(m) Trusts (Scotland) Act 1921 and the statutory power would not be construed to be exercisable in a dispositive manner. An example of an administrative exercise of the power might be the waiver of rent in one year in order to make it more likely that the tenant will be able to pay rent in subsequent years.

If the particular power is dispositive, the power is arguably consistent with an interest in possession. It is not a power to withhold income: it is a power to prevent income arising. This is consistent with the scheme of the Act: s.15 IHTA 1984.

(1) A departure power is one which, if exercised, will cause the trust to cease satisfying the relevant conditions.

(2) A disqualifying power is one the existence of which, whether or not actually exercised, prevents the trust from satisfying the relevant conditions.

Power to permit beneficiary to occupy or use trust property rent free

16.15 We have already noted that a power to permit beneficiaries to use or occupy trust property is dispositive. The power raises difficulties for special IHT trusts.

It is often a condition that the income of the settled property is applied for the benefit of the beneficiary (or accumulated). So long as trust property is enjoyed in kind, it will not produce income. How does the condition operate then? It is considered that the word "income" in the income condition should be taken to refer to the use or enjoyment of trust property rent free; for such use and enjoyment is analogous to income.[25] If this is correct, the effect of the income condition is that trust property may only be enjoyed in kind by the beneficiary. A power to allow other beneficiaries to enjoy trust property on favourable terms is a disqualifying power and breaches the condition.

Similar considerations apply to powers to allow beneficiaries to use chattels, and powers to make interest free loans; and to a power to charge property as security for debts and liabilities of beneficiaries.

Power to use income to pay life insurance premiums

16.16 Suppose trustees have power to pay life insurance premiums out of income. Textbooks record a theoretical argument that this power may breach the income condition but nobody believes it.[26] Nevertheless the safer course is

---

[25] As Lord Oliver said in *City of London Building Society v Flegg* [1988] AC 54 at 83: "The beneficiary's possession or occupation is no more than a method of enjoying in specie the rents and profits pending sale in which he is entitled to share" (in relation to a beneficiary under a trust for sale). An economist would regard the right to occupation as "income": Kay and King, *The British Tax System* (5th edn, 1990). While of course legal and economic concepts of income do differ, it is suggested that the law may have regard to economists in this situation at least. HMRC agree: IHT Manual 16066.

[26] The argument is that:

(1) The payment of a life insurance premium out of income will not (usually) be the application of income for the exclusive benefit of the beneficiary; and
(2) the payment of a life insurance premium does not amount to the "accumulation" of income.

Support for this view could be drawn from *Bassil v Lister* (1851) 9 Hare 177, 68 ER 464 discussed in *Carver v Duncan* 59 TC at 166, but it is not convincing.

that trustees should not be given power to pay life insurance premiums out of income. The absence of this power is not significant in practice.[27]

Protection clauses

16.17 In an ideal world a drafter would know exactly what provisions were permitted in a trust which was intended to qualify as an IP or an IHT special trust. In practice there are inevitably a few doubtful areas. This has led to "protection clauses" (or "safety net" clauses) intended to restrict the terms of a trust so as to satisfy the relevant tax conditions. These clauses have become common since the introduction of capital transfer tax in 1975.

It goes without saying that a protection clause is no substitute for analysing the statutory provisions and framing the trust accordingly. A protection clause is not an essential drafting technique. In the drafts in this book the clauses are not relied upon: their omission would not affect the operation of any of the trusts. However, there is perhaps a possibility that HMRC might argue that some provision (which the drafter had judged to be satisfactory) breached the relevant conditions. The practice in this book is to include the clause in all types of trusts except standard discretionary trusts.[28]

Drafting and construction of protection clauses

16.18 One sometimes sees in practice a wide protection clause which if literally construed has an extremely restrictive effect which was certainly unintended by the drafter. The question whether such clauses should be literally construed is therefore one of general importance—though of course in any particular case, much will depend on the exact wording. As an example consider this clause:

> *None of the trusts, powers and discretions conferred upon or vested in the Trustees shall be capable of exercise in any way such as will or may directly or indirectly prevent Section 71A [or 71D] of the Inheritance Tax Act 1984 from applying or continuing to apply to the Trust Fund.*

Literally construed, this prevents trustees exercising their power of advancement to transfer trust property to the beneficiary![29] It is submitted that clauses of this type should not be so literally construed. Otherwise the express power of advancement (typically found elsewhere in the trust) is rendered virtually otiose. This construction makes more sense in the context of the scheme of the IHTA 1984.

---

[27] The same result can generally be achieved by first accumulating the income, turning it into capital, and then investing the capital in the insurance policy.
[28] In a discretionary trust there are no uncertain conditions to be satisfied.
[29] Since s.71A (or 71D) ceases to apply to property so advanced.

The moral is that one should not make protection clauses unduly wide. The approach in this book is to apply the restrictions of the protection clause only to what are intended to be the administrative powers of the trust. The safety net clause is there in case unintended dispositive powers have found their way in. No advantage can be seen in imposing any restriction on the beneficial provisions. In the case of a simple IP trust, this is plainly unnecessary. In the case of special trusts, which are more complex, the imposition of a protection clause on the beneficial provision may lead to uncertainty.

We have already mentioned the distinction between disqualifying and departure powers. There is no need for a protection clause to restrict departure powers.[30] Unfortunately the drafting of the clause distinguishing between the two types of power is somewhat cumbersome.[31] The form in this book does not discriminate and applies to both sorts of power. Our protection clause is therefore wider than it strictly need be. This does not matter since the clause—restricted as it is to administrative provisions—is only for the avoidance of doubt and has no discernible practical effect.

Interest in possession protection clause

16.19 Where it is important to have an IP for IHT purposes, (e.g. an IPDI trust) the form used in this book is as follows:

> The powers conferred by this schedule[32] shall not be exercisable so as to prevent a Beneficiary from being entitled to an interest in possession in Trust Property (within the meaning of the Inheritance Tax Act 1984).

It is not strictly necessary to define "interest in possession" which is a familiar term in English law. But the IHTA 1984 gives a special meaning to the phrase,[33] so a referential definition is desirable.

It is not necessary to say: "the IHTA 1984 *or any modification or re-enactment thereof*" as those words are implied.[34]

It is not necessary to include this form in a lifetime IP trust made after 22 March 2006, because the IP is not recognized for IHT purposes, but no harm is done if it is included.

---

[30] Richard Oerton first pointed this out in "Safety Net Clauses" Trusts & Estates 66 (1992).
[31] The Oerton form was in outline:

> "If during any period the mere existence of any powers given to the Trustees in relation to this settlement would be enough (without their exercise) to prevent (and would be the only thing preventing) the conditions stated in s.71 IHTA 1984 from being satisfied in respect of the property comprised in the trust or some part of it then during that period those powers shall be restricted (in relation to that property or that part) so far as may be necessary to avoid that result."

[32] This will be the schedule of administrative powers in the precedents used in this book.
[33] Section 50 IHTA 1984. The expression is used in the CGT legislation and in the 1925 property legislation without definition.
[34] Sections 17, 23 Interpretation Act 1978.

"No conflict" clause

16.20 One sometimes sees forms like these:

> *The provisions of the schedule below shall not take effect so as to conflict with the beneficial provisions of this settlement.*
>
> *Nothing in the schedule hereto shall authorise any of the Trust Fund or income to be dealt with in a manner inconsistent with the beneficial provisions applicable to the Trust Fund.*

The effect of this "no conflict" clause naturally depends on what is in "the schedule" to which it refers. The provisions will be largely administrative in nature. "Administrative" and "beneficial" provisions are mutually exclusive categories. Administrative provisions aid beneficial provisions and do not conflict with them or destroy them. This is bolstered by a presumption, a rule of construction—which does not need to be stated expressly in a trust—that provisions contained in a section of a trust dealing with administration would be administrative and would not be construed to conflict with beneficial provisions.[35] It is considered, therefore, that administrative provisions are not affected by the no conflict clause.[36] The schedule will generally contain some dispositive provisions which do conflict and would be restricted by the clause.

This form is intended to perform the same task as a protection clause, and it would have that effect. In an IP trust, the form will prevent powers in the schedule from being exercised in a way which would prevent the life tenant from having an interest in possession. Where there is a protection clause as in the precedents in this book, there is no need for a no-conflict clause. The no-conflict clause is wider than a protection clause and it prevents any conflict between the powers in the settlement and the beneficial provisions (even a conflict which does not breach IP conditions).[37] It may impose some significant (and probably unintended) restrictions.[38] The form is also too vague to be satisfactory and it is not used in this book.

---

[35] This presumption is supported by common sense, and authority: *IRC v Miller* [1987] STC 108 at 112; *Inglewood v IRC* [1983] STC 133 at 139.

[36] But provisions properly classified as "administrative" may nonetheless affect a beneficiary's entitlement very substantially; and in such cases some might argue that there is a "conflict".

[37] Suppose the schedule contains a power to release powers. The no-conflict clause would restrict this to a power to release administrative powers. It could not be used to release a power of appointment.

[38] For instance, suppose (i) a beneficial provision directs trustees to pay income to A; and (ii) a power in the schedule (subject to the no-conflict clause) permits trustees to allow beneficiaries to reside in trust property. The power could not be used to allow beneficiaries (other than A) to reside, as that would conflict with the beneficial provisions; 16.11 (Power to permit beneficiary to occupy or use trust property rent free).

Suppose the schedule (subject to the no-conflict clause) confers on the trustees a power of advancement. It is suggested that the power of advancement could be used and that would not "conflict" with the beneficial provisions. This is consistent with the comment in *Inglewood v IRC* [1983] STC 133 that the power of advancement is "like an administrative power". But the contrary is arguable. Compare *Re Batty* [1952] Ch 250 where the power of advancement is described as "confiscatory".

CGT protection clause

16.21 *The powers conferred by this schedule shall not be exercisable so as to cause the settlement to be an accumulation or discretionary settlement (within the meaning of section 5 of the Taxation of Chargeable Gains Act 1992).*

This clause is obsolete. It related to the foolish rule (introduced in 1988 and abolished 10 years later) that an accumulation or discretionary trust paid CGT at a higher rate than an IP trust. Where the form is still used (for instance under the first edition of the STEP Standard Provisions) no harm is done.

A & M protection clause

16.22 Paragraph 14 of the STEP Standard Provisions provides an A&M protection clause:

These provisions shall not have effect . . . so as to prevent the conditions of section 71(1) Inheritance Tax Act 1984 from applying to Trust Property.

This clause is obsolete now that A&M trusts have been abolished. Where the form is used, however, no harm is done as the words have no effect.

CHAPTER 17

TYPES OF WILL TRUSTS

Types of will trusts: terminology

17.1 This chapter considers the many different types of will trust, their qualifying conditions, and tax treatment. These trusts can be divided into two classes:

(1) *Standard IHT Trusts*: A trust which does not qualify for any special IHT treatment, and so is taxed with 10-year and exit charges.[1] This category includes an ordinary IP trust.

(2) *Special IHT Trusts*, the most important of which are:

    (a) *IPDI Trust*: A trust within s.49A IHTA 1984 (Immediate post-death interests)
    (b) *Bereaved Minors Trust*: A trust within s.71A IHTA 1984
    (c) *Age 18-to-25 Trust*: A trust within s.71D IHTA 1984
    (d) *Disabled trusts*: discussed at 24.1 (Disabled trusts).

These are not subject to 10-year and exit charges. A discretionary will trust can within two years be converted into any of the above.

We use the labels "Bereaved Minors trust" and "Age 18-to-25 trust" with reluctance:

- "Age 18-to-25 trust" is a misleading description for a trust which falls within s.71D. "Age 0-to-25 trust" would be more accurate.
- "Bereaved Minors trust" is a tolerably accurate description of trusts within s.71A, but that term also fits trusts within s.71D.

However practitioners must use technical terminology of one kind or another. The alternative terms are "Section 71A trusts" and "Section 71D

---

[1] Chapter 3, Part 3 IHTA 1984

trusts", but on balance it seems better to stick with the terms used in the IHTA 1984.

The terms "standard" and "special" trusts are non-statutory and are also less than ideal:

- "Standard" trusts might more accurately be called "relevant property trusts"[2] but that label is not very helpful.
- "Special" trusts are all those which are not "standard": they may not be very special! These are sometimes called "privileged" trusts but that is inapt as the "special" trusts will sometimes pay more tax than standard trusts.

Spouses: terminology

For almost all practical purposes a civil partner and a spouse are in the same position. However, the legislation distinguishes between the two in its terminology and the words "spouse" and "marriage" do not (in the absence of special context) include a civil partner or civil partnership. So in this book:

(1) "Spouse" means either a spouse or a civil partner.

(2) "Single" refers to an individual who is neither married nor a civil partner.

(3) "Cohabitees" refers to an individual and partner who are unmarried and not civil partners.

17.2

IPDI trusts: qualifying conditions

The IPDI conditions are straightforward. The main condition is that a beneficiary has an interest in possession.[3] We follow the example of the legislation and call this beneficiary, the life tenant, "L". This condition must be satisfied at all times since L became beneficially entitled to the interest in possession.[4] L may be a minor.[5] In addition:

17.3

---

[2] The trust property is "relevant property" as defined in s.58 IHTA 1984.
[3] Section 49A IHTA 1984. For this requirement, see 14.3 (Interest in possession income clause) and 16.1 (Provisions inconsistent with IP and IHT special trusts.)
[4] Section 49A(5) IHTA 1984
[5] See 14.17 (Life tenant a minor)

254   Types of Will Trusts

(1) The settlement must be effected by will or intestacy.[6] A lifetime trust cannot be an IPDI.

(2) L must become beneficially entitled to the interest in possession immediately on the death of the testator;[7] hence *immediate post-death interest*. But a discretionary will trust may within two years be converted into an IPDI trust.[8]

(3) The trust is not a Bereaved Minors trust (this will not in practice happen) and not a disabled trust.[9] The regimes for these types of trust have priority.

The IPDI trust may have an overriding power of appointment, giving considerable flexibility.

Why use IPDI trusts?

17.4   *IHT advantages & disadvantages.* The IPDI is an estate-IP, so the property is treated for IHT purposes as if it belonged to the life tenant. The trust property will be subject to tax on L's death, unless the value of the estate is within the nil rate band, or an exemption applies. The spouse exemption will in principle apply on the death of the testator if L is the testator's spouse. This will generally be better than:

(1) the standard IHT trust regime of 10 year and exit charges, or

(2) an Age 18-to-25 trust (which suffers the 4.2% charge).

CGT advantages & disadvantages. There is a tax-free uplift on death of L, the life tenant.[10] Conversely there is no CGT hold-over relief to defer the CGT charge on the termination of the trust during L's lifetime (except for business/agricultural property). Age 18-to-25 trusts seem better because they do offer CGT hold-over relief.[11] This drawback is not as significant as may at first appear. So long as the trust endures there is no need for

---

[6] Section 49A(2) IHTA 1984. It is considered that a gift by will to an existing trust can satisfy this condition, but this issue does not arise for wills in the form in this book.

[7] Section 49A(3) IHTA 1984.

[8] Under s.144 IHTA 1984. What if a testator dies and the beneficiary is *en ventre sa mere* or born in the following two years? An unborn child cannot have an interest in possession. It is considered that a discretionary trust followed by an interest in possession for the beneficiary (once born) qualifies as an IPDI under s. 144 IHTA 1984.

[9] Disabled trusts are discussed in 24.1 (Disabled trusts)

[10] Sections 72, 73 TCGA 1992. This assumes that the administration of the testator's estate is complete when the life tenant dies.

[11] Assuming the beneficiary is UK resident and does not become non-resident in the following 6 years.

hold-over relief. Also, if hold-over relief is needed, it can up to a point (for property within the nil rate band) be obtained by creating a short term discretionary period.

Income tax advantages. IP trusts are better than discretionary trusts for income tax purposes.

Terms of IPDI trust after death of life tenant

The IPDI trust will confer a life interest on the life tenant, "L", subject to an overriding power of appointment. **17.5**

The position after the death of L depends on whether L is married/a civil partner. On the death of a life tenant who is single, there should normally be a discretionary trust.[12]

On the death of a life tenant who is married, there is a stark choice to be made:

(1) The trust fund may pass to the surviving spouse absolutely; or

(2) The trust property may continue to be held in trust.[13]

If L's spouse was disabled when the testator died, there is a third choice: to confer an IP on L's spouse.

Route (1) qualifies for the IHT spouse exemption.[14] Of course this route is only a practical solution if the spouse is a suitable person to receive the trust fund absolutely. Route (2) does not qualify for the spouse exemption. IHT is payable on the death of L and so 60% of the fund passes to the next generation.[15] There is an old jibe[16] that IHT is a voluntary tax paid by those who distrust their heirs more than they dislike the Revenue. This was formerly a half-truth; from 2006 (read "spouse" for "heirs") it is reasonably accurate.

The correct choice depends on the individual circumstances. Either route qualifies for the CGT uplift on the death of L.

---

[12] This gives flexibility. If the trust is would up after the death of the life tenant, this discretionary trust gives rise to a trivial exit charge, but the price is worth paying.
[13] Of course, lifetime planning offers further choices:
   (1) There could be an absolute appointment to L, following which L could confer an IPDI by will on his spouse. Then the property qualifies for the spouse exemption on the death of L. This course has a possible CGT downside: it loses (or at least reduces) the benefit of the CGT uplift on the death of L and instead incurs a CGT charge on the appointment to L.
   (2) The life tenant's interest could be revoked during his lifetime (creating either a PET or a chargeable transfer, depending on how it was done).
[14] Assuming the spouse is UK domiciled.
[15] Unless the spouse of L is disabled at the time of L's death.
[16] Roy Jenkins, *Hansard*, 19 March 1986, col.325.

This decision must be made during the lifetime of L. It cannot be altered after his death.[17] It is not necessary to make the *final* decision when drafting the will of the testator: it is necessary to make a *provisional* decision, i.e. one which can be changed subsequently (during the lifetime of L). The provisional decision made here is to forego the spouse exemption, and keep the trust property in the settlement. This is more often likely to be the final choice.

The provisional decision may be changed by executing an appropriate deed of appointment during the lifetime of L to confer an absolute interest on L's surviving spouse. The deed should normally be revocable during the lifetime of L. That is a matter which may usefully be considered when L makes his own will.

Age 18-to-25 trusts: qualifying conditions

17.6 The conditions here are complicated and much more restrictive.

The relief applies to trusts under the will of a parent of a beneficiary under the age of 25. A lifetime trust cannot be an Age 18-to-25 trust. Only parents may create an Age 18-to-25 trust.

The main condition is in s.71D(6) IHTA 1984 and needs to be set out in full:

> (a) that the [beneficiary who has not yet attained 25] ("B"), if he has not done so before attaining the age of 25, will on attaining that age become absolutely entitled to—
>
> (i) the settled property,
> (ii) any income arising from it, and
> (iii) any income that has arisen from the property held on the trusts for his benefit and been accumulated before that time,
>
> (b) that, for so long as B is living and under the age of 25, if any of the settled property is applied for the benefit of a beneficiary, it is applied for the benefit of B, and
>
> (c) that, for so long as B is living and under the age of 25, either—
>
> (i) B is entitled to all of the income (if there is any) arising from any of the settled property, or
> (ii) no such income may be applied for the benefit of any other person.

Although s.71D(6) IHTA is drafted by reference to a single beneficiary (i.e. B), HMRC apply the principle that the singular includes the plural

---

[17] Sections 142, 144 IHTA 1984 do not apply to settled property.

and so take B to include all beneficiaries within the relevant class provided they are alive at the date the s.71D trust takes effect and are under the age of 25.[18] It is permitted to have an overriding power of appointment which complies with these conditions.

It is also permitted to have the statutory power of advancement, and to extend it to the whole of the trust fund.

A trust satisfying the IPDI conditions is not an Age 18-to-25 trust: the IPDI regime has priority. But subject to that, an Age 18-to-25 trust may confer an interest in possession.[19]

What is the position if a parent has more than one child under 25? In the discussion below, it is assumed there are three children, A, B, and C. What can be done with the income and capital of each child's share? There are two approaches to this question: these may be called "share-by-share approach" and "the global approach".

(1) The share-by-share approach is to direct that:

   (a) The income and capital income of A's share may be applied only for the benefit of A.
   (b) Likewise B's share may be applied only for the benefit of B; and likewise for C's share.

(2) The global approach is to direct that:

   (a) The income and capital of A's share may be applied for the benefit of A or B or C (while under 25).
   (b) Likewise, B's share and C's share may be applied for the benefit of A or B or C (while under 25).

HMRC accept that the global approach is permitted in an Age 18-to-25 trust. So it is unnecessary for a parent by will to fix each child's share. While the child is under the age of 25, the income and capital may be used for any of the other children under that age. However, the child's share cannot be altered after he has reached 25. He must become entitled to the income and capital at that age. IPDI trusts are preferable, since although the income is fixed, capital may be used for any of the children or any other beneficiary irrespective of their ages.

---

[18] See www.step.org/attach.pl/1893/3568/s71Dguidance.
[19] It is an interesting question whether s.144(3) IHTA 1984 applies if a beneficiary under an Age 18-to-25 trust attains an IP within two years of the testator's death. But this question does not arise in this book. Age 18-to-25 trusts are not used.

Why use Age 18-to-25 trusts?

17.7 *IHT advantages and disadvantages.* Age 18-to-25 trusts offer two IHT advantages:

(1) There is no IHT charge on the death of a beneficiary under the age of 18. Since the possibility of a child dying under the age of 18 is in practice extremely remote, this is not a significant advantage.

(2) There is no ten-year charge or exit charge while the beneficiary is under 18; and the exit charge between the ages of 18 and 25 is based on that seven-year period (so the maximum charge at current rates is 4.2% of the trust fund). This seems like an advantage because it is better than the standard IHT trust treatment of ten year and exit charges. However it is much less favourable than IPDI trusts, where:

(a) the IHT charge arises on the death of the life tenant; and
(b) there is scope for IHT planning during his life.

If desired, the IHT risk of death under 25 for an IPDI could be covered by insurance. The cost of insurance against death under 25 would be far cheaper than the 4.2% IHT charge on the Age 18-to-25 trust. This is for the obvious reason that death under 25 is extremely rare. (In order to understand the rules, it is worth bearing in mind that although the 4.2% charge is *called* "inheritance tax", it is not in any meaningful sense an inheritance tax.[20] It is a tax on trusts, or if you prefer, a penalty for using trusts. It does not reflect the tax advantage of Age 18-to-25 trusts (as set out above). If it did, the rate would be far less than 4.2%.)

The only circumstance we can see in which an Age 18-to-25 trust may be useful is the somewhat theoretical case where:

(1) a parent dies leaving a child under 25, and

(2) the child himself has such a seriously impaired life expectancy that he will (or is almost certain to) die under the age of 25.

CGT advantages and disadvantages. Age 18-to-25 trusts do offer CGT hold-over relief on a termination of the trust.[21] As mentioned above, this relief is not as significant as may at first appear. So long as the trust endures there is no need for the relief.

---

[20] Contrast the income tax charge on pre-owned assets, which is not a tax on income: it is a penalty for carrying out certain types of IHT planning: see *Taxation of Foreign Domiciliaries*, James Kessler QC, Key Haven Publications, 7th edn, 2008, para.51.37.
[21] Section 260 TCGA 1992.

Bereaved Minors trusts

Bereaved Minors trusts can be dealt with quite briefly as there are no circumstances in which they will actually be useful. The main condition is set out in s.71A IHTA 1984: **17.8**

> (a) that the bereaved minor, if he has not done so before attaining the age of 18, will on attaining that age become absolutely entitled to—
>
> > (i) the settled property,
> > (ii) any income arising from it, and
> > (iii) any income that has arisen from the property held on the trusts for his benefit and been accumulated before that time,
>
> (b) that, for so long as the bereaved minor is living and under the age of 18, if any of the settled property is applied for the benefit of a beneficiary, it is applied for the benefit of the bereaved minor, and
>
> (c) that, for so long as the bereaved minor is living and under the age of 18, either—
>
> > (i) the bereaved minor is entitled to all of the income (if there is any) arising from any of the settled property, or
> > (ii) no such income may be applied for the benefit of any other person.

Why not to use Bereaved Minors trusts

The main reason why Bereaved Minors trusts will not be used is that parents will not want their children to become entitled to substantial sums at the age of 18. But even if a parent was content to allow that, an Age 18-to-25 trust is better, because it allows the option of postponing vesting of capital until 25 (or indeed later).[22] If the capital is in fact distributed at the age of 18, there is no IHT charge. A Bereaved Minors trust is less flexible, and offers no corresponding advantage.

"Express Wills"

The will drafting software "Express Wills" (published by Sweet & Maxwell) allows users to incorporate the will trusts from this book. This **17.9**

---

[22] By exercise of a power of advancement.

software is sophisticated and easy to use. It is not, of course, foolproof, but a useful tool and timesaver.

Will trusts and lifetime trusts: drafting differences

17.10   A will trust is of course a different matter from a lifetime trust. It takes effect in different circumstances—the testator *ex hypothesi* being dead at the time—and there are specific rules which apply only to wills. Tax considerations are different. These factors, however, do not cause many differences between the drafting of will trusts and lifetime settlements.

A handful of minor drafting points:

- One refers to the "testator" rather than the settlor. ("Testator" will serve for both sexes and "testatrix" is now obsolete.[23])

- Accumulation and perpetuity periods run from the date of the testator's death.

- The will has no settlor exclusion clause; for the settlor *ex hypothesi* will not benefit from his own will.

- The will is traditionally drafted in the first person, so one refers to "my trustees" instead of "the trustees", "my residuary estate", etc.; a convention of no significance and not fully adopted in this book.

- There are conventionally no recitals in wills; these are unnecessary in a lifetime settlement, so their omission does not matter. It follows that there is no testatum ("now this deed witnesses ...") whose purpose is to indicate where the recitals end and the body of the document begins.

The great distinction in common practice is that a lifetime trust is generally a lengthy document, drawn up with some care; a will trust is too often a short document and drawn up without much thought. This is usually the explanation of deficiencies of wills met in practice, as well as the routine absence of good drafting techniques, such as a definition clause or the use of a schedule of administrative provisions.[24] This practice has been castigated[25] but still continues. The drafter's first duty is to produce a will

---

[23] Following *Garner's Modern Legal Usage* (2nd edn, 1995, entry under "Testatrix").
[24] Perhaps in the past the use of schedules was discouraged by the rule that the will had to be signed at the "foot or end thereof", but that rule has been abolished, and it is now clear that a will may be signed either before or after the schedule: s.9 Wills Act 1837 as amended by the Administration of Justice Act 1982.
[25] "Trusts appear in wills as well as in lifetime settlements, and of course they need to be drafted with as much skill and care in either place; yet by tradition, solicitors and public alike seem to treat settlements as being specialised and difficult and wills as being so easy that they can be drafted by

that suits his client's needs. However the drafter (and authors of drafting books) must recognise commercial reality and seek to devise forms of wills which are technically adequate and approach the simplicity that the client would like to see.

Foreign trustees

17.11 In very large estates serious consideration should be given to the appointment by the will of non-resident trustees and (especially where there are foreign domiciled beneficiaries) non-resident executors.[26] This offers the possibility of substantial tax savings.

Survivorship clauses

17.12 A survivorship clause is one which provides that the spouse must survive the testator by a period (commonly 28 days) in order to benefit under the will.

These clauses do no harm provided:

(1) The survivorship period must be short enough not to delay or hinder administration. Twenty-eight days is OK; six months probably about the limit; anyway s.92 IHTA 1984 sets a six-month limit or you may lose the IHT spouse exemption).

(2) The estates of each spouse should contain sufficient assets for each to utilise their nil rate band.[27]

But what is the reason for the clause?

The testator's concern may be that his spouse will survive him, take under his will, and then die shortly after, so his residuary estate effectively passes under the will of the spouse. But if that is his concern, a survivorship clause is not a good solution since the spouse may just survive the

---

almost anyone and given away with packets of cornflakes..." (Richard Oerton, *New Law Journal* 19 February 1993, p.246.) Will trusts are in fact harder to draft than lifetime settlements, as the drafter has to look ahead to the time of the death of the testator and cater for a wider variety of circumstances.

[26] See *Taxation of Foreign Domiciliaries,* James Kessler QC, Key Haven, 7th edn, 2008, Chapters 52 (Estates of Deceased Person CGT) and 53 (Estates of Deceased Persons IT).

[27] Otherwise the NRB of the surviving spouse may be lost. E.g. suppose H has a estate of £1m and W has nothing. H dies and W dies shortly after, so the gift to W in H's will fails because of the survivorship clause. W's NRB is not utilised. A deed of variation would then be necessary to solve the problem.

28-day (or whatever) period and then die shortly after, and exactly the same problem still arises.

Usually the testator will be happy that his property passes under his spouse's or civil partner's will if he dies first. Usually the beneficiaries would be the same whoever dies first.

If the testator is not happy with this (e.g. in cases of remarriage with separate children from each marriage) then he ought to give the spouse an IPDI and direct where the capital is to go after her death.

For this reason, survivorship clauses are not used in the wills in this book.

Gift by will to existing trust[28]

17.13   The will precedents in this book do not make gifts to existing trusts. However, such gifts are sometimes made. Some concern has been caused by the view expressed by one commentator, that one cannot make gifts by will to existing trusts. The following discussion may therefore be of interest.

The leading cases in this area are *Re Edwards*[29] and *Re Schintz*.[30] It is submitted that the rules of law which emerge from these cases are as follows:

(1) A testator cannot make a gift by will to trustees to hold on the terms of a trust made after the will.[31]

(2) A testator cannot make a gift by will to trustees to hold on the terms of a trust

   (a) made before the will, but
   (b) affected by an appointment made after the execution of the will (and before the testator's death).[32]

Whether a particular gift is of this type is a matter of construction.[33]

---

[28] See also 21.6 (Power to accept additional funds).
[29] [1948] Ch 440.
[30] [1951] Ch 870.
[31] This breaches s.9 Wills Act 1837 (unless the trust is executed with the formalities of a will).
[32] Unless the power of appointment is exercised in a way which satisfies the formalities of the Wills Act 1837, which would require that the testator signed it in the presence of two witnesses. That is not, of course, the position for powers of appointment in common form. The reported cases concern powers of appointment exercisable by the testator. But in principle the same should apply to powers of appointment exercisable by trustees.
[33] Suppose the gift is "to the Trustees of the [name] trust, to hold on the terms of that trust".
It is considered that this clause as worded will result in the gift being held by the trustees on the terms of the Trust as it stood at the time of the will. For while a will "speaks and takes effect" from the time of the testator's death, as far as descriptions of property are concerned, it does not "speak and take effect" from the time of death for other purposes: see s.24 Wills Act 1837. Thus

If a testator purports to make a gift of this type then the gift might be entirely void;[34] or else it may take effect as a gift to the trustees to hold on the terms which had effect at the time the will was made (ignoring the subsequent appointment). In that case the power of appointment may then remain exercisable after the death of the testator.

(3) A testator can make a gift by will to trustees to hold on the terms of a trust made before the will. That trust may confer powers of appointment exercisable (in relation to the estate of the testator) after the death of the testator. This is often done. If (while the testator is still alive) the trustees of a trust make an appointment altering the terms of the trust, it would be necessary to make a new will.[35] This is a trap easily overlooked.

Watch out if a will makes a gift to a trust which holds two or more funds on distinct terms: remember to specify to which fund the gift is made, or how it is shared between the funds.

---

the reference in the will to "the terms of the trust" should be taken to mean the terms of the trust at the time the will was made, so the gift is valid. The cases are reviewed in *Thomas on Powers* (1st edn, Sweet & Maxwell, 1998), 2–19 to 2–38.

[34] As in *Re Jones* [1942] Ch 328.

[35] Assuming the intention is that the property passing under the will should pass to the terms of the trust as affected by the appointment.

CHAPTER 18

WILL DRAFTING AFTER THE FINANCE ACT 2008

Introduction

18.1 This chapter considers:

(1) The important development of the FA 2008, transferable nil rate bands.[1]

(2) What are the most suitable forms of will for different classes of testator.

(3) The drafting and construction of NRB gifts.

18.2 Basic IHT planning for spouses requires that each should make full use of the nil rate band. The IHT nil rate band (NRB) for 2008/09 is £312k and will rise to £325k in April 2009 and to £350k in April 2010 so use of both nil rate bands may save more than £140,000 tax.

Section 8A IHTA 1984 allows the transfer of NRBs between spouses (and civil partners—all references in this chapter to spouses include civil partners.) This relief applies if the surviving spouse dies on or after 9 October 2007. It does not matter when the first spouse died.[2] The relief therefore applies to any widow/widower or surviving civil partner living on 8 October 2007.

---

[1] We are grateful to Sheena Grattan, co-author of Drafting Trusts & Will Trusts in Northern Ireland, whose work on transferable nil rate band is incorporated in this chapter.

[2] For civil partners, the first death must necessarily have occurred on or after 5 December 2005 (the date of commencement of the Civil Partnership Act 2004).

Classic NRB trusts

18.3 Care has always been needed to ensure that spouses make full use of the NRB on the death of the first spouse to die. Before the introduction of transferable NRBs, this was generally achieved by a NRB discretionary trust in the will. The standard form was:

(1) a legacy of an amount equal to the NRB made to a discretionary trust.

(2) residue to the survivor absolutely or to an IPDI trust for her benefit.

The surviving spouse was a beneficiary of the NRB trust and so could continue to benefit from the entire estate. We refer to this as **"the classic NRB trust"**.

In order for the NRB trust to have effect the spouses had to equalise their estates or at least arrange that each estate held assets of a value equal to the NRB.[3]

The administration of NRB trusts is complicated, and is discussed in the next chapter.

Will drafting after the Finance Act 2008

18.4 NRB trusts are now redundant in most cases. The introduction of transferable NRBs means that the first spouse can leave everything to the survivor (or to an IPDI trust for the survivor). The survivor's estate can take advantage of two NRBs. The NRB of the first to die is not in principle wasted.

It has been suggested that NRB trusts might be preferable to using the transferable allowance, but in normal cases their advantages are tenuous:

(1) The transferable NRB may be abolished in the future; but this seems unlikely. In any case, the continued efficacy of debt and charge schemes cannot be guaranteed.

(2) The benefit of the NRB trust will exceed the benefit of the transferred NRB *if* the value of the assets held in the trust (or the associated debt or charge) is greater than the value of the transferred NRB at the time of the second death; but predicting these future values is impossible, so this is not a practical consideration.

---

[3] Note that transfers made specifically to use the nil rate band have an impact on the implementation of debt or charge arrangements: see Appendix 4 (NRB debt and charge arrangements: tax analysis).

(3) Classic NRB trusts may be useful where a married couple wants to create long term trusts (i.e. trusts which will continue following the second death). The first to die could leave everything to the survivor who could then establish a discretionary trust of two NRBs. The NRBs are not wasted on either death. However, the survivor's NRB is only increased for the purpose of the charge to tax on her death. So only one NRB will be available for the purpose of future IHT charges on the trust (i.e. the 10-yearly and exit charges). Two separate NRB trusts will eliminate any IHT charges in the first 10 years and reduce future charges. But in practice (like more elaborate planning involving pilot trusts) we do not expect this will often be worthwhile.

Married clients should generally opt for the simpler and cheaper route of transferable NRBs. So far as possible they should leave their NRB intact on the first death so it is transferred to the surviving spouse.

How transferable NRBs work

18.5 In short, the amount of the NRB on the death of the second spouse to die is increased by the percentage of the NRB which was not used on the first death. The percentage is calculated by:

- taking the NRB in force on the first death; and
- seeing how much of it, expressed as a percentage, was used up by the first spouse on his death.[4]

Example:
H dies in 2002/03 when the NRB is £250,000. He leaves £125,000 to his son and the residue to his wife W.
W dies in 2010/11 when the NRB is £350,000. H only used 50% of his NRB. The NRB available on W's death is increased by 50%, that is, to £525,000.

Same facts save that H left everything to W. H used 0% of his NRB. The NRB available on W's death will be increased by 100%, that is, to £700,000.

The NRB is only increased for the purpose of reducing the charge to IHT which is payable on the death of the second to die.[5] Obviously the

---

[4] Section 8A IHTA. HMRC have published tables showing the NRBs for IHT capital transfer tax and estate duty going back to August 1914: *www.hmrc.gov.uk/cto/customerguide/page15.htm*. Gifts made by the first spouse to die within seven years of his death reduce the NRB in the usual way.
[5] Section 8A(3) IHTA.

transferred NRB is available for the purpose of reducing the IHT on free property in the estate of the second to die, but it is also available for:

- failed PETs made by the second to die within 7 years of her death[6]
- settled property in which the second to die enjoyed an estate IP
- property subject to the gift with reservation provisions.

It does not matter whether there were sufficient assets on the first death to utilise the NRB, so it is not necessary for married couples to equalise their estates.

NRB claims

A claim must be made for the relief; we refer to this as a "**NRB claim**". 18.6
Section 8B IHTA provides:

(1) A claim under section 8A above may be made—
   (a) by the personal representatives of the survivor within the permitted period, or
   (b) (if no claim is so made) by any other person liable to the tax chargeable on the survivor's death within such later period as an officer of Revenue and Customs may in the particular case allow.

The NRB claim is normally made by the personal representatives of the second spouse to die though if they fail to do so it could in principle be made by a beneficiary of the estate or by the recipient of a failed PET.

A NRB claim is made by completion of a form[7] which should be sent to HMRC with the IHT 200. The time limit for a NRB claim (the "permitted period") is usually two years from the end of the month in which

---

[6] It is not obvious from the statute that this is correct. Tax on a failed PET is not strictly a charge to tax on the death (even though in the absence of the death there is no charge.) However when the Opposition (briefed by the Law Society) made the point, Jane Kennedy (Financial Secretary to the Treasury) stated in Parliament that the wording is "sufficient to encompass lifetime transfers on which an IHT charge subsequently crystallises on death"; *Hansard* 13 May 2008 col.172. That should be sufficient to resolve the ambiguity.
Relief is not available against tax payable at the time of a lifetime chargeable transfer (but there is no reason to make such a transfer.)

[7] Form IHT 216 accessible on *www.hmrc.gov.uk/CTO/iht216.pdf*.

the death of the second to die occurred[8] (there is provision for late claims but this should not be relied on).[9]

The PRs of the second to die need to provide the following documents to support their NRB claim: the death certificate of the first spouse to die; the marriage certificate, a copy of the will; a copy of any deed of variation; a copy of the grant of probate.

The PRs of the first to die should calculate how much of the NRB is transferable and ensure that they pass on to the surviving spouse (or his solicitor) sufficient documents and information to permit the surviving spouse's PRs to make a NRB claim in due course. This will include copies of: the IHT 200 return; the deceased's will; any deeds of variation; valuations of any assets which pass (under the will or intestacy or in the case of jointly held property by survivorship) other than to the surviving spouse; evidence to support the availability of reliefs such as APR and BPR where the relievable assets pass to someone other than the surviving spouse.

Solicitors can expect to do much chasing of copy documents for their long widowed clients! Remember to heed HMRC's warning about the importance of looking after one's documents: "The information and documents about the claim could be very valuable … and it will be important to keep them safe."[10]

HMRC will refuse to agree the amount of the transferable NRB on the first death.[11] HMRC may therefore reopen valuations/eligibility for reliefs on the occasion of the second death.[12]

Transfer of NRB in cases of remarriage

18.7 Where one spouse dies and the surviving spouse remarries, it is possible to acquire the NRBs of more than one deceased spouse. No distinction is drawn between the deceased's original NRB and the transferred NRBs of any predeceasing spouses. However this only applies up to a limit of one additional NRB.

---

[8] "Permitted period" is defined in s.8A(3) IHTA:

"In subsection (1)(a) above "the permitted period" means—

(a) the period of two years from the end of the month in which the survivor dies or (if it ends later) the period of three months beginning with the date on which the personal representatives first act as such, or
(b) such longer period as an officer of Revenue and Customs may in the particular case allow.

[9] See IHT Manual para.43006 for the circumstances in which HMRC admit late claims.
[10] See HMRC's "Transferable nil rate bands—Frequently asked questions" accessible on *www.hmrc.gov.uk/cto/rate-bands.pdf*.
[11] IHT Manual para.43050
[12] Section 274 TCGA 1992.

Example:
H1 dies leaving everything to his wife W. W thus acquires a 2nd NRB.
W marries H2.
W dies in 2010/11. W left £350k to her son and residue to H2. The NRB available on the death of H2 will be increased by 100% to £700,000.

Same facts save that W left everything to H2. The NRB available on the death of H2 will be increased by 100% to £700,000. Half the double NRB of W (representing the NRB of H1) is wasted.

Two NRB claims are needed: (1) a claim on the death of W and (2) a claim on the death of H2. The NRB claim on the death of W may in some cases be made late (at the time of the death of H2)[13] but it would be better practice to make that NRB claim at the time of the death of W.

Untransferable NRB problems

The rule that one is not allowed more than two nil rate bands raises various problems when spouses have remarried, which we call "**untransferable NRB problems**". Consider the following cases:

18.8

	Testator ("T")	Spouse ("W")
Case 1	One NRB	Two NRBs
Case 2	Two NRBs	One NRB
Case 3	Two NRBs	Two NRBs

Case one: T has one NRB and W already has two NRBs

If T gives his entire estate to W (not using his own NRB) then *all* his own NRB is entirely wasted. The problem is exactly as in the bad old days before transferable nil rate bands.

In this case the best form of will for T is a legacy of the single NRB to a classic NRB trust, with a gift of residue to W (or to an IPDI for her benefit). In this way T uses his NRB which is otherwise lost. T and W must equalise their estates (or at least make sure that T has assets to use his NRB).[14]

---

[13] Section 8B(2) IHTA.
[14] An alternative is to make simple gifts of the single NRB to the children absolutely. This avoids the hassle of the classic NRB trust. It is only satisfactory if W is sufficiently provided for and the children are financially competent to receive the money.

The above is a slight simplification: in many cases W will have more than one but less than two full NRBs.[15] So the best form of will for T is a legacy to the NRB trust which uses up the *untransferable* NRB (which may be the entire NRB amount or something smaller); and the residue is given to W (so as to top up her NRB to a double NRB.)

Case two: T has two NRBs and W has one NRB

If T gives his entire estate to W (not using his double NRB) then *half* of his double NRB is wasted. The position is similar—not identical—to the bad old days before transferable nil rate bands.

In this case the best form of will is for T to make a legacy equal to the single NRB to a classic NRB trust, with a gift of residue to W or to an IPDI for her benefit. In this way one half of T's double NRB is used by the gift to the trust and the other half is used by the transfer to W who will acquire a double NRB.[16] As above, T and W must equalise their estates (or at least make sure that T the assets needed to make the gift to the NRB trust.)

In many cases T will have more than one but less than two full NRBs. In that case the best form of will for T is a legacy to the NRB trust which uses up the untransferable NRB, and the residue is given to W (so as to give her a double NRB.)

Case three: T and W each have two NRBs

If T gives his entire estate to W, all of his double NRB is wasted. The position is comparable—but not identical—to the bad old days before transferable nil rate bands.

In this case it is not immediately obvious what is the best form of will.

The best solution will generally be for T to give a legacy equal to the *double* NRB to a classic NRB trust, with a gift of residue to W or to an IPDI for her benefit. In this way the double NRB of T is fully used. As above, T and W must equalise their estates (or at least make sure that T has assets to use his double NRB).

In many cases T and W will each have more than one but less than two full NRBs. In that case the best form of will for T is a legacy to the NRB trust which uses up the untransferable NRB (which may be the double NRB amount or something smaller); and the residue is given to W (so as to top up her NRB to a double NRB.)

---

[15] That is, only part of the NRB of W's former spouse may have been transferred to W, either because the will of W's former spouse made other gifts chargeable to IHT or because W's former spouse made lifetime chargeable gifts within seven years of death (failed PETs).

[16] As above, an alternative is to make simple gifts of a single NRB to the children absolutely.

The double NRB 10-year charge problem

The drawback is that the NRB trust (which will hold assets up to the amount of the double NRB) will suffer a small 10-year charge on the 10-year anniversary of the death of T.[17] We refer to this as the "**double NRB 10-year charge problem**". But the amount of that charge will not be significant compared to the future IHT saving on the death of W.

One way to avoid the 10-year problem is:

(1) to make simple gifts of a *single* NRB to the children absolutely, and

(2) to give a legacy equal to the single NRB to a classic NRB trust.

Of course it is only satisfactory if W is sufficiently provided for and the children are financially competent to receive the money.[18]

It is suggested that the standard will in this case ought to ignore the double NRB 10-year charge problem and give the full double NRB legacy to a NRB trust. If appropriate, a post-death appointment under s.144 IHTA within two years of the death can distribute some or all of the fund of the NRB trust. Part II of this book contains a precedent reducing a double NRB legacy to a single NRB legacy: **Form NRB Appointment 3.**

Why not use a Deed of Variation?

A form of will which is possible but slightly risky for estates with an untransferable NRB problem is one giving the estate to the surviving spouse absolutely. Of course the survivor could make a deed of variation after the death, so as to use the nil rate band. However, for various reasons the survivor may not make (or may be unable to make) the necessary arrangements.[19] It would be safer to make the NRB gift by will. In practice we suspect it will often happen that the entire estate is given to the surviving spouse, and the matter will have to be put right by a deed of variation. Where the exact IHT position is not known for certain when the DoV is executed, the documentation should employ a formula similar to that used in the draft wills in this book.

---

[17] In short, the NRB trust does not enjoy the benefit of a transferred NRB. So a trust with £624k assets anticipates a 10-year charge at an effective rate of 1%, = £6,240 tax (at 2008/09 rates). The use of lifetime pilot trusts may avoid the double NRB 10-year charge problem, but the amounts involved could only barely justify the additional trouble and cost.

[18] As above, an alternative is to make simple gifts of the double NRB amount to the children absolutely.

[19] A further problem is that a trust made by deed of variation is within the scope of the income tax settlement provisions. However, this problem would not affect typical NRB trusts as the NRB trust usually has no income; and even in other cases it does not greatly matter if the settlement provisions apply. Indeed, it will often be better if they do apply.

Commentary: let's abolish untransferable NRB problems

The introduction of transferable NRBs—a reform which this book advocated for many years—is very welcome. It is unfortunate that sometimes NRBs remain untransferable and NRB trusts will continue to be needed for most testators who remarry after the death of their first spouse, and for spouses of those testators. The removal of the double NRB limit would be a useful simplification of the law. The only objection to this reform can be the loss of tax paid by the estates of those unaware of (or who choose not to take advantage of) existing possibilities for tax planning. IHT payable on the second nil rate band of a remarried testator may fairly be described as a voluntary tax.

Choice of will trusts: overview

18.9 There are seven forms of will trust which will usually be the most satisfactory choices in any normal but reasonably substantial estate:

(1) *Discretionary will trust.* This is the most suitable form for a testator who is single. It can within two years of death be converted into any other form of trust. **Will 1** of the Precedents.

(2) *IPDI for surviving spouse.* This is the generally the best form for a married testator. It allows full transfer of the NRB. **Will 2** of the Precedents.

The next four wills are for where the testator faces the untransferable NRB problem:

(3) *Absolute gift of untransferable NRB; residue to IPDI trust for surviving spouse.* This form is appropriate for a testator facing the untransferable NRB problem if:

   (a) the family assets are sufficiently large that the surviving spouse does not need access to the untransferable NRB; and
   (b) the beneficiaries who receive the untransferable NRB gift (typically the testator's children) are adult and settled in life so it is appropriate to give them the sum absolutely. **Will 3** of the Precedents.

(4) *Classic NRB trust for untransferable NRB; residue to IPDI trust for surviving spouse.* This form is appropriate for a testator facing the untransferable NRB problem if it is not appropriate to give the surviving spouse an absolute interest. **Will 4** of the Precedents.

(5) *Classic NRB trust for untransferable NRB; residue to surviving spouse absolutely.* This is an alternative to form (4) where the testator:

   (a) has a smaller estate; or
   (b) wants simplicity; or
   (c) where it is desired to create an IPDI for the next generation(s). (If the spouse has an IPDI, as in will (4), a subsequent interest in possession does not qualify as an IPDI.)

   Will 5 of the Precedents.

(6) *Classic NRB trust for untransferable NRB; residue to surviving spouse absolutely or to discretionary trust (if no surviving spouse).* Better than Will 5, though more complex, this provides appropriate flexibility if the spouse does not survive. This is generally the best form if the family is united and it is appropriate to give the surviving spouse an absolute interest. **Will 6** of the Precedents.

Lastly for the single testator:

(7) *Classic NRB trust; residue to cohabitee absolutely.* **Will 7** of the Precedents.

Best form of will for single testator

The best form of will where a testator is single, and wishes to benefit his family or other individuals, is generally a discretionary will trust of the entire residuary estate. This allows the decision what to do with the property to be made after the death.[20] So long as s.144 IHTA 1984 remains in force, the testator need not in principle revise his will to take into account changes in circumstances or tax law. This is even more important following the FA 2006, since the current state of the law cannot be regarded as stable. We would regard this as preferable to an IPDI and far preferable to an Age 18-to-25 trust. The drafting is straightforward: see **Will 1** in the precedents.

A possibility for a cohabitee is a NRB trust with an absolute gift of residue to the testator's partner: see **Will 7**. Classic NRB trusts may be useful where it is desired to make provision for unmarried cohabitees or relatives (remember the elderly home-sharing Burden sisters).[21] The transferable NRBs do not apply in this case. IHT is in principle payable on the first cohabitee's death. The advantage of a will creating a NRB trust is that it avoids or reduces "bunching"—the additional IHT payable on the

18.10

---

[20] Section 144 IHTA 1984.
[21] *Burden v UK* [2008] STC 1305, ECHR (Grand Chamber).

second death which would arise if the first cohabitee gives everything by will to his partner. Of course the same result can be achieved by a simple discretionary will trust followed later by a deed of appointment. One could save more IHT by giving more than the nil rate sum to the discretionary trust, and indeed one would normally save the most by giving the entire estate to the discretionary trust. But then the discretionary trust does itself become subject to 10-year charges. Where the balance of advantage comes beyond a NRB gift will depend on many factors: obviously values and life expectancy of the cohabitee are the key factors, but there are other matters, such as cash flow, administration costs, and the completely unforeseeable issue of what the law will be at the time of the second death. So the NRB trust should be the starting point, because that costs nothing (beyond modest administration costs).

Best form of will for testator who is married or a civil partner

18.11 Where the testator is married, a discretionary will trust of the residuary estate is not the preferred choice, as:

(1) The process of obtaining probate is easier if the surviving spouse has an IPDI in the entire estate.[22]

(2) The almost inevitable execution of a deed of appointment involves additional legal work and expense.

The most appropriate form of will for a testator who is married is in principle as follows:

---

[22] Under a discretionary will trust IHT must be paid up front in order to obtain probate; and the tax is then reclaimed after execution of the appointment in favour of the spouse. Occasionally in practice the IHT Account is completed on the basis that an appointment in favour of a spouse will be made and IHT is not paid up front. In the past this led to no worse sanction than admonition: ("I trust you will take note of this for future cases": CTO General Examination Manual, Vol.2, reference SL 64). This practice does not seem to be mentioned in the present IHT Manual. But correct practice should be followed, since otherwise (i) the solicitor involved is submitting an incorrect return, which should never be done knowingly; and (ii) there remains a risk of penalties if the appointment is not made because (say) the surviving spouse unexpectedly dies.

The problem can in principle be avoided by an appointment creating an IPDI executed before obtaining probate. See s.144(3) IHTA 1984. An appointment before probate is in principle possible as a matter of trust law.

It is not necessary to wait three months from the death of the testator before creating an IPDI. The "three-month trap" survives in an attenuated form as it remains necessary to wait three months:

(1) In order to obtain the spouse exemption on an *absolute* appointment to a spouse; or
(2) In order to obtain IHT charity relief on an appointment to charity.

If an absolute appointment to a spouse or charity is made within three months, no IHT relief is available. See s.144(1) IHTA 1984, as (somewhat over-literally) expounded in *Frankland v IRC* [1997] STC 1450.

Either:

(1) Absolute gift of the entire estate to the surviving spouse.

Or:

(2A) Personal chattels to the surviving spouse absolutely;[23]

(2B) Residue to pass to will trust under which:

   (a) the spouse has an IPDI;
   (b) subject to that there is a discretionary trust.

In either case:

(1) There is no IHT on the death of the testator if the spouse survives him.[24]

(2) The surviving spouse acquires the testator's available NRB.

Before 2006, route 2 (life interest for surviving spouse) was better than route 1 (absolute gift to surviving spouse). At first sight, the FA 2006 altered the balance. It seems that each route has advantages and disadvantages:

(1) The advantage of an absolute gift to a spouse is that the surviving spouse can create an IPDI in favour of children/grandchildren on her death. A grandchildren's IPDI takes property out of the scope for IHT for two generations, which is as far as anyone can look ahead. But this assumes that the testator can accept the property law consequences of allowing his spouse absolute ownership.

(2) An IPDI for the surviving spouse avoids that problem, so the surviving spouse cannot consume the capital or prevent it from passing as the testator wants on her death. But if the spouse is given an IPDI, the next generation cannot have an IPDI under the same trust.

In fact, however, if the will creates an IPDI, the executors can review the position after the death of the testator. If appropriate they can appoint the trust property to the surviving spouse absolutely.[25] That allows us to return

---

[23] This must be the most convenient course unless the chattels include particularly valuable items.
[24] Section 18 IHTA 1984 (spouse exemption). This exemption does not apply if a UK domiciled testator leaves a foreign domiciled spouse: s.18(2). See on foreign domiciliaries generally James Kessler QC, *Taxation of Foreign Domiciliaries*, 7th edn, 2008, Key Haven Publications.
[25] There is no CGT cost in this if it is done during the administration period as the beneficiary acquires "as legatee": see s.62 TCGA 1992. If the property is transferred from the IPDI trust to the surviving spouse absolutely after the end of the administration period, there is a disposal for CGT purposes, see s.71 TCGA 1992, which may give rise to a CGT charge. But conferring a general power of appointment on the spouse/life tenant will solve this problem as this avoids the CGT charge on terminating a trust, and the interest created under the general power is an IPDI. HMRC accept that: STEP/CIOT Statement August 2008 Question 15, accessible on www.step.org.

back to route 2 if desired. A will creating an IPDI is therefore the more flexible, and so the better, option. The form is **Will 2**.

Where untransferable NRB problems arises, classic NRB trusts remain useful for a married testator.

Married testator: provision for children by will

18.12   What if the testator does not wish to give his spouse the entire estate or an IPDI in the entire estate? The testator may want to provide benefits on his death to his children (or other chargeable beneficiaries, i.e. not the spouse or UK charities). The usual case is where the testator has remarried and wishes to make substantial gifts to his children by his first marriage.

The simple course is a direct gift by will to the children. If the amount of the chargeable gift is *less* than the available nil rate band, this is satisfactory and although slightly less than ideal[26] it will generally be the best course as it is the simplest.

If the amount of the gift is *more* than the available nil rate band, this course should be avoided as it gives rise to unnecessary IHT on the death of the testator.[27] There are two better ways to deal with this situation:

(1) The testator may give a short IP to his spouse (e.g. to pay income to her for three months) and subject to that for (say) the children absolutely.

(2) Alternatively the testator could give a revocable life interest to the spouse and leave a letter of wishes requesting the trustees to make an appropriate appointment in favour of (say) the children.

In either case:

(1) There will be no IHT on the death of the testator if the spouse survives him/her as the IHT spouse exemption will apply.[28]

(2) The termination of the interest of the surviving spouse later will (if the drafting is right) be a PET.

---

[26] The gift will have the effect of reducing the NRB which can be transferred for use on the surviving spouse's death. It would be (slightly) better to make a gift of the entire estate to the spouse, transferring the NRB to her; and the spouse makes gifts to the children (which would be PETs). But in practice the advantage is not usually worth the complication involved.

[27] If this bad form of will is made it is possible to put matters right by a deed of variation, but this may involve a good deal of legal work and expense.

[28] Section 143 IHTA 1984 will not override the IHT spouse exemption: *Harding v IRC* [1997] STC (SCD) 321. The only complication is the loss of the nil rate band of the surviving spouse if she dies within seven years of the PET: see 29.12 (Arrangement for loss of nil rate band in case of death within 7 years).

Either of solutions (1) and (2) is satisfactory and it does not matter much which is chosen. The former solution is suggested where smaller sums are involved and the latter where larger sums are involved because it gives more flexibility. That course does however require the testator to rely wholly on his executors.

A simpler solution (for a united family) is to give the entire estate to the spouse absolutely and for the spouse to make gifts to the children. However:

(1) This does of course require the testator to rely wholly on his spouse.

(2) Section 143 IHTA raises a problem. This provides:

> Where a testator expresses a wish that property bequeathed by his will should be transferred by the legatee to other persons, and the legatee transfers any of the property in accordance with that wish within the period of two years after the death of the testator, this Act shall have effect as if the property transferred had been bequeathed by the will to the transferee.

Thus if the testator expresses a wish, and the spouse acts on it within two years, IHT is charged as if the gift were made by the testator (with consequent loss of the NRB) and if the values exceed the NRB a charge to tax on the death of the testator. One could avoid this problem by waiting two years, but that postpones the date when the 7-year PET period begins to run.

The nil rate formula

18.13 It cannot be known what the nil rate band will be at the time of the death; or how much of it will be available in the circumstances of the testator. Since testators do not want to review their wills each year, normal practice is to give a legacy of a sum of money fixed by a formula to equal the available nil rate band. This is easy enough in principle:

> "The Nil Rate Sum" means the maximum amount of cash which I can give on the terms of the Nil Rate Fund without incurring any liability to Inheritance Tax on my death.

The difficulty with the formula is its uncertainty. Quite apart from the possibility of a transferred NRB, discussed below, the NRB might be increased substantially: the Conservative Party promised to increase the NRB to £1m.[29] It may be substantially reduced. So the will should be drafted so that it still works satisfactorily even if the amount of the nil rate

---

[29] In addition, the nil rate sum may effectively increase if the testator owns business or agricultural property at the time of his death, or if he acquires a foreign domicile.

sum turns out to be substantially more or less than expected. This is best achieved in the following manner:

(1) The nil rate legacy should be given to *a discretionary trust for the benefit of all the family of the testator.* Except in very substantial estates, where the spouse would not need the nil rate sum, it should not be given to the children absolutely, or to a trust for the benefit of the family excluding the spouse. Thus no member of the testator's family need be prejudiced by an unexpected increase in the nil rate band.

(2) Other legacies in the will should be given priority to the nil rate sum. Thus other legatees will not be prejudiced by an unanticipated increase in the nil rate band.[30]

The nil rate sum is therefore defined in the following manner:

(1) "The Nil Rate Sum" means the maximum amount of cash which I can give on the terms of the Nil Rate Fund without incurring any liability to Inheritance Tax on my death, but subject to the following clauses.

(2) The Nil Rate Sum shall be nil if:

(a) Inheritance Tax has been abolished at the time of my death; or
(b) I am not married[31] at the time of my death; or
(c) The amount of the Nil Rate Sum would otherwise be less than £5,000.

(3) Any other legacy given by my will or any codicil shall be paid in priority to the Nil Rate Sum.

To reduce the Nil Rate Sum to the untransferable Nil Rate Sum, we say:

(1) "**The Untransferable Nil Rate Sum**" means the maximum amount of cash which I can give on the terms of the Nil Rate Sum:

(a) without incurring any liability to Inheritance Tax on my death; and
(b) without reducing the amount by which the Nil Rate Band applicable on the death of my Spouse would (apart from

---

[30] An alternative is to put a cap on the formula, so the amount given will not exceed a specified amount. This approach is adopted in Will 3.
[31] If the testator is a civil partner say: "I am not a Civil Partner at the time of my death". Of course paragraph (2)(b) is not appropriate for a cohabitee (Will 6).

this clause) be increased under section 8A Inheritance Tax Act 1984,

but subject to the following clauses.

(2) It shall be assumed that:

(a) any claim which may increase the Untransferable Nil Rate Sum shall be made[32]; and
(b) My Spouse will not remarry or enter into a civil partnership after my death.[33]

(3) My executors shall make a claim under section 8B Inheritance Tax Act 1984.

In the case where a testator with a double NRB wishes to create a NRB trust of a single NRB add:

(4) The Nil Rate Sum shall not exceed the Nil Rate Band Maximum at the time of my death. "The Nil Rate Band Maximum" here means the amount shown in the second column in the first row of the Table in Schedule 1 Inheritance Tax Act (upper limit of portion of value charged at rate of nil %) and in the first column in the second row of that Table (lower limit of portion charged at next rate).[34]

The amount of the Nil Rate Sum may be uncertain because:

(1) the testator may make a gift of an asset (within seven years of his death) the value of which is uncertain; or

(2) he may make gifts where it is unclear whether an IHT relief applies (such as the normal expenditure exemption or business property relief).

---

[32] That is, one must assume that the PRs of the surviving spouse will make any possible claim for the transferable NRB.
[33] This addresses the position if (1) H1 dies with a will in our book's form. (2) W has not previously married, so only has one NRB, so one would think that the untransferable NRB of H is £0. So far this is straightforward. (3) W then swiftly marries H2, say, while the estate of H1 is in the course of administration. (4) H2 dies, say, while the estate of H1 is in the course of administration, and leaves his entire estate to W. In the absence of this sub clause, could the executors of H1 say that the estate of W has a double NRB (because of the death of H2) so that there is an untransferable NRB given to the NRB trust after all? If that is right, perhaps the executors of H1 could or should always wait (maybe indefinitely) and see if W remarries. They may say that they will not know whether they have an untransferable NRB until the death of W. This sub-clause precludes that argument.
[34] The drafting is based on s.8A(7) IHTA.

It is suggested that the executors should have power to determine the issue for the beneficiaries and the following precedent is based on s.22(3) TA 1925:

> My executors may ascertain and fix the amount of the Nil Rate Sum so as to bind all persons interested under this Will if the executors have discharged the duty of care set out in section 1(1) Trustee Act 2000.

Construction of traditional nil rate band formula where transferable NRB applies

18.14 Suppose:

(1) A testator ("T") has a double NRB, because T's first spouse ("W1") predeceased T and left her entire estate to T.

(2) T married W2.

(3) T leaves a will in the form in the 8th edition of this book (a standard pre-2008 form) giving a legacy ("the NRB legacy") to a NRB trust of "*the maximum amount of cash which I can give on the terms of the Nil Rate Fund without incurring any liability to Inheritance Tax on my death*" and the residue to W2 (or to an IPDI for W2).

Effect of NRB claim

Assume that T's executors make a NRB claim. What is the amount of the NRB legacy: is it the amount of the single NRB or the double NRB? The answer is that it is the amount of the double NRB, for that amount is "the maximum amount of cash" which T can give to the trust.[35]

In the drafting of T's Will one should say this expressly, not for the avoidance of doubt (for we see little room to doubt) but to save the reader from having to ask the question.

---

[35] This is confirmed (if confirmation is needed) by consideration of s.8A(2) IHTA 1984. This defines the amount M as "the maximum amount that could be transferred by a chargeable transfer made (under section 4 above) on the person's death if it were to be wholly chargeable to tax at the rate of nil per cent (assuming, if necessary, that the value of the person's estate were sufficient but otherwise having regard to the circumstances of the person)." It is clear from s.8A(6)(a) IHTA that the transferred NRB is taken into account in computing M. It is not logical to construe similar words in a will differently.

HMRC also agree with this view: IHT Manual para.43053.

The contrary view has been suggested, on the grounds that a will speaks from death, so anything that happens after death (such as a claim for the transfer of the NRB) must be disregarded. But the statutory rule is actually that a will shall "speak and take effect as if it had been executed immediately before the death of the testator"; Section 24 Wills Act 1837. The statutory provision does not support the view that one should disregard post death events if relevant under the terms of the will.

The power to make a NRB claim

In this situation the decision to make a NRB claim is very significant: the claim does not affect the amount of IHT payable on the death of T (there is none either way) but it doubles the size of the NRB legacy (received by the NRB trust) and correspondingly decreases the residuary estate (received by the widow).

In general, a claim can only be made by the PRs of T.[36] In the absence of any provision in the will, T's executors have a discretion whether or not to make the NRB claim.

A NRB claim made by the PRs must be made by all the PRs[37] so if W2 is an executor she has effective power to veto the NRB claim. It is considered that the power of W2 to make (or refuse) a NRB claim should be regarded as a semi-fiduciary power so that other beneficiaries could only challenge a decision not to make a NRB claim where there is bad faith; for W2 to consult her own interests in deciding whether or not to allow a NRB claim to be made is not bad faith.

If W2 is not an executor, the executors will have to balance the conflicting interests of W2 against those of the trust in deciding whether or not to make the NRB claim. In practice since W2 will be a beneficiary of the NRB trust, it should not be problematic to make the claim, and it would normally be in the interest of the beneficiaries as a whole to make the NRB claim (that is why the NRB trust is set up in the first place).

The issue is most likely to be problematic where:

(1) T has children of his first marriage who are beneficiaries of the NRB trust; and
(2) W2 has children from her first marriage who are not beneficiaries of the NRB trust.

In that case the effect of the claim is to transfer a NRB amount from W2 to the trust, so in principle providing a long term benefit for the children of T and depriving the children of W2 (assuming they would benefit under W2's will). The solution may be to add the children of W2 to the NRB trust and make an appropriate appointment before making the claim.

It is suggested that in the drafting of the Will one should expressly require the PRs to make the NRB claim, so as to avoid these difficulties.

Once one has made the claim, the executors then face the untransferable NRB charge problems. Assuming that W2 has only a single NRB, it will be desirable for the executors of T:

---

[36] The beneficiaries of the NRB trust could not make a claim as they are not a person liable to tax on the death. It is theoretically possible the recipient of a failed PET might be able to make a claim but that will not often happen.

[37] HMRC agree: IHT 216 provides: "All those who will be applying for a grant of representation/Confirmation to the deceased's estate must sign."

(1) to claim the transferable NRB.

(2) to transfer half of the double NRB legacy to W. Then W will acquire the double NRB on her death, and the double NRB legacy on the death of T is not wasted. Part II of this book contains a precedent.

Terms of classic NRB trust

18.15 There are two possibilities:

(1) The nil rate sum may be held on a long-term discretionary trust. This was the usual course prior to the FA 2006.

(2) The nil rate sum may be held:
   (a) on a discretionary trust for the period of two years;
   (b) thereafter the surviving spouse may have an IP. This will not be an IPDI, so it will not be an estate IP for IHT purposes.[38] The nil rate fund will not be in the estate of the surviving spouse.

The nil rate sum will normally consist of non-income producing assets so it does not make any practical difference which solution is adopted, but solution (1) is marginally easier to draft, and solution (2) raises the problem of the disabled person trap if the surviving spouse was disabled when the testator died.[39] So the precedents in this book set out a simple discretionary trust.

There are two ways to give the nil rate sum to a discretionary trust:

(1) The nil rate sum may be given to a lifetime trust in existence at the time the will is made. In practice this normally involves creating one (or two) trusts (known as "pilot trusts") with a nominal trust fund.

(2) The nil rate sum may be held on terms set out in the will.[40]

---

[38] Provided that the surviving spouse is not a disabled person (in the IHT sense) at that time.
[39] See 26.7 (Disabled person trap).
[40] It is not necessary to say:

"I give the Nil Rate Sum to the Trustees to hold on the terms set out below"

Such forms go back to before the Land Transfer Act 1897 when real property did not vest automatically in executors, so a testator had to devise it expressly to trustees, if he wanted to create a trust. So even for land the form has been unnecessary for a century. The meaning of the will is plain enough without it: if the trustees are directed to hold the Nil Rate Sum on trust, that is what they must do. But these words are reluctantly added to the wills in the 7th and subsequent editions of this book because experience showed their absence caused some confusion.

Married testator with business or agricultural property 283

It makes little difference which is chosen, from a trust or a tax viewpoint.[41] The forms in this book make the gift to a discretionary trust declared in the will, which seems the easier course.

The will may also provide that the spouse will have an interest in possession in the residuary estate. The drafter then has another choice:

(1) The will may create two separate trusts, a trust of the nil rate sum and a trust of the residuary estate.

(2) The will may create one single trust with two funds, a nil rate fund and a residuary fund (generally called "sub-funds").

It makes little difference from a trust or a tax viewpoint, and the balance of convenience favours a single trust with two funds.

For the administration of NRB trusts, see the next chapter (Administering NRB trusts).

Alternative to nil rate band trusts

18.16 An alternative to a NRB trust is an absolute gift of a share of the family home to children. This is fine from an IHT viewpoint. It loses the CGT private residence exemption (but that is less important than IHT). The surviving spouse has slightly less security of possession (e.g. on the insolvency of a child). In practice this is not usually done.

Married testator with business or agricultural property

18.17 One difficulty with drafting a will involving business or agricultural property is that the drafter can have no idea what IHT relief will apply to that property at the time of the testator's death. There is no reason to think that the present rules are destined to endure.

From an IHT viewpoint the ideal form of will for a testator who is married, whose estate includes business or agricultural property, is as follows:

1. A discretionary trust consisting of:

   (1) all property qualifying for 100% business property relief;

---

[41] Note in particular that s.80 IHTA 1984 will apply to the fund in which the surviving spouse has an IPDI. In consequence, briefly, that fund is treated as being comprised in a trust (i) made when the surviving spouse dies, or when her interest terminates, and (ii) which is treated as a separate trust from the nil rate band trust.

(2) property qualifying for less than 100% relief (up to the nil rate band).

2. An IPDI for the spouse for the remainder.

Unfortunately the drafting is frightfully complicated because the draft must deal with (i) assets qualifying for 100% relief, (ii) assets qualifying for 50% relief, (iii) restrictions on relief under s.112 IHTA 1984 (excepted assets). The result is not appropriate except for clients whose estates are sufficiently large to justify more than usual care.

For ordinary estates, the better course is to use a discretionary will trust, which is simple and nearly as satisfactory. (Some practitioners avoid this course because of the risk that s.144 IHTA 1984 may be abolished. But it is considered that the risk of this is remote; if it happened the worst that would follow would be that the testator has to make a new will.)

Bad form of will for testator with business or agricultural property

A testator with agricultural or business property should not make a nil rate band gift in common form. A gift of "the maximum amount of cash which I can give on the terms of the Nil Rate Fund without incurring any liability to inheritance tax on my death" will not have the expected effect because of the application of s.39A IHTA 1984.

Best forms of will making substantial gifts to charity

18.18 Will drafting is straightforward if the entire estate (or the entire estate above the nil rate band) passes to UK charities; but there are many difficult questions if the testator wishes to share his estate between charities and individuals who receive more than the nil rate band. There is much scope for maximising the tax reliefs. Care is also needed for foreign charities. For these problems, and suggested solutions, see James Kessler's *Taxation of Charities*.[42]

Best form of will for foreign domiciled testator

18.19 A testator not domiciled in the UK with a substantial estate in England or Wales should make two wills:

---

[42] James Kessler QC and Setu Kamal, 6th edn, 2007, Key Haven Publications, for details see *www.kessler.co.uk*.

(1) A will governed by English law to deal with property situate in the UK. This should be drafted by English lawyers in the first instance but reviewed by lawyers in the country of the testator's domicile.

(2) A will governed by the law of his domicile, to govern all other property. Such a will should be considered even if there is no such property.

While a single English will could be made which deals with UK and foreign property, there is a risk that problems may arise through ignorance of requirements of the law of domicile. Conversely a foreign will may deal with UK situate property[43] but the IHT complications are such that the foreign will must be reviewed by UK lawyers; and it is easier to have a separate English will made for the purpose.[44]

The English will, where the testator is married, should normally give an interest in possession to the spouse; and if appropriate a nil rate band discretionary trust. In other cases, a simple discretionary will trust is probably the best form for the English will.[45]

The English will should contain a governing law clause: see 27.1 (Governing law, place of administration and jurisdiction clauses). Both wills should contain declarations of the testator's domicile.[46] In case there is any doubt where the property is situated, the trustees of each will

---

[43] The Wills Act 1963 makes this easier: inter alia a will executed in accordance with the law of domicile is treated as properly executed.

[44] It is tempting not to bother. Those who are so tempted should read *McGowan v Hamblett* 8 ITELR 943. Here a New Zealand will disposed of English land. The drafter fell into the *Benham* trap (leaving property in equal shares to a spouse and other beneficiaries without considering the IHT implications). A small cost in UK legal advice at the time of the will would have made the entire litigation unnecessary.

[45] For a full discussion of the tax issues for wills of foreign domiciliaries see *Taxation of Foreign Domiciliaries*, 7th edn, 2008, Key Haven Publications, Ch.46 (IHT on death: wills and IOVs).

[46] The declaration will be evidence, though not necessarily cogent evidence, of the testator's domicile. This is obvious on principle but if authority is needed, see *IRC v Bullock* 51 TC 522 at p.540: "The declaration as to domicile contained in the Appellant's will is also a matter to be taken into account, although the weight to be attributed to it must depend on the surrounding circumstances." This evidence is much more cogent if the will briefly sets out the facts which justify foreign domicile (rather than simply stating that the testator is domiciled in any particular state). The declaration should be drafted according to the individual's circumstances, and not taken from a standard precedent. Three examples:

"I declare that my domicile is and continues to be the Province of Nova Scotia, Canada, where I was born and brought up, to which Province I intend to return and remain permanently upon my wife's death." (The form used in the *Bullock* case.)

"I declare that (i) although I have resided in England since [*date*] I do not have, and have never had the intention of residing there permanently, and (ii) it is my intention on my retirement to return to my home in Bermuda and to cease to reside in the United Kingdom; and I am domiciled in Bermuda accordingly."

"I declare that:

(1) I was born in and have a domicile of origin in England.
(2) I have resided in Bermuda since [*date*] and intend to reside there permanently.

Accordingly I am and intend to remain domiciled in the Bahamas."

should have power to determine the issue in a manner which binds the beneficiaries.

Best form of will for UK domiciled testator with foreign domiciled spouse

18.20 Where a UK domiciled testator has a foreign domiciled spouse, the usual IHT spouse exemption does not apply.[47] The choice for the will lies between a discretionary will trust or an absolute gift to the foreign domiciled spouse. Which is better? Either way, there is a charge to IHT on the death of the testator. But if the property is given to the spouse, it is outside the scope of IHT thereafter, so long as it is not UK situate. If the property is given to a will trust, it remains within the scope of IHT, it is not excluded property, as the will trust has a UK domiciled settlor. So at first sight, the absolute gift seems better. Having said that, if property goes into the discretionary will trust and out to the spouse again within two years, the IHT position is just the same as a direct gift: s.144 IHTA 1984. And it may be desired to pass the property to others, perhaps giving it to the next generation (particularly if not UK domiciled). Also when the testator make the will, one won't usually know the domicile position at the time of the death. If the spouse lives long enough, she may become deemed UK domiciled for IHT purposes. All things considered, the discretionary will trust seems the more flexible and safer course for the will, in a routine case. In most cases, the will trust is likely to be wound up within two years. But the only cost is the cost of the deed of appointment. Of course, the impact of the law of the domicile of the spouse would also need to be considered.

Existing wills containing a classic NRB trust

18.21 There are of course many existing wills containing a NRB trust. Even if the testator has already died, it may still be possible to take advantage of the transferable NRB. There are three scenarios to consider:

For an example of a bald declaration of domicile being (rightly) disregarded, see *Reddington v MacInnes* [2002] ScotCS 46 accessible on *www.bailii.org*. (If those drafting that will had considered domicile more carefully, the litigation might have been avoided.)

[47] Apart from the (almost) nominal £55,000 spouse exemption, which will sometimes be available but often that will have been used up before the death. See *Taxation of Foreign Domiciliaries* James Kessler QC, Key Haven Publications, 6th edn, Ch.41 (UK domiciliary married to foreign domiciliary).

Scenario One: Both spouses died before 9 October 2007

The NRB is not transferable. The first spouse to die had to make use of his or her own nil rate band by way of a classic NRB trust or absolute gift. If this was not effected by the will it is still possible to execute a deed of variation within two years of the first death. This can be done on the "double death" situation—so long as the instrument of variation is executed within two years of the death of the first spouse to die. This will therefore remain important until 9 October 2009.

Scenario Two: Surviving spouse is still alive; first spouse has died

The principles are the same whether the first spouse died before or after 9 October 2007. If the first spouse to die has left everything to the surviving spouse the full nil rate band is transferable.

What if the first to die had a will incorporating a standard NRB trust? If still within two years of death (and remember the first three-month trap)[48] the trustees can appoint the trust assets in favour of the surviving spouse and this will be treated for IHT purposes as if the assets had simply been left to the surviving spouse outright.[49] This is not possible if the two years have expired from the death (but a debt or charge or appropriation scheme should by then have been put in place.)

Scenario Three: Both spouses dead; surviving spouse died on or after 9 October 2007

Suppose H died in 2005/06 when the NRB was £275,000. W died on 12 October 2007. H's will gave the NRB to a discretionary trust and the residue to W. W's executors are alert to the fact that if husband had not used any of his NRB, her estate would benefit from £600,000 (rather than £575,000).

The appointment out within two-year route has been closed since W died before any distribution could be made to her from the NRB trust (whereupon she ceased to be an object of the trustees' powers). Is it possible to vary the husband's will to eliminate the NRB trust? The class of beneficiaries in a standard form NRB trust includes minor or unborn beneficiaries so this would not be possible.[50] Is it possible to appoint out to adult beneficiaries who then make the variation? In authors view, the answer is, yes, though care must be taken with the drafting.

---

[48] See fn.22 above.
[49] See s.144 IHTA 1984. This is confirmed—if confirmation is necessary—by HMRC's guidance (para.15) accessible at *www.hmrc.gov.uk/pbr2007/it-nil-rate-guide.pdf*.
[50] Except with an application to the Court under the VTA 1958 which is not likely to be cost effective.

Both spouses still alive

Both parties are still alive and have wills creating NRB trusts. Should they make new wills? No: codicils could be made to revoke the NRB gifts but that can (as noted above) just as well be done after the death by an appointment within s.144 IHTA. Part II of this book contains a precedent: **Form NRB Appointment 1.**

CHAPTER 19

ADMINISTRATION OF NIL RATE BAND TRUSTS

Introduction

This chapter deals with the administration of NRB trusts in the limited cases where they remain useful after FA 2008: Wills 4–7 in this book.[1] It is assumed that the testator is survived by his spouse.[2] There are five ways to proceed:

(1) Raise the nil rate sum (2008/09, £312,000) to hold on the terms of the NRB trust. Alternatively appropriate assets to that value to the trust. The trust is then administered like any other normally funded trust.

(2) Appropriate a share in the family home to the trust.

(3) The loan scheme (discussed below).

(4) The charge scheme (discussed below).

(5) Waive the NRB legacy (in whole or in part).

Appropriation of share of family home

The simplest course is to appropriate to the NRB trust:

(1) the whole of the testator's interest in the family home (if its value is less than the nil rate sum); or

19.1

19.2

---

[1] See Chapter 18 (Will Drafting after the FA 2008)
[2] Wills 4–6 deal with a married testator. Will 7 concerns cohabitees. This chapter refers to a "spouse" (the term is understood to include civil partner) but the same applies to a cohabitee in a Will 7 case.

(2) a share of the family home with a value equal to the nil rate sum (if the value of the testator's interest exceeds the nil rate sum).

HMRC have contended—though with limited enthusiasm—that the surviving spouse occupying the property has an interest in possession in it.[3] But it does not matter after the FA 2006 whether this is right or wrong, as long as:

(1) the appropriation is not within two years of the death[4]; and

(2) the surviving spouse is not "disabled" (in the IHT sense) at the time of the death of the testator.

The recommended method of dealing with NRB gifts is, therefore:

(1) to wait two years from the death of the testator;

(2) to appropriate to the trust the testator's interest in the family home (or a share of that interest if it is worth more than the nil rate sum). There is no SDLT on this appropriation.[5] To facilitate this we have provided in the draft wills in this book that the appropriation may rely on the probate valuation.

(3) to appoint an IP in favour of the surviving spouse. The appointment has no IHT effect but will ensure that CGT principal private residence relief is available to the NRB trustees when the property is eventually sold. This is discussed in detail in Appendix 6.

Part II of this book contains a precedent deed of appropriation and appointment.

This seems the best course, where it is possible, because it is simplest. In particular:

(1) It avoids the complex tax issues raised by the debt and charge schemes including SDLT and s.103 FA 1986 (see Appendices 4 and 5).

(2) It avoids Limitation issues raised by the debt and charge schemes (see below).

(3) It avoids the problem that the debt may become irrecoverable.

---

[3] There are strong arguments against this view, which HMRC have at least on some occasions accepted. A full discussion is outside the scope of this book: see "Splitting Up the Family", *Taxation*, Vol.137 (1996) p.113 accessible on *www.kessler.co.uk*. See also *Judge (PRs of Walden decd) v IRC* [2005] STC (SCD) 863. HMRC did not argue that the trustees (who were unaware that they even had a discretion to allow her to occupy) conferred an estate-IP on the spouse.

[4] A discretionary trust may be converted into an IPDI trust within two years by operation of s.144 IHTA 1984.

[5] Paragraph 3A Sch.3 FA 2003

Position if house worth less than nil rate sum

If the testator's interest in the home is worth less than the nil rate sum and the testator has additional assets in his estate, the question arises how to deal with the balance. The choice is:

(1) *Waive the balance of the legacy to the NRB trust.* This is the easiest course. It may be less efficient for IHT: it loses the benefit of part of the testator's nil rate band, and it may increase IHT on the second death. But in practice this may not matter, or the amount involved may not be worth worrying about.

(2) *Appropriate further assets to the NRB trust and deal with the trust like any other funded trust.* This is administratively inconvenient.

(3) *Leave the money owed to the NRB trust outstanding, as a debt from the surviving spouse.* This is the debt or charge arrangement. The advantages are:

   (a) It is not necessary to invest and administer the nil rate fund separately, incurring additional investment and accountancy costs.
   (b) The nil rate fund will not produce income, and so it will not be necessary to pay tax at the trust rate or dividend trust rate.[6]

In practice the appropriation of the home interest to the NRB trust will normally suffice. However, the debt will sometimes be an attractive supplement in addition.

If the surviving spouse was "disabled" (in the IHT sense) when the testator died it is not desirable to appropriate the family home to the trust. In this (relatively rare) case, the debt or charge scheme should be operated for the entire nil rate sum.

Trust law issues

The trustees must have power to make the arrangements. (A family trustee may be prepared to act in breach of trust; a professional trustee could not do so.) The will should pave the way for arrangements of this kind by including appropriate powers, and these are contained in will forms 4–7.[7]

19.3

19.4

---

[6] This problem can be avoided if the NRB trust becomes interest in possession in form.
[7] Sometimes the will contains a NRB discretionary trust but no express power to make the debt or charge arrangements. In this case an exercise of the overriding power of appointment under the will trust can generally confer the necessary power: see 11.2 (Power of appointment).

The arrangement must not be a sham. Properly executed arrangements will not be a sham. It does not matter that the debt from the surviving spouse remains outstanding. It does not matter that the trustees follow the wishes of the spouse if they consider (as trustees generally will) it is appropriate to do so.[8] It might be different if (say) the spouse were (mis)advised not to bother about the documentation as the funds were "yours really".

The professional advisers must explain to the spouse:

1. Their (limited) rights as beneficiary under the discretionary trust.
2. Their duties as executor and trustee (if appointed executor and trustee).
3. The terms of the debt or charge (if any).
4. An appropriate risk warning. This would make the following points. The arrangement has been accepted by HMRC since at least the 1990s. While it is possible they may change their minds there is (in our view) no sound basis for them to do so. There is also some risk that an IHT ten-year charge may arise, of a more than nominal amount (e.g. because rates or values change). But any ten-year charge will be far less than the IHT saving. It is also conceivable that new legislation may stop the scheme, but even if that happens it is most unlikely that the tax position will be worse than if nothing is done.

That advice should be recorded in writing.

There is no difficulty in the same solicitors acting for the executors and the surviving spouse, as long as both parties agree to that. An explanation must likewise be given to the other executors and trustees (unless they are solicitors and do not need this).

We discuss the tax issues in Appendices 4–5.

Implementation of debt scheme

19.5 The following deals with the position where:

---

[8] *Re the Esteem Settlement* [2004] WTLR 1 [2003] JLR 188 at para.165 accessible on *www.jerseylaw.je*. Kessler, "What is (and what is not) a Sham" (1999) OITR, vol.9, p.125 accessible on *www.kessler.co.uk*. In 2003 this aspect received attention because of comments of Peter Twiddy, former head of IR (Capital Taxes), but this was not followed up by action. See the Trust Discussion Forum thread "NRB Loans: CTO Sham Attack", on *www.trustsdiscussionforum.co.uk*.

(1) it is not desired to appropriate the family home to the trust (e.g. where the surviving spouse was disabled (in the IHT sense) when the testator died); or

(2) the nil rate sum is not wholly satisfied by an appropriation of the testator's interest in the family home, and the debt (or charge) arrangement is used for the balance.

There is an important difference between Wills 4 and 5–7 which affects the implementation of the debt scheme.

(1) Under Will 4, the residue of the estate is retained by the executors in their capacity as the trustees (who hold on trusts under which the surviving spouse has an IPDI.)

(2) Under Wills 5–7, the residue is transferred to the surviving spouse absolutely and the executors will eventually drop out of the picture.

This affects the way that the legacy of the nil rate sum ("NRS") is dealt with.

Implementation of debt/charge scheme in a Wills 5–7 case

In the Wills 5–7 case there are two ways of dealing with the NRS:

(1) The spouse may promise to pay the NRS personally: she then receives the entire unencumbered residuary estate but incurs a debt which will be deductible for IHT on her death. This is known as "the debt scheme".

(2) The NRS may be charged on the testator's property (so the spouse does not incur a debt; she does not receive the entire unencumbered estate; but the assets she does acquire from the estate are reduced in value by the charge on the testator's property). The documentation and implementation is rather more complicated. This is known as "the charge scheme".

The debt scheme is easier than the charge scheme: the documentation and implementation of the charge scheme is rather more difficult. However, in some cases s.103 FA 1986 makes the debt scheme ineffective so the charge scheme is the only option (or Will 4 should be used).

Implementation of debt scheme in a Will 4 case

Under Will 4, there is a simpler solution. The NRS may simply be left unpaid. There would be an agreement (under clause 11 of Will 4) which dealt with index-linking. One does not need a debt agreement imposing a personal liability on the trustees of the residuary estate, or a charge. The NRS is a liability of the residuary estate and deductible for IHT. Section 103 FA 1986 is not a problem in a Will 4 case.

Liability for breach of trust if NRS becomes irrecoverable

In the Will 4 case, the trustees of the NRS could not possibly be liable for breach of trust if the NRS becomes unrecoverable (i.e. the debt is left outstanding and the residuary estate becomes insolvent). The reason is that the beneficiaries interested in the capital of the NRS are the same as the beneficiaries interested in the capital of the residuary estate. Leaving the debt outstanding is an action which favours the capital beneficiaries of the residuary estate, so what they lose on one side they gain on the other. Hence an exclusion clause such as in cl.8.4 of Will 5 (cl.9.4 of Will 6) is not needed for Will 4.

Wills 5–7 contain an exclusion clause to cover this case. It is not really needed; the power to lend is a dispositive power, it is intended to be used to benefit the spouse.

Administration of the NRB trust

19.6 The NRB trust will be within the scope of IHT 10-year charges.[9] In practice no IHT charge will arise because the value of the trust fund (the interest in the home and/or the benefit of the debt) should fall within the nil rate band. If the asset is a share in the house, it should be valued on a discounted basis.[10] Nevertheless, it will be necessary to complete the form IHT100.

The trustees have discretions which they should review as often as appropriate. If the circumstances of the spouse change, it may be appropriate to call in the debt (if any) of the spouse. For instance, if the spouse moves into residential care accommodation and the land is sold. On any occasion when the spouse makes a new will, or if she remarries, the position should generally be reviewed. In the absence of these special circumstances, it is sufficient to review the position every 10 years when an IHT return falls due.

---

[9] These arise on the 10-year anniversaries of the death of the testator: see ss.64 and 83 IHTA 1984.
[10] See 20.5 (Valuation).

Limitation considerations

The trustees must not allow the debt (if any) to become statute-barred. **19.7**
Section 8 Limitation Act 1980 provides:

> An action upon a speciality shall not be brought after the expiration of 12 years from the date on which the cause of action accrues.

The Spouse Undertaking in this book is a "speciality" since it is made by deed. The cause of action "accrues" when the deed is made.[11] This applies even though the intention of the parties may be that the spouse should not pay for many years. The only way to avoid the Limitation Act applying, therefore, is that the spouse must acknowledge the trustees' claim.[12] Then the 12-year period starts running again from the date of acknowledgement.[13] The convenient time to deal with this would be on the 10-year anniversary when the IHT return goes in.[14]

Subsequent sale of property

No difficulty arises on the sale of the property. If the property has been **19.8**
appropriated to the trust, CGT private residence relief will in principle apply.[15] The proceeds of sale will be received by the trustees and the surviving spouse in proportion to their joint ownership. The trustees may

---

[11] *Re George* (1890) 44 Ch. D 627; *Re Brown* [1893] 2 Ch. 300.
[12] Section 6 Limitation Act 1980 allows an extension of time for certain contracts of loan. However the Spouse Undertaking is not a contract of loan. An alternative to acknowledgement is repayment of the debt in part (£1 would suffice). Another solution is that the debt should be on terms that it is not payable on demand, but this raises possible IHT and income tax problems.
[13] See s.29(5) Limitation Act 1980. The acknowledgement must be in writing and signed by the debtor.
[14] If the debt does accidentally become statute-barred, the result may not be disastrous. HMRC accept that a statute-barred debt of a deceased person is allowable for IHT purposes provided that it is paid: see IHT Manual para.28384. So as long as the debt is actually paid to the trustees of the NRB trust by the executors of the spouse, after the death of the spouse, the IHT deduction is available. Difficulties would arise, however, if the executors refused to make the payment. They would refuse to make the payment if the beneficiaries under the will of the spouse were different from the beneficiaries under the NRB trust. (That might well happen. It is quite likely to happen if a spouse remarries after the death of the testator. It might also happen if a spouse's marriage to the testator was a second or subsequent marriage.)

To let the debt become statute-barred is in principle a breach of trust. If the spouse is a trustee of the NRB Trust, she will not be allowed to gain by her own breach of trust. Her estate would be required to reimburse the nil rate trustees. That would in principle solve the problem, though this claim too might conceivably become statute-barred. It would be better that the debt does not become statute-barred and this need not be considered any further.

[15] The appointment of an IP in favour of the surviving spouse ensures that PPR is available to the NRB trustees when the property is eventually sold: see s.225 TCGA 1992. This is discussed in detail in Appendix 6.

consider calling in their loan (if any) at that point, turning the trust into a conventionally funded trust. That might be especially appropriate if, for instance, the surviving spouse goes into residential care. The trustees and spouse may apply the proceeds of sale in a new property if appropriate.

Winding up the NRB trust after the death of the spouse

19.9 The NRB trust will normally be wound up after the death of the spouse. The trustees of the NRB trust should review the position at that time. The property will normally be sold. The trustees may:

1. Call in the debt (if any), and

    (1) retain the funds on the terms of the discretionary trust, or
    (2) appoint new trusts, or appoint the capital out to beneficiaries.[16]

2. The trustees may transfer the debt to beneficiaries (who may themselves release it or call it in as they wish).

3. The trustees may release[17] the debt if this is for the benefit of beneficiaries of the discretionary trust. (This depends primarily on whether the residuary legatee of the spouse's will is also a beneficiary of the discretionary trust. That will normally (but not always) be the case.)

Tax implications of repayment or release of the debt

19.10 See Appendix 4: NRB debt and charge arrangements: tax analysis.

---

[16] The appointment will in principle give rise to an IHT exit charge: s.65 IHTA 1984. However no IHT charge will in practice arise because the values will fall within the nil rate band exemption. It will be necessary to put in an IHT return.

[17] A release of the debt should be made by deed (though a release in writing may be valid under the Bills of Exchange Act 1882).

CHAPTER 20[1]

WILLS AND CARE FEE PLANNING

Introduction

A person who goes into permanent residential care is normally required to pay all or part of the care home fees.[2] The payment depends on the amount of capital he or she has. If this can be minimised, more capital will be preserved for the next generation. This chapter concerns the use of will trusts to protect the family home and other assets from becoming part of the assessable capital.   **20.1**

In the following, the testator is called "the first to die" or "the deceased"; and the person who may go into residential care "the survivor", and they are together referred to as "a couple". The couple will normally be spouses, civil partners or cohabitees but similar principles apply when anyone wishes to make provision by will for a person who may go into permanent residential care. We assume that the couple own living accommodation ("the house") in England or Wales.

The term sometimes used for this arrangement is "protective property trust".

Why use will trusts?

For the purposes of assessing care home fees, a person's capital is the market value of his assets, but it does not include property in which he has a life interest.   **20.2**

If the couple own the house as joint tenants then, on the first death, the survivor will become entitled to the whole interest in the house by survivorship. The survivor's capital will include the value of the house. The same applies where the couple own the house as tenants in common (or

---
[1] We are grateful to Sarah Dunn who prepared a first draft of this chapter.
[2] For a detailed analysis of this subject, see "Coldrick on Care Home Fees", David Coldrick (2005, Ark Group).

the first to die owns the entire beneficial interest) if the first to die leaves his interest to the survivor absolutely.

The first to die could leave his interest in the house to others, perhaps the children, bypassing the survivor altogether, but that would generally leave the survivor insufficiently provided for. It also loses CGT private residence relief.

If, instead, the first to die leaves his or her interest in the house on trust for the survivor for life, then the deceased's interest will not become part of the capital of the survivor. (The survivor's own share in the house will form part of his capital. However, the value of that share will be less, usually much less, than 50% of the value of the whole. We return to the question of valuation below.)

If the house is owned under a joint tenancy, this must of course be severed while both parties are alive. This can be done simply by serving a notice of severance. The couple should be advised to do this at the time the will is drafted.

Types of trust

20.3 There are three types of will trust used for this purpose:

(1) The survivor may have an IPDI in the deceased's interest in the house.

(2) The survivor may have an IPDI in the whole estate of the deceased (Will 2).

(3) A nil rate band discretionary trust; residue to the survivor for life or absolutely; and provision for implementation of the charge or debt scheme (Wills 4–7).

If the couple's combined estates significantly exceed one IHT nil rate band,[3] then option (3) is best. Unless a nil rate band trust is used, the nil rate band of the first to die will be wasted, so additional and unnecessary inheritance tax will be payable on the second death. For inheritance tax purposes, the property in the IPDI trust forms part of the survivor's estate. This is in contrast to the rule for care home fees, where not even the actual value of the life interest is taken into account. The debt or charge scheme, if properly implemented, reduces the value of the estate for inheritance tax and care fee purposes.[4]

The first and second options are appropriate for estates where inherit-

---

[3] £300,000 for 2007/08.
[4] See Chapter 19 (Administration of NRB Trusts).

ance tax is not a concern (because the total value of both estates is not significantly more than the nil rate band). Normally option (2) will be the better one. It excludes from the assessable capital of the survivor not only the deceased's share in the house but also his other assets. However, option (1) is appropriate where the deceased's assets other than the house are relatively low in value. If he has a few thousand pounds in the bank and nothing else, it is not worth the extra cost of administering this as trust property, particularly if it is likely to be exhausted by the deceased's funeral expenses or the survivor's living expenses before the survivor needs permanent care.

Assessing liability to pay

The first step is to determine whether the person's capital: 20.4

(1) exceeds £21,500;[5]

(2) does not exceed £21,500 but does exceed £13,000; or

(3) does not exceed £12,500.

Ability to pay is then assessed as follows:

(1) *Capital exceeds £21,500*

　　The person is liable to pay for his accommodation at the full rate. So long as his capital remains above £21,500, there is no assessment of his income.

(2) *Capital between £13,000£21,500*

　　The person's liability to pay is calculated primarily by reference to his weekly income. From this is deducted the amount per week which he is deemed to need for his personal requirements, currently £20.45.[6] Added to his weekly income is a further amount of deemed income based on his capital. For every £250 of capital he has in excess of £13,000, he is treated as receiving an additional £1 income per week.

(3) *Capital under £13,000*

　　No account at all is taken of capital which does not exceed £13,000. The person's liability to pay is based on his weekly income after

---

[5] Regulation. 3 National Assistance (Sums for Personal Requirements and Assessment of Resources) (Amendment) (England) Regulations 2007) ("the 2007 Regs").
[6] Section 22(4) NAA 1948; Reg.2 of the 2007 Regs.

deducting the amount he is deemed to need for his personal requirements.

There are detailed rules for assessing income which are outside the scope of this book. In assessing capital, there are four important points for present purposes.

First, the general rule is that capital which a person possesses is assessed at its current market value. Valuation is discussed further below.

Second, certain capital is disregarded altogether. Such capital is not assessed whatever its value. The most relevant "capital disregards" are discussed below.[7]

Third, capital which a person no longer possesses may be treated as his and assessed as if it were his.[8]

Fourth, if the person's level of assessable capital changes, this must be taken into account. A person who has capital in excess of £20,500 when he goes into care will be obliged to pay care home fees at the full rate. If his capital is only a few thousand pounds above that figure, his expenditure on care home fees alone will bring it below the threshold within a few weeks or months. When that happens, his automatic liability to pay at the full rate ends. Ability to pay must now be reassessed in accordance with (2) above (weekly income plus deemed income from capital) until such time as his capital falls below £13,000, when his remaining capital will be ignored.

Where the survivor has capital of her own in excess of £21,500, care fees planning may still be worthwhile. If there is any prospect that his or her own capital (leaving aside anything inherited from the first to die) will fall below £21,500, perhaps after a few years of payment of care home fees, then it will usually be in the family's interest for the first to die to give his interest in the house to a trust so that, at least, is protected from care home fees.

Valuation

20.5   The valuation provisions are in the National Assistance (Assessment of Resources) Regulations 1992 ("NAARR"). Regulation 23(1) NAARR sets out the general rule:

> ... subject to regulation 27(2), capital which a resident possesses in the UK shall be calculated at its current market or surrender value (whichever is the higher), less—

---

[7] See 20.6 (Capital disregards).
[8] See 20.7 (Deprivation of capital).

VALUATION

(a) where there would be expenses attributable to sale, 10%; and
(b) the amount of any incumbrance secured on it.

If the survivor owns the entire beneficial interest in the house, then reg.23(1) is straightforward to apply. The value of the house is its market value less (a) 10% for sale expenses and (b) the amount of any incumbrances (typically a mortgage but also a nil rate band debt charged on the property).

The position is more complicated where:

(1) the survivor owns a share in the house ("the survivor's share"); and

(2) the other share is held on the terms of the will trust ("the settled share"). Regulation 27(2) provides:

> Where a resident [of a nursing home] and one or more other persons are beneficially entitled in possession to any interest in land—
>
> (a) the resident's share shall be valued at an amount equal to the price which his interest in possession would realize if it were sold to a willing buyer, less 10 per cent and the amount of any incumbrance secured solely on his share of the whole beneficial interest; and
> (b) the value of his interest so calculated shall be treated as if it were actual capital.

This requires one to ascertain the market value of the survivor's share. That value will in principle be less than 50% of the value of the whole house.

The amount by which it is less will depend upon how soon a purchaser of the survivor's share can realise the value of his interest by forcing a sale of the house. This will depend on whether those interested in the settled share possess rights of occupation because if they do the court may have no power to order a sale, or if it does have power it is not likely to order a sale.[9]

Section 12(1) TLATA 1996 provides:

> A beneficiary who is beneficially entitled to an interest in possession in land subject to a trust of land is entitled by reason of his interest to occupy the land at any time if at that time—
>
> (a) the purposes of the trust include making the land available for his occupation (or for the occupation of beneficiaries of a class of which he is a member or of beneficiaries in general), or
> (b) the land is held by the trustees so as to be so available.

In order to apply this one needs to bear in mind that there are two distinct trusts here:

---

[9] See *Smith on Plural Ownership* (OUP, August 2004) at pp.122 and 156.

(1) "the trust of land", the trust which arose when the couple acquired the house jointly.[10]

(2) the will trust, which holds the settled share (under which the survivor will initially have an interest in possession, though that may be altered by exercise of an overriding power of appointment).

Rights of occupation under s.12(1)(a) TLATA 1996 depend on the purpose of the trust of land, which is normally[11] the purpose of the couple at the time the trust of land was created, i.e. when the house was jointly acquired. In the typical case, the purpose will be for them to live there together as their joint home and, normally, for the survivor to live there after one has died. This purpose will normally continue if the survivor goes into care in circumstances where he or she may return to the house. However, once it becomes clear that the survivor is in permanent care, this purpose is exhausted. It appears that no-one then has a right to occupy.

The purpose *might* extend to enabling an adult child who lives at the house to remain there after the death of one or both of the parents, but that would be unusual.

In the absence of that unusual situation, where:

(1) the deceased has died and left his share in the house to a will trust; and

(2) the survivor has moved into a home;

it is considered that a purchaser of the survivor's share *would* in principle be able to obtain a sale of the house.

Suppose the trustees of the will trust exercise their overriding power so as to terminate the survivor's interest in possession in the settled share and confer a life interest on an adult child. Could the child then acquire a right to occupy and thus reduce the value of the survivor's share? If the trustees of land actually make the land available for occupation by the child, then the child can acquire a right to occupy under s.12(1)(b) TLATA 1996.[12] The will trustees cannot unilaterally alter the purposes of the trust of land but the purposes can be altered if the will trustees and the survivor together agree. However, this can only happen if the land is suitable for the child's occupation. That will not be the case if the child is an adult with no intention of moving into his parents' house. In the typical case, the children will be in late middle age with their own homes when the surviving parent goes into permanent care. In those circumstances, the

---

[10] Since all jointly owned land is held in trust: s.36 LPA 1925.
[11] The purposes of the trust of land may change after creation of the trust, if the change represents a new purpose of all beneficial co-owners. For instance, a couple may originally buy the house as a rental investment, and later move into the property. But that will be rare.
[12] See *Smith* (above) at pp.161–167.

child will not acquire a right of occupation even if he is given an interest in possession in the settled share. A purchaser of the survivor's share could in principle force a sale. In practice that will normally be the position. But this is an area which is highly fact-sensitive.

If the trust of land trustees do not wish to sell, a purchaser of the survivor's share will have to make an application to the court before he can realise the value of his interest. The application should succeed but there is no certainty. This fact alone should substantially depress the value of the survivor's share. Apparently some local authorities have on occasion accepted that the value of the survivor's share of the house is nominal on the grounds that a child has a right to occupy for life.[13] In most cases, it is unlikely that the child does have that right. This does not mean that the discount in the value of that share is insignificant. A purchaser would be reluctant to buy a share in land which could only be turned to account by making an application to the court. The irrecoverable costs of such an application will often represent a significant proportion of the value of the share.

If the value of the survivor's share is above £21,500, the use of a will trust is still normally worthwhile. Suppose that the house is worth £200,000 and is owned by a couple as tenants in common without a mortgage. The first to die leaves his or her share on life interest trusts for the survivor. Suppose that the survivor's share is valued at £30,000. After deducting 10% for the costs of sale, the survivor's capital is assessed at £27,000. His other capital is worth less than £13,000.

Initially, the survivor is liable to pay the care home fees in full because his capital (including his share in the house) exceeds £21,500.[14] However, he may be able to defer payment of all or part of his obligation to pay in return for a local authority charge over his beneficial interest in the house.[15] The local authority is not obliged to enter into this arrangement ("a deferred payment agreement"). It is entitled to do so if the house is or was previously occupied by the survivor as his or her only or main residence.[16]

In practice, local authorities often enter into these agreements. The alternative is to try to enforce the survivor's liability for fees by forcing a sale of his or her half share. This is unlikely to be a better option for the local authority.

If the survivor and the local authority enter into a deferred payment agreement, the payments which are deferred are the difference between (1) the survivor's total liability for fees and (2) the amount of that liability if his interest in the home were disregarded. In the example above, amount (2) will be solely based on the survivor's income. This is all he will have

---

[13] See discussion on the Trusts Discussion Forum at *www.trustsdiscussionforum.co.uk*.
[14] See (1) at 20.4 (Assessing liability to pay).
[15] See s.55 Health and Social Care Act 2001, the National Assistance (Residential Accommodation) (Relevant Contributions) (England) Regulations 2001 (SI 2001/3069).
[16] The Health and Social Care Act 2001 (Commencement No.2) (England) Order 2001 (SI 2001/3167).

to pay. The remainder of his liability to pay fees in full will be deferred and charged on the house.

That charge is an incumbrance on the survivor's share in the house. Once the amount of the charge has reached £14,000, the value of his beneficial interest for the purposes of reg.27(2) NAARR will be £13,000. This is because his interest is valued at its market value (£30,000) less 10% for expenses (£3,000) and less the amount secured on it (£14,000). Once this position has been reached, the survivor's ability to pay will be assessed by reference to his or her income alone. The heirs will ultimately inherit 93% of the value of the property (a house worth £200,000 subject to a charge of £14,000, and thus with a net value of £186,000). In contrast, if the deceased had left his or her share to the survivor absolutely, up to £187,000 of the value of the property could be spent on care home fees, with the heirs inheriting only £13,000.

Capital disregards

20.6 Certain capital is ignored in determining a person's capital resources. The most important disregard for our purposes is:

> The value of the right to receive any income under a life interest or from a [Scottish] liferent.[17]

If the survivor has a life interest in the deceased's share in the house, i.e. the settled share, this will simply be left out of account.

There are many other capital assets which are disregarded.[18] The following disregards will sometimes apply to the survivor's share in the house:

(1) A dwelling occupied by a person who is only temporarily resident in the care home;[19]

(2) A dwelling still occupied by the partner of the care home resident (including a former partner from whom the claimant is neither estranged nor divorced); and

(3) A dwelling still occupied by a relative or family member who is either over 60, incapacitated, or a child under 16 whom the resident is liable to maintain.[20]

This is not an exhaustive list.

---

[17] Income Support (General) Regulations 1987 Sch.10 para.13, incorporated into Sch.4 NAARR, which lists the items of capital to be disregarded, by para.11.
[18] Schedule 4 NAARR.
[19] Paragraph 1 Sch.4 NAARR.
[20] Paragraph 2 Sch.4 NAARR.

Deprivation of capital

Regulation 25(1) NAARR provides: **20.7**

> A resident may be treated as possessing actual capital of which he has deprived himself for the purpose of decreasing the amount that he may be liable to pay for his accommodation.

This rule is not directly relevant to the will planning discussed in this chapter. It explains why it is important to do this planning by will. A person cannot put his own interest in a property into a life interest trust and thereby avail himself of the "disregard" for property in which he has a life interest. The deprivation rule overrides the disregard of a life interest. It treats the property given away (whether into a life interest trust, to children, or otherwise) as actual capital of the disponor. The deprivation rule is not relevant to will planning because the survivor has not deprived himself of property belonging to the deceased.

This notional capital is reduced each week by reference to the additional care home fee liability for that week attributable to the notional capital.

According to the local authority guidance,[21] the deprivation rule will apply even if reducing liability for care home fees was not the sole or main purpose of the deprivation. It is sufficient that it was a significant purpose.[22] This is probably over-generous to the local authority. Similar wording ("for the purpose of") is used in s.423(3) Insolvency Act 1986 (transactions defrauding creditors).[23] The courts have held that a person only enters into a transaction "for the purpose of" one of the prohibited ends if his "dominant intention" was to achieve that end.[24] It is suggested that the same test applies to the deprivation rule.

Administration of the will trust after the survivor goes into care

This section considers the position where the first to die has given his **20.8** share of the home to an IPDI trust and the survivor goes into permanent

---

[21] Charging for Residential Accommodation Guide ("CRAG"), Department of Health; at the time of writing the 2008 version is in draft, accessible on *www.dh.gov.uk/en/Publicationsandstatistics/ Publications/PublicationsPolicyAndGuidance/DH_086008*.
[22] See CRAG at 6.062 to 6.063.
[23] "Where a person has entered into [a transaction at an undervalue], an order shall only be made if the court is satisfied that it was entered into by him for the purpose—
   (a) of putting assets beyond the reach of a person who is making, or may at some time make, a claim against him, or
   (b) of otherwise prejudicing the interests of such a person in relation to the claim which he is making or may make."
[24] *Chohan v Saggar* [1994] BCC 134, [1994] 1 BCLC 706 accessible on *www.kessler.co.uk*.

care. The trustees have to consider what to do with the house. There are six main options:

(1) Sell the whole house to a third party.

(2) The survivor sells his or her share at a discounted price:
   (a) to the children, or
   (b) to the will trustees.

   The purchase price may either be paid or left outstanding as an interest free loan.

(3) Let the house.

(4) Leave the house empty.

(5) Children or other relatives move into occupation rent free.

(6) The survivor gives his or her share to the will trustees.

Option (1) is the least desirable from the perspective of care home fees. When the house is sold, the survivor will become entitled to half of the proceeds. The discount in the value of the share (for care home fees purposes) is lost. Thereafter, his or her liability will be assessed by reference to the cash proceeds and not the (lower) value of the half share.

Option (2) will be attractive if the survivor can justify selling at the discounted value. The discount will not then be lost. The children (in conjunction with the trustees) will be able to realise the value of the house by selling it or letting it. The trustees should consider terminating the survivor's interest in possession in the settled share. Otherwise, half of the rental income or income from the proceeds of sale will be taken into account in assessing the survivor's care fees. The deprivation of capital rule will not apply on the termination of the survivor's interest by the trustees.[25] There is a SDLT cost if the sale price exceeds the SDLT threshold.

If the amount for which the share is sold to the children is too low, the local authority may invoke the deprivation of capital rule. Perhaps the survivor could have negotiated a higher price on account of the fact that the value of the share to the children is much higher, particularly if they are in a position to procure a sale of the whole house. This risk may be greater if the children have to borrow to buy the survivor's share, clearly intending to discharge it out of the proceeds of a subsequent sale.

Under Option (3) the survivor's half share in the rental income will be taken into account as income. The survivor's interest in possession in the settled share should be terminated so that this is not also taken into account (see option (2) above).

---

[25] See 20.7 (Deprivation of capital).

Option (4) is could be sensible if the survivor may return to live in the house. Otherwise, it is not an attractive long term option.

If the children want to move in to the house, then option (5) is likely to maximise the discount in the value of the survivor's share. However, it is rare for the children to wish to do this.

If the survivor gives his or her share to the will trustees, option (6), the deprivation of capital rule will in principle apply. The survivor will treated as possessing the actual capital of which he has deprived himself or herself.[26] That capital is valued in accordance with normal rules. It is valued as though it were still owned by the survivor. It is considered that the discount for jointly held property will be available.[27] The capital is to be valued "as if it were actual capital which [the survivor] does possess".[28]

If the share were sold or given to the children, there would be a CGT downside. The children will have a low base cost and no principal private residence relief. It is suggested that the best course is that the survivor should give or sell the share to the trustees of the will trust. The trustees will then have three years from the date when the survivor moved out to sell the whole house with the benefit of full principal private residence relief. Those who are concerned about care home fees and who look ahead might do this well before the survivor goes into a home.

---

[26] See 20.7 (Deprivation of capital).
[27] Regulation. 25(5).
[28] Regulation. 25(5).

CHAPTER 21

ADMINISTRATIVE PROVISIONS

Introduction

21.1 The administrative powers of trustees conferred by the general law are broadly but not wholly satisfactory. The Trustee Act 2000 improved matters considerably, but the general law still imposes restrictions (sometimes complex and bureaucratic) intended to reduce the risk of mismanagement.[1] The statutory powers of investment and delegation are good examples. This approach is well intentioned but misguided. Where the general law of trusts fails, it falls to the drafter to ensure that the trust has the administrative provisions needed to allow trustees to manage the trust fund in the best way; and to find a fair balance between trustees and beneficiaries when their interests conflict.

It is convenient to place all the provisions dealing with the administration of the trust in a schedule.[2]

Unnecessary provisions

Provisions duplicating the Trustee Acts

21.2 Where the general law already confers powers on trustees, no purpose is served in repeating the terms of the statute at length in the trust. This is often found in trust deeds: probably the drafter is following precedents unrevised since the enactment of the Trustee Act 1925 or its nineteenth-century predecessors. Common examples are the power to apportion blended funds[3] and power to ascertain and fix valuations.[4]

---

[1] Law Com., Report No. 260, para.2–19 (*Trustees' Powers and Duties*) accessible on www.lawcom.gov.uk
"The law must aim to achieve a balance between two factors—
(1) the desirability of conferring the widest possible investment powers, so that trustees may invest trust assets in whatever manner is appropriate for the trust; and
(2) the need to ensure that trustees act prudently in safeguarding the capital of the trust."
[2] Paragraph. 10.31 (Schedule of administrative provisions).
[3] Section 15(b) TA 1925.
[4] Paragraph. 21.46 (Power of appropriation).

Power to insure

Trustees have full power to insure trust property.[5]   21.3
It is quite common to provide that trustees should not be liable for any loss that may result from a failure to take out insurance. In this book a provision of this kind is intentionally omitted. It is considered that trustees should be expected to give proper consideration to the question of whether or not to insure trust property. Proper reasons for not taking out insurance may include cost and difficulties of funding. They would not of course be liable for loss if, having considered the matter, they reasonably decided not to insure.[6]

Power to vary investments

The Trustees may vary or transpose the investments for or into others of any nature hereby authorised.   21.4

Wherever trustees have a power to invest, they have by implication power to sell any trust property and invest or reinvest the proceeds.[7] This provision is still found in some precedents. Perhaps it is thought worthwhile to express clearly what would otherwise only be implied; perhaps the form is retained under the influence of obsolete statutory precedent.[8] The provision was sometimes incorporated into the trust-for-sale clause, now happily obsolete. More logically, it is sometimes given the status of a separate power. In any event, it is certainly unnecessary; especially where there is a general power of management.

Power to add powers

Some trusts give trustees power to confer additional administrative   21.5
powers. In the precedents in this book such a power is unnecessary. The powers conferred expressly are comprehensive. For good measure the power of appointment can be used to confer additional administrative powers.[9] The power to add powers would do no harm;[10] but the possibility of the power being usefully invoked is so remote that it merits no place in a standard draft.

---

[5] Section 19 TA 1925.
[6] This is the view of the Law Commission: Law Com., Report No.260, *Trustees' Powers and Duties*, para.6–8, accessible on *www.lawcom.gov.uk*.
[7] *Re Pope* [1911] 2 Ch 442.
[8] Section 1(1) Trustee Investments Act 1961. The contemporary provisions in the TA 2000 have no equivalent.
[9] Paragraph. 11.2 (Power of appointment).
[10] It might be objected that the extent of the power is unclear: the borderline between administrative and dispositive powers is not a precise one. But the *existence* of the power would not give rise to difficulties; and questions of doubt should not arise in practice.

Power to accept additional funds or onerous property

21.6 The Trustees may accept such additional money or investments or other property as may be paid or transferred to them upon the trusts hereof by the settlor or by any other person (including property of an onerous nature) the acceptance of which the Trustees consider to be in the interest of the beneficiaries.

Trustees do not need express power to accept additions to the trust fund.[11] (If anyone doubts this, let him ask: what remedy would there be for a breach of trust of this kind?)

The power as regards onerous property needs more consideration. The expression "onerous property" suggests property which may give rise to a liability, such as a lease with tenants' covenants, or shares which are not fully paid up or contaminated land.[12] "Accepting" such property suggests that on acquiring the property, the trustees become liable for leasehold covenants, calls on the shares, or subject to duties imposed on the owner of the land.

The trustees could use trust funds to purchase such property. On what basis could it possibly be said that they were not entitled to accept such property if given to them? Possibly the onerous property may have no value or a negative value: it may (in common parlance) be a liability. In that case the trustees could not properly accept it as a gift (unless authorised in specific terms to accept onerous property to the benefit of the "donee" and to the detriment of the trust fund). It is therefore considered that a general power to accept additional property is unnecessary in a standard draft.[13]

Powers relating to accounts and audits

21.7 For all practical purposes the powers in the Trustee Act 1925 are sufficient, and no special provision is required.[14]

Powers to deal with shares and debentures

21.8 Section 10(3) of the Trustee Act 1925 gave trustees a general power to deal with securities:

> Where any securities of a company are subject to a trust, the trustees may concur in any scheme or arrangement)

---

[11] Paragraph. 10.41 (Definition of "the trust fund").

[12] The expression "onerous property" is not a term of art. Contrast the more elaborate definition of "onerous property" in s.178 Insolvency Act 1986.

[13] The power may be useful in the context of tax avoidance arrangements where it may be particularly important that added property forms part of the trust to which it is added. This is not sufficiently common to merit a place in a standard draft. See also 17.13 (Gift by will to existing trust).

[14] Section 22(4) TA 1925 provides that trustees may arrange audited accounts every three years or more often if it is reasonable to do so. The power is wide enough to allow trustees to have accounts audited every year if they wish, or produce unaudited accounts, or for a dormant trust, not to produce any accounts at all.

(a) for the reconstruction of the company;
(b) for the sale of all or any part of the property and undertaking of the company to another company;
(bb) for the acquisition of the securities of the company, or of control thereof by another company;
(c) for the amalgamation of the company with another company;
(d) for the release, modification, or variation of any rights, privileges or liabilities attached to the securities or any of them;

in like manner as if they were entitled to such securities beneficially ...

"Securities" here meant shares and stocks, but (arguably) not debentures.[15] Some drafters therefore set out at length in their drafts the terms of s.10(3) TA 1925 but with one extension: the term "securities" is defined to include "debentures". This is here called "the extended s.10(3) power".

Is the extended s.10(3) power needed? It is thought not. The only reason for s.10(3) is that the proposed arrangements might cause the trustees to acquire new assets in place of their old securities. Those new assets might not be authorised investments. This is the problem which the s.10(3) power was intended to meet.[16]

It follows that where (as is now the case) the trustees have a wide power of investment they do not need the s.10(3) power at all; a fortiori they do not need any extension of the power to deal with debentures. This was recognised by the Trustee Act 2000 which repealed s.10 in its entirety. For good measure, the general power of management would cover this situation. In this book, therefore, the extended s.10(3) power is not adopted.

Power to repair and maintain trust property

Trustees have power to repair and maintain trust property.[17] It is not necessary to make express provision.   **21.9**

Unnecessary forms relating to administrative powers

"Powers not restricted by technical rules"

These powers shall not be restricted by any technical rules of interpretation. They shall operate according to the widest generality of which they are capable.   **21.10**

This form is not desirable: see 4.13 (Construction not restricted by technical rules).

---

[15] Section 68(13) TA 1925.
[16] Wolstenholme and Cherry, *Conveyancing Statutes* (13th edn, 1972) Vol.4, p.10.
[17] *Re Hotchkys* (1886) 32 Ch D 408 at 416–417; s.6 TLATA 1996.

Restricting administrative powers to perpetuity period

21.11 Administrative powers are not subject to the rule against perpetuities and need not be restricted to the perpetuity period.[18]

The following form is therefore unnecessary (though occasionally seen):

> Any powers set out in Schedule 1 which are not powers to do acts in the administration of the Trust Fund for the purposes of section 8(1) of the Perpetuities and Accumulations Act 1964 shall be exercisable only during the Trust Period.

If the schedule just contains administrative powers, this is only stating what would in any case be the position. If the schedule contains dispositive provisions, the clause has some effect, but (unless there is something unusual in the schedule) it would normally be sufficient to rely on "wait and see" to avoid any perpetuity difficulty here.

21.12 *"In addition to the statutory powers"*

One sometimes sees a form that the powers of the trustees conferred by the trust shall be in addition to the powers conferred by statute or by law. This is unnecessary.[19]

Trustees entitled to expenses of exercising powers

21.13 The exercise of a power may involve expense. One sometimes sees an express provision authorising the trustees to incur that expense. Even the parliamentary drafter is not above this practice.[20] However, trustees have a general power to reimburse themselves for all expenses properly incurred when acting on behalf of the trust.[21] Individual "charging" provisions are therefore unnecessary.

A further issue is whether the expenses should be paid out of income or capital. In the precedents in this book this is dealt with in a separate clause so it is not necessary to address this question in any individual power.

Trustees not liable for loss from exercising powers

This is otiose: see 6.17 (Construction of trustee exemption clauses).

---

[18] Section 8(1) PAA 1964.
[19] Section 69(2) TA 1925 already provides that the powers conferred by statute shall be in addition to the powers conferred by the trust.
[20] Section 23(1) TA 1925 (repealed): "Trustees ... may, instead of acting personally, employ and pay an agent ... and shall be entitled to be allowed and paid all charges and expenses so incurred ...".
[21] Section 31 TA 2000; *Dowse v Gorton* [1891] AC 190.

Other provisions

Some provisions are not permitted in trusts intended to qualify as IP or IHT special trusts. Such powers must be avoided in trusts of the appropriate type; they may be included in discretionary trusts. See 16.1 (Provisions inconsistent with IP and IHT special trusts). For provisions authorising trustees to act negligently, see 6.17 (Construction of trustee exemption clauses). For power to change the name of a trust, see 10.18. For power to change the perpetuity period, see 9.5 (Trust period and perpetuity period distinguished). **21.14**

Void powers

Power to decide between income and capital

The following power was held to be void[22]: **21.15**

> The trustees may:
>
> (1) determine what articles pass under any specific bequest
> (2) determine whether any moneys are to be considered as capital or income
> (3) determine all questions and matters of doubt arising in the execution of the trusts of my will
>
> and every such determination whether made upon a question actually raised or only implied in the acts or proceedings of the trustees shall be conclusive and binding upon all persons interested under my will.

Accordingly trustees were not entitled, despite the clear terms of this power, to decide whether the proceeds of a sale of timber constituted capital or income. Danckwerts J. said:

> the insertion of a clause of this kind ... is not desirable, because it is likely to mislead equally trustees and beneficiaries as to their true position and rights; and, therefore, it would be far better if a clause of this kind was omitted.

So trustees should not be given power to decide whether a sum received by them is income or capital; or whether expenditure is of an income or capital nature. These questions must be decided by the courts; even though it has been said that the courts have not made a particularly good job of

---

[22] This was invalid as an attempt to oust the jurisdiction of the court: *Re Wynn* [1952] Ch 271. The power set out here is a simplification of the actual form used in *Wynn*. Other parts of the clause (not set out here) repeat provisions of the TA 1925 and were otiose. The division into sub-clauses as set out in the text above is not in the original draft. If the drafter in *Wynn* had divided his long clause into subclauses it would have been easier for him to consider their implications.

answering them.[23] This principle does not prohibit powers which allow trustees to treat income as capital, or vice versa; see 21.27 (Provisions relating to the income/capital distinction).

Power to determine questions of fact or law or "matters of doubt"

21.16   The general rule is that trustees should not be given power to determine questions of law. Plainly it is a mistake—though once a common form—to give trustees power to determine "questions and matters of doubt".

Trustees may in principle be given power to determine questions of fact. The classic example is a power to make valuations. There is a statutory precedent for this.[24]

In practice many questions are difficult to classify as "fact" or "law". The drafter must tread warily in this area. To be safe, no-one should be given power to determine the meaning of expressions used in a trust. Nor, which is similar, should anyone have power to determine whether a condition of the trust is satisfied. But in special cases the courts will permit this.[25] If the point is likely to be important the general practitioner should seek specialist advice. This book does not employ any provisions using this technique.

Power to make determinations subject to jurisdiction of court

21.17   The Trustees may (subject to the jurisdiction of the Court) determine whether receipts and liabilities are to be considered as capital or income, and whether expenses ought to be paid out of capital or income. The Trustees shall not be liable for any act done in pursuance of such determination (in the absence of fraud or negligence) even though it shall subsequently be held to have been wrongly made.

---

[23] J.A. Kay, *Is Complexity in Taxation Inevitable?* (IFS Working Paper 57, February 1985) accessible on www.kessler.co.uk. Kay is an economist; but few lawyers would disagree. There is a good argument that *Wynn* should not be followed by a modern court, but the drafter should not proceed on that basis. *Wynn* was followed in *Wendt v Orr* [2004] WASC; 26 [2005] WTLR 223; 6 ITELR 989 (reversed on other grounds on appeal). Interestingly, in *Richardson v FCT* (2001) 48 ATR 101; [2001] FCA 1354 the Full Federal Court treated as valid, for the purposes of argument, a power "to determine" whether any real or personal property or any increase or decrease in amount number or value of any property or holdings of property or any receipts or payments from for or in connection with any real or personal property shall be treated as and credited or debited to capital or to income ...". *Re Wynn* and similar authorities were not brought to the Court's attention. A good study of the older cases is Gover, *A Concise Treatise on the Law of Capital and Income as Between Life Tenant and Remainderman* (sadly the most recent edition is 1933). But modern market practices have blurred the distinction still further.

[24] Section 22(3) TA 1925. Section 5 Trustee Investments Act 1961 (repealed) is another example.

[25] The Court brushed aside a provision that "my trustees shall be the sole judges of what the term 'advancement in life' may signify" where the trustees exercised the power in self-interest: *Molyneux v Fletcher* [1898] 1 QB 648. But the Courts respected a provision that the question whether a person belonged to "the Jewish Faith" be determined by the Chief Rabbi: *Re Tuck* [1978] Ch 49. The logical basis for this area of law has yet to be fully worked out. This is not the place to summarise the tentative solutions proposed in the cases. The practitioner is fortunate that this area has sparked considerable academic interest and a correspondingly large literature; perhaps equally fortunately, the point arises only rarely in practice.

This is a power to determine doubtful capital/income issues, but only so far as the law allows. This is not objectionable, but it is of no effect, so long as *Wynn* is good law. This clause was found in earlier editions of this book. Now that *Wynn* has been followed, there seems to be no point at all in this clause. The clause does contain an exclusion of liability for trustees who make erroneous determinations but the general trustee exclusion clause in this book will cover that point.

Power exercisable with consent of court

21.18 The drafter should not direct that any power or provision in the trust should depend on the consent of the court. Such provisions are void.[26]

Which powers should the drafter include?

21.19 It is hard to predict exactly what powers trustees will need, because trustees in different circumstances need different powers. Trusts designed to hold investments, a residence, or shares in a family company each have different requirements.

When drafting administrative provisions two considerations lead the drafter to a policy of all-inclusion. First, circumstances may change. It is easy to see that trust property of one sort may be sold and other property acquired. So broad provisions should be included regardless of current needs. The second motive is the desire for a standard form of trustees' powers; so the drafter can run off his trusts and wills without *too* much consideration of individual circumstances. And since the client pays for the drafter's time and trouble, this consideration is neither selfish nor lazy.

What is the drafter to do? One course is to put every conceivable power in every trust. The first edition of this book (1992) proposed a compromise solution: two standard forms of trustees' administrative powers; a longer form and a short form. The longer form would contain every power which might possibly be desired. In simpler trusts a shorter form would be preferred. One need not pack a wetsuit to cross the Sahara.

---

[26] *Re Hooker* [1955] Ch 55.

STEP Standard Provisions

21.20 A better course is now available in simple cases. This is to use the standard provisions promulgated by the Society of Trust and Estate Practitioners (STEP).[27] A lengthy schedule may then be replaced by the words:

> The standard provisions of the Society of Trust and Estate Practitioners (1st ed.) shall apply.

Standard forms of this type are not an innovation. Standard forms in conveyancing and company documentation are taken for granted. Standard precedents in trust and will drafting are not unknown.[28] The standard form shortens the length of a document; reduces the risk of unfortunate omissions or inclusions; and the lawyer familiar with the standard form will save a considerable amount of time.

On the other hand, if the provisions are set out at length, the material is immediately available for the reader; he need not turn to a separate document to find out the terms of the trust.

Where is the balance of advantage? The best course is to use the STEP Provisions in simple matters, and to set out an express schedule of provisions in more substantial ones. The standard provisions are now very widely used in exactly this sort of situation. The course for which there was absolutely no justification is where the drafter failed to provide adequate provisions. This happened far too often in will drafting before the Trustee Act 2000. The typical will is only two pages long. Now after the Trustee Act 2000 a trust governed by the general law is more or less adequate. Nevertheless the lot of the beneficiaries under such wills would be improved if the wills included the STEP Provisions by reference.[29] This led Professor John Adams to describe the provisions as "quite the most exciting development for private client drafters for several decades"; and Ralph Ray to describe them as "an enormous asset".[30]

---

[27] The text is set out in Appendix 1, which also discusses some points about their use. The text is also published in booklet form (Sweet & Maxwell); *Precedents for the Conveyancer* (Looseleaf); *Wills, Probate and Administration Service* (Looseleaf); *Encyclopaedia of Forms and Precedents* (5th edn, 1997), Vol.40(1), p.249; *Administration of Trusts* (looseleaf); and is accessible on *www.step.org*.

[28] E.g. s.33 TA 1925 (protective trusts); s.179 LPA 1925; the Statutory Will Forms 1925; s.11 Married Woman's Property Act 1882; Law Society's Standard Conditions of Sale; s.7 Agricultural Holdings Act 1986.

[29] Such wills generally contain absolute gifts, rather than trusts; but trusts for minors may come about under s.33 Wills Act 1837.

[30] *Taxation*, Vol.138, p.348.

Standard administrative provisions

We can now turn to consider the standard administrative provisions. **21.21**

Power of investment

In the absence of an express power of investment, trustees may invest in any investment[31] except land outside the United Kingdom.[32] **21.22**

The exception is well meant but misguided. The Law Commission states:

> The concept of the trust is not universally recognised and, even in those jurisdictions that do recognise trusts, the law does not necessary give effect to the safeguards for the protection of the interests of beneficiaries against the claims of third parties that apply in England and Wales.[33]

The Law Commission Report is surely rare if not unique in that it contains a refutation and repudiation of its own position: the Scottish Law Commission observe in the following page of the same report:

> Trustees are subject to a duty of care at common law in the exercise of their functions. This duty requires them to consider the risk associated with purchasing immovable property in a foreign country that does not recognise trusts (such as claims by personal creditors of the trustees, and rights of succession on their death) in the same way as it requires them to weigh the risks of investing in securities in developing countries, for example, or the more volatile sectors of the British economy.[34]

Quite so. Accordingly, the form used here extends the power of investment. The form used in this book is as follows:

(1) The Trustees may make any kind of investment that they could make if they were absolutely entitled to the Trust Fund. In particular the Trustees may invest in land in any part of the world and unsecured loans.

(2) The Trustees are under no obligation to diversify the Trust Fund.

(3) The Trustees may invest in speculative or hazardous investments but this power may only be exercised at the time when there are at least two Trustees, or the Trustee is a

---

[31] On the meaning of "investment" see Andrew Hicks, "The TA 2000 and the modern meaning of 'investment'" [2001] TLI 203 accessible on *www.kessler.co.uk*.
[32] Section 3 TA 2000.
[33] Law Com., Report No.260, *Trustees' Powers and Duties*, para.2.42 accessible on *www.lawcom.gov.uk*.
[34] Law Com. Report No.260, *Trustees' Powers and Duties*, para.2.46. The Trustee Act (Northern Ireland) 2001 also follows the Scottish reasoning and contains no exceptions for foreign land.

company carrying on a business which consists of or includes the management of trusts.

The opening sentence echoes the statutory power.[35] The specific extension to unsecured loans is only for the avoidance of doubt.[36] It is unlikely that trustees would ever want to invest in unsecured loans, but on balance it is preferable to give them clear power to do so if they wish.

There is no rule which requires trustees to diversify trust investments. The rule is that trustees must consider the need for diversification (so far as is appropriate to the circumstances of the trust). Sub-clause (2) is therefore not strictly necessary.[37] Some drafters exclude the duty to *consider* the need for diversification[38] but that is wrong in principle.

21.23 Although wide, the power of investment is restricted by the usual principles applying to fiduciary[39] powers (supplemented by statutory provisions which merely state what the general law would in any case have implied). Accordingly:

> (1) *Duty to maximise return.* The trustees must aim to seek the best return for the beneficiaries, judged in relation to the risks of the investments in question. For instance, they should not invest merely to accommodate the wishes of the settlor.[40]
>
> (2) *Prudence.* Trustees must in principle be prudent in their choice of investments. This does not mean they must avoid risk altogether, but no more than a "prudent degree of risk" is acceptable. Trustees must avoid "hazardous" or "speculative" investments unless the trust deed confers express authority to do so.

Should the drafter alter this rule? In some cases the settlor or beneficiaries will be entrepreneurs and the trust fund will be invested in their business. In these cases a power to invest in hazardous or speculative investments will be necessary. In other cases the trust fund is a "nest egg" for the beneficiaries and the settlor would not want the trustees to indulge in anything approaching speculation.

What is the drafter to do? The precedents in this book include a clause

---

[35] A power to invest "in such investments as the trustees think fit" was held to be unlimited without any additional words: *Re Harari* [1949] 1 All ER 430; *Re Peczenick* [1964] 2 All ER 339. For another statutory precedent see s.34 Pensions Act 1995.
[36] *Khoo Tek Keong v Ch'ng Joo Tuan Neoh* [1934] AC 529. The decision was based on the curious ground that a secured loan is, but an unsecured loan is not, an "investment". The concept of "investment" is much wider than it used to be, and this ground of the decision would not now be adopted in the UK.
[37] Section 4(3)(b) TA 2000.
[38] TA 2000 does not state expressly that the duty can be excluded but this should be implied: cf. 21.35 (Occupation and use of trust property).
[39] On the fiduciary nature of a power despite the "absolute owner" form, see 6.21 ("Absolute owner" and "beneficial owner" clauses).
[40] *Cowan v Scargill* [1985] Ch 270.

authorising speculative investments subject to a two-trustee safeguard, though it should be deleted in appropriate cases.[41]

(3) *Duty to select suitable investments.* The trustees must have regard to the suitability of the investment to the trust. See s.4(3)(a) Trustee Act 2000. Some drafters direct that this section should not apply, but that is not done here. Plainly, trustees should try to select suitable investments; where the power is expressly excluded the duty of the trustees could hardly be different.

(4) *Duty to obtain and consider proper investment advice so far as necessary and appropriate.*[42] This, again, does no more than spell out the implications of a fiduciary power in our era of investment sophistication and complexity, and it is not sensible to alter this rule.

Matters not belonging in an investment clause. An investment clause sometimes confers a power to acquire residential property for a beneficiary to occupy, but this is not the logical place for that power. The acquisition of a residence for that purpose is not an "investment". The matter is more appropriately covered in a separate clause. Likewise questions of wasting assets, non-income producing assets and joint property are best dealt with in separate clauses. On power to vary investments, see 21.4 (Power to vary investments). On the formula "whether producing income or not", see 21.33 (Balance between income and capital). No express power is needed to acquire insurance policies as an investment.

Power of joint purchase

The form used in this book is as follows: 21.24

> The Trustees may acquire property jointly with any person and may blend Trust Property with other property.

Trustees may wish to acquire property jointly with others or to merge two trust funds together. It is considered that the general power of investment is wide enough to authorise this,[43] but the point is made expressly for the avoidance of doubt.

---

[41] It is best to resist the temptation to specify the circumstances in which hazardous investments may be made. Even if speculative investments are authorised, the trustees remain under a general duty to seek the best return for the beneficiaries, judged in relation to the risk involved.
[42] Section 5 TA 2000.
[43] This was the view of the Law Commission: Law Com. Report No.260, *Trustees' Powers and Duties*, para.2.28. For the position in the absence of such wide general powers, see *Webb v Jonas* (1888) 39 Ch D 660. In *Re Harvey* [1941] 3 All ER 284 the absence of such a power was solved by an application under s.57 TA 1925. There is a power in s.15(b) TA 1925 to apportion blended funds.

The clause refers to "acquiring property" rather than "investing in property". The common case of joint property will be the purchase of a residence jointly by trustees and a beneficiary; such a purchase may not, strictly, amount to an "investment".

General power of management and disposition

21.25 The form used in this book is as follows:

> The Trustees may effect any transaction relating to the management or disposition of Trust Property as if they were absolutely entitled to it.[44]

Statute has conferred on trustees general powers in relation to land in England and Wales.[45] This general power is therefore still needed for personal property and for land outside England and Wales.

One could attempt to specify and authorise every conceivable form of disposition. This leads to a thesaurus of legal terminology:

> The Trustees may retain or sell, exchange, convey, lease, mortgage, charge, pledge, licence, grant options over and otherwise conduct the management of any real or personal property comprised in the trust fund …

Section 57 Trustee Act 1925 and s.64 Settled Land Act 1925 are the basis for other precedents to the same effect.

Power to improve trust property

21.26 The Trustees may develop or improve Trust Property in any way. Capital expenses need not be paid out of income under section 84(2) of the Settled Land Act 1925, if the Trustees think fit.

Trustees normally have power under the general law to make improvements.[46]

Improvements would normally be paid out of capital. Under the general law the trustees may in some cases, and must in other cases, recoup the cost of improvements gradually out of income. This is supposed to be done by instalments over a period of up to 25 years.[47] In practice it will be rare

---

[44] On the interpretation of the phrase "as if they were absolutely entitled" see 6.21 ("absolute owner" and "beneficial owner" clauses).
[45] Section 6(1) TLATA 1996. The draft clause is loosely based on this section.
[46] In the case of land in England and Wales, under s.6(1) TLATA 1996; in other cases improvement expenditure may be authorised as an "investment" under the power of investment.
[47] Section 84(2)(a) (b) SLA 1925. It is considered that this rule continues to apply after the TLATA 1996. By implication, this must plainly be permitted under the rule against accumulations, and

for the trustees to want to do this. The power is here retained, but the trustees are given a discretion in the matter: recoupment out of income is not compulsory.

It is quite common to find extended provision allowing the cost of improvement to be paid directly out of income:

> The Trustees may apply capital **or income** of the Trust Fund in the improvement or development of Trust Property.

This raises problems. The power to use income for improvements is dispositive in nature, and inconsistent with an interest in possession.[48] The power amounts to accumulation for the purposes of the rule against accumulation and will not be valid after the accumulation period.[49] A clause of this kind is best avoided.

Provisions relating to the income/capital distinction

Under a trust it is frequently necessary to decide whether a receipt or an item of expenditure is one of income or capital. In principle this is a matter of law, to be decided by the courts if need be. A provision that the trustees can decide such questions is void as it ousts the jurisdiction of the court: see 21.15 (Power to decide between income and capital). This is a shame, as it cannot be said that the courts have made a particularly good job of elucidating this troublesome distinction. Fortunately there is another drafting technique which has the same effect and which does not "oust the jurisdiction of the Court". This is a provision which directs trustees (or empowers trustees at their discretion) to treat an income receipt as if it were capital, or to treat a capital receipt as if it were income. It is a question of construction whether a clause confers a power to determine whether a receipt is income or capital (void) or a power to treat income as capital (valid). In practice of course it is easy to devise a clause which is unambiguous and valid, if one bears these principles in mind.[50]

21.27

---

consistent with an interest in possession. There is a difference between this sort of gradual recoupment and paying the entire cost out of one year's income. The position is analogous to sinking funds: see 21.31 (Sinking funds).
[48] The question arises whether the power would be a "departure" power or a "disqualifying power". This would depend on the words used, but in the absence of any clear indication in the wording, the latter is the better view. See 16.9 (IP trusts: "departure" v "disqualifying" powers).
[49] *Vine v Raleigh* [1891] 2 Ch 22.
[50] This paragraph was cited with approval in *Morgan Trust Company of the Bahamas Limited v DW*, Supreme Court of the Bahamas, Butterworths Offshore Service Cases, Vol.2, p.31.

322 ADMINISTRATIVE PROVISIONS

Power to pay capital expenses out of income

21.28 The form used in this book is:

> The Trustees may pay taxes and other expenses out of income although they would otherwise be paid out of capital.

This is an important power, for two reasons:

(1) It is sometimes unclear whether expenses should be paid out of capital or income;[51] using this power the trustees do not have to decide the point.

(2) It is sometimes convenient to pay out of income expenses which are strictly capital expenses.

The Trustee Act 2000 has effected a significant change here. Formerly trustees had to pay capital expenses out of capital and income expenses out of income. Now it is considered they have a discretion.[52] The contrary view is arguable,[53] so it remains best to confer an express power.

This power is permitted for IP and IHT Special trusts, as it is administrative, see 16.4 (Power to pay capital expenses out of income). It is submitted that the rule against accumulations does not apply to this power because it is administrative.[54]

---

[51] The only modern case is *Carver v Duncan* 59 TC 125. Here the House of Lords (obiter) took a very restrictive view of what constitutes an income expense. An expense is capital if it is incurred for the benefit of the estate as a whole. Annual investment management charges are on this test a capital expense! The position will be clearer when *HMRC v Clay* [2008] STC 928 is final.

[52] To explain the law it is convenient to start with the power of insurance. The trustees have power to pay insurance premiums out of the "trust funds"; this expression means any income or capital funds of the trust: see s.19(5) TA 1925 (as amended by TA 2000). (This overrides the natural meaning of "Trust Funds", which is "Trust Capital".) Plainly, trustees can pay insurance premiums out of income or capital as they think fit. This is what the Law Commission intended: Law Com. Report 260, *Trustees' Powers and Duties*, para.6.6 accessible on www.lawcom.gov.uk.

Now, s.31 TA 2000 authorises a trustee to be reimbursed out of "trust funds" for any expenses properly incurred when acting on behalf of the trust. "Trust funds" is likewise defined as "income or capital funds of the trust": s.39(1) TA 2000. So the trustees must have the same discretion in relation to expenses generally.

It is surprising that this significant change was made without express discussion in the Law Commission paper; it appears to have been unintentional. However, it is the only natural construction. It is consistent with many other statutory provisions, e.g. s.22(4) TA 1925. It is also a highly satisfactory result as the former law was complex, uncertain, unworkable, and ignored in practice. The old case law is still relevant as showing what is the position in the absence of an exercise of the trustees' powers. (*Carver v Duncan* 59 TC 125 would still be decided the same way, though slightly different reasoning is needed to reach the same conclusion.)

[53] It is preferred by *Lewin on Trusts* (18th edn, 2008), 25–67. The consequence of the view adopted here is not as extreme as the horrified editors of *Lewin* suggest, because the power must be exercised in the context of the general duty on trustees to hold a fair balance between life tenant and remainderman.

[54] This is consistent with the principles in 16.2 (Significance of administrative/dispositive distinction) and supported by the Trustee Act 2000 (see fn.52 above). However, in *Re Rochford* [1965] Ch 111 at 123 the line was expressed slightly differently (though in practice there would rarely

Power to apply trust capital as income

The form in this book is as follows: **21.29**

> The Trustees may apply Trust Property as if it were income arising in the current year. In particular, the Trustees may pay such income to an Income Beneficiary for the purpose of augmenting his income.
> **"Income Beneficiary"** here means a Beneficiary to whom income of the Property is payable (as of right or at the discretion of the Trustees).

This power might be useful if trustees are unsure whether a receipt or an expense is one of income or capital. However it may also be needed for tax planning purposes. Suppose trustees wish to transfer trust capital to a beneficiary. Under the trusts in this book there are two ways to achieve this:

(1) The trustees may use their overriding power to advance the capital to the beneficiary.

(2) The trustees may use this power to treat the capital as income; and then pay that "income" to the beneficiary.[55]

From a practical, property law point of view there is no difference. Either way, the beneficiary simply receives the same property. There is, however, an important difference for tax. In the first case the receipt is one of capital;[56] in the other case it is a receipt of income.[57] If it is income, the beneficiary will suffer income tax, so a capital receipt will normally be preferred. However, there will be circumstances where it is better to have an income receipt. The common case would be where the trustees have accumulated income and paid tax at the trust rate or dividend trust rate: an income receipt allows the beneficiary to reclaim that tax.[58]

---

be any difference between the two approaches). On the one hand, it was said, there may be "some liability for a comparatively small amount—say counsel's fees for an opinion given to the trustees—which would normally be payable out of capital but trustees would probably have no difficulty in paying it out of income, without having to resort to anything which could be described as an accumulation of income." On the other hand, it was said, the capital liabilities may be "far too large to be paid out of any income payable to the next income beneficiary which would come to the hands of the trustees before the first date upon which such beneficiary might normally expect to receive a payment of income from the trust." The second category (not the first) was said to be subject to the rule against accumulations, so a power to use income to pay expenses in this category would not be exercisable after the accumulation period had expired. This is not, however, a drafting issue and there is nothing the drafter should do about it.

[55] It is assumed the Beneficiary is an "Income Beneficiary" as defined in the clause.
[56] *Stevenson v Wishart* 59 TC 740.
[57] That might not, exceptionally, be the case where the larger part of the trust fund is disposed of in this way. For the mere use of the label "income" is not determinative: see *Jackson's Trustees v IRC* 25 TC 13.
[58] Section 496 ITA 2007 (assuming the beneficiary does not pay tax at the higher rate). There are also complex tax avoidance schemes which call for such powers. On the IHT position, see SP E6.

In short, it will sometimes be better for a beneficiary to receive a sum as income; sometimes he should receive it as capital. It is desirable that the trustees should have power to achieve either result; so they can decide between income or capital as appropriate. The general law only allows this choice in restricted circumstances.[59]

The decision to apply trust funds as income should be documented by an appropriate trustee resolution.

Rent: income or capital receipt?

21.30 Under the general law rent is income. Under SLA settlements (now obsolescent), in the exceptional case of mining leases granted under the statutory power, rent was partly income and partly capital.[60] This explains why one occasionally sees in old trust deeds a provision to reverse the SLA rule:

> *No part of any mining or other rent shall be set aside as capital;*
> or
> *"Income of the trust fund" includes the net rents and profits of all land held in the Trust Fund.*

These forms are now obsolete because the mining rent under a trust of land will in principle now be regarded as wholly income, not partly capital.[61]

Some old precedents provide that:

> *No part of any mining or other rent shall be set aside as capital* **unless and until and except to such extent as the Trustees in each or any case may think fit so to set aside the same.**

Rather than this narrow form it would be better to have a general power to create a sinking fund (into which this power would be subsumed).

Sinking funds

21.31 Income may be set aside and invested to answer any liabilities which in the opinion of the Trustees ought to be borne out of income or to meet depreciation of the capital value of any Trust Property. In particular, income may be applied for a leasehold sinking fund policy.

---

[59] Income accumulated during a beneficiary's minority under s.31 TA 1925 can be applied as income during the beneficiary's minority, so long as his interest continues. The power lapses when the beneficiary attains 18, or dies.
[60] Section 47 SLA 1925.
[61] According to Gover, *Capital and Income* (3rd edn, 1933), this already was the position under a trust for sale, after 1925; until 1997 that was perhaps debatable; but since the repeal of s.28 LPA 1925, it is reasonably clear that s.47 SLA 1925 treatment does not apply to trusts of land.

This form would allow trustees to accumulate a sinking fund to replace wasting assets such as a lease. This is an administrative power, permitted in any form of trust.[62] The power is not affected by the rule against accumulations.[63] While such a power would not often be used, it may just occasionally be desirable. The draft is based on statutory precedent.[64]

Equitable apportionment

There are three cases where trustees must under the general law treat income as if it were capital, or capital as if it were income. These are sometimes called the rules of equitable apportionment[65]:

Disposal of unauthorised reversionary investment. Where trustees hold an unauthorised investment which produces little or no income (e.g. a reversionary interest), they should generally sell it; the life tenant then receives some of the capital proceeds of sale to compensate him for the income which he did not receive during the period that the trustees held the asset. This rule is known as the rule in *Howe v Earl of Dartmouth*.

Disposal of unauthorised wasting investment. Likewise, where trustees hold a wasting investment (e.g. a short lease) they should sell it; in the meantime some of the income is treated as capital to compensate the remainderman for the wasting nature of the asset concerned. This is known as the rule in *The Earl of Chesterfield's Trusts*.

Payment of debts. Where a testator leaves debts which are not paid immediately out of the estate, the life tenant may receive income from capital in fact required for payment of the debts. Part of that income should be treated as capital and used towards payment of the debts. This is known as the rule in *Allhusen v Whittell*.

The calculations involved are so complex that the costs and administrative difficulties are quite out of proportion to any advantage that arises. It is hardly surprising that the rules are excluded in all well drafted trusts, and if not excluded are more honoured in the breach than in the observance.[66]

There are two common methods of excluding the rules. The first is to exclude the rules by name:

21.32

---

[62] 16.5 (Retention of income to provide for liabilities or depreciation of a capital asset).
[63] Because the rule against accumulation does not apply to administrative provisions: see 16.2 (Significance of administrative/dispositive distinction). *Re Gardiner* [1901] 1 Ch 697.
[64] *Re Harlbatt* [1910] 2 Ch 553. Form 8(7)(b) of the Statutory Will Forms 1925 accessible at www.kessler.co.uk. The power is also probably conferred (in relation to land) by s.6(1) TLATA 1996, but it is helpful to state it expressly.
[65] This name is unhelpful. The rules have nothing in common with the rules of apportionment under the Apportionment Act 1870, known as the statutory apportionment rule, discussed at para.19.54 (Statutory apportionment).
[66] Law Reform Committee, 23rd Report, *The Powers and Duties of Trustees*, Cmnd. 8733 (1982) paras 3.26 *et seq*.

The equitable rules of apportionment shall not apply to this Settlement;

or:

The rule in Howe v The Earl of Dartmouth *in all its branches shall not apply to this Settlement.*

The other technique is to say that income should be treated as income:

The income of the Trust Fund shall, however the property is invested, be treated and applied as income.[67]

Now, under trusts in this book, the trustees have a wide power of investment which includes power to acquire wasting and non-income producing assets.[68] Such assets are therefore authorised investments. The rules in *Howe v Earl of Dartmouth* and *The Earl of Chesterfield's Trusts* cannot apply. It is unnecessary to exclude them.[69] Likewise, the rule in *Allhusen v Whittell* does not apply to lifetime trusts, where trustees borrow under an express power. Accordingly, provisions of this type are unnecessary. It has been suggested that following the Trusts of Land and Appointment of Trustees Act 1996 the rule in *Allhusen v Whittell* has ceased to apply even to wills; but this is doubtful and it is still desirable to exclude the rule in wills if only for the avoidance of doubt.

One sometimes sees a provision that it is for the trustees to decide whether or not to apply the rules. This is open to various objections. In particular, in trusts with wide powers of investment the clause is otiose or its effect is unclear.

The balance between income and capital

21.33 The following form is used in this book:

(1) The Trustees may acquire:

(a) wasting assets
(b) assets which yield little or no income

for investment or any other purpose.[70]

(2) The Trustees are under no duty to procure distributions from a company in which they are interested.

---

[67] This precedent is derived from Statutory Wills Forms 1925, Form 8.
[68] See 21.33 (The balance between income and capital). It is doubtful whether the rules apply at all after the abolition of authorised lists of investment in the TA 2000. Ford & Lee (Principles of the Law of Trusts, at 11150) suggest that the rule survives but in a modified form: the trustee must still consider the appropriateness of the trust investments for maintaining a fair balance between the life tenant and must determine an appropriate accounting procedure to maintain a fair balance between the different classes of beneficiary.
[69] Re Nicholson [1909] 2 Ch 111; Re Van Straubenzee [1901] 2 Ch 779. But see Robert Mitchell, "Trusts for Sale in Wills—Excess Baggage" [1999] *The Conveyancer* 84, for another view.
[70] The words "or any other purpose" are needed, for instance, to authorise the acquisition of a short lease for the residence of a beneficiary.

(3) Generally, the Trustees are under no duty to hold a balance between conflicting interests of Beneficiaries.

It is a general principle that trustees should maintain a fair balance between beneficiaries interested in income and capital. Two consequences arise.

1. Investment policy.

Trustees should invest the trust fund so as to produce a reasonable amount of income and to protect the capital values of the trust fund.[71] It would be wrong to invest the entire trust fund in a non-income producing asset (e.g. an insurance policy) or in a building society account (leading to capital depreciation owing to inflation). A fortiori this precludes an investment of the entire trust fund in a wasting asset (such as a short lease). The rule is flexible. For instance, where a life tenant is in special need of income, trustees might adopt an investment policy which will increase his income at some expense to capital.[72]

This rule seems sensible enough; is it wise to exclude it? On balance, it is better to do so. There may be occasions where, for good reasons, trustees would like complete freedom either to invest in wasting assets—perhaps completely depriving the remainderman of his capital—or in non-income-producing assets—perhaps completely depriving the life tenant of his income. For instance, the life tenant may be in state residential accommodation and find that all her income is taken to pay the cost of her care.[73]

Decisions on these matters are better left to the good sense of the trustees rather than the general principles—however flexible—of trust law.

A standard form in old fashioned investment clauses authorises trustees to purchase investments "whether producing income or not". It is considered that this form does not affect the overriding duty to act fairly.[74] It addresses the (now rejected)[75] view that an asset not yielding income is not an "investment" at all. Since it is clear that "investments" does nowadays include assets not yielding income, this form serves no purpose and should not be used.

2. Management of company held by trust.

The same principle governs the management of the trust fund. Where trustees exercise control over a company, they should adopt a dividend policy which is fair to all. The rule could be inconvenient, especially if

---

[71] *Re Dick, Lopes-Hume v Dick* [1891] Ch 423.
[72] *Nestle v National Westminster Bank* [1993] 1 WLR 1260 at 1279.
[73] See Chapter 20 (Wills and Care Fee Planning).
[74] *Lewin on Trusts* (18th edn, 2008) 35–75 inclines to the same view, though it describes this as "a moot point", and offers other explanations of the purpose of the words.
[75] *Marson v Morton* 59 TC 381.

the trust property consists of shares in a family company, and it seems best to exclude it.

Demergers

21.34 Where a company whose shares are held by a trust carries out an indirect demerger, the shares received are treated as trust capital, which is plainly right. Where there is a direct demerger, however, the demerged shares will be treated as income, which is equally plainly wrong.[76] This could be altered by appropriate drafting.[77] Direct demergers are not uncommon.[78] It is easy to criticise the present rule but hard to frame a better one. Any fixed rule would be complex and to some extent arbitrary and unsatisfactory. One might say that a demerger specifically within s.213(3) ICTA 1988 is to be a capital receipt. This would not work for foreign companies and a recasting of the tax rules (bound to happen sooner or later) could lead to unforeseeable results and uncertainties for the trust. A very wide discretion in the trustees might be thought to be dispositive rather than administrative. One might possibly give the trustees a narrow discretion, such as:

> *A dividend from a company which in the opinion of the Trustees is a capital receipt in economic reality shall be treated as a capital receipt.*

On balance, however, the drawbacks of the present law are preferable to the uncertainties raised by such a clause. Statutory law reform inspired by the Trust Law Committee may eventually solve the problem better than the drafter can. Specific provisions might be considered, however, for a trust in anticipation of a direct demerger which is of more than ordinary significance for the trust. This specific provision need refer only to the company concerned, and can be drafted so as to be an administrative provision for tax purposes.[79]

---

[76] "Direct" and "indirect" demergers are transactions of the kind described by (a) and (b) respectively of s.213(3) ICTA 1988. See *Sinclair v Lee* [1993] Ch 497; the law is discussed in more detail in the Trust Law Committee Consultative Paper on Capital and Income of Trusts (June 1999) accessible on *www.kcl.ac.uk/depsta/law/tlc/consult.html*.
[77] *Bouch v Sproule* (1887) 12 App.Cas. 385.
[78] They include the Hanson demergers (1995) and GUS/Burburry (2005).
[79] 16.7 (Capital/income and apportionment provisions).

Occupation and use of trust property

The form used in this book is as follows: **21.35**

(1) The Trustees may acquire any interest in property anywhere in the world for occupation or use by an Income Beneficiary.

(2) The Trustees may permit any Income Beneficiary to occupy or use Trust Property on such terms as they think fit.

(3) "**Income Beneficiary**" here means a Beneficiary to whom income of the Property is payable (as of right or at the discretion of the Trustees).

(4) This paragraph does not restrict any right of Beneficiaries to occupy land under the Trusts of Land and Appointment of Trustees Act 1996.

Trustees have a statutory power to acquire land for a beneficiary's occupation, but the power is not completely comprehensive.[80] An unrestricted power is desirable, and sub-clause (1) sets this out.

Where trustees hold land, a life tenant has certain statutory rights of occupation.[81] These could be excluded by the drafter.[82] The rules are, however, quite satisfactory, and this precedent retains them: sub-paragraph (4). Where these rules do not apply (e.g. discretionary trusts, or property other than land) then the matter is left to the trustees' discretion. This would probably be the position in any event, but it seems best to cover it expressly.

This power should be made subject to the consent of the protector where there is one.

The draft clause covers both land and chattels; it seems unnecessary to deal with these in separate clauses. The clause rests loosely on statutory **21.36**

---

[80] The statutory power only applies to freehold or leasehold land in the UK: s.8 TA 2000. On the wisdom of purchasing land outside the UK see 21.22 (Power of investment).

Re Power [1947] Ch 572 is sometimes cited as authority for the proposition that a common form power of investment never permits trustees to purchase a residence for a beneficiary because a residence is not an "investment". More accurately, the position is considered to be that the acquisition of a residence *may* not be an investment, and so may be outside the scope of a common form power of investment, but this depends on the circumstances of the acquisition. But after the TA 2000 the issue could only arise in unusual circumstances, e.g. if trustees wish to purchase property for occupation by a person who is not a beneficiary (at a rent or rent free with the consent of a life tenant).

[81] Section 12 TLATA 1996.

[82] In some cases the provisions of the TLATA are expressly subject to contrary terms in a trust (e.g. ss.8, 11); in some cases the provisions expressly override any expression of contrary intent (e.g. s.4). In ss.12 and 13, however, there is no guidance in the statute either way. It is considered that these statutory rules can be excluded by the drafter. It is a fundamental principle of trust law that it is up to the settlor to decide what rights to confer under the trust. Restrictions on freedom of disposition should not be lightly inferred. (However, this question is academic. The statutory right of occupation is so limited that in circumstances where it confers a right of occupation trustees acting reasonably would almost invariably exercise their power to let the beneficiaries into occupation in any event.)

precedent.[83] Some precedents detail the terms on which the beneficiaries may use the property (e.g. "on such terms as to payment of rent, repair, decoration, insurance, etc."). The formulae end with a general power ("and such terms generally as the trustees think fit") which must include all that has gone before; nothing is gained.

Some drafters follow the statutory precedent and add that trustees shall not be liable for loss. Presumably, the fear is that one beneficiary will drop the Ming vase; and another will sue the trustees. Now, if the trustees are acting properly and within their powers, it is hard to see that they are liable. And in any case, should not the vase have been insured? The matter is adequately dealt with by the general provision discussed at 6.17 (Construction of trustee exemption clauses).

In IP trusts the restriction to "Income Beneficiaries" could be simplified by saying "Income Beneficiary" means a beneficiary entitled to an interest in possession in the trust property; but that would cease to be appropriate if the trust ceased to be IP in form. In discretionary trusts the restriction may be omitted.

To the extent that the power is dispositive, it should strictly be restricted to the trust period. However, it is better to leave the "wait and see" rule to have this effect rather than to complicate the drafting by saying this expressly.

Loans to beneficiaries

21.37 The form used in this book is as follows:

> The Trustees may lend trust money to an Income Beneficiary. The loan may be interest free and unsecured, or on such terms as the Trustees think fit. "Income Beneficiary" here means a Beneficiary to whom income of the money is payable (as of right or at the discretion of the Trustees).

Trustees should have power to make loans to beneficiaries on favourable terms. Such loans may be convenient in practice and tax efficient. This clause authorises trustees to do this. It is uncertain to what extent such loans would be proper in the absence of express authority.[84]

This power should be made subject to the consent of the protector where there is one.

21.38 Express mention is given in the draft to unsecured loans in view of the

---

[83] Section 8 TA 2000; s.47(1)(iv) AEA 1925.
[84] The power of investment will authorise loans by way of investment. Loans on favourable terms raise more problems. In *Re Laing* [1899] 1 Ch 593 trustees had power to invest trust funds "upon personal credit without security". It was assumed that trustees, under this clause, could lend (presumably interest free) to the life tenant.

general suspicion of unsecured loans expressed in the context of trustees' power of investment.[85]

Some drafters provide that no loan should be made to the settlor. This is not necessary. The settlor exclusion clause will prohibit loans on favourable terms. No harm arises from the mere possibility that loans could be made on arm's length terms. The actual making of the loan may have severe tax consequences: but that is a matter for the trustees to consider at the time of the loan.

In IP trusts the restriction to income beneficiaries could be simplified by saying

> "Income Beneficiary" means a beneficiary entitled to an interest in possession in the trust property.

However, that would cease to be appropriate if the trust ceased to be interest in possession in form. In discretionary trusts the restriction may be omitted.

To the extent that the power is dispositive, it should strictly be restricted to the trust period. However, it is better to leave the "wait and see" rule to have this effect rather than to complicate the drafting by saying this expressly.

Trust property as security for beneficiaries' liabilities

The form used in this book is as follows: 21.39

> The Trustees may charge Trust Property as security for any debts or obligations of an Income Beneficiary. "Income Beneficiary" here means a Beneficiary to whom income of the Trust Property is payable (as of right or at the discretion of the Trustees).

An alternative to the trustees lending money to a beneficiary is for them to provide security so he can borrow more easily elsewhere. This requires express authorisation.

This power should be made subject to the consent of the protector where there is one.

The restriction to income beneficiaries is the same as the power to apply trust capital as income.

Power to trade

The form used in this book is as follows: 21.40

> The Trustees may carry on a trade, in any part of the world, alone or in partnership.

---

[85] *Khoo Tek Keung v Ch'ng Joo Tuan Neoh* [1934] AC 529.

Trustees cannot properly carry on a trade without express power.[86]

In practice trustees rarely carry on a trade, though trading trusts offer some tax[87] and commercial[88] advantages. The inclusion of the power does no harm, whereas it is conceivable that its absence may be regretted. The standard practice is to include this power in all cases.

The draft is concise, self-explanatory and, it is thought, comprehensive. There is little trust law on the subject but there is a company law precedent.[89]

Some drafters authorise the trustees to carry on a trade *or business*. The word "business" is wider than the word "trade".[90] It is hard to see what this adds. If it is a business of making or holding investments, there is already ample authority for that in the power of investment. It is not necessary to give trustees an express indemnity against the trust fund for trading debts properly incurred by them.[91]

Power to borrow

21.41 The form used in this book is as follows:

> The Trustees may borrow money for investment or any other purpose. Money borrowed shall be treated as Trust Property.

The general law gives trustees power to borrow for some purposes.[92] Trustees do not have an unrestricted power to borrow, and, in particular, trustees may not borrow money for investment purposes.[93]

It is thought that trustees may be entrusted with unrestricted powers

---

[86] A standard form power of investment is wide but does not confer a power to "invest" in a trade: *Re Berry* [1962] Ch 97.
[87] The IHT and CGT system generally favours trade over investment, a partial reversal of the 19th-century aristocratic prejudice against trade. (Income tax is now heading the opposite way.) However, the distinction the law draws between trade and investment is (inevitably) a formal one, and often the same economic result can be achieved by an "investment" or in a form which the law regards as a trade. For instance, trustees holding land used by a trader may arrange to trade in partnership with the occupier of the land so as to qualify for 100% IHT business property relief, or for CGT roll-over and entrepreneurs reliefs. This is easy if the land (often farmland) is occupied by a beneficiary, but may be possible even if the occupier is unconnected with the trust.
[88] A trading trust with a corporate trustee enjoys an element of limited liability without public disclosure of trading accounts.
[89] Section 31(1) Companies Act 2006.
[90] *American Leaf Blending Co. Sdn Bhd v Director-General of Inland Revenue* [1978] STC 561.
[91] Paragraph. 21.13 (Trustees entitled to expenses of exercising powers).
[92] Section 71 SLA 1925; s.212 IHTA 1984; s.16(1) TA 1925; s.39(1) AEA 1925. The Law Commission suggest (Law Com. Report No.260, *Trustees' Powers and Duties*, para.2–44) that s.8(1) TA 2000 authorises trustees to purchase land with the aid of a mortgage, but the contrary view is arguable.
[93] *Re Suensen Taylor* [1974] 1 WLR 1280, [1974] 3 All ER 397.

to borrow money, especially since loans made to trustees offer tax advantages.[94]

... *For investment or for any other purpose.* It is desirable specifically to override the case which held that trustees' statutory power to borrow does not allow trustees to borrow in order to invest.

The draft is drawn from s.71 of the Settled Land Act 1925. Some drafters say that the trustees may borrow ... *On such terms as the trustees think fit.* These words (not found in statutory precedents) are strictly unnecessary; there is certainly no authority to suggest any need for a lengthier formula such as "on such terms and conditions relating to interest, capital" and so on.

In this book a power to give security is dealt with separately.[95]

Delegation

The Trustee Act 2000 allows trustees to delegate to an agent, but imposes many restrictions, some understandable, others quixotic.[96] Four matters cannot be delegated:

21.42

(a) dispositive powers;[97]

(b) power to decide whether payments should be made out of income or capital;

(c) power of appointing new trustees;

(d) power of delegation, use of nominee.

A beneficiary cannot be appointed an agent.[98] This is in striking contrast to many other statutory provisions which recognise that it may be appropriate for a beneficiary to act as trustee.[99]

Trustees may not delegate the following matters unless it is "reasonably necessary" to do so:

---

[94] An individual would not receive tax relief on interest paid unless the loan is eligible for relief under the restrictive conditions of Pt.IX ICTA 1988. Interest paid by trustees effectively enjoys higher rate tax relief; for a trustee does not pay higher rate tax, and a beneficiary would pay higher rate tax only on the net amount of income received from the trust (i.e. income after interest has been paid). *Murray v IRC* 11 TC 133; *Macfarlane v IRC* 14 TC 538. The settlement provisions counteract the tax advantages in some circumstances.
[95] Paragraph. 21.45 (Power to give security for trustees' liabilities).
[96] Section 11 TA 2000. Further rules apply to charitable trusts (not discussed here).
[97] Paragraph. 16.2 (Significance of administrative/dispositive distinction).
[98] The expression "beneficiary" is undefined and in some cases it is unclear who is a "beneficiary". See 5.18 (Definition of "Beneficiaries").
[99] See the references in 6.3 (Beneficiaries as trustees).

(a) power to sub-delegate;

(b) limitation of liability of agent;

(c) permitting agent to act in potential conflicts of interest.

There must be considerable doubt as to what constitutes "reasonable necessity".

Further restrictions apply to "asset management functions". Here we have the regulator's delight: written agreements and policy statements. Applied to trusts as a whole, will the benefit of all this paper outweigh the cost? The answer is by no means obvious; it might perhaps benefit from research but is probably unresearchable.[100]

In the absence of sound research the drafter must rely on intuition and it is submitted that trustees can be trusted with a general and unrestricted power of delegation. All these restrictions on the power of delegation are needless complications. Policy statements, for instance, may be regarded as good practice but should not be compulsory regardless of circumstances. If they are fit to be trustees they are fit to decide how to delegate.

The technical question then arises of whether these restrictions can be overridden by the drafting and, if so, what wording is required. The TA 2000 has used a variety of drafting techniques to impose the restrictions, which causes some unnecessary complexity and confusion.

The restriction that certain functions are not "delegable" and the restriction on delegating to beneficiaries, apply only to the statutory power of delegation. These restrictions do not apply if the trust confers its own power of delegation, e.g. as in the STEP standard form ("a trustee may delegate ... any of his functions to any person"). It is reasonably clear that the same applies to the restriction relating to joint delegation and the three matters which can only be delegated if reasonably necessary.

This leaves the restrictions relating to asset management functions. It is considered the same applies. Section 15 Trustee Act 2000 (Asset management functions: special restrictions) only imposes its restrictions on the statutory power of delegation. So if a trust confers an express power of delegation, whether before or after the Act, s.15 does not apply and there is no duty to prepare a policy statement. But the contrary view has been suggested.[101] However, even if any of these restrictions apply at all to express powers of delegation, they only apply subject to contrary intent

---

[100] Written policy statements are however the spirit of the age, and it is likely that trust practitioners will see more of them before the tide turns. The Charity Commission, for instance, now recommends charity trustees should "develop a written policy" on how to deal with conflicts of interest relating to trustee remuneration (CC 11, Payment of Charity Trustees, Sept 2000), a charity reserves policy (RS3, 1993), a risks policy (Charities/Accounts and Reports) Regs 2000); etc.

[101] This view regards s.15 TA 2000 as a self-standing section, not only applicable to the statutory power. But the context would seem to be against this.

in the trust itself. The restrictions can be excluded by express words or by implication.[102]

Ideally one would set out at length exactly what is authorised, but the length of the clause would be out of proportion to the importance of the issue. Accordingly, the precedents in this book adopt the shorthand of an exclusion by reference to the specific statutory provisions. This leads to a simple form of draft:

> A Trustee or the Trustees jointly (or other person in a fiduciary position) may authorise any person to exercise all or any functions on such terms as to remuneration and other matters as they may think fit. None of the restrictions on delegation in ss.12 to 15 Trustee Act 2000 shall apply.

This draft is drawn from s.11 Trustee Act 2000. There are many other statutory precedents.[103] This clause applies to trustees and other fiduciaries. This would allow the settlor to delegate his power to appoint new trustees.[104] On the use of the words "functions" as shorthand for "trusts, powers and discretions" see 7.4 (Powers and duties: terminology). It is not necessary to add the words "anywhere in the world".[105]

Some drafters begin the clause with phrases such as:

Notwithstanding any rule of law or equity to the contrary ...
Notwithstanding the fiduciary nature of the Trustees' powers ...

What can be the purpose of this? It acknowledges that the general rule (that trustees may not delegate their powers) is overridden; but the general rule can be overridden by any clear words: no particular form is needed.[106] By this formula the drafter vaunts his superiority to the rule of equity; but the additional words add nothing of substance.[107]

---

[102] Even this has been doubted, at least in the very early days of the TA 2000, in relation to s.15 TA 2000! But the idea that Parliament should intend these petty restrictions on delegation to override the intention of the settlor is absurd. It is also contrary to the approach of the Court in *Re Turner* [1937] Ch 15 and *LRT Pension Trustees v Hatt* [1993] Pensions Law Reports, accessible on www.kessler.co.uk, in which apparently mandatory statutory words were held in context to apply subject to contrary intent.

[103] Section 25 TA 1925; s.23(2) (repealed); s. 29 LPA 1925, now replaced by s.9 TLATA 1996; s.10 Powers of Attorney Act 1971; s.3(3) Enduring Powers of Attorney Act 1985 (repealed); articles 71 and 72 of Table A of the Companies (Tables A to F) Regulations 1985; art. 25 Trusts (Jersey) Law 1984.

[104] The settlor could not delegate this power under any of the statutory powers of delegation applicable to trustees.

[105] See the discussion on similar wording in 6.33 (Appointment of new trustees).

[106] See (if authority is needed) *Pilkington v IRC* [1964] AC 612. Although s.25 TA 1925 uses this form, it is not found in other statutory powers of delegation, listed above.

[107] One drafter has even provided a clause beginning: "notwithstanding any rule of law or equity *or otherwise* ..."! One wonders what other rules the drafter had in mind.

Nominees and custodians

21.43 The form used in this book is as follows:

> (1) The Trustees may appoint a person to act as their nominee in relation to such of the assets of the trust as they may determine. They may take such steps as are necessary to secure that those assets are vested in the nominee.
>
> (2) The Trustees may appoint a person to act as custodian in relation to such of the assets of the trust as they may determine. The Trustees may give the custodian custody of the assets and any documents or records concerning the assets. The Trustees are not obliged to appoint a custodian of securities payable to bearer.
>
> (3) The Trustees may appoint a person to act as nominee or custodian on such terms as to remuneration and other matters as they may think fit.

It is often convenient to use a nominee or custodian. This can save time, paperwork and expense, especially on a change of trustees or on the sale of securities dealt with on the stock exchange. It also reduces the cost of investment management.

In *Mason v Fairbrother* [108] Judge Blackett-Ord V.C. considered:

> ... a proviso about a nominee being a bank or something like that. But in my view that is an undesirable complication. I will simply authorise the trustees to appoint a nominee or nominees to hold any investment in the fund. That is a power that the trustees can exercise in proper circumstances and if they misuse it, they will be liable.

Quite so. All such attempts to safeguard trust property by fettering trustees' powers are misguided. This form (based on the statutory wording) overrides the elaborate restrictions on the statutory powers set out in ss.16–20 Trustee Act 2000.

Power to give indemnities

21.44 The form used in this book is as follows:

> The Trustees may indemnify any Person for any liability relating to this Settlement.

Of course trustees may give indemnities without authorisation by the trust. The purpose of express authorisation is to permit the trustees:

> (1) to reimburse themselves out of the trust fund if the indemnity is called upon; and

---

[108] [1983] 2 All ER 1078 at 1087. (This was an application for additional powers under s.57 TA 1925.)

(2) to use their powers of mortgage and charge so as to secure the indemnity on the trust fund.

In the absence of an express power other statutory powers would sometimes authorise indemnities (but not always).[109]

Power to give security for trustees' liabilities

21.45 The form used in this book is as follows:

> The Trustees may mortgage or charge Trust Property as security for any liability incurred by them as Trustees (and may grant a floating charge so far as the law allows).

The duty of trustees being to preserve trust property, they need express authority to mortgage it. The ability to mortgage trust property as security for trustees' liabilities is useful. The general law allows trustees to mortgage trust property for certain purposes only, but there seems no reason for any restrictions.

The drafter may append the power to mortgage trust property as an ancillary to various powers where security may be needed (power to borrow; power to give indemnities, etc.). It is easier to put in a single self-standing paragraph to achieve this end. The concept of liabilities incurred "as trustees" follows statutory precedent.[110]

A floating charge is possible under English law, except in relation to personal chattels.

Power of appropriation

21.46 The form used in this book is as follows:

> The Trustees may appropriate Trust Property to any person or class of persons in or towards the satisfaction of their interest in the Trust Fund.

Trustees need a power of appropriation to allow a division of the trust fund into separate shares, if desired. The powers conferred by the general law are inadequate.[111]

---

[109] See Chapter 31 (Indemnities for trustees).
[110] Section 26(1) TA 1925.
[111] (1) Section 41 AEA 1925 confers the power on personal representatives, but not on trustees.
(2) Section 7 TLATA 1996 confers a power of appropriation in relation to land in England or Wales.
(3) Section 15(b) TA 1925 confers power to sever and apportion "blended trust funds or property". It is submitted that this gives trustees power to appropriate whenever trustees

The draft is based on the statutory precedent.

This form authorises appropriation to a settled share, since the beneficiaries of the settled share are a "class of persons".

The statutory power of appropriation normally requires the consent of the beneficiary concerned. If the power is set out independently it is unnecessary, even for the avoidance of doubt, to say: "without the consent of any person...".

Where trustees have this power, they may ascertain the value of the property by qualified agents; and a valuation made by the trustees is binding on the beneficiaries. It is not necessary to say this expressly.[112]

Receipt by charities

21.47 The form used in this book is as follows:

> Where Trust Property is to be paid or transferred to a charity, the receipt of the treasurer or appropriate officer of the charity shall be a complete discharge to the Trustees.

This form solves a possible administrative difficulty where trust property is payable to a charitable trust, or an unincorporated charitable association. In such cases the trustees would strictly need to investigate who could give them a valid receipt.

This is a provision of marginal significance. It is obviously unnecessary if the trust does not include charitable beneficiaries. It is unnecessary where trust property is to be transferred to a charitable company; most large charities are now incorporated. Omission of the clause is unlikely to matter: in the unlikely event that trust funds were accidentally paid to the wrong person, and then stolen, the trustees' own conduct would not usually cause them to be liable for breach of trust.

The draft is drawn loosely from statutory precedents.[113]

---

hold trust property in undivided shares — so the power overlaps with (1) and (2) above. This is significant since this power (unlike the above) does not require any beneficiary to consent.
- (4) The extent to which the common law allows appropriation is unclear. The old cases are discussed in *Kane v Radley-Kane* [1999] Ch 274.
- (5) Section 188 LPA 1925 confers a further power on the Court, in relation to chattels. If one is going to court an application could also be made under the Variation of Trusts Act 1958—though perhaps not under s.57 TA 1925, see 16.8 (Power of appropriation).

The Law Reform Committee, 23rd Report, *The Powers and Duties of Trustees*, Cmnd. 8733 (1982) para.4.42 recommended that trustees should have a wide statutory power of appropriation and this would be a desirable reform. It would simplify the law, shorten trust documents and help beneficiaries whose trusts are not well drafted. There is, however, no current prospect of reform.

[112] Section 22(3) TA 1925.
[113] Sections 14, 63(2) TA 1925; Statutory Will Forms 1925, Form 4 accessible on *www.kessler.co.uk*; s.95 SLA 1925. Some extend this form to apply not only to the "treasurer or appropriate officer"

Release of rights and powers

The form used in this book is as follows: **21.48**

> The Trustees (or other persons in a fiduciary position) may by deed release wholly or in part any of their rights or functions and (if applicable) so as to bind their successors.

This clause gives trustees power to release their powers.[114] It would also allow the settlor to release his power of appointing new trustees. This has become a standard provision in modern practice, though it is not strictly needed: the trustees' overriding powers could be exercised so as to have the same effect as a release.[115]

The power could be used to change the structure of the trust fundamentally. Where there is a protector the exercise of this power should require his consent.

The general question of when and which categories of power can be released under the general law has attracted a difficult case law, which is fortunately largely redundant. There is little in the cases relevant to drafting. The first limb of our draft clause is self-evident, and the second for the avoidance of doubt only. The words "wholly or in part" would be implied in any case and could be omitted.[116] Some drafters authorise trustees to enter into a contract not to exercise their powers. This is implied in any event,[117] and it is hard to conceive of a case where such a power would be useful.

Some drafters begin the clause with phrases such as:

Notwithstanding any rule of law or equity to the contrary . . .

Notwithstanding the fiduciary nature of the trustees' powers . . .

This acknowledges that the general rule (that trustees may not release their powers) is to be overridden. But this general principle can be overridden by any clear form of words.[118]

---

of the charity, but any person "appearing to be" treasurer or officer. It is difficult to see that this makes much difference in practice, particularly since trustees will generally have the defence to a breach of trust conferred by s.61 TA 1925 and (in the precedents in this book) a defence that they have not been negligent.

[114] Fiduciary powers cannot be released in the absence of an express power to release them: *Re Wills* [1964] Ch 219. Section 155 LPA 1925 misleadingly appears to authorise trustees to release powers; but it does not have that effect.

[115] *Muir v IRC* [1966] 1 WLR 1269.

[116] *Re Evered* [1910] 2 Ch 147.

[117] *Ibid.*

[118] See (if authority is needed) *Muir v IRC* [1966] 1 WLR 1269. See 21.42 (Delegation) where similar comments apply.

Ancillary powers

21.49 The form used in this book is as follows:

> The Trustees may do anything which is incidental or conducive to the exercise of their functions.

On a fair construction this form should never make any practical difference,[119] but it may dispel doubts raised by any arguments in favour of a narrow construction of trustees' powers. The form simplifies the drafting of the other administrative powers, since one need not scatter forms of this kind in all the other powers. There are trust and company law precedents.[120]

Provisions relating to minors

21.50 The form used in this book is:

> Where the Trustees may apply income for the benefit of a minor, they may do so by paying the income to the minor's parent or guardian on behalf of the minor, or to the minor if he has attained the age of 16. The Trustees are under no duty to enquire into the use of the income unless they have knowledge of circumstances which call for enquiry.

Payment of income to parent or guardian

Trustees may, under the general law, pay funds belonging to a child to the person who has parental responsibility for that child.[121] It is therefore not necessary to say that trustees may pay income to the parent or guardian of a child.[122] In the draft in this book, the important part of the clause is the

---

[119] The courts ought to apply to the construction of trustees' powers the principle well established in company law, that whatever may fairly be regarded as incidental to or consequent upon a company's objects ought not to be held ultra vires: *Att. Gen. v Great Eastern Railway Co* (1880) 5 App.Cas. 473 at 478.
[120] Section 15 Contrast TA 1925; s.31(1) Companies Act 2006; Sch.1 para.23 Insolvency Act 1986; s.33(5)(d) National Heritage Act 1983; s.111 Local Government Act 1972. Case law records that local authorities have not had much success in trying to justify under this section acts (swaps, trading in land) not otherwise within their powers.
[121] Section 3(3) Children Act 1989. The Act sensibly changed the law. Previously, a guardian had power to give a receipt on behalf of a minor but a parent did not.
[122] One often sees a clause which says that trustees may pay income to a parent of a minor. Presumably such drafts have not been revised since the Children Act 1989 Act. See "The Property of Minors under English Law", Denker and Haworth, [2004] PCB 376. That clause is not entirely without effect. It would authorise trustees to make a payment to a parent who did not have parental responsibility for the child. This may happen, for instance, in the case of an illegitimate child. But the point is of trivial importance.

second sentence. This deals with the question of what responsibility the trustees should have to ensure that income is properly used by the parent or guardian: this is discussed at 6.32 (Excluding duty to supervise parents and guardians).

Payment of income to child

A minor cannot normally give a receipt for trust money.[123] It might possibly be convenient to relax this rule though in practice the point is unlikely to be important. This form does not give the child a right to demand payment: the trustees may choose whether or not to pay to him.[124]

Power to retain income of child

The form used in this book is: **21.51**

> Where Trustees may apply income for the benefit of a minor, they may do so by resolving that they hold that income on trust for the minor absolutely and:
> (1) The Trustees may apply that income for the benefit of the minor during his minority.
> (2) The Trustees shall transfer the residue of that income to the minor on attaining the age of 18.
> (3) For investment and other administrative purposes that income shall be treated as Trust Property.

This power is intended to facilitate elementary income tax planning for children who are beneficiaries of discretionary trusts.

For income tax purposes one might like children to have an income of their own, so as to use their personal allowances. This offers a worthwhile annual tax saving. Where the beneficiaries are not children of the settlor, trustees can deal with trust income in the following ways:

(1) The trustees may accumulate it. The income will be subject to tax at the rates set out in s.479 ITA 2007 (the trust rate and the dividend trust rate).[125]

(2)(a) The trustees may spend it for the benefit of the minor children.
  (b) The trustees may retain the income on trust for the child by exercising this special power.[126]

---

[123] In the unlikely event that he or she is married, a minor can give a receipt for (1) trust income (s.21 LPA 1925); and (2) accumulated income payable to the minor under s.31(2)(i) TA 1925.
[124] *Re Somech* [1957] Ch 165.
[125] It may be possible to reclaim this tax by making income payments to the beneficiary in later years, but the beneficiary's personal allowance in the earlier years is lost.
[126] The child might become entitled to quite a substantial sum at 18, a result the parents may not view with enthusiasm.

In both these cases the income is effectively[127] taxed as the child's income (and up to the personal allowance, escapes tax altogether). The power to retain income for a child is therefore a useful means of obtaining the tax advantage without spending the income.

Where the beneficiary is an unmarried minor child of the settlor, s.629 ITTOIA 2005 counteracts the tax advantage in situation (2). This is done by providing that the child's income should be treated as the income of the parent.[128]

Administrative provision for mentally handicapped beneficiaries

21.52 Where the terms of a trust require trustees to pay funds to a mentally handicapped beneficiary they should pay the funds to his attorney under a lasting power of attorney which relates to his property and affairs or to a deputy appointed by the court under the Mental Capacity Act 2005 whose powers include taking possession or control of this property. Where:

(1) it is not desired to appoint a deputy (because of the expense); and

(2) the beneficiary cannot appoint an attorney (because he does not have the necessary mental capacity),[129]

it is submitted that the trustees may properly retain the funds and invest them as nominee for the beneficiary, or apply the funds for the direct benefit of the beneficiary. However it is desirable to have an express power to confirm this. The form used in this book is self-explanatory:

---

[127] Since the trust is not IP in form (see 14.17 (Life tenant a minor)) the tiresome procedures set out in ss.479 and 496 ITA 2007 must be followed: (1) The trustees will pay tax at the rate set out in s.479 ITA 2007. (2) On exercise of the power, the retained income becomes the beneficiary's income: *Stevenson v Wishart* [1987] STC 266; *Spens v IRC* 46 TC 276. (3) Tax is then reclaimed by the beneficiary under the credit system of s.496 ITA 2007. (The exercise of the power to retain counts as a "payment" for the purposes of s.496 ITA 2007. The word "payment" in s.496 ITA 2007 has a wide meaning: see *IRC v Berrill* 55 TC 429 at 444.) The position is less advantageous for dividend income.

[128] It follows that a teenage marriage is an effective if drastic way round the anti-avoidance provision. The section applies in a more attenuated form where the trust was made before 9 March 1999 (for which see the fourth edition of this book para.15–055, accessible on *www.kessler.co.uk*).

[129] The capacity needed to create a Lasting Power of Attorney must be assessed by reference to the principles set out in ss.2 and 3 of the Mental Capacity Act 2005. Thus, the donor must be able to understand the information relevant to the decision, retain that information, use or weigh that information as part of the process of making the decision and communicate his decision. It is thought that the information relevant to the creation of a Lasting Power of Attorney will be similar to that considered relevant in *Re K* [1988] Ch 310.

Mentally Handicapped Beneficiary

Where income or capital is payable to a Beneficiary who does not have the mental capacity to appoint an attorney under a lasting[130] power of attorney which relates to his property and affairs, the Trustees may (subject to the directions of the Court or a deputy appointed under the Mental Capacity Act whose powers include receiving such income or capital) apply that income or capital for his benefit.

Where this form has not been used, trustees may be able to use a power of appointment or advancement to confer this power on themselves.

Power to disclaim[131]

21.53 The form used in this book is as follows:

> A Person may disclaim his interest in this Settlement wholly or in part.

This is an IHT motivated provision.

On the death of a life tenant with an estate IP, trust property will often pass to his widow/civil partner: this will normally postpone an IHT charge.

There are circumstances where this would not be desirable. It may be better that some or all of the trust property should pass directly to the next generation, so as to take advantage of the life tenant's nil rate band. The difficulty is that the drafter cannot know at the time the trust is made whether this will be the case or not. In the case of non-settled property, issues of this kind can be resolved after death by means of a deed of variation; but deeds of variation are not available for settled property.[132]

The use of a disclaimer offers an answer to this problem. It allows the question of whether the spouse/civil partner should take an interest in the trust property to be resolved after death. Section 93 IHTA 1984 provides:

> Where a person becomes beneficially entitled to an interest in settled property but disclaims the interest, then, if the disclaimer is not made for a consideration in money or money's worth, the Inheritance Tax Act 1984 shall apply as if he had not become entitled to the interest.

Thus if the surviving spouse/civil partner becomes entitled to an interest in the settled property on the death of the life tenant, and it is desired to utilise the deceased's nil rate band, she simply may disclaim her interest.

---

[130] Since October 2007 (when the Mental Capacity Act 2005 took effect) it is no longer possible to create an enduring power of attorney. However, such powers created before that date remain valid and must be registered with the Public Guardian in accordance with the Act.
[131] On this topic see Oerton and Wood, *Capital Taxes News & Reports* (1989), p.17.
[132] Section 142(5) IHTA 1984. There is no good reason for this discrimination against settled property; but there is little prospect of law reform.

The usual rule is that an individual must disclaim the entire interest in property given to him; he cannot disclaim part. That rule derives from a presumption that the donor so intended. It is therefore possible to authorise a beneficiary to disclaim an interest in part.[133] The IHT relief applies to a partial disclaimer as well as to a complete disclaimer.[134]

It is considered that the IHT relief applies when a person becomes entitled to an absolute interest in settled property, as well as when she becomes entitled to a lesser interest.

Statutory apportionment[135]

21.54 Under the general law, income is where possible treated as accruing from day to day as it is earned. It is not income of the day it happens to be received. This means that when there is any change of entitlement to income, the income may need to be apportioned and:

(1) one part treated as income received before the change would have been treated and

(2) the other part treated as income received after the change.

The implications of this are somewhat surprising and the matter is best illustrated by examples.

Example 1

Application of statutory apportionment rule on death of life tenant

Trustees hold a trust fund on trust for A for life, remainder to B. A dies on 30 April 1992. In 1993 the trustees receive a dividend for the calendar year 1992.

(1) One-third of the dividend will be apportioned to the period before A's death (and so paid to A's estate).

(2) The remaining two-thirds is apportioned to the period after A's death and so paid to B.

---

[133] *Guthrie v Walrond* (1883) 22 Ch D 573.
[134] This appears to be HMRC's view; see SP E18 and HMRC correspondence published in *Tolley's Practical Tax*, June 28, 1989.
[135] See 21.32 (Equitable apportionment) for the entirely distinct rules known unhelpfully as "equitable apportionment"

Example 2

Application of statutory apportionment rule on death of testator

The testator dies on 30 April 1992. By his will his residuary estate is held on trust for B for life with remainder over. In 1993 the executors receive a dividend for the calendar year 1992.

(1) One-third of the dividend is apportioned to the period before the testator's death, and is retained by the executors as trust capital (just as any sums actually received by the testator before his death would have become trust capital).

(2) B will be entitled to the remaining two-thirds.[136]

The apportionment rule is intended to operate fairly between the different beneficiaries (or their estates). The rule produces a fairness which is expensive and inconvenient. The sums involved are usually small. Like motorists with the urban speed limit, trustees ignore the apportionment rule if they feel they can do so safely. So common is this practice that the rule is scarcely if ever observed. Where figures are large, and the rule has not been excluded by a trust, the question occasionally arises whether the application of the rule can be overridden by the appropriate exercise of a common form power of appointment: i.e. can a deed of appointment deal with income not yet payable, but which time apportioned would accrue before the date of the appointment? It is submitted that the answer is yes; but views may differ.

It is plainly desirable to avoid this pedantry and direct that the statutory apportionment rule should not apply. Instead income is treated as accruing when payable to the trustees: in the three examples above all the dividends would be paid to B. This is also the view of a very distinguished Law Reform Committee who recommended effective abolition of the rule.[137] Fortunately the apportionment rule can be reversed without difficulty in trust law[138] or tax law.[139] The form used in this book is as follows:

> Income and expenditure shall be treated as arising when payable, and not from day to day, so that no apportionment shall take place.

The drafting echoes the language of the statute. It is not appropriate to say:

> *This settlement shall be construed as if the Apportionment Act 1870 had not been enacted.*

---

[136] For an example of application of statutory apportionment rule on an A&M beneficiary attaining an interest in possession, see the 7th edn of this book, para.20.54
[137] Law Reform Committee, 23rd Report, *The Powers and Duties of Trustees*, Cmnd. 8733 (1982), para.3.39.
[138] Section 7 Apportionment Act 1870 directs that the provisions of the section do not apply in any case where it is expressly stipulated that no apportionment shall take place.
[139] Paragraph. 16.7 (Capital/income and apportionment provisions).

Interest was apportioned under the common law. The 1870 Act merely brings other types of income into line. It is unnecessary to refer to the 1870 Act or its predecessor the Apportionment Act 1834.[140]

Power for trustees to apply the apportionment rules?

Sometimes the trustees are given the power to decide for themselves whether or not to apply the apportionment rules. Thus in the examples above the trustees would pay the dividends to B but with power:

(1) on the facts of Example 1, to pay one-third of the dividend to A's estate; and

(2) on the facts of Example 2, to retain one-third of the dividend as capital.

It is possible to envisage circumstances where trustees might desire to do this, but in practice it would probably never happen. It is suggested that the form is not worth the trouble and accordingly it is not used in this book.[141]

Trustee remuneration

21.55 In the absence of any specific provision, the position is governed by the Trustee Act 2000. For trusts other than charities a trust corporation can always charge.[142] A trustee acting in a professional capacity can also charge, but subject to the safeguard that he is not a sole trustee and each other trustee has agreed in writing.[143] Should a professional trustee rely on this? It is considered that an "agreement" with the other trustees may be irrevocable (so that the professional trustee is not at risk if the other trustee later tries to change his mind). However, if the other trustee dies the surviving sole trustee could not charge until he has appointed a second trustee who will consent to his charges. Where two trustees are partners in the same partnership it is considered that one could consent to the charges of the other but the contrary is faintly arguable (because the trustee benefits from his own consent).[144] While little difficulty should arise in practice from

---

[140] The 1834 Act was repealed in 1977, so forms referring to that Act are obsolete.
[141] The tax implications of this power are also of concern. On the facts of examples (1) and (2) would one third of the dividend be within the scope of s.479 ITA 2007 since it is income payable at the discretion of the trustees? The answer is probably no, since the power is merely administrative: see 16.2 (Significance of administrative/dispositive distinction).
[142] Section 29(1) TA 2000.
[143] Section 29(2) TA 2000.
[144] It is even arguable that the same applies where there is a third trustee who also consents.

the statutory rule, however, the form allowing trustees to charge without consent has long been used and few difficulties seem to have arisen. The precedents in this book therefore retain the traditional form. The drafting echoes the statutory wording.[145]

> (1) A trustee acting in a professional capacity is entitled to receive reasonable remuneration[146] out of the Trust Fund for any services that he provides to or on behalf of the Trust.
>
> (2) For this purpose, a trustee acts in a professional capacity if he acts in the course of a profession or business which consists of or includes the provision of services in connection with
>
>> (a) the management or administration of trusts generally or a particular kind of trust, or
>> (b) any particular aspect of the management or administration of trusts generally or a particular kind of trust.

It is fair that lay trustees, such as members of the family of the settlor, should not charge for their services. If they do not want to do the work, they may appoint professional agents to do it for them. But this will need to be reconsidered in special cases.

An old and traditional formula authorises charges to be made by:

> *Any trustee being a solicitor or other person engaged in a profession or business ...*

This is wider than the clause used in this book. There need be no connection between the trustee's business and the trust. Under this form, any self-employed person, carrying on a trade or profession, will be able to charge; the window cleaner just as well as the solicitor. A trustee who is a company director can charge for work done since he is engaged in the business of his company. A trustee who is an employee is likewise "engaged" in the business of his employer or in the business of being an employee.[147] Even (say) a part-time nanny is "engaged" in the business of being a nanny. There is some sense in allowing a trustee to charge in all these cases. If the trustee were not involved in his duties as trustee, he would have more time to devote to, and might therefore expect more profit from, his other business. The test is to ask what the typical settlor or testator would want, and on this basis the traditional wording is thought to be rather wide as a standard form.

---

[145] For other statutory precedents see s.42 TA 1925; Sch. 11, para. 6 School Standards and Framework Act 1998.

[146] Section 29(3) TA 2000 defines "reasonable remuneration" but in such general terms as to add nothing to one's understanding, so it is not necessary or appropriate to set out the definition in the draft.

[147] This natural reading is also supported by the reference to the "business" of the directors in art. 89 of Table A of the Companies (Tables A to F) Regulations 1985 and *Ronbar Enterprises* v *Green* [1954] 2 All ER 266 (discussing comparable wording in a covenant in restraint of trade).

Standard charges and conditions

21.56 Another standard form provides:

> *A corporate trustee shall have the rights benefits and remuneration set out in its published terms and conditions for the time being* ...

As far as remuneration is concerned, it is suggested that the normal remuneration clause is quite sufficient. It will allow reasonable remuneration; if the corporate trustee cannot justify its charges as reasonable, the drafter should hesitate to provide a form which might allow them.

As far as the other "conditions" are concerned, the drafter should himself deal with such matters and should not leave the matter to subsequent negotiation. Standard conditions drafted on behalf of corporate trustees will naturally give the trustees the most generous exemption clause.[148] Experience suggests that there will be no difficulty in finding corporate trustees prepared to act without these clauses.

Some commentators take the view that a reference to scale fees or conditions of a trust corporation in a will may be ineffective to incorporate a scale or conditions which are variable in the future.[149]

Fees to be agreed at time of appointment

A common form provides:

> [1] The trustees are entitled to charge and be paid out of the Trust Fund such remuneration as at or prior to their appointment may have been agreed upon in writing between the trustees and the person or persons making such appointment.
>
> [2] Notwithstanding the foregoing it is expressly declared that any corporate body which by its constitution is entitled to undertake the office of Trustee may as such Trustee as aforesaid act on its terms and conditions (including the right to remuneration and the incidence thereof) in force at the date hereof as if such terms and conditions were set out herein provided always that if and so often as the Trustee shall from the date hereof publish new terms and conditions in which its rates or modes of charging remuneration or both shall be different from those in force at the date hereof the Trustee shall thereafter be entitled to remuneration in accordance with such new terms and conditions in substitution therefore (only so far as concerns remuneration for those previously in force).

---

[148] See 6.17 (Construction of trustee exemption clauses).
[149] Williams, Mortimer and Sunnucks, *Executors, Administrators and Probate* (19th edn, 2008), 5–07. Under the usual rules of incorporation by reference this is strictly correct. But the courts would probably not strike down what has become common conveyancing practice.

It has been held (despite the word "notwithstanding"!) that clause (1) prevails over (2), for there is no point in agreeing fees if the trustee is free to resile from the agreement later.[150] It is suggested the better basis for the decision is that a trustee who agrees fees is not free to change them later (at least without giving reasonable advance notice). But in this book this wording is not used.

Commissions and bank charges

The form used in this book is: **21.57**

> A person may retain any reasonable commission or profit in respect of any transaction or service relating to this Settlement even though that was procured by an exercise of fiduciary powers (by that person or some other person) provided that:
>
> (a) The person would in the normal course of business receive and retain the commission on such transaction.
> (b) The receipt of the commission or profit shall be disclosed to the Trustees.

The form is self-explanatory. On basic principles this could not be done without authorisation.[151] It could be omitted if the drafter is seeking to be concise.

Excursus: trustee charging clauses [152]

The burden of history rests heavily on the construction of trustee charging **21.58** clauses. In earlier times there was a plenitude of persons with the leisure and resources to take on unremunerated trusteeships. In those days it was natural that the courts would regard charging clauses with suspicion, and construe them strictly. Of course times have changed. Professional trustees, who charge, have ceased to be the exception and have become the norm. On reading the older cases, this must be borne in mind: thoughtless citation of dicta from the old cases will give an entirely misleading impression.

---

[150] *Mackie v BCB Trust Co Ltd* [2006] WTLR 1253 (Supreme Court of Bermuda).
[151] Authority is not needed for this proposition but see *Marley v Mutual Security Merchant Bank and Trust Co Limited* [1995] CLC 261 and (belatedly) [2001] WTLR 483 accessible on www.kessler.co.uk.
[152] A transcript has also been seen—presumably prepared by a rueful litigant—which referred to a "trustee chagrin clause".

Layman's work

21.59 A charging clause is taken (in the absence of contrary intent) to include charges for layman's work: s.28(2) Trustee Act 2000. [153]

Informing the client

21.60 The old cases laid down that a drafter should not include a charging clause of the kind used in this book except under express instructions given by the client himself with full knowledge of its effect.[154] This made sense at a time when the client would not expect trustees to charge. Nowadays no client of testamentary capacity will expect professional trustees to work for nothing. Further, charging clauses are generally implied by statute. Accordingly this rule has ceased to apply. Having said that, it is the solicitor's duty to explain the draft to the client, and an explanation of the charging clause would follow as part of that in any event.

Remuneration of corporate trustee

21.61 One commentator formerly expressed the view that a charging clause only authorised companies (as opposed to individuals) to charge if this was expressly authorised. It is considered this was based on a misreading of a case on the construction of a specific charging clause.[155] However, no-one could take this view now; the Trustee Act 2000 implied charging clauses for a trustee acting in a professional capacity plainly apply to companies and individuals.

---

[153] Some commentators expressed the view that before the TA 2000 an express charging clause authorised charges for professional work but not layman's work unless this was expressly stated. It is considered that this view was based on a misreading of some antique cases on the construction of specific charging clauses. The point is now academic but for a discussion see the fourth edition of this work at para.15.062. Section 28(2) only applies where the trustee is a trust corporation or acting in a professional capacity. However, where lay trustees are authorised to charge, the rule excluding charges for layman's work cannot on any view be considered to apply. For charitable trusts see 21.55 (Trustee remuneration).

[154] *Re Chapple* (1882) 27 Ch 584; *Re Sykes* [1909] 2 Ch 241. There is no contemporary authority on the point, except the delphic comment of Vinelott J. in *Re Orwell* [1982] 3 All ER 177 at 179: "*It has been said* that a wider form of charging clause entitling a solicitor trustee to charge ought not to be included except under express instructions given by the client himself with full knowledge of its effect." (Emphasis added; the first four words are surely significant.)

[155] The point is now academic but for a discussion see the fourth edition of this work at para.15.064.

Trustee remuneration clause: dispositive or administrative?

Status of remuneration clause for purposes of succession law

It was formerly the case that: **21.62**

(1) The charging clause did not take effect in a will if the trustee—the "beneficiary" of the charging clause (or his spouse)—was a witness. Likewise if the witness was a partner or the spouse of a partner of the trustee.

(2) The benefit of the clause would abate if the estate was insufficient for payment in full.

(3) The clause would not take effect if the estate was insolvent.

This was because the charging clause was a beneficial[156] provision for these purposes. Now these rules have been reversed in relation to professional trustees.[157]

Status of remuneration clause for other purposes

By contrast, a remuneration clause is administrative for the following purposes: **21.63**

(1) The courts' jurisdiction to secure proper administration of a trust: the court has inherent jurisdiction to authorise trustee remuneration (though it has no jurisdiction to alter beneficial interests).[158]

(2) The rule against perpetuities: the remuneration clause is outside the scope of that rule.[159]

(3) All tax purposes;[160] no one has ever doubted that a trustee remuneration clause may be included in an IP trust and any IHT special trust and does not infringe the conditions for such trusts. If the settlor

---

[156] See 16.1 (Administrative/dispositive/beneficial). If these matters had first come before the courts today, when trustees charging clauses are the norm, the matter would have been decided differently. But the law is now settled.

[157] Section 28(2) TA 2000. The old law still applies in relation to charging clauses for the benefit of lay trustees. It is a pity the Law Commission did not adopt the simpler solution of abrogating the old law entirely. The point does not arise in the precedents in this book, which do not authorise lay trustees to charge.

[158] *Re Duke of Norfolk* [1982] Ch 61.

[159] This is mentioned expressly in s.8 PAA 1964: the drafter plainly had the authorities in mind and was aware that he needed to deal with this power expressly, as it would not otherwise have been clear whether the power was to be classified as an administrative power, outside the perpetuity rule, or as a dispositive power, within it.

[160] Section 90 IHTA 1984 (trustees annuities) is an exception.

receives remuneration, this is not a benefit for the IHT reservation of benefits rules,[161] or, by parity of reasoning, for the income tax or CGT settlement provisions.

(4) Charity law: see 24.9 (Remuneration of charity trustees).

Reviewing this list it is obvious that the succession law cases are anomalous and explicable only for historic reasons. Thus for all other purposes it is submitted that a modern court should regard the remuneration clause as administrative.

Can the settlor charge if he is a trustee but there is a settlor exclusion clause?

21.64 The reader will recall that a trust will generally contain a settlor exclusion clause:

> ... no power conferred by this Settlement shall be exercisable for the benefit of the Settlor or the spouse or Civil Partner of the Settlor ...

It is considered that the settlor exclusion clause does not prevent remuneration of a settlor or spouse/civil partner. This is because (looking at the matter broadly) the settlor or spouse/civil partner has gained no advantage: he has worked for his remuneration. The alternative basis for reaching this conclusion is that the payment is administrative and not dispositive. On any view, it is not necessary to say expressly that the settlor and spouse/civil partner cannot charge remuneration.

Trustee/director remuneration

21.65 The form used in this book is as follows:

> The Trustees may make arrangements to remunerate themselves for work done for a company connected with the Trust Fund.

Where trustees hold a majority of shares in a company they cannot receive remuneration for work done for the company. Where trustees have a

---

[161] HMRC rightly accept this: see the IHT Manual 14394:

> "The donor may be, or become, a trustee of the settlement of the gifted property. So may the donor's spouse or civil partner. This is not of itself regarded as a reservation of benefit. The spouses or civil partners hold the property in a fiduciary capacity only and are required to deal with it in accordance with their fiduciary duties. The position is the same even if the donor and spouse or civil partner are entitled to payment for their services as trustees provided the remuneration is not excessive. This is despite the Court's decision in Oakes v Commissions of Stamp Duties for NS Wales [1954] AC 57.

HMRC sensibly ignore the old Australian estate duty decision to the contrary, *Oakes*. The same applies to trustee/director remuneration clauses discussed below.

minority shareholding, it seems that they should use their trust votes to oppose their own remuneration. This rule would prevent trustees from working for companies connected with the trust; hardly desirable. The general rule must therefore be reversed by express provision in the trust.

How should this be done? It is said that the standard trustee remuneration clause does not itself allow trustees to charge a company for work done for that company.[162] A common form is:

> The Trustees may enter into a contract with and be remunerated as a director or other officer or employee or as agent or adviser of any company at any time or in any way connected with the Trust Fund and retain as the Trustees' absolute property any remuneration received in that capacity notwithstanding that his office or employment may have been obtained in right or by means or by reason of his position as one of the Trustees or any shares, stock, property, rights or powers belonging to or connected with the Trust Fund.

The more succinct form used in this book is derived from a precedent upheld in *Re Llewellin*.[163] The judge observed that it was not necessary to state in express terms that the trustees "are not to be liable to account to the trust for the remuneration derived from their office"; that followed as a matter of necessary implication.

---

[162] *Re Gee* [1948] Ch 284. The reasoning is unconvincing and perhaps the point may come to be reviewed by the courts.
[163] [1949] Ch 225.

CHAPTER 22

BARE TRUSTS

Terminology

22.1 A "bare trust" (in short)[1] is one where trustees hold property on trust for one or more beneficiaries absolutely.
I use the following terminology:

(1) A *single* bare trust is one where the trustees hold property on trust for a single beneficiary absolutely.

(2) A *joint* bare trust is one where the trustees hold property on trust for more than one beneficiary ("joint beneficiaries") absolutely.

(3) A *substantive* trust is one which is not a bare trust.

Why use bare trusts?

22.2 Bare trusts may be used in two cases:[2]

(1) A settlor may make a gift to a bare trust rather than a substantive trust.

---

[1] More precisely, the term "bare trust" has various meanings, but private client practitioners use the word specifically to mean a trust of property:
  (1) within s.60 TCGA 1992 (nominee property, not settled property for CGT purposes), and
  (2) not within s.43 IHTA 1984 (not settled property for IHT purposes).

The CGT and IHT definitions are not the same, but in practice they usually amount to the same. That is the sense adopted here. In the past the expression was used in a variety of quite different senses. The old cases are assembled in *Re Blandy Jenkins* [1917] 1 Ch 46 but this is now of historic interest only.

[2] This list is not exhaustive. Another use of a bare trust is a "blind trust" under which politicians transfer assets to nominees to (hopefully) avoid conflicts of interest. See Ministerial Code: A Code of Ethics and Procedural Guidance for Ministers, accessible on *www.cabinetoffice.gov.uk/ propriety_and_ethics/ministers*.

(2) Existing A&M trusts may be converted into bare trusts (before 2008) to avoid ten-year charges.

Tax advantages

A bare trust is not a "settlement" for IHT purposes and so is outside the standard IHT trust regime. A gift to a bare trust is a PET. The trust fund is in the estate of the beneficiaries.

The gains of a bare trust are the gains of the beneficiaries for CGT purposes, so it is possible to use the beneficiaries' CGT annual allowances. This is not such a significant advantage for a single bare trust. However, where the settlor has a number of children, or grandchildren, the CGT advantage of a joint bare trust for all of them becomes substantial.

The income of the bare trust is the income of the beneficiaries (unless the beneficiaries are minor children of the settlor).

22.3

Non-tax aspects of bare trusts

Beneficiary attains 18

If a sole beneficiary attains 18, he can call for the fund to be transferred to him. If a joint beneficiary attains 18, he can call for his share of the trust fund to be transferred to him if it is easily divisible.[3]

However, the beneficiary may agree not to call for the property to be transferred to him. On attaining the age of 18, a beneficiary may be invited to sign an agreement along the following lines:

22.4

> Dear [trustees]
>
> In return for your continuing to act as trustees, I agree not to call for my share of the [name of trust] bare trust to be transferred to me until I reach the age of 21, or I have given the trustees one month's notice in writing, whichever shall be the later.
> Signed ...

Death of beneficiary

There are two possibilities:

---

[3] Not if the trust fund is land: *Crowe v Appleby* 51 TC 457; or a majority shareholding: *Lloyds Bank v Duker* [1987] 1 WLR 1324; or an insurance policy. Policies are normally issued in clusters, and a beneficiary entitled to (say) a one quarter share of ten policies could in principle call for at least two of them.

(1) Sole beneficiary of a single bare trust. On the death of the beneficiary under the age of 18, his share must pass under the intestacy rules, in principle, to his parents. After the age of 18 his share will pass accordingly to his Will (or intestacy).

(2) On the death of a beneficiary of a joint bare trust:

   (a) If the beneficiary's share is held as tenant in common, the position is as (1) above.
   (b) If the beneficiary's share is held as joint tenant, it passes by survivorship to the other beneficiaries.

Whether the share is held as joint tenant or tenant in common depends on the drafting.[4]

Power of advancement

A bare trust may contain a power of advancement; the statutory power will normally be implied.[5] This allows the trustees to apply capital of each beneficiary's share for the benefit of the beneficiary.

It would authorise the trustees to transfer the beneficiary's share to a new, substantive trust, if this is for the benefit of the beneficiary.[6] This can be done at any time, if there are good reasons why it would benefit the beneficiary to transfer the funds to a substantive trust under which he could not spend the capital. This would include situations where:

(1) A beneficiary is about to become bankrupt.

(2) A beneficiary is about to divorce.

(3) A beneficiary is about to die.

The creation of the substantive trust is not in principle a transfer of value for IHT purposes.[7] It is considered that the beneficiary is the settlor for tax purposes, but the contrary is arguable.[8]

Power to appropriate and to mix funds

The trustees may have power:

---

[4] A joint tenant could sever the joint tenancy and create a tenancy in common, but in practice we expect that will not often happen.
[5] *CD v O* [2004] EWHC 1036 [2004] WTLR 751; the correct name is *CD v O* but the case is reported under the name *D v O* in 7 ITELR 63; the report in [2004] 3 All ER 780 uses both names in different places.
[6] See 11.11 (Power of advancement used to create new trusts).
[7] Because the beneficiary does not make a disposition, unless s.3(3) IHTA 1984 is in point.
[8] See Taxation of Foreign Domiciliaries, 7th edn, 2008, Ch.54 (Who is the settlor?).

(1) to blend funds of joint beneficiaries together;

(2) to appropriate assets to a beneficiary.

Draft bare trust

Investment companies have for some time offered standard forms of a single bare trust to use for their own funds. That should be satisfactory as the drafting is straightforward. However, in practice, advisors may prefer their own drafting.[9] Here is a precedent of a joint bare trust:

22.5

> This settlement is made [date] between:
>
> 1 [Name of settlor] of [address] ("the Settlor") of the one part and
>
>   2 2.1 [Name of first trustee] of [address] and
>
>   2.2 [Name of second trustee] of [address]
> ("the Original Trustees") of the other part.
>
> Whereas
>
> (A) The Settlor has [ten] grandchildren now living ("the Grandchildren") namely
>
>   (1) [name] who was born on [date].
>
> *[continue with each grandchild on a new line]*
>
> (B) This Settlement shall be known as the [Name-of-Settlor Settlement 2006].
>
> Now this deed witnesses as follows:
>
> 1 **Definitions**
>
> In this settlement:
>
>   1.1 **"The Trustees"** means the Original Trustees or the trustees of the settlement for the time being.
>
>   1.2 **"The Trust Fund"** means:
>
>   1.2.1 property transferred to the Trustees to hold on the terms of this Settlement; and
>
>   1.2.2 all property from time to time representing the above.
>
>   1.3 **"Trust Property"** means any property comprised in the Trust Fund.
>
> 2 The Trust Fund shall be held on trust for the Grandchildren as beneficial joint tenants absolutely.[10]
>
> 3 Section 32 Trustee Act 1925 (Power of Advancement) shall apply with the following modification: the words "one-half of" in section 32(1) shall be deleted.[11]

---

[9] For the difficulties of standard forms, see 23.2 (Insurance company standard form).

[10] This wording creates a joint tenancy: see 22.4 (Non-tax aspects of bare trusts). If a tenancy in common is desired, say: " ... for the Grandchildren in equal shares absolutely".

[11] This is the wording of the STEP standard provision. It seems better to use the statutory power, since no-one could suggest that could prevent a trust from being a bare trust.

4 Appointment of Trustees

The power of appointing trustees is exercisable by the Settlor during [his] life and by will.

5 Further Provisions

The provisions set out in the schedule below shall have effect.

The beneficiaries of the bare trust should not be a party to the deed.[12]

Additions to bare trust

22.6 If the bare trust is intended to benefit children or grandchildren equally, the settlor may wish to add property to it after another child or grandchild is born. This may be done by a transfer of property to the trustees together with a declaration of trust:

> To [names of trustees]
> **[Name of Bare Trust]**
> I have transferred [specify property] to you. I direct you to hold that property:
> (1) on the terms of the [name of bare trust] but as if references to the "grandchildren" were references to all my grandchildren now living (including [name] who was born on [*date: specify those born after date of bare trust*])
> (2) in such shares so as to ensure that each grandchild's share in the Trust Fund is equal.

If the settlor is concerned to provide for further grandchildren who may be born after his death, he may enter into a lifetime covenant or make provision by his will.

---

[12] See 10.8 (Who should be parties).

CHAPTER 23

TRUSTS OF LIFE INSURANCE POLICIES

Introduction

This chapter considers straightforward life insurance policies, i.e. policies which pay a sum of money on death. Different considerations apply to: **23.1**

(1) Seven-year reducing policies to cover the risk of IHT on a PET. These should usually be given to the donee of the PET.
(2) Policies to pay a sum on survival to a specified age or prior death. The complication here is that the policyholder may want to give away the death benefit but retain the other benefit. More bespoke drafting is needed.
(3) Policies (often called bonds) which contain only a nominal element of life insurance. In substance these are simply investments wrapped up in a life insurance package, and they do not require any particular form of trust.
(4) Pension schemes (which may of course confer death benefits).

A life insurance policy should not normally[1] be kept by the life assured. For the proceeds of the policy (which *ex hypothesi* the life assured will not live to see) would be subject to IHT on his death. A policy could be given to the individual's children or to a bare trust for them. It is often more appropriate to transfer it to a trust for the benefit of the individual's children and widow.

Insurance company standard form

The drafter of a trust for a life policy has an easy option; this is to adopt the standard form supplied free of charge[2] by the insurance company **23.2**

---

[1] One exception is when the policy is to be security for a loan taken out by the life assured.
[2] A charge would be an offence: see 2.11 (Formal qualifications for the drafter).

concerned. This is generally more or less adequate.[3] But even where all possible care is taken on behalf of the insurance company, the forms suffer from a number of defects. First, they are standardised. The drafter had to devise a single form which was short, comprehensible, and which requires a minimum of subsequent attention. This is by no means easy. Second, the insurance company standard documentation is drafted to deal with one policy only, but where a client has a number of policies it is convenient to use a single trust (or possibly a series of similar trusts) but not to use separate trusts in different forms. The reader will not be surprised that the insurance company's forms come supplied with a stiff disclaimer so if problems do arise, an action against the insurance company may not be easy.[4]

How much more satisfactory to draft a proper trust drafted with the individual's circumstances in mind. If there is some other trust in the family, that may be a suitable trust to hold the life insurance policy; one should not multiply trusts unnecessarily.

Trusts created pursuant to contract of insurance

23.3 The contract with the insurance company (and the policy provided pursuant to that contract) may provide that the policy is from its inception to be held on trust.[5] It is necessary to check that this is not the case, so that the client owns his policy and can transfer it into a trust.

Trust created over existing policy

23.4 There are two usual methods to create a trust of a life insurance policy belonging to the client:

---

[3] But there are (or at least have been) a few rotten eggs in this basket. It usually takes many years for the problem to emerge (which conveniently helps the company's limitation defence to any claim). For instance, *Pappadakis v Pappadakis* [2000] 1 WTLR 719 accessible on *www.kessler.co.uk* discloses some shoddy practice in Abbey Life in the 1980s.

[4] Another short cut, mentioned here for completeness, is to express the life insurance to be "effected for the benefit of the individual's wife and children." This is a short form, which brings into effect a primitive trust for those objects: s.11 Married Women's Property Act 1882. The form of 1882 would not today be regarded as adequate. It would be better to use the life insurance company's standard form.

[5] This is a convenient way of creating trusts in the life insurance company standard form. The question whether particular wording created a trust is discussed in a number of cases, summarised in *Re Foster* [1966] 1 WLR 222. A shameful, unnecessary case law because competent drafting should always make it plain whether or not a trust is intended. The absence of modern case law suggests this lesson may have been learned.

(1) *Declaration of trust by settlor:*

    (a) the settlor executes a declaration of trust, under which he declares that he holds the policy on trust;

    (b) it is then usual (not strictly essential but convenient) for the settlor to appoint one or more additional trustees to act with him.[6]

(2) *Transfer to trustees to hold on trust:*

    (a) the settlor (and trustees) execute a trust deed; and

    (b) the settlor assigns the policy to the trustees.[7]

The simplest course is that:

(1) the trust is not set out in the contract or the terms of the policy

(2) the settlor and trustees execute the trust;[8] and

(3) in a separate deed, the settlor assigns the policy to the trustees.

IHT implications of using a trust

When the policy is transferred to the trust it will normally have relatively little value. So a gift of the policy to the trust will not usually[9] give rise to IHT, because of the annual exemption or the nil rate band.[10] The payment

23.5

---

[6] This appointment may be:

    (i) set out in the deed of declaration of trust; or
    (ii) set out in a separate deed of appointment.

Either way, the appointment has the effect of an assignment of the policy to the new trustees: s.40 Trustee Act 1925. Notice should be given to the insurance company.

[7] This assignment may be:

    (1) set out in the trust deed, or
    (2) set out in a separate deed.

Notice should be given to the insurance company.

[8] Of course if the trust exists already and new policies are to be assigned to it, then only a simple deed of assignment will be required.

[9] The only exceptions are if the settlor has made a substantial chargeable transfer in the last seven years; or if the "normal expenditure" IHT exemption will not apply on payment of the premiums.

[10] This assumes that:

    (1) the settlor has made no chargeable transfers in the seven years prior to creating the trust; and

    (2) the settlor assigns the policy to the trust as soon as it is taken out; or if there is a delay, the settlor is not so ill or so old that he is likely to die soon (making the policy a valuable asset);

    (3) the policy is paid out of annual premiums and not by a single substantial one-off payment.

If these assumptions were wrong there might be an IHT charge on the transfer of the policy to a trust.

of regular premiums for the life insurance policy will normally be an exempt transfer.[11]

The gift of the policy to the trust will not give rise to a gift with reservation provided that the owner of the policy is excluded from benefit under the trust. Likewise, the payment of premiums will not give rise to a gift with reservation for IHT purposes provided that the person who pays the premiums is excluded from benefit under the trust. Thus in a simple case where the settlor takes out the policy and pays the premiums, the settlor must be excluded from benefit. Strictly speaking, his spouse/civil partner need not be excluded. The usual course is to exclude settlor and spouse/civil partner, but not the widow/surviving civil partner of the settlor.

The position is different where a couple take out a joint policy, payable on the death of the survivor of the two of them. In such cases the premiums will normally be paid by the couple jointly, and the policy would belong to them jointly. It is then necessary to exclude them both from the trust; see 10.11 (Form where trust made by joint settlors).

Ten-year charges and exit charges during lifetime of settlor

23.6 The trust will be within the IHT trust regime of 10-year charges and exit charges. The amount of the 10-year charge would normally[12] be nil if the value of the trust property (the policy) falls within the nil rate band at that time. That will be the case if:

(1) the death benefit is within the nil rate band, or

(2) the life assured is in good health on the 10-year anniversary.[13]

The trustees should therefore review the position shortly before each 10-year anniversary.[14] The amount of an exit charge before the first 10-year anniversary would be nil, so a 10-year charge can be avoided if necessary by an appropriate appointment. It would only be desirable to make some appointment at that stage if the settlor is old or in very poor health at that time and the policies have a value above the nil rate band.

It is just possible that the settlor might die unexpectedly immediately before the 10-year anniversary. In that case there could be a charge on the 10-year anniversary. The maximum rate is 6% but normally the rate will

---

[11] Section 21 IHTA 1984 (normal expenditure out of income). It follows that s.67 IHTA 1984 (added property) will not apply in computing 10-year charges.
[12] Assuming the settlor had not made chargeable transfers in the last seven years.
[13] Note for completeness that s.167 IHTA 1984 has specific rules on the valuation of life policies. However, in practice this section will not make a great deal of difference.
[14] To avoid the necessity for this, insurance company standard forms usually confer interests in possession on the children of the settlor. This works passably well, but the flexibility of a discretionary trust will usually be slightly better.

be much less or nil. That risk is an acceptable price to pay for the significant advantage of flexibility offered by the trust.

Tax returns

No IHT return is normally[15] required on the creation of the trust. IHT returns would be required on:

23.7

(1) subsequent 10-year anniversaries; and

(2) on the termination of the trust.

If this was accidentally overlooked (which perhaps often happens when the trust fund is small and the charge nil) the maximum penalty is £100.[16] No other returns are required while the trust has no taxable income or gains.

Advantages of multiple discretionary trusts

A client who has created a trust over a life policy may wish to take out another policy to increase his life cover. The question arises whether he should use the same trust for both policies or create a new trust.

23.8

A single trust is all that is needed where the total death benefit of all policies in the trust is within the nil rate band. The trust is in principle outside the scope of IHT because the exit and 10-year charges are nil.

The advantage of separate trusts is that each will have in effect its own nil rate band, so 10-year charges and exit charges which would apply to a more substantial discretionary trust (above the nil rate band) will be reduced or avoided. This assumes that the law remains broadly as it now is, which (following the 2006 reforms) is a questionable assumption. The disadvantage is complexity and additional administration costs. Also, other trusts made by the same settlor will enjoy a smaller CGT annual exemption, though in practice this may not concern many settlors.

Everyone would prefer to use a single trust for all of a client's policies. But it depends on the circumstances and values involved. If the total death benefit of all policies is less than £300,000, say, then a single trust is certainly preferable. In such cases there need not normally be any significant 10-year or exit charge. As the values increase, the balance of advantage shifts to some extent towards separate trusts. If the death benefit exceeds

---

[15] This assumes that:

(1) the value transferred by any gift to the trust (together with all previous chargeable transfers within the 12 months) does not exceed £10,000; and
(2) the total chargeable transfers made during the 10 years preceding the transfer does not exceed £40,000.

For this purpose potentially exempt transfers may be ignored: they are not "chargeable transfers". See 29.13 (Returns and other matters).

[16] Section 245 IHTA 1984. One hopes that HMRC would charge no penalty in practice.

£1 million then multiple trusts would be better. For cases in between, the answer depends on how much trouble and expense one is prepared to take in order to optimise the tax position. The tax problem is not so much the 10-year charges during the lifetime of the client (which will usually be nil or manageable, as explained above). The advantage of multiple trusts is very long term: if one single trust is used, and has a very substantial trust fund, the trustees will be reluctant to keep the trust once the policies mature, after the death of the settlor. This is because the IHT cost of doing so (the 10-year charges) will make this unattractive.[17] If there are a number of separate trusts, the 10-year charges will be much reduced or nil, and this would allow the trustees to let the trusts remain.

A similar question arises if the client is taking out substantial life cover, say £1 million. It would best from a tax point of view to create four separate trusts, each holding separate policies for £¼ million rather than one single policy. The question is whether the costs incurred will justify the long-term IHT saving. As a rule of thumb it is suggested that the balance of advantage favours the use of multiple separate trusts (each with a trust fund within the nil rate band) only if the total sum insured exceeds £1 million. In practice that will be rare. If there is to be more than one trust, care is needed in the execution of the arrangements. The trusts should not be identical in form.[18] They should not commence on the same day.[19]

Some drafting points

23.9 Trusts of life insurance policies tend to be held in store and not reviewed for many years. Standard forms of life insurance companies often contain a "missing trustee" form. This may help solve a problem which no doubt arises occasionally in practice:

> Where one trustee ("the Missing Trustee") cannot be found and the other trustees ("the Remaining Trustees") have made all reasonable efforts to trace him, the

---

[17] At 2006/07 rates some sample computations of the IHT 10-year charge are as follows:

Value of trust fund on TYA	£400,000	£700,000	£1,000,000	£2,000,000
Tax rate	1.70%	3.6%	4.3%	5.15%
10-year charge	£7,000	£25,000	£43,000	£103,000

[18] In *Rysaffe v IRC* [2002] STC 872 five settlements identical in all but formal respects were held to be separate settlements but "it would have been clearer if there had been a few differences between them at the outset" (para.25). An HMRC argument based on associated operations was also rejected.

[19] This aggregates the IHT charge: see ss.62, 66(4)(c) IHTA 1984. A settlement commences when property first becomes comprised in it: s.60 IHTA 1984. In *Rysaffe v IRC* [2002] STC 872 the settlor wrote a single cheque for £50 to his solicitors. The judge found, on the basis of evidence not set out in the judgment, that £10 became comprised in the five settlements on separate days. It would have been clearer to write five separate cheques, banked on separate days.

Remaining Trustees being not less than two in number or a company may by deed discharge the Missing Trustee. A recital in that deed stating that the Missing Trustee cannot be found and that the Remaining Trustees have made all reasonable efforts to trace him shall be conclusive evidence in favour of any person dealing with the Trustees in good faith.

It would be sensible to appoint a professional trustee younger than the settlor, along with the settlor (if desired) and a friend or member of the family (if desired).

Some standard forms provide:

No lien shall be created on the policy as a result of any payment of a premium by the Settlor.

This does no harm but is not necessary. The question of whether a payment of a policy premium (or any other sum for the trust) creates a right to reimbursement (by a lien) is not determined by the terms of the trust. It is determined by the intention of the payer at the time of the payment. In normal circumstances one would assume that the intention of the settlor paying a premium was to benefit the trust, and the settlor did not intend he should have a right of reimbursement.[20]

Precedent trust for life policy

The standard discretionary trust will be appropriate with modification of the accumulation period. **23.10**

This settlement is made [date] between:

1. [Name of settlor] of [address] ("the Settlor") of the one part and

    2. 2.1 [Name of first trustee] of [address] and

    2.2 [Name of second trustee] of [address]
    ("the Original Trustees") of the other part.

Whereas:

1. The Settlor has [two] children:

    1.1 [Adam Smith] ("[Adam]") who was born on [date] and

    1.2 [Mary Smith] ("[Mary]") who was born on [date].

2. This Settlement shall be known as the [John Smith Discretionary Settlement 1998].

Now this deed witnesses as follows:

---

[20] *Re Smith* [1937] Ch 636, *De Vigier v IRC* 42 TC 24 at 40 (lien intended); *Re Roberts* [1946] Ch 1 (no lien intended).

1. Definitions

In this settlement:

1.1 **"The Trustees"** means the Original Trustees or the trustees of the settlement for the time being.

1.2 **"The Trust Fund"** means:

    1.2.1 property transferred to the Trustees to hold on the terms of this Settlement; and

    1.2.2 all property from time to time representing the above.

1.3 **"Trust Property"** means any property comprised in the Trust Fund.

1.4 **"The Trust Period"** means the period of 80 years beginning with the date of this Settlement. That is the perpetuity period applicable to this Settlement under the rule against perpetuities.

1.5 **"The Accumulation Period"** means the period of 21 years beginning with the death of the Settlor.[21]

1.6 **"The Beneficiaries"** means:

[set out standard definition]

1.7 **"Person"** includes a person anywhere in the world and includes a Trustee.

2. Trust Income

Subject to the Overriding Powers below:

2.1 The Trustees may accumulate the whole or part of the income of the Trust Fund during the Accumulation Period. That income shall be added to the Trust Fund.

2.2 The Trustees shall pay or apply the remainder of the income to or for the benefit of any Beneficiaries, as the Trustees think fit, during the Trust Period.

3. Overriding Powers

The Trustees shall have the following powers ("Overriding Powers"):

[set out standard overriding powers]

4. Default Clause

Subject to that, the Trust Fund shall be held on trust for [Adam and Mary in equal shares — or specify default trusts as appropriate] absolutely.

5. Appointment of Trustees

5.1 The power of appointing trustees is exercisable by the Settlor during [his] life and by will.

---

[21] On the use of this accumulation period, see 15.8 (Other accumulation periods?).

5.2 Where one trustee ("the Missing Trustee") cannot be found and the other trustees ("the Remaining Trustees") have made all reasonable efforts to trace him, the Remaining Trustees being not less than two in number or a company may by deed discharge the Missing Trustee. A recital in that deed stating that the Missing Trustee cannot be found and that the Remaining Trustees have made all reasonable efforts to trace him shall be conclusive evidence in favour of any person dealing with the Trustees in good faith.

6. Further Provisions

The provisions set out in the schedule below shall have effect.

For a shorter form, omit the schedule and say instead of the above:

"The standard provisions of the Society of Trust and Estate Practitioners (1st Edition) shall apply with the deletion of paragraph 5. Section 11 Trusts of Land and Appointment of Trustees Act 1996 (consultation with beneficiaries) shall not apply."]

[Set out form to exclude settlor and (if desired) spouse/civil partner[22]]

In witness, [etc.]

THE SCHEDULE: FURTHER PROVISIONS

[Here set out the administrative provisions suitable to the discretionary settlement.]

---

[22] Since the trust of the policy means no income or gains, it may be satisfactory to exclude the settlor (for IHT reasons) and not the spouse/civil partner.

CHAPTER 24

CHARITABLE TRUSTS[1]

Introduction

24.1 Charities take a variety of forms and can be categorised in different ways. A distinction should be drawn between:

(1) a charity set up by an individual as a vehicle for his personal charitable donations (here called a "family charity"); and

(2) a charity of a more specialist or independent nature.

A family charity is generally a fairly standard piece of drafting. Part 2 of this book contains a precedent.

Other types of charity vary widely and need more bespoke drafting. An unincorporated association or a company would often be a more suitable vehicle than a trust. The standard drafts of the Charity Law Association and of the Charity Commissioners are a useful drafting resource for these.[2]

An alternative to a client creating his own family charitable trust is to use the services of the Charities Aid Foundation.[3] This charity manages charitable funds on behalf of clients under agreement which place the client in a position similar to a charitable trustee. For smaller funds the cost ought to be lower.

---

[1] On charity tax generally, see *Taxation of Charities*, Kessler and Kamal (6th edn, 2007, Key Haven).
[2] Obtainable from www.charitylawassociation.org.uk and www.charitycommission.gov.uk.
[3] www.cafonline.org.

Some general comments

The draft should normally confer a power to expend capital: permanent endowment is a terrible nuisance. **24.2**

Some drafts contain a good deal of material implied by law, e.g. an express duty to prepare accounts. That is perhaps useful for a charity with lay trustees who may not have access to legal advice and might mistake the legal position. It should not be necessary for a standard family charity with a solicitor acting as trustee.

Remember that fundraising literature is important—as donations may be held on the terms of that literature and not on the terms of the trust! An appalling prospect if drafted by fundraisers and not reviewed by a lawyer.

If a charitable trust is in a non-standard form, it is advisable to register it with the Charity Commission before making substantial gifts to it.

It used to be common in the draft to define "charitable" to mean "exclusively charitable according English law" but this is not now necessary in an English law trust, as it is implied in any event.[4]

Name

A charitable trust needs a name, under which it will be registered: s.3(3) Charities Act 1993. **24.3**

The Charity Commission will rightly object if an existing charity has the same name, and discourage use of names of former charities.[5] With 180,000 registered charities there is a real possibility of accidental duplication of names! So check the Charity register online before choosing a name.

Charities which are not family charities do occasionally like to change their name. The Charity Commission have recommended the form:

> The charity shall be called XXX but the trustees may by resolution change the charity's name from time to time. *Before doing so they must obtain the written approval of the Charity Commissioners for England and Wales for the new name.*

It is considered the words in italics should be omitted. The Charity Commission have certain powers to require a new name[6] but there is no point in spelling this out in the deed or in extending their powers so that no name change can take place without their approval. But this point is almost completely theoretical.

---

[4] Section 1 Charities Act 2006.
[5] See *www.charitycommission.gov.uk/supportingcharities/OGS/index018.asp.*
[6] Section 6 Charities Act 1993.

Trustees

24.4 The Charity Commission states:

> It is for each organisation to decide what number of charity trustees best meets its needs. As a general guide, every charity usually has at least 3 charity trustees and most charities find that between 3 and 9 trustees is adequate.[7]

In practice one could expect the Charity Commission to object to a charity having a single trustee, or two related trustees (e.g. husband and wife).

In the case of a family charity, the settlor will want the power to appoint new trustees and no provisions are needed for trustees' meetings. Where the charity is more of an independent organisation, the trustees of the charity will usually appoint their successors. In that case there should be a provision that:

> A trustee may be appointed or discharged by resolution of a meeting of the charity trustees.

This brings in the relatively informal method of appointment and retirement of trustees authorised by s.83 Charities Act 1993. There should also be a power for charity trustees to resign:

> A Trustee may resign by giving notice in writing to the other Trustees. On receipt of such notice the retiring Trustee shall cease to be a Trustee provided that there shall be remaining at least two persons to act as Trustees or a Trust Corporation (within the meaning of the Trustee Act 1925).

Where there are more than three trustees, a quorum clause is desirable. The Charity Commission guidance on the point seems sensible: "If there are 3, 4 or 5 charity trustees we would suggest that the quorum should be 2, but if there are 6 or more charity trustees, we would suggest that the quorum should be stated as "3, or one third of all the current charity trustees, whichever is more".[8]

Table A articles offer precedents for a quorum clause and regulation of trustees' meetings.[9]

Exclusion of settlor and non-charitable purposes

24.5 Notwithstanding anything else in this deed, no power conferred by this Charitable Trust shall be exercisable, and no provision shall operate so as to allow Trust Property or its income:

---

[7] See publication CC22 Choosing & Preparing a Governing Document, April 2008, para.60.
[8] See CC22 Choosing & Preparing a Governing Document, April 2008, para.66.
[9] See arts 88 and following of Table A of the Companies (Tables A to F) Regulations 1985.

(1) to become payable to or applicable for the benefit of the Settlor or the spouse or Civil Partner of the Settlor
(2) to be applied for any purpose that is not Charitable.

This is a useful precaution. Contrast 16.17 (Protection clauses). There is no need for a settlor exclusion clause[10] but one is generally included and it can do no harm. Certainly do not have an extended one!

Rule against accumulation

The rule against accumulations was invented with private trusts in mind, but there is no express exemption for charitable trusts. The better view is that the rule does not apply, though a trust to accumulate income in perpetuity fails for the different reason that it is not charitable.[11] The alternative view is that trustees of a charitable trust cannot "accumulate" income after a specified period. Nevertheless, any charity has an implied power to hold income in reserve for any period of time, instead of expending it promptly, if it is in the charity's best interests to do so. This power may be exercised after the accumulation period has expired. This is not "accumulation" but merely "retention" of income.[12] The course adopted in the precedent in this book is to say that charity trustees can accumulate for 21 years and such further period as the law allows. In practice they can then accumulate (call it "retention" if you like) indefinitely.

24.6

Administrative provisions for charities

The Charity Commission model charitable trust introduces its powers with the words:

24.7

> In addition to any other powers they have, the Trustees may exercise any of the following powers in order to further the objects (but not for any other purpose).

---

[10] Normally, a payment to or for the benefit of the settlor would not be a charitable payment and so impossible; exceptionally, it might be possible (e.g. if the settlor becomes destitute) but such a payment would not breach s.624 ITTOIA 2005.
[11] *Re Armstrong, Perpetual Trust v Bishop of Christchurch* 8 ITELR 222. This is not however the view adopted in the Law Commission's draft perpetuities and accumulations bill.
[12] The alternative view is expressed by the Charity Commission: see para.32 of CC19 (Charities' Reserves) accessible on *www.charitycommission.co.uk*; and the Law Commission also accept this view: Report No.251, (The Rules Against Perpetuities and Excessive Accumulations), paras10.18 accessible on *www.lawcom.gov.uk*. This does read quite a significant exception into the statutory rule against accumulation (or at least gives the word "accumulation" a more limited meaning that one might expect). But neither of these consider the relevant New Zealand authorities, and the distinction between retention and accumulation (in the context of a charitable trust) is meaningless. The alternative view is merely grasping at straws to avoid the wholly impractical conclusion that charitable trusts have to distribute all their income after the accumulation period has expired.

This is not strictly necessary but is now standard wording.

The administrative powers should be conservatively drawn. Starting with the standard form in this book, the following amendments are suggested.

> A statutory power of investment, without the provisions disapplying the obligation to diversify the Trust Fund or permitting speculative or hazardous investments.
>
> No power of joint investment.
>
> Limited powers relating to capital and income.
>
> No provisions about use of trust property.
>
> Only the statutory powers of nominees and custodians.
>
> No exemption for supervision of company. A trustee exemption clause is consistent with charitable status and was formerly a standard form. Many registered charitable trusts contain such clauses. The clause is not however appropriate to a charity and nowadays the Charity Commission are likely to object to its inclusion.
>
> No provisions dealing with waiver, disclaimer or statutory apportionment.
>
> No power to change the proper law.[13] Express powers to appoint foreign trustees or to carry on the administration outside the UK are not generally appropriate to a charity. (The statutory power can be used to appoint a foreign trustee if this is actually appropriate to the circumstances of the charity.)

Trading

24.8   The Charity Commission model charitable trust provides the trustees have power:

> to raise funds. In exercising this power, the Trustees must not undertake any substantial permanent trading activity ...

The Charity Commission say:

> Our view is that any charity may trade within the limits of this exemption, provided that the governing document does not generally prohibit non-

---

[13] A trust without a UK proper law would not normally qualify as a charity for tax or charity law purposes: see *Taxation of Charities*, Kessler and Kamal (6th edn, 2007, Key Haven).

primary purpose trading. The familiar provision which, in the context of conferring a power to raise funds, prohibits "substantial" trading should not be treated as prohibiting trading which falls within [the exemption for small trades— s.46 FA 2000].[14]

While in practice that should resolve doubts about the meaning of "substantial" we prefer the following wording:

> The Trustees may carry on any Qualifying Trade either alone or in partnership.
> A "Qualifying Trade" here means a trade the profits of which would qualify for any income tax exemption given to Charities.

Remuneration of charity trustees

A charity trustee has a statutory entitlement to receive "remuneration" for providing services to the charity in the absence of an express power provided that certain conditions are met.[15] In broad terms, the conditions are that: **24.9**

(1) the number of trustees receiving payment must be in a minority;

(2) the amount paid must be reasonable and set out in a written agreement between the trustee and the charity; and

(3) the governing document must not contain any specific provision forbidding this type of payment.[16]

However, this entitlement does not extend to "remuneration for services provided by a person in his capacity as a charity trustee".[17] It is therefore

---

[14] OG 63 B2—10 April 2003 accessible on *www.charity-commission.gov.uk/supportingcharities/ogs/ g063b002.asp*.
[15] Section 73A Charities Act 1993 as inserted by the Charities Act 2006.
[16] See subsections 73A(2)–(6).
[17] See section 73A(7)(a)). The Charity Commission's guidance summarises the law and the distinction between services provided by a trustee in his personal capacity and as trustee as follows:

> While there is a general power to pay a trustee for providing services, there is no such general power to pay a trustee for carrying out trustees duties. Charities cannot do this unless they have a suitable authority, either in the charity's governing document or one provided by us or the Court ...
> Paying a trustee for the provision of a service usually involves a charity making a one-off or occasional payment to a trustee who is to provide it with a specific service that is quite separate from his or her normal trustee duties. Many charities already have a specific power to do this in their governing documents. If not, they can usually rely on the power contained in the 1993 Act ...
> In contrast, payment for trustee means that a trustee receives payment from a charity for carrying out his or her normal trustee duties. In some cases, payment will be made on a continuous basis whenever these duties are carried out; or it may take the form of a periodic or annual allowance; or it may be made on an occasional basis, intended to reflect only a certain aspect of the trustee role, or to enable a trustee to attend a specific meeting ...

suggested that most charitable trusts should still have a power to remunerate professional trustees. Even if there is no immediate intention to use the power, trustee remuneration may become appropriate in the future.

A trustee remuneration clause is consistent with charitable status: the clause does not prevent what would otherwise be a charitable trust from qualifying as a charity, for charity law or tax law purposes. This is accepted by the Charity Commission:

> Where a charity is being set up the trusts may include a provision for the remuneration of the trustees. Provided that this provision is couched in terms which tie the nature and level of remuneration to the services undertaken by the trustee (even as trustee) we shall not object to its inclusion in the charity's trust deed.[18]

It is suggested that the restrictions set out below should be included in the trustee remuneration clause in normal cases:

(1) The majority of trustees should not be remunerated.

(2) A trustee must withdraw from a meeting where his remuneration is under discussion.

This follows the policy of the Charities Act 2006. It helps to avoid the risk of laxity (or worse) in the remuneration of charity trustees. The Charity Law Association model draft imposes further safeguards.

A charging clause in a charitable trust should expressly authorise charging for services capable of being provided by a lay trustee.[19] Trustee Act 2000 s.28(3) enacts a presumption that professional trustees of a charitable trust cannot charge for non- professional work. This should be reversed in the wording of the charging clause.

Trustee/director remuneration. A charity may own a non-charitable subsidiary; either because a private company has been given to the charity, or in order to avoid income tax on trading income.[20] If the trustees are directors of that company, they will need express authorisation in the trust in order to be paid remuneration for work done for the company: see 21.65

Crucially, there is no general power in charity law for trustee boards to make such payments, and normally they cannot do so unless their governing document specifically allows it, or unless they have authority from the Commission or the Court.

See CC11 (Trustee expenses and payments), June 2008, accessible on *www.charity-commission.gov.uk/publications/cc11.asp*.

[18] Decisions of the Charity Commissioners Vol.2 p.14 (April 1994). The same view is taken in the Trustee Remuneration Consultation Document, Charity Commission, September 1999 and booklet CC11 (Trustee Expenses and Payments). This view is also supported by s.30 TA 2000.

[19] In the absence of such a clause the power for a charity trustee to charge for lay services is governed by the unnecessarily complex rules of s.28 TA 2000. For the position for non-charitable trusts see 21.59 (Layman's work).

[20] *Taxation of Charities* (Kessler and Kamal, 6th edn, 2007, Key Haven) Ch.8 (Trading Companies held by Charities).

(Trustee/director remuneration). It is submitted that the law is the same as for direct trustee remuneration: the standard clause authorising retention of trustee remuneration is consistent with charitable status though some restrictions along the lines of trustee remuneration would be wise. The Charity Commission now accept this view,[21] though in the past they have refused to register a charity with such a clause.

Insurance for claims against charity trustees

The law should distinguish between:

(1) Insurance where the proceeds belong to the trust fund. This is permitted under general trust law, or at least, under the general power of management used in this book.[22]

(2) Insurance where the proceeds belong beneficially to the trustees. This is not permitted under general trust law except in special cases.[23] However charity trustees now have statutory power to take out insurance indemnifying them against the risk of personal liability arising from:

(1) breach of trust or duty in their capacity as trustees; and
(2) any negligence, default, breach of duty or breach of trust committed by them while acting as directors or officers of a charitable company or any company carrying out activities on behalf of the charity

provided certain conditions are met.[24]

The statutory duty of care in the TA 2000 applies to the trustees when making the decision to take out insurance.[25]

---

[21] See the Charity Commission's booklet CC 35 (Trustees, trading and tax) section D15 provides:

"A charity trustee cannot be paid for his or her services as a director or employee of the charity's trading subsidiary unless either [1] *unless the governing document of the charity specifically provides for this* or [2] there is some other specific authority, such as an order from the Charity Commission."

(Emphasis added)

[22] All insurance of this class may benefit trustees, in the sense that they are personally liable for claims (with an indemnity against the trust fund) and so concerned to ensure that the trust fund is solvent, but that should not matter.

[23] The case law is thin but there have been two cases in category (2). A £525 missing beneficiary insurance policy was permitted in the case of *Re Evans* [1999] 2 All ER 777 in circumstances where an application to the Court for directions would have given rise to far greater expense. By contrast, insurance was not permitted to cover (i) far fetched claims of (non-fraudulent) breach of trust and (ii) claims by overlooked beneficiaries which could be dealt with by a notice under s.27 TA 1925: *Kemble v Hicks* [1999] OPLR 1 [1999] Pens. LR 287 accessible on *www.kessler.co.uk*.

[24] See s. 73F Charities Act 1993.

[25] Section 73F(5).

The trustees must be satisfied that the insurance is in the "best interests" of the charity.[26] The Charity Commission's guidance on this is that:

> The trustees must be clear their decision to purchase TII is based on a genuine need, and that risks and potential liabilities have been identified that justify spending charity funds on insurance cover. They should ensure the cost is reasonable, and will not be a drain on the charity's finances, or in any way adversely affect its activities. They will need to be satisfied the insurance policy they take out is suitable for the charity, and that they are clear on the extent of insurance cover—after taking expert advice if necessary.[27]

The insurance policy must include a clause to ensure that it will **not** cover:

(1) liability in respect of fines imposed in criminal proceedings, or penalties arising from regulatory action;

(2) liability arising from defending criminal proceedings in which the trustee is convicted of fraud, dishonesty, or wilful or reckless misconduct; and

(3) liability arising out of conduct which the trustee knew, or should have known, was not in the interests of the charity.[28]

We suggest that the statutory power to insure is sufficient.

Procedure after execution of charitable trust

24.10 The steps to be taken are set out in the HMRC Guidance Note for Charities.[29] The Charity Commission refuse to register a charity unless it contains some funds, but nominal funds will suffice. So some funds must be transferred to the trustees before the application for registration. The draft charity trust in this book takes into account drafting comments made by the Charity Commission. The Commission could take further points in particular cases, but in practice this should not happen.

Transfers to the charity are exempt from stamp duty and SDLT.[30]

---

[26] Section 73F(4)
[27] See the Information Sheet (Trustee Indemnity Insurance) accessible at *www.charity-commission.gov.uk/supportingcharities/ogs/g100c004.asp*.
[28] Section 74F(2)
[29] Sections 2.3–2.5 accessible on *www.hmrc.gov.uk/charities*.
[30] See 29.14 (Stamp duty and SDLT) and *Taxation of Charities* (Kessler and Kamal, 6th edn, 2007), Key Haven, Ch.5 (Stamp duties).

Charitable will trusts

It is possible to create a charitable trust by will or to make a gift by will to an existing charitable trust. It is good practice to create a lifetime trust (if need be, a pilot trust with a nominal trust fund) and make a gift to it by will. The trust can then be registered and its charitable status will not be in dispute when the will takes effect: this will simplify the administration of the estate and avoid the risk that the trust may fail. This should not be necessary if the trust is in an absolutely standard form.

22.11

CHAPTER 25

TRUSTS OF DAMAGES

This chapter is concerned with trusts set up to hold damages, sometimes called "personal injury trusts". Different (though overlapping) considerations apply depending whether the claimant is (1) an adult with mental capacity, (2) a child under 18, or (3) a person lacking mental capacity.

Benefit "disregard" of trust of damages

25.1 Trusts of damages have welfare benefit advantages.[1] For the purposes of income support, one must disregard:

> Where the funds of a trust are derived from a payment made in consequence of any personal injury to the claimant, the value of the trust fund and the value of the right to receive any payment under that trust.[2]

This applies whether the claimant is an adult, child or patient. Any form of trust will satisfy this; even a bare trust.[3]

Trust of damages for adult with mental capacity

25.2 An adult with mental capacity can of course transfer his damages to a trust if he wants this advantage. He has a free choice what sort of trust to create.

It is suggested that the most appropriate form for a fund producing

---

[1] On this topic generally, see *Coldrick on Personal Injury Trusts* (3rd edn, 2007, Ark Group).
[2] Paragraph 46 and Sch.10 para.12 Income Support (General) Regulations 1987. Similar exemption applies for other benefits.
[3] This follows from the words of the regulation and no authority is needed. Some further support could be drawn from a curate's egg of a Social Security Commissioner's decision, CIS 368/1994, [1996] 3 JSSL D136 and *Ryan v Liverpool Health Authority* [2002] Lloyd's Rep Med 23 at para.25, accessible on *www.kessler.co.uk*.

income is normally a discretionary trust, of which the settlor is a beneficiary. The settlor may be one of the trustees.

The benefit "disregard" does not apply for tax purposes. The income tax and CGT settlement provisions will apply to the trust, but for a client of modest means that will happily be a more satisfactory result than if they did not apply. The gift to the settlement is a chargeable transfer so the sum given should not exceed the nil rate band. The gift will also be a gift with reservation for IHT, but this is not a problem if the entire estate of the settlor can be expected to fall within the nil rate band.

For property not producing income, an IP trust for the settlor or a bare trust may be preferable.

For property in excess of the nil rate band, an IP trust or bare trust would be preferable (if appropriate, investing the fund in non-income producing assets). An IHT disabled persons trust (where possible) may be better: see 26.8 (IHT deemed IP trust for disabled beneficiary).

Jurisdiction to transfer child's damages to bare trust

The problem for a child is how to create a trust, if one is desired, as the child lacks legal capacity to do so himself. Rule 21.11 of the Civil Procedure Rules 1998 provides: **25.3**

(1) Where in any proceedings—

(a) money is recovered by or on behalf of or for the benefit of a child or patient; or
(b) money paid into court is accepted by or on behalf of a child or patient, the money shall be dealt with in accordance with directions given by the court under this rule and not otherwise.

(2) Directions given under this rule may provide that the money shall be wholly or partly
[a] paid into court and invested or
[b] otherwise dealt with.

(Paragraphing added.)

It is submitted that rule 21.11(2)[b] empowers the court to direct the payment of money to a bare trust, that is, a trust where the trustees hold property on trust for the minor beneficiary absolutely.[4] This rule does not empower the court to order the payment of the money to a substantive trust (i.e. a trust which is not a bare trust, for instance, a trust under which the principal beneficiary is only entitled to the income of the fund during his life, with remainder to some other beneficiary after his death).[5]

---

[4] A bare trust involves in a sense a delegation of the Court's power to deal with the funds, but such delegation is a method of "dealing with" the funds and so authorised.

[5] There are two reasons for reaching this conclusion:

(1) Rule 21.11(2)[a] is an administrative (not dispositive) power. So 21.11(2)[b] "otherwise dealt with" should be construed *ejusdem generis* so that only administrative matters can be

A precedent bare trust for child

25.4 The following precedent is proposed:

This Trust is made [date] by

(1) [Name of first trustee] of [address] and

(2) [Name of second trustee] of [address]

("the Original Trustees").

Whereas:

(A) [Name of Judge] ordered on [date] [set out terms of Order]

(B) This Trust shall be known as the [Peter Smith Trust 2006]

Now this deed witnesses as follows:

1. Definitions

In this settlement:

(1) "**The Trustees**" means the Original Trustees or the trustees of the settlement for the time being.

(2) "**The Trust Fund**" means:

(a) Property transferred to the Trustees to hold on the terms of this Trust; and

(b) All property from time to time representing the above.

(3) "**Trust Property**" means any property comprised in the Trust Fund.

(4) "**[Peter]**" means [Peter Smith] of [address].

(5) "**Person**" includes a person anywhere in the world and includes a Trustee.

2. Trust Income and Capital

(1) The Trustees may pay or apply the income of the Trust Fund to or for the education, maintenance or benefit of [Peter] and shall hold the remaining income on trust for [Peter] as an accretion to the Trust Fund absolutely.

(2) The Trustees shall hold the capital of the Trust Fund on trust for [Peter] absolutely.

3. Power of Advancement

Section 32 Trustee Act 1925 shall apply with the deletion of proviso (a).

4. Appointment of Trustees

The power of appointing trustees is exercisable by the Trustees.

---

dealt with. The payment to a bare trust is an administrative matter but payment to a substantive trust would be dispositive.

(2) *Allen v Distillers Co Ltd* [1974] QB 384 reached this conclusion in relation to identical wording in RSC Ord. 80.12, stating as the general rule that the Court has no power to order a substantive settlement of a child's property.

5. Further Provisions

The provisions set out in the schedule below shall have effect.

In witness, [etc.]

The Schedule: Administrative Provisions

[The administrative provisions should be conservatively drawn. Starting with the standard form in this book, the following amendments are proposed:

Use the first sentence of the standard form power of investment only.

The following administrative provisions should be deleted as inappropriate to a bare trust of this kind: income and capital: subclause 1.5.4; supervision of companies; appropriation; payment to charities; conflict of interest; power to appoint foreign trustees.]

Consequences of using bare trust

The consequences of using a bare trust are as follows: 25.5

(1) If the child attains 18, and has mental capacity, he can call for the fund to be transferred to him.

(2) On the death of the child under the age of 18 the fund must pass under the intestacy rules, in principle, to his parents. After the age of 18 the fund will pass according to the will of the child. The Court of Protection could of course make a will for an adult who does not have mental capacity to do so himself.

(3) For tax purposes the fund is treated as the child's, so that he is subject to tax on trust income and gains, and the funds form part of his estate for IHT.

A bare trust satisfies the benefits "disregard", and meets the administrative need of finding a manager for the funds during the minority of the beneficiary. The court would normally appoint solicitors to act as trustees.[6] The trust is not really satisfactory for a fund of any size since it is not appropriate that the child should be given power over a large fund on attaining the age of 18.

---

[6] It would not normally be appropriate to appoint parents to act as trustees, because of the conflict of interest and risk of breach of trust, though there is no real objection to parents acting as trustees jointly with a solicitor. (Theoretically parents could seek to have the funds transferred to them by virtue of their powers over the children's property conferred by s.3 Children's Act 1989. In such cases trustees should seek the guidance of the court, and it is suggested that the court would have a discretion whether or not to allow the parents control of the funds.)

Exercising the power of advancement to turn a bare trust into a substantive trust

The bare trust may contain a wide power of advancement. This would authorise the trustees to transfer the funds to a new substantive trust if this is for the benefit of the beneficiary.[7] That is a matter which could be considered further (at any time after the creation of the trust and in particular before the beneficiary's 18th birthday) if there are good reasons why it would benefit the beneficiary to transfer the funds to a substantive trust under which he could not spend the capital.

Creation of a substantive trust of child's damages by compromise

25.6 If:

(1) the parties agree a compromise of the claim;

(2) the terms of the compromise include the transfer of funds to a substantive trust; and

(3) the compromise is for the benefit of the child

then the court can approve the terms of the compromise, even though the court has no power to order the creation of a substantive trust on its own initiative.

An appropriate form of trust would be somewhat narrower than the standard trusts used elsewhere in this book. If the child is not disabled (in the IHT sense) the following is suggested:[8]

(1) Accumulation & Maintenance trusts while the child is under the age of 25 (that is, power to maintain the child and to accumulate surplus income).

(2) A life interest to the child on attaining the age of 25.

(3) Power of advancement in favour of the child.

(4) On the child's death the fund would be held:

   (a) on such terms as the child may appoint; subject to which
   (b) on the intestacy rules; subject to which
   (c) for such charities concerned with disabilities similar to those suffered by the child as the trustees shall select.

---

[7] *CD v O* [2004] EWHC 1036; See 11.11 (Power of advancement used to create new trusts)
[8] A draft along these lines was used for Thalidomide victims: *Allen v Distillers Co* [1974] QB 384.

The consequence of such a trust would be:

(1) The trust is subject to 10-year charges on a standard IHT trust, but there is no IHT charge on creation of the trust because the child does not make a transfer of value.

(2) From the point of view of state benefits, the trust income and capital may not be regarded as the child's income and capital (except to the extent that the fund is used to pay income to the child).

(3) For CGT and income tax the position would depend on whether the child would be regarded as settlor for tax purposes. It is considered that the child would not be a settlor.[9]

(4) When the child attains 18—even if he has mental capacity—he cannot call for the fund to be transferred to him because it is not his fund.

If the child is disabled in an IHT sense, the alternative is an actual or deemed IP trust, avoiding the ten year charges but (in principle) incurring an IHT charge on the death of the child instead.[10]

Trusts for minors: commentary

Minors may be awarded damages of several million pounds. No-one would make a gift of such a sum on terms that the minor becomes absolutely entitled to it at the age of 18. At the very least, entitlement should be deferred to the age of 25. Fortunately this result can be achieved by indirect methods under the present law. It is suggested that the court ought to have jurisdiction to create appropriate trusts directly.[11]

Trusts of damages for person lacking mental capacity

There are two methods of setting up a trust. The court has power to make a settlement for a person lacking capacity.[12] The parties to litigation may

---

[9] See *Taxation of Foreign Domiciliaries*, James Kessler, 7th edn (2008 Key Haven), 54.27 (Settlement made by compromise of claim of minor/person lacking capacity).
[10] 26.6 (actual estate-IP for disabled beneficiary); 26.8 (IHT deemed IP for disabled beneficiary).
[11] The court had some power to do this under the Infant Settlements Act 1855, until its repeal by the Family Law Reform Act 1969. For damage limitation by trustees, see 5.1 (Too much money).
[12] Sections 16, 18(h) Mental Capacity Act 2005. It is considered that the person lacking capacity is the "settlor" of a settlement created under this power. See *Taxation of Foreign Domiciliaries*, James Kessler, 7th edn, 2008 para.54.26 (Trust made by court for person lacking capacity).

create a settlement under a compromise; this needs the consent of the Court of Protection.[13]

Award under Criminal Injuries Compensation Scheme

There is jurisdiction for an award under the Criminal Injuries Compensation Scheme to be transferred to a settlement.[14]

---

[13] See the Court of Protection Practice Note on the settlement of personal injury awards to patients, 15th November 1996, set out in the White Book (Civil Procedure), para. 6B-119.

[14] Section 3(1)(d) Criminal Injuries Compensation Act 1995; The Criminal Injuries Compensation Scheme 2001 r.50.

CHAPTER 26

TRUSTS FOR DISABLED BENEFICIARIES

Mentally handicapped beneficiaries

Trusts are the traditional means of providing for a mentally handicapped beneficiary. It is plainly inadvisable to transfer funds absolutely to a person who is not well able to manage them. If a mentally handicapped person with assets in his own name is unable to manage his property or appoint an attorney under a lasting power for this purpose, it would generally be necessary for a deputy to be appointed to act for him under the Mental Capacity Act 2005. The appointment of a deputy inevitably imposes formal procedures and may involve substantial costs and should be avoided where possible.   **26.1**

Choosing provisions for disabled beneficiaries

For administrative provisions see 21.52 (Administrative provisions for mentally handicapped beneficiaries). Drafting beneficial provisions for the benefit of the disabled is more difficult than normal because account must be taken of two additional considerations: welfare benefits and tax reliefs.   **26.2**

Welfare benefits

This is a daunting topic, nearly as large as income tax, and even more volatile. When advising on wills or lifetime gifts for persons qualifying for benefit the adviser must consider the impact on benefits. It is not possible to examine this topic in detail but two general propositions will be made: **26.3**

(1) The benefit system discourages gifts of capital (beyond a small limit) to any person claiming means tested benefits.

(2) The benefit system penalises beneficiaries who receive trust income, withdrawing benefits pound for pound. Accordingly beneficiaries on

means tested benefits should not be life tenants if the trust fund produces income: the trusts should generally be discretionary in form.[1]

Tax reliefs for disabled beneficiaries

26.4 In this area tax planning and trust drafting are so interwoven that it is not possible to discuss one without the other.

There are now nine tax reliefs for disabled beneficiaries which can be categorised as follows:

(1) IHT dependent relative relief

(2) IHT reliefs for disabled beneficiaries:

    (a) actual estate-IP
    (b) deemed estate-IP

(3) IHT reliefs for prospectively disabled settlor:

    (a) actual estate-IP
    (b) deemed estate-IP

(4) CGT full annual allowance

(5) CGT hold-over relief

(6) Income tax/CGT transparency for:

    (a) disabled beneficiary
    (b) orphan beneficiary

These reliefs have a variety of disability and drafting requirements.

IHT dependent relative relief

26.5 A lifetime gift is not a transfer of value (and so is broadly outside the scope of IHT) if:

(1) it is made in favour of a dependent relative of the donor, and

(2) it is reasonable provision for his care or maintenance.[2]

---

[1] The *possibility* of benefit under discretionary trusts does not at the present time affect means tested benefits. It has in the past and may again in the future. The risk is greater for trusts qualifying for IHT and CGT disabled person's reliefs. There is little the drafter can sensibly do to anticipate such changes in the law. The *provision* of benefits from a trust may or may not affect welfare benefits, depending on the circumstances.

[2] Section 11(3) IHTA 1984.

The disability requirement here is in the term "dependent relative".[3]

The drafting requirement is that the disposition must be "in favour of" that relative. Trusts which satisfy any of the other reliefs discussed below will usually be suitable.

Is it worth qualifying for this relief? Unless the donor is old, insurance against the risk of death within seven years of the gift is usually cheap. Then the relief is not worth the trouble. However in the case of an elderly donor (or in any case where insurance against the IHT on death within seven years is expensive) the relief is valuable and should be used.

Actual estate-IP for disabled beneficiary

The conditions for this relief are relatively straightforward. The relief applies to:

26.6

> an interest in possession in settled property to which a disabled[4] person becomes beneficially entitled on or after 22nd March 2006.[5]

We take this to mean that the relief applies where the beneficiary is disabled when the property is transferred into the settlement. The relief is not lost if the beneficiary later ceases to be disabled, and the relief is not applicable if the beneficiary becomes disabled after the settlement is made.

What is the position if a beneficiary acquires an interest in reversion, which later falls into possession? For instance suppose:

(1) Year 1, S makes a gift to A for life, remainder to B for life, with remainder over. B has an interest which is a reversionary interest.

(2) Year 2, A dies and B's interest becomes an interest in possession.

It is considered that for the purposes of this relief, B's interest is a "disabled person's interest" if B is disabled (in the IHT sense) in year 1, on the death of A. It is irrelevant whether or not he is disabled in year 2, when the interest falls into possession.[6] In the case of a will trust, it is not clear whether

---

[3] The definition is in s.11(6) IHTA 1984:

"dependent relative" means, in relation to any person—

(a) a relative of his, or of his spouse or civil partner, who is incapacitated by old age or infirmity from maintaining himself, or
(b) his mother or his father or his spouse's or civil partner's mother or father."

[4] See Appendix 7 for a definition of this term.
[5] See s.89B(1)(c) IHTA 1984. The relief is not needed for an interest in possession to which a disabled person became entitled before 22 March 2006, because the (rather more generous) transitional rules apply.
[6] See s.89B(2) and 89(4) IHTA 1984.

the relevant time is the time of death or the time that the administration is complete. A strict construction favours the later view, but a purposive construction favours the former view, and it is suggested that a purposive construction is to be preferred. What matters is whether the beneficiary is disabled at the time of the testator's death.

The effect of the relief is that the beneficiary's interest in possession, called a "disabled person's interest", is an estate-IP for IHT purposes.[7] In consequence:

(1) The trust property is in the estate of the life tenant.

(2) The trust is not subject to the standard IHT regime of ten year and exit charges.

The practical consequences of this relief are important:

(1) A settlor may provide for a disabled beneficiary by making a lifetime gift to an IP trust for his benefit.

(2) The termination of any estate-IP (e.g. an IPDI) may be followed by this "disabled person's interest" so as:

　(a) to qualify for the spouse/civil partner exemption, if applicable; or
　(b) the termination of the life tenant's interest during his lifetime, followed by the disabled person's interest, would in principle be a PET.

Disabled Person Trap

26.7　The relief for a disabled person's interest therefore poses a trap. Suppose, after 2006, a lifetime gift is made to a settlement for A for life, remainder to B for life. A's interest is not an estate-IP and the trust is a standard IHT trust, subject to ten-year charges. But if B is disabled when the trust is made, then the property falls into the estate of B, and subject to IHT at the rate of 40% on B's death. The only solution in these cases is to provide that B's interest in possession should not come into effect if it would be a disabled person's interest. This means it is, in many circumstances, wholly impractical ever to give an interest in possession to an elderly disabled life tenant.

---

[7] See s.89B(1)(c) and s.52(3A)(b) IHTA 1984.

Actual estate-IP for prospectively disabled settlor

26.8 A settlor who is actually disabled (in the IHT sense) may make a gift to a settlement under which he has an interest in possession and qualify for the relief set out above. The following relief applies to a settlor who is prospectively[8] disabled—that is, in due course he expects to become disabled (in the IHT sense). The relief is not important, and is only mentioned here for completeness.

The condition for the relief is that:

(1) the settlor has an interest in possession; and

(2) if any of the settled property is applied during the lifetime of the settlor for the benefit of a beneficiary, it is applied for the benefit of the settlor. (It would appear, nevertheless, that there is some scope for overriding powers of appointment.)

The effect of the relief is that the settlor's interest in possession is an estate-IP for IHT purposes: it qualifies as a "disabled person's interest".[9] But in practice it will generally be more convenient to create a lasting power of attorney in respect of the settlor's property and affairs, than to create a life interest trust of this restrictive kind. For then on the death of the settlor it is possible to create an IPDI, which is impossible if one takes advantage of this (apparent) relief.

IHT deemed IP for disabled beneficiary

26.9 Under a deemed IP trust:[10]

(1) The disabled beneficiary is treated as having an interest in possession for IHT purposes.[11]

(2) A gift to the trust is in principle a PET for IHT purposes.[12]

---

[8] For the full meaning of this term, see Appendix 7.
[9] Section 89A IHTA 1984
[10] Our terminology for a trust which satisfies the conditions of s.89 IHTA 1984. The trusts are there called "trusts for disabled persons". The term "disabled trust" is used in s.3A IHTA 1984. But that terminology is inadequate to distinguish between the many different types of trusts which carry some kind of disability relief.
[11] Section 89(2) IHTA 1984.
[12] Section 3A IHTA 1984. If the disabled beneficiary makes the gift, or if IHT dependent relative relief applies, the gift is not of course a transfer of value for IHT so there is no PET.

These rules are compulsory: it is not possible to disclaim them by making an election.

A deemed interest in possession is a mixed blessing. The trust is not subject to IHT 10-year and exit charges under the standard IHT trust regime. This seems like an advantage. However, the property is in the estate of the disabled beneficiary and in principle suffers IHT on the death of the disabled beneficiary. If the disabled beneficiary has an *actual* estate-IP in the trust property the IHT position is the same and it is better for CGT: the trust qualifies for the CGT tax free uplift on the death of the beneficiary. The deemed IP trust allows the practical advantage of accumulating trust income without loss of means-tested benefits, but at the cost of the CGT uplift on death.

The conditions are as follows:

(1) *Disability requirement* The beneficiary must be disabled (in the IHT sense).[13] This condition need only be satisfied at the time of the gift to the trust. It does not matter if the beneficiary later ceases to be disabled.

(2) *Drafting requirement* The terms of the trust must provide:

   (a) during the life of the disabled beneficiary, no interest in possession in the settled property subsists, and
   (b) not less than half of the settled property which is applied during his life is applied for his benefit.

Condition (b) is the same as the condition for CGT full annual allowance. Unfortunately condition (a) is different and must be satisfied throughout the disabled beneficiary's life. The condition is therefore incompatible with the condition for a full CGT annual allowance trust.[14] Condition (2)(a) prevents one from allowing any person (even the disabled person) an interest in possession, so if the decision is made to use a deemed IP trust, it is impossible later to move to a disabled estate-IP trust.[15]

IHT deemed IP for prospectively disabled settlor

26.10 This relief applies where a settlor who is prospectively disabled (in the IHT sense) creates a trust similar to the deemed IP trust for a disabled beneficiary. We can see almost no circumstances in which a well advised settlor would possibly want to create such a trust, which loses the benefit of CGT

---

[13] The definitions of "disabled" are discussed in Appendix 7.
[14] Unless accumulation is possible throughout the life of the disabled beneficiary. That would be the case if (1) a suitable foreign proper law is chosen or (2) the disabled beneficiary is the settlor.
[15] Unless an application is made under the Variation of Trusts Act 1958.

uplift on death, as well as the possibility of creating an IPDI on death. This can therefore be regarded as a dead-letter relief.

CGT full annual allowance

All trusts qualify for a CGT annual allowance. Normally this is set at one half the amount of the individual's allowance (2008/09 £9,600 ÷ 2 = £4,800). Certain trusts for disabled beneficiaries enjoy the full and not the half allowance. This tax advantage is therefore worth £1,864 in a year in which a trust realises chargeable gains. It is not a very significant tax relief. **26.11**

The conditions are as follows:

(1) *Disability requirement:* The beneficiary must be "disabled" (in the CGT sense).[16]

(2) *Drafting requirement:* The terms of the trust must provide that, during the lifetime of the disabled beneficiary:

    (a) not less than half of the property[17] which is applied is applied for the benefit of the disabled beneficiary, and

    (b) [i] the disabled beneficiary is entitled to not less than half of the income arising from the property, or

        [ii] no such income may be applied for the benefit of any other person.[18]

A trust loses the benefit of this relief if the disabled beneficiary dies or ceases to be disabled. A trust does not qualify for the relief unless it is known at the outset that condition (2)(b) will be satisfied *throughout* the life of the disabled beneficiary.[19] Thus trust income must be (i) (at least as to half) paid to or applied for the benefit of the disabled beneficiary; or (ii) accumulated. After the accumulation period[20] at least half the trust income must be applied for the benefit of the disabled beneficiary and so he must have an interest in possession.

Mixed trusts

The CG Manual provides: **26.12**

---

[16] Schedule 1 para.1(1)(6) TCGA 1992. For the definitions of "disabled", see Appendix 7.
[17] "The property" means the capital of the trust fund.
[18] This is a roundabout way of saying that the income must be accumulated. HMRC accept this: CG Manual 18061.
[19] HMRC take this view: CG Manual 18061A.
[20] But see 15.9 (Strategies for trustees after accumulation period has expired).

18067. Mixed settlements
It is possible that only part of a settlement may fulfil the qualifying conditions. For example, the trust may secure that during the lifetime of the disabled person the income and any capital applied of a specified fund is to be applied as described above. If the fund itself meets the conditions, then the trustees of the settlement are entitled to the main exemption. Paragraph 1(1) refers to "settled property" and not to "all the settled property comprised in the settlement."

By way of contrast if the disabled beneficiary is entitled to an undivided share of the property, as in the example in CG18064, then the tests are to be applied to the whole of the settled property. So if there are three life tenants, each entitled to one-third of the income, and one is disabled, the conditions are not met.

This is surprising but there it is. Accordingly one way to draft a trust qualifying for a full CGT annual allowance is to split the trust fund into two parts:

(1) A specified fund which is restricted to satisfy the conditions. It may be most convenient to provide that the disabled beneficiary is life tenant of this fund.

(2) The balance may be held on whatever trusts seem most appropriate.

CGT hold-over relief

26.13 Section 169B TCGA 1992 disapplies hold-over relief on a gift to a settlor-interested trust. There is an exemption for disabled trusts: section 169D TCGA 1992. Trusts qualifying for either the full CGT annual allowance or IHT deemed IP will qualify for this relief. The relief applies in a case where a disabled beneficiary makes a gift to a settlement under which he is the principal beneficiary (which will not happen in practice).[21]

Income tax/CGT transparency: disabled beneficiary

26.14 The FA 2005 introduced an extraordinarily complex code of income tax and CGT reliefs for two types of trust: trusts for disabled beneficiaries and for orphans. The reliefs for the two types of trust are the same, but the requirements are entirely different and it is necessary to consider them separately.

---

[21] See 26.7 (Actual estate-IP for prospectively disabled settlor)

This relief is referred to (slightly inaccurately) as income tax/CGT transparency.

Two elections are required for the reliefs to apply: a vulnerable person election (made once) and an annual claim by the trustees (made in their tax return). The vulnerable person election is (technically) irrevocable but since it is supplemented by an annual claim, the relief is effectively an optional one. A vulnerable person election without an annual claim is of no effect.[22]

Disability requirement: the beneficiary must be disabled (within the Income tax definition).[23]

Drafting requirement:

The requirements are in s.34 FA 2005 and we set them out as a paraphrase cannot do them justice: **26.15**

34 Disabled persons

(1) For the purposes of this Chapter where property is held on trusts for the benefit of a disabled person those trusts are qualifying trusts if they secure that the conditions in subsection (2) are met—

(a) during the lifetime of the disabled person, or
(b) until the termination of the trusts (if that occurs before his death).

(2) Those conditions are—

(a) that if any of the property is applied for the benefit of a beneficiary, it is applied for the benefit of the disabled person, and
(b) either that the disabled person is entitled to all the income (if there is any) arising from any of the property or that no such income may be applied for the benefit of any other person.

This is different from the CGT full annual allowance relief as it need only apply until the termination of the trusts. On the other hand all the trust income must be applied for the disabled beneficiary or accumulated. This allows a wide overriding power of appointment (perhaps best to draft it in a form which refers to "terminating the trusts" which take effect in default). However, if you do that you cannot qualify for IHT deemed IP treatment or a full CGT annual allowance. The section continues:

---

[22] Nevertheless if a vulnerable person election is in effect, trustees must inform HMRC within 90 days if:

(1) the person ceases to be a vulnerable person,
(2) the trusts cease to be qualifying trusts, or
(3) the trusts are terminated.

Section 37 FA 2005. Readers may wish to contemplate how this relates to Government promises to reduce regulation (e.g. 2005 Budget: "The Government wants to increase the emphasis at the heart of the regulatory process upon the simplification and removal of regulations...").

[23] For full details, see s.38 FA 2005. The definitions of "disabled" are discussed in Appendix 7.

(3) The trusts on which property is held are not to be treated as failing to secure that the conditions in subsection (2) are met by reason only of [statutory or similar powers of advancement].

(4) The reference in subsection (1) to the lifetime of the disabled person is, where property is held for his benefit on trusts of the kind described in section 33 of the Trustee Act 1925 (protective trusts), to be construed as a reference to the period during which such property is held on trust for him.

Income tax/CGT tax transparency: orphan beneficiary

26.16   We mention this only for completeness as its practical importance is minimal.

Income tax/CGT transparency applies to certain trusts for the benefit of a person one or both of whose parents have died. Statute calls this a "relevant minor"; we use the (slightly inaccurate) term "orphan".

Three types of trust will qualify:

(1) Trusts under the intestacy rules.

(2) Trusts under the will of a deceased parent of the orphan.

(3) Trusts under the Criminal Injuries Compensation Scheme.

The conditions are in short:[24]

(a) that the orphan will, on attaining the age of 18, become absolutely entitled to the property and its income,

(b) that, until that time, for so long as the orphan is living, if any of the property is applied for the benefit of a beneficiary, it is applied for the benefit of the orphan, and

(c) that, until that time, for so long as the orphan is living, either—

(i) the orphan is entitled to all the income (if there is any) arising from any of the property, or

(ii) no such income may be applied for the benefit of any other person.

Since no sensible parent will want an 18-year-old to become entitled to a substantial sum, this can in practice be regarded as another dead-letter relief.

---

[24] For full details, see s.35 FA 2005.

Effect of income tax/CGT transparency relief

The relief is wonderfully complex, and a full discussion would require a book to itself. In short, trustees will pay tax at the rate applicable if the beneficiary had received the trust income and gains.[25] The tax saving *could* be as much as £5,000 per year because of the stiff tax rates applied to small discretionary trusts, but it will generally be far less than that, and after allowing for the professional costs involved it would be surprising if there were any overall saving.

It is possible for a claim for the relief to increase tax liabilities. This may happen if the individual realises gains of his own, because the trust loses its CGT annual allowance if a claim is made.

Settlor-interested settlements do not qualify for this relief[26] but the settlement provisions have the same effect.

26.17

Disabled beneficiaries: conclusion

How then should one provide for disabled beneficiaries?

26.18

Small funds

The amounts involved may be too small to justify a trust. The best course then must be to seek a suitable individual who will take the funds and (without obligation) use them for the beneficiary.

If no suitable individual is found, a scheme operated by Mencap[27] may be considered. Under this scheme an individual creates a discretionary trust, with a nominal trust fund, and bequeaths additional funds by will. The Mencap trust company acts as trustee. Mencap only administers trusts set up under its standard form and does not act with co-trustees (though it does of course work with the family of the individual). Charges are raised on a non-profit making basis. Administrative costs should therefore be less than for comparable private trusts. The minimum trust fund is £10,000.

26.19

Substantial funds: provision by will

The uncertainties are so great that the most sensible form of will must be a discretionary will trust: this course allows the important decisions to be deferred until after the death of the testator.

26.20

---

[25] See ss.26 to 32 FA 2005.
[26] Section 25 FA 2005.
[27] *www.mencap.org.uk*.

Substantial funds: lifetime provision

26.21 Where sums involved are within the IHT nil rate band (or twice that amount, if husband and wife are making gifts) then the best course would be to make a gift to a discretionary trust.

Where sums involved are large, and means tested benefits not a consideration, and the beneficiary is disabled in the IHT sense, the best course will generally be to create an actual estate-IP trust.

Should one use standard form IP or discretionary trusts; or make amendments in order to satisfy the conditions for (1) income tax/CGT transparency or (2) full CGT annual allowance? This course would somewhat limit the trustees' flexibility but for CGT that drawback could be minimised by creating a trust with two separate funds for point (2), see 26.12 (Mixed trusts). It is a question of how much trouble and expense one is prepared to take in order to optimise the tax position:

(1) Where a trust accumulates income, and the disabled beneficiary has no other income or gains, income tax/CGT transparency is just about worthwhile.

(2) If both the beneficiary and the trust realise chargeable gains annually, a full CGT annual allowance is just about worthwhile.

It is possible to envisage circumstances where the IHT deemed IP Trust is the most suitable form of trust, but in practice this is not often likely to be the case: only where a trust has a beneficiary with a good life expectancy, claiming benefits, where the fund is so large that IHT ten-year changes are a serious burden.

Where the settlor cannot expect to survive seven years, it is important to take trouble for the gift to qualify for IHT dependent relative relief.

Commentary

26.22 What is needed is a single, coherent set of rules for income tax, IHT and CGT. We had hoped that this might emerge from the 2003–05 review on the taxation of trusts! The FA 2005 is a textbook example of disproportionate complexity arising from well meant tinkering; after the FA 2006 the position can only be described as a shambles; but there it is.

CHAPTER 27

GOVERNING LAW, PLACE OF ADMINISTRATION AND JURISDICTION CLAUSES

The governing law

A trust must have a "governing law"[1] whose significance is as follows: 27.1

(1) The law governs the validity, construction, effect and administration of the trust.[2] But only occasionally will the many differences between trust jurisdictions matter in practice to a well-drafted trust.

(2) It cannot be a breach of trust to comply with rules of the governing law relating to tax, a settlor's (or beneficiary's) right of recovery for tax, or exchange control. It may be a breach of trust to comply with other countries' rules on such matters.[3]

(3) The law is occasionally relevant for tax.[4]

---

[1] A note on terminology. The terms "applicable law" and "governing law" and "proper law" are synonymous. All of them have found favour with statutory drafters. "Governing law" is the term used in modern offshore legislation: e.g. the Bahamian Trusts (Choice of Governing Law) Act 1989; Cayman Islands Trusts Law. "Applicable law" is the term used in the Hague Convention. "Proper law" has been used twice in English statutes: s.22 FA 1949 (estate duty); s.304 Copyright, Designs & Patents Act 1988 (trust for Great Ormond St Hospital). As noted in *Philipson-Stow v IRC* [1961] AC 727 the word "proper" is somewhat inapt. "Governing law" is the best term as it is the most transparent term of the three.
[2] Hague Convention on the Law Applicable to Trusts (hereafter "the Hague Convention") implemented by the Recognition of Trusts Act 1987. Article 8 explains the meaning of this phrase in some detail.
[3] "It is difficult to see how the will trustees could possibly be in breach of trust in complying with the provisions of that system of law which the testator, by necessary implication, selected to regulate the rights of the parties under the trusts constituted by his will." *Re Cable* [1977] 1 WLR 7 at 23. See also *Re Latham* [1962] Ch 616.
[4] This is rare, which is not surprising, since the settlor has power to choose the governing law. However:

(4) The law is one factor (no more) in determining whether a Court has or will exercise jurisdiction over the trust.[5]

(5) The law is one factor (no more) in determining the situs of an equitable interest under the trust.[6]

Selection of English governing law

27.2 The settlor of a lifetime trust may in principle choose any governing law which recognises trusts.[7] The same applies to a trust created by will.[8]

If no express choice is made a trust is governed by the law with which it is most closely connected.[9] So in the usual case it is unnecessary for the drafter expressly to select the governing law. A trust with English settlor and beneficiaries, English trustees and trust property will, by clear implication, be governed by English law. Where there is a foreign element—for instance where the settlor and the trustees are not all domiciled and resident in England—then the trust should expressly direct which governing

---

(1) Some IHT double tax treaties apply different rules depending on the governing law of the trust: see Taxation of Foreign Domiciliaries, 7th edn, Ch.45 (IHT Planning Before and After a Change of Domicile).
(2) The source of a life tenant's income (for UK tax purposes) will normally be the underlying assets. However, if the law (unlike English law) does not give the life tenant the right to the trust income as it arises, but only the right to a sum from the trustees, then the "source" will be the trust. This is significant for the remittance basis and "source-ceasing" tax planning. See James Kessler QC, *Taxation of Foreign Domiciliaries* (7th edn, 2008, Key Haven Publications), para.10.16 (Income from trusts: identifying the source).
(3) The governing law may be relevant for foreign law or tax purposes.

[5] See 27.6 (Exclusive jurisdiction clause). For the purposes of the Civil Jurisdiction and Judgments Act 1982 and the 1968 Brussels Convention, a trust is "domiciled" in England if English Law "is the system of law with which the trust has its closest and most real connection". The governing law chosen is an important factor (but not, it is submitted, a conclusive factor) in applying this test.

[6] The situs of an equitable interest is not usually important, but it could matter, e.g. in ascertaining the jurisdiction whose rules govern dispositions of the equitable interest (matters such as formality, capacity, intestacy); or for tax. On situs see James Kessler QC, *Taxation of Foreign Domiciliaries* (7th edn, 2008, Key Haven Publications), Chs 55 and 56 (Situs of Assets for IHT and CGT).

[7] Hague Convention Art.6; this was also broadly the position at common law: Dicey and Morris, *The Conflict of Laws* (14th edn, 2006), Ch.29. There is a good discussion of the older cases in *Dymond's Death Duties* (15th edn, 1975), p.1286. For exceptions see below.

[8] The law governing a trust created by the will must be distinguished from:

(1) Formalities (governed by the Wills Act 1963).
(2) The material or essential validity of the will (governed by the domicile of the testator).
(3) The administration of the estate (governed by the law from which the administrator derives his authority.

There is no freedom to alter these. See *Tod v Barton* [2002] WTLR 469.

[9] Hague Convention, Art.7 (which further explains the concept of "closely connected"). The same principle applies at common law: *Chellaram v Chellaram* [1985] Ch 409 at 431 and *Chellaram v Chellaram (No.2)* [2002] 3 All ER 17, para.166.

law is to apply. Otherwise it may be difficult to identify the governing law.[10] A draft for a lifetime trust[11] is:

> English law governs the validity of this Settlement, and its construction, effects and administration.[12]

It is not correct to say: "the law of the United Kingdom": different legal systems apply in Scotland and Northern Ireland. In the past, those sensitive to regional nationalism would refer to "the law of England and Wales".[13] Since the Government of Wales Act 1998, the law of England and Wales may differ, though this seems unlikely in relation to trust law.

Selection of foreign governing law

A settlor may choose a foreign governing law. This opens an agreeable prospect: a free market in legal systems, where the settlor (or his advisers) may select whichever offers the most suitable rules and institutions for his purposes. 27.3

The selection of a foreign governing law might offer the following advantages:

Freedom from restrictive rules of English trust law. The drafter of a discretionary trust will find himself tempted to select a foreign jurisdiction to avoid the absurdities of the rule against accumulations.

Taxation. In practice tax advantages will be rare: see 27.1 (The governing law).

Protection from expropriation. A foreign governing law would be a defence against enforcement (in foreign jurisdictions) of future English confiscatory legislation. The possibility of such legislation seems remote.

---

[10] Dicey and Morris, *The Conflict of Laws*, assembles many authorities illustrating the courts' travails in determining the governing law in the absence of a choice of law clause; all unnecessary had the drafter specified the law.

[11] In a will the form "This will takes effect in accordance with English law" was held to be an effective choice of law in relation to such aspects as are governed by attestator's choice. *Tod v Barton* [2002] WTLR 469. But it would be better to be more explicit and say:

> "This Will takes effect in accordance with English law. In particular, English law governs the validity of the settlement constituted by this Will, and its construction, effects and administration. The English Courts have exclusive jurisdiction in any proceedings involving rights or obligations under that settlement."

[12] The wording is derived from Art.8 of the Hague Convention.

[13] Since s.4 Welsh Language Act 1976 abolished the earlier rule that statutory references to England included Wales, the Parliamentary drafter has referred to "the law of England and Wales" much more often than "the law of England".

Ease of administration. If foreign trustees are appointed, they may prefer their local law to govern their trust. The retention of English governing law is unlikely ever to be a serious handicap to trust administration.

These are somewhat tenuous advantages. There is also a drawback to the selection of a foreign governing law. A person dealing with the foreign-law trust may need to familiarise himself with the local law or seek local professional advice; or very likely, both. The choice of a foreign governing law may give rise to extra expense.

The freedom to select a foreign governing law is not absolute: the choice of a foreign governing law may be ineffective if "manifestly incompatible with public policy".[14] Would the English courts hold that the selection of a foreign governing law is contrary to public policy simply because the foreign law does not have our statutory rule against accumulations? The answer is plainly, no.[15]

In determining whether United Kingdom public policy requires the rejection of an express selection of a foreign governing law, some commentators suggest that a relevant factor would be whether the foreign governing law has any real connection with the trust. Thus they recommend that where a foreign governing law is selected, the initial trustees or trust property should be in the same jurisdiction. It is then harder still to question the governing law of the trust. While this might be adopted as a precaution it is not in our view necessary.[16]

It is in principle possible to arrange that the law of one jurisdiction should govern the validity of a trust, and the law of another jurisdiction should govern its administration.

---

[14] Hague Convention, Art.18.

[15] It is impossible to contend that avoidance of the rule against accumulations would be "manifestly incompatible with public policy". The Law Commission have recommended the abolition of the rule against accumulations (and indeed canvassed the case for abolition of the rule against perpetuities). See "The Rules against Perpetuities and Excessive Accumulations, Law Com 251, accessible on *www.lawcom.gov.uk*. The Government have accepted the recommendation, and most jurisdictions have never had, or have repealed, the rule. Even though the rule was regarded as an important rule of public policy when introduced in 1800, notions of public policy change with the passage of time: contrast the attenuation of the law of maintenance: *Bevan Ashford v Yeandle* [1999] Ch 239. The Hague Convention has altered the common law rule under which the selection of a foreign governing law could not prevent the rule against accumulations applying to land in England, freehold or even leasehold: *Freke v Lord Carbery* (1873) LR 16 Eq. 461.

[16] Difficulties and absurdities arise if (contrary to our firm view) the English Courts were to hold that a trust is governed by English law, notwithstanding an express selection of a foreign governing law. The foreign jurisdiction would almost certainly take the view that the same trust was governed by its law. (Some foreign trust laws state this expressly—e.g. s.4 Bahamian Trusts (Choice of Governing Law) Act 1989: "A term of a trust expressly declaring that the laws of the Bahamas shall govern the trust is valid, effective and conclusive regardless of any other circumstance." But the same conclusion would generally be reached at common law.) The resulting battle of jurisdictions might be determined by factors such as residence of trustees and situs of trust assets. So if an Irish law trust more than 21 years old decided to invest in English land, the trustees would suddenly be unable to accumulate income and a beneficiary may acquire an interest in possession! These difficulties go to show that the Courts should not impose English trust law against the principles of the Hague Convention.

The conclusion is that the drafter of a UK resident trust should not in normal circumstances select a foreign governing law.

Power to change the governing law

A power to change the governing law of a trust is valid in English law.[17]   27.4
A change of governing law may significantly alter the effect of a trust. For example, a change of proper law may be used to do the following:

(1) Override the English law restriction that the statutory power of advancement is limited to one half of the trust fund.[18] (This may be useful in the surprising number of trusts that include a power to change the governing law but do not extend the statutory power of advancement.)

(2) Extend the accumulation[19] and perpetuity[20] periods.

(3) Confer on the court power to vary the trust without the consent of the beneficiaries.[21]

(4) Make an action for breach of trust harder to pursue.

(5) An income receipt under English law may be regarded as a capital receipt under a foreign law (or vice versa).[22]

(6) Reverse the rule that references in the trust to "children" include illegitimate and adopted children.[23]

(7) Make a settlor's statutory indemnity for tax harder to enforce.[24]

---

[17] Hague Convention, Art.10 envisages such a power, subject to the public policy considerations of Art.18. This view was adopted in *Chellaram v Chellaram (No.2)* [2002] 3 All ER 17.
[18] There is no such restriction in Art.38(5) Trusts (Jersey) Law 1984 or s.24 Trustee Act 1975 (Bermuda).
[19] See 15.9 (Strategies after accumulation period expires).
[20] For instance the Cayman Islands have a 150-year perpetuity period and Jersey has abolished the rule against perpetuities altogether.
[21] e.g. s.412 (a) and s.416 of the US Uniform Trust Code:

"The court may modify the administrative or dispositive terms of a trust or terminate the trust if, because of circumstances not anticipated by the settlor, modification or termination will further the purposes of the trust. To the extent practicable, the modification must be made in accordance with the settlor's probable intention. ... To achieve the settlor's tax objectives, the court may modify the terms of a trust in a manner that is not contrary to the settlor's probable intention. The court may provide that the modification has retroactive effect."

Likewise Arts 910 para.5 and 932a para.165 of the Liechtenstein *Personen und Gesellschaftrecht*.
[22] See Capital and Income in Trusts: Classification and Apportionment, Law Com Consultation Paper 175 (2004) paras 5.4–5.8.
[23] See 5.22 (Illegitimate beneficiaries); 5.23 (Adopted beneficiaries).
[24] There are too many such rights to compile a complete list, but the most important is Sch. 5 para.6 TCGA 1992. The questions raised by such indemnities have become very important since the reforms of the FA 1998, but have not yet been fully explored in the Courts.

Should trustees be given power to change the governing law? The power may well be useful once the trust is more than 21 years old, if the trustees wish to accumulate income.[25] The following draft is proposed:

> The Trustees may during the Trust Period by deed with the consent of the Settlor during his life or of two Beneficiaries after his death declare that from the date of such declaration:
>
> (1) The law of any Qualifying Jurisdiction governs the validity of this Settlement, and its construction, effects and administration, or any severable aspect of this Settlement; and
> (2) The courts of any Qualifying Jurisdiction have exclusive jurisdiction in any proceedings involving rights or obligations under this Settlement.
>
> In this paragraph a "Qualifying Jurisdiction" is one which recognises trusts (as defined in the Hague Convention on the Law Applicable to Trusts and on their Recognition).

The power to change the governing law should be subject to the safeguard that it should only be exercised with the consent of the protector, settlor or two beneficiaries.

Sometimes the trustees are given power to make alterations in the terms of the trust which are consequential to the change in the governing law, but this only duplicates the standard overriding powers.

Sometimes the power is made subject to the condition that no part of the trust should become unenforceable in the new jurisdiction; but this raises difficult questions as to what is meant by "part of a trust" and "unenforceable". Sometimes the power is made subject to the condition that all (or substantially all) the terms of the trust should be capable of taking effect in the new jurisdiction. However, the purpose of changing the governing law may be precisely to alter the effect of the terms of the trust. It is suggested that the only appropriate restriction should be that the new governing law is one which recognises trusts.

Sometimes the power is made subject to the condition that the trust should not be revocable in the new jurisdiction. It is of course important that the power to change the governing law cannot be exercised to allow the settlor or his spouse/civil partner to benefit from the settled property (assuming they are meant to be excluded from the trust, as will usually be the case); or to prevent the trust from qualifying as an interest in possession trust (if appropriate). However the usual settlor exclusion clause and protection clause will ensure that this is the case and no additional wording is needed.[26]

---

[25] See 15.9 (Strategies for trustees after the accumulation period expires).
[26] HMRC lost an argument along these lines before the Special Commissioners: *IRC v Schroder* [1983] STC 480 at p.489. There was, wisely, no appeal on this point.

Place of administration of trust

The form used in this book is as follows: **27.5**

> The Trustees may carry on the administration of this Settlement anywhere they think fit.

The place of administration[27] of the trust is relevant for some tax and minor conflict of law issues.[28]

Trustees can as a matter of general principle carry on the administration of a trust wherever they think fit.[29] The clause is therefore strictly unnecessary. However if it is desired to move the place of administration to a new jurisdiction, it is good practice to exercise this power by formal resolution.[30]

The choice of place of administration does not significantly affect the beneficiaries' rights. It is unnecessary to require a protector's consent to the exercise of the power or to restrict the power in any way.

---

[27] "Place of administration" is one of a cluster of concepts expressed in slightly different ways, with slightly different nuances of meaning. Contrast:

1. "Central management and control of the trust estate" which is relevant for trust residence for Australian tax purposes.
2. The "place of effective management" of a trust which is relevant to determine trust residence for the purpose of double tax treaties using the OECD Model. This concept is not quite the same as "place of administration" as the emphasis is on "top management".

[28] The place of administration does *not* determine the law applicable to matters of administration: *Chellaram v Chellaram* [1985] Ch 409; Hague Convention, Art.8. (This needs stressing as the contrary view was once generally held, and still survives in some textbooks.) However:

1. The place of administration is relevant in deciding whether a Court has (or will exercise) jurisdiction over the trust: see *Chellaram v Chellaram*. In some foreign trust laws the point is made expressly: e.g. Art.5(d) Trusts (Jersey) Law 1984 ("the Court has jurisdiction where ... administration of any trust property of a foreign trust is carried on in Jersey.")
2. "The place of administration of the trust designated by the Settlor" is relevant to ascertain the applicable law of the trust, if no applicable law has been chosen expressly: Hague Convention Art. 7.
3. The place of administration may be relevant to a clause in a trust which refers to the place of administration (this book does not use that drafting technique).
4. The place of administration is not relevant for UK trust taxation after 2007, but it is relevant for some foreign tax purposes (e.g. Ireland retains the old UK CGT rules).

[29] We cannot find authority for this proposition, but only since it has never been questioned. Of course in practice it would be normal for administration to be carried on where the trustees are resident.

[30] The resolution is no more than a step in the right direction. What matters is not where the trustees intend, or are required to carry on the administration, but where it is actually done. Contrast *Unit Construction v Bullock* [1960] AC 351; 38 TC 712.

Exclusive jurisdiction clause

27.6 In the absence of an exclusive jurisdiction clause, the English Court has jurisdiction to administer a trust with English governing law,[31] or a foreign governing law.[32] The English Court has jurisdiction under the VTA 1958 to vary a trust with a foreign governing law though "where there are substantial foreign elements in the case ... the Court must consider carefully whether it is proper for it to exercise the jurisdiction".[33]

Various international conventions provide that an exclusive jurisdiction clause is effective:

> The court or courts of a Contracting State on which a trust instrument has conferred jurisdiction shall have exclusive jurisdiction in any proceedings brought against a settlor, trustee or beneficiary, if relations between these persons or their rights or obligations under the trust are involved.[34]

In jurisdictions which are not party to these Conventions, a Court has a discretion to disregard an exclusive jurisdiction clause but only does so in exceptional cases.[35]

The recommended practice is to include an exclusive jurisdiction clause where there is an express selection of governing law, but not otherwise. The wording should be based on the Conventions:[36]

---

[31] A claim form may be served outside England and Wales on a claim to execute trusts which "ought to be executed according to English law": r.6.20(11) Civil Procedure Rules 1998.
[32] *Re Cable* [1977] 1 WLR 7.
[33] *Re Paget* [1965] 1 WLR 1046.
[34] EU Council Regulation on Jurisdiction and the Recognition and Enforcement of Judgments in Civil and Commercial Matters 44/2001 Art.22(4) Brussels and Lugano Conventions on Jurisdiction and the Enforcement of Judgments in Civil and Commercial Matters Art.17(2).
[35] *Koonmen v Bender* 6 ITELR 568, 4 Butterworths Offshore Trust Cases 774, [2004] TLI 44, [2007] WTLR 293 at [49]. The discretion to disregard the clause may be exercised slightly more readily if the claim is by beneficiaries, not the settlor: *Capricorn v Compass* [2001] JLR 205, accessible on www.jerseylegalinfo.je.
[36] *Koonmen v Bender* (above) discussed a form commonly used in offshore trusts:

> "(1) 'The Proper Law' means the law to the exclusive jurisdiction of which the rights of all parties and the construction and effect of each and every provision of this settlement shall from time to time be subject and by which such rights, construction and effect shall be construed and regulated. ...
> (2) Proper law. This settlement is established under the laws of Anguilla and subject and without prejudice to any transfer of the administration of the trusts hereof to any change in the Proper Law and to any change in the law of interpretation of this settlement duly made according to the powers and provisions hereinafter declared the Proper Law shall be the law of Anguilla which said Island shall be the forum for the administration hereof."

The drafting is muddled. Clause (1) purports to be a definition of "proper law" but is actually a substantive provision. It also purports to give exclusive jurisdiction to a "law" instead of to a court. Clause (2) uses the expression "forum of administration" which is (as noted below) ambiguous. But the court rightly held (at [45]to [48]) that the correct construction was that this is an exclusive jurisdiction clause. There is no strict rule for construing exclusive jurisdiction clauses (comparable to exclusion clauses in contracts).

The English Courts have exclusive jurisdiction in any proceedings involving rights or obligations under this Settlement.

Proper law and exclusive jurisdiction clauses do not exclude the UK jurisdiction to vary trusts on divorce.[37] However, the English court order will need to be enforced against the trustees in the foreign jurisdiction; some jurisdictions will (generally) recognise an order of the English court but others may not.[38]

"Forum of administration"

Old precedents used to specify a governing law and, separately, a "forum of administration" of the settlement.[39] The purpose of the latter was:

(1) To specify the country whose courts had jurisdiction over administration.

(2) To specify the law governing matters of administration.

Now, however:

(1) The issue of jurisdiction is better dealt with in a form based on the Brussels Convention.

(2) The governing law governs matters of administration.[40]

---

[37] *C v C* [2005] Fam 250 paras 27–43, also reported under the name of *Charalambous v Charalambous* [2004] WTLR 1061. See 5.12 (Variation of settlement on divorce).
[38] For the position in Jersey, see *CI Law Trustees Ltd v Minwalla* [2006] WTLR 821. In *T v T* [1996] 2 FLR 357 foreign trustees were joined as parties to English matrimonial proceedings. See 5.12 (Variation of settlement on divorce).
[39] There was likewise power to alter the governing law and, separately, power to alter the forum of administration, e.g. the trust in *Chellaram v Chellaram* [1985] Ch 409 at p.419: "a power for the trustees by deed to declare that the settlement shall take effect in accordance with the law of some other place in any part of the world *and that the forum for the administration hereof shall thenceforth be the laws of that place.*"
[40] The form goes back to the time when it was thought that

(1) the governing law only governed issues of validity and construction; but
(2) the place of administration (or "forum of administration") governed issues of administration.

Since 1987 at least it has been clear that the governing law in principle determines issues of administration along with everything else; see above.

Therefore it is not now appropriate or meaningful[41] for the drafter to specify a "forum of administration" in addition to specifying a governing law and a place of exclusive jurisdiction.

---

[41] The expression "forum of administration" is often used in a way where it is unclear whether the meaning is (i) Courts with jurisdiction over administration; (ii) law governing administration; or (iii) place where administration is carried on. The drafter of s.89(3) Cayman Islands Trust Law (2001 revision) wanted to include (i) and (iii), referring to a provision that "the Islands *or the courts of the Islands* are the forum for the administration of the trust". *Dymond's Death Duties* (15th edn, 1973), p.1299 states that in the older cases the term was used to refer to what is now called the proper law. This lack of clarity is a reason to avoid the expression.

CHAPTER 28

RESTRICTING RIGHTS OF BENEFICIARIES

This chapter discusses techniques intended to restrict rights of beneficiaries. None of them are used in the precedents in this book.

Restrictions on disclosure of information

A settlor may wish to restrict rights of information in different ways and for different reasons: **28.1**

(1) So that individual beneficiaries are not entitled to find out what other beneficiaries receive.

(2) So that younger beneficiaries do not find out about the trust until they reach a more mature age.

(3) So that distant "fall back" beneficiaries who are not (in practice) likely to receive benefits do not receive any information.

There are two main ways in which a beneficiary may obtain information:

(1) in the case of a will, the rule is that all wills are open to public inspection;

(2) in any case, from the right of a beneficiary to information from the trustees.

A third method is by seeking disclosure in the course of litigation. The drafter cannot, however, restrict the Court's power to order disclosure in the course of litigation.

Disclosure of Will

28.2 A Will is a public document.[1] However, one can avoid disclosure by using a secret trust.[2] Although the Will is open to inspection, the Will itself will only show that there is a gift of the residuary estate to the executors. The reader of the Will may guess that there is a secret trust, but he will not find out its terms from the Will. Of course, the actual beneficiary of the secret trust will be entitled to information about their trust.

The value of the testator's estate will, however, be disclosed to the public. If it is desired to avoid that disclosure, the client might create one or more trusts during his lifetime. This might be a trust under which the client has an interest in possession, with power to advance capital to him. The trust fund will not in principle form part of his free estate. So its value will not be included in the value of his free estate, which is the value that is made public. However in most cases the tax cost makes this proposal impractical.

Beneficiary's right to trust information[3]

The general law position

28.3 The Court has a discretion to require trustees to disclose information to beneficiaries (including mere objects of trustees' powers). This discretion is based on the essential requirement of a valid trust, that trustees must be under an effective obligation to deal with the trust fund for the benefit of beneficiaries.[4] Duties to disclose are part of the irreducible core obligations of trustees which cannot be excluded.[5] A clause which purports to remove or exclude the right to information entirely will be ignored as inconsistent with a trust.[6] The fact that a protector has a right to information is merely a factor that the Court may take into account in deciding whether

---

[1] Section 124 Supreme Court Act 1981; rule 58 Non-contentious Probate Rules 1987.
[2] An alternative to a secret trust is a "half secret trust". That is, a gift to the executors combined with a direction in the Will that the executors are to hold the property on appropriate trusts. The Will itself will not say what the terms of these trusts are. Some commentators take the view that this type of trust rests on the principle of "incorporation by reference". If that is so then the underlying trust documentation should be publicly available with the Will. To avoid this uncertain question a fully secret trust is preferable to a half secret trust.
[3] See International Trust Laws (Jordan Publishing, looseleaf) section B7 (Disclosure of Information by Trustees, Campbell and Hilliard).
[4] *Schmidt v Rosewood Trust* [2003] 2 AC 709.
[5] See "Trustees Duty to Provide Information to Beneficiaries", Lightman J. [2004] PCB 23, accessible on *www.judiciary.gov.uk/publications_media/speeches/pre_2004/jl211003.htm*.
[6] The only way to restrict information may be to select a proper law with statutory restrictions on information rights.

to grant disclosure to a beneficiary. It cannot be used to justify removing beneficiaries' information rights.[7]

It is considered that a restriction on information rights in a trust deed would not have any effect.[8]

Practical means of restricting information rights

One viable route is to arrange that:

(1) Each beneficiary has a settlement creating appropriate trusts for the benefit of that beneficiary and (say) his future family.[9]

(2) Each settlement is a separate settlement for trust law purposes.

(3) Each beneficiary is not a beneficiary under the other settlements.

Since a beneficiary of one settlement is not a beneficiary under the other settlements, he cannot be entitled to information about the other settlements.

Where confidentiality of a statement of wishes is important it is suggested that the statement should be expressed to be confidential and give reasons for confidentiality (if not obvious). If appropriate the settlor might record two statements of wishes; one to be disclosed, the other expressed to be confidential, and setting out the further confidential material. This procedure places the maximum obstacles in the way of a beneficiary seeking disclosure. However a letter of wishes will normally be disclosed as a matter of good administration and refusal to disclose might encourage disappointed beneficiaries to litigate.[10]

No named beneficiaries or unascertainable default beneficiary

Some drafters make it hard to ascertain who the default beneficiaries will be. They hoped this would weaken claims to information or to the trust fund. But *Schmidt v Rosewood* shows that this technique does not help. The furthest that we would go down this road would be to provide that the default beneficiary should be "such charities as the trustees shall determine".

28.4

---

[7] *Schmidt v Rosewood Trust* [2003] 2 AC 709.
[8] See *Bathurst v Kleinwort Benson (Channel Islands) Trustees* Royal Court of Guernsey [2007] WTLR 959 accessible on www.guernseybar.com at [126] to [129]. If restrictions are desired (they can after all do no harm) then Article 33 Trust (Guernsey) Law 1989 is a suitable precedent.
[9] Or, of course, if appropriate, a beneficiary may be given his share absolutely.
[10] *Scott v National Trust* [1998] 2 All ER 705 and *Breakspear v Ackland* [2008] WTLR 777.

Sometimes the default beneficiary is expressed to be:

> *The persons who would have been entitled to the settlor's estate (and in the share or amounts and for the interest in and for which such persons respectively would have become so entitled thereto) under the law relating to the distribution of the moveable estate of a person dying intestate under the law in force in the jurisdiction of the proper law of the trust at the expiration of the trust period if the settlor had died on that date (but after the death of any other person dying on that date) wholly intestate and domiciled in the jurisdiction of the proper law of this trust without leaving any spouse him surviving and possessed only of an absolute beneficial interest in the net proceeds of sale and conversion of the trust fund.*

This form will often breach the rule against perpetuities.

Some tax lawyers have suggested that an appropriate default beneficiary might be the Chancellor of the Exchequer on the expiry of the trust period. Some academics propose the Warden of All Souls. But since there is (one may assume) no genuine intention to benefit the Chancellor or the Warden, this might be regarded by a hostile Court as a sham.[11]

A variant of this idea is that there should be no beneficiaries named in the trust deed at all. The risk that a hostile court would regard this as a sham is greater than ever.

Extension of powers of disclosure

28.5 We have seen a form authorising disclosure to Government departments:

> *The Trustees may make such disclosures concerning this Trust or Trust Property (including disclosure of any direct or indirect beneficial interests therein and of any dealings therein) as may be properly required by any competent authority or person whether or not such disclosure may be enforced upon the Trustees.*

No-one has ever doubted that the general law allows trustees to disclose information properly required; this form is only appropriate in foreign jurisdictions where the local law imposes greater secrecy requirements.

No-Contest Clauses

28.6 A no-contest clause is one which provides that a beneficiary forfeits his interest if he contests a will or trust. The clauses are fairly common in offshore trusts.[12] The object is to discourage litigation by beneficiaries.

---

[11] It should not be held to be a sham, applying the well established case law test; but hostile courts have sometimes applied a looser test of sham. See Kessler, "What is (and what is not) a Sham" (1999) OITR, vol.9, p.125 accessible on *www.kessler.co.uk*.

[12] This fact is stated in *AN v Barclays Private Bank and Trust (Cayman) Ltd* 9 ITELR 630, [2007] WTLR 565 (Cayman Islands Grand Court) at [33].

The clauses are not much used in England, but they may catch on here. They are not included in the precedents in this book: it is suggested they should not be a standard form.

There are many forms that the clause may take. There are also many reported cases, though most of them are antique or only marginally relevant. The only two recent cases (hereafter *Nathan*[13] and *AN*[14]) are not enough to deal with all the issues which arise, the more so because they are not consistent on all points, and the former concerned a home-made will with bodged drafting.

Certainty

A no-contest clause must meet a requirement of certainty. The test of certainty here is that one can know from the outset the exact event the happening of which will result in forfeiture.[15] It seems clear on principle, and authority confirms, that the following conditions meet the certainty test:

(1)(a) *If a beneficiary contests or disagrees with my will.*[16]

These words "encompass any proceedings which might result in an alteration of the dispositions made by the will."[17]

(1)(b) *If a beneficiary contests the validity of this deed and the trust created under it.*[18]
(1)(c) *If a beneficiary contests the validity of any conveyance of property to the trustees.*[19]

Form 1(c) is more far reaching than forms 1(a) or (b). If the beneficiary is successful in a 1(a)(b) case the entire trust or will is set aside, the forfeiture clause becomes irrelevant. Whereas if a beneficiary successfully contests the validity of *one* conveyance to the trust, the forfeiture clause might still take effect in relation to other conveyances which may not have been contested.

(1)(d) *If a beneficiary takes any steps whatever (whether directly or indirectly) to contest [any of the above].*[20]
(1)(e) *If a beneficiary* unreasonably *does any of the above [i.e. contests etc.].*[21]

---

[13] *Nathan v Leonard* [2003] 1 WLR 827.
[14] *AN v Barclays Private Bank and Trust (Cayman) Ltd* 9 ITELR 630, [2007] WTLR 565 (Cayman Islands Grand Court).
[15] *AN* at [72]; *Nathan* at [17].
[16] *Nathan* at [17] to [19]. The will in fact referred to a beneficiary who "*wishes to* contest or disagree". But the Judge (rightly) held that the words "wishes to" (in context) added nothing.
[17] *Nathan* at [19]. "*Contests and disagrees*" obviously includes a claim under the Inheritance (Provision for Family and Dependants) Act 1975. See *Nathan* at [16]; but it is clear both on principle and on authority that such a claim also "contests" the will; see (if authority is needed) *Re Gaynor* [1960] VR 640 (Supreme Court of Victoria).
[18] *AN* at [50].
[19] *AN* at [50].
[20] *Evanturel v Evanturel* (1874) LR 6 PC 1, cited *AN* at [51].
[21] *AN* at [98].

Form 1(e) is in fact considerably less certain than forms 1(a) to 1(d). However the certainty test is not applied that strictly.[22] Further, the concept of reasonableness is deeply embedded in the law and should be regarded as sufficiently certain. It hardly seems a wise policy to authorise no-contest clauses for unreasonable contests, and to strike down clauses restricted to reasonable contests.

> *(2) If a beneficiary [unreasonably] challenges the decision of the trustees or the protector.*

I refer to forms 1(a) to (e) validity-contest clauses, and I refer to form (2) as an administration-contest clause.

AN held that form (2) was uncertain without the word "reasonably" but became sufficiently certain if that word was included.[23] It is difficult to see how the word "reasonably" renders an uncertain clause more certain. The Judge was quite right to say that the clause is invalid without the word "reasonable" but the ground for invalidity is repugnancy and not uncertainty. But what matters here is that form (2) (restricted to reasonable challenges) meets the certainty requirement.

Repugnancy, ouster and public policy

No-contest clauses have been challenged on the grounds of repugnancy, ouster and public policy. The repugnancy argument is that a no-contest clause is inconsistent with the terms of any gift to a beneficiary. The ouster argument is that the clause ousts the jurisdiction of the Court. The public policy argument is that the clause should be held void as contrary to public policy. There is a large element of overlap between these three arguments.

There are of course examples of clauses which are:

(1) void for repugnancy (e.g. restrictions on alienation);

(2) void for ousting the jurisdiction of the Court;[24] or

(3) void for public policy (e.g. a forfeiture on marriage or bankruptcy).

None of these examples are close to a no-contest clause.

The public policy issue on no-contest clauses is a battle between two conflicting public interests, freedom of disposition[25] (the settlor's property rights) *v* freedom of beneficiaries to litigate over those rights. The Courts decided in the 19th century to uphold no-contest clauses of type (1) above,

---

[22] *Sifton v Sifton* [1938] AC 656 at 671: "It must be ascertainable whether the provision has taken effect or not; not that it must be ascertained in fact by the person affected, or even ascertainable by him without difficulty ...".

[23] *AN* at [52] to [58] especially at [58].

[24] e.g. *Re Wynn* [1952] Ch 271.

[25] I use this term to include freedom of testation.

the laisser-faire spirit of those times weighing in favour of freedom of disposition. But the 19th-century cases have (quite rightly) been followed and it is well settled that those no-contest set up clauses (forms 1(a) to (e) above) are valid and not made void by rules relating to repugnancy, ouster or public policy.

A different public policy argument was raised in *Nathan*, which did not arise in the 19th century, that no-contest clauses in wills should be void as deterring an application under the Inheritance (Provision for Family and Dependants) Act 1975. This was (we think convincingly) rejected.[26] Of course, this point applies to wills but not (normally) to lifetime settlements.

The position is different for administration-contest clauses (form (2) above). There is an irreducible core of obligations owed by trustees to beneficiaries. If the beneficiaries cannot make *any* challenge to the trustees' actions or decisions, there is no trust. An unrestricted administration-contest clause clearly is repugnant (ie inconsistent) with a trust.[27]

Construction of no-contest clauses

It is said that no-contest clauses (like all forfeiture clauses) should be strictly construed.[28] This is no doubt so, but in well drafted clauses this should make no difference, because the meaning should be clear and the result should be the same whether the construction is strict or benevolent.

In *AN* the no-contest clause provided:

Whosoever contests the validity:

(1) of this deed and the Trust created under it,
(2) of the provisions of any conveyance of property by any person or persons to the Trustee to form and be held as part of the Trust Fund, and
(3) of the decisions of the Trustee and/or of the Protector

shall cease to be a Beneficiary of any of these Trusts and shall be excluded from any benefits direct or indirect deriving from the Trust Fund.[29]

Read literally, subclause (3) is void and (since it is not easy to sever the void part) the whole clause must fail. The Judge construed (or stretched) the clause to mean "whoever *unjustifiably*[30] contests ... etc." Thus the validity of the clause (in this emasculated form) could be upheld.

---

[26] Sidney Ross is less convinced: see "Forfeiture Clauses in Wills" *Trust Quarterly Review* Vol.1 Issue 1 (2003) accessible to STEP members on *www.step.org* [56] to [60], but his analogy with s.34(1) Matrimonial Causes Act 1973 is not a close one. The position is different in Canada and Australia: *Re Chester* (1978) 19 SASR 247.
[27] This proposition is self-evident, but if authority is needed see *AN* at [92].
[28] *AN* at [35] and [39].
[29] Needless to say, the paragraphing is added for greater clarity.
[30] The Judge explained "justifiably" to mean: bona fide, not frivolous or vexatious, and with *probabilis causa litigandi*, a good cause for litigation. See *AN* [98] to [102]. But that only expresses the common sense meaning of "justifiable".

The learned Judge was, with respect, on more doubtful ground when he held[31] that *validity-contest* clauses (forms 1(a) to (e) above) are to be construed as only applying to challenges which are both unsuccessful and unjustifiable (even if this is not expressly stated). The better view is that taken in *Nathan*, which the Judge in *AN* did not cite. The correct approach is to construe a no-contest clause. It may be right to construe it as applying only to unsuccessful challenges, but if not the clause (if valid) takes effect whether the challenge succeeds or fails.[32]

Gift-over requirement

The no-contest clause must operate by way of forfeiture of the interest in the defaulting beneficiary and a gift over of his interest to somebody else.[33] This has been called the *in terrorem* rule but that label is not apt and even if it were, English would be preferable. I suggest it should be called "the gift-over requirement". In the common form discretionary trust, the gift-over requirement is met in relation to the class of discretionary beneficiaries. If any of the beneficiaries are in default, they are excluded and the "gift-over" is to the others in the class. If (in practice unlikely) *all* the class were in default, then the default clause of the trust would take effect. But (in the absence of an express gift-over) a no-contest clause would not affect the fixed interest of the default beneficiary.

The rule against perpetuities

A no-contest clause must satisfy the rule against perpetuities. But even if that rule is not satisfied, the clause will normally be saved by the wait and see rule.

Relief from forfeiture

In *AN* the Judge held that the Court had jurisdiction to grant relief from forfeiture.[34] In *Nathan* the point was left open.[35] But this is not a drafting issue as the drafter cannot exclude jurisdiction (if it exists) or confer it (if it does not).

---

[31] See *AN* at [90]–[91] and [94].
[32] See *Nathan* at [24] to [26] especially at [26].
[33] *AN* at [30].
[34] *AN* at [104] to [123]. Since the no-contest clause (as construed) applied only to beneficiaries who litigated unjustifiably, a case for relief from forfeiture must be rare, but that does not affect the general principle. An example might be a minor beneficiary acting through an incompetent or conflicted representative.
[35] See *Nathan* at [28] to [31] but relief would not have been granted even if there were jurisdiction to grant it on the facts of that case.

Drafting a no-contest clause

If a no-contest clause is to be used, the following is suggested, loosely based on *AN*:

> Whereas the Settlor wishes so far as consistent with a valid trust to avoid and prevent litigation and disharmony between Beneficiaries and the Trustees, the Settlor therefore directs as follows:
>
> *(1) If a Beneficiary takes any legal proceedings to set aside or contest the validity of this deed/will or the trust created under it, he shall cease to be a Beneficiary and shall be excluded from any benefit from the Trust Fund. This sub-clause applies to all proceedings whether or not justifiable or successful.*
>
> *(2) If a Beneficiary takes any legal proceedings to set aside or contest the validity of:*
>
> *(a) any part of this deed/will or*
> *(b) any conveyance or transfer or declaration of trust by which property becomes part of the Trust Fund*
>
> *he shall cease to be a Beneficiary and shall be excluded from any benefit from the Trust Fund. This sub-clause shall not apply if the Beneficiary is wholly successful in the legal proceedings, but otherwise shall apply to all proceedings whether or not bought in good faith and with good cause.*
>
> *(3) (a) If a beneficiary unjustifiably takes any legal proceedings to contest any act or decision of the Trustees [or of the Protector][36] he shall cease to be a Beneficiary and shall be excluded from any benefit from the Trust Fund.*
>
> *(b) For this purpose proceedings are unjustifiable unless at all times conducted in good faith and with good cause.*
>
> *(4) This clause shall not apply to proceedings instigated with the prior consent in writing [of the Settlor],[37] [of the Protector][38] or of any trustee or any director of a corporate trustee.*
>
> *(5) This clause shall not apply unless proceedings commence before the end of the Trust Period.*
>
> *(6) If any sub-clause of this clause is void, it shall be regarded as severable and such sub-clauses that are not void shall take effect.*

The object of this rather complex clause is to find a balance between the conflicting needs of beneficiaries and trustees, and not to skirt too close to the limits of what trust law allows.

The recital may be relevant to the Court's jurisdiction to grant relief from forfeiture, if that exists, though the point should be self-evident.

Clause (1) concerns challenges to the entire trust. The unsuccessful beneficiary is excluded here (if he is successful there is of course no trust from which to exclude him).

---

[36] Omit if no Protector.
[37] Omit in will.
[38] Omit if no Protector.

Clause (2) concerns challenges to part of the trust. So far as successful, there is no trust and if successful the beneficiary does not become excluded from the rest of the trust. It does seem wrong that if a trust is in fact void in part, no-one could effectively say so. The sanction is, therefore, exclusion unless the beneficiary is successful. That should make a beneficiary pause before instigating proceedings. It is considered that this clause is valid, though (as noted above) the contrary would be arguable. But to restrict the clause to "justifiable" actions would substantially reduce its effect.

Clause (3) applies to acts and decisions of the trustees. It is restricted to unjustifiable litigation, in accordance with *AN*. One might (just) get away with restricting the clause to unsuccessful litigation, but the result is bound to be litigation on the validity of the clause. The aim of a no-contest clause is to *reduce* litigation. If the settlor wants more than permitted by this clause, he should create a trust using a governing law with a statutory regime such as Cayman Island Star Trusts.

Non-assignment clauses

28.7 *No person interested under this trust may sell pledge assign or encumber his interest under this trust.*

This provision is void in English law, though some foreign trust laws permit it. A similar result can be achieved: see 5.4 (A better solution).

CHAPTER 29

EXECUTION OF WILLS AND TRUST DEEDS

This Chapter sets out the procedures to be carried out once a draft has reached its final form.

Review of draft

The counsel of perfection is as follows. Every document should be reviewed twice after it has reached its final form. The penultimate review should be made by the drafter, at least 24 hours after he last examined the document. This enables him to apply a fresh mind to his work. The final review should be made by a person other than the drafter. Where counsel has prepared the draft, this duty rests on his instructing solicitor. A draft produced in-house should be reviewed by another member of the firm. He should have the text of the document printed out in its final form ready for execution. It is no cynical asperity to observe that the existence of this peer review concentrates the mind of the drafter himself.

29.1

Bear in mind the text:

Whoever thinks a faultless piece to see
Thinks what ne'er was, nor is, nor ne'er shall be.

In the case of a female settlor or beneficiary, care needs to be taken to replace "his" with "her", and "widower" for "widow". (Complete avoidance of personal pronouns may render this unnecessary, at the cost of clumsy phraseology.)

Special care needs to be taken where drafts have been amended or errors corrected. In such a case the drafter should review a mental checklist that:

(1) the revised clause fits properly into its context;

(2) the revision does not infringe the rule against perpetuities;

(3) the revision does not infringe the rule against accumulations;

(4) the clauses are renumbered as necessary, and references to clause numbers in the deed are systematically revised.

An omission of text is a remarkably difficult error to spot. This is an error as old as writing itself[1] but it still remains prevalent in the age of the word processor. A prime example from the author's experience is a trust for a beneficiary "if he shall attain the vesting age"; the vesting age not being defined.

Review and approval by parties

29.2 All parties should understand the document they are signing. They should have an explanation of it and an opportunity to comment on it in draft. They should have the opportunity to take independent advice, and in some circumstances independent advice may be essential. The execution of a document which any party has not understood is the recipe for disaster. One might have thought this was so obvious it did not need saying, but the law reports show otherwise.[2]

Use and misuse of precedents

29.3 Standard drafts should be subjected to the same review procedure: they are not immune from error. Published precedents (this book included) should be reviewed with some suspicion: quite apart from the possibility of error, they may not be entirely suitable for the particular case. This advice is as old as precedent books themselves.[3]

Caution! Word processor at work

29.4 The Solicitors Indemnity Fund have issued this warning[4]:

> It is dangerous to place too much reliance upon equipment in the office. The fact that a document has been produced by a word processor does not obviate

---

[1] There is a well-known biblical example at 1 Samuel 14.41.
[2] For a spectacular example of such a disaster, see *Anker-Peterson v Christensen* [2002] WTLR 313.
[3] "Here is good counsell and advice given, to set down in conveyances every thing in certaintie and particiularitie, for certaintie is the mother of quietnesse and repose, and incertaintie the cause of variance and contentions; and for obtaining of the one, and avoyding of the other, the best meane is, in all assurances, to take counsell of learned and well-experienced men, and not to trust only without advice to a precedent." *Coke upon Littleton* 212a (1628)
[4] *Law Society's Gazette*, December 10, 1997, Vol.94, p.34. Jokes about computerised drafting were circulated at least two centuries ago; see Campbell's anecdote of Lord Eldon accessible on *www.kessler.co.uk*.

the need to check the document carefully, as shown in the two examples below.

The indemnified law firm received instructions to prepare a lease of premises on behalf of a client. The client required the lease to contain an upwards only rent review. A draft lease was produced with commendable speed with the assistance of a word processor. The draft was not checked. It was taken for granted that the draft was correct. In fact a section of the rent review clause was omitted. No one knew why. The effect of the omission was to create an upwards and downwards rent review clause.

The second example shows just how extreme the problem can be. A draft lease generated by the word processor was in fact patent nonsense. It contained every provision available in the precedent. The landlord was to maintain the structure, the tenant was to maintain the structure; the landlord was to insure, the tenant was to insure; the term was for five, ten, fifteen and twenty years. A cursory inspection would have revealed the problem.

To avoid this type of claim ...

- Do not assume that a document generated by a word processor is correct.
- Always check the document both in draft form and when engrossed.
- Remember that it is the responsibility of the fee earner, not the secretary, to ensure the draft is correct.

We set out the Solicitors Indemnity Fund view at length because the ad-men would have us think otherwise.[5] The reader must choose who to believe.

The clearer drafting style advocated in this book renders errors slightly less likely to occur, and slightly easier to spot; but (thankfully) it seems unlikely that the computer will render unnecessary a sharp eye and a clear mind on the part of the drafter.

Printing

The size of paper used was originally a vast and inconvenient desk size sheet. This gradually reduced to A3 and then to an elongated A4. Nowadays the standard A4 size is always used. The reason is probably that

29.5

---

[5] "Encyclopaedia of Forms & Precedents on CD-ROM has transformed the way we work. Previously time consuming tasks are now effortless ... drafts and re-drafts of documents are a thing of the past" (from advertising material).

the office printers are set up for A4. Whatever the reason, it is a welcome change as standard A4 size is more convenient for the file.

Single or double spacing is a matter of style only.

A firm of solicitors traditionally puts its name and address on the backsheet or title page of a document, a sign of professional pride in authorship and a useful reference if, many years later, it becomes necessary to investigate the background.

As far as the written letters of the document are concerned, there are two concerns: natural decay and fraudulent alterations.

Natural decay

29.6 Any trust may need to be examined for as long as a century so the document must be durable. The important factor is not the ink or toner, but the quality of paper. If the paper is not acid free, there is a danger of the letters falling off in course of time. Acid free paper must be used for the document itself and for the envelope or package in which it is stored. A paper supplier can advise.

Fraudulent alterations

29.7 The possibility of fraudulent alteration of an existing will or trust seems remote. Quite apart from the practical difficulties inherent in such forgery, a comparison with other copies or drafts would be likely to reveal the fraud.

An old-fashioned protection against fraudulent alteration was the practice of lining in the space from the end of a sentence to the right-hand margin; this is thought to be unnecessary and is no longer standard practice.

Procedure on execution of a lifetime settlement

29.8 There are a number of further procedures to set in motion after the execution of a trust deed.

(1) Transfers of trust property to trustees

29.9 Trust property must be transferred to the trustees (or their nominees) or the trust will generally be ineffective. Each type of property must be transferred by the appropriate method.

ASSET	METHOD OF TRANSFER
Cash	Transfer to bank account in name of trustees
Shares registered in name of settlor	Stock transfer form and entry on company register; consider need for consents from shareholders, directors or liquidator
Assets held by nominee	Written direction to nominee signed by beneficial owner
Registered land (unmortgaged)[6]	Land Transfer form, and entry at Land Registry; restriction on the register;[7] consider need for landlord's consent (for a lease)
Unregistered land (unmortgaged)[8]	Conveyance and application to register land; consider need for landlord's consent (for a lease)
Chattels	Deed of assignment
Life assurance policy	Deed of assignment and notice to Insurer
Equitable interest under an existing trust	Deed of assignment and notice to trustees of the existing trust

Transfers must be carried out without delay. Time for the purposes of the seven-year IHT period only begins to run when the trust property is transferred; and if the settlor died before the transfer the trust would not take effect.

(2) Statement of wishes

A statement of wishes is desirable where the trustees have a wide discretion. That applies to every precedent in this book. See 7.15 (Statement of wishes). 29.10

(3) Arrangements for payment of IHT on gift in case of death within seven years[9]

A lifetime gift to a disabled trust may be a PET and so an IHT charge may arise if the donor does not survive seven years. This tax charge is primarily the liability of the trustees.[10] The possibilities are as follows. 29.11

---

[6] For land subject to a mortgage, see 8.4 (Land subject to mortgage).
[7] Schedule 4, Form A Land Registration Rules 2003.
[8] For land subject to a mortgage, see 8.4 (Land subject to mortgage).
[9] See 13.5 (Trustees to pay tax on gift to trust).
[10] There is a lacuna in the statute here. Sections 199 and 205 IHTA 1984 state that the settlor's personal representatives and the trustees (and for good measure some beneficiaries) are all liable against HMRC to pay the IHT on a failed PET. The legislation does not spell out who—as between them—is primarily liable to pay the tax. Someone must bear the primary liability. It is inconceivable that the burden of tax will rest on whichever person HMRC choose to assess, so

(1) The donor may take out insurance against the risk of the IHT charge. He should give the policy to the donee (trustees).

(2) The donor may wish to provide in his will that tax should be paid out of his estate (rather than by the donee, as would otherwise have been the case).

(3) The donee may accept the risk of the IHT charge accruing if the settlor dies within seven years. Alternatively the donee may take out insurance.

(4) Arrangements for loss of nil rate band in case of death within seven years

29.12 If the donor dies within seven years of the gift, the donor's estate will, in principle, lose the benefit of the nil rate band. This problem is quite distinct from (3) above (IHT payable on the gift itself). The tax burden falls on the donor's estate (or if the donor makes subsequent gifts, the tax burden falls on the subsequent donees). The amount of IHT in issue cannot be ascertained at the time of the gift, although one could make an educated guess.

Very occasionally the donee is required to give an indemnity in respect of this tax. This would require careful bespoke drafting to suit the circumstances. This problem would normally arise only when a parent needs to provide for children from different marriages.

---

the question who bears the primary liability must be inferred as best one can from the provisions. The inference from ss.204(8) and 212 IHTA 1984 is that the trustees are primarily liable. Where the tax is paid by some other person, it is submitted that he has the right in equity to recover from the person who is primarily liable. See Emily Campbell "The Burden of Inheritance Tax on Lifetime Transfers" [1998] PCB 58 accessible on *www.kessler.co.uk*. However, this question is fairly academic. The IHT Manual, paras 30042, 30044 provide:

"You should treat the following persons as primarily liable [to IHT on a failed PET]:
– the transferee, or
– where the property is settled by the transfer, the trustees.

Where there are indications that there may be difficulties in collecting from the transferee or trustees (e.g. where the transferee has dealt with the property given, or is out of the jurisdiction, or the settlement has been wound up and the trust property distributed), you should consider whether, exceptionally, any other persons may be liable under s.199(1)(c) and (d) IHTA 1984 and, if so, take early action to collect from them ...

You must remember that the facility to have recourse to the transferor's personal representatives is not to be regarded as a soft option. We are to make all the attempts at recovering from the persons liable under s.199(1) IHTA 1984 that we would presently contemplate in a similar situation against any liable person."

In circumstances where HMRC choose not to collect tax from the trustees, the unfortunate person who does pay the tax is likely to find his right of indemnity against the trustees hard to enforce.

Some commentators suggest that the donor should seek an express indemnity from the donee in respect of tax due on a failed PET. An express indemnity is not needed in ordinary circumstances. In particular, an express indemnity is never needed on a gift to a settlement with reputable trustees.

(5) Returns and other matters

Once the trust has been completely constituted, a number of returns and other matters need attention: **29.13**

- (i) *Form 41G (Trust)*. This should be sent to the appropriate[11] HMRC Trust Tax Office to set up a trust record. This is not necessary if the trust will receive no income or gains for the long or medium term (e.g. a trust of a life insurance policy). It is also possible to complete Form 41G but request that a dormant trust should not receive annual SA returns.

- (ii) *IHT account*. An account (Form IHT 100) is needed when a gift is made to an IHT standard trust.[12] The duty rests on the transferor and the trustees (so that each may be liable to penalties in the case of default). No account is required for a gift to an estate-IP trust but appropriate records should be kept in case of death within seven years. If the donor dies within seven years of his gift the PET is disclosed in the executor's account.

- (iii) *Returns for non-resident trust*. Further returns are required for non-resident trusts.[13]

- (iv) *CGT claim for hold-over relief or losses*. A claim may be needed for CGT hold-over relief. The election is made by the settlor alone: the trustees will not be parties to it. A further claim may be made under SP 8/92 to avoid a valuation.[14] A claim is also needed if an allowable loss arises on the disposal to the trust. These claims are usually dealt with in the settlor's tax return.

- (vi) *Review will*. The donor should review his will as a matter of course following any substantial gift, to confirm that the terms of the will are still appropriate.

- (vii) *Inform beneficiaries*. An adult beneficiary who has an interest in possession should be informed of his interest. This is particularly relevant if the fund does not produce income. Concealment may be taken as evidence of a sham.

- (viii) *Diarise important deadlines*. For a standard IHT trust, diarise the next ten year anniversary. If appropriate, diarise dates that beneficiaries

---

[11] The HMRC Trusts Settlements and Estates Manual, para.1420 (The Correct Trust Office) explains how the work is shared around the trust offices.
[12] Section 216 IHTA 1984. The Inheritance Tax (Delivery of Accounts) (Excepted Transfers and Excepted Terminations) Regulations 2002 provide a de minimis exception which may apply in the case of a chargeable transfer of £10,000 or less, but that will not normally apply except for trusts of life insurance policies, or cases of 100% Business Property Relief.
[13] Section 218 IHTA 1984; Sch. 5A TCGA 1992.
[14] "Capital Gains Tax: Hold-Over Relief and SP 8/92" (April 1997, Tax Bulletin 28).

become absolutely entitled. Also diarise the date six months before each deadline, to allow time for action.

Stamp duty and SDLT

29.14 A will is not subject to stamp duty or SDLT. The following applies to lifetime settlements only. It is assumed that there is no consideration for the transfer to the settlement.

(1) SDLT is not normally[15] charged on a transfer of land in the UK for no consideration. The FA 2008 removed the need for trustees to self-certify that no land transaction is required.[16] (Note the trap that the assumption of liability for an outstanding debt, e.g. a mortgage, is consideration for SDLT purposes.)

(2) Stamp duty only applies to "instruments relating to stock and marketable securities".[17] The FA 2008 abolished the £5 fixed duty which previously applied to:

   (a) "a transfer of property otherwise than on sale" (although no duty was payable if the instrument was certified exempt)[18]; and
   (b) "a declaration of any use or trust of or concerning property unless the instrument constitutes a transfer on sale".[19]

The abolition of the £5 fixed duty was advocated by this book for many years.[20] Thus, a transfer of property to a settlement will normally be exempt and the trustees will not usually need to self-certify.

---

[15] One exception is where the transferee is a company connected with the transferor: s.53 FA 2003. S.54 FA 2003 confers relief for a transfer to a corporate trustee:

   (1) where the company holds the property as trustee in the course of a business carried on by it that consists of or includes the management of trusts;
   (2) where the transferor is connected with the company only because he is settlor of the trust.

There is a (narrow) SDLT trap here, because it is (just) possible that a transfer to a corporate trustee could not qualify for this exemption and so give rise to a SDLT charge on market value.

[16] See s.77 FA 2003 as amended by FA 2008.
[17] Section 125(1) FA 2003.
[18] S.99 and Sch. 32 FA 2008 removes the former charging provision in para.16, Sch.13 FA 1999. Category L of the Stamp Duty (Exempt Instruments) Regulations 1987 provided the exemption.
[19] FA 2008, s.99, Sch.32 removes the former charging provision in para.17, Sch.13 FA 1999.
[20] In addition, FA 2008, s.100 removed the need to have a document adjudicated and stamped which would formerly have been subject to the charge (abolished in 1985) on "any conveyance or transfer operating as a voluntary disposition *inter vivos*".

A deed of appointment exercising an overriding power is not subject to stamp duty.[21]

Procedure on execution of a will

To ensure that the formalities of execution are correctly followed, the proper course is that at least one of the witnesses of the will should be a solicitor. The client may not wish to visit the solicitor's office, or to pay the cost of a solicitor visiting him. In such a case a letter should be sent to the client setting out the reasons why it is better to execute the will in the presence of a solicitor, with a recommendation to follow this course. If the client refuses to do so his refusal should be recorded in writing. Subsequently the client may be advised in writing of the formalities for execution of a will, and left to carry them out. The solicitor should then check that the will appears on its face to have been properly executed if it is returned to him.[22]

29.15

The client should be advised to execute a Lasting Power of Attorney along with his will. Two forms have been prescribed. One (LPA PA) must be used where the power relates to the donor's property and affairs and the other (LPA PW) where it relates to his personal welfare. It is not possible for a single LPA to cover both these areas. The forms are available from the Office of the Public Guardian. An LPA confers no authority until it has been registered with the Public Guardian. However, it can be registered at any time after it has been created. It is possible to grant LPAs relating to property and affairs, but not personal welfare, that are effective while the client still has capacity. However, the client will usually intend that the LPA should only operate from the onset of mental incapacity. If so, a restriction should be inserted into form LPA PA at section 6. The following wording is based on s.20(1) of the Mental Capacity Act 2005:

> my attorney(s) does not have power to make a decision on my behalf in relation to a matter concerning my property and affairs if he knows or has reasonable grounds for believing that I have capacity I relation to the matter.

Earlier (revoked) wills should be marked as revoked by the new will.

The author is grateful to John Hawes for the following sage advice:

> I have for many years now kept (or my secretary has) a perpetual diary in which the execution of every client's will is noted for review three years ahead. Every month during a quiet moment my secretary gets out the diary and prepares a standard letter saying, in effect, are you still alive and here's a copy of your will

---

[21] The fixed charge on "Deed of any kind whatsoever" was abolished by s.85 FA 1985.
[22] *Esterhuizen v Allied Dunbar Assurance* [1998] 2 FLR 668 accessible on *www.kessler.co.uk*.

in case you want to change it. Please tick the appropriate box in the attached form and send it back in the SAE. At the same time, my secretary notes the diary for another three years ahead. This is good for the clients, it keeps my records straight if clients have moved and it is also good and cheap marketing as it reminds the clients that you are their solicitor.[23]

Tax reviews after execution of trust

29.16 It is of course the general duty of the trustees to mitigate so far as possible the taxation of the trust. They should review the tax position at regular intervals.

In particular, the IHT position should be reviewed:

(1) if it seems likely that the settlor will not survive seven years from the time he creates the trust. It may be possible to mitigate the tax charge on his gift to the trust;

(2) on the death of a life tenant of an estate-IP trust;

(3) shortly before a 10-year anniversary of an IHT standard trust.

The CGT position should be reviewed:

(1) in good time before the trustees realise substantial gains;

(2) before a beneficiary becomes absolutely entitled to trust property.

Trustees who are not specialists in these matters may seek specialist advice.[24]

---

[23] It is important to frame the letter so that the client is not led to believe that a "watching brief" is being kept over his tax affairs if there has been no express retainer for such. The Guidance published by the Law Society's Standards and Guidance Committee (printed in the Society's *Probate Practitioner's Handbook*) includes the following statement: "Without specific instructions from the client, a retainer for will preparation would not entail the solicitor in maintaining any such 'watching brief', but it is possible for a solicitor by his or her conduct to change a retainer so that a client comes to have a reasonable expectation that such a watching brief will be maintained. Solicitors would be well-advised to ensure that these matters are clear between themselves and their clients." See e.g. *Hines v Willans* (1997) reported belatedly [2002] WTLR 299.

[24] Details from *www.revenue-bar.org*.

CHAPTER 30

APPOINTMENT AND RETIREMENT OF TRUSTEES

Powers of appointment/retirement

30.1 The position is more complicated than necessary because there are three statutory powers, which are differently worded. The powers are:

(1) *Replacement* of trustee,[1] i.e. appointment of new trustee(s) in place of a trustee who:

   (a) dies;
   (b) remains out of the UK for more than 12 months;
   (c) wishes to retire or refuses to act; or
   (d) is unfit to act or incapable of acting.

(2) Appointment of *additional* trustee (without replacing a trustee).[2]

(3) *Retirement* of trustee (without a new appointment).[3]

We refer to the replacement/additional trustee powers together as "appointment of new trustees"; we refer to all three powers together as "appointment/retirement of trustees".

The person with power to appoint new trustees is:

(1) the person nominated for the purpose in the trust document; or

(2) if there is no such person, or no such person able and willing to act, then the surviving trustees, or the personal representatives of the last surviving trustee.[4]

---

[1] Section 36(1) TA 1925.
[2] Section 36(6) TA 1925.
[3] Section 39 TA 1925.
[4] Section 36(1) TA 1925.

In the discussion in this chapter:

(1) We refer to a person within (1) as "the appointor". (In the drafts it is unnecessary to use that term.)

(2) We assume either there is an appointor within (1) or the power is vested in the trustees (in which case we say there is no "nominated appointor"). We do not consider appointments where there is no nominated appointor and the sole trustee lacks capacity.[5]

Review by new trustees before accepting trusteeship

30.2   A person asked to become a trustee should consider before accepting office whether he will be able to perform the duties properly, and disclose any facts which may affect the trusteeship. This applies for instance where the new trustee intends to use trust powers to benefit himself (even assuming he can properly do so)[6] or where he may be subject to some restriction which stops him selling trust assets.[7]

Can the trustee be remunerated under a trustee remuneration clause or by statute?[8] (A problem here is exceptional, but it needs to be checked.) Will the trust have liquid assets to pay the remuneration? If not, indemnities may be a solution.

A power of dismissal is acceptable unless combined with a power to divest trust property; if there is a problem on this aspect, perhaps seek indemnities. A problem here is exceptional, but it needs to be checked.

Is there any reason to think the trust has been badly administered? If so the prospective trustee should consider what he is taking on. His duties will include investigating past administration. Also, a new trustee is (quite unfairly) personally liable for unpaid CGT, income tax and SDLT liabilities of the trust regardless of the value of the trust assets.[9] Indemnities could be a solution.

---

[5] See practice direction 9G—applications to appoint or discharge a trustee accessible on *www.publicguardian.gov.uk/docs/09G_-_Trustees_PD.pdf.*
[6] *Galmerrow Securities v National Westminster Bank* TLI Vol.14 (2000) p.158 at 172; [2002] WTLR 125.
[7] See 6.6 (Accountants as trustees), 6.7 (Director of listed company as trustee), 6.8 (Insider dealing and trusteeship).
[8] See 21.55 (Trustee remuneration).
[9] Section 151 FA 1989; para.5 Sch.16 FA 2003.

Review by appointor and retiring trustees before appointing new trustees or retiring

The person with the power of appointing new trustees should satisfy himself that the new trustees are suitable persons to be appointed. 30.3

Likewise a retiring trustee should satisfy himself that the trust will have appropriate trustees after his retirement.

Drafting an appointment/retirement of new trustees

First of all one must review the will or trust deed[10] to ascertain: 30.4

(1) the appointor (usually the settlor or the protector if there is one);

(2) any express provisions on appointments (e.g. old settlements often say that the settlor or beneficiaries may not be trustees).

(3) minimum number of trustees. Remember the possible two-trustee requirement if there are less than two trustees after the appointment.[11] Old settlements sometimes require three trustees as a minimum.

Take care if beneficiaries are appointed trustees: some settlements (particularly offshore settlements) say that trustees are excluded from benefit.

Check the chain of earlier appointments to confirm that current trustees are validly appointed.

If there have been earlier indemnities by beneficiaries (e.g. against an act which was a possible breach of trust) this needs review. New indemnities may be needed. Review earlier indemnities given by present trustees to former trustees; and review Money Laundering requirements.

The consent of the Court of Protection is sometimes[12] needed to exercise

---

[10] Documentation supplemental to the will or trust deed may also be relevant, but that would be exceptional.

[11] See 6.37 (Two-trustee requirement).

[12] The relevant provisions (though sensible) are slightly intricate and it is better to set them out than to paraphrase. Section 36 TA 1925 provides:

(1) Where a trustee ... is ... is incapable of acting ... then,

(a) the person or persons nominated for the purpose of appointing new trustees by the instrument, if any, creating the trust; or
(b) if there is no such person, or no such person able and willing to act, then the surviving or continuing trustees or trustee for the time being, or the personal representatives of the last surviving or continuing trustee;

may, by writing, appoint one or more other persons ... to be a trustee or trustees in the place of the trustee ... being incapable...

the power to replace a trustee who lacks mental capacity and has an interest in possession in trust property.[13]

If new trustees are separately represented, then the draft will normally be done by solicitors for the new trustees; the retiring trustee should check it himself or make it plain that he is relying on them to act on his behalf.

Title of deed

The term "deed of appointment" is ambiguous as it could be a deed exercising an overriding power of appointment. So call the document "deed of appointment of new trustees"[14] or "deed of retirement".

Parties

The parties are in principle:[15]

(1) The appointor; if (as is common) the settlor is the appointor, we prefer to call him "the Settlor" in the drafting.

(2) The new trustees.

(3) The retiring trustees.

(4) The continuing trustees.

If a trustee is being replaced on the grounds that he

(a) remained out of the UK for more than 12 months;

(b) refuses to act; or

(c) is unfit to act or is incapable of acting

he need not strictly be a party[16] but the better practice is to include him if practical, to avoid possible dispute later.

---

(9) Where a trustee lacks capacity to exercise his functions as trustee, and is also entitled in possession to some beneficial interest in the trust property, no appointment of a new trustee in his place shall be made by virtue of *paragraph (b) of subsection (1) of this section*, unless leave to make the appointment has been given by the Court of Protection.

(Text as amended by Mental Capacity Act 2005). So if (as is usual) the power appointing new trustees is vested in the settlor, then during the settlor's life Court of Protection consent is not needed because the power of appointment is exercisable under s.36(1)(a). After the settlor's death the power is (usually) exercisable by the trustees under s.36(1)(b), so consent is needed.

[13] For the procedure and precedents see Procedure Note 8 (Appointing new trustees) accessible on www.guardianship.gov.uk. (This book does not give precedents for this situation.)

[14] This title may be used if there is an appointment and retirement.

[15] There may be an overlap between these categories; it is not necessary to include a person more than once.

[16] *Re Stoneham* [1953] Ch 59.

Useful recitals

(1) Set out entire chain of trusteeship, i.e. *x* died; *y* retired and *z* appointed by deed of appointment dated ... etc. This is a good discipline. Once done it can be reused in later appointments. If there has been a problem here, the sooner it is identified the better.[17]

(2) The deed of appointment is supplemental to the settlement and relevant supplemental deeds.[18]

(3) The [*appointor*] has the power of appointing new trustees (refer to clause but preferably cite the clause): another good discipline.

(4) A retiring trustee desires to retire.[19]

(5) In the case of appointment by PRs of the last surviving trustee, appropriate details.

Useless recitals

Don't say, "the appointor is desirous of exercising the power of appointing new trustees". Would he execute the deed if he did not want to?

It is quite common to set out the trust fund in a schedule to the deed, but this is probably more trouble than it is worth (unless doubts have arisen as to the identity of the trust fund).

Don't say, "it is the intention to transfer the trust fund to the new trustees". That is obvious and otiose, as s.37(1)(d) Trustee Act 1925 deals with this.[20]

The CGT charge on the emigration of a UK trust can be collected from a former trustee if at the time of his retirement there is a proposal to appoint non-resident trustees.[21] Some drafters put in a recital that "there is no proposal that the trustees might become neither resident nor ordinarily resident in the UK." But either such proposal exists or it does not, a recital in the deed of appointment of new trustees has no significant effect, and is not considered worthwhile in a normal case.

Provisions of deed

The operative clause, which effects the appointment and retirement, should copy the wording of ss.36(1), 36(6) or 39 TA 1925. Thus: **30.5**

---

[17] For a horror story, see *Yudt v Leonard Ross & Craig* Ch 24 July 1998.
[18] See 12.4 (Useful recitals).
[19] In a deed of retirement this is necessary to comply with the conditions of s.39 TA 1925 (though it should be implied by a signature to a deed of retirement). In a deed of appointment this is not strictly necessary under s.36(1) TA 1925, but it is good practice.
[20] The form is unnecessary in the body of the deed: see 30.6 (Unnecessary clauses in deed of appointment).
[21] Section 82 TCGA 1992.

Replacement (settlor is appointor)

> In exercise of the power conferred by s.36(1) Trustee Act 1925, the Settlor appoints the New Trustee to be a Trustee in place of the deceased/retiring Trustee.

Replacement (no nominated appointor)

> In exercise of the power conferred by s.36(1) Trustee Act 1925, the Trustees appoint the New Trustee to be a Trustee in place of the deceased/retiring Trustee.

Retirement (settlor is appointor)

> In exercise of the power conferred by s.39 Trustee Act 1925, the Retiring Trustee retires from the Settlement. The Continuing Trustees and the Settlor consent to the discharge of the Retiring Trustee, and to the vesting in the Continuing Trustees alone of the trust property.

Retirement (no nominated appointor)

> In exercise of the power conferred by s.39 Trustee Act 1925, the Retiring Trustee retires from the Settlement. The Continuing Trustees consent to the discharge of the Retiring Trustee, and to the vesting in the Continuing Trustees alone of the trust property.

Appointment of additional trustee (settlor is appointor)

> In exercise of the power conferred by s.36(6) Trustee Act 1925, the Settlor appoints the New Trustee to be an additional Trustee.

Appointment of additional trustee (no nominated appointor)

> In exercise of the power conferred by s.36(6) Trustee Act 1925, the Continuing Trustees appoint the New Trustee to be an additional Trustee.

The precedents in this book include two sample deeds of appointment of new trustees, and the companion CD contains nine precedents (not printed as there is so much duplication).

Unnecessary clauses in deed of appointment

30.6 An appointment of trustees of an English law trust will by implication be governed by English law and the same law will govern subsidiary matters in the deed such as indemnities. It is not necessary to include a proper law clause but some may think it is advisable for the avoidance of doubt if there is a foreign element (e.g. a non-UK party).

The Retiring Trustees will promptly do all matters things deeds and documents necessary for completing the transfer of the trust property into the names of the New Trustees

This is in principle otiose as the retiring trustees are under a duty to do this anyway: s.37(1)(d) Trustee Act 1925. However it implies a waiver of the trustees' lien, and that could make a difference. The best practice is to include the clause when there is a trustee indemnity, and not to include it where there is no trustee indemnity; but (except in the rare case where the trustee needs to rely on his lien) the clause makes no practical difference.[22]

Vesting trust property in new trustees

A deed of appointment/retirement of trustees operates to convey to the new trustees any unregistered land in England and Wales subject to the trust, and the right to any debt or other chose in action. This does not apply to mortgages, most leases, or shares.[23] Following the appointment of new trustees, trust property must be transferred to the new trustees by the appropriate method and nominees and creditors etc. must be notified:

30.7

ASSET	FORM OF TRANSFER	NOTICE TO
Bank account	None needed	Bank
Shares	Stock transfer form; entry on company register; consider need for consent from co-shareholders, directors or liquidator	None
Assets held by nominee	None needed	Nominee
Registered freehold land (unmortgaged)	Land Transfer form; entry at Land Registry	Tenant (if any)
Registered leasehold land	As above; consider need for landlord's consent	Landlord Sub-tenant (if any)

---

[22] The form is also sometimes found as an unnecessary recital: see 30.4 (Useless recitals)
[23] Section 40 TA 1925.

ASSET	FORM OF TRANSFER	NOTICE TO
Unregistered freehold land (unmortgaged)	Application to register land	Tenant (if any)
Unregistered leasehold land	As above; consider need for landlord's consent	Landlord Sub-tenant (if any)
Chattels	None needed	Person in possession of chattels
Life assurance policy	None needed	Insurer
Equitable interest under another trust	None needed	Trustees of other trust

If the trustees are registered for VAT, give notice to HMRC.

Stamp Duty and SDLT

30.8 A deed of appointment of new trustees is exempt from stamp duty (even if the trust property includes stock or marketable securities).

The FA 2008 abolished the £5 fixed duty which was previously applied to a stock transfer form transferring stock or marketable securities to the new trustees. There is no need to self-certify.

A transfer of land to new trustees does not give rise to SDLT,[24] but needs a self-certificate.

---

[24] SDLT Manual 31745 provides:

Changes in the composition of trustees of a continuing settlement [November 2005]

For stamp duty land tax purposes we treat trustees of a settlement as a single and continuing body of persons, as we do for CGT. It follows that for a continuing settlement a change in the composition of trustees is not a land transaction.

This means in particular that there is no charge on such an occasion where trust property is secured by a mortgage or other borrowing."

CHAPTER 31

INDEMNITIES FOR EXECUTORS AND TRUSTEES

Introduction

This chapter considers indemnities[1] which trustees may seek in various circumstances: **31.1**

(1) Trustees may seek indemnities on transferring trust property to beneficiaries (individuals or new trusts) absolutely entitled under the terms of the trust or will.

(2) Retiring trustees may seek indemnities from new trustees.

In the discussion below "current trustees" means the trustees seeking an indemnity and "new trustees/beneficiaries" are those giving the indemnities.

It is necessary to distinguish between:

(1) indemnities conferred by law ("trust law indemnities");
(2) indemnities conferred by specific agreement of new trustees or beneficiaries ("express indemnities").

Trust law indemnities

Section 31 TA 2000 provides a trust law indemnity: **31.2**

---

[1] We use the word "indemnities" widely, to include any right of recovery conferred on trustees. Where the context permits "trustees" includes executors and former trustees. Indemnities on the appointment of separate trustees over a separate part of the trust fund are particularly complicated and not dealt with here.

A trustee—

(a) is entitled to be reimbursed from the trust funds, or
(b) may pay out of the trust funds,

expenses properly incurred by him when acting on behalf of the trust.[2]

Right of trustees to retain trust property as security

31.3   Trustees have a lien over trust property to support their indemnity. The lien is the personal right of the trustees. They may properly retain all or part of the trust property unless reasonable provision is made to ensure that their liabilities will be met.[3]

Right of trustee to refuse to retire

31.4   In general, retiring trustees need only retire if they "desire to be discharged".[4] A trustee is certainly acting properly if he refuses to retire on the grounds that to do so would expose him to liabilities which he would not have if he continued to be a trustee.[5]

The trustees' right to refuse to retire and the trustees' lien provide more or less the same level of protection for the retiring trustees. (In practice it may be more convenient for trustees not to retire than to retire but retain the property.)

Right of executors

31.5   Section 36(10) AEA 1925 provides:

A personal representative may, as a condition of giving an assent or making a conveyance, require security for the discharge of any such duties, debt, or

---

[2] "Trustee" here includes "executor": see s.68(17) TA 1925.
[3] *X v A* [2000] 1 All ER 490; [2000] WTLR 11.
[4] Section 36 TA 1925.
[5] This proposition is supported by:
   (1) *Re Pauling (No.2)* [1964] Ch 303;
   (2) common sense; and
   (3) the statutory provision: It is inherent in the word "desire" that a trustee can have regard to his own wishes and private interests in deciding whether or not he "desires" to be discharged.

liability ... and an assent may be given subject to any legal estate or charge by way of legal mortgage.

Right of former trustees

31.6 A former trustee has a trust law indemnity against the trust fund in the hands of new trustees or beneficiaries.[6]

In particular, since former trustees with unsatisfied trust liabilities have an interest in the trust fund, the new trustees owe a duty to them. It would be a breach of trust for the new trustees to distribute to beneficiaries in a manner which will prejudice known claims of the retiring trustees against the trust fund. Though of course this duty must be balanced against the conflicting duties to other beneficiaries; thus trustees might take a reasonable view and make a distribution.

Limits on trust law indemnities

31.7 Notwithstanding all these rights, it is a truism that a trustee is a fiduciary; that he must act in the interests of the beneficiaries; that he must not make a profit out of the trusteeship.[7] These principles suggest that a trustee is not entitled to seek a financial profit or advantage from exercising the rights set out above. The law is therefore as follows:

(1) Trustees may offer to retire or transfer trust assets only on terms which ensure that they are left in no worse position than they would be if they continued to be trustees or hold trust assets.

(2) Trustees may not properly threaten

   (a) to refuse to retire; or
   (b) to refuse to transfer trust property, holding on to their lien; or
   (c) to refuse to advance or appoint trust property to beneficiaries

---

[6] See *Re Spurling* [1966] 1 WLR 920; *Re Pauling (No.2)* [1964] Ch 303; and the Trust Law Committee paper ("the Proper Protection by Liens Indemnities or Otherwise of Those who Cease to be Trustees") accessible on *www.kcl.ac.uk/schools/law/research/tlc/consult.html*.

[7] Except where the trust instrument so provides; which is not relevant here. Trustee remuneration for work involved in the course of retiring is of course different. In principle the Court would exercise its power to remove a trustee who demanded a sum in return for retiring.

demanding terms which leave them in a better position than if they continued to be trustees.[8]

Are express indemnities needed?

31.8 Trustees do not need express indemnities if trust law indemnities give sufficient protection.

The trust law indemnity is usually more valuable than an unsecured express indemnity which is only as good as the solvency of the trustee or beneficiary who gives it. An express indemnity should be sought only where there is some reason to think it is necessary. There should be some liabilities to justify an indemnity, and a reason to think that the trust law indemnities may be inadequate. The fact that the beneficiary is not in the same country as the current trustees may be a valid reason.

Negotiating indemnities

31.9 The first step is to identify any potential claims and liabilities of trustees. It is in everyone's interest that these should be known by all parties. It is not possible to compile a full list, but the following are the most common issues:

- IHT on PET by life tenant on termination of estate interest in possession within seven years.[9]

- IHT on PET by settlor on gift to estate IP trust within seven years (less common after 22 March 2006).

- CGT on current year gains even (unfairly) gains accruing after a retirement.

---

[8] Authority is not needed as this proposition is self-evident. But for examples see *ATC (Cayman) Ltd v Rothschild Trust Cayman Ltd* 9 ITELR 36 at [25]: "It can seldom if ever be appropriate for a trustee to exert undue pressure to secure its own entitlements, to the detriment of its beneficiaries, by withholding the entire or very large portions of the trust fund." Likewise *Re the Carafe Trust* [2005] JLR 159 [2006] WTLR 1329, 8 ITELR 29 accessible on www.jerseylaw.je at [37]:

"A retiring trustee is entitled to be paid its fees before retiring. However, fee disputes often arise. In those circumstances, a trustee is entitled to security for its disputed fees. But it is not entitled to exert improper pressure to agree the fees by withholding the entire trust fund; nor is it entitled to security over the whole trust fund. An escrow arrangement of the nature proposed gives the retiring trustee all the security to which it is entitled."

Likewise *Virani v Guernsey International Trustees Ltd* at [59] (Trustees tactical intransigence to obtain a better identity penalised by indemnity costs order).

[9] If this is covered by insurance, the current trustees may consider retaining the policies in their own names. In calculating the tax exposure, one cannot assume that agricultural or business property relief will apply, as a subsequent sale may disapply the relief: s.113A, 124A IHTA 1984.

- CGT on migration within subsequent 12 months if there is a proposal to migrate the trust (in practice exceptional).[10]
- Unpaid CGT following a hold-over to a beneficiary who becomes non-resident and fails to pay within 12 months.[11]
- Claims by the settlor for reimbursement of tax under statutory indemnities[12]
- Contractual liabilities of current trustees: possibilities include liabilities under leases; warranties and indemnities on share sale agreements; and derivative contracts (options, futures, etc.) which trustees may enter into in the course of managing trust investments.
- Trustees fees.

Conflicts of interest

There is a potential conflict between the current trustees (who may want as generous an indemnity as possible) and new trustees or beneficiaries (who want to give a limited indemnity). If the parties are separately represented, the matter is straightforward; but that is rare. **31.10**

There are many permutations. In cases where solicitors act for current trustees and beneficiaries/new trustees (despite a potential of conflict between two sets of clients) it is considered that in a straightforward case the solicitors may act for both parties with written consent.[13] However, in cases where:

(1) solicitors are the current trustees (potential conflict of interest between themselves and beneficiaries/new trustees); or

(2) there is some other more difficult problem (eg the problem of indemnities from more than one beneficiary)

solicitors should not act for both sides.

---

[10] See 30.4 (Drafting an appointment/retirement of new trustees). The change is in some cases overridden by EU law. See the next fn.
[11] Section 168(7) TCGA 1992. This charge is overridden by EU law if the beneficiary moves to another Member State: see the EU Commission Communication "Exit Taxes" 19 December 2006 COM (2006) 825 accessible on www.*ec.europa.eu/taxation_customs/resources/documents/taxation/COM(2006)825_en.pdf* discussed Taxation of Foreign Domiciliaries, 6th edn (2007) Ch.5 (Exit Charges).
[12] Section 78 and Sch.5 para.6 TCGA 1992; ss.538 and 646 ITTOIA 2005.
[13] Solicitors Code of Conduct rule 3.02(1). The parties have a substantially common interest, namely, their interest in good administration of the trust. The code of conduct is accessible on *www.sra.org.uk*.

Solicitors should make it clear for whom they are acting and the terms of their retainer. If the solicitors are (or are only acting for) the current trustees, they should write to the new trustees/beneficiaries along these lines: *"We consider these are normal and proper indemnities for you to give. However we cannot advise you on this aspect as we are acting for the current trustees. If you have any doubts we recommend you seek independent advice."*

For younger beneficiaries, especially, watch undue influence.

Indemnity from beneficiaries

31.11 Indemnities from beneficiaries are more straightforward than indemnities from new professional trustees. If a single beneficiary receives the entire trust fund, he will normally be content to give an indemnity binding his estate, without limit of amount, without limit of time, for all liabilities properly incurred by the trustees. The risks in doing so are normally theoretical[14] and the cost and inconvenience of drafting to cater for the risk exceeds any advantage that might result.

Suppose a single beneficiary receives part of the trust fund absolutely, the trustees retaining the other part. In this case no indemnity should normally be necessary, as the trustees have recourse to the retained funds. But (exceptionally) if an indemnity is needed, it should be limited to liabilities attributable to the distributed funds.

A problem arises in the case of multiple beneficiaries. Suppose three beneficiaries, A, B and C receive the entire trust fund absolutely. An uncapped indemnity to the current trustees by A is quite a different matter from an indemnity which is limited to liabilities relating to A's share of the fund. It is suggested that the indemnity ought to be so limited. If that is problematic (e.g. B is financially insecure) then the trustees ought to deal with the matter by obtaining security for liabilities relating to B's share: they should not expect A to shoulder the risk of B's default. In practice, in straightforward cases, this may be ignored for the sake of simplicity, but this course requires the beneficiaries to take a risk which should be noted, understood and accepted.

Indemnity from new trustees

31.12 Of course new trustees can give an express indemnity to the current trustees if they wish. The important question is whether they can later seek

---

[14] The risk being that (1) a claim may be made against the trustee which exceeds the value of the entire trust fund and (2) the loss might have fallen on the trustee instead of the beneficiary, but for the unlimited extent of the indemnity.

reimbursement from the trust fund for sums they have to pay out under that indemnity.[15] This requires that they have power to give the indemnity and exercise it properly.[16]

Power is usually conferred expressly by the trust. The power is properly exercised if it is given in the context of an agreement under which:

(1) the new trustees indemnify the current trustees against trust liabilities; and in return

(2) the retiring trustees abandon their lien and transfer the trust property to the new trustees.[17]

The new trustees may be fair but cannot be generous to the current trustees. New trustees cannot in principle recover from the trust fund for payments they have to make under express indemnities if a reasonably careful trustee would not have given the indemnity.[18] This raises the question: what is a reasonable indemnity? The starting point is to say:

> The New Trustee covenants with the Retiring Trustee to indemnify it against all costs and expenses (including tax and interest) incurred
>
> (1) in its capacity as trustee or by reason of having acted as Trustee of the Settlement; or
> (2) by reason of or in connection with entering into or exercising rights under this deed.

Indemnity for breach of trust

An indemnity for breach of trust by the current trustees will not normally be reasonable. The following limitation is recommended:

31.13

> This indemnity applies only to liabilities in respect of which
>
> (1) the retiring trustees are entitled to reimbursement out of the Trust Fund or
> (2) would have been so entitled had they continued to be trustees.

---

[15] The liability of the new trustees under an express indemnity is personal unless (unusually) the deed provides otherwise; see 21.44 (Power to give indemnities).

[16] Section 15(f) TA 1925 would provide such a power in some cases: see Paul Matthews "Indemnities for retiring trustees", OTPR (1990) Vol.1, Issue 2, p.27 accessible on *www.kessler.co.uk*.

[17] See *ATC (Cayman) v Rothschild* [2007] WTLR 951 (Cayman Islands Grand Court) in which it was held that the new trustees indemnified the retired trustees by undertaking to the effect that it would withhold a certain sum of moeny and not allow the trust funds to be depleted below that amount for a specified period and this was held to be a proper exericse of the express power and not a fetter on the trustees' discretions.

[18] The amendment to s.15 TA 1925 by the TA 2000 is significant here. New trustees cannot give express indemnities that damage the trust fund in a situation where they have acted negligently but in good faith. A decision to give over-generous indemnities may conceivably be a defensible commercial decision, e.g. if it is to facilitate a retirement and reduce costs.

Time limit to indemnity

31.14 In the absence of special circumstances, it is suggested that indemnities given by new trustees should expire after a fixed time. This makes administration easier on subsequent appointments of new trustees or distributions of trust capital. Six years (as the usual limitation period) seems appropriate. The following clause is recommended:

> This indemnity applies only to liabilities notified to the New Trustees in writing within six years from the date of this deed.

Cap on amount payable under indemnity

31.15 If the amount of the indemnity is unlimited, the new trustees are personally at risk if their trust fund is worth less than the claim. This will not be acceptable to professional new trustees.

The indemnity could be capped so that it is limited to the amount of the trust fund at the time that the trustees have to make a payment under the indemnity (so the trust fund is never worth less than the claim.)

The difficulty is that capital distributions to beneficiaries will reduce the value of the indemnity. It is difficult to see the point of an express indemnity on such terms since it gives the current trustees nothing more than they are entitled to under the trust law indemnity.

The indemnity could provide that in the event of capital distributions, the new trustees are released from liability under the indemnity to the extent that the beneficiary receives assets and enters into a similar indemnity for the current trustees. This solution is fair but complicated and expensive. If however the indemnity is time limited (see above) the complications are bearable since after six years the indemnity can be ignored. An alternative is to say:

> The liabilities of any person under this Deed to any indemnified person shall not exceed the sums
>
> (1) available from the Trust Fund to the person liable; or
> (2) which would have been available from the Trust Fund to the person liable if he had acted with reasonable care to that indemnified person.

This forces a trustee to have regard to the interests of the retiring trustees and may discourage him recklessly distributing the trust fund (which of course he should not do in any event).

Death of new trustee

The current trustees may want an indemnity which binds the estate of the person giving the indemnity. However this would complicate the administration of his estate, and would not be acceptable to a professional trustee. Moreover, in practice, the enforcement of the indemnity may be difficult. So the better course is that the indemnity does not bind the estate of a deceased person. This does not affect corporate trustees of course. The following clause is recommended:

31.16

> On the death of a New Trustee (not being sole trustee) the personal representatives of the deceased New Trustee shall be discharged from all liability under this indemnity.

Retirement of new trustee

The current trustee may want an indemnity which continues after the retirement of a new trustee. However that would not be acceptable to the new trustee, since he will no longer have direct control over the trust fund. The fairer course is that the new trustee should be released on retirement provided that the continuing trustees are liable. The following clause is recommended:

31.17

> If a New Trustees ceases to be a trustee (otherwise than on death) that New Trustee shall be discharged from all liability under this indemnity, if the persons who are trustees immediately after the New Trustee ceases to be a trustee enter or have entered into a covenant with the Retiring Trustees in terms similar to this Deed.

Multiple trustees

If a *share* of a trust fund is given to trust A (with other shares given to beneficiaries or other trusts), then in principle the trustees of trust A should *not* give an indemnity for liabilities which are attributable to other shares. At the very least, if they give such an indemnity, it should be subordinated to the liability of the other shares, and that liability may need to be secured to protect trust A.

31.18

Security for indemnity

It will always be in the interest of the current trustees that their indemnity is secured. However, security brings inconvenience and additional costs.

31.19

New trustees should hesitate to agree to security unless there is some good reason. In practice indemnities are usually given without security. A power to demand security if that becomes necessary, e.g. if anticipated liabilities exceed 50% of trust assets, may be a fair compromise.

Proper law and jurisdiction clause

31.20 If all the parties are in England and Wales a proper law and jurisdiction clause should not be necessary.

PART 2

PRECEDENTS

PRECEDENTS FOR LIFETIME TRUSTS

INTEREST IN POSSESSION TRUST FOR ADULT BENEFICIARY

This settlement is made [date] between:

1 [Name of settlor] of [address] ("the Settlor") of the one part and
2 2.1   [Name of first trustee] of [address] and
   2.2   [Name of second trustee] of [address]
("the Original Trustees") of the other part.

Whereas this Settlement shall be known as the [name-of-settlor Settlement 2008].
Now this deed witnesses as follows:

1 Definitions

In this settlement:

1.1 **"[Adam]"** means [Adam Smith] the [son] of the Settlor.
1.2 **"The Beneficiaries"** means:
    1.2.1 The descendants of the Settlor.
    1.2.2 The Spouses of the descendants of the Settlor.
    1.2.3 The Surviving Spouses of the descendants of the Settlor.
    1.2.4 The Surviving Spouse of the Settlor.
    1.2.5 Any Person or class of Persons added to the class of Beneficiaries by the Trustees by deed with the consent in writing of:
        1.2.5.1 the Settlor or

1.2.5.2 two Beneficiaries (if the Settlor has died or has no capacity to consent).

1.3 **"Spouse"** includes a civil partner within the meaning of section 1 Civil Partnership Act 2004 and a person is a **"Surviving Spouse"** whether or not they have remarried or entered into another civil partnership.

1.4 **"Person"** includes a person anywhere in the world and includes a Trustee.

1.5 **"The Trustees"** means the Original Trustees or the trustees of this Settlement for the time being.

1.6 **"The Trust Fund"** means:

1.6.1 property transferred to the Trustees to hold on the terms of this Settlement; and

1.6.2 all property from time to time representing the above.

1.7 **"The Trust Period"** means the period of 80 years beginning with the date of this Settlement. That is the perpetuity period applicable to this Settlement under the rule against perpetuities.

1.8 **"Trust Property"** means any property comprised in the Trust Fund.

2 Trust Income

Subject to the Overriding Powers below:

2.1 The Trustees shall pay the income of the Trust Fund to [Adam] during [his] life.

2.2 Subject to that, if [Adam] dies during the Trust Period, the Trustees shall pay the income of the Trust Fund to [Adam]'s surviving spouse or surviving Civil Partner during his or her life.

2.3 Subject to that, during the Trust Period, the Trustees shall pay or apply the income of the Trust Fund to or for the benefit of any Beneficiaries as the Trustees think fit.[1]

---

[1] It would be possible to put in a power to accumulate income during the accumulation period. However, by the time that Adam (and his spouse) have died, the 21-year accumulation period will in all probability have expired, so the clause would not have any eVect, and it is simpler not to have it. The same result can be achieved by use of the overriding powers.

3 Overriding Powers

The Trustees shall have the following powers ("Overriding Powers"):

3.1 *Power of appointment*

3.1.1 The Trustees may appoint that they shall hold any Trust Property for the benefit of any Beneficiaries, on such terms as the Trustees think fit.

3.1.2 An appointment may create any provisions and in particular:

3.1.2.1 discretionary trusts;

3.1.2.2 dispositive or administrative powers; exercisable by any Person.

3.1.3 An appointment shall be made by deed and may be revocable or irrevocable.

3.1.4 An appointment may provide for accumulation of income within the period of 21 years from the date of this settlement, or such longer period as is permitted by law.

3.2 *Transfer of Trust Property to another settlement*

3.2.1 The Trustees may by deed declare that they hold any Trust Property on trust to transfer it to trustees of another settlement, wherever established, to hold on the terms of that settlement, freed and released from the terms of this Settlement.

3.2.2 The Trustees shall only exercise this power if:

3.2.2.1 every Person who may benefit is (or would if living be) a Beneficiary; or

3.2.2.2 with the consent in writing of
(a) the Settlor, or
(b) two Beneficiaries (after the death of the Settlor).

3.3 *Power of advancement*

The Trustees may pay or apply any Trust Property for the advancement or benefit of any Beneficiary.

3.4 The Overriding Powers shall be exercisable only:

3.4.1 during the Trust Period; and

3.4.2 at a time when there are at least two Trustees, or the Trustee is a company carrying on a business which consists of or includes the management of trusts.

4 Default Clause

Subject to that, the Trust Fund shall be held on trust for [Adam or specify default trusts as appropriate] absolutely.

5 Appointment of Trustees

The power of appointing trustees is exercisable:

5.1 by the Settlor during [his] life and by will, and after [his] death

5.2 by [Adam] after [he] has reached the age of 25 during his life and by will.

6 Further Provisions

The provisions set out in the schedule below shall have effect.
[For a shorter form, say instead of the above:

"The standard provisions of the Society of Trust and Estate Practitioners (1st Edition) shall apply with the deletion of paragraph 5. Section 11 Trusts of Land & Appointment of Trustees Act 1996 (consultation with beneficiaries) shall not apply."

And omit the schedule.]

7 Exclusion of Settlor and Spouse

Notwithstanding anything else in this Settlement, no power conferred by this settlement shall be exercisable, and no provision shall operate so as to allow Trust Property or its income to become payable to or applicable for the benefit of the Settlor or the Spouse of the Settlor in any circumstances whatsoever.

8 Irrevocability

This Settlement is irrevocable.
In witness, [etc.]

THE SCHEDULE: FURTHER PROVISIONS

[Here set out the administrative provisions suitable to an IP trust settlement: see *"Administrative provisions for lifetime settlement"* below. This is set out in full on the CD.]

DISCRETIONARY TRUST

This settlement is made [date] between:

1 [Name of settlor] of [address] ("the Settlor") of the one part and
2 2.1   [Name of first trustee] of [address] and
   2.2   [Name of second trustee] of [address]

("the Original Trustees") of the other part.

Whereas:

1 The Settlor has [two] children:

   1.1 [Adam Smith] ("[Adam]") who was born on [date] and
   1.2 [Mary Smith] ("[Mary]") who was born on [date].

2 This Settlement shall be known as the [Name-of-settlor Settlement 2008].

Now this deed witnesses as follows:

1 Definitions

In this settlement:

1.1 **"The Accumulation Period"** means the period of 21 years beginning with the date of this Settlement.

1.2 **"The Beneficiaries"** means:

   1.2.1 The descendants of the Settlor.
   1.2.2 The Spouses of the descendants of the Settlor.
   1.2.3 The Surviving Spouses of the descendants of the Settlor.
   1.2.4 The Surviving Spouse of the Settlor.
   1.2.5 Any Person or class of Persons added to the class of Beneficiaries by the Trustees by deed with the consent in writing of:

1.2.5.1 the Settlor or

1.2.5.2 two Beneficiaries (if the Settlor has died or has no capacity to consent).

1.3 **"Spouse"** includes a civil partner within the meaning of section 1 Civil Partnership Act 2004 and person is a **"Surviving Spouse"** whether or not they have remarried or entered into another civil partnership.

1.4 **"Person"** includes a person anywhere in the world and includes a Trustee.

1.5 **"The Trustees"** means the Original Trustees or the trustees of this Settlement for the time being.

1.6 **"The Trust fund"** means:

1.6.1 property transferred to the Trustees to hold on the terms of this Settlement; and

1.6.2 all property from time to time representing the above.

1.7 **"The Trust Period"** means the period of 80 years beginning with the date of this Settlement. That is the perpetuity period applicable to this Settlement under the rule against perpetuities.

1.8 **"Trust Property"** means any property comprised in the Trust Fund.

2 Trust Income

Subject to the Overriding Powers below:

2.1 The Trustees may accumulate the whole or part of the income of the Trust Fund during the Accumulation Period. That income shall be added to the Trust Fund.

2.2 The Trustees shall pay or apply the remainder of the income to or for the benefit of any Beneficiaries, as the Trustees think fit, during the Trust Period.

3 Overriding Powers

The Trustees shall have the following powers ("Overriding Powers"):

3.1 *Power of appointment*

3.1.1 The Trustees may appoint that they shall hold any Trust Property for the benefit of any Beneficiaries, on such terms as the Trustees think fit.

3.1.2 An appointment may create any provisions and in particular:

3.1.2.1 discretionary trusts;

3.1.2.2 dispositive or administrative powers; exercisable by any Person.

3.1.3 An appointment shall be made by deed and may be revocable or irrevocable.

3.2 *Transfer of Trust Property to another settlement*

3.2.1 The Trustees may be deed declare that they hold any Trust Property on trust to transfer it to trustees of another settlement, wherever established, to hold on the terms of that settlement, freed and released from the terms of this Settlement.

3.2.2 The Trustees shall only exercise this power if:

3.2.2.1 every Person who may benefit is (or would if living be) a Beneficiary; or

3.2.2.2 with the consent in writing of

(a) the Settlor, or

(b) two Beneficiaries (after the death of the Settlor).

3.3 *Power of advancement*

The Trustees may pay or apply any Trust Property for the advancement or benefit of any Beneficiary.

3.4 The Overriding Powers shall be exercisable only:

3.4.1 during the Trust Period; and

3.4.2 at a time when there are at least two Trustees, or the Trustee is a company carrying on a business which consists of or includes the management of trusts.

4 Default Clause

Subject to that, the Trust Fund shall be held on trust for [Adam and Mary in equal shares – or specify default trusts as appropriate] absolutely.

5 Appointment of Trustees

The power of appointing trustees is exercisable by the Settlor during [his] life and by will.

6 Further Provisions

The provisions set out in the schedule below shall have effect.[1]

7 Exclusion of Settlor and Spouse

Notwithstanding anything else in this Settlement, no power conferred by this settlement shall be exercisable, and no provision shall operate so as to allow Trust Property or its income to become payable to or applicable for the benefit of the Settlor or the Spouse of the Settlor in any circumstances whatsoever.

8 Irrevocability

This Settlement is irrevocable.

In witness, [etc.][1]

THE SCHEDULE: FURTHER PROVISIONS

[Here set out the administrative provisions suitable to a discretionary trust: see *"Administrative provisions for lifetime settlement"* below. This is set out in full on the CD.]

---

[1] *For a shorter from, say instead:*

"The standard provisions of the Society of Trust and Estate Practitioners (1st Edition) shall apply with the deletion of paragraph 5. Section 11 Trusts of Land & Appointment of Trustees Act 1996 (consultation with beneficiaries) shall not apply."

And omit the schedule.

CHARITABLE TRUST

This Charitable Trust is made [date] between

1 [Name] of [address] ("the Settlor") of the one part and
2 2.1 [Name] of [address] and
   2.2 [Name] of [address]

("the Original Trustees") of the other part.

Now this deed witnesses as follows:

1 Definitions

In this Deed:

1.1 **"The Accumulation Period"** means the period of 21 years beginning with the date of this Trust.

1.2 **"Charity"** means any institution which:

   1.2.1 is a charity for the purposes of the Charities Act 2006; or

   1.2.2 which is established under the law of Scotland or Northern Ireland, and to which the Commissioners for Her Majesty's Revenue and Customs have given intimation, which has not subsequently been withdrawn, that tax relief will be due in respect of income of the body which is applicable and applied to charitable purposes only.

1.3 **"Civil Partner"** has the same meaning as in section 1 Civil Partnership Act 2004.

1.4 **"Person"** includes a person anywhere in the world and includes a Trustee

1.5 **"The Trustees"** means the Original Trustees or the trustees of this Charitable Trust for the time being.

1.6 **"The Trust Fund"** means:
    1.6.1 Property transferred to the Trustees to hold on the terms of this Charitable Trust and
    1.6.2 Property from time to time representing the above.

1.7 **"Trust Property"** means any property comprised in the Trust Fund.

2 Name of Charitable Trust

This Charitable Trust shall be known as the [name of settlor] Charitable Trust or by such name as the Trustees shall determine.

3 Trust Income

3.1 Subject to the Powers over Capital below, the Trustees shall pay or apply the income of the Trust Fund to such Charities or for such charitable purposes as the Trustees think fit.

3.2 The Trustees may accumulate any part of the income of the Trust Fund during the Accumulation Period or such other period as may be permitted by law.

4 Powers over Capital

The Trustees shall have the following powers:

4.1 Power of appointment:
    4.1.1 The Trustees may appoint that they shall hold any Trust Property on such charitable trusts as the Trustees think fit.
    4.1.2 An appointment may create any provisions and in particular:
        4.1.2.1 discretionary trusts
        4.1.2.2 dispositive or administrative powers
        exercisable by any Person, but at all times this Charitable Trust shall remain a Charity.
    4.1.3 An appointment shall be made by deed and may be revocable or irrevocable.

4.1.4 The Trustees shall send to the Charity Commissioners a copy of any appointment (but failure to do this shall not invalidate the appointment).

4.2 Power of advancement

The Trustees may pay or transfer any Trust Property to any Charity and may apply any Trust Property for any charitable purposes.

5 Further Provisions

The provisions set out in the schedule below shall have effect in furtherance of the charitable purposes of this Charitable Trust but not otherwise.

6 Exclusion of settlor and non-charitable purposes

Notwithstanding anything else in this deed, no power conferred by this Charitable Trust shall be exercisable, and no provision shall operate so as to allow Trust Property or its income:

6.1 to become payable to or applicable for the benefit of the Settlor or the spouse or Civil Partner of the Settlor; or

6.2 to be applied for any purpose that is not charitable.

7 New Trustees

The power of appointing trustees is exercisable by the Settlor during his life or by will

IN WITNESS ETC.

THE SCHEDULE

[Here set out administrative provisions appropriate to a charity; see 24.7 (Administrative provisions for charities). This is set out in full on the CD.]

WILL 1
DISCRETIONARY WILL TRUST

I, [Name of testator] of [address] declare this to be my last Will.

1 I revoke all my earlier testamentary dispositions.

2 Appointment of Executors

I appoint:

  2.1 [Name] of [address] and

  2.2 [Name] of [address]

  to be my executors and Trustees.

3 Personal Chattels

I give my personal chattels (as defined in section 55 of the Administration of Estates Act 1925) to my [Spouse] absolutely.

4 [Other legacies, appointment of guardians, etc., follow here.]

5 Residuary Estate

  5.1 My executors shall:

    5.1.1 pay my debts, funeral and testamentary expenses, legacies and Inheritance Tax on all property which vests in them; and
    5.1.2 hold the remainder ("my Residuary Estate") as set out below.

  5.2 Debts, funeral and testamentary expenses, legacies and Inheritance Tax shall be payable out of the capital of my estate (subject to the Trustees' administrative powers relating to capital and income).

6 Definitions

In this Will:

6.1 **"The Accumulation Period"** means the period of 21 years beginning with the date of my death.

6.2 **"The Beneficiaries"** means:

    6.2.1 My Spouse.[1]
    6.2.2 My descendants.
    6.2.3 The Spouses of my descendants.
    6.2.4 The Surviving Spouses of my descendants.
    6.2.5 Any Person or class of Persons added to the class of Beneficiaries by the Trustees by deed with the consent in writing of two Beneficiaries.
    6.2.6 [Any favoured charity].
    6.2.7 At any time during which no descendant of mine is living:

        6.2.7.1 [*specify "fall back" beneficiaries if desired, e.g. nieces and nephews and their families*]
        6.2.7.2 [*any company, body or trust established for charitable purposes only*].

6.3 **"Spouse"** includes a civil partner within the meaning of section 1 Civil Partnership Act 2004 and a person is a **"Surviving Spouse"** whether or not they have remarried or entered into another civil partnership.

6.4 **"Person"** includes a person anywhere in the world and includes a Trustee.

6.5 **"The Trustees"** means my executors or the trustees for the time being.

6.6 **"The Trust Fund"** means:

    6.6.1 my Residuary Estate and
    6.6.2 all property from time to time representing the above.

6.7 **"The Trust Period"** means the period of 80 years beginning with the date of my death. That period is the perpetuity period applicable to this Will under the rule against perpetuities.

6.8 **"Trust Property"** means any property comprised in the Trust Fund.

---

[1] Omit reference to "my spouse" if testator is not married.

7 Trust Income

Subject to the Overriding Powers below:

7.1 The Trustees may accumulate the whole or part of the income of the Trust Fund during the Accumulation Period. That income shall be added to the Trust Fund.

7.2 The Trustees shall pay or apply the remainder of the income to or for the benefit of any Beneficiaries, as the Trustees think fit, during the Trust Period.

8 Overriding Powers

The Trustees shall have the following powers ("Overriding Powers"):

8.1 *Power of appointment*

8.1.1 The Trustees may appoint that they shall hold any Trust Property for the benefit of any Beneficiaries, on such terms as the Trustees think fit.

8.1.2 An appointment may create any provisions and in particular:

8.1.2.1 discretionary trusts;
8.1.2.2 dispositive or administrative powers;

exercisable by anyPerson.

8.1.3 An appointment shall be made by deed and may be revocable or irrevocable.

8.2 *Transfer of Trust Property to another settlement*

8.2.1 The Trustees may by deed declare that they hold any Trust Property on trust to transfer it to trustees of another settlement, wherever established, to hold on the terms of that settlement, freed and released from the terms of this Will.

8.2.2 The Trustees shall only exercise this power if:

8.2.2.1 every Person who may benefit is (or would if living be) a Beneficiary; or
8.2.2.2 with the consent in writing of two Beneficiaries.

8.3 *Power of advancement*

The Trustees may pay or apply any Trust Property for the advancement or benefit of any Beneficiary.

8.4 The Overriding Powers shall be exercisable only:

    8.4.1 during the Trust Period; and

    8.4.2 at a time when there are at least two Trustees, or the Trustee is a company carrying on a business which consists of or includes the management of trusts, or when the power to appoint additional Trustees cannot be exercised.

9 Default Clause

Subject to that, the Trust Fund shall be held on trust for [my children Adam and Mary in equal shares—or specify default beneficiaries as appropriate] absolutely.

10 Standard Provisions

The Standard Provisions of the Society of Trust and Estate Practitioners (1st Edition) shall apply with the deletion of paragraph 5. Section 11 of the Trusts of Land and Appointment of Trustees Act 1996 (consultation with beneficiaries) shall not apply.
 [Alternatively say: "The provisions set out in the Schedule below shall have effect" and set out the provisions in full in the schedule. The CD with this book has the form.]

Signed by [name of testator] to give effect to this Will,
in the presence of two witnesses present at the same time,
who have each signed this Will in the presence of the Testator.

[Signature of Testator]

Date

1st Witness
Address

2nd Witness
Address

WILL 2
LIFE INTEREST FOR SURVIVING SPOUSE/CIVIL PARTNER

I, [Name of testator] of [address] declare this to be my last Will.

1 I revoke all my earlier testamentary dispositions.

2 Appointment of Executors

I appoint:

    2.1 [Name] of [address] and

    2.2 [Name] of [address]

to be my executors and Trustees.

3 Personal Chattels

I give my personal chattels (as defined in section 55 of the Administration of Estates Act 1925) to my Spouse absolutely.
[Other legacies, appointment of guardians, etc., follow here.]

4 Residuary Estate

    4.1 My executors shall:

        4.1.1 pay my debts, funeral and testamentary expenses, legacies and Inheritance Tax on all property which vests in them; and

        4.1.2 hold the remainder ("my Residuary Estate") as set out below.

    4.2 Debts, funeral and testamentary expenses, legacies and Inheritance Tax shall be payable out of the capital of my estate (subject to the Trustees' administrative powers relating to capital and income).

5 Definitions

In this Will:

5.1 **"The Accumulation Period"** means the period of 21 years beginning with the date of my death.

5.2 **"The Beneficiaries"** means:

5.2.1 My Spouse.
5.2.2 My descendants.
5.2.3 The Spouses of my descendants.
5.2.4 The Surviving Spouses of my descendants.
5.2.5 Any Person or class of Persons added to the class of Beneficiaries by the Trustees by deed with the consent in writing of two Beneficiaries.
5.2.6 [*Any favoured charity*].
5.2.7 At any time during which no descendant of mine is living:

5.2.7.1 [*specify "fall back" beneficiaries if desired, e.g. nieces and nephews and their families*]
5.2.7.2 [*any company, body or trust established for charitable purposes only*].

5.3 **"Spouse"** includes a civil partner within the meaning of section 1 Civil Partnership Act 2004 and a person is a **"Surviving Spouse"** whether or not they have remarried or entered into another civil partnership.

5.4 **"Person"** includes a person anywhere in the world and includes a Trustee.

5.5 **"The Trustees"** means my executors or the trustees for the time being.

5.6 **"The Trust Fund"** means:

5.6.1 my Residuary Estate; and
5.6.2 all property from time to time representing the above.

5.7 **"The Trust Period"** means the period of 80 years beginning with the date of my death. That period is the perpetuity period applicable to this Will under the rule against perpetuities.

5.8 **"Trust Property"** means any property comprised in the Trust Fund.

6 Trust Income

Subject to the Overriding Powers below:

6.1 The Trustees shall pay the income of the Trust Fund to my Spouse during [her] life.

6.2 Subject to that, the Trustees may accumulate the whole or part of the income of the Trust Fund during the Accumulation Period. That income shall be added to the Trust Fund.

6.3 Subject to that, during the Trust Period, the Trustees shall pay or apply the income of the Trust Fund to or for the benefit of any Beneficiaries as the Trustees think fit.

7 Overriding Powers

The Trustees shall have the following powers ("Overriding Powers"):

7.1 *Power of appointment*

7.1.1 The Trustees may appoint that they shall hold any Trust Property for the benefit of any Beneficiaries, on such terms as the Trustees think fit.

7.1.2 An appointment may create any provisions and in particular:

7.1.2.1 discretionary trusts;
7.1.2.2 dispositive or administrative powers;

exercisable by any Person.

7.1.3 An appointment shall be made by deed and may be revocable or irrevocable.

7.2 *Transfer of Trust Property to another settlement*

7.2.1 The Trustees may by deed declare that they hold any Trust Property on trust to transfer it to trustees of another settlement, wherever established, to hold on the terms of that settlement, freed and released from the terms of this Will.

7.2.2 The Trustees shall only exercise this power if:

7.2.2.1 every Person who may benefit is (or would if living be) a Beneficiary; or
7.2.2.2 with the consent in writing of two Beneficiaries.

7.3 *Power of advancement*

The Trustees may pay or apply any Trust Property for the advancement or benefit of any Beneficiary.

7.4 The Overriding Powers shall be exercisable only:

7.4.1 during the Trust Period; and

7.4.2 at a time when there are at least two Trustees, or the Trustee is a company carrying on a business which consists of or includes the management of trusts, or when the power to appoint additional Trustees cannot be exercised.

8 Default Clause

Subject to that, the Trust Fund shall be held on trust for [my children Adam and Mary in equal shares—or specify default beneficiaries as appropriate] absolutely.

9 Standard Provisions

The Standard Provisions of the Society of Trust and Estate Practitioners (1st Edition) shall apply with the deletion of paragraph 5. Section 11 of the Trusts of Land and Appointment of Trustees Act 1996 (consultation with beneficiaries) shall not apply.

[Alternatively say: "The provisions set out in the Schedule below shall have effect" and set out the provisions in full in the schedule. The CD with this book has the form.]

Signed by [name of testator] to give effect to this Will,
in the presence of two witnesses present at the same time,
who have each signed this Will in the presence of the Testator.

[Signature of Testator]

Date

1st Witness
Address

2nd Witness
Address

WILL 3
LIFE INTEREST FOR SURVIVING SPOUSE/CIVIL PARTNER WITH ABSOLUTE GIFT OF NIL RATE SUM

I, [Name of testator] of [address] declare this to be my last Will.

1 I revoke all my earlier testamentary dispositions.

2 Appointment of Executors

I appoint:

    2.1 [Name] of [address] and

    2.2 [Name] of [address]

to be my executors and Trustees.

3 Personal Chattels

I give my personal chattels (as defined in section 55 of the Administration of Estates Act 1925) to my Spouse absolutely.

4 Gift of Untransferable Nil Rate Sum

    4.1 I give the Untransferable Nil Rate Sum to [my children in equal shares] absolutely.[1]

    4.2 **"The Untransferable Nil Rate Sum"** here means the maximum amount of cash which I can give on the terms of this clause:

---

[1] It is not necessary to include a provision for lapse (children predeceasing testator leaving issue) because s.33 Wills Act 1837 does this. An express provision for lapse could be put in the clause, to make the position clear to a lay reader, but the form is complex. We prefer to omit it. A provision for lapse would be appropriate if gift is not to children or descendants of the testator (e.g., a gift to a class including stepchildren).

4.2.1 without incurring any liability to Inheritance Tax on my death; and

4.2.2 without reducing the amount by which the Nil Rate Band applicable on the death of my Spouse would (apart from this clause) be increased under section 8A Inheritance Tax Act 1984,

but subject to the following clauses.

4.2.3 It shall be assumed that:

4.2.3.1 any claim which may increase the Untransferable Nil Rate Sum shall be made; and

4.2.3.2 my Spouse will not remarry or enter into a civil partnership after my death.

4.2.4 My executors shall make a claim under section 8B Inheritance Tax Act 1984.[2]

4.2.5 The Untransferable Nil Rate Sum shall be nil if:

4.2.5.1 Inheritance Tax has been abolished at the time of my death; or

4.2.5.2 I am not [married] at the time of my death.

4.2.6 Any other legacy given by my will or any codicil shall be paid in priority to the Untransferable Nil Rate Sum.

4.2.7 My executors may ascertain and fix the amount of the Untransferable Nil Rate Sum so as to bind all persons interested under this Will if the executors have discharged the duty of care set out in section 1(1) Trustee Act 2000.

4.2.8 The Untransferable Nil Rate Sum shall not exceed £1,000,000.[3]

[Other legacies, appointment of guardians, etc., follow here.]

5 Residuary Estate

5.1 My executors shall:

5.1.1 pay my debts, funeral and testamentary expenses, legacies and Inheritance Tax on all property which vests in them; and

5.1.2 hold the remainder ("my Residuary Estate") as set out below.

---

[2] This sub-clause is only needed if the testator (having survived a previous spouse) has more than 1 nil rate band: the will should impose a duty so a claim must be made.

[3] Since this is a simple absolute gift of the untransferable nil rate sum, this clause does not contain a £5,000 de minimis provision (intended to prevent a trust of a very small trust fund).

5.2 Debts, funeral and testamentary expenses, legacies and Inheritance Tax shall be payable out of the capital of my estate (subject to the Trustees' administrative powers relating to capital and income).

6 Definitions

In this Will:

6.1 **"The Accumulation Period"** means the period of 21 years beginning with the date of my death.

6.2 **"The Beneficiaries"** means:

    6.2.1 My Spouse.
    6.2.2 My descendants.
    6.2.3 The Spouses of my descendants.
    6.2.4 The Surviving Spouses of my descendants.
    6.2.5 Any Person or class of Persons added to the class of Beneficiaries by the Trustees by deed with the consent in writing of two Beneficiaries.
    6.2.6 [*Any favoured charity*].
    6.2.7 At any time during which no descendant of mine is living:

        6.2.7.1 [specify *"fall back"* beneficiaries *if desired, e.g. nieces and nephews and their families*]
        6.2.7.2 [*any* company, *body* or trust *established for charitable purposes only*].

6.3 **"Spouse"** includes a civil partner within the meaning of section 1 Civil Partnership Act 2004 and a person is a **"Surviving Spouse"** whether or not they have remarried or entered into another civil partnership.

6.4 **"Person"** includes a person anywhere in the world and includes a Trustee.

6.5 **"The Trustees"** means my executors or the trustees for the time being.

6.6 **"The Trust Fund"** means:

    6.6.1 my Residuary Estate; and
    6.6.2 all property from time to time representing the above.

6.7 **"The Trust Period"** means the period of 80 years beginning with the date of my death. That period is the perpetuity period applicable to this Will under the rule against perpetuities.

6.8 **"Trust Property"** means any part of the Trust Fund.

6.9 **"The Nil Rate Band"** means the upper limit specified in Schedule 1 Inheritance Tax Act 1984.

7 Residuary Estate

Subject to the Overriding Powers below:

7.1 The Trustees shall pay the income of the Trust Fund to my Spouse during [her] life.

7.2 Subject to that, the Trustees may accumulate the whole or any part of the income of the Trust Fund during the Accumulation Period. That income shall be added to the Trust Fund.

7.3 Subject to that, during the Trust Period, the Trustees shall pay or apply the income of the Trust Fund to or for the benefit of any of the Beneficiaries as the Trustees think fit.

8 Overriding Powers

The Trustees shall have the following powers ("Overriding Powers"):

8.1 *Power of appointment*

8.1.1 The Trustees may appoint that they shall hold any Trust Property for the benefit of any Beneficiaries, on such terms as the Trustees think fit.

8.1.2 An appointment may create any provisions and in particular:

8.1.2.1 discretionary trusts;
8.1.2.2 dispositive or administrative powers;

exercisable by any Person.

8.1.3 An appointment shall be made by deed and may be revocable or irrevocable.

8.2 *Transfer of Trust Property to another settlement*

8.2.1 The Trustees may by deed declare that they hold any Trust Property on trust to transfer it to trustees of another settlement, wherever established, to hold on the terms of that settlement, freed and released from the terms of this Will.

8.2.2 The Trustees shall only exercise this power if:

8.2.2.1 every Person who may benefit is (or would if living be) a Beneficiary; or
8.2.2.2 with the consent in writing of two Beneficiaries.

8.3 *Power of advancement*
   The Trustees may pay or apply any Trust Property for the advancement or benefit of any Beneficiary.

8.4 The Overriding Powers shall be exercisable only:

   8.4.1 during the Trust Period; and
   8.4.2 at a time when there are at least two Trustees, or the Trustee is a company carrying on a business which consists of or includes the management of trusts, or when the power to appoint additional Trustees cannot be exercised.

9 Default Clause

Subject to that, the Trust Fund shall be held on trust for [my son Adam - or define the default beneficiary as appropriate] absolutely.

10 Standard Provisions

The Standard Provisions of the Society of Trust and Estate Practitioners (1st Edition) shall apply with the deletion of paragraph 5. Section 11 of the Trusts of Land and Appointment of Trustees Act 1996 (consultation with beneficiaries) shall not apply.

[Alternatively say: "The provisions set out in the Schedule below shall have effect" and set out the provisions in full in the schedule. The CD with this book has the form.]

Signed by [name of testator] to give effect to this Will,
in the presence of two witnesses present at the same time,
who have each signed this Will in the presence of the Testator.

[Signature of Testator]

Date

1st Witness
Address

2nd Witness
Address

WILL 4
LIFE INTEREST FOR SURVIVING SPOUSE/CIVIL PARTNER WITH NIL RATE BAND DISCRETIONARY TRUST

I, [Name of testator] of [address] declare this to be my last Will.

1 I revoke all my earlier testamentary dispositions.

2 Appointment of Executors

I appoint:

    2.1 [Name] of [address] and

    2.2 [Name] of [address]

to be my executors and Trustees.

3 Personal Chattels

I give my personal chattels (as defined in section 55 of the Administration of Estates Act 1925) to my Spouse absolutely.
   [Other legacies, appointment of guardians, etc., follow here.]

4 Residuary Estate

    4.1 My executors shall:

        4.1.1 pay my debts, funeral and testamentary expenses, legacies and Inheritance Tax on all property which vests in them; and

        4.1.2 hold the remainder as set out below.

    4.2 Debts, funeral and testamentary expenses, legacies and Inheritance Tax shall be payable out of the capital of my estate (subject to the Trustees' administrative powers relating to capital and income).

5 Definitions

In this Will:

5.1 **"The Accumulation Period"** means the period of 21 years beginning with the date of my death.

5.2 **"The Beneficiaries"** means:

5.2.1 My Spouse.
5.2.2 My descendants.
5.2.3 The Spouses of my descendants.
5.2.4 The Surviving Spouses of my descendants.
5.2.5 Any Person or class of Persons added to the class of Beneficiaries by the Trustees by deed with the consent in writing of two Beneficiaries.
5.2.6 [*Any favoured charity*].
5.2.7 At any time during which no descendant of mine is living:

5.2.7.1 [*specify "fall back" beneficiaries if desired, e.g. nieces and nephews and their families*]
5.2.7.2 [*any company, body or trust established for charitable purposes only*].

5.3 **"Spouse"** includes a civil partner within the meaning of section 1 Civil Partnership Act 2004 and a person is a **"Surviving Spouse"** whether or not they have remarried or entered into another civil partnership.

5.4 **"The Nil Rate Fund"** means:

5.4.1 the Untransferable Nil Rate Sum; and
5.4.2 all property from time to time representing the above.

5.5 **"The Untransferable Nil Rate Sum"** means the maximum amount of cash which I can give on the terms of the Nil Rate Fund:

5.5.1 without incurring any liability to Inheritance Tax on my death; and
5.5.2 without reducing the amount by which the Nil Rate Band applicable on the death of my Spouse would (apart from the gift of the Untransferable Nil Rate Sum made in my Will) be increased under section 8A Inheritance Tax Act 1984,

but subject to the following clauses.

5.5.3 It shall be assumed that:

5.5.3.1 any claim which may increase the Untransferable Nil Rate Sum shall be made; and

5.5.3.2 my Spouse will not remarry or enter into a civil partnership after my death.

5.5.4 My executors shall make a claim under section 8B Inheritance Tax Act 1984.[1]

5.5.5 The Untransferable Nil Rate Sum shall be nil if:

5.5.5.1 Inheritance Tax has been abolished at the time of my death; or

5.5.5.2 I am not [married] at the time of my death; or

5.5.5.3 The amount of the Untransferable Nil Rate Sum would otherwise be less than £5,000.

5.5.6 Any other legacy given by my will or any codicil shall be paid in priority to the Untransferable Nil Rate Sum.

5.5.7 My executors may ascertain and fix the amount of the Untransferable Nil Rate Sum so as to bind all persons interested under this Will if the executors have discharged the duty of care set out in section 1(1) Trustee Act 2000.

5.6 **"Person"** includes a person anywhere in the world and includes a Trustee.

5.7 **"The Trustees"** means my executors or the trustees for the time being.

5.8 **"The Trust Fund"** means:

5.8.1 the remainder of my estate after deducting the Nil Rate Fund and any other legacies; and

5.8.2 all property from time to time representing the above.

5.9 **"The Trust Period"** means the period of 80 years beginning with the date of my death. That period is the perpetuity period applicable to this Will under the rule against perpetuities.

5.10 **"Trust Property"** includes any part of the Trust Fund and the Nil Rate Fund.

5.11 **"The Nil Rate Band"** means the upper limit specified in Schedule 1 Inheritance Tax Act 1984.

6 Nil Rate Fund

I give the Untransferable Nil Rate Sum to the Trustees.[2] During the lifetime of my Spouse and subject to the Overriding Powers below:

---

[1] This sub-clause only needed if the testator (having survived a previous spouse) has more than 1 nil rate band: the will should impose a duty so a claim must be made.

[2] This sentence was not included in earlier editions of this book because it is not necessary. However experience suggests that it may be easier to follow if it is there.

6.1 The Trustees may accumulate the whole or any part of the income of the Nil Rate Fund during the Accumulation Period. That income shall be added to the Nil Rate Fund.

6.2 Subject to that, during the Trust Period, the Trustees shall pay or apply the income of the Nil Rate Fund to or for the benefit of any of the Beneficiaries as the Trustees think fit.

6.3 Subject to that, the Trustees shall add the Nil Rate Fund to the Trust Fund.

7 The Trust Fund

Subject to the overriding powers below:

7.1 The Trustees shall pay the income of the Trust Fund to my Spouse during [her] life.

7.2 Subject to that, the Trustees may accumulate the whole or any part of the income of the Trust Fund during the Accumulation Period. That income shall be added to the Trust Fund.

7.3 Subject to that, during the Trust Period, the Trustees shall pay or apply the income of the Trust Fund to or for the benefit of any of the Beneficiaries as the Trustees think fit.

8 Overriding Powers

The Trustees shall have the following powers ("Overriding Powers"):

8.1 *Power of appointment*

8.1.1 The Trustees may appoint that they shall hold any Trust Property for the benefit of any Beneficiaries, on such terms as the Trustees think fit.

8.1.2 An appointment may create any provisions and in particular:

8.1.2.1 discretionary trusts;
8.1.2.2 dispositive or administrative powers;

exercisable by any Person.

8.1.3 An appointment shall be made by deed and may be revocable or irrevocable.

8.2 *Transfer of Trust Property to another settlement*

    8.2.1 The Trustees may by deed declare that they hold any Trust Property on trust to transfer it to trustees of another settlement, wherever established, to hold on the terms of that settlement, freed and released from the terms of this Will.

    8.2.2 The Trustees shall only exercise this power if:

        8.2.2.1 every Person who may benefit is (or would if living be) a Beneficiary; or

        8.2.2.2 with the consent in writing of two Beneficiaries.

8.3 *Power of advancement*

The Trustees may pay or apply any Trust Property for the advancement or benefit of any Beneficiary.

8.4 The Overriding Powers shall be exercisable only:

    8.4.1 during the Trust Period; and

    8.4.2 at a time when there are at least two Trustees, or the Trustee is a company carrying on a business which consists of or includes the management of trusts, or when the power to appoint additional Trustees cannot be exercised.

9 Default Clause

Subject to that, the Trust Fund shall be held on trust for [my son Adam—or define the default beneficiary as appropriate] absolutely.

10 Standard Provisions

The Standard Provisions of the Society of Trust and Estate Practitioners (1st Edition) shall apply with the deletion of paragraph 5. Section 11 of the Trusts of Land and Appointment of Trustees Act 1996 (consultation with beneficiaries) shall not apply.

[Alternatively say: "The provisions set out in the Schedule below shall have effect" and set out the provisions in full in the schedule. The CD with this book has the form.]

11 Additional Provisions relating to Nil Rate Fund

Where during the lifetime of my Spouse there are separate sets of Trustees for the Nil Rate Fund and the Trust Fund:

    11.1 The Trustees of the Nil Rate Fund may allow the payment of the Untransferable Nil Rate Sum to be postponed for such period as they think fit and in such case no Trustee shall be personally liable for payment of the Untransferable Nil Rate Sum except to the extent that he can recover such liability from the Trust Fund.

11.2 If payment is postponed beyond one year from my death, the Untransferable Nil Rate Sum shall carry interest at the rate applicable to legacies (or shall be on such other terms as the trustees of the Trust Fund and the trustees of the Nil Rate Fund shall agree).

11.3 The Trustees of the Nil Rate Fund may waive payment of interest which has accrued and is payable before such interest is paid.

11.4 The Trustees of the Nil Rate Fund may waive the payment of the whole or any part of the Untransferable Nil Rate Sum.

11.5 The provisions of this clause shall not be exercisable so as to prevent a Person from being entitled to an interest in possession in the Trust Fund.

11.6 The provisions of this clause shall not be exercisable so as to give any Person an interest in possession in the Nil Rate Fund.

Signed by [name of testator] to give effect to this Will,
in the presence of two witnesses present at the same time,
who have each signed this Will in the presence of the Testator.

[Signature of Testator]

Date

1st Witness
Address

2nd Witness
Address

WILL 5
NIL RATE BAND DISCRETIONARY TRUST; RESIDUE TO SURVIVING SPOUSE/CIVIL PARTNER ABSOLUTELY

This precedent is intended for smaller estates. Where, after deduction of the nil rate band, there remains a substantial residue, it would generally be better to provide that the residue should be held on trust for the spouse/CP for life; not absolutely

I, [Name of testator] of [address] declare this to be my last Will.

1 I revoke all my earlier testamentary dispositions.

2 Appointment of Executors

I appoint:

    2.1 [Name] of [address] and

    2.2 [Name] of [address]

to be my executors and Trustees.

[Other legacies, appointment of guardians, etc., follow here.]

3 Definitions

In this Will:

    3.1 **"The Accumulation Period"** means the period of 21 years beginning with the date of my death.

    3.2 **"The Beneficiaries"** means:

        3.2.1 My Spouse.
        3.2.2 My descendants.

3.2.3 The Spouses of my descendants.

3.2.4 The Surviving Spouses of my descendants.

3.2.5 Any Person or class of Persons added to the class of Beneficiaries by the Trustees by deed with the consent in writing of two Beneficiaries.

3.2.6 [*Any favoured charity*].

3.2.7 At any time during which no descendant of mine is living:

    3.2.7.1 [*specify "fall back" beneficiaries if desired, e.g. nieces and nephews and their families*]

    3.2.7.2 [*any company, body or trust established for charitable purposes only*].

3.3 **"Spouse"** includes a civil partner within the meaning of section 1 Civil Partnership Act 2004 and a person is a **"Surviving Spouse"** whether or not they have remarried or entered into another civil partnership.

3.4 **"The Nil Rate Fund"** means:

3.4.1 the Untransferable Nil Rate Sum; and

3.4.2 all property from time to time representing the above.

3.5 **"The Untransferable Nil Rate Sum"** means the maximum amount of cash which I can give on the terms of the Nil Rate Fund:

3.5.1 without incurring any liability to Inheritance Tax on my death; and

3.5.2 without reducing the amount by which the Nil Rate Band applicable on the death of my Spouse would (apart from the gift of the Untransferable Nil Rate Sum made in my Will) be increased under section 8A Inheritance Tax Act 1984,

but subject to the following clauses.

3.5.3 It shall be assumed that:

    3.5.3.1 any claim which may increase the Untransferable Nil Rate Sum shall be made; and

    3.5.3.2 my Spouse will not remarry or enter into a civil partnership after my death.

3.5.4 My executors shall make a claim under section 8B Inheritance Tax Act 1984.[1]

3.5.5 The Untransferable Nil Rate Sum shall be nil if:

    3.5.5.1 Inheritance Tax has been abolished at the time of my death; or

---

[1] This sub-clause is only needed if the testator (having survived a previous spouse) has more than 1 nil rate band: the will should impose a duty so a claim must be made.

3.5.5.2 I am not [married] at the time of my death; or

3.5.5.3 The amount of the Untransferable Nil Rate Sum would otherwise be less than £5,000.

3.5.6 Any other legacy given by my will or any codicil shall be paid in priority to the Untransferable Nil Rate Sum.

3.5.7 My executors may ascertain and fix the amount of the Untransferable Nil Rate Sum so as to bind all persons interested under this Will if the executors have discharged the duty of care set out in section 1(1) Trustee Act 2000.

3.6 **"Person"** includes a person anywhere in the world and includes a Trustee.

3.7 **"The Trustees"** means my executors or the trustees for the time being.

3.8 **"The Trust Period"** means the period of 80 years beginning with the date of my death. That is the perpetuity period applicable to this Will under the rule against perpetuities.

3.9 **"Trust Property"** means any part of the Nil Rate Fund.

3.10 **"The Nil Rate Band"** means the upper limit specified in Schedule 1 Inheritance Tax Act 1984.

4 Nil Rate Fund

I give the Untransferable Nil Rate Sum to the Trustees.[2] Subject to the Overriding Powers below:

4.1 The Trustees may accumulate the whole or any part of the income of the Nil Rate Fund during the Accumulation Period. That income shall be added to the Nil Rate Fund.

4.2 Subject to that, during the Trust Period, the Trustees shall pay or apply the income of the Nil Rate Fund to or for the benefit of any of the Beneficiaries as the Trustees think fit.

4.3 Subject to that, the Nil Rate Fund shall be held on trust for [my son Adam – or define the default beneficiary as appropriate] absolutely.

5 Overriding Powers

The Trustees shall have the following powers ("Overriding Powers"):

---

[2] This sentence was not included in earlier editions of this book because it is not necessary. However experience suggests that it may be easier to follow if it is there.

5.1 *Power of appointment*

   5.1.1 The Trustees may appoint that they shall hold any Trust Property for the benefit of any Beneficiaries, on such terms as the Trustees think fit.
   5.1.2 An appointment may create any provisions and in particular:

   5.1.2.1 discretionary trusts;
   5.1.2.2 dispositive or administrative powers;

   exercisable by any Person.
   5.1.3 An appointment shall be made by deed and may be revocable or irrevocable.

5.2 *Transfer of Trust Property to another settlement*

   5.2.1 The Trustees may by deed declare that they hold any Trust Property on trust to transfer it to trustees of another settlement, wherever established, to hold on the terms of that settlement, freed and released from the terms of this Will.
   5.2.2 The Trustees shall only exercise this power if:

   5.2.2.1 every Person who may benefit is (or would if living be) a Beneficiary; or
   5.2.2.2 with the consent in writing of two Beneficiaries.

5.3 *Power of advancement*

   The Trustees may pay or apply any Trust Property for the advancement or benefit of any Beneficiary.

5.4 The Overriding Powers shall be exercisable only

   5.4.1 during the Trust Period; and
   5.4.2 at a time when there are at least two Trustees, or the Trustee is a company carrying on a business which consists of or includes the management of trusts, or when the power to appoint additional Trustees cannot be exercised.

6 Residuary Estate

6.1 My executors shall:

   6.1.1 pay my debts, funeral and testamentary expenses, legacies and Inheritance Tax on all property which vests in them; and
   6.1.2 hold the remainder ("my Residuary Estate") on trust for my Spouse absolutely. [It may be desired to provide for a simple gift over if the Spouse does not survive. Also see will form 6.]

6.2 Debts, funeral and testamentary expenses, legacies and Inheritance Tax shall be payable out of the capital of my estate (subject to the Trustees' administrative powers relating to capital and income).

7 Standard Provisions

The standard provisions of the Society of Trust and Estate Practitioners (1st Edition) shall apply with the deletion of paragraph 5. Section 11 of the Trusts of Land and Appointment of Trustees Act 1996 (consultation with beneficiaries) shall not apply.
[Alternatively say: "The provisions set out in the Schedule below shall have effect" and set out the provisions in full in the schedule. The CD with this book has the form.]

8 Additional Provisions relating to Nil Rate Fund

8.1 In this clause "**The Nil Rate Trustees**" means the trustees of the Nil Rate Fund.

Spouse may undertake to pay Untransferable Nil Rate Sum personally

8.2

    8.2.1 My executors may require the Nil Rate Trustees to accept a written undertaking from my Spouse.

    8.2.2 That undertaking shall be to pay the Untransferable Nil Rate Sum (or, if less, the value of my Residuary Estate at the time of the undertaking) to the Nil Rate Trustees on demand. The undertaking may include any other terms and in particular:

        8.2.2.1 fixed or floating security;
        8.2.2.2 interest;
        8.2.2.3 index linking the sum payable.

    8.2.3 That undertaking will be in substitution for payment of the Untransferable Nil Rate Sum by the executors to the Nil Rate Trustees. My executors shall be under no further liability in relation to the Untransferable Nil Rate Sum.

Executors may charge residuary estate instead of paying Untransferable Nil Rate Sum directly

8.3

    8.3.1 My executors may charge all or part of my Residuary Estate with the payment of all or part of the Untransferable Nil Rate Sum to the Nil Rate Trustees on demand.

    8.3.2 That charge may be a fixed or floating charge. It may include any other terms and in particular:

        8.3.2.1 interest;

        8.3.2.2 index linking the sum payable.

    8.3.3 To the extent of the amount charged on the property (and regardless of the value of the property charged):

        8.3.3.1 the charge will be in substitution for payment of the Untransferable Nil Rate Sum by the executors to the Nil Rate Trustees; and

        8.3.3.2 my executors shall be under no further liability in relation to the Untransferable Nil Rate Sum.

    8.3.4 When my executors give an assent of the property charged, my Spouse shall not thereby become personally liable for the sum charged.

Untransferable Nil Rate Sum may be left outstanding

8.4 The Nil Rate Trustees may refrain from calling in the Untransferable Nil Rate Sum (or exercising any rights in relation to the Untransferable Nil Rate Sum) for as long as they think fit. They may waive the payment of any income or capital due in respect of the Untransferable Nil Rate Sum. They shall not be liable if my Spouse becomes unable to make any payment or if a security becomes inadequate or for any other loss which may occur through exercising any power given by this clause.

8.5 The powers given by this clause are exercisable even though my executors and the Nil Rate Trustees are the same persons.

8.6 My Spouse shall not be the sole Nil Rate Trustee.

8.7 The provisions of this clause shall not be exercisable so as to give any Person an interest in possession in the Nil Rate Fund.

8.8 The Untransferable Nil Rate Sum shall carry interest at the rate applicable to legacies from the third anniversary of my death (if still outstanding at that time).

8.9 Any asset appropriated in or towards satisfaction of the Untransferable Nil Rate Sum within three years of my death may be valued for the purpose of the appropriation at its value at the time of my death.

Signed by [name of testator] to give effect to this Will,
in the presence of two witnesses present at the same time,
who have each signed this Will in the presence of the Testator

[Signature of Testator]

Date

1st Witness
Address

2nd Witness
Address

WILL 6
NIL RATE BAND DISCRETIONARY TRUST RESIDUE TO:
(1) SURVIVING SPOUSE/CIVIL PARTNER ABSOLUTELY
(2) DISCRETIONARY TRUST (IF NO SURVIVING SPOUSE/CP)

I, [Name of testator] of [address] declare this to be my last Will.

1 I revoke all my earlier testamentary dispositions.

2 Appointment of Executors

I appoint:

    2.1 [Name] of [address] and

    2.2 [Name] of [address]

to be my executors and Trustees.

[Other legacies, appointment of guardians, etc., follow here.]

3 Residuary Estate

    3.1 My executors shall:

        3.1.1 pay my debts, funeral and testamentary expenses, legacies and Inheritance Tax on all property which vests in them; and

        3.1.2 hold the remainder ("my Residuary Estate") as set out below.

    3.2 Debts, funeral and testamentary expenses, legacies and Inheritance

Tax shall be payable out of the capital of my estate (subject to the Trustees' administrative powers relating to capital and income).

4 My executors shall hold my Residuary Estate on trust for my Spouse if [she] survives me absolutely.

5 Definitions

In this Will:

5.1 **"The Accumulation Period"** means the period of 21 years beginning with the date of my death.

5.2 **"The Beneficiaries"** means:

5.2.1 My Spouse.
5.2.2 My descendants.
5.2.3 The Spouses of my descendants.
5.2.4 The Surviving Spouses of my descendants.
5.2.5 Any Person or class of Persons added to the class of Beneficiaries by the Trustees by deed with the consent in writing of two Beneficiaries.
5.2.6 [*Any favoured charity*].
5.2.7 At any time during which no descendant of mine is living:

5.2.7.1 [*specify "fall back" beneficiaries if desired, e.g. nieces and nephews and their families*]
5.2.7.2 [*any company, body or trust established for charitable purposes only*].

5.3 **"Spouse"** includes a civil partner within the meaning of section 1 Civil Partnership Act 2004 and a person is a **"Surviving Spouse"** whether or not they have remarried or entered into another civil partnership.

5.4 **"The Untransferable Nil Rate Sum"** means the maximum amount of cash which I can give on the terms of the Trust Fund:

5.4.1 without incurring any liability to Inheritance Tax on my death; and
5.4.2 without reducing the amount by which the Nil Rate Band applicable on the death of my Spouse would (apart from the gift of the Untransferable Nil Rate Sum made in my Will) be increased under section 8A Inheritance Tax Act 1984,

but subject to the following clauses.

5.4.3 It shall be assumed that:

- 5.4.3.1 any claim which may increase the Untransferable Nil Rate Sum shall be made; and
- 5.4.3.2 my Spouse will not remarry or enter into a civil partnership after my death.
- 5.4.4 My executors shall make a claim under section 8B Inheritance Tax Act 1984.[1]
- 5.4.5 The Untransferable Nil Rate Sum shall be nil if:
  - 5.4.5.1 Inheritance Tax has been abolished at the time of my death; or
  - 5.4.5.2 I am not [married] at the time of my death; or
  - 5.4.5.3 The amount of the Untransferable Nil Rate Sum would otherwise be less than £5,000.
- 5.4.6 Any other legacy given by my will or any codicil shall be paid in priority to the Untransferable Nil Rate Sum.
- 5.4.7 My executors may ascertain and fix the amount of the Untransferable Nil Rate Sum so as to bind all persons interested under this Will if the executors have discharged the duty of care set out in section 1(1) Trustee Act 2000.

5.5 **"Person"** includes a person anywhere in the world and includes a Trustee.

5.6 **"The Trustees"** means my executors or the trustees for the time being.

5.7 **"The Trust Fund"** means:

- 5.7.1 if my Spouse survives me, the Untransferable Nil Rate Sum only; and
- 5.7.2 if my Spouse does not survive me, my Residuary Estate; and
- 5.7.3 all property from time to time representing the above.

5.8 **"The Trust Period"** means the period of 80 years beginning with the date of my death. That is the perpetuity period applicable to this Will Trust under the rule against perpetuities.

5.9 **"Trust Property"** means any part of the Trust Fund.

5.10 **"The Nil Rate Band"** means the upper limit specified in Schedule 1 Inheritance Tax Act 1984.

---

[1] This sub-clause is only needed if the testator (having survived a previous spouse) has more than 1 nil rate band: the will should impose a duty so a claim must be made.

6 Trust Fund

I give the Trust Fund to the Trustees.[2] Subject to the Overriding Powers below:

6.1 The Trustees may accumulate the whole or any part of the income of the Trust Fund during the Accumulation Period. That income shall be added to the Trust Fund.

6.2 Subject to that, during the Trust Period, the Trustees shall pay or apply the income of the Trust Fund to or for the benefit of any of the Beneficiaries as the Trustees think fit.

6.3 Subject to that, the Trust Fund shall be held on trust for [my son Adam—or specify default beneficiary as appropriate] absolutely.

7 Overriding Powers

The Trustees shall have the following powers ("Overriding Powers"):

7.1 *Power of appointment*

7.1.1 The Trustees may appoint that they shall hold any Trust Property for the benefit of any Beneficiaries, on such terms as the Trustees think fit.

7.1.2 An appointment may create any provisions and in particular:

7.1.2.1 discretionary trusts;
7.1.2.2 dispositive or administrative powers;

exercisable by any Person.

7.1.3 An appointment shall be made by deed and may be revocable or irrevocable.

7.2 *Transfer of Trust Property to another settlement*

7.2.1 The Trustees may by deed declare that they hold any Trust Property on trust to transfer it to trustees of another settlement, wherever established, to hold on the terms of that settlement, freed and released from the terms of this Will.

7.2.2 The Trustees shall only exercise this power if:

7.2.2.1 every Person who may benefit is (or would if living be) a Beneficiary; or

---

[2] This sentence was not included in earlier editions of this book because it is not necessary. However experience suggests that it may be easier to follow if it is there.

7.2.2.2 with the consent in writing of two Beneficiaries.

7.3 *Power of advancement*

The Trustees may pay or apply any Trust Property for the advancement or benefit of any Beneficiary.

7.4 The Overriding Powers shall be exercisable only:

7.4.1 during the Trust Period; and
7.4.2 at a time when there are at least two Trustees, or the Trustee is a company carrying on a business which consists of or includes the management of trusts, or when the power to appoint additional Trustees cannot be exercised.

8 Standard Provisions

The standard provisions of the Society of Trust and Estate Practitioners (1st Edition) shall apply with the deletion of paragraph 5. Section 11 of the Trusts of Land and Appointment of Trustees Act 1996 (consultation with beneficiaries) shall not apply.

[Alternatively say: "The provisions set out in the Schedule below shall have effect" and set out the provisions in full in the schedule. The CD with this book has the form.]

9 Additional Provisions relating to Nil Rate Sum

9.1 In this clause "**The Nil Rate Trustees**" means the trustees of the Untransferable Nil Rate Sum.

Spouse may undertake to pay Untransferable Nil Rate Sum personally

9.2

9.2.1 My executors may require the Nil Rate Trustees to accept a written undertaking from my Spouse.
9.2.2 That undertaking shall be to pay the Untransferable Nil Rate Sum (or, if less, the value of my Residuary Estate at the time of the undertaking) to the Nil Rate Trustees on demand. The undertaking may include any other terms and in particular:

9.2.2.1 fixed or floating security;
9.2.2.2 interest;
9.2.2.3 index linking the sum payable.

9.2.3 That undertaking will be in substitution for payment of the Untransferable Nil Rate Sum by the executors to the Nil Rate Trustees. My executors shall be under no further liability in relation to the Untransferable Nil Rate Sum.

Executors may charge residuary estate instead of paying Untransferable Nil Rate Sum directly

9.3
9.3.1 My executors may charge all or part of my Residuary Estate with the payment of all or part of the Untransferable Nil Rate Sum to the Nil Rate Trustees on demand.
9.3.2 That charge may be a fixed or floating charge. It may include any other terms and in particular:

9.3.2.1 interest;
9.3.2.2 index linking the sum payable.

9.3.3 To the extent of the amount charged on the property (and regardless of the value of the property charged):

9.3.3.1 the charge will be in substitution for payment of the Untransferable Nil Rate Sum by the executors to the Nil Rate Trustees; and
9.3.3.2 my executors shall be under no further liability in relation to the Untransferable Nil Rate Sum.

9.3.4 When my executors give an assent of the property charged, my Spouse shall not thereby become personally liable for the sum charged.

Untransferable Nil Rate Sum may be left outstanding

9.4 The Nil Rate Trustees may refrain from calling in the Untransferable Nil Rate Sum (or exercising any rights in relation to the Untransferable Nil Rate Sum) for as long as they think fit. They may waive the payment of any income or capital due in respect of the Untransferable Nil Rate Sum. They shall not be liable if my Spouse becomes unable to make any payment or if a security becomes inadequate or for any other loss which may occur through exercising any power given by this clause.

9.5 The powers given by this clause are exercisable even though my executors and the Nil Rate Trustees are the same persons.

9.6 My Spouse shall not be the sole Nil Rate Trustee.

9.7 The provisions of this clause shall not be exercisable so as to give any Person an interest in possession in the Nil Rate Fund.

9.8 The Untransferable Nil Rate Sum shall carry interest at the rate applicable to legacies from the third anniversary of my death (if still outstanding at that time).

9.9 Any asset appropriated in or towards satisfaction of the Untransferable Nil Rate Sum within three years of my death may be valued for the purpose of the appropriation at its value at the time of my death.

Signed by [name of testator] to give effect to this Will,
in the presence of two witnesses present at the same time,
who have each signed this Will in the presence of the Testator.

[Signature of Testator]

Date

1st Witness
Address

2nd Witness
Address

WILL 7
NIL RATE BAND DISCRETIONARY TRUST; RESIDUE TO PARTNER (NOT SPOUSE/CIVIL PARTNER) ABSOLUTELY

*Note: This precedent is intended for a testator who is not married or a civil partner. Where, after deduction of the nil rate band, there remains a substantial residue, it would generally be better to provide that the entire residue should be held on discretionary will trusts (**Will 1**).*

I, [Name of testator] of [address] declare this to be my last Will.

1 I revoke all my earlier testamentary dispositions.

2 Appointment of Executors

I appoint:

    2.1 [Name] of [address] and

    2.2 [Name] of [address]

to be my executors and Trustees.

[Other legacies, appointment of guardians, etc., follow here.]

3 Definitions

In this Will:

    3.1 **"The Accumulation Period"** means the period of 21 years beginning with the date of my death.

    3.2 **"The Beneficiaries"** means:

        3.2.1 My Partner.

3.2.2 My descendants.
3.2.3 The Spouses of my descendants.
3.2.4 The Surviving Spouses of my descendants.
3.2.5 Any Person or class of Persons added to the class of Beneficiaries by the Trustees by deed with the consent in writing of two Beneficiaries.
3.2.6 [*Any favoured charity*].
3.2.7 At any time during which no descendant of mine is living:

    3.2.7.1 [*specify "fall back" beneficiaries if desired, e.g. nieces and nephews and their families*]

    3.2.7.2 [*any company, body or trust established for charitable purposes only*].

3.3 **"Spouse"** includes a civil partner within the meaning of section 1 Civil Partnership Act 2004 and a person is a "**Surviving Spouse**" whether or not they have remarried or entered into another civil partnership.

3.4 **"The Nil Rate Fund"** means:

    3.4.1 the Nil Rate Sum; and

    3.4.2 all property from time to time representing the above.

3.5

    3.5.1 **"The Nil Rate Sum"** means A–B where:

        3.5.1.1 A is the upper limit specified in Schedule 1 Inheritance Tax Act 1984 applicable to the chargeable transfer made on my death; and

        3.5.1.2 B is the aggregate of the values transferred by any chargeable transfers made by me in the period of seven years ending with the day of my death, disregarding transfers made on that day;

    but subject to the following clauses.

    3.5.2 The Nil Rate Sum shall be nil if:

        3.5.2.1 Inheritance Tax has been abolished at the time of my death; or

        3.5.2.2 The amount of the Nil Rate Sum would otherwise be less than £5,000.

    3.5.3 Any other legacy given by my will or any codicil shall be paid in priority to the Nil Rate Sum.

    3.5.4 My executors may ascertain and fix the amount of the Nil Rate Sum so as to bind all persons interested under this Will if the executors have discharged the duty of care set out in section 1(1) Trustee Act 2000.

3.6 **"My Partner"** means [*specify name of partner*].

3.7 **"Person"** includes a person anywhere in the world and includes a Trustee.

3.8 **"The Trustees"** means my executors or the trustees for the time being.

3.9 **"The Trust Period"** means the period of 80 years beginning with the date of my death. That is the perpetuity period applicable to this Will under the rule against perpetuities.

3.10 **"Trust Property"** means any part of the Nil Rate Fund.

4 Nil Rate Fund

I give the Nil Rate Sum to the Trustees.[1] Subject to the Overriding Powers below:

4.1 The Trustees may accumulate the whole or any part of the income of the Nil Rate Fund during the Accumulation Period. That income shall be added to the Nil Rate Fund.

4.2 Subject to that, during the Trust Period, the Trustees shall pay or apply the income of the Nil Rate Fund to or for the benefit of any of the Beneficiaries as the Trustees think fit.

4.3 Subject to that, the Nil Rate Fund shall be held on trust for [my son Adam – or define the default beneficiary as appropriate] absolutely.

5 Overriding Powers

The Trustees shall have the following powers ("Overriding Powers"):

5.1 *Power of appointment*

5.1.1 The Trustees may appoint that they shall hold any Trust Property for the benefit of any Beneficiaries, on such terms as the Trustees think fit.

5.1.2 An appointment may create any provisions and in particular:

5.1.2.1 discretionary trusts;

---

[1] This sentence was not included in earlier editions of this book because it is not necessary. However experience suggests that it may be easier to follow if it is there.

5.1.2.2 dispositive or administrative powers; exercisable by any Person.

5.1.3 An appointment shall be made by deed and may be revocable or irrevocable.

5.2 *Transfer of Trust Property to another settlement*

5.2.1 The Trustees may by deed declare that they hold any Trust Property on trust to transfer it to trustees of another settlement, wherever established, to hold on the terms of that settlement, freed and released from the terms of this Will.

5.2.2 The Trustees shall only exercise this power if:

5.2.2.1 every Person who may benefit is (or would if living be) a Beneficiary; or

5.2.2.2 with the consent in writing of two Beneficiaries.

5.3 *Power of advancement*

The Trustees may pay or apply any Trust Property for the advancement or benefit of any Beneficiary.

5.4 The Overriding Powers shall be exercisable only

5.4.1 during the Trust Period; and

5.4.2 at a time when there are at least two Trustees, or the Trustee is a company carrying on a business which consists of or includes the management of trusts, or when the power to appoint additional Trustees cannot be exercised.

6 Residuary Estate

6.1 My executors shall:

6.1.1 pay my debts, funeral and testamentary expenses, legacies and Inheritance Tax on all property which vests in them; and

6.1.2 hold the remainder ("my Residuary Estate") on trust for my Partner absolutely. [It may be desired to provide for a simple gift over if the Partner does not survive.]

6.2 Debts, funeral and testamentary expenses, legacies and Inheritance Tax shall be payable out of the capital of my estate (subject to the Trustees' administrative powers relating to capital and income).

7 Standard Provisions

The standard provisions of the Society of Trust and Estate Practitioners (1st Edition) shall apply with the deletion of paragraph 5. Section 11 of the

Trusts of Land and Appointment of Trustees Act 1996 (consultation with beneficiaries) shall not apply.

[Alternatively say: "The provisions set out in the Schedule below shall have effect" and set out the provisions in full in the schedule. The CD with this book has the form.]

8 Additional Provisions relating to Nil Rate Fund

8.1 In this clause "**The Nil Rate Trustees**" means the trustees of the Nil Rate Fund.

Surviving Partner may undertake to pay Nil Rate Sum personally

8.2

    8.2.1 My executors may require the Nil Rate Trustees to accept a written undertaking from my Partner.

    8.2.2 That undertaking shall be to pay the Nil Rate Sum (or, if less, the value of my Residuary Estate at the time of the undertaking) to the Nil Rate Trustees on demand. The undertaking may include any other terms and in particular:

        8.2.2.1 fixed or floating security;

        8.2.2.2 interest;

        8.2.2.3 index linking the sum payable.

    8.2.3 That undertaking will be in substitution for payment of the Nil Rate Sum by the executors to the Nil Rate Trustees. My executors shall be under no further liability in relation to the Nil Rate Sum.

Executors may charge residuary estate instead of paying Nil Rate Sum directly

8.3

    8.3.1 My executors may charge all or part of my Residuary Estate with the payment of all or part of the Nil Rate Sum to the Nil Rate Trustees on demand.

    8.3.2 That charge may be a fixed or floating charge. It may include any other terms and in particular:

        8.3.2.1 interest;

        8.3.2.2 index linking the sum payable.

    8.3.3 To the extent of the amount charged on the property (and regardless of the value of the property charged):

        8.3.3.1 the charge will be in substitution for payment of the Nil Rate Sum by the executors to the Nil Rate Trustees; and

- 8.3.3.2 my executors shall be under no further liability in relation to the Nil Rate Sum.
- 8.3.4 My executors may transfer the property charged to my Partner who shall not thereby become personally liable for the sum charged.

Nil Rate Sum may be left outstanding

- 8.4 The Nil Rate Trustees may refrain from calling in the Nil Rate Sum (or exercising any rights in relation to the Nil Rate Sum) for as long as they think fit. They may waive the payment of any income or capital due in respect of the Nil Rate Sum. They shall not be liable if my Partner becomes unable to make any payment or if a security becomes inadequate or for any other loss which may occur through exercising any power given by this clause.
- 8.5 The powers given by this clause are exercisable even though my executors and the Nil Rate Trustees are the same persons.
- 8.6 My Partner shall not be the sole Nil Rate Trustee.
- 8.7 The provisions of this clause shall not be exercisable so as to give any Person an interest in possession in the Nil Rate Fund.
- 8.8 The Nil Rate Sum shall carry interest at the rate applicable to legacies from the third anniversary of my death (if still outstanding at that time).
- 8.9 Any asset appropriated in or towards satisfaction of the Nil Rate Sum within three years of my death may be valued for the purpose of the appropriation at its value at the time of my death.

Signed by [name of testator] to give effect to this Will,
in the presence of two witnesses present at the same time,
who have each signed this Will in the presence of the Testator.

[Signature of Testator]

Date

1st Witness
Address

2nd Witness
Address

PRECEDENTS FOR ADMINISTRATIVE PROVISIONS

Lifetime Trusts

The following material is the basis for the schedule of administrative provisions in a lifetime trust when the STEP Standard Provisions are not used. The equivalent for a will is available on the CD ROM with this book (not printed in the book for reasons of space).

1 Additional powers

The Trustees have the following additional powers:

1.1 Investment

1.1.1 The Trustees may make any kind of investment that they could make if they were absolutely entitled to the Trust Fund. In particular the Trustees may invest in land in any part of the world and unsecured loans.

1.1.2 The Trustees are under no obligation to diversify the Trust Fund.

1.1.3 The Trustees may invest in speculative or hazardous investments but this power may only be exercised at the time when there are at least two Trustees, or the Trustee is a company carrying on a business which consists of or includes the management of trusts.

1.2 Joint property

The Trustees may acquire property jointly with any Person and may blend Trust Property with other property.

1.3 General power of management and disposition

The Trustees may effect any transaction relating to the management or disposition of Trust Property as if they were absolutely entitled to it.

1.4 Improvement

The Trustees may develop or improve Trust Property in any way. Capital expenses need not be repaid out of income under section 84(2) of the Settled Land Act 1925, if the Trustees think fit.

1.5 Income and capital

1.5.1 The Trustees may acquire:

    1.5.1.1 wasting assets and
    1.5.1.2 assets which yield little or no income
        for investment or any other purpose.

1.5.2 The Trustees are under no duty to procure distributions from a company in which they are interested.

1.5.3 The Trustees may pay taxes and other expenses out of income although they would otherwise be paid out of capital.

1.5.4 Generally, the Trustees are under no duty to hold a balance between conflicting interests of Beneficiaries.

1.5.5 Income may be set aside and invested to answer any liabilities which in the opinion of the Trustees ought to be borne out of income or to meet depreciation of the capital value of any Trust Property. In particular, income may be applied for a leasehold sinking fund policy.

1.6 Application of trust capital as income[1]

The Trustees may apply Trust Property as if it were income arising in the current year. In particular, the Trustees may pay such income to an Income Beneficiary as his income, for the purpose of augmenting his income.

    "Income Beneficiary" here means a person to whom income of the Property is payable (as of right or at the discretion of the Trustees).

---

[1] Variant for lifetime Discretionary Settlement

The above administrative provisions are suitable for any type of settlement. In a lifetime discretionary settlement they could be simplified by the following changes:
Clauses 1.6 and 1.7; the phrase "income beneficiary" could be replaced by "Beneficiary" and the definition of "income beneficiary" may be deleted.
In a will creating a discretionary trust the same amendment could be made, but the author would be inclined to retain the text unaltered.

1.7 Use of trust property[2]

1.7.1 The Trustees may acquire any interest in property anywhere in the world for occupation or use by an Income Beneficiary.

1.7.2 The Trustees may permit an Income Beneficiary to occupy or enjoy the use of Trust Property on such terms as they think fit.

1.7.3 The Trustees may lend trust money to an Income Beneficiary. The loan may be interest free and unsecured, or on such terms as the Trustees think fit. The Trustees may charge Trust Property as security for any debts or obligations of an Income Beneficiary.

1.7.4 **"Income Beneficiary"** here means a Person to whom income of the Property is payable (as of right or at the discretion of the Trustees).

1.7.5 This paragraph does not restrict any right of Beneficiaries to occupy land under the Trusts of Land and Appointment of Trustees Act 1996.

1.8 Trade

The Trustees may carry on a trade, in any part of the world, alone or in partnership.

1.9 Borrowing

The Trustees may borrow money for investment or any other purpose. Money borrowed shall be treated as Trust Property.

1.10 Delegation

A Trustee or the Trustees jointly (or other Person in a fiduciary position) may authorize any Person to exercise all or any functions on such terms as to remuneration and other matters as they think fit. A Trustee (or other Person in a fiduciary capacity) shall not be responsible for the default of that Person (even if the delegation was not strictly necessary or convenient) provided he took reasonable care in his selection and supervision. None of the restrictions on delegation in sections 12 to 15 Trustee Act 2000 shall apply.

---

[2] For discretionary settlements, see n.1 above.

1.11 Nominees and custodians

1.11.1 The Trustees may appoint a Person to act as their nominee in relation to such of the assets of the trust as they may determine. They may take such steps as are necessary to secure that those assets are vested in the nominee.

1.11.2 The Trustees may appoint a Person to act as custodian in relation to such of the assets of the trust as they may determine. The Trustees may give the custodian custody of the assets and any documents or records concerning the assets. The Trustees are not obliged to appoint a custodian of securities payable to bearer.

1.11.3 The Trustees may appoint a Person to act as nominee or custodian on such terms as to remuneration and other matters as they may think fit.

1.12 Place of administration

The Trustees may carry on the administration of this Settlement anywhere they think fit.

1.13 Indemnities

The Trustees may indemnify any Person for any liability relating to the Settlement.

1.14 Security

The Trustees may mortgage or charge Trust Property as security for any liability incurred by them as Trustees (and may grant a floating charge so far as the law allows).

1.15 Supervision of company

The Trustees are under no duty to enquire into the conduct of a company in which they are interested, unless they have knowledge of circumstances which call for inquiry.

1.16 Appropriation

The Trustees may appropriate Trust Property to any Person or class or Persons in or towards the satisfaction of their interest in the Trust Fund.

1.17 Receipt by charities

Where Trust Property is to be paid or transferred to a charity, the receipt of the treasurer or appropriate officer of the charity shall be a complete discharge to the Trustees.

1.18 Release of powers

The Trustees (or other Person in a fiduciary position) may be deed release wholly or in part any of their rights or functions and (if applicable) so as to bind their successors.

1.19 Ancillary powers

The Trustees may do anything which is incidental or conducive to the exercise of their functions.[3]

2 Minors

2.1 Where the Trustees may apply income for the benefit of a minor, they may do so by paying the income to the minor's parent or guardian on behalf of the minor, or to the minor if he has attained the age of 16. The Trustees are under no duty to inquire into the use of the income unless they have knowledge of circumstances which call for inquiry.

2.2 Where the Trustees may apply income for the benefit of a minor, they may do so by resolving that they hold that income on trust for the minor absolutely and:

2.2.1 The Trustees may apply that income for the benefit of the minor during his minority.
2.2.2 The Trustees shall transfer the residue of that income to the minor on attaining the age of 18.
2.2.3 For investment and other administrative purposes that income shall be treated as Trust Property.

---

[3] **Variant for Discretionary Settlement**
In a discretionary settlement the trustees could be given the following additional powers: to be inserted at the end of cl.1, i.e. after cl.1.19.
1.20 Waiver
The Trustees may waive the payment of income before it becomes due.
1.21 Insurance Policies
The Trustees may pay premiums of any insurance policy out of income

3 Mentally handicapped beneficiary

Where income or capital is payable to a Beneficiary who does not have the mental capacity to appoint an attorney under a lasting power of attorney which related to his property and affairs, the Trustees may (subject to the directions of the Court or a deputy appointed under the Mental Capacity Act whose powers include receiving such income or capital) apply that income or capital for his benefit.

4 Disclaimer

A Person may disclaim his interest in this Settlement wholly or in part.

5 Apportionment

Income and expenditure shall be treated as arising when payable, and not from day to day, so that no apportionment shall take place.

6 Conflicts of interest

6.1 In this paragraph:
- 6.1.1 **"Fiduciary"** means a Person subject to fiduciary duties under the Settlement.
- 6.1.2 **"An Independent Trustee"**, in relation to a Person, means a Trustee who is not:
    - 6.1.2.1 a brother, sister, ancestor, descendant or dependent of the Person;
    - 6.1.2.2 a spouse or Civil Partner of paragraph .1.2.1 above, or a spouse or Civil Partner of the Person;
    - 6.1.2.3 a company controlled by one or more of any of the above.

6.2 Subject to subparagraph .3 below a Fiduciary may:
- 6.2.1 enter into a transaction with the Trustees, or
- 6.2.2 be interested in an arrangement in which the Trustees are or might have been interested, or

6.2.3 act (or not act) in any other circumstances;
 even though his fiduciary duty under the Settlement conflicts with other duties or with his personal interest.

6.3 Subparagraph .2 above only has effect if:

6.3.1 the Fiduciary first discloses to the Trustees the nature and extent of any material interest conflicting with his fiduciary duties, and

6.3.2 there is in relation to the Fiduciary and Independent Trustee in respect of whom there is no conflict of interest, and he considers that the transaction arrangement or action is not contrary to the general interest of the Settlement.

6.4 The powers of the Trustees may be used to benefit a Trustee (to the same extent as if he were not a Trustee) provided that there is in relation to that Trustee an Independent Trustee in respect of whom there is no conflict of interest.

7 Absolute discretion clause

7.1 The powers of the Trustees may be exercised:

7.1.1 at their absolute discretion; and
7.1.2 from time to time as occasion requires.

7.2 The Trustees are not under any duty to consult with any Beneficiaries or to give effect to the wishes of any Beneficiaries.

8 Trustee remuneration

8.1 A Trustee acting in a professional capacity is entitled to receive reasonable remuneration out of the Trust Fund for any services that he provides[4] to or on behalf of this Settlement.

8.2 For this purpose, a Trustee acts in a professional capacity if he acts in the course of a profession or business which consists of or includes the provision of services in connection with:

8.2.1 the management or administration of trusts generally or a particular kind of trust, or

---

[4] In the case of a will, continue "in connection with this will, or to or on behalf of any Settlement made by this Will."

8.2.2 any particular aspect of the management or administration of trusts generally or a particular kind of trust.

8.3 The Trustees may make arrangements to remunerate themselves for work done for a company connected with the Trust Fund.

9 Commissions and bank charges

9.1 A Person may retain any reasonable commission or profit in respect of any transaction relating to this Settlement even though that commission or profit was procured by an exercise of fiduciary powers (by that Person or some other Person) provided that:

9.1.1 The Person would in the normal course of business receive and retain the commission or profit on such transaction.
9.1.2 The receipt of the commission or profit shall be disclosed to the Trustees.

9.2 A bank may make loans to the Trustees and generally provide banking services upon its usual terms and shall not be liable to account for any profit so made even though the receipt of such profit was procured by an exercise of fiduciary powers (by the bank or some other Person).

10 Liability of trustees

10.1 The duty of reasonable care (set out in s.1, Trustee Act 2000) applies to all the functions of the Trustees.

10.2 A Trustee shall not be liable for a loss to the Trust Fund unless that loss was caused by his own fraud or negligence.

10.3 A Trustee shall not be liable for acting in accordance with the advice of Counsel, of at least ten years' standing, with respect to the settlement. The Trustees may in particular conduct legal proceedings in accordance with such advice without obtaining a Court Order. A Trustee may recover from the Trust Fund any expenses where he has acted in accordance with such advice.

10.4 The above sub-paragraph does not apply:

10.4.1 if the Trustee knows or has reasonable cause to suspect that the advice was given in ignorance of material facts;
10.4.2 if proceedings are pending to obtain the decision of the court on the matter;

10.4.3 in relation to a Trustee who has a personal interest in the subject matter of the advice; or

10.4.4 in relation to a Trustee who has committed a breach of trust relating to the subject matter of the advice.

10.5 The Trustees may distribute Trust Property or income in accordance with this Settlement but without having ascertained that there is no Person who is or may be entitled to any interest therein by virtue of a relationship unknown to the Trustees. The Trustees shall not be liable to such a Person unless they have notice of his claim at the time of the distribution.

10.6 This paragraph does not prejudice any right of any Person to follow property or income into the hands of any Person, other than a purchaser, who may have received it.

11 Appointment and retirement of trustees

11.1 A Person may be appointed Trustee of the Settlement even though he has no connection with the United Kingdom.

11.2 A Trustee may be discharged even though there is neither a trust corporation nor two Persons to act as trustees provided that there remains at least one trustee.

12 Change of governing law

The Trustees may during the Trust Period by deed with the consent of the Settlor during his life or of two Beneficiaries after his death declare that from the date of such declaration:

12.1 The law of any Qualifying Jurisdiction governs the validity of this Settlement, and its construction, effects and administration, or any severable aspect of this Settlement; and

12.2 The courts of any Qualifying Jurisdiction have exclusive jurisdiction in any proceedings involving rights or obligations under this Settlement.

In this paragraph a "Qualifying Jurisdiction" is one which recognises trusts (as defined in the Hague Convention on the Law Applicable to Trusts and on their Recognition).

13 Interest in possession protection clause

The provisions of this schedule shall not have effect so as to prevent a Person from being entitled to an interest in possession in Trust Property (within the meaning of the Inheritance Tax Act 1984).[5]

---

[5] This clause is only appropriate when an IP matters for IHT purposes (e.g. an IPDI trust). It can be deleted fro a discretionary trust or an ordinary lifetime IP trust (an IHT standard trust); see 16.19 (IP protection clause).

FORM NRB APPOINTMENT 1
(WINDING UP NRB TRUST)

This deed is intended to wind up an unwanted NRB discretionary trust. The trust fund is appointed to the surviving spouse absolutely.

It is assumed:

*(1)	The testator died leaving a NRB will trust in the form of Will 5 or Will 6 in the 8th or earlier edition of this book (gift of NRB sum to classic NRB trust: balance to spouse absolutely).*

*(2)	The spouse of the testator survived the testator (and is living at the time of the appointment.)*

*(3)	There is no untransferable NRB problem; see 18.8 (Untransferable NRB problems).*

*(4)	It is sensible from a property law viewpoint to transfer the funds to the surviving spouse absolutely.*

Time limits: this deed should be executed more than three months after but less than 2 years after the death of the testator.

This deed of appointment is made [date] by

(1) [Name] of [address] and

(2) [Name] of [address]

   (together called "the Present Trustees").

WHEREAS:

(A) This Deed is supplemental to the will ("the Will") made [date] by [name] ("the Testator").

(B) The Testator died on [date].

(C) Clause ... confers on the Trustees the following power ("the Power of Appointment"):

   [set out the power].

(D) The Present Trustees are the present trustees of [the Nil Tate Fund] [The Trust Fund]. [*Will 5 refers to the Nil Rate Fund and Will 6 refers to the Trust Fund*]

NOW THIS DEED WITNESSES as follows:

1. In this deed, [the Nil Rate Fund] [The Trust Fund] has the same meaning as in the Will.
2. In exercise of the Power of Appointment the Present Trustees irrevocably appoint that they hold the [the Nil Rate Fund] [The Trust Fund] upon trust for [name of spouse] absolutely.

In witness *etc*

FORM NRB APPOINTMENT 2 (REDUCING GIFT TO NRB TRUST TO UNTRANSFERABLE NRB)

This deed is intended to reduce a gift to a NBR discretionary trust to the untransferable NRB. The rest of the NRB gift is appointed to the surviving spouse absolutely.

It is assumed:

(1) The testator died leaving a NRB will trust in forms 5 or 6 in the 8th or earlier edition of this book.

(2) The widow of the testator survived the testator (and is living at the time of the appointment.)

(4) It is sensible from a property law viewpoint to transfer funds to the surviving spouse absolutely.

Time limits: this deed should be executed more than three months after but less than 2 years after the death of the testator.

This deed of appointment is made [date] by

(1) [Name] of [address] and

(2) [Name] of [address]

(together called "the Present Trustees").

WHEREAS:

(A) This Deed is supplemental to the will ("the Will") made [date] by [name] ("the Testator").

(B) The Testator died on [date].

(C) Clause ... confers on the Trustees the following power ("the Power of Appointment"):

[set out the power].

(D) The Present Trustees are the present trustees of [the Nil Rate Fund] [The Trust Fund]. [*Will 5 refers to the Nil Rate Fund and Will 6 refers to the Trust Fund*]

NOW THIS DEED WITNESSES as follows:

1. In this deed:

   1.1 **"The Untransferable Nil Rate Sum"** means the maximum amount of cash which the Testator can give on the terms of [the Nil Rate Fund] [The Trust Fund]:

   1.1.1 without incurring any liability to Inheritance Tax on [his] death; and

   1.1.2 without reducing the amount by which the Nil Rate Band applicable on the death of [name of spouse] would (apart from the gift of the Nil Rate Sum made in the Will as affected by this deed) be increased under section 8A Inheritance Tax Act 1984,

   But subject to the following clauses.

   1.1.3 It shall be assumed that:

   1.1.3.1 any claim which may increase the Untransferable Nil Rate Sum shall be made; and

   1.1.3.2 [name of spouse] of the testator will not remarry or enter into a civil partnership after my death.

   1.1.4 My executors have made or shall make a claim under section 8B Inheritance Tax Act 1984.[1]

   1.1.5 "Nil Rate Band" means the upper limit specified in Schedule 1 Inheritance Tax Act 1984.

2. In exercise of the power of Appointment the Present Trustees irrevocably appoint that they hold the [the Nil Rate Fund] [The Trust Fund] apart from the Untransferable Nil Rate Sum upon trust for [name of spouse] absolutely.

3. Subject to that the Will shall stand.

In witness *etc*

---

[1] This sub-clause is only needed if the testator (having survived a previous spouse) has more than 1 nil rate band: the will should impose a duty so a claim must be made.

FORM NRB APPROPRIATION AND APPOINTMENT

This deed is intended to carry out a NRB appropriation scheme. The testator's interest in the family home (or part of it) is appropriated to the trustees in satisfaction of the NRB legacy and a life interest is appointed to the surviving spouse.
It is assumed:
(1) The testator died leaving a classic NRB trust with balance to spouse absolutely in the forms of Will 5 or 6 in the 9th or earlier editions of this book.
(2) It is not desired to wind up the NRB trust.
(3) The widow of the testator survived the testator (and is living at the time of the appointment and not disabled in the IHT sense.)

Time limits: this deed should be executed more than 2 years and less than 3 years after the death of the testator.

This deed is made [date] between

(1) [Name] of [address] ("the Spouse") and

(2) (a) [Name] of [address] and

(3) (b) [Name] of [address]

   (together called "the Present Trustees").

WHEREAS:

(A) This deed is supplemental to the will ("the Will") made [date] by [name] ("the Testator").

(B) The Testator died on [date] and probate was granted on [date] by the [name] registry to the Present Trustees.

(C) The Present Trustees are the present trustees of [the Nil Rate Fund] [the Trust Fund]. [*Will 5 refers to the Nil Rate fund and Will 6 refers to the Trust Fund*]

(D) The Testator's estate includes the property described in clause 1.2 below.

(E) The STEP standard provisions (incorporated by clause [ ][1] confer on the Present Trustees a power of appropriation ("the Power of Appropriation").

(F) Clause [ ][2] of the Will provides:

> "Any asset appropriated in or towards satisfaction of the Nil Rate Sum within three years of my death may be valued for the purpose of the appropriation at its value at the time of my death"

(G) Clause [ ][3] of the Will confers on the Present Trustees the following power ("the Power of Appointment"):

[set out power]

NOW THIS DEED WITNESSES as follows:

1. In this deed:

    1.1 "The Trustees" means the trustees for the time being of the [Nil Rate Fund] [the Trust Fund].

    1.2 "The Property" means [a [specify] share in][4] the property described in the schedule below.

    1.3 ["The Nil Rate Sum"]["The Untransferable Nil Rate Sum"], ["the Nil Rate Fund"]["the Trust Fund"] and "Overriding Powers" have the same meaning as in the Will. [The 9th edition refers to the Untransferable Nil Rate Sum and the 8th and earlier editions to the Nil Rate Sum; Will 5 refers to the Nil Rate Fund and Will 6 refers to the Trust Fund in all editions]

2. In exercise of the Power or Appropriation the Present Trustees appropriate the Property [in][5] [towards][6] satisfaction of [the Untransferable Nil Rate Sum] [the Nil Rate Sum] [the Nil Rate Sum].

3. For the purposes of this appropriation the Property shall be valued at its value at the time of the Testator's death.

4. In exercise of the Power of Appointment the Present Trustees revocably appoint that they hold [the Nil Rate Fund] [the Trust Fund] on the following terms.

---

[1] The STEP provisions are incorporated by clause 7 of Will 5 and clause 8 of Will 6.
[2] The provision is set out in clause 8.9 of Will 5 and clause 9.9 of Will 6.
[3] The power of appointment is set out in clause 5.1 of Will 5 and clause 7.1 of Will 6.
[4] Include wouds in squared brackets if the value of the testator's interest exceeds the nil rate sum.
[5] Include "in" and delete "towards" if the value of the testator's interest exceed the nil rate sum.
[6] Include "towards" and delete "in" if the value of the testator's interest is within the nil rate sum

3. Subject to the Overriding Powers the Trustees shall pay the income of [the Nil Rate Fund] [the Trust Fund] to the Spouse during [her] life.

5. The Present Trustees and the Spouse declare that they hold their interests in the property described in the Schedule below so as to be available to the Spouse for [her] occupation under section 12 of the Trusts of Land and Appointment of Trustees Act 1996.

6. The Spouse undertakes to keep the property described in the schedule below insued and in good repair and meet all outgoings relating to that property.

7. The Trustees may, during the Trust Period, by deed wholly or partly revoke the appointment contained in this deed.

8. Subject to that, the Will shall stand.

In witness *etc*

THE SCHEDULE:

[SPECIFY DETAILS OF PROPERTY]

NIL RATE BAND DISCRETIONARY TRUST: SPOUSE UNDERTAKING

This precedent is for purpose of the arrangements discussed at Chapter 19 (NRB debt arrangements) if it is not desired to wind up the nil rate trust, or to use the appropriation or charge arrangement. It assumes the Will is drafted in form 5 in the current edition of this book. Of course one must review the actual Will in each case. This precedent is for a spouse; amendments for a Civil Partner will be needed, if appropriate.

This Deed is made [date] between;

1 [Name of Spouse] of [address] ("the Spouse") of the one part and
2 (a) [Name] of [address] and
  (b) [Name] of [address]

("the Executors") of the other part.[1]

Whereas:

(A) This Deed is supplemental to the will ("the Will") made [date] by [name] ("the Testator").

(B) The Testator died on [date] and probate was granted on [date] by the [name] registry to the Executors.

(C) Clause [8.2] of the Will provides:

"[8.2.1] My executors may require the Nil Rate Trustees to accept a written undertaking from my spouse.

[8.2.2] That undertaking shall be to pay the Nil Rate Sum (or, if less, the value of my Residuary Estate at the time of the undertaking) to the Nil Rate Trustees on demand. The undertaking may include any other terms and in particular:

---

[1] The executors and the trustees are the same persons and they should not be regarded as separate parties.

[8.2.2.1] fixed or floating security;
[8.2.2.2] interest;
[8.2.2.3] index linking the sum payable.

[8.2.3] That undertaking will be in substitution for plyment of the Nil Rate Sum by the executors to the Nil Rate Trustees. My executors shall be under no further liability in relation to the Nil Rate Sum."

[*Where a avaluation of the residuary estate is needed[2] add:*]

(D) Section 22(3) Trustee Act 1925 provides:

"Trustees may, for the purpose of giving effect to the trust ... (by duly qualified agents) ascertain and fix the value of any trust property in such manner as they think proper, and any valuation so made shall be being upon all persons interested under the trust if the trustees have discharged the duty of care set out in section 1(1) of the Trustee Act 2000."]

[*Where there is uncertainty over the amount of the Nil Rate Sum[3] add:*]

(E) Clause 3.5.7 of the Will provides:

"My Executors may ascertain and fix the amount of the Nil Rate Sum so as to bind all persons interested under this Will if the Executors have discharged the duty of care set out in section (1) Trustee Act 2000."]

Now this deed witnesses as follows:

1. In this deed:

    1.1 **"The Nil Rate Sum"** and **"the Nil Rate Trustees"** have the same meaning as in the Will.
    1.2 "The **Index Linked Nil Rate Sum**" means A + (A x B) where:

        1.2.1 A is the lesser of the Nil Rate Sum and the value of the residuary estate on the date of this deed.[4]
        1.2.2 B = (RD − RI)/RI (rounded to the nearest third decimal place).
        1.2.3 RI is the Retail Prices Index for the month that this agreement is executed.
        1.2.4 RD is the Retail Prices Index for the month before

---

[2] Because the residuary estate is or may be worth less than the nil rate sum (as defined). The undertaking is to pay the lesser of the nil rate sum and the value of the residuary estate: see Recital C

[3] E.g. because the testator has made gifts within seven years of death, and it is not clear what their value is, or whether they qualify for an IHT relief such as the normal expenditure exemption.

[4] This can be simplified depending on the facts of the case. If the value of the residuary estate exceeds the amount of the nil rate sum, simply say: A is the Nil Rate Sum. If the value of the residuary estate is less thatn the amount of the nil rate sum, say: A is the value of the residuary estate at the date of the deed.

the month in which the Index Linked Nil Rate Sum is paid.[5]

1.3 **"The Retail Prices Index"** means:

1.3.1 the general index of retail prices (for all items) published by the Office for National Statistics, or

1.3.2 if that index is not published for a relevant month, any substituted index or index figures published by that Office,

1.3.3 subject to that, the substituted index or index figures which the Nil Rate Trustees (acting reasonably) think appropriate.[6]

2. [*if appropriate (see recital D): The Executors ascertain and fix the value of the residuary estate at the date of this deed as £xxx*]

3. [*if appropriate (see recital E): The Executors ascertain and fix the amount of the Nil Rate Sum as £xxx*]

4. The Spouse undertakes to pay the Index Linked Nil Rate Sum on demand to the Nil Rate Trustees.

5. The Spouse is entitled to pay the Index Linked Nil Rate Sum at any time.

6. Interest is not due on the Index Linked Nil Rate Sum.[7]

7. The benefit of this spouse undertaking may be assigned on the appointment of new trustees or on a distribution of trust property to a beneficiary for no consideration but subject to that shall not be assignable.

8. In consideration of the Spouse undertaking to pay the Index Linked Nil Rate Sum, the Executors require the Nil Rate Trustees to accept that unsertaking in substitution for payment of the Nil Rate Sum by the Executors to the Nil Rate Trustees.

In witness *etc.*

---

[5] The index linking provision is drawn from s.54 TCGA 1992.
[6] The definition of the RPI is drawn from s.989 ITA.
[7] We have considered providing in the documentation for interest to accrue on the spouse's debt (rolled up during the life of the spouse). This is attractive from an IHT viewpoint but it raises IT problems and on balance we think it better not to do this.

NIL RATE BAND DISCRETIONARY TRUST: CHARGE OVER HALF SHARE OF LAND

This precedent is for the purpose of the arrangements discussed at Chapter 19 (NRB charge arrangements) if it is desired not wind up the NRB trust, or to use the appropriation or debt arrangement. It assumes the Will is drafted in form 5 in the current edition of this book. Of course one must review the actual Will in each case. For an additional clause where the amount of the Nil Rate Sum is uncertain, see recital E and clause 3 of the spouse NRB undertaking. Following execution there should be restriction on the Land Register in form A schedule 1 Land Registration Rules 2003.

This Equitable Charge is made [date] by:

1 [Name] of [address] and

2 [Name] of [address]

("the Executors").

Whereas:

(A) This Deed is supplemental to the will ("the Will") made [date] by [name] ("the Testator").

(B) The Testator died on [date] and probate was granted on [date] by the [name] registry to the Executors.

(C) The estate of the Testator includes the property described in the schedule below.

(D) Clause [8.3] of the Will provides:

"8.3.1 My executors may charge all or part of my Residuary Estate with the payment of all or part of the Nil Rate Sum to the Nil Rate Trustees on demand.

8.3.2 That charge may be a fixed or floating charge. It may include any other terms and in particular:

8.3.2.1 interest;
8.3.2.2 index linking the sum payable.

8.3.3 To the extent of the amount charged on the property (and regardless of the value of the property charged):

8.3.3.1 the charge will be in substitution for payment of the Nil Rate Sum by the executors to the Nil Rate Trustees; and

8.3.3.2 my executors shall be under no further liability in relation to the Nil Rate Sum."

Now this deed witnesses as follows.

1. In this deed:

   1.1 **"The Nil Rate Sum"** and **"the Nil Rate Trustees"** have the same meaning as in the Will.

   1.2 **"The Index Linked Nil Rate Sum"** means A + (A x B) where:

   1.2.1 A is the Nil Rate Sum

   1.2.2 B = (RD − RI)/RI (rounded to the nearest third decimal place).

   1.2.3 RI is the Retail Prices Index for the month that this agreement is executed.

   1.2.4 RD is the Retail Prices Index for the month before the month in which the Index Linked Nil Rate Sum is paid.[1]

   1.3 **"The Retail Prices Index"** means:

   1.3.1 the general index of retail prices (for all items) published by the Office for National Statistics, or

   1.3.2 if that index is not published for a relevant month, any substituted index or index figures published by that Office,

   1.3.3 subject to that, the substituted index or index figures which the Nil Rate Trustees (acting reasonably) think appropriate.[2]

2. The Executors charge the property specified in the Schedule with the payment of [all][3] the Index Linked Nil Rate Sum.

---

[1] The index linking provision is drawn from s.54 TCGA 1992.
[2] The definition of the RPI is drawn from s.989ITA.
[3] If the Nil Rate Sum exceeds the value of the charged property, there is a choice:
(1) A part of the Nil Rate Sum is charged on the property, and the balance is paid to the NRB trustees. This maximizes the IHT advantages.
(2) The whole of the Nil Rate Sum is charged on the property and nothing is paid to the NRB trustees. This wastes some of the testator's available nil rate band. On the death of the spouse, and

Payment shall fall due forthwith on demand by the Nil Rate Trustees or forthwith on notice given to the Nil Rate Trustees by the beneficial owner of the property subject to this charge.

3. Interest is not due on the Index Linked Nil Rate Sum.

In witness *etc.*

The Schedule:
The one half share of the Testator in [specify details of property]

IHT deduction for the charge cannot (in short) exceed the then value of the charged property. However it is administratively convenient.

APPOINTMENTS OF NEW TRUSTEES

There follow tow sample precedent appointments of new trustees. The disc contains a more comprehensive list of precedents not printed here as there is much duplication between them. For possible indemnities see Chapter 31.

Retirement and appointment of new trustee: Settlor is appointor

This deed of appointment of new trustees is made [date] between

(1) [Name] of [address] ("the Settlor") or the first part

(2) (a) The Settlor[1] and

(b) [Name] of [address]

("the Continuing Trustees") of the second part[2]

(3) [Name] of [address] ("the New Trustee") of the third part and

(4) [Name] of [address] ("the Retiring Trustee") of the fourth part.

WHEREAS:

(A) This deed is supplemental to the following:

(1) A settlement ("the Settlement") made [date] between (1) the Settlor and (2)(a) the Settlor (b) [name of other original trustee] [*(c) continue with names of other original trustees, if any*].

(2) A deed of appointment made [date] by [parties]. [*set out all deeds of appointment and retirement of trustees*]

---

[1] It is assumed in this draft that the settler is one of the two continuing trustees.
[2] It is not strictly necessary for the continuing trustees to be parties as their consent is not needed to an appointment by the settler, but it is common practice to make them parties.

(B) Clause ... of the Settlement confers on the Settlor the power of appointing new trustees.

(C) The Retiring Trustee wishes to retire from the Settlement.

Now this deed witnesses as follows:

In exercise of the power conferred by *s*.36(1) Trustee Act 1925, the Settlor appoints the New Trustee to be a Trustee in place of the Retiring Trustee.

In witness etc

Appointment of new trustee after death of trustee: Trustees are appointors

This deed of appointment of new trustees is made [date] between

(1) (a) [Name] of [address] and

   (b) [Name] of [address]

   ("the Continuing Trustees") of the first part and

(2) [Name] of [address] ("the New Trustee") of the second part.

WHEREAS:

(A) This deed is supplemental to the following:
   (1) A settlement ("the Settlement") made [date] between (1) [name] ("the Settlor") and (2)(a) the Settlor (b) [name of other original trustee] [*(c) continue with names of other original trustees, if any*].
   (2) A deed of appointment made [date] by [parties] [*set out all deeds of appointment and retirement of trustees*]

(B) Clause ... of the Settlement confers on the Settlor the power of appointing new trustees but the Settlor died on [data].

(C) [Name] ("the Deceased Trustee") died on [date].

Now this deed witnesses as follows:

In exercise of the power conferred by s.36(1) Trustee Act 1925, the Continuing Trustees appoint the New Trustee to be a Trustee in place of the Deceased Trustee.

In witness etc

Retirement without appointment of new trustee: Trustees are appointors

This deed of retirement is made [date] between

(1) (a) [Name] of [address]

(b) [Name] of [address]

("the Continuing Trustees") of the first part and

(2) [Name] of [address] ("the Retiring Trustee") of the second part.

WHEREAS:

(A) This deed is supplemental to the following:
 (1) A settlement ("the Settlement") made [date] between (1) [name] ("the Settlor") and (2)(a) the Settlor (b) [name of other original trustee] [(c) continue with names of other original trustees, if any].
 (2) A deed of appointment made [date] by [parties]

[Set out all deeds of appointment and retirement of trustees]

(B) Clause ... of the Settlement confers on the Settlor the power of appointing new trustees but the Settlor died on [date].

(c) The Retiring Trustee wishes to retire from the Settlement.

Now this deed witnesses as follows:

In exercise of the power conferred by s.39 Trustee Act 1925, the Retiring Trustee retires from the Settlement. The Continuing Trustees consent to the discharge of the Retiring Trustee, and to the vesting in the continuing Trustees alone of the trust property.

In witness *etc*.

APPENDIX 1

STANDARD PROVISIONS OF THE SOCIETY OF TRUST AND ESTATE PRACTITIONERS

The text of the 1st Edition of the STEP Standard Provisions is as follows:

1. INTRODUCTORY

1(1) These Provisions may be called the standard provisions of the Society of Trust and Estate Practitioners (1st Edition).

1(2) These Provisions may be incorporated in a document by the words:–
> The standard provisions of the Society of Trust and Estate Practitioners (1st Edition) shall apply

or in any manner indicating an intention to incorporate them.

2. INTERPRETATION

2(1) In these Provisions, unless the context otherwise requires:-

(a) **Income Beneficiary,** in relation to Trust Property, means a Person to whom income of the Trust Property is payable (as of right or at the discretion of the Trustees).

(b) **Person** includes a person anywhere in the world and includes a Trustee.

(c) **The Principal Document** means the document in which these Provisions are incorporated.

(d) **The Settlement** means any settlement created by the

Principal Document and an estate of a deceased Person to which the Principal Document relates.
- (e) **The Trustees** means the personal representatives or trustees of the Settlement for the time being.
- (f) **The Trust Fund** means the property comprised in the Settlement for the time being.
- (g) **Trust Property** means any property comprised in the Trust Fund.
- (h) **A Professional Trustee** means a Trustee who is or has been carrying on a business which consists of or includes the management of trusts or the administration of estates.

2(2) These Provisions have effect subject to the provisions of the Principal Document.

3. ADMINISTRATIVE POWERS

The Trustees shall have the following powers:

3(1) Investment

(a) The Trustees may invest Trust Property in any manner as if they were beneficial owners. In particular the Trustees may invest in unsecured loans.
(b) The Trustees may decide not to diversify the Trust Fund.

3(2) Management
The Trustees may effect any transaction relating to the management administration or disposition of Trust Property as if they were beneficial owners. In particular:

(a) The Trustees may repair and maintain Trust Property.
(b) The Trustees may develop or improve Trust Property.

3(3) Joint property

The Trustees may acquire property jointly with any Person.

3(4) Income and capital
The Trustees may decide not to hold a balance between conflicting interests of Persons interested in Trust Property. In particular:

(a) The Trustees may acquire

(i) wasting assets and
(ii) assets which yield little or no income
for investment or any other purpose.

(b) The Trustees may decide not to procure distributions from a company in which they are interested.
(c) The Trustees may pay taxes and other expenses out of income although they would otherwise be paid out of capital.

3(5) *Accumulated income*
The Trustees may apply accumulated income as if it were income arising in the current year.

3(6) *Use of trust property*
The Trustees may permit an Income Beneficiary to occupy or enjoy the use of Trust Property on such terms as they think fit. The Trustees may acquire any property for this purpose.

3(7) *Application of trust capital*
The Trustees may:

(a) lend money which is Trust Property to an Income Beneficiary without security, on such terms as they think fit,
(b) charge Trust Property as security for debts or obligations of an Income Beneficiary, or
(c) pay money which is Trust Property to an Income Beneficiary as his income, for the purpose of augmenting his income

Provided that:—

(i) the Trustees have power to transfer such Property to that Beneficiary absolutely; or

(ii) the Trustees have power to do so with the consent of another Person and the Trustees act with the written consent of that Person.

3(8) *Trade*
The Trustees may carry on a trade, in any part of the world, alone or in partnership.

3(9) *Borrowing*
The Trustees may borrow money for investment or any other purpose. Money borrowed shall be treated as Trust Property.

3(10) *Insurance*
The Trustees may insure Trust Property for any amount against any risk.

3(11) *Delegation*
A Trustee may delegate in writing any of his functions to any Person. A Trustee shall not be responsible for the default of that Person (even if the delegation was not strictly necessary or expedient) provided that he took reasonable care in his selection and supervision.

3(12) *Deposit of documents*
The Trustees may deposit documents relating to the Settlement (including bearer securities) with any Person.

3(13) *Nominees*
The Trustees may vest Trust Property in any Person as nominee, and may place Trust Property in the possession or control of any Person.

3(14) *Offshore administration*
The Trustees may carry on the administration of the trusts of the Settlement outside the United Kingdom.

3(15) *Payment of tax*
The Trustees may pay tax liabilities of the Settlement (and interest on such tax) even though such liabilities are not enforceable against the Trustees.

3(16) *Indemnities*
The Trustees may indemnify any Person for any liability properly chargeable against Trust Property.

3(17) *Security*
The Trustees may charge Trust Property as security for any liability properly incurred by them as Trustees.

3(18) *Supervision of company*
The Trustees are under no duty to enquire into the conduct of a company in which they are interested, unless they have knowledge of circumstances which call for enquiry.

3(19) *Appropriation*
The Trustees may appropriate Trust Property to any Person or class of Persons in or towards the satisfaction of their interest in the Trust Fund.

3(20) *Receipt by charities*
Where Trust Property is to be paid or transferred to a charity, the receipt of the treasurer or appropriate officer of the charity shall be a complete discharge to the Trustees.

3(21) *Release of powers*
The Trustees may by deed release any of their powers wholly or in part so as to bind future trustees.

3 (22) *Ancillary powers*
The Trustees may do anything which is incidental or conducive to the exercise of their functions.

4. POWERS OF MAINTENANCE AND ADVANCEMENT

Sections 31 and 32 Trustee Act 1925 shall apply with the following modifications:

(a) The Proviso to section 31(1) shall be deleted.

(b) The words one-half of in section 32(1)(a) shall be deleted.

5. TRUST FOR SALE

The Trustees shall hold land in England and Wales on trust for sale.

6. MINORS

6(1) Where the Trustees may apply income for the benefit of a minor, they may do so by paying the income to the minor's parent or guardian on behalf of the minor, or to the minor if he has attained the age of 16. The Trustees are under no duty to enquire into the use of the income unless they have knowledge of circumstances which call for enquiry.

6(2) Where the Trustees may apply income for the benefit of a minor, they may do so by resolving that they hold that income on trust for the minor absolutely and:

(a) The Trustees may apply that income for the benefit of the minor during his minority.

(b) The Trustees shall transfer the residue of that income to the minor on attaining the age of 18.

(c) For investment and other administrative purposes that income shall be treated as Trust Property.

7. DISCLAIMER

A Person may disclaim his interest under the Settlement wholly or in part.

8. APPORTIONMENT

Income and expenditure shall be treated as arising when payable, and not from day to day, so that no apportionment shall take place.

9. CONFLICTS OF INTEREST

9(1) In this paragraph:

(a) **A Fiduciary** means a Person subject to fiduciary duties under the Settlement.
(b) **An Independent Trustee**, in relation to a Person, means a Trustee who is not:

   (i) a brother, sister, ancestor, descendant or dependent of the Person;
   (ii) a spouse of the Person or of (i) above; or
   (iii) a company controlled by one or more of any of the above.

9(2) A Fiduciary may:

(a) enter into a transaction with the Trustees, or
(b) be interested in an arrangement in which the Trustees are or might have been interested, or
(c) act (or not act) in any other circumstances
even though his fiduciary duty under the Settlement conflicts with other duties or with his personal interest;

Provided that:–

(i) The Fiduciary first discloses to the Trustees the nature and extent of any material interest conflicting with his fiduciary duties, and
(ii) there is an Independent Trustee in respect of whom there is no conflict of interest, and he considers that the transaction arrangement or action is not contrary to the general interest of the Settlement.

9(3) The powers of the Trustees may be used to benefit a Trustee (to the same extent as if he were not a Trustee) provided that there is an Independent Trustee in respect of whom there is no conflict of interest.

10. POWERS OF TRUSTEES

The powers of the Trustees may be exercised:

(a) at their absolute discretion; and

(b) from time to time as occasion requires.

11. TRUSTEE REMUNERATION

11(1) A Trustee who is a solicitor or an accountant or who is engaged in a business may charge for work done by him or his firm in connection with the Settlement, including work not requiring professional assistance. This has priority to any disposition made in the Principal Document.

11(2) The Trustees may make arrangements to remunerate themselves for work done for a company connected with the Trust Fund.

12. LIABILITY OF TRUSTEES

12(1) A Trustee (other than a Professional Trustee) shall not be liable for a loss to the Trust Fund unless that loss was caused by his own fraud or negligence.

12(2) A Trustee shall not be liable for acting in accordance with the advice of Counsel of at least five years standing, with respect to the Settlement, unless, when he does so:

(a) he knows or has reasonable cause to suspect that the advice was given in ignorance of material facts; or

(b) proceedings are pending to obtain the decision of the court on the matter.

13. APPOINTMENT AND RETIREMENT OF TRUSTEES

13(1) A Person may be appointed trustee of the Settlement even though he has no connection with the United Kingdom.

13(2) A Professional Trustee who is an individual who has reached the age of 65 shall retire if:—

    (a) he is requested to do so by his co-trustees, or by a Person interested in Trust Property; and
    (b) he is effectually indemnified against liabilities properly incurred as Trustee.

On that retirement a new Trustee shall be appointed if necessary to ensure that there will be two individuals or a Trust Corporation to act as Trustee.

In this sub-paragraph Trust Corporation has the same meaning as in the Trustee Act 1925.

This sub-paragraph does not apply to a Professional Trustee who is:

    (a) a personal representative
    (b) the settlor of the Settlement or
    (c) a spouse or former spouse of the settlor or testator.

14. PROTECTION FOR INTEREST IN POSSESSION AND ACCUMULATION AND MAINTENANCE SETTLEMENTS

These Provisions shall not have effect:–

(a) so as to prevent a Person from being entitled to an interest in possession in Trust Property (within the meaning of the Inheritance Tax Act 1984);

(b) so as to cause the Settlement to be an accumulation or discretionary settlement (within the meaning of section 5 Taxation of Chargeable Gains Act 1992);

(c) so as to prevent the conditions of section 71(1) Inheritance Tax Act 1984 from applying to Trust Property.

COMMENTARY ON THE STANDARD PROVISIONS[1]

How should the standard provisions be incorporated?

It would be possible to set the provisions out at length. However, the better course is to use a short form.

The following is suggested as a standard form:

---

[1] This commentary does not form part of the standard provisions.

Standard provisions
The standard provisions of the Society of Trust and Estate Practitioners (1st Ed.) shall apply with the deletion of paragraph 5. Section 11 of the Trusts of Land & Appointment of Trustees Act 1996 (consultation with beneficiaries) shall not apply.

No difficulty arises if the standard provisions are incorporated in full without amendment. However, this form makes two minor changes following the Trusts of Land and Appointment of Trustees Act 1996:

(1) Delete standard provision clause 5 ("the Trustees shall hold land in England and Wales on trust for sale"). While this certainly does no harm, it is now unnecessary.

(2) Exclude section 11 of the Act (which imposes duties of consultation inappropriate to substantive trusts).

No amendments are needed in the light of the Trustee Act 2000 or Finance Act 2006, though certain provisions have become unnecessary. STEP will in due course bring out a second edition of the Standard Provisions.

When should the standard provisions be used?

The standard provisions are suitable for inclusion in any normal will or settlement.

In the case of a simple will, some of the provisions may be unnecessary. The drafter is recommended to incorporate the provisions by the short form. To pick and choose among the provisions loses many of the advantages of a standard form. It is a waste of professional time; and runs the risk of accidental omissions.

Are the standard provisions comprehensive?

The Standard Provisions form a comprehensive code of administrative provisions, and in the view of STEP it is not necessary to amend them except in relation to the Trusts of Land and Appointment of Trustees Act 1996.

What should one tell the client?

Many clients would probably not want a detailed explanation of the standard provisions. They would only wish to know that "This is a standard way of providing the executors with a number of technical and routine provisions they need to administer the estate properly."

The STEP Technical Committee have confirmed that no notice is required under the STEP practice rule relating to Trustee Exemption clauses (because the Standard Provisions do not contain any provisions the effect of which is to limit or exclude liability for negligence).

Obtaining probate of a will including the Standard Provisions

A will including the STEP provisions is to be proved in the usual way. It is not necessary to prove the text of the provisions, or to refer to the provisions in the oath.[2]

Duplication of the provisions

Practitioners may duplicate the standard provisions in any way. (Publishers should contact STEP for a formal licence agreement.)

---

[2] Practice Direction of the Principal Registry of the Family Division, April 4, 1995; Circular of Secretary to Principal Registry, May 17, 1995 accessible on *www.kessler.co.uk*. Likewise there is no difficulty if an English grant is resealed in a foreign jurisdiction. However, where a grant of a will is made in a foreign jurisdiction the registrar may require a certified copy of the Standard Provisions. If this is anticipated it would be better not to incorporate the STEP Standard Provisions, but a certificate if needed can be obtained from STEP.

APPENDIX 2

ANNOTATED BIBLIOGRAPHY

General Precedent Works

Butterworths Encyclopaedia of Forms & Precedents covers a broad range of precedents, but includes detailed coverage of trusts and will trusts.

There are three heavy reference works which are now out-of-date. *Hallett's Conveyancing Precedents* (Sweet & Maxwell, 1965) was used in its day for many discretionary trusts, a few of which still exist. *Key and Elphinstone's Precedents in Conveyancing* (Sweet & Maxwell, 15th edn, 1953) and *Prideaux Precedents in Conveyancing* (Stevens, 25th edn, 1958) might still be useful if one wishes to search for old authorities.

Trust Precedents

Practical Trust Precedents (Sweet & Maxwell, also on CD).

Looseleaf is an unsuitable format for trust precedents,[1] but the following may be noted:

Potter & Monroe, *Tax Planning* (Sweet & Maxwell). Principally a work of tax planning, but also includes precedents.

Precedents for the Conveyancer (Sweet & Maxwell).

---

[1] An abbreviated dyslogy. A user who wants to find what was said about a precedent he has used will in due course find the relevant looseleaf pages have been discarded. Trust precedent books need to remain available for later reference. Looseleaf books impose an immoderate burden on the author and an undue administrative burden in the office. They are expensive. One cannot comfortably open looseleaf works in the armchair. The CD Rom will ultimately replace them.

Will Precedents

Among many are:
Wills, Probate & Administration Service (Butterworths, looseleaf).

Style

Legal drafting is by no means insulated from the broader issues of prose composition. Anyone interested in understanding our subject in this context should read first of all George Orwell's magnificent ground breaking essay, *Politics and the English Language* (1946; included in Penguin's *Essays of George Orwell*). Its influence on current thinking (e.g. the Clinton Memorandum on plain English[2]) is readily apparent.

The movement for plain legal English is an international one, and legal drafting in England is also subject to international trends. The rewrite of tax legislation here was preceded by Australian and New Zealand rewrites. Appendix 3 offers some US and Canadian references.

There is good guidance to be found in Garner, *A Dictionary of Modern Legal Usage* (OUP, 2nd edn, 1995). This is on the model of Fowler's *Modern English Usage* addressed to legal drafting and legal writing generally and well worth having on the bookshelf.

Mellinkoff, *The Language of the Law*, 1963, is an excellent scholarly and historical study, also useful on the usage of particular words.

Drafting techniques

There are many books devoted to legal drafting in general. They are of limited practical use because most of a drafter's time is spent not with generalities, but with the specific rules of law affecting the subject matter of the draft. The interested reader is recommended to begin with Piesse, *The Elements of Drafting* (The Law Book Co, 10th edn, 2004). This is short and has a good bibliography.

General Principles of Construction

Trust law textbooks scarcely deal with construction, leaving the field to textbooks on wills which traditionally devote a short chapter to it. The condensed treatment tends to suggest a specious consistency of judicial

---

[2] Accessible on *http://govinfo.library.unt.edu/npr/library/direct/memos/memoeng.html*.

attitude. Lord Denning, *The Discipline of Law* (1st edn, 1979) (Part One, The Construction of Documents), good holiday reading, shows the opposite is the truth.

Hawkins on the Construction of Wills (5th edn, 2000) contains a fascinating chapter on general principles and does not fall into that trap. He is unusual in drawing into a legal textbook the philosophical distinction (used by Frege and later adopted by Russell and Wittgenstein) of *sense* and *reference*, which I often find helpful.[3] Unfortunately this is spoilt by an overemphasis on s.21 Administration of Justice Act 1982, which does not in my view represent "a triumph of the intentional approach" (if it did, there would be a marked difference between wills and lifetime trusts, which has never been suggested).

Those who try first Lewison's *Interpretation of Contracts* (Sweet & Maxwell, 4th edn, 2007) are rarely disappointed. This work now has a rival: *The Construction of Contracts*, Gerard McMeel, OUP, 2007.

Meaning of particular words and phrases

Hawkins and all the textbooks on wills offer chapters on gifts to classes of persons; words describing relationships; and the like. It is usually worth looking at more than one; each deals with aspects that the other does not. *Stroud's Judicial Dictionary* (6th edn, 2000) and Saunders, *Words & Phrases Legally Defined* (3rd edn, 1988) might sometimes be useful.

Plain Legal English Guides

The movement for plain legal English has produced a considerable polemical literature.[4] This includes:

Mark Adler, *Clarity for Lawyers* (The Law Society, 2nd edn, 2006).

Richard Wydick, *Plain English for Lawyers* (5th edn, Carolina Academic Press, 2005).

Michele Asprey, *Plain English for Lawyers* (Federation Press, 3rd edn, 2003).

Peter Butt & Richard Castle, *Modern Legal Drafting* (2nd edn, CUP, 2006).

---

[3] Wilberforce J. found the distinction (independently?) in *Fitch Lovell v IRC* [1962] 1 WLR 1325.
[4] Those interested should join the worthwhile association "Clarity"; see *www.clarity-international.net/*.

History of the Plain English movement

The Plain English movement dates back to the 1960s and has an interesting history. Butt & Castle has a chapter on this, as does Christopher Williams, *Tradition and Change in Legal English* (Peter Lang, 2005) p.168.

Foreign Law Trusts

Drafting Trusts and Will Trusts in Australia, Kessler & Flynn (Thomson, 2008).
Drafting Trusts and Will Trusts in Canada, Kessler & Hunter (Butterworths, 2nd edn 2007).
Drafting Cayman Island Trusts, Kessler & Pursall (Kluwer, 2006).
Drafting Trusts and Will Trusts in the Channel Islands, Kessler & Matthams (Sweet & Maxwell, 2006).
Drafting Trusts and Will Trusts in Northern Ireland, Kessler & Grattan (Butterworths, 2nd edn 2007).
Drafting Trusts and Will Trusts in Singapore, Kessler & Lee (Sweet & Maxwell, 2007).

Statutory Drafting Manuals

Many states and international organisations have put their in-house drafting manuals online. See *Legislative Drafting Guide: A Practitioner's View* by Kenneth Rosenbaum accessible *www.fao.org/Legal/prs-ol/lpo64.pdf* which has a long list of these.

APPENDIX 3

USEFUL WEBSITES

UK Government Sites

www.bailii.org UK cases.
www.statutelaw.gov.uk UK statutes.
www.lawcom.gov.uk Law Commission. Includes recent Law Com. reports including LC260 (Trustees' Powers and Duties) and LC251 (Rules Against Perpetuities and Excessive Accumulations).

www.charitycommission.gov.uk Charity Commission. Their Register of Charities is useful for checking names and details of English charities.

www.oscr.org.uk OSCR Scottish Charity Regulator. Their Register of Charities is useful for checking names and details of Scottish charities

www.landreg.gov.uk English Land Registry. Includes Land Registry practice guides, guide 8 (Execution of Deeds) has many useful forms for trust drafting

www.jerseylaw.je Jersey cases and statutes.

UK Non-Government Sites for Trusts

www.kessler.co.uk James Kessler's website. Includes free updates on this book and an archive of material referred to in this book.

www.trustsdiscussionforum.co.uk Trusts Discussion Forum. Opportunity to subscribe, and archive.

www.venables.co.uk Delia Venables' legal resources. Start here for UK legal links.

www.kcl.ac.uk/schools/law/research/tlc/ Trust Law Committee. Includes report on creditors of trustees and valuable consultation papers on capital/income, trustee exemption clauses and trustee indemnities.

International Sites for Trusts

www.hcch.net Hague Conventions including Convention on Trusts, with lists of contracting states.

International Sites relevant for drafting

www.plainlanguage.gov Website of the Plain Language Action Network. This is a US government group working to improve communications from the federal government to the public. They believe better communications "will increase trust in government, reduce government costs, and reduce the burden on the public". Ambitious, but who is to say they are wrong? Plain English issues extend beyond legal drafting to writing of all kinds. Take a look at their guidance document: *Writing User-Friendly Documents.*

www.hkreform.gov.hk/en/lawlinks/content.htm Good starting point for non-UK legal links

APPENDIX 4

NRB DEBT AND CHARGE ARRANGEMENTS: TAX ANALYSIS

Introduction

This appendix considers the tax aspects of entering into NRB debt and charge schemes. It will be rare for these schemes to be entered into after the FAs 2006 and 2008.[1] However, the issues discussed in this appendix remain important for the many existing schemes. Administration and winding up the scheme are discussed at Chapter 19 (Administration of NRB trusts).

App 4.1

The issues discussed in this appendix only arise for the debt and charge arrangements. If (which is usually preferred) the executors appropriate a share in the family home to the NRB trust, the SDLT issue does not arise, and the other issues only arise so far as there is a debt in addition to the appropriation.

Tax is often very fact sensitive. The analysis in this appendix is based on the following assumptions:

1. A testator has died leaving a Will in forms 5 to 7 of this book and is survived by his spouse.[2] (For Will 4, see below.)

2. The testator owned the whole of the family home, or a share of the family home as a tenant in common. We refer to this as "the land". The land is not subject to a mortgage[3] and is situated in England or Wales.

---

[1] NRB trusts are redundant in most cases after FA 2008 (see Chapter 18). In the limited cases where they remain useful, the best course will usually be to appropriate the testator's interest in the family home (or a share of that interest) to the NRB trust (see Chapter 19 (Administration of NRB Trusts).

[2] Wills 5–6 deal with a testator who is married/a civil partner. Will 7 concerns cohabitees. In this appendix references to spouses include civil partners, and what we say of spouses also applies to a cohabitee in a Will 7 case.

[3] Alternatively any mortgage or charge will be paid off by the executors before the execution of the spouse undertaking or charge.

3. The nil rate band ("NRB") sum given by the Will to the NRB trust is not satisfied by a payment or transfer of assets from the estate. Instead the spouse gives an undertaking ("the spouse undertaking") or the executors execute the charge ("the executors charge") along the lines of the forms in this book. The undertaking or charge is made within one year of the death of the testator.[4]

Further consideration is needed if the estate of the testator at his death includes property qualifying for IHT business or agricultural property relief (unless that property is the subject of a specific gift).[5]

HMRC accept that the pre-owned assets rules do not apply to these arrangements.[6]

Inheritance tax on death of spouse

Debt Scheme

App 4.2 The liability under the spouse undertaking will in principle be deductible for IHT purposes from the estate of the spouse on her death. See s.5(3) IHTA 1984. Section 5(5) IHTA 1984 restricts the deduction unless the debt is incurred for full consideration. In the form in this book the consideration for the debt is (as the drafting makes clear) that the executors require the trustees of the discretionary trust to accept the undertaking in substitution for the NRB legacy: that will be full consideration.

Section 103 FA 1986 disallows certain liabilities for IHT purposes. This is an intricate section which is not considered in detail here.[7] There is only one point relevant for present purposes. HMRC take a point under s.103 where the discretionary trust includes property derived from the spouse who has incurred the liability. A typical case is where:

(1) the family home formerly belonged to H absolutely.

---

[4] The complication of delay is that interest accrues on the NRB legacy after one year from the death of the testator. If the undertaking is made shortly after the year, any interest can be ignored as *de minimis*. It would cost more to deal with the interest in the documentation than the amount of interest would justify. Once the amount of interest becomes more substantial, say, more than £5,000, it would need to be considered. Either the nil rate trustees would waive their right to interest (the simplest solution) or else the amount of the spouse's debt could be increased to allow for the interest. This problem is avoided by providing that interest does not accrue on a NRB legacy for three years.

[5] See 18.17 (Married testator with business or agricultural property).

[6] "Pre-owned Assets, Technical Guidance" 17 March 2005 appendix 1; for a discussion of pre-owned assets see *Taxation of Foreign Domiciliaries*, 7th edn, Key Haven Publications, Chapter 51 (Pre-Owned Assets).

[7] For a detailed analysis see *Taxation of Foreign Domiciliaries*, James Kessler, Key Haven Publications, 7th edn, 2008 para.44.3 (s.103 FA 1986).

(2) H during his lifetime gave a half share to W.

(3) W died first, and gave the NRB sum to a NRB trust.

(4) H executes the spouse undertaking and incurs the debt to the trust.

In such a case H's debt is disallowed for IHT purposes under s.103.[8] In these circumstances the charge arrangement should be used instead.

Charge Scheme

The liability under the executors charge will be deductible from the value of the charged property for IHT purposes, on the death of the surviving spouse. The deduction is the lesser of the value of the asset charged and the amount outstanding under the charge at the time of the death. Section 103 does not apply in the case of a charge for two reasons:

(1) Section 103 only applies to liabilities made by the debtor: it does not apply to the executors charge, which is made by the executors, not by the survivor herself.

(2) Point (1) does not help where a spouse is sole executor, as then she *does* make the disposition which creates the encumbrance.[9] But even in this case, s.103 does not apply because (under the documentation in this book) the disposition is not made for consideration.

Some commentators have expressed the view that the spouse should not be one of the executors (or if appointed should not take out a grant), where a nil rate band debt or charge scheme is to be used, but this is unacceptable for most clients and is in any event unnecessary.

Section 5(5) IHTA 1984 also does not apply.

Interest in possession in nil rate sum

The spouse must not acquire an interest in possession in the trust fund (the nil rate sum) within two years of the death of the testator.[10] Otherwise the entire advantage of the debt or charge arrangement is lost. The circumstances in which a beneficiary of a discretionary trust may acquire an interest in possession in an interest free debt have not been fully worked out by the courts. The solution proposed before 2006 is that the debt is index linked and:

---

[8] *Phizackerley v IRC* [2007] STC (SCD) 328.
[9] The counter-argument is that the surviving spouse creates the encumbrance in a different capacity.
[10] From 2006 it does not matter if the spouse/CP acquires an IP after 2 years, unless the spouse is "disabled" in the IHT sense at the time that the testator died.

(1) In a case where the spouse is absolutely entitled to the residuary estate (Wills 5–7) she should not be sole trustee of the nil rate trust. (Appoint an additional trustee if necessary on completion of administration.)

(2) In the case where the surviving spouse has a life interest in the residuary estate (Will 4) there should be separate persons as trustees of the nil rate sum and trustees of the residuary estate.[11]

If this is done, it is considered impossible for HMRC to maintain that the spouse has an interest in possession.[12] But from 2006 these precautions are not strictly necessary unless the surviving spouse is "disabled" (in the IHT sense).

Stamp duty land tax

The nature of SDLT

App 4.3 The fundamental features of SDLT are as follows:

(1) SDLT is charged on "land transactions".[13] If there is no Land Transaction there will be no SDLT.

(2) A "Land Transaction" means any "acquisition" of a "chargeable interest".[14]

(3) "Chargeable Interest" means (in short):

(a) an interest in land; or
(b) the benefit of an obligation affecting the value of an interest in land.

It does not include a "security interest" (as defined).[15]

---

[11] Under the will they will usually be the same persons, but this can be altered on completion of administration by a suitable appointment of new trustees.

[12] An interest in possession is a present right to present enjoyment: *Pearson v IRC* [1980] STC 318. The spouse does not have an interest in possession for two reasons:

(1) The survivor does not have the "right" to enjoyment of the trust fund (the benefit of the debt). Her "enjoyment" is precarious. The Courts have never decided the point, but this is right in principle, and to some extent supported by comments in *Swales v IRC* [1984] 413 at p. 421.

(2) The survivor does not have "enjoyment" of the nil rate sum. Because of the index linking, she must repay more than the benefit she receives. It is not like an interest-free loan.

It should by no means be conceded that an interest in possession need exist in the absence of all these precautions. In practice HMRC appear not to take the point.

[13] Section 42(1) FA 2003.
[14] Section 43(1) FA 2003.
[15] Section 48 FA 2003.

SDLT on Debt Scheme

We need to consider what are the rights of the parties immediately before and immediately after the spouse undertaking.

For convenience we refer to the executors (of the estate) and the trustees (of the discretionary trust) as separate persons; in practice they will usually be the same persons, but that makes no difference to the position.

Immediately before the undertaking the position is as follows:

(1) The trustees are pecuniary legatees. They are *prima facie* entitled to a cash sum from the estate. That right may be satisfied by certain things other than cash. It may be satisfied by:

(a) an appropriation of assets of the estate *in specie*;[16] or
(b) the spouse undertaking.

Nevertheless the trustees' right is in principle a right to a cash sum. They can recover that sum and nothing else unless and until the executors chose to exercise one of their powers to give them something else. That sum is payable out of, and so a charge on, the residuary estate: see s.34 Administration of Estates Act 1925. We refer to this as "the trustees' rights under the will". If the trustees' rights can be regarded as an interest in land the rights are a "security interest" for SDLT purposes. This is not a Chargeable Interest.

(2) The surviving spouse is entitled to the residuary estate subject to the trustees' rights.

(3) The executors hold the assets subject to the obligation to give effect to the above.

After the undertaking the position is as follows:

(1) the trustees are now entitled to a cash sum from the spouse under the spouse undertaking; the trustees' rights under the will have been extinguished.

(2) the spouse is still entitled to the residuary estate; the estate is now free from the trustees' rights under the will;

(3) the executors hold the assets with the obligation to give effect to the above.

What, therefore, has the spouse undertaking changed? The spouse has *not* become entitled to receive the land by virtue of the undertaking. She was entitled to receive the land before. What has happened is that her

---

[16] See 21.46 (Power of appropriation).

entitlement has ceased to be subject to the burden of the trustees' rights under the will. Her undertaking has freed the land from the burden of paying the NRB legacy.

SDLT on spouse undertaking

The execution of the spouse undertaking does not involve the acquisition of a Chargeable Interest, so there is no SDLT on the occasion of making the undertaking. If the spouse "acquires" an interest in the land at all, what she acquires is by virtue of the release or destruction of the trustees' rights under the will which is not a Chargeable Interest.[17]

The position is different if the spouse agrees to *purchase* an interest in the land from the executors, i.e.

(1) she promises to pay a sum to (or at the direction of) the executors and

(2) the executors promise to transfer the land to her.

SDLT would be payable in the event of such a purchase. However the transaction here would not be carried out in that way.[18]

A separate argument that there is no SDLT on the making of the spouse undertaking may be based on the (daft but well established) principle that a beneficiary of an estate in the course of administration has no interest in the assets of the estate.[19] However, it is not necessary to rely on this argument, which, in any event, may not help in the (less usual but pos-

---

[17] Of course, the destruction of the trustees' rights under the will is not, strictly, an "acquisition" of any interest by the spouse. However s.43(3)(b) FA 2003 provides that the surrender or release of a chargeable interest is regarded as the "acquisition" of that interest by any person whose interest or right is benefited or enlarged by the transaction.

[18] It might be argued that there is no economic difference between:
(1) the surviving spouse purchasing an interest in the land from the executors, and
(2) the survivor giving the undertaking in order to procure the release of the trustees' right under the will.
However "What is the relevant consideration may depend on the terms and form of the transaction adopted by the parties. The parties to a proposed transaction frequently can achieve the same practical and economic result by different methods... If the question is raised what method has been adopted and the transaction is in writing, the answer must be found in the true construction of the document or documents read in the light of all the relevant circumstances." See *Spectros International v Madden* 70 TC 349 at 374 approved in *Garner v Pounds Shipowners and Shipbreakers* 72 TC 561. This comment applies here. Moreover, there *is* a difference between:
(1) The surviving spouse giving the undertaking to procure the release of the trustees' right under the will (which is what happens here); and
(2) The survivor purchasing the interest in the land from the trustees.
An unsatisfied creditor of the estate would be entitled to be paid (if necessary) out of a sale of the land in case (1) but not in case (2).
It follows that the CGT case of *Passant v Jackson* 59 TC 230 has no relevance here. That was a case where a beneficiary *purchased* an interest in land from the executors.

[19] *Lord Sudeley v AG* [1897] AC 11; *CSD v Livingston* [1965] AC 694.

sible) case where the deceased's estate is fully administered before the debt scheme is carried out.

SDLT on transfer of land from executors to spouse following spouse undertaking

Subsequently, in the course of administration of the estate, the executors will transfer the testator's interest in the land to the spouse (as the residuary legatee entitled under the Will of the testator). This is done by means of an "assent". This is a Land Transaction because at this point the spouse acquires a Chargeable Interest (an interest in land). However there is no SDLT on this Land Transaction.

SDLT is charged on the "Chargeable Consideration". If there is no "Chargeable Consideration" there is no SDLT. Chargeable Consideration is defined:

> The chargeable consideration for a transaction is, except as otherwise expressly provided, any consideration in money or money's worth given for the subject-matter of the transaction, directly or indirectly, by the purchaser[20]...

The spouse's undertaking is not "consideration" given for the spouse's acquisition of the land from the executors. Consideration is a contractual term: it means what the spouse pays for.[21] The spouse undertaking here is given in consideration of the executors exercising their power and the extinction of the trustees' rights under the will. It may be said that the spouse would not receive the land unless she gave the undertaking.[22] But even if receiving the land were a *consequence* of the spouse's undertaking, it would not be in *consideration* of it. The spouse acquires the land as residuary legatee, and not as purchaser. The reason that she does so is because the land forms part of the residuary estate of the testator of which the spouse is residuary legatee. If the spouse has acquired any interest in land for consideration, what she has acquired is a security interest and not a Chargeable Interest.

It may be said that the spouse has given consideration for the land transaction "indirectly". But if the above analysis is right then she has not given consideration for the land transaction (the assent) either directly or indirectly.[23]

---

[20] Schedule 4 para.1 FA 2003. The spouse is the "purchaser" (as defined); see s.43(4) FA 2003.
[21] *C&E Comms v Apple & Pear Development Council* [1996] STC 383 at 389; *R v Braithwaite* [1983] 1 WLR 385 at 391.
[22] This is only the case if one assumes the estate has insufficient assets to meet the NRB sum without recourse to the land, and if one assumes (implausibly) that the charge scheme would not have been used.
[23] The correct construction of the definition of "Chargeable Consideration" is this: it applies where:
  (1) consideration is given directly by a purchaser, or
  (2) it is given indirectly by a purchaser (e.g. the purchaser gives funds to A and A uses the funds to pay the consideration to the vendor).

If this argument were wrong, then prior to 1 December 2003 the same arrangement would have been subject to stamp duty. But nobody suggested that that was the case.

If this argument were wrong, then when land is held on trust for A for life remainder to B, and B purchases A's interest, there is double SDLT: on the purchase and again on a later conveyance from the trustees to B.

Paragraph 3A Schedule 3 FA 2003 provides a separate reason that there is no SDLT on the transfer to the spouse:

> (1) The acquisition of property by a person in or towards satisfaction of his entitlement under or in relation to the will of a deceased person, or on the intestacy of a deceased person, is exempt from charge.
> (2) Sub-paragraph (1) does not apply if the person acquiring the property gives any consideration for it, other than the assumption of secured debt.
> (3) Where sub-paragraph (1) does not apply because of sub-paragraph (2), the chargeable consideration for the transaction is determined in accordance with paragraph 8A(1) of Schedule 4.
> (4) In this paragraph—
> "debt" means an obligation, whether certain or contingent, to pay a sum of money either immediately or at a future date, and
> "secured debt" means debt that, immediately after the death of the deceased person, is secured on the property.

However, it is not necessary to rely on this (which would not help in a case where the NRB gift was made by instrument of variation).

HMRC view

HMRC's view is set out in their SDLT Manual.[24] They say:

> The transfer of an interest in land, whether to a residuary beneficiary or to any other person, and whether in satisfaction of an entitlement under a Will or not, is a land transaction for SDLT purposes. The question is whether the transferee gives any chargeable consideration for the transfer.

This is correct. The statement continues:

> Very often a beneficiary gives no chargeable consideration for the transfer of land under a Will. However transactions in connection with NRB Trusts *may* result in the beneficiary giving chargeable consideration.

One can test the matter with this theoretical example. Suppose under the will (or deed of variation) the trustees do not receive a pecuniary legacy: they are given an interest in the land, say, a lease. Suppose the surviving spouse then pays for the extinction of that interest. That would be the "acquisition" of a "chargeable interest" so it would be a Land Transaction subject to SDLT. However, when the executors subsequently assent the land to the survivor, nobody would say that there is *another* charge to SDLT at that point. For the consideration that the survivor gave in this case would not be for that land transaction.

[24] SDLTM04045 (scope: how much is chargeable). HMRC published their view in a statement on 12 November 2004 repeated verbatim in SDLT Newsletter no.4, December 2004.

(Emphasis added.)
This is correct if one is allowed to stress the word "may". The statement continues:

> The commonest examples of such transactions, and their SDLT consequences, are as follows:
> [1] [a] The NRB trustees accept the surviving spouse's promise to pay in satisfaction of the pecuniary legacy and
>   [b] in consideration of that promise land is transferred to the surviving spouse.
> The promise to pay is chargeable consideration for SDLT purposes.

This assumes that the transfer is in consideration of the spouse's promise. Of course it could be, and if it is then the SDLT charge applies. In the documentation in this book the transfer is not in consideration of that promise for the reasons set out above. It is difficult to comment further in the absence of any analysis in the HMRC statement.
The statement continues:

> [2][a] The NRB trustees accept the personal representatives' promise to pay in satisfaction of the pecuniary legacy[25] and
> [b]   land is transferred to the surviving spouse in consideration of the spouse accepting liability[26] for the promise.
> The acceptance of liability for the promise is chargeable consideration for SDLT purposes. The amount of chargeable consideration is the amount promised (not exceeding the market value of the land transferred).

We agree that if this happened, then of course there is chargeable consideration for SDLT purposes. But once again that is not the way things are done in this book (or in any other).
The statement continues:

> [3] Land is transferred to the surviving spouse and the spouse charges the property with payment of the amount of the pecuniary legacy. The NRB trustees accept this charge in satisfaction of the pecuniary legacy. The charge is money's worth and so is chargeable consideration for SDLT purposes

Since no-one has and, probably, no-one ever will carry out their NRB arrangements in precisely this way, it is not necessary to comment.
For these reasons it is considered clear that no SDLT arises in the case of the debt scheme.
The statement concludes with a comment on the charge scheme:

---

[25] The author of these words is confused. It would be pointless for the NRB trustees to "accept the PR's promise to pay in satisfaction of the pecuniary legacy" since the pecuniary legacy is itself an obligation of the PR's to pay.
[26] It is not strictly possible for the spouse to "accept liability" for the PR's promise. Presumably what is meant in contract law terms is a novation under which the trustees are released from their liability and the spouse undertakes a new one.

[4][a] The personal representatives charge land with the payment of the pecuniary legacy.

[b] The personal representatives and NRB trustees also agree that the trustees have no right to enforce payment of the amount of the legacy personally against the owner of the land for the time being.[27]

[c] The NRB trustees accept this charge in satisfaction of the legacy.

[d] The property is transferred to the surviving spouse subject to the charge.

There is no chargeable consideration for Stamp Duty Land Tax purpose[s] provided that there is no change in the rights or liabilities of any person in relation to the debt secured by the charge.

The conclusion of HMRC that there is no SDLT on the execution of the charge is correct and not contentious.

FA 2004 Sch.4 para.8 has no impact on the debt or the charge scheme.

SDLT: Conclusion

There are two ways to proceed. The first is to follow the suggestion of HMRC statement (4) and use the charge scheme rather than the debt scheme. The charge scheme does have the attraction that documentation falls within the precise wording of the HMRC statement and the SDLT position is not contentious. On the other hand there are two drawbacks:

(1) Conveyancing on the subsequent sale of the property is made slightly complicated. However the problems are soluble.[28]

(2) The amount of the deduction for the charge on the death of the spouse is limited to the value of the land charged, not the value of the residuary estate of the deceased survivor. This is not a problem if the land charged is worth the amount of the nil rate sum or more, but it is a serious problem if the land charged is worth less than the nil rate sum. The only solution is to use the debt scheme as well as the charge scheme. For example, if a testator dies leaving a half share of land worth £150,000 and assets of £80,000 then there will be a charge on £150,000 and a spouse undertaking for £80,000.

---

[27] This is misconceived because under no circumstances would the trustees have a right to enforce payment of the amount of the legacy personally against the owner of the land unless the owner of the land had undertaken liability to pay.

[28] If the surviving spouse purchases a new property of equal or greater value than the asset charged, a new charge can be made over that property. If the survivor does not purchase a new property (perhaps moving into residential care) she can enter into a debt scheme at that point. If the survivor purchases a new property of lesser value than the value of the asset charged, it may be necessary to do both.

The alternative is to rely on the analysis set out in this appendix and to use the debt scheme as would have been done before. We think the SDLT position is clear and this is an entirely acceptable course. On balance, we think it is to be preferred. Indeed, we would be surprised if this view was ever seriously challenged. The only problem is that the (relatively) small sums of SDLT at stake in individual cases would make it difficult for a taxpayer to manage the dispute: costs would exceed the sums at stake. However we would be sufficiently confident in the correctness of the analysis in this appendix to offer to act on a pro bono or contingency basis if this view is challenged in respect of a spouse undertaking in the form in this book.

Capital gains tax on execution of the spouse undertaking

App 4.4 The execution of the spouse undertaking does not give rise to any capital gains tax. Neither the executors nor the spouse dispose of any asset when they execute the undertaking. The trustees of the discretionary trust do not dispose of an asset giving rise to a chargeable gain because of the general rule that satisfaction of a cash legacy does not give rise to capital gains tax in the hands of the legatee.[29] HMRC have in practice accepted this.

Will 4 cases

App 4.5 In Will 4, the residuary estate is held on interest in possession trusts, and the NRB sum remains unpaid: see 19.5 (Implementation of debt scheme.) There is no difficulty in obtaining the deduction under s.103 FA 1986 and no question of SDLT.

---

[29] Either s.62(4)(b) or s.251 TCGA 1992 provides relief here. It may also be said that the trustees do not, at that stage, exist for CGT purposes (the estate still being in the course of administration).

APPENDIX 5

TAX ON PAYMENT OF INDEX LINKED NIL RATE SUM

In the draft spouse undertaking in this book, the spouse undertakes to pay to the trustees an amount called the Index Linked Nil Rate Sum, which is, the nil rate sum increased by the retail price index. In the draft charge, the executors charge property (the testator's interest in the land) with payment of the index linked nil rate sum.

This appendix deals with the question of whether the trustees are subject to tax on the indexation element when this amount is paid.

These comments only apply to the drafts in this book. It is possible that a drafter unfamiliar with the tax rules could create a debt on which interest accrues (income-taxable if interest paid); or possibly, a deeply discounted security (income-taxable on disposal); or a debt on a security (CGTable on disposal).

Income tax: Interest

App 5.1 HMRC have on occasion argued that the indexation element is interest and subject to income tax. This appendix discusses the issue in detail.

The following propositions are well established:

(1) Someone who lends money faces various losses or risks of losses, for which he would normally require compensation or consideration, in return for making the loan:

   (a) Loss of the benefit of use of the money while the loan is outstanding.
   (b) The risk that the lender will not recover all the money owing due to insolvency of the borrower.
   (c) The risk that the money which the lender does recover will

not be worth as much as when it was lent due to inflation or other changes in the value of currency.

(2) Compensation for (a) is classified as interest and subject to income tax when received. Compensation for risks (b) and (c) may either take the form of additional interest or it may be a capital receipt ("capital"). If it is capital it is not subject to income tax. The only difficulty is to tell which it is; this depends on the contract and surrounding circumstances.

(3) So if

(a) the loan is at a reasonable commercial rate of interest, and
(b) the supplement is identified as compensation for the capital risk because of the risk of insolvency of the borrower

then the supplement is capital:

> "A lends £100 to B at a reasonable commercial rate of interest and stipulated for payment of £120 at the maturity of the loan. In such a case it may well be that A requires payment of the £20 as compensation for the capital risk; or it may merely be deferred interest. If it be proved that the former was the case by evidence of what took place during the negotiations, it is difficult to see on what principle the £20 ought to be treated as income [ie, it is capital]."[1]

This was in fact the case in *Lomax v Peter Dixon*, where the loan to a Finnish company in 1930 faced the risk that it would not be repaid in the event of a Russian invasion:

> "The element of capital risk was quite obviously a serious one, and the parties were entitled to express it in the form of capital rather than in the form of interest if they bona fide so chose."[2]

(4) The same applies if:

(a) the loan is at a reasonable commercial rate of interest, and
(b) the supplement is compensation for the capital risk of *inflation* (reduction in the value of money).

Lord Greene gives the example of repayment linked to gold prices:

> "A good example of the difficulty is to be found in the contracts of loan which used to be made on a gold basis when the currency had left, or was expected to leave, the gold standard.[3] In such contracts the amount to be repaid was fixed by reference to the price of gold ruling at the repayment date, and if the currency depreciated in terms of gold, there

---

[1] *Lomax v Peter Dixon* 25 TC 353 at p.363.
[2] *Lomax v Peter Dixon* 25 TC 353 at p.365.
[3] Lord Greene is writing in 1943: Britain had come off the gold standard in 1931.

was a corresponding increase in the amount of sterling to be repaid at the maturity of the loan. It could scarcely be suggested that this excess ought to be treated as income when the whole object of the contract was to ensure that the lender should not suffer a capital loss due to the depreciation of the currency."[4]

The same principle applies to RPI indexation:

"The Inland Revenue wish to clarify the tax position regarding corporate stock issued on an indexed basis and bearing a reasonable commercial rate of interest. ... Although the precise tax treatment must have regard to the terms of any contract between the parties, in general if the indexation constitutes a capital uplift of the principal on redemption to take account of no more than the fall in real value because of inflation the lender ... will be liable only to CGT on the uplift... [i.e. the uplift is capital not interest].[5]

(5) If a *commercial* loan does not provide for interest, then any supplement paid on repayment of the loan is regarded as interest:

"But in many cases mere interpretation of the contract leads nowhere. If A lends B £100 on the terms that B will pay him £110 at the expiration of two years, interpretation of the contract tells us that B's obligation is to make this payment; it tells us nothing more. The contract does not explain the nature of the £10. Yet who could doubt that the £10 represented interest for the two years? The justification for reaching this conclusion may well be that, *as the transaction is obviously a commercial one*, the lender must be *presumed to have acted on ordinary commercial lines* and to have stipulated for interest on his money. In the case supposed, the £10, if regarded as interest, is obviously interest at a reasonable commercial rate, a circumstance which helps to stamp it as interest."[6]

The same applies if a commercial loan is at a low rate of interest: the supplement may be regarded as further interest. A possible example is *IRC v Thomas Nelson & Sons*: interest on the loan was payable at 3% which was "a remarkably low rate for an unsecured loan of this kind". The supplement was held to be interest.[7]

In the light of these clear cases, what is the position with the index linked sum? The key to the answer is to appreciate that this is not a commercial transaction. The loan is a transaction between friendly, connected persons, the executors and the spouse. The charge is a unilateral transac-

---

[4] *Lomax v Peter Dixon* 25 TC 353 at p.363.
[5] Press Release 25 June 1982 [1982] STI 270 approved *R v IRC Ex. p. MFK* [1989] STC 873 at p.877d.
[6] *Lomax v Peter Dixon* 25 TC 353 at p.362. *Davies v Premier Investment* 27 TC 27 is a straightforward example.
[7] 22 TC 175. However there was a second feature of the supplement which gave it the character of income: the amount paid increased with the length that the loan was outstanding, in the manner of interest.

tion, though the executors have in mind the interests of two parties, the spouse and the trustees of the NRB trust. In each case the indexation element is less than market rate interest: the object is that the spouse should pay less than the commercial cost of borrowing. The object of indexation is not to obtain a profit: it is so as not to incur a loss due to inflation. It is the paradigm of a capital receipt.

If the agreement had included market rate interest *and* an indexation element, the indexation element would be capital. The fact that the interest is dropped because of the element of bounty or gratuitous intent does not turn what would otherwise be capital into income.

HMRC must rely on proposition (4): that if a *commercial* loan does not provide for interest, then the supplement paid on repayment of the loan is regarded as interest because "the lender must be presumed to have acted on ordinary commercial terms." This reason does not apply here because the spouse undertaking or charge is not commercial.

It is true that Lord Greene says:

> "Where no interest is payable as such, different considerations will, of course, apply. In such a case ... a 'premium' will normally, if not always, be interest. But it is not necessary or desirable to do more than to point out the distinction between such cases and the case of a contract similar to that which we are considering."[8]

Here is some comfort for HMRC. But Lord Greene is at all times considering commercial loans, and he rightly qualified this broad statement so it applies "normally" but not necessarily "always".

For these reasons there is no income tax charge on payment of the index linked nil rate sum.

If this were held to be wrong, one could avoid the charge on interest from arising by waiving the debt, or the indexation element, after the death of the debtor. Interest is not taxable if it is waived before payment.[9]

Income tax: Deeply discounted securities

If the benefit of the spouse undertaking or charge is a deeply discounted security, the profit is subject to IT under s.427 ITTOIA 2005. However, this only applies if the agreement constitutes a "security" within the meaning of these provisions. Clearly, not every debt is a security, there must be something more. "Security" is not defined and bears its normal commercial meaning. For the meaning of the phrase it is more appropriate to turn to commercial law than to tax cases.

App 5.2

---

[8] *Lomax v Peter Dixon* 25 TC 353 at p.3657.
[9] *Dewar v IRC* 19 TC 361.

Interests in Securities (Benjamin, 2000) states (para.1.03, 1.10):

"Securities are a type of transferable financial asset. The meaning of the term 'securities' has varied over time.[10] Originally the term was used to denote security interests (such as mortgages and charges) supporting the payment of a debt or other obligation. In the early modern period, companies and government agencies began to raise capital from the public by issuing transferable debt obligations, the repayment of these debt obligations was secured on the assets of the issuer.[11] By a process of elision, these secured debt obligations came to be known as 'securities'.[12] Since late medieval times, commercial companies have raised funds by issuing participations or shares. In the Victorian era the transferability of these shares under the general principles of company law was put beyond doubt. As shares became more readily transferable, their functional likeness to debt securities became clearer, and both forms of investment became known as 'securities'. More recently, the term 'securities' has been extended to include units in investment funds and other forms of readily transferable investment. . . .[13]
Transferability is an essential characteristic of securities.[14]

Gore-Browne on Companies states at 17.3 [footnotes in original]::

"The term 'security' has no precise legal meaning, but is traditionally used to describe 'something which makes the enjoyment or enforcement of a right more secure or certain'.[15] Consequently, the term 'debt security' traditionally describes an instrument, given by the debtor in addition to the original debt, and either containing an additional promise or constituting evidence of the debt, designed to make the creditor's burden easier to discharge.[16] One major example of such an instrument is obviously one which creates security, but the creation of security is not essential. It appears to be enough that the instrument acknowledges a liability in a form which makes its enforcement easier or more convenient. Thus promissory notes and certificates for unsecured loan stock

---

[10] 'The word [securities] is not a term of art, but only a word of description. It is a commercial word which will vary with the history of commerce': *Re Rayner* [1904] 1 Ch 176, per Vaughan Williams L.J. at 185.
[11] Such secured corporate debt obligations are called debentures.
[12] See *Re Smithers* [1939] Ch 1015 per Crossman J. at 1017–1020.
[13] The connotation of a security interest has now been lost: 'finally, we do not consider there is any requirement for a security to confer a proprietary interest in the fund or assets to which it relates': letter, Dilwyn Griffiths, HM Treasury, to Iain Saville, CRESTCo, 19 July 2000.
   See also *Re Douglas' Will Trusts, Lloyds Bank v Nelson* [1959] WLR 744 per Vaisey J. at 749: 'I am prepared to make a declaration that "securities" includes any stocks or shares or bonds by way of investment'. See the discussion of the meaning of the term in *Re Rayner* [1904] 1 Ch 176 per Romer L.J. at 189, per Stirling L.J. at 191.
[14] Indeed, the repackaging of relatively illiquid assets into readily transferable assets is known as 'securitisation'.
[15] Jowitt's *Dictionary of English Law* (2nd edn, 1977. (Cf. *Singer v Williams* [1921] 1 AC 41 at 49 (per Viscount Cave L.C.), 57 (per Lord Shaw), 59 (per Lord Wrenbury) and 63 (per Lord Phillimore): the comments are probably distinguishable as being primarily concerned with distinguishing securities from possessions (for income tax purposes).
[16] See *The British Oil and Cake Mills Ltd v IRC* [1903] 1 KB 689 at 697 to 698 per Stirling LJ: *Jones v IRC* [1895] 1 QB 484 at 494 per Collins J.; *Brown, Shipley & Co v IRC* [1895] 2 QB 598.

are 'securities',[17] and the term is now commonly used to describe virtually any form of financial instrument issued in connection with a loan.[18]

Further, a "deeply discounted security" is one where the amount payable *on maturity* is or might be an amount involving a deep gain. Since the spouse's debt on the spouse undertaking is payable on demand, the debt matures immediately it is made.[19] Hence the debt (even it is a security) is not a "deeply discounted security".[20]

In its normal sense the word "security" can apply to a debt owed by an individual as well as a company. However here it is considered that the provisions apply only to corporate debt. The securities must be issued, and the word "issued" is only appropriate to a corporate issuer, i.e. a company can issue shares or debentures, but an individual does not "issue" a security. In *Hansard* it is stated that the provisions apply only to corporate debt.[21]

Capital Gains Tax

Section 251(1) TCGA provides: App 5.3

> Where a person incurs a debt to another, whether in sterling or in some other currency, no chargeable gain shall accrue to that (that is the original) creditor or his personal representative or legatee on a disposal of the debt, except in the case of the debt on a security ...

Thus no chargeable gain arises on a disposal of the debt. The spouse undertaking clearly gives rise to a debt; it is considered that the rights of the trustees under the charge are likewise within the relief of s. 251.

The relief does not apply if the debt is a "debt on a security". The fact (inter alia) that the debtor is entitled to repay the debt at any time is inconsistent with the status of "debt on a security": see *Taylor Clark International v Lewis* 71 TC 226.

---

[17] See *Speyer Brothers v IRC* [1908] AC 92; *Rowell v IRC* [1897] 2 QB 194.
[18] The term 'security', and variations of it, are also specifically defined for certain statutory and regulatory purposes: see e.g. Criminal Justice Act 1993, s.54, Sch.2; Taxation of Chargeable Gains Act 1992 s.132(3)(b); Financial Services Act 1986 s.142(7); Banking Act 1987 (Exempt Transactions) Regulations 1997 SI 1997/817, *The Listing Rules* (the London Stock Exchange); Trustee Act 1925 s.68(1), para.(13); Income and Corporation Taxes Act 1988 s.710; Insolvency Act 1986 s.248. See also *Bristol Airport Plc v Powdrill* [1990] Ch 744; *Taylor Clark International ltd v Lewis (Inspector of Taxes)* [1997] STC 499.
[19] See *Edwards v Walters* [1896] 2 Ch 157 following *Re George* (1890) 44 Ch D 627.
[20] We are grateful to Rory Mullen for this observation.
[21] *Hansard* 26/4/1996 col. 1360 (Lord Mackay: "Clauses 80 to 105 cover the measures in this Bill which relate to the taxation of corporate debt.") *http://hansard.millbanksystems.com/lords/1996/apr/26/finance-bill*.

Conclusion

App 5.4 For these reasons there is in our view no tax on the payment of the index linked sum. The amount of tax at stake in any one case is likely to be small but (to avoid cases settling by reason of the costs of defending what is right) we would be prepared to act on a pro bono basis if this were challenged in relation to a document drafted in the form in our book.

APPENDIX 6

SHARE OF HOUSE IN TRUST: CGT PRIVATE RESIDENCE RELIEF

This appendix considers the availability of CGT private residence relief ("PPR relief") where a share in a dwelling house is held in a trust. The issue typically arises where:

(1) The testator and his spouse (or civil partner—all references in this chapter to spouses include civil partners) own the family home ("the property") as tenants in common.

(2) T dies and is survived by his spouse.

(3) T leaves a will establishing a NRB trust (or of course the same position can be reached by a deed of variation);

(4) The executors appropriate the testator's share in the family home to the trust in satisfaction of the NRB legacy;

(5) The appropriation is made more than two years after the testator's death (in order to avoid any argument that the surviving spouse acquired an IPDI, which is an estate-IP)[1];

(6) The surviving spouse continues to occupy the property.

If the property is sold, a gain will accrue to the surviving spouse and the trustees. The gain accruing to the spouse will qualify for private residence relief (it is assumed all the conditions for that relief are met). The question is whether the gain accruing to the trustees also qualifies for relief.

The availabilty of the relief is especially important given that no tax-free uplift will be available on the death of the surviving spouse (as would be the case if she had an estate-IP).[2]

---

[1] This will not prevent an estate-IP if the surviving spouse is disabled (in the IHT sense) at the time of the death of the testator. It is assumed that the spouse is not disabled.
[2] Section 72(1A) TCGA 1992.

Relief for individuals

App 6.1 Sections 222–224 TCGA provide PPR relief for individuals. So far as relevant s.222(1) provides:

> This section applies to a gain accruing to an individual so far as attributable to the disposal of, or of an interest in—
>
> (a) a dwelling-house or part of a dwelling-house which is, or has at any time in his period of ownership been, his only or main residence, or
> (b) land which he has for his own occupation and enjoyment with that residence as its garden or grounds up to the permitted area.

Section 222 is headed *Relief on disposal of private residence* but in fact the relief is conferred by s.223 (which is headed *Amount of relief*). For present purposes it is sufficient to set out s.223(1):

> No part of a gain to which section 222 applies shall be a chargeable gain if the dwelling-house or part of a dwelling-house has been the individual's only or main residence throughout the period of ownership, or throughout the period of ownership except for all or any part of the last 36 months of that period.

Relief for trustees

App 6.2 Of course this by itself would not help trustees, as s.222 applies where a gain accrues to an *individual*, and trustees are not an individual. However the relief is extended by s.225 TCGA. So far as relevant this provides:

> [1] Sections 222 to 224 shall also apply in relation to a gain accruing to the trustees of a settlement
> [2] on a disposal of settled property being an asset within section 222(1)
> [3] where, during the period of ownership of the trustees, the dwelling-house or part of the dwelling-house mentioned in that subsection has been the only or main residence of a person entitled to occupy it under the terms of the settlement,
> [4] and in those sections as so applied—
> (a) references to the individual shall be taken as references to the trustees except in relation to the occupation of the dwelling-house or part of the dwelling-house ...

The condition in s.225[3] is:

> during the period of ownership of the trustees, the dwelling-house ... mentioned in that subsection has been the only or main residence of a person entitled to occupy it under the terms of the settlement.

The word "during" is capable of bearing two meanings. It could mean "throughout" the trustees' period of ownership. Here, however, it clearly means "at some point" in their ownership (otherwise the apportionment provision in s. 223(2) TCGA could never apply).

The PPR provisions in ss. 222–224 apply to trusts subject to the modifications of s.225[4]. Amended as s.225[4] requires, s.222[1] provides:

> (1) This section applies to a gain accruing to an individual [*the trustees*] so far as attributable to the disposal of, or of an interest in—
>
> (a) a dwelling-house or part of a dwelling-house which is, or has at any time in his [*the trustees'*] period of ownership been, his [*the individual's*] only or main residence, or
>
> (b) land which he has [*the trustees have*] for his [*the individual's*] own occupation and enjoyment with that residence as its garden or grounds up to the permitted area.

As noted above, PPR relief is conferred by s.223. Amended as s.225[4] requires, s.223(1) provides:

> No part of a gain to which section 222 applies shall be a chargeable gain if the dwelling-house or part of a dwelling-house has been *the individual's* only or main residence throughout the period of ownership, or throughout the period of ownership except for all or any part of the last 36 months of that period ...

The reference to "individual" here must be to the beneficiary since it is a reference in relation to the occupation of the residence.

If the residence has not been the beneficiary's only or main residence throughout the trustees ownership, only a fraction of the gain is exempt: s.223(2) TCGA. However in the circumstances which we are envisaging, the residence will be the beneficiary's residence throughout the period of ownership of the trustees.

Amount of relief

Section 223(1) TCGA provides that no part of the gain is chargeable if the *beneficiary* occupied the property as his/her only or main residence throughout the *trustees'* period of ownership. As long as the surviving spouse occupied the property since death (which will normally have been the case), PPR relief is in principle available in full, i.e. without any apportionment of the gain.

Section 223 does not require that the beneficiary is *entitled* to occupy throughout the trustees' period of ownership. Rather the requirement is that the beneficiary has in fact *occupied* it throughout that period.

Entitlement to occupy

The relief is only available to the trustees if, at least at some point during their ownership of the residence, a beneficiary is "entitled to occupy ... under the terms of the settlement": s.225[3] TCGA. This raises the question whether the surviving spouse is entitled to occupy.

App 6.3

It has been suggested[3] that as a matter of land law the spouse is not entitled to occupy; trustees in the circumstances envisaged in this appendix cannot have power to allow any beneficiary to occupy the property. An express power is invalid. If this is right, the surviving spouse does not and cannot occupy "under the terms of the settlement" and PPR relief is not available.

Rights of occupation are governed by the TLATA.[4] Section 12(1) TLATA provides:

> A beneficiary who is beneficially entitled to an interest in possession in land subject to a trust of land is entitled by reason of his interest to occupy the land at any time if at that time—
>
> (a) the purposes of the trust include making the land available for his occupation (or for the occupation of beneficiaries of a class of which he is a member or for the beneficiaries in general) or
>
> (b) the land is held by the trustees so as to be so available.

The first question is whether the NRB trust is a "trust of land". A trust of land is "any trust of property which consists of or includes land".[5] "Land" includes a "right, privilege or benefit in, over, or derived from land".[6] The NRB trust holds a right in land so it is a trust of land.[7] There may of course be two (or more) rights or interests in the same physical land, in which case there may be two (or more) trusts holding those rights, each of which are trusts of land. That is in fact the case here, since the surviving spouse holds the legal title to the land,[8] which is also a trust of land, but that does not matter.

The surviving spouse is "a beneficiary".[9] The next question is whether she is "beneficially entitled to an interest in possession in land subject to a trust of land." Since the spouse will have an interest in possession (see below) in the NRB trust, she clearly meets this condition.

Lastly, we note that the conditions in s.12(a)(b) TLATA are met. Accordingly the surviving spouse has a right to occupy the land under s.12 TLATA.[10]

---

[3] Chamberlain and Whitehouse, *Trust Taxation—Planning After the Finance Act 2006*, at paras 28.16 and 31.25

[4] This point is considered in more detail in *Taxation of Foreign Domiciliaries*, James Kessler, 7th edn, 2008, para.5.22 (Co-ownership defence to living accommodation charge).

[5] Section 1 TLATA 1996.

[6] Section 205(1)(ix) LPA incorporated by s.23(2) TLATA.

[7] TLATA repealed the words "but not an undivided share in land" which had previously appeared in that section: s.25(2), Sch.4 TLATA. It is therefore clear that the expression "trust of land" used in TLATA includes a trust holding a share in land.

[8] It is assumed that legal title was vested in the testator and the spouse during their joint lifetimes; on the death of the testator legal title would pass to the surviving spouse by survivorship.

[9] Section 22 TLATA 1996.

[10] For completeness, the right to occupy land can be restricted under s.12(2) or s.13 TLATA 1996, but these provisions will not apply here.

We consider that any argument that the surviving spouse has no right to occupy the land under the terms of the NRB trust is misconceived.

Section 12 TLATA requires that the beneficiary has an IP in the trust's share of the land. This means that the surviving spouse should be given an IP in the NRB trust's share (which is otherwise held on discretionary trusts). This is easy enough. The trustees can appoint a life interest in it at the time of the appropriation. The interest will not be an IPDI so no IHT consequences will follow. Part II of this book contains a precedent.

If TLATA is a problem it would prevent trustees claiming PPR relief in all cases where the trustees hold a share in land (even a 99% share), not just NRB trusts. This is a startling proposition! HMRC do not as far as we are aware seriously take this point.

Another (bad) argument

One other argument that is much more easily dismissed is that PPR relief is unavailable because the right of the surviving spouse to occupy derives from her own half share in the home, rather than the NRB trust. Section 225 TCGA does not require that the beneficiary is *only* entitled to occupy it by virtue of her/his entitlement under the settlement. It is enough that the surviving spouse would (ignoring any other rights she may have) be entitled to occupy the property under the terms of the settlement.

Summary

In summary, it is safe to appropriate the testator's share in the family home to the NRBDT provided:

App 6.4

(1) the appropriation is made 2 years or more after the death of the testator;[11]

(2) the surviving spouse is not disabled in the IHT sense at the time of the death of the testator); and

(3) the surviving spouse is given an interest in possession in the trust fund.

This course will ensure that PPR relief is available to the trustees when the property is eventually sold. This arrangement avoids the complex issues raised by the debt/charge arrangements and is in our view the most convenient way to administer a NRB trust.

---

[11] The appointment could be made within 2 years if the spouse has moved out of the property.

APPENDIX 7

DEFINITIONS OF "DISABLED PERSON"

Definition for IHT Purposes

App 7.1 The definition is in s.89 IHTA 1984. There are seven categories of disabled person.

Category 1: No mental capacity

A person who is incapable, by reason of mental disorder within the meaning of the Mental Health Act 1983 of administering his property or managing his affairs.

The Mental Health Act 1983 only applies in England, and was repealed in 2007 by the Mental Capacity Act 2005, but its (commonsense) definition of "mental disorder[1]" will continue to apply for tax purposes.

Category 2 and 3: Attendance or disability living allowance

A person in receipt of an attendance allowance under:

(1) s.64 Social Security Contributions and Benefits Act 1992 or
(2) s.64 SSCB (Northern Ireland) Act 1992.

A person in receipt of a disability living allowance under:

(1) s.71 Social Security Contributions and Benefits Act 1992 or
(2) s.71 SSCB (Northern Ireland) Act 1992

by virtue of entitlement to the care component at the highest or middle rate.

---

[1] "Mental illness, arrested or incomplete development of mind, psychopathic disorder and any other disorder or disability of mind": s.1 Mental Health Act 1983.

Definitions of "disabled person" 563

The person must receive the benefit, not merely be entitled to claim it. The IHT Manual para.42805 summarises the requirements of these benefits:

The attendance allowance is payable only to a person who
— is age 65 or over
— satisfies prescribed conditions as to residence and presence in Great Britain or Northern Ireland, and
— is not entitled to the care component of a disability living allowance, and
— is so severely disabled mentally or physically that he requires from another person:

> frequent attention throughout the day (or prolonged or repeated attention at night) in connection with his bodily functions, or continual supervision throughout the day or night in order to avoid substantial danger to himself or others.

A person is entitled to the care component of a disability living allowance at the highest or middle rate if he
— satisfies prescribed conditions as to residence and presence in Great Britain or Northern Ireland, and
— is so disabled that

> he requires frequent attention throughout the day, or for a significant portion of the day, in connection with his bodily functions, or
> he cannot prepare a cooked main meal for himself if he has the ingredients, or
> he requires continual supervision throughout the day in order to avoid substantial damage to himself or others.

For further details and application forms, see *www.direct.gov.uk/disability-aa* and *www.direct.gov.uk/disability-dla*.

The remaining categories concern those who nearly qualify for one of these allowances, but fail on certain grounds.

Category 4: Renal patients

A person who would have been in receipt of attendance allowance under section 64 of either of the Acts mentioned in subsection (4)(b) above had provision made by regulations under section 67(1) or (2) of that Act (non-satisfaction of conditions for attendance allowance where person is undergoing treatment for renal failure in a hospital or is provided with certain accommodation) been ignored.

Section 65(2) SSCBA applies where the claimant is suffering from renal failure and is undergoing a particular form of treatment. Paragraphs 5(2) and (3) SS (Attendance Allowance) Regulations 1991 allow a person having such treatment at least twice a week to be deemed (in some circumstances) to satisfy one of the attendance conditions. Section 67(1) allows for regulations which limit the scope of this concession. The regulations drawn under this particular section are paragraphs 5(3) and (4) of of the SS (AA) Regulations 1991. The effect of this category is to ignore these paragraphs for the purposes of IHT.

Category 5: Patients for whom accommodation is provided:

A person who would have been in receipt of disability living allowance by virtue of entitlement to the care component at the highest or middle rate had provision made by regulations under section 72(8) of either of the Acts mentioned in subsection (4)(c) above (no payment of disability living allowance for persons for whom certain accommodation is provided) been ignored.

Category 6 and 7: Non-residents

(a) *A person who would have been in receipt of attendance allowance under section 64 of either of the Acts mentioned in subsection (4)(b) above—*

  (i) *had he met the conditions as to residence under section 64(1) of that Act, and*

  (ii) *had provision made by regulations under section 67(1) or (2) of that Act been ignored.*

(b) *A person who would have been in receipt of a disability living allowance by virtue of entitlement to the care component at the highest or middle rate—*

  (i) *had he met the prescribed conditions as to residence under section 71(6) of either of the Acts mentioned in subsection (4)(c) above, and*

  (ii) *had provision made by regulations under section 72(8) of that Act been ignored.*

Definition for CGT

App 7.2 Only categories (1) to (3) above qualify as disabled persons for CGT reliefs: Sch.1 para.1 TCGA 1992 (full annual allowance) and s.169 TCGA 1992 (holdover relief).

Definition for IT/CGT transparency

App 7.3 Categories (1) to (5) above qualify as disabled persons for IT/CGT transparency: s.38 FA 2005.

APPENDIX 8

NOTES ON THE TRANSLATION OF WILL PRECEDENTS INTO WELSH

By Ian Sydenham

I am very happy to have prepared the Welsh precedents for this edition of *Drafting Trusts & Will Trusts*. The precedents are to be found on the CD with this book.

The Welsh Language Act 1993 established the principle that in the conduct of public business and the administration of justice in Wales, the English and Welsh languages should be treated on a basis of equality.[1] It is pleasing that there is a general awareness not only of the existence of Welsh as a living language but also of the need for legal precedents.

While the number of Welsh speakers continues to grow and the language is used more and more in everyday and commercial life it is an unfortunate fact that it is not as broad as English in terms of vocabulary. This can, however, be a positive advantage for translation since it imposes a discipline of not using several words where one will do. There is therefore possibly less of a need to ensure that the precedents are written in "plain Welsh" as opposed to "plain English" because to complicate them would require more work.

Welsh precedents do, I think, suffer from a different problem. In common with other legal and technical documents which have been translated into or, more rarely, produced in Welsh the precedents use a technical vocabulary which may be unfamiliar even to fluent readers. There is the risk that using Welsh documents can be simply too much effort. I remember considerable difficulty in reading through the Civil Procedure Rules in Welsh. The result is that translations can be seen as an end in themselves with the production of the items rather than their actual use being the main goal. We do hope that this will not be the case with these precedents and that they will be of use to practitioners rather than

---

[1] See the preamble to and ss. 3, 5 Welsh Language Act 1993.

mere curiosities. Within Wales it should be possible to conduct matters in Welsh if the parties desire and it is of course straightforward to prove a Will which is written in Welsh.

One interesting grammatical aspect of Welsh (in common with Celtic and some other languages[2]) is its use of mutations where the first letter of a word (or sometimes the whole word or part of the preceding word) may change. This is why the Welsh word for Wales is *Cymru* but road signs say *Croeso i Gymru*. This did give some pause for thought when considering defined terms since the initial, capitalised, letter will change depending on the context. I have decided to simply capitalise the mutated initial letter on the basis that the meaning remains clear. Similarly, where the precedent includes options I have not mutated, considering the options somewhat outside of the main text.

A second interesting issue is the disparity between Welsh spoken in North Wales and that in South Wales. A good number of words and terms do vary and it not simply a case of one being the correct form and the other a regional variation. As the precedents are technical I hope that this will not be too relevant. I do not think that I have been particularly parochial although this may just be a North Walian bias meaning that I have not appreciated where I have done so.

As with any translation it has not been possible to simply change the precedents from English to Welsh in exactly the same form. Many words can be translated in more than one way while retaining a similar meaning. A translation back into English would inevitably therefore differ in look from the original precedents but not, I hope, by very much or, in terms of meaning, at all.

This does however give rise to a problem in ensuring consistency, particularly when translating technical terms which are likely to have been included in government documents or legislation. It would be quite possible to translate a standard English term such as, for example, "interest in possession", in several different ways, each of which would convey a similar meaning. However, as HMRC in their Welsh language forms and guidance use a particular translation I felt it desirable to use the term already in use.

In that regard I found both HMRC and The Probate Service to have very useful websites containing a large number of translated documents. Considering these has, I hope, helped to produce a desirable standardisation in the translation of technical terms.

I do not doubt that my translations can be improved upon and would welcome any suggestions for doing so.

Ian Sydenham TEP
Hill Dickinson LLP
Ian.Sydenham@hilldickinson.com

---

[2] Classical Hebrew is another example.

INDEX

Absolute discretion
  trustees and, 7.10
Accumulation and maintenance trusts
  changes required to, 1.5
Accumulation period
  expiry of, 15.9
  extension of, 15.8
  length of, 15.8
  provision for, 15.7
  rule against, 15.6
Administrative powers
  meaning of, 16.1
  significance of, 16.2
  trustees' powers and, 16.3
Administrative provisions
  See also **Drafting style**; **Exceptions**; **Inconsistent provisions**
  accepting additional funds, 21.6
  accounts and audit, 21.7
  additional powers, taking, 21.5
  ancillary powers, 21.49
  applying trust capital, 21.29
  apportionment, 21.54
  appropriation, power of, 21.46
  bank charges, 21.57
  beneficiaries liabilities, security for, 21.39
  borrow, power to, 21.41
  capital expenses, 21.28
  charities, receipts by, 21.47
  commission, 21.57
  consent of court, 21.18
  custodians, 21.43
  debts, payment of, 21.32
  delegation, 21.42
  demergers, 21.34
  determining doubtful capital or income, 21.17, 21.27

  disclaim interest, 21.53
  disposition, powers of, 21.25
  equitable apportionment, 21.32
  expenses of trustees, 21.13
  extent of, 21.1
  fees, 21.56
  indemnities, power to give, 21.44
  insure, power to, 21.3
  investment policy, 21.33
  investment powers, 21.22–21.23
  joint purchase powers, 21.24
  liability for losses, 31.13
  loans to beneficiaries, 21.37
  matters of doubt, 21.16
  matters of law, 21.16
  mentally handicapped beneficiaries, 21.52
  minors, provisions relating to, 21.50–21.51
  nominees, 21.43
  onerous property, 21.6
  power to borrow, 21.41
  power to insure, 21.3
  power to trade, 21.40
  power to vary investments, 21.4
  repair and maintain trust property, 21.9
  restricting powers to perpetuity period, 21.11
  restrictions on provisions, 21.14
  rights and powers, release of, 21.48
  shares and debentures, 21.8
  sinking funds, 21.31
  standard charges and conditions, 21.56
  statutory apportionment, 21.54
  STEP provisions, 21.20
  trade, power to, 21.40
  trust property, 21.26, 21.39
  trustee charging clauses, 21.58–21.61

trustee remuneration, 21.55, 21.62–21.65
trustees' liabilities, security for, 21.45
trustees' powers, 21.19
unnecessary forms, 21.10
unnecessary provisions, 21.2
unsecured loans, 21.38
void powers, 21.15

Annuity
purchase of, 16.6

Anti-alimony
forms of trust, 5.15

Appointment
powers of, 7.22, 7.25, 7.33

Appropriation
power of, 16.8

Backdating
the gods and, 9.6

Bare trusts
See also **Disabled people**
additions to, 22.6
advancement, power of, 22.4
death of beneficiary, 22.4
draft, 22.5
funds,
    power to mix and appropriate, 22.4
non-tax aspects of, 22.3
terminology, 22.1
use of, 22.2

Beneficiaries
additional, 5.41, 5.49
adopted, 5.23
anti-alimony clauses, 5.15
anti-creditor clauses, 5.8
approach to, 5.1
assisted reproduction and, 5.25
charities as, 5.36, 5.46
children, 5.20
children of x and y, 5.21
civil partners, 5.29, 5.30, 5.31
civil partnerships, 5.13
consultation with, 7.18
default clause, 5.48
definition of, 5.18
dependants, 5.43
descendants, 5.20
distant relatives, 5.47
divorce of,
    creation of trusts, 5.14
    claim in the event of, 5.9
    equitable interest of, 5.10
    trust as a financial resource, 5.11
    variation of settlement on, 5.12
employees of, 5.43
"fall back," 5.45–5.47
foreign charities, 5.38
foreign domiciled, 5.16
gender of, 5.27
illegitimate, 5.22
insolvency of,
    bankruptcy proceedings and, 5.5–5.7
    tax consequences, 5.6, 5.7
interest free loan,
    power to lend, 7.20
limited extension of class of, 5.50
marriage settlements, 5.13
marriage under 18, 5.17
meaning, 5.49
minors as, 5.2
non-charitable companies, 5.37
power to add, 5.39
power to exclude, 5.40
powers of consent, 7.23
profligacy, 5.2
protective trusts, 5.3
restricting rights of, 28.1
settlor as, 5.31
    lifetime trust, 5.33
    surviving spouse of, 5.33
shares in family companies, 5.44
spouse,
    drafting points, 5.30
    meaning of, 5.32
    separated, 5.35
    settlor and, 5.31
    status of, 5.28
    surviving, 5.33
    testator of, 5.34
step-children, 5.24
surrogate children, 5.26
taxation of class of,
    entrepreneurs' relief, 5.51
    offshore trusts, 5.51
    remittance based planning, 5.51
    re-investment relief, 5.51
trustees' powers, 5.1, 5.2
trust property,
    use of, 7.20

Bible
drafting error in, 30.1
punctuation in, 2.2

Care fees planning
capital,
    between £13,000 and £21,500, 20.4

deprivation of, 20.7
disregards, 20.6
exceeds £21,500, 20.4
under £13,000, 20.4
deferring obligation to pay, 20.5
generally, 20.1
liability to pay, 20.4
right of occupation, 20.5
valuation provisions, 20.5
will trusts,
  administration after survivor goes into care, 20.8
  types of, 20.3
  use of, 20.2

Charitable trusts
accumulation,
  rule against, 24.6
administrative provisions, 24.7
charitable will trusts, 24.11
charity trustees,
  insurance for claims against, 24.9
  remuneration of, 24.9
execution of,
  procedure after, 24.10
foreign charities, 5.38
generally to, 24.1–24.2
name, 24.3
non-charitable purposes, 24.5
settlor,
  exclusion of, 24.5
trading, 24.8
trustees, 24.4

Children
administrative provisions, 21.50–21.51
beneficiaries,
  minors as, 5.2
bereaved minors trust, 17.1, 17.8
step-children, 5.24
surrogate children, 5.26
trust for minors, 25.7

Civil partner
meaning of, 5.30, 5.32

Civil partnerships
beneficiaries as, 5.13, 5.29, 5.30, 5.31
settlement,
  variation of, 5.13

Client
duty to, 2.1
elderly, 2.2
ill, 2.2

Consent
See also **Appointment**
completely beneficial, 7.33

powers of, 7.23, 7.24, 7.33
semi-fiduciary, 7.33
wholly personal, 7.23

Criminal injuries compensation scheme
award under, 25.9

Damages, trusts of
See also **Bare trusts**; **Disabled people**
adult with mental capacity, 25.2
bare trust,
  consequences of using, 25.5
  precedent for, 25.4
  transfer to, 25.3
benefit disregard, 25.1
child's damages,
  creation of a substantive trust, 25.6
  precedent for bare trust, 25.4
  transfer to bare trust, 25.3
claim,
  compromise of, 25.6
criminal injuries compensation scheme,
  award under, 25.9
mental capacity,
  adult with, 25.2
  person lacking, 25.8
trust for minors, 25.7

Deed of advancement
execution of,
  procedure after, 12.15

Deed of appointment
drafting of, 12.1, 12.3, 12.6
drafting transfers to another settlement, 12.8
example of, 12.7
execution of,
  procedure after, 12.15
instructing counsel, 12.2
parties, 12.3
power to transfer to another settlement, 12.9
resolutions of advancement,
  drafting, 12.11
  examples of, 12.12
  transfer property from one settlement to another, 12.14
  transfer property to two different settlements, 12.13
royal lives clause, 12.5
settled advances,
  drafting of, 12.10
time limits, 12.6

useful recitals, 12.4
useless recitals, 12.4
Deed of resettlement
execution of,
procedure after, 12.15
Disabled people
actual estate–IP for disabled
beneficiary, 26.6
actual estate–IP for prospectively
disabled settlor, 26.8
capital gains tax,
full annual allowance, 26.11
hold–over relief, 26.13
transparency, 26.14, 26.17
choosing provisions for, 26.2
complexity of rules for, 26.22
deemed IP trust,
inheritance tax on, 26.9
prospectively disabled settlor,
26.10
disability requirement, 26.9
drafting requirements, 26.9, 26.11,
26.14
income tax, 26.14, 26.17
inheritance tax dependant relative
relief, 26.5
interest in possession, 26.7
mentally handicapped beneficiaries,
26.1
mixed settlements, 26.12
mixed trusts, 26.12
orphan beneficiary, 26.16
provision for,
lifetime provision, 26.21
small funds, 26.19
substantial funds, 26.20
tax reliefs, 26.4
welfare benefits, 26.3
Discretionary trusts
accumulation period,
expiry of, 15.9
extension of, 15.8
length of, 15.8
provision for, 15.7
rule against, 15.6
beneficiaries, 15.11
income,
accumulation of, 15.5
clause for, 15.3
distribution of, 15.4
waiver of, 15.12
meaning of, 15.1
powers of, 15.12

structure of, 15.10
use of, 15.2
Dispositive powers
meaning of, 16.1
significance of, 16.2
trustees' powers and, 16.3
Disqualifying powers
use of, 16.9, 16.14
Divorce
creation of trusts, 5.14
claim in the event of, 5.9
equitable interest of, 5.10
marriage settlements, 5.12
trust as a financial resource, 5.11
variation of settlement on, 5.12
Domicile
foreign beneficiaries, 5.16
foreign domicile of settlor, 10.19
foreign domiciled spouse, 18.20
foreign domiciled testator, 18.19
foreign trustees, 17.11
UK domiciled testator,
foreign domiciled spouse, with,
18.20
Drafting style
See also **Administrative powers;
Exclusion clauses**
addresses, 3.12
age, 3.13
and/or, 3.16
archaic expressions, 3.18
artificial rules of construction, 3.21,
3.23
brevity and, 3.8
but, 3.16
capitals, use of, 3.3
civil claims and, 2.13
class closing rule, 3.22
clause headings, 3.19
clauses, use of, 3.5, 3.10
court's approach to, 2.3
coverture, 3.25
cross-references, 3.24
dates 3.11
deemed, 3.17
entails, 3.27
for her separate use, 3.26
gender, 3.15
incorporation by reference, 3.20
indentation, 3.6
numbers, 3.9
obsolete forms, 3.25
passive voice, 3.7

plain English, 3.1
plural, 3.14
prolix expressions, 3.18
provided that, 3.16
punctuation, 3.2
qualifications and, 2.11
sentence length, 3.4
singular and plural, 3.14
sources for, 2.6–2.10
treated as, 3.17
trusts for sale, 3.28

Exclusion clauses
See also **Administrative powers;
Drafting style**
actual benefit, 13.8
additional and indirect settlors, 13.15
anti-avoidance provisions, 13.1
capital gains hold-over relief, 13.2
coverage of, 13.12
dependent children, 13.2, 13.22
drafting of, 13.13
inheritance tax and, 13.1
interest in settlement, 13.1
joint settlors, 13.14
limitations on, 13.12
marrying the settlor, 13.20
no reservation of benefit, 3.18
no resulting trust to settlor, 13.21
prohibition on loans to settlor, 13.19
reciprocal arrangements, 13.9
reference to spouse in, 13.16
trustees to pay costs of setting up the trust, 13.4
trustees to pay tax on gift to trust, 13.5
unnecessary provisions in, 13.17
use of, 13.10, 13.11

Execution of wills and trusts
See also **Trustees**
alterations after, 29.7
approval by parties, 29.2
checking documents, 29.4
inheritance tax,
　payment of, 29.11
lifetime settlements, 29.8
nil rate band,
　arrangements for loss of, 29.12
printing of wills, 29.5
procedure for, 29.15
returns and other matters, 29.13
review of draft, 29.1, 29.2
stamp duty, 29.14

stamp duty land tax, 29.14
statements of wishes, 29.10
tax reviews after, 29.16
transfer of trust property following, 29.9
use and misuse of precedents, 29.3

Finance Act 2006
changes made to, 1.2
existing trusts and, 1.5
impact of, 1.1
policy issues and, 1.3
trusts after, 1.4

Foreign domicile
See **Domicile**

Governing law
exclusive jurisdiction clause, 27.6
foreign law, 27.3
forum of administration, 27.7
law and jurisdiction, 31.20
place of administration of trust, 27.5
power to change, 27.4
requirement for, 27.1
selection of, 27.2

Hancock v Watson
use of rule in, 3.23

Inconsistent provisions
administrative powers,
　meaning of, 16.1
　significance of, 16.2
　trustees' powers and, 16.3
annuity,
　purchase of, 16.6
apportionment, 16.7
appropriation,
　power of, 16.8
borderline cases, 16.3
capital asset,
　depreciation of, 16.5
capital expenses,
　power to pay out of income, 16.4
departure,
　powers of, 16.9, 16.14
dispositive powers,
　meaning of, 16.1
　significance of, 16.2
　trustees' powers and, 16.3
disqualifying powers, 16.9, 16.14
income,
　power to waive, 16.13

572 INDEX

insurance premiums,
    power to pay out of income, 16.10, 16.16
interest free loans, 16.12
interest in possession,
    existence of, 16.2
    protection clause, 16.19
liabilities,
    retention of income to provide for, 16.5
life assurance premiums, 16.6
no conflict clause, 16.20
partly paid shares,
    applying income in the purchase of, 16.6
    subscription of, 16.6
protection clauses,
    accumulation and maintenance trusts, 16.22
    capital gains tax, 16.21
    drafting and construction of, 16.18
    interest in possession, 16.19
    need for, 16.17
    no conflict clause, 16.20
special trusts, 16.2, 16.14
tax law, 16.2
test for, 16.3
trust property,
    applying income to improve or develop, 16.6
    power to permit beneficiary to occupy or use, 16.11, 16.15
    rent free use, 16.11

Information
beneficiary's right to trust, 28.3
disclosure of,
    extension of powers of, 28.5
    restriction on, 28.1
    will, 28.2
no contest clauses, 28.6
no named beneficiary, 28.4
non assignment clauses, 28.7
restricting rights to, 28.3
unascertainable default beneficiary, 28.4

Insolvency
bankruptcy proceedings and, 5.5–5.7
tax consequences, 5.6, 5.7

Insurance premiums
See also **Life insurance**
power to pay out of income, 16.10, 16.16

Interpreting trust documents
background, 4.3
construction,
    technical rules and, 4.13
    trusts, of, 4.12
    wills of, 4.12
declarations of intent, 4.3
deemed intention, 4.5.1
ejusdem generis, 4.10
generally, 4.1, 4.2, 4.11
inadmissibility rules, 4.6
intention and meaning, 4.5
intention irrelevant, 4.5.2
meaning of documents, 4.4
meaning of words, 4.4
noscitur a sociis, 4.10
objective meaning, 4.5
objective principle,
    arguments for and against, 4.8
    generally, 4.5
    inadmissibility rules and, 4.6
    literal construction, 4.7
    rectification and, 4.9
precedent and, 4.10
previous negotiations, 4.3
subjective intention, 4.5

IP trusts
changes required to, 1.5

Landlord
consent of, 8.3

Lassence v Tierney
use of rule in, 3.23

Life insurance policies
drafting points, 23.9
existing policies and, 23.4
exit charges, 23.6
inheritance tax and, 23.5
insurance company standard form, 23.2
multiple discretionary trusts, 23.8
overriding powers, 23.10
precedent trust for life policy, 23.10
tax returns, 23.7
ten–year charges, 23.6
trustees,
    appointment of, 23.10
trusts of,
    creation of, 23.3, 23.4
    generally, 23.1

Lifetime interest in possession trusts
accumulation of income, 14.11
beneficiary,
    powers of, 14.7

categories of, 14.1
children,
   life interest to, 14.6
civil partner,
   life interest to, 14.6
death of principal beneficiary,
   discretionary trusts, 14.6
   perpetuity and, 14.9
   provisions after, 14.6
death of,
   surviving civil partner, 14.10
   surviving spouse, 14.10
default trusts, 14.4
divorce,
   interest of ex-spouse, 14.8
income clause, 14.3
income for life, 14.5
life tenants,
   entitlement at specified age, 14.16
   minor or child beneficiaries, 14.17
   provision for, 14.12–14.15
overriding powers, 14.4
perpetuity problem, 14.9
reversionary interest, 14.6
settlor, for, 14.18
structure of, 14.4
trust income, 14.4
use of, 14.2
waste,
   impeachment for, 14.19
widow,
   bad forms, 14.8
   describing the, 14.8
   life interest to, 14.6

Lifetime settlement
creation of, 10.2

Limitation Act
avoiding application of, 19.7

Marriage settlements
See also **Civil partnerships**; **Divorce**
settlements,
   existing settlements, 5.13
   test for, 5.13
   under 18, 5.17

Mental capacity
adult with, 25.2
person lacking, 25.8

Money laundering
suspicion of, 2.12

Mortgagee
consent of, 8.4

Nil rate band trusts
administration of, 19.1, 19.6
breach of trust,
   liability for, 19.5
capital gains tax, 19.8
debt scheme,
   implementation of, 19.5
family home,
   appropriation of share of, 19.2
house worth less than nil rate sum, 19.3
Limitation Act,
   avoiding application of, 19.7
sale of property, 19.8
spouse,
   death of, 19.9
   duties as executor and trustee, 19.4
   rights as beneficiary, 19.4
tax implications, 19.10
trust law issues, 19.4
winding up the trust, 19.9

Nominees
use of, 7.32

Overriding powers
See also **Power of advancement**; **Power of appointment**; **Power of resettlement**
categories of, 11.1
exercising, 12.1
existence of, 11.1
principal function of, 11.1

Perpetuities
beneficiaries' interests, 9.7
clauses for, 9.3
confusion over dates, 9.4
curtailing the trust period, 9.5
dispositive powers, 9.6
expressions covering perpetuity, 9.3
failure to remain within the period, 9.8
non–charitable trust, 9.2
period of perpetuity, 9.3
rule against,
   future of, 9.9
   generally, 9.1

Power of advancement
advanced beneficiaries, 11.11
advanced trusts, 11.11
creation of new trusts, 11.11
form of, 11.8
power to pay or transfer to beneficiary, 11.9
settled advancement, 11.11

statutory power and, 11.8, 11.11
use of, 11.11
Power of appointment
See also **Deeds of appointment**
advances to beneficiary, 11.10
clause for, 11.2
construction, 11.5
delegation, 11.5
form of, 11.2
Hallett precedent, 11.4
in such manner in all respects, 11.5
Joicey power, 11.5
problem with narrow powers of, 11.5
respective, 11.3
unnecessary provisions in, 11.3
Power of resettlement
form of, 11.6
use of, 11.7
Protection clauses
accumulation and maintenance trusts, 16.22
capital gains tax, 16.21
drafting and construction of, 16.18
interest in possession, 16.19
need for, 16.17
no conflict clause, 16.20
Protector
consent of, 7.29
death of, 7.29
duties of, 7.29
office of, 7.29
powers of, 7.29
retirement of, 7.29
settler as, 7.29
tax implications, 7.29
trustee and, 6.16

Residential care
See **Care fees planning**
Royal lives
clause, 9.2, 12.5

Settlor
beneficiary as, 5.31
benefit under a resulting trust, 13.6
default clause,
content of, 13.23
correcting errors in, 13.26
drafting of, 13.24
requirement for, 13.27
satisfying the tax requirement, 13.24
unnecessary provisions in, 13.25

excluding the, 13.3
exclusion clauses,
actual benefit, 13.8
additional and indirect settlors, 13.15
anti-avoidance provisions, 13.1
capital gains hold-over relief, 13.2
coverage of, 13.12
dependent children, 13.2, 13.22
drafting of, 13.13
inheritance tax and, 13.1
interest in settlement, 13.1
joint settlors, 13.14
limitations on, 13.12
marrying the settlor, 13.20
no reservation of benefit, 3.18
no resulting trust to settlor, 13.21
prohibition on loans to settlor, 13.19
reciprocal arrangements, 13.9
reference to spouse in, 13.16
trustees to pay costs of setting up the trust, 13.4
trustees to pay tax on gift to trust, 13.5
unnecessary provisions in, 13.17
use of, 13.10, 13.11
lifetime trust, 5.33
power to benefit, 13.7
powers of consent, 7.24
protector, as, 7.29
sole trustee, as, 7.27
surviving spouse of, 5.33
trustee, as, 6.2
trustee remuneration, 13.12
weighted majority and, 7.28
Shares
partly paid, 16.6
Special trusts
clauses for, 16.2, 16.14
Spouse
See also **Divorce**
lifetime transfer, 5.33
meaning of, 5.32
powers of appointment, 7.25
separated, 5.35
surviving, 5.33
testator, of, 5.34
will,
beneficiary of, 5.34, 5.35

Trust deed
administrative provisions, 10.31

backdating, 10.6
beneficial provisions, 10.28
beneficiaries,
    schedule of, 10.32
capitalisation, 10.33
commencement date, 10.5
consent of trustees, 10.24
date, 10.4
declaration of trust, 10.2
definitions,
    clause for, 10.36, 10.45
    define as you go, 10.35
    exhaustive, 10.37
    implied by law, 10.44
    inclusive, 10.37
    making, 10.34
    means and includes, 10.37
    purpose and use of, 10.33
    standard, 10.39
    unnecessary forms of, 10.38, 10.43
    use in text of, 10.45
intention to transfer additional property to trustees, 10.23
irrevocability, 10.25, 10.48
irrevocably witnesses, 10.26
joint settlors, 10.11
nominal settlor, 10.14
order of, 10.1
parties,
    describing the, 10.9
recitals,
    background, 10.15
    foreign domicile of settlor, 10.19
    lack of legal effect of, 10.20
    name of trust, 10.17
    power to change name of, 10.18
    principal beneficiaries, 10.16
schedule of trust property, 10.30
settlor as one of the trustees, 10.10
settlor as sole trustee, 10.12
statement of purpose of the trust, 10.21
successive interests,
    drafting, 10.46
    subject to that, 10.47
testatum, 10.26
testimonium clause, 10.29
title, 10.3
transfer of trust property to trustees, 10.22
transfer to trustees, 10.2
trust fund,
    definition of, 10.41
trust property,
    definition of, 10.42
trustees,
    definition of, 10.40
witnesseth, 10.26

Trust property
agricultural property relief and, 8.7
applying income to improve or develop, 16.6
business property, 8.7
chattels, 8.6
inheritance tax,
    sale of property and, 8.7
land subject to mortgage, 8.4
leasehold property, 8.3
life insurance, 8.5, 23.1
particular assets, 8.1
power to permit beneficiary to occupy or use, 16.11, 16.15
property situated outside the UK, 8.8
rent free use, 16.11
shares and securities, 8.2

Trustees
See also **Administrative provisions**; **Trustees' functions**
accountants as, 6.6
actual fraud and, 6.17
additional,
    appointment of, 6.38
appointment of, 6.12, 6.33, 6.34, 6.35, 30.1–30.6
beneficiary as, 6.3, 6.16
choice of, 6.2
clause for, 6.14
conflicts of interest, 6.13, 31.10
conscious wrongdoing, 6.17
corporate, 6.5
counsel's advice,
    litigation, on, 6.30
    relying on, 6.30
custodian, 6.9
director of listed company as, 6.7
dishonesty and, 6.17
dismissal of, 6.40, 7.30
exemption clauses,
    construction of, 6.17
    drafting of, 6.25
    duty to disclose, 6.24
    insertion of, 6.23
    use of, 6.26
    validity of, 6.22
family companies,
    excluding duty to supervise, 6.31

flee clauses, 6.12
fiduciary,
   conflicts, 6.15
   meaning, 6.16
foreign, 6.10, 6.35
former, 7.31, 31.6
fraud,
   prevention of, 6.13
free from responsibility for loss, 6.18
indemnities,
   beneficiaries, from, 31.11
   breach of trust, for, 31.13
   cap on amount payable under, 31.15
   generally, 31.1
   lien over trust property, 31.3
   limits on, 31.7
   multiple trustees, 31.18
   negotiating, 31.9
   new trustees, from, 31.12
   security for, 31.19
   time limit on, 31.14
   trust law and, 31.2
insider dealing and trusteeship, 6.8
managing, 6.9
multiple, 31.18
new trustees,
   death of, 31.16
   retirement of, 31.17
   review of, 30.2
   stamp duty and, 30.8
   stamp duty land tax, 30.8
   vesting property in, 30.7
no liability for loss, 6.19
number of, 6.1, 6.37
offshore, 6.10
order of names, 6.11
parents and guardians,
   excluding duty to supervise, 6.32
personal and fiduciary conflicts, 6.15
professional, 6.4
protector and, 6.16
removal of trust property, 7.31
resignation of, 6.39
retirement of, 6.36,
   procedure for, 30.1–30.5
   refusal to, 31.4
settlor as, 6.2
spouse as, 6.2
standard of care, 6.27
strict liability,
   exclusion of, 6.28
successor,
   appointment of, 6.42

unknown beneficiaries,
   exclusion of claims by, 6.29
weighted majority, 7.28
willful default, 6.17

Trustees' functions
See also **Overriding powers**
absolute discretion, 7.10, 7.11
"as the trustees shall see fit",
   meaning, 7.10
appointment of new trustees, 7.17
authorities, 7.4
beneficiaries,
   consultation with, 7.18
checks on powers of trustees, 7.21
control of, 7.12, 7.19, 7.26
drafting duties, 7.5
drafting powers, 7.5
duties and powers,
   distinguishing between, 7.2, 7.3
freedom of action, 7.10
functions,
   meaning, 7.4
guidance of, 7.12
majority decisions, 7.13
powers,
   appointment, of, 7.22, 7.25, 7.33
   consent, of, 7.23, 7.24, 7.33
   control on, 7.20
   exercise of, 7.7, 7.9
   meaning, 7.4
   time limits on, 7.8
protector,
   consent of, 7.29
   office of, 7.29
   settler as, 7.29
statement of wishes,
   content of, 7.15
   drafting of, 7.16
   execution of, 7.16
substantial trust company,
   exercise by, 7,14
terms to describe duties, 7.4
time limits, 7.8
trust corporation,
   exercise by, 7.14
two trustee rule, 7.14

Trusts
fixed period, 9.1
flexibility of, 2.4
policy of government, 1.1
simplicity of, 2.5
time limits on, 9.1

Waste
   Eve J. admits not understanding, 13.19
   impeachment for, 13.19

Will drafting
   See also **Care fee planning**
   after Finance Act 2008, 18.1
   nil rate bands,
      deed of variation, 18.8
      NRB claim, 18.6
      remarriage and, 18.7
      transferable, 18.5
      untransferable problems, 18.8,
      use of, 18.2
   nil rate band trusts,
      classic trusts, 18.3, 18.4
      redundancy of, 18.4

Will trusts
   See also **Care fee planning**; **Nil rate band trusts**; **Will drafting**
   age 18–25 trusts,
      capital gains tax, 17.7
      inheritance tax, 17.7
      qualifying conditions, 17.6
      use of, 17.7
   agricultural property and, 18.17
   bereaved minors trust,
      use of, 17.8
   best form for,
      civil partner, 18.11
      married testator, 18.11
      single testator, 18.10
   business property and, 18.17
   charity,
      substantial gifts to, 18.18
   choice of, 18.9
   express wills, 17.9
   foreign domiciled spouse, 18.20
   foreign domiciled testator, 18.19
   foreign trustees, 17.11
   gift by will to existing trust, 17.13
   IPDI trusts,
      capital gains tax, 17.4
      death of life tenant and, 17.5
      income tax, 17.4
      inheritance tax, 17.4
      overriding power of enjoyment, 17.5
      qualifying conditions, 17.3
      terms of, 17.5
      trust passing to spouse, 17.5
      use of, 17.4
   lifetime trusts,
      drafting differences, 17.10

married testator,
   provision for children by will, 18.12
nil rate band,
   alternative to, 18.16
   classic trust, 18.15
   construction of traditional formula, 18.14
   discretionary trusts and, 18.15
   effect of claim, 18.14
   existing wills, 18.21
   formula for, 18.13
   power to make claim, 18.14
   untransferable nil rate sum, 18.13
   use of, 18.21
nil rate sum,
   gift to lifetime trust, 18.15
   long-term discretionary trust, 18.15
spouse,
   both deceased before 9 October 2007, 18.21
   death of first spouse, 18.21
   interest in possession of, 18.15
   surviving spouse died on or after 9 October 2007, 18.21
   terminology, 17.2
survivorship clauses, 17.12
types of,
   bereaved minors trust, 17.1
   section 71A trusts, 17.1
   section 71D trusts, 17.1
   special IHT trusts, 17.1
   standard IHT trusts, 17.1
UK domiciled testator,
   foreign domiciled spouse, with, 18.20

Words and phrases
   See also **Drafting style**; **Exceptions**
   absolute owner, 6.20
   actual fraud, 6.17
   as the trustees think fit, 7.10
   at any time, 7.9
   authorities, 7.4
   beneficial owner, 6.21
   conscious wrongdoing, 6.17
   discretion, 7.4
   free from responsibility for loss, 6.18
   from time to time, 7.9
   functions, 7.4
   made on the parties to the marriage, 5.13
   no liability for loss, 6.19

powers, 7.4
settlement, 7.4
shall, 7.6
trust as a synonym of settlement, 7.4

trust corporation, 7.14
trust for sale, 7.4
willful default, 6.17
willful fraud, 6.17

THE COMPANION CD

Instructions for Use

Introduction

These notes are provided for guidance only. They should be read and interpreted in the context of your own computer system and operational procedures. It is assumed that you have a basic knowledge of WINDOWS. However, if there is any problem please contact our help line on 0845 850 9355 who will be happy to help you.

CD Format and Contents

To run this CD you need at least:

- IBM compatible PC with Pentium processor
- 8MB RAM
- CD-ROM drive
- Microsoft Windows 95

The CD contains data files of the clauses in this book. It does not contain software or commentary.

Installation

The following instructions make the assumption that you will copy the data files to a single directory on your hard disk (e.g. C:\Drafting Trusts and Will Trusts).

Open your **CD ROM drive**, select and double click on **setup.exe** and follow the instructions. The files will be unzipped to your **C drive** and you will be able to open them up from the new **C:\Drafting Trusts and Will Trusts** folder there.

LICENCE AGREEMENT

Definitions

1. The following terms will have the following meanings:

"The PUBLISHERS" means SWEET & MAXWELL LIMITED, incorporated in England & Wales under the Companies Acts (Registered No. 28096) whose registered office is 100 Avenue Road, London NW3 3PF, (which expression shall, where the context admits, include the PUBLISHERS' assigns or successors in business as the case may be) of the other part (on behalf of Thomson Reuters (Legal) Limited incorporated in England & Wales under the Companies Acts (Registered No. 1679046) whose registered office is 100 Avenue Road, London NW3 3PF)

"The LICENSEE' means the purchaser of the work containing the Licensed Material.

"Licensed Material" means the data included on the disk;

"Licence" means a single user licence;

"Computer" means an IBM-PC compatible computer.

Grant of Licence; Back-up Copies

2.(1) The PUBLISHERS hereby grant to the LICENSEE, a non-exclusive, non-transferable licence to use the Licensed Material in accordance with those terms and conditions.

(2) The LICENSEE may install the Licensed Material for use on one computer only at any one time.

(3) The LICENSEE may make one back-up copy of the Licensed Material only, to be kept in the LICENSEE's control and possession.

Proprietary Rights

3. (1) All rights not expressly granted herein are reserved.

(2) The Licensed Material is not sold to the LICENSEE who shall not acquire any right, sale or interest in the Licensed Material or in the media upon which the Licensed Material is supplied.

(3) The LICENSEE, shall not erase, remove, deface or cover any trademark, copyright notice, guarantee or other statement on any media containing the Licensed Material.

(4) The LICENSEE shall only use the Licensed Material in the normal course of its business and shall not use the Licensed Material for the purpose of operating a bureau or similar service or any online service whatsoever.

(5) Permission is hereby granted to LICENSEES who are members of the legal profession (which expression does not include individuals or organisations engaged in the supply of services to the legal profession) to reproduce, transmit and store small quantities of text for the purpose of enabling them to provide legal advice to or to draft documents or conduct proceedings on behalf of their clients.

(6) The LICENSEE shall not sublicense the Licensed Material to others and this Licence Agreement may not be transferred, sublicensed, assigned or otherwise disposed of in whole or in part.

(7) The LICENSEE shall inform the PUBLISHERS on becoming aware of any unauthorised use of the Licensed Material.

Warranties

4. (1) The PUBLISHERS warrant that they have obtained all necessary rights to grant this licence.
   (2) Whilst reasonable care is taken to ensure the accuracy and completeness of the Licensed Material supplied, the PUBLISHERS make no representations or warranties, express or implied, that the Licensed Material is free from errors or omissions.
   (3) The Licensed Material is supplied to the LICENSEE on an "as is" basis and has not been supplied to meet the LICENSEE's individual requirements. It is the sole responsibility of the LICENSEE to satisfy itself prior to entering this Licence Agreement that the Licensed Material will meet the LICENSEE's requirements and be compatible with the LICENSEE's hardware/software configuration. No failure of any part of the Licensed Material to be suitable for the LICENSEE's requirements will give rise to any claim against the PUBLISHERS.
   (4) In the event of any material inherent defects in the physical media on which the licensed material may be supplied, other than caused by accident abuse or misuse by the LICENSEE, the PUBLISHERS will replace the defective original media free of charge provided it is returned to the place of purchase within 90 days of the purchase date. The PUBLISHERS' entire liability and the LICENSEE's exclusive remedy shall be the replacement of such defective media.
   (5) Whilst all reasonable care has been taken to exclude computer viruses, no warranty is made that the Licensed Material is virus free. The LICENSEE shall be responsible to ensure that no virus is introduced to any computer or network and shall not hold the PUBLISHERS responsible.
   (6) The warranties set out herein are exclusive of and in lieu of all other conditions and warranties, either express or implied, statutory or otherwise.
   (7) All other conditions and warranties, either express or implied, statutory or otherwise, which relate in the condition and fitness for any purpose of the Licensed Material are hereby excluded and the PUBLISHERS shall not be liable in contract, delict or in tort for any loss of any kind suffered by reason of any defect in the Licensed Material (whether or not caused by the negligence of the PUBLISHERS).

Limitation of Liability and Indemnity

5. (1) The LICENSEE shall accept sole responsibility for and the PUBLISHERS shall not be liable for the use of the Licensed Material by the LICENSEE, its agents and employees and the LICENSEE shall hold the PUBLISHERS harmless and fully indemnified against any claims, costs, damages, loss and liabilities arising out of any such use.
   (2) The PUBLISHERS shall not be liable for any indirect or consequential loss suffered by the LICENSEE (including without limitation loss of profits, goodwill or data) in connection with the Licensed Material howsoever arising.
   (3) The PUBLISHERS will have no liability whatsoever for any liability of the LICENSEE to any third party which might arise.
   (4) The LICENSEE hereby agrees that
      (a) the LICENSEE is best placed to foresee and evaluate any loss that might be suffered in connection with this Licence Agreement,
      (b) that the cost of supply of the Licensed Material has been calculated on the basis of the limitations and exclusions contained herein; and
      (c) the LICENSEE will effect such insurance as is suitable having regard to the LICENSEE's circumstances.
   (5) The aggregate maximum liability of the PUBLISHERS in respect of any direct loss or any other loss (to the extent that such loss is not excluded by this Licence Agreement or otherwise) whether such a claim arises in contract or tort shall not exceed a sum equal to that paid at the price for the title containing the Licensed Material.

Termination

6. (1) In the event of any breach of this Agreement including any violation of any copyright in the Licensed Material, whether held by the PUBLISHERS or others in the Licensed Material, the Licence Agreement shall automatically terminate immediately, without notice and without prejudice to any claim which the PUBLISHERS may have either for moneys due and/or damages and/or otherwise.
   (2) Clauses 3 to 5 shall survive the termination for whatsoever reason of this Licence Agreement.
   (3) In the event of termination of this Licence Agreement the LICENSEE will remove the Licensed Material.

Miscellaneous

7. (1) Any delay or forbearance by the PUBLISHERS in enforcing any provisions of this License Agreement shall not be construed as a waiver of such provision or an agreement thereafter not to enforce the said provision.
   (2) This Licence Agreement shall be governed by the laws of England and Wales. If any difference shall arise between the Parties touching the meaning of this Licence Agreement or the rights and liabilities of the parties thereto, the same shall be referred to arbitration in accordance with the provisions of the Arbitration Act 1996, or any amending or substituting statute for the time being in force.